ABEL ROOT, SR.

OF BOLIVAR, NEW YORK

ABEL ROOT, SR.

OF BOLIVAR, NEW YORK AND HIS DESCENDANTS

William A. Paquette, Ph.D.
Professor of History

New Dominion Press • Norfolk • Virginia

Abel Root, Sr. of Bolivar, New York and His Descendants

Published by:

New Dominion Press
New Dominion Media/New Dominion Press
1217 Godfrey Avenue, Norfolk, Virginia 23504-3218
www.NewDominionPress.com

First Printing: October 2020.

Cover design, Graphics Design, and Typography by New Dominion Press

Publisher's Cataloging-in-Publication Data
provided by Five Rainbows Cataloging Services

Names: Paquette, William A., 1947- author.
Title: Abel Root, Sr. of Bolivar, New York and his descendants / William A. Paquette.
Description: Norfolk, VA : New Dominion Press, 2020. | Includes references and index.
Identifiers: LCCN 2020917804 | ISBN 978-1-7331292-5-1 (paperback)
Subjects: LCSH: Root family. | Root, Abel, active 18th century-19th century--Family. | Bolivar (Allegany County, N.Y.) | New York (State)--Emigration and immigration. | Immigrants--New York (State)| England--Emigration and immigration--History--19th century- 20th century. | Genealogy. | Biography. | BISAC: REFERENCE / Genealogy & Heraldry. | HISTORY / United States / State & Local / Middle Atlantic (DC, DE, MD, NJ, NY, PA).
Classification: LCC CS90 .P41722 2018 (print) | DDC 929.2/089114--dc23.

First Edition

In Memory Of

Cookie 2008 – 2019

My Beloved Chocolate Himalayan who sat, slept, ate, and meowed at my desk while I researched and wrote this genealogy, but who died from stomach cancer on February 1, 2019.

DEDICATION

Dorothy Root Paquette
My Mother

Who developed my sense of family,
And who encouraged me to write.

Table of Contents

Preface

It has been thirty years since I published *The Root Family of Bolivar, New York.* In thirty years, the Internet has taken users to web sites, which offered a tremendous array of genealogical resources making it apparent that my 1990 publication needed significant updating. The result is *Abel Root, Sr. of Bolivar, New York, and His Descendants.*

Abel Root, Sr. and his wife, Penelope Cartwright Root, with five children: Abel, Jr., David, Bishop, Penelope, and Franklin, moved to Scio in Allegany County, New York in 1822 from Unadilla in eastern New York State. In 1824 the Root family moved to Bolivar township establishing a farm across the road from Maple Lawn Cemetery. Their youngest child, James Harlow Root, was the first recorded birth in Bolivar in 1825. The 1879 *History of Allegany County, New York* documents Abel Root, Sr.'s 1845 departure to Illinois with his wife. The reasons for moving to Illinois are unknown. All six children remained in Allegany County where each one married, raised a family, and was buried. Unfortunately, what happened to Abel Root, Sr. still remains a mystery. No death record or burial location can be found. The 1850 US Census lists his wife, Penelope, living with son Franklin Root in Angelica, New York. Penelope Root Cartwright was buried in Maple Lawn Cemetery in 1851 in an unmarked grave. Between 1845 and 1850 Abel Root, Sr. must have died but documentation remains elusive.

Abel Root, Jr. had six children, five of whom survived to adulthood. All five married and their lines of descent are documented to the present day. David Cartwright Root had four children. His youngest son died at Andersonville Prison, Georgia and his eldest daughter married but died without issue. The line of descent of David Root's eldest son, Albert Root, is well documented in this genealogy and includes an impressive list of creative and artistic talent. The line of descent of David Root's youngest daughter remains incomplete. Truman Bishop Root had ten children, five sons and five daughters. All ten children married. The eldest son, David B. Root, died without issue and a younger son, Bryant Hebron Root, married but his line ended with the deaths of his grandchildren. A younger daughter, Mary Root, married and had two children, both of whom predeceased her without living issue. Lines of descent for the other seven children are well documented. Huldah Penelope Root Kellogg bore seven children before dying in 1851. Her only daughter predeceased her. One son died at the start of the Civil War and two sons died in the Civil War, all unmarried and without issue. One son disappeared in the 1870s and cannot currently be traced. Two sons married and had issue. Francis Albertus Kellogg moved to Shinglehouse, Pennsylvania where his descendants became one of the most prolific of the Root lines. The line of descent of the other son, Royal Jaspar Kellogg, has been more difficult to trace and his line of descent is still incomplete. Franklin B. Root had three children, two daughters and one son. The eldest daughter, Frances Root, disappears from documentation after 1865. The youngest daughter, Florence Root, married twice but never had issue. Franklin Root's son, George Root, married but his line seems to have ended with the death of his granddaughter. James Harlow Root had two children, twins, a son and a daughter, by his second wife. James Root's son, Harlie Root, had two sons and one daughter. Although there are some references that both sons married, no documentation could be found to prove that and Harlie Root's documented line survives through his daughter, Sarah Margaret Root. James Root's daughter, Hattie Root, married and had three children but only the youngest married and this line survives with just one remaining descendant. My goal has been to bring each line to at least the year 2000 and I believe I have come close to that objective.

The original Abel Root, Sr. homestead across from Maple Lawn Cemetery was given to their youngest son, James. Their two eldest sons, Abel, Jr. and David, were farmers in the hamlet of Kossuth just east of Bolivar along highway 417 where oil was later discovered. Son, Bishop Root, was a carpenter by profession as was his brother, Franklin Root. Franklin moved to Angelica in 1849 to work on the County Jail and stayed there. Penelope Root Kellogg's husband, Loring, was a lumberman in Bolivar township and the youngest Root child, James Harlow, was a local village businessman and farmer. The pastoral harmony enjoyed by Bolivar and the Root family ended with the advent of the Civil War. Abel Root, Sr.'s grandsons, Lyman, David, Albert, and Asa Root, and James and Elmer Kellogg all volunteered to join the Union army as did grandsons-in-law, Addison Evans and Alonzo Crandall. Asa Root and Elmer and James Kellogg died in the Civil War and both David and Albert Root and Addison Evans and Alonzo Crandall suffered from war injuries the rest of their lives.

During the 1860s the first migration of Root family members out of Bolivar and Allegany County began. The reasons remain unknown, but I suggest that it was the desire to seek better economic opportunities or to just start over somewhere else. The first grandchildren to leave were Minerva Root Holly after her separation and divorce from her husband along with her sister and brother-in-law, Mary Jane and Elmer Barber. They relocated to Detroit, Michigan. David Root's youngest daughter and son-in-law, Elosica and Addison Evans, moved to Missouri and his eldest son, Albert Root, went to Washington, D. C. Mary Root Rew, a younger daughter of Bishop, and her husband Justice took their two children to Kansas, while Penelope's two surviving sons, Francis and Royal, sought new economic opportunities in Pennsylvania. Franklin Root's only son and his widowed youngest daughter moved to Iowa.

The discovery of oil in the 1880s brought an economic boom to Allegany County keeping the Root family in Bolivar. Financial success led to more Root owned businesses. The history of the State Bank of Bolivar is a history of Root financial success as the first president was James Curtiss, husband of Huldah Root. Later bank presidents included Christopher Garthwait, husband of Elizabeth Root, and Asa Prentice Root. Many Root family members were employed as clerks at the State Bank of Bolivar (now the Key Bank) including Agnes M. Evans, Elmer Garthwait, Glen Garthwait, George A. Root, Edwin Milford Root, and Cecelia Cawley Root. Root family members were either employed in the oil industry, a business associated with the oil industry, or with railroads who hauled oil, making this narrative a parallel history of the *Black Gold* boom that came to Allegany County and lasted eighty years.

The first decade of the 20th century witnessed a slow downturn in the oil industry, which continued over the next sixty years until oil production virtually ceased, and which gradually took Root family members decade after decade away from Bolivar, Allegany County, and New York State as they searched for economic opportunities. Many continued to find employment in the oil industry and their journeys led them to Kansas, Oklahoma, and Texas. Some believed California was a better state for creative success. This was particularly true for descendants of David Cartwright Root. Only a few Root descendants, including one holding the Root name, remain in Bolivar today. Migration to find economic opportunity is as much a part of the Root family narrative as it is a part of the history of the United States and the fulfillment of the *American Dream.* Departure from Bolivar never severed family ties to the community. Many Root descendants returned to visit the region Abel Sr. settled as recounted in newspaper articles in the *Bolivar Breeze.*

Even though my research still leaves unanswered questions, some exciting discoveries have been made. I found Penelope Root, the daughter of Abel, Sr. and Penelope Cartwright Root. The daughter was known as Huldah Penelope Root. She married Loring Kellogg, had seven children, but died in 1851 and was buried in Bolivar's Maple Lawn Cemetery. I have been able to trace most of her descendants to Shinglehouse, Pennsylvania where they resided for generations. I found more information on Minerva Root Holly Neff, the eldest daughter of Abel Root, Jr., but her death and burial information are still unknown. I have traced the descendants of her son, Judson Holly, to the year 2000 in the Detroit area, but I was unable to document what happened to two other of Minerva Root Holly's children.

My assumption that Root descendants in the 19th century remarried because of the death of their spouse proved to be way off the mark. Roots divorced or moved to another state where documentation about divorce may not have been requested. Minerva Root Holly's first husband, Daniel Holly, did not die permitting her remarriage. Each remarried with Daniel Holly moving to Olean, New York and Minerva to Detroit. Arthur Lew Root and his wife, Lydia Cowles, divorced with each one taking a second spouse. Truman Bishop Root and his wife Polly Mead Root divorced and each remarried although there is argument for and against Bishop's second marriage. Divorce in the 19th century carried a significant stigma and was difficult to get from the courts, particularly if the wife sought the divorce. New York State did grant divorce, and for a time banned remarriage by either partner. Therefore, the number of Root presumed divorces and remarriages was a surprise. Currently, divorce records are the hardest documents to find and few states, including New York State, have released them. Therefore, while it is assumed that a divorce was granted to a Root family member, I could not find any documentation to prove these divorces were given.

The research for this book uncovered a number of significant scandals. I decided that if the scandalous information surfaced in documents or newspaper accounts, I was obligated to present it in the biographies. If the information was hearsay, I did not include it in the genealogical narratives. This family history was greatly helped by the *Bolivar Breeze*, a weekly newspaper published from 1890 to 1965, being online with a search by name capability. Newspaper articles have provided a much more in-depth biography for many Root descendants. Ancestry.com continues to add more documentation and that website was a great assist in updating the Root biographies listed in the 1990 genealogy and the new biographies added to this publication. Ebay.com proved an interesting resource where I purchased documents on the bankruptcy of the J. H. Root and Son store in Bolivar in 1898 and cancelled checks signed by a number of Root family members.

One major feature of this new publication is the inclusion of a ***Reference*** list after each individual biography. This enables the reader to learn where the biographical information came from and how the documentation can be easily found and used for genealogical society membership applications. The number of photographs has increased. This is particularly true for the line of David Cartwright Root. The Lily Dale Historical Association in Lily Dale, New York was the beneficiary of the David and Marietta Tyler Root family archive donated by Agnes and Alice Evans, the granddaughters of David Root. Lily Dale provided permission for the use of the photographs for David Root and his family for which I am grateful. The archive includes a photograph of Asa Wallace Root who died in Andersonville prison. Lily Dale has possession of the three-volume diary Asa W. Root wrote during the Civil War until his death in 1864 along with letters he and his brother Albert Root wrote to their parents.

Photocopied documents used in this genealogy will be donated to an Allegany County museum to aid future researchers along with the correspondence from Root family members that formed a vital part of the 1990 publication. I regret that most of the Root family members who provided information and lent photographs for the 1990 edition have passed. However, they are relisted in this edition along with new Root family members who helped update the genealogy. Root artifacts in my possession include the original Civil War discharge document for Lyman E. Root, silver plated napkin rings for Almira Reed Root, his wife, and their daughter Lola, the rose gold and diamond cufflinks of Ernest Jerome Root and a monogrammed platter from the dinner service of Ernest J. Root and his wife, Belle Fuller Root. They, too, will be donated to a County museum along with select items of furniture dating back to the Civil War era. However, the identity of Ella whose name was monogrammed on a baby cup with the date December 25, 1873, remains unknown. All burials with the last name of Root in Bolivar's Maple Lawn Cemetery are related with the exception of the burial for an Ella Root. Genesee Township Historian Jean Milliman solved this mystery. Ella was the daughter of Allentown, New York residents Jonathan Richardson and Ada Woodard Richardson. Ella, born 1891, married Frank Marion Root of Michigan, died April 20, 1969, and was buried with her mother in Maple Lawn Cemetery. Currently, no linkage connects Ella to the Root or Richardson families who are subjects in this narrative.

My maternal grandparents, Leo C. and Ethel Bernard Root, resided in Allentown, New York from 1945 until their respective deaths. Residing on White Hill Road outside Allentown, New York was the Ralph Root family. Some members of both families resembled each other, but there was no clear documentation that they were related. Ralph Root and Leo Root both worked for the Bradley Producing Company. Research on the Root genealogy reveals that Leo C. Root was descended from

Thomas Roote who settled Hartford, Connecticut in 1637. Ralph Root was descended from John Roote who settled Farmington, Connecticut. The Farmington Roote line migrated to Connecticut from Massachusetts in 1640. Currently, it cannot be proven that these two lines are related. Three Roote brothers settled Salem, Massachusetts and those lines are also separate from the Hartford and Farmington, Connecticut lines. The most famous Root in American History remains Secretary of State and Nobel Peace Prize Winner, Elihu Root (1845-1937). Elihu Root was the great-great-great-great-great grandson of John Roote of Badby, England. John Roote accompanied his brother, Thomas, from whom we are descended, to Connecticut in 1637. Therefore, Elihu Root would have been a seventh cousin of his contemporary Bolivar Root cousins, Lyman, Hiram, Albert, Asa, Erastus, David, Bryant, Sidney, Lew, George, and Harlie.

I am delighted that the lines of descent of the Holly, Kellogg, Withey, Hulbert, and Richardson lines are now so complete. Unfortunately, even with the assist of the Internet it was not possible to find living descendants for a number of contributors to the 1990 edition. I believe my research in the 1980s was easier just using the telephone with an information search. Some current descendants did not want their data updated so those requests were honored.

It is important to remember that documenting a family's past is fraught with documentation issues. Except for New England, birth, marriage, and death records are difficult to find because states did not require documentation be kept by localities and counties until long after the Civil War. New York State did not mandate documentation for vital statistics until 1881. Divorce records are a challenge to find anywhere. Even New England vital statistics records contain errors. A case in point listed in this genealogy concerns the first wife of Solomon Root (#18). Connecticut marriage documents record that Solomon Root and Rachel Corrier were married April 16, 1772. However, Connecticut death records list Rachel Corrier Root's death as February 23, 1772. How could Solomon Root marry a woman already dead, but who gave him a daughter the same day she died? I suggest that Solomon and Rachel were married April 16, 1772 but Rachel died February 23, 1773, not 1772. Solomon remarried to Mary Hendee September 3, 1773, which leads me to believe that he quickly remarried to have a wife and mother for his six-month old daughter. Researching one's genealogical past is both fun, challenging, and confusing.

Enjoy the greatly revised Root genealogy. The 1990 Edition had 148 pages of genealogical information and 61 photographs. The 2020 edition has 540 pages of family narratives and 259 pictures. Please excuse any mistakes as none were intended. Perhaps in your reading you will discover that a friend, classmate, or neighbor is actually a relative!

William A. Paquette, Ph. D.
Professor of History

Part I | The Genealogy

Abel Root Sr. of Bolivar, New York

<u>Abbreviations:</u>

about	=	a.
aged	=	ae.
born	=	b.
died	=	d.
married	=	m.
no further information	=	***nfi.***
more information under a person's number	=	***f.***

1.

Thomas Roote, son of John Roote and Ann Russell of Badby, England, b. January 16, 1605, d. July 17, 1694; m. name of wife not known.

Thomas Roote came to the United States in 1637 and was among the first settlers of Hartford, Connecticut where he owned a considerable amount of land. He moved to Northampton, Massachusetts in 1654. Mr. Roote was employed as a farmer and a cloth weaver. Thomas Roote served as a parish deacon. All of his children were born in Hartford, Connecticut.

Children:

2. I. ***Joseph Roote***, b. a. 1640, d. April 19, 1711, m. (1) December 30, 1660 Hannah Hayes; m. (2) Mary Holton Bart. Joseph Roote had eight children by his first wife.

3. II. ***Thomas Roote***, b. a. 1644, d. January 28, 1691; m. (1) Abigail Alvord, b. October 6, 1647; m. (2) Mary Kirkland Hart. Thomas Roote had five children by his first wife.

4. III. ***John Roote***, b. January 10, 1646, d. September 19, 1677; m. a. 1676 Mehitable Hinsdale. John Roote was killed by Indians. He had one son.

5. IV. ***Jonathan Roote***, d. December 25, 1741; m. March 22, 1680 Ann Hull, d. September 4, 1746. They had six children.

6. V. ***Hezekiah Roote***, d. September 29, 1690; m. July 12, 1682 Mehitable Friary, b. 1664, d. November 7, 1689. They had four children.

7. VI. ***Jacob Roote, f.***

8. VII ***Sarah Roote***, m. March 20, 1679.

Reference: Root, James Pierce, *Root Genealogical Records, 1600-1870.* New York: R. C. Root, Anthony & Co., 1870.

7.

Jacob Roote, son of Thomas (1), b. Hartford, Connecticut, d. August 9, 1731; m. February 2, 1680 Mary Friary, b. July 24, 1662, d. February 8, 1744.

Jacob Roote was mentioned in the list of Northampton, Massachusetts freemen for February 8, 1678. He was among the first settlers of Hebron, Connecticut where he moved in 1705. His farm remained in the family for 125 years. His wife was the daughter of Sampson and Mary Daniel Friary of Deerfield, Massachusetts. All ten of their children were born in Northampton. Five of them are listed below. They resided in Hebron, Connecticut.

Children:

9. I. ***Joanna Root***, b. November 5, 1681, d. 1725; m. December 7, 1703 Samuel Pomeroy of Northampton. They had three children.

10. II. ***Daniel Root, f.***

11. III. ***Jacob Root***, b. June 15, 1687, d. 1766, ae 79 years; m. Sarah Goodale. He resided in Marlborough, Connecticut, but later relocated. They had nine children.

12. IV. ***Mary Root***, b. November 24, 1689, d. October 15, 1735, ae 45 years; m. Nathaniel Mann February 1, 1713. They had one child.

13. V. ***Margaret Root***, b. October 1691, d. June 1793 ae 101 years; m. (1) June 25, 1727 John Warner; m. (2) a Miss Trumbull. They resided in Marlborough, Connecticut.

Reference: Root, James Pierce, *Root Genealogical Records, 1600-1870.* New York: R. C. Root, Anthony & Co., 1870.

10.

Daniel Root, son of Jacob (7), grandson of Thomas (1), b. Northampton, Massachusetts October 2, 1694; m. January 14, 1714, his wife's name is not known. The town record stated that his wife was 18 years and one day on her wedding day. They resided in Hebron, Connecticut.

Children:

14. I. ***Daniel Root, f.***

15. II. ***Ebenezer Root***, b. May 22, 1717, d. March 13, 1777, ae. 59 years; m. August 25, 1737 Rachel Skinner. They resided in Hebron, Connecticut and had seven children.

16. III. ***Rachel Root***, b. December 28, 1721; m. September 7, 1737 Zerubbabel Rollo.

Reference: Root, James Pierce, *Root Genealogical Records, 1600-1870.* New York: R. C. Root, Anthony & Co., 1870.

14.

Deacon Daniel Root, son of Daniel (10), grandson of Jacob (7), b. Hebron, Connecticut February 11, 1715, d. April 21, 1763, ae 48; m. Hannah, last name not known. They resided in Hebron, Connecticut.

Children:

17. I. ***Daniel Root***, b. March 2, 1746, d. 1826 ae. 80 years; m. (1) September 14, 1769 Mindwell Root, b. June 28, 1748; m. (2) Widow Gillet. He had six children and moved to Franklin, New York.

18. II. ***Solomon Root, f.***

19. III. ***Hannah Root***, b. January 5, 1751.

20. IV. ***Joshua Root***, b. July 8, 1753; m. September 28, 1775 Sarah Chapman. They had eleven children.

21. V. ***Naomi Root***, b. April 9, 1756.

22. VI. ***Ezekiel Root***, b. September 12, 1759; m. November 13, 1764 Deborah Buck. They had three children.

23. VII ***Benjamin Root***, b. May 22, 1762, d. May 31, 1762.

Reference: Root, James Pierce, *Root Genealogical Records,* 1600-*1870.* New York: R. C. Root, Anthony & Co., 1870.

18.

Solomon Root, son of Daniel (14), grandson of Daniel (10), b. Hebron, Connecticut May 19, 1749, death date not known; m. (1) Hebron, Connecticut, April 16, 1772, Rachel Corrier, d. February 23, 1773; m. (2) Hebron, Connecticut, September 3, 1733, Mary Hendee of Coventry, Connecticut, b. Coventry, Connecticut January 14, 1750, d. Madison, New York July 28, 1838.

They resided in Hebron, Connecticut; then moved to Madison and Unadilla, New York. Mary Hendee Root was buried in Madison Village Cemetery in Madison, New York. It is not known where Solomon Root was buried. Their son, Solomon Root, was buried with his family in Madison Village Cemetery. Son Justus Root and his family were buried in the Indian Opening Cemetery in Madison, New York.

Children: (by first marriage)

24. I. ***Rachel Root***, b. February 23, 1773; m. a Mr. Littlefield.

Children: (by second marriage)

25. I. ***Solomon Root***, b. January 5, 1774; resided in Madison, New York.

26. II. ***Elijah Root***; resided in Oneida, Michigan.

27. III. ***Benjamin Root***. It is believed he resided in Pennsylvania.

28. IV. ***Abel Root**, f.*

29. V. ***Ezekiel Root***; resided in Orleans, New York.

30. VI. ***John Root***; resided in Monroe County, Michigan.

31. VII. ***Justus Root***, b. September 12, 1790, d. February 2, 1867, ae. 76 years; m. March 24, 1816 Sarah Griswold, b. October 23, 1798, b. October 23, 1798, d. September 9, 1862, ae. 63 years. They resided in Bouckville, New York and had nine children.

32. VIII. ***Polly Root.***

33. IX. ***Lydia Root***; m. a Mr. Smith.

Reference: Root, James Pierce, *Root Genealogical Records, 1600-1870.* New York: R. C. Root, Anthony & Co., 1870; Connecticut Marriage Index 1620-1926; Madison Village Cemetery Records, Madison, New York; Indian Opening Cemetery Records, Madison, New York.

28.

Abel Root, Sr., son of Solomon (18), grandson of Daniel (14), birth place not known, birth date not known but after 1774 and before 1790, place of death not known, death date not known but after 1845; m. place of marriage not known, marriage date not known, Penelope Cartwright b. Rhode Island October 7, 1782, d. Angelica, New York 1851.

It is not known how, when or where Abel Root and Penelope Cartwright met. Their first two children, Abel Jr. and David, were born in Rensselaer County, New York. The second two children, probably twins, Truman and Huldah Penelope, were born in Oneida County. Son Franklin Root was born in Madison County, New York and their last child, James H. Root, was born in Bolivar, New York. Abel Root, Sr. resided in 1810 in Berlin, Rensselaer County, New York with his wife and two eldest sons. In 1819, Abel Root, Sr. explored the area around Bolivar, New York. Abel Root and his family were recorded in the 1820 United States Census for Madison, New York. In February 1822, they moved to Scio in Allegany County from Unadilla, New York. In 1824, Abel Root moved his family to nearby Bolivar where their youngest son was born. Abel Root, Sr. purchased lot 54 in Bolivar Township, the area west of the intersection of the highways linking Bolivar to Richburg and Wellsville near Maple Lawn Cemetery on April 25, 1823. Abel Root, Sr. and his family were recorded in the 1830 United States Census for Bolivar, New York. Their eldest son, Abel, Jr., was recorded separately as he had married and started his own family by 1830. In the 1840 United States Census, Abel, Sr. was still residing in Bolivar with his wife, daughter Huldah Penelope and youngest son James. Abel, Sr. and his wife moved to Illinois in or after 1845. The reason is unknown, but all six of their children remained in Bolivar.

By 1850 Penelope Cartwright Root returned to Allegany County residing with her son Franklin and his wife in Angelica, New York as recorded in the 1850 United States Census. Penelope died in 1851 and was buried in an unmarked grave in Bolivar's Maple Lawn Cemetery. It is possible that Abel Root, Sr. was deceased by 1850 but no documentation can be found for his death or burial site. Abel Root, Sr.'s death year has been incorrectly recorded by some as having occurred in 1836 in Sweden, Monroe County, New York. The Abel Root of Sweden, New York was the son of William Root of Hebron, Connecticut and a distant relative, but he is not Abel Root, Sr. of Bolivar. Penelope Cartwright Root was the daughter of Bryant Cartwright, Jr. (1739-1817), a veteran of the Revolutionary War, and Elizabeth Hall (1740-1837), both of Hopkinton, Rhode Island. Penelope was a descendant of Edward Cartwright of Dittisham, Devonshire, England who settled Nantucket Island in 1672. The Cartwrights were Sabbatarian Baptists, later known as Seventh Day Adventists. It is believed that Penelope Cartwright Root's great-grandmother, Ruth West Cartwright, was a direct descendant of Lady Mary Boleyn, sister of Queen Anne Boleyn, second wife of Henry VIII. Penelope's brothers, Bryant III, Jabez, William, Theodaty, and Samuel and sister Elizabeth all settled in Allegany County.

Children:

34. I. ***Abel Root, Jr.**, f.*

35. II. ***David Cartwright Root**, f.*

36. III. ***Truman Bishop Root**, f.*

37. IV. ***Huldah Penelope Root**, f.*

38. V. ***Franklin B. Root**, f.*

39. VI. ***James Harlow Root**, f.*

References: Root, James Pierce, *Root Genealogical Records, 1600-1870.* New York: R.C. Root, Anthony and Co., 1870; United States Federal Census Records: 1810, 1820, 1830, 1840, 1850; Western New York Land Transactions, 1825-1835; Rhode Island, Births, 1636-1930; Mack, Stanley, *The Family and Ancestors of Earl Cartwright and Dorothy Maria Beaman of Nantucket, Massachusetts and Some of His Descendants.* Duluth, Minnesota, 1936; Beers, F. W., *History of Allegany County, NY, 1806-1879.* New York: F. W. Beers & Co., 1879; undated letter from Hattie Root Homer (daughter of James Harlow Root) to Alice and Agnes Evans; Maple Lawn Cemetery Records, Bolivar, New York.

First Generation of Descent from Abel Root, Sr.

34.

Abel Root, Jr., son of Abel, Sr. (28), grandson of Solomon (18), b. Rensselaer County, New York a. 1807, d. Bolivar April 9, 1878 ae. 71 years; m. (1) Polly or Mary Polly Scott in 1826, b. a. 1806, d. Bolivar January 28, 1875 from congestion of the brain; m. (2) place and date unknown, Frances E. (Bancroft).

Abel Root, Jr. and his younger brothers were among the first settlers of the hamlet of Kossuth, just east of Bolivar along a stream that bears the name *Root Hollow Creek.* Abel purchased land in lot 46 of Bolivar Township on February 6, 1827, an area between Bolivar village and Kossuth. He later bought land in lot 38 in Kossuth. The 1875 New York State Census recorded that Abel Root, Jr.'s farm consisted of 110 acres with seventeen acres each in unimproved land and woodland, fourteen acres plowed, thirty-five acres in pasture, and fifteen acres in meadow. The farm produced thirty tons of hay, fifty bushels of wheat and 275 bushels of oats. Fifteen cherry trees produced six bushels of fruit while fifty apple trees produced 90 bushels of apples. The farm processed three barrels of cider, fifteen gallons of molasses, and 60 pounds of maple sugar. Abel Root's farm had twenty-eight sheep producing 84 pounds of wools. There were seven milking cows, one bull, and one heifer producing six gallons of milk and 200 pounds of butter. The rest of the farm animals included two horses, five pigs, and a large number of chickens. The farm was valued at $3000 with an additional $500 the value of farm dwellings. Livestock was valued at $535, tools at $170 in value, and the sale of farm products for 1875 amounted to $245.

In the 1830 United States Census Abel Root, Jr. resided on his farm with his wife, a daughter, and an unnamed male teenager who may have been a farm helper. The 1840 US Census records Abel, Jr. and his wife residing at their farm with three daughters and two sons. In the 1850 US Census Abel Root's eldest daughter had married and left home leaving two sons and two daughters at home along with a worker, Andrew Howard. The New York State Census for 1855 records the Root household comprising Abel, his wife, sons Lyman and Hiram, daughter Mary Jane, and niece Charlotte Root (daughter of Truman Bishop Root). Daughter Elizabeth Root Withey died just before the 1860 US Census. In 1860 residing with Abel and Polly Root were son Hiram, son-in-law Charles Withey and grandchildren Charles S, Emma, and Jesse Withey. Charles Withey remarried by the time of the 1865 New York State Census leaving just two Withey grandchildren, Emma and Jesse, residing with Abel and Polly Root. Abel and Polly Root resided alone in the 1870 US Census.

With Polly death's in 1875, Abel Root continued to reside on the farm with his grandsons, Jesse Withey and Elmer Holly (son of Minerva Root Holly), and granddaughter Emma Withey Sawyer and her husband Rufus Sawyer. Abel Root was one of the original trustees of Bolivar's United Methodist Church. Polly or Mary Polly Scott was the daughter of John Scott, Sr., born in Pepperell, Massachusetts January 18, 1877, d. March 22, 1850 in Bolivar and his second wife, Jane Polly Rogers Scott, b. a. 1778 and died September 21, 1847 in Bolivar. No graves are recorded for Mrs. Root's parents in Maple Lawn Cemetery. Polly Scott Root had two sisters, Samantha and Caroline, and six brothers, Benjamin, John Jr., Elias, Hiram, Erastus, and Horace. She had a half-sister, also named Polly, and two half-brothers, Jonathon and James, from her father's first marriage to Freelove Boyden. Polly's brother Elias was the father of four daughters, Asenath, Philura, Polly, and Helen, and five sons, Alanson, Leander, Erastus, Sanford, and Edgar. Elias' five sons and four sons-in-law all served in the Civil War and survived. Polly Root's nephew, Sanford Scott, married Mary Martin Scott who was affectionately known in the Bolivar community as *Aunt Mate* and was Bolivar's last Union widow dying in 1940. Abel Root, Jr. remarried sometime after the June 1, 1875 New York State Census.

The mention of a second wife surfaces in Abel Root, Jr.'s 1876 will. For three decades this author could not find any further reference to *Frances E. Root*. I offer a circumstantial case suggesting that Frances E. Bancroft was the second wife of Abel Root, Jr. Recently, a grave for Frances E. Bancroft, wife of A. E. Root, was revealed among the records for Union Cemetery in Fort Edward, New York near the Vermont border and next to Rensselaer County, New York where Abel Root, Jr. was born. She was born in Fort Edward on April 6, 1857, which means that she would have been about nineteen years of age if she was the one who married Abel, Jr. Frances died December 25, 1887 in Fort Edward and except for her tombstone; there is no mention or surviving documentation of her marriage to A. E. Root. I did not learn the middle name of Abel Root, Jr., but the middle name of his eldest son, Lyman, was Eleasure, which could have been Abel's as well. The family of Frances E. Bancroft Root's father was from Hartford, Connecticut where the Root family originally settled and her mother's family was from Rhode Island where the Cartwrights resided. The 1880 US Census lists Frances under her maiden name residing with her widowed mother. Even though considerable distance separated Washington County, New York from Allegany County, New York, it was possible that the families kept in touch either with each other or with other friends and/or family who suggested Frances E. Bancroft to Abel Root, Jr. as a wife as part of a financial arrangement. Frances' father was already deceased and the Bancroft family was not financially well off.

Abel Root, Jr. was living alone and needed someone to take care of him. Frances E. Root, as the widow, received 1/3 of Abel Root, Jr.'s estate. The rest of the estate was divided among his four surviving children with specific household bequests to his two surviving daughters, Minerva Root Hawley Neff and Mary Jane Root Barber, grandson Jesse Withey, granddaughter Emma Withey Sawyer, and daughter-in-law Almira Reed Root. Son Lyman E. Root and Edwin Kilbury were the estate's executors. The bequest to Almira Root, wife of Lyman Root, was a dresser with mirror, which survives going to Leo Root, Almira's grandson then to his daughter Dorothy Root Paquette, and now to this author. Abel Root, Jr. and (Mary) Polly Root were buried in Bolivar's Maple Lawn Cemetery. Their markers were restored by the author.

Children (all from first marriage):

40. I. ***Minerva Root, f.***

41. II. ***Elizabeth Root, f.***

42. III. ***Lyman Eleasure. Root, f.***

43. IV. ***Mary Jane Root, f.***

44. V. ***Hiram James Root, f.***

45. VI. ***Jamila Root***. Mentioned in a letter from Alice Evans to Asa P. Root dated June 4, 1931 from Lily Dale, New York that Jamila was scalded to death. There is a third burial in the Abel Root plot, but without a marker. It is possible that the burial with Abel and Polly Root was Jamila's.

References: US Census Records: 1830, 1840, 1850, 1860, 1870; New York State Census Records: 1855, 1865, 1875. Maple Lawn Cemetery Records, Bolivar, New York; Union Cemetery Records, Fort Edward, New York; Western New York Land Transactions, 1825-1835; New York Wills and Probate Records, 1659-1999 (May 27, 1878); Beers, F. W., *History of Allegany County, NY, 1806-1879.* New York: F. W. Beers & Co., 1879; June 4, 1931 letter from Alice Evans to Asa P. Root of Bolivar.

35.

David Cartwright Root, son of Abel, Sr. (28), grandson of Solomon (18), b. Rensselaer County, New York November 30, 1808, d. Bolivar, New York July 14, 1890; m. Marietta Tyler February 26, 1830, b. place unknown, February 26, 1815, d. Bolivar, New York May 10, 1887.

David Root resided with his father until 1829 when he purchased land on lot 38 in Kossuth across the highway from the farm of his eldest brother, Abel Root, Jr. He took up residence there in 1831. In 1880 David Cartwright Root's farm consisted of 115 acres valued at $2000 with an additional $50 in value for farm equipment and $260 in value for farm livestock. The farm produced 2,250 gallons of milk and 350 pounds of butter. The annual sale of products from the David Root farm amounted to $525 in 1879. The farm straddled both sides of the highway (state highway 417) extending along the north side to Harry Parker and Thomas Richardson farms. Along the southern boundary of the farm gushed a splendid spring of pure cold water known as *Cold Spring*. The farm was leased for oil and at one time the property boasted dozens of successfully drilled wells with derricks. Marietta Root impressed people with her intimacy with departed spirits who communicated through her while Mrs. Root was in a trance and also informed her where both oil and water were located. All of Mrs. Root's oil and water well predictions resulted in producing water or oil wells. The family of six remained an intact family unit until the 1852 marriage of the eldest daughter Huldah to James Curtiss of Bolivar.

Huldah would be the only child of David and Marietta Root to remain a Bolivar resident. The Civil War claimed their youngest son, Asa, but the eldest son, Albert, returned home after the Civil War residing in Ceres, New York until his first wife died. Albert moved to Washington, DC in 1872 taking up permanent residence there until his death. Their youngest daughter, Elosica, and her husband, Addison Evans, left Bolivar in 1870 for Missouri and Illinois. Elosica and her twin daughters moved back to Bolivar after the death of Addison Evans. David Cartwright Root was known in the family as *Uncle David.* His obituary described him as one of the gentlest and easy-going men in the area who was well liked by everyone. Marietta Tyler Root was the daughter of Christopher and Polly Cowles Tyler; one of Bolivar, New York's founding families, as were the Roots.

The Tyler family resided in Friendship, New York in 1820, which included Bolivar. They relocated to Hinsdale, New York by 1830 as noted in the US Census and to Keating, Pennsylvania by1840 when another US Census was taken. Marietta was one of at least seven children born to Christopher and Polly Tyler. Two of Marietta's siblings, Hannah and Chester, died young and were buried in Bolivar's Maple Lawn Cemetery along with her parents. A sister, Alceba, and two brothers, Stowell and Nathaniel, and their families settled in Farmers Valley, Pennsylvania. The fate of Marietta's oldest brother, Amasa Tyler, remains undocumented. Marietta was described by her contemporaries as a kindly old woman with an established reputation as a root and herb doctor and a successful mid-wife. She collected the roots, herbs, leaves, and barks used in the preparations of her medicines and many residents of Bolivar Township praised their gratitude for the ministrations from her generous hands. She was an ardent spiritualist. Spiritualism was practiced by her daughters Huldah Curtiss and Elosica Evans and later by her granddaughters Agnes and Alice Evans. In 1883 spiritualists made their headquarters with Huldah Root Curtis.

It is not known if the death of David and Marietta's youngest son, Asa Wallace Root, in Andersonville Prison in 1864 during the Civil War, increased the family's interest in Spiritualism in order to contact Asa after his death, but it was probable. Both daughters and the two granddaughters were sometime residents of Lily Dale, New York the center of Spiritualism, where communication with the departed was believed more easily facilitated with the living. A number of descendants of David and Marietta Root professed to have psychic abilities, among them the late Tracy Rose Root Martin. Mr. and Mrs. Root were buried in Bolivar's Maple Lawn Cemetery.

Children:

46. I. ***Huldah Jane Root, f.***

47. II. ***Albert Lovice Root, f.***

48. III. ***Asa Wallace Root, f.***

49. IV. ***Elosica Hannah Root, f.***

References: US Census: 1840, 1850, 1860, 1870, 1880; New York State Census: 1855, 1865, 1875. Maple Lawn Cemetery Records, Bolivar, New York; Beers, F. W. *History of Allegany County, New York, 1806-1879.* New York: F.W. Beers & Co., 1879; *Bolivar Breeze, 1891-1965*, selected issues; *Christopher Tyler* by Dr. William Paquette, BRAG Newsletter, April 2015.

36.

Truman Bishop Root, son of Abel, Sr. (28), grandson of Solomon (18), b. Oneida County, New York February 12, 1812, d. Bolivar, New York June 6, 1892, ae. 80 years, 3 months, and 10 days from rheumatoid conditions and apoplexy; m. a. 1835 (1) probably Bolivar, date unknown, Polly Mead, b. Cherry Valley, New York March 11, 1815, d. Bolivar, New York April 22, 1894, divorced, date unknown; (2) place unknown, date unknown, Annie Smith Moore, b. place not known, b. April 5, 1813, d. Bolivar, New York April 11, 1892.

Truman Bishop Root's name has been incorrectly transcribed as *Freeman B. Root.* Careful examination of the cursive handwriting reveals that the *T* in Truman was incorrectly recorded as an *F* and the lines of the *u* were read as two *es*. Over time Truman Bishop Root was usually referred to as Bishop Root. Truman Bishop Root was the twin brother of his sister, Huldah Penelope Root Kellogg. No record exists of Bishop Root owning land. He worked as a farmer and as a carpenter. During the marriage of Bishop and Polly Root, ten children were born. Sometime after the July 1860 US Census was recorded, Bishop and Polly Root separated and divorced. No document of divorce can currently be found. New York State law made it very difficult to divorce. The grounds for divorce in the mid-19th century were habitual drunkenness, adultery, non-age, bigamy, insanity, fraud, and physical incapacity. Divorce decrees were granted by the New York State Legislature and denied either party the right to remarry. No information currently exists to clarify the circumstances surrounding the divorce of Bishop and Polly Root.

Descendants of Annie Smith Moore contest the legitimacy of her remarriage to Bishop Root. According to the New York State Census taken in June of 1865, Bishop had remarried to Annie Smith Moore and she was listed in that census as Annie Root. Polly Mead Root also remarried to Horace Hitchcock of Bolivar. Their date and place of remarriage are unknown. The 1865 New York State Census records Bishop Root married and residing with him, his wife Annie, and two of her children, Mary Moore and James Moore. In the 1870 US Census Anna is listed under the name Root, but she no longer resided with Bishop Root. She resided with her daughter and son-in-law William and Margaret Moore Smith in West Clarksville, New York. The last census for which Anna's name appeared was the 1880 US Census and she lived with the same daughter and son-in-law, but in Portville, New York and she was recorded under the name Moore. Annie and her first husband, James Moore, had nine children. There was some dispute among Annie Smith Moore's descendants as to whether or not her first husband, James Moore, was really deceased permitting her remarriage. Moore descendants, who believed that James Moore was alive after 1850, could not find a document of divorce for James and Annie Smith Moore in Allegany County, New York or in Potter and Jefferson Counties in Pennsylvania. A James Moore residing in Jefferson County Pennsylvania after 1850 had married a Tirza Kinne. Anna died in Bolivar on April 11, 1892 at the home of daughter Louise Jane Moore Mead and she was buried in Bolivar's Maple Lawn Cemetery.

Correspondence on ancestry.com indicated that descendants of Anna Smith Moore retain correspondence about the family's genealogy written by Annie Moore, but nothing in those letters referred to her marriage to Bishop Root. Polly Mead Root and Horace Hitchcock could not be found in the 1865 New York State Census. Both are listed in the 1870 US Census and as husband and wife. Polly and Horace Hitchcock are both listed in the 1875 New York State Census and the 1880 US Census. Horace, born in 1812, was previously married to Betsey Dowd who died May 1, 1863 and was buried in Maple Lawn Cemetery. Horace and Betsey Hitchcock had six children. Horace, a widower, was legally free to remarry. Horace Hitchcock disappeared on September 29, 1888. He suffered from dementia and frequently disappeared for a day or two before coming back home. In September he disappeared and did not return. A search found his body. Horace had three bullet holes in his head, two below the right eye and one in the forehead. The Smith and Wesson, which killed him, was found inside his coat pocket.

The newspaper, the *Allegany Democrat,* called the death a suicide. Horace Hitchcock's death date was October 17, 1888. The death was never investigated, but the question remains how could someone shoot themselves three times in the head and put the revolver neatly into their breast coat pocket? Bishop Root died on June 6, 1892 in Bolivar last residing with his eldest daughter Elizabeth Root Garthwait. Polly Mead Root Hitchcock died at the home of her daughter, Mrs. Olivia Pire, on April 22, 1894. She had been living with the Pire family at least since the 1892 New York State Census. Polly's obituary identifies her as Mrs. Polly Hitchcock, names her ten children, but made no mention of either marriage or any of her step-children. Polly and Bishop Root were buried together with a shared tombstone in Bolivar's Maple Lawn Cemetery.

Children (all from first marriage):

50. I. ***Elizabeth A. Root, f.***

51. II. ***David Buel Root, f.***

52. III. ***Bryant Hebron Root, f.***

53. IV. ***Arzulla D. Root, f.***

54. V. ***Erastus F. Root, f.***

55. VI. ***Charlotte Root, f.***

56. VII. ***Sidney Leroy Root, f.***

57. VIII. ***Mary A. Root, f.***

58. IX. ***Olivia Root, f.***

59. X. ***Arthur Llewellyn Root, f.***

References: US Census: 1840, 1850, 1860, 1870, 1880; New York State Census: 1855, 1865, 1875, 1892; *The Curious Case of Bishop Root* by Dr. William Paquette, BRAG Newsletter, July 2013; *Bolivar Breeze, 1891-1965*, selected issues; *The Allegany Democrat*, October 3, 1888; NYS Death Certificates: Bishop Root, Annie Moore; F. W. Beers, *History of Allegany County, New York, 1806-1879.* New York: F. W. Beers & Co., 1879.

37.

Huldah Penelope Root, daughter of Abel, Sr. (28), granddaughter of Solomon (18), b. Oneida County, New York February 11/12, 1812, d. Bolivar, New York July 29, 1851 ae. 39 years, 5 months, 18 days; m. Bolivar, New York November 12, 1836 Loring Grant Kellogg, b. Bolivar, New York May 3, 1814, d. Bolivar, New York April 16, 1858.

Huldah Penelope Root Kellogg and Loring Grant Kellogg were buried in Bolivar's Maple Lawn Cemetery with markers in evidence. In the few surviving documents about the children of Abel Root, Sr. and Penelope Cartwright Root, Huldah Penelope Root was referred to as Penelope Root. Other than her name no information about this daughter of Abel, Sr. and Penelope could be found thirty years ago. Given her birth date, Huldah Penelope Root was a twin sister of Truman Bishop Root, although no mention of fraternal twins in this generation was ever mentioned. Loring Grant Kellogg was a lumberman and farmer who resided in Bolivar.

In 1855 his lumber business was valued at $1500 and had four employees. The mill was powered by water and produced over 200,000 boards. He was a member of the Methodist Episcopal Church and in politics a Whig. Huldah and Loring Kellogg had seven children. The Kellogg family was not recorded on the 1850 US Census. The cause of Huldah Penelope Root Kellogg's death in 1851 is not known. Loring Grant Kellogg remarried April 4, 1852 to Wirt, New York resident Hepzibah Lord, b. 1810, d. 1889. Hepzibah Lord Kellogg was buried in the Dimmick Cemetery in Richburg, New York. They had two sons. Loring Wallace Kellogg, b. Wirt, New York July 10, 1853 and Abram Kellogg, b. Wirt November 30, 1854. The 1855 New York State Census does not record Loring Grant Kellogg, his second wife, their children, or his children from his first marriage except for son Jasper Kellogg who was listed as a boarder with his maternal uncle, James H. Root.

The 1856 State Census for Iowa records Loring (Lorain), his second wife, his children from his first marriage: Ebenezer, Orlando, Albert, James, and Elmer, and his two sons from his second marriage: Wallace and Abram. It is not known why Loring Kellogg moved to Iowa, but he owned a farm in Oakland, Iowa while there. Their time in Iowa was brief because Loring Kellogg died in Bolivar just two years later. Why most of the Kellogg family returned to the Bolivar by 1858 is not known. In the 1860 US Census Hepzibah and her sons Wallace and Abram were in Wirt, New York residing with her parents. Loring Kellogg's sons from his first marriage, Ebenezer and Jasper lived with James H. Root in Bolivar who was their maternal uncle. Elmer resided with his paternal grandfather in Friendship, New York. Orlando and James Kellogg remained in Iowa. Francis Albertus was not recorded in the 1860 US Census. Loring Wallace Kellogg, known as Wallace, never married and was last recorded alive in the 1925 New York State Census residing in Wirt, New York with the Roy Woodard family. Abram Kellogg moved to Shinglehouse, Pennsylvania, married and raised a family there. His death date is not known, but there is a marker in Maple Grove Cemetery in Shinglehouse for him. It is believed that Abram's half-brother, Francis Albertus and his wife Abigail, were buried in unmarked graves in the Abram Kellogg lot.

Children:

60. I. ***Ebenezer Abel Kellogg***, b. Bolivar September 23, 1837, d. Bolivar, April 1861 unmarried and was believed buried in Maple Lawn Cemetery in Bolivar, but this cannot be confirmed. In the 1860 US Census he resided with his maternal uncle, James H. Root.

61. II. ***Orlando Ives Kellogg***, b. Bolivar May 12, 1839, d. date and place unknown; married in Clinton, Iowa, but disappeared in the 1870s.

62. III. ***Francis Albertus Kellogg, f.***

63. IV. ***James Fayette Kellogg, f.***

64. V. ***Elmer D. Cass Kellogg, f.***

65. VI. ***Royal Jasper Kellogg, f.***

66. VII. ***Huldah Francelia Kellogg***, b. Bolivar November 9, 1847, d. Bolivar September 15, 1850, ae. two years, ten months, and seven days and was buried in Maple Lawn Cemetery with her parents with a separate marker.

References: US Census: 1840, 1850, 1860; New York State Census: 1855; Iowa State Census: 1856; US Selected Federal Census Non-Population Schedules, 1850-1880; Maple Lawn Cemetery Records, Bolivar, New York; Hopkins, Timothy, *The Kelloggs in the Old World and the New*. San Francisco, California: Sunset Press, 1903; *Finding Penelope Root* by Dr. William Paquette, BRAG Newsletter, October 2014.

38.

Franklin B. Root, son of Abel, Sr. (28) and grandson of Solomon (18), b. Madison County, New York March 1818, d. Bolivar, New York May 10, 1905 from influenza and cardiac failure; m. (1) date and place not known, but by 1850, Jane Voakes or Vokes, b. England March 7, 1828, d. Angelica, New York October 23, 1889 from organic heart disease ae. 61 years, 7 months, and 16 days; m. (2) Belfast, New York September 20, 1896 Mrs. Abigail Patterson, b. February 1838, d. after 1900 and before Franklin Root's death in 1905.

In an 1895 interview with the *Bolivar Breeze*, Franklin Root remembered that when the Root family came to Bolivar in 1819 there were only six families living along the wood's road between Ceres and Friendship, New York. Bolivar consisted of six log houses. The settlers found ample deer, small game, and trout to sustain them. In 1849, after thirty years of residence in Bolivar, Franklin Root moved from Bolivar to Angelica to work as a carpenter on the construction of the Allegany County Jail when

Angelica was the county seat of Allegany County. He remained in Angelica the rest of his life where he was always employed in the carpentry trade. Frank Root does not appear on the 1840 US Census. In the 1850 US Census Frank Root resided with his first wife and his mother in Angelica. By the time of the 1855 New York State Census, Frank and Jane Root had two daughters, Frances and Florence. In the 1860 US Census their family had increased to include a son, George. The Root family remained at five people in the 1865 New York State Census. Daughter Frances E. Root cannot be traced after the 1865 New York State Census and was not listed in the 1870 US Census. Daughter Florence was a widow living at home in the 1880 US Census. By the time of the 1892 New York State Census, Franklin Root resided alone. His first wife had died in 1889 and his children Florence and George had moved out of New York State.

The Root family resided at 44 Olean Street in Angelica on three acres of land valued at $1500 in 1870 with farm animals adding an additional $100 in value. Franklin Root died at the home of his great-niece, Libbie Root Ennis, on Boss Street in Bolivar while visiting family and friends in the community in 1905. He was a widower at the time of his passing and was buried in Angelica in the Until the Dawn of the Day Cemetery without a marker in evidence. Frank Root's first wife was the daughter of George Voakes who was born in England and in the 1850 US Census resided in Caneadea, New York where he farmed. The identity of Jane's mother is not known, but her mother was also born in England. George Voakes remarried to Esther Bacon before the 1850 US Census. George Voakes died November 7, 1852 and was buried in an unmarked grave in Allen Cemetery in Allegany County. Esther Bacon Voakes died January 17, 1864 and was buried in Wilcox Cemetery in Genoa, New York. Jane and her three sisters were mentioned in Esther Bacon Voakes' will with each step-daughter receiving $150 and a portion of household goods. Jane Voakes Root was buried in the Angelica's Until the Dawn of the Day Cemetery with a marker in evidence. There was a third burial in the lot, but that person's identity is not known. Abigail Patterson, Frank's second wife, was previously married to Delbert Patterson, a blacksmith from Cuba, New York. Delbert and Abigail Patterson only appear on the New York State Census records for 1855, 1865, and 1892 and cannot be located in any US Census records. It is assumed that Mr. Patterson died sometime after 1892 and before Abigail's second marriage in 1896. Abigail's maiden name is not known and currently there is no evidence of any children from her first marriage. Abigail's death date and place of burial are not known.

Children (all from first marriage):

67. I. ***Frances E. Root***, b. a. 1852 Angelica, New York. She was recorded in the New York State Census Records for 1855 and 1865 and the US Census for 1860. No further information can be found on Frances E. Root. It is possible that the third burial in the Franklin and Jane Root lot is for Frances E. Root although there is no documentation to support this conclusion.

68. II. ***Florence Root**, f.*

69. III. ***George H. Root, f.***

References: US Census: 1850, 1860, 1870, 1880, 1900; New York State Census: 1855, 1865, 1875, 1892; New York State Marriage Index, 1881-1967: 1896; New York State Death Index, 1880-1956: 1889, 1905; US Selected Federal Census Non-Population Schedules, 1850-1880, 1870; *Bolivar Breeze, 1891-1965*, selected issues; Until the Day of the Dawn Cemetery Records, Angelica, New York; Beers, F. W. *History of Allegany County, New York, 1806-1879*. New York: F. W. Beers & Co., 1879; New York Wills and Probate Records 1859-1999 for Esther Voakes.

39.

James Harlow Root, son of Abel, Sr. (28), grandson of Solomon (18), b. Bolivar April 1825, d. Olean, New York June 17, 1903; m. (1) probably Bolivar Mary W., last name not known, b. England August 23, 1825, d. Bolivar, New York April 5, 1863 ae. 37 years, 7 months, and 13 days; m. (2) 1864 Desdemona Procter Patridge or Partridge, b. Andover, New York, August 23, 1827, d. Olean, New York February 2, 1902.

James Harlow Root was the first recorded birth in Bolivar, New York. For many years he owned and operated a dry goods store, J. H. Root & Son, on Main Street across from the Masonic Temple; a location later occupied by Stimson and Bell Hardware. In February 1896, the store had undergone an extensive renovation. A partition was erected separating the main store from a carpet room in the back. The front area measured 30 feet by 60 feet and the carpet room measured 30 feet by 30 feet. The store's new look included wall paper, oak woodwork, and Welsh back lighting. The business office was located to the left of the main entrance. Unfortunately, the expensive renovations may have contributed to the store's bankruptcy a mere two years later on June 30, 1898. Surviving court documents from the following creditors: Western Union Telegraph Company of Bolivar, New York, Harriet H. Eaton, Dr. J. H. Wasson, William H. Smith, Isaac Beir and William Gormly, and Lewis P. Ross detail the unpaid items and their value in the bankruptcy law suit. The business was placed into the receivership of Wilbur P. Cook by court order September 25, 1899. Wilber P. Cook gave a final accounting to the Allegany County Court in Friendship, New York on July 27, 1900. The building was sold under a foreclosure sale October 19, 1899 to Hoyt and Cowles for $1,485. The amount covered the mortgage and the expenses of the foreclosure. J. H. Root had already retired by the time of the sale. His son, Harlie J. Root, accepted a mercantile job with Maston & Co. of Buffalo, New York in January 1899 and sold his Bolivar residence and a vacant lot on Friendship Street for $700. For many years James Harlow Root served the Bolivar community as first secretary for the Bolivar Cemetery Association. There is little information about Mr. Root's first wife. They did not have any children and were first recorded as a married couple in the 1850 US Census. Between 1850 and 1863, when Mrs. Root died, James and Mary Root took in several of his Kellogg nephews whose parents died young. Mrs. Mary Root was buried in the oldest section of Bolivar's Maple Lawn Cemetery with a marker in evidence.

James Harlow Root's second wife was Desdemona Proctor Patridge or Partridge from Wellsville, New York. Desdemona was the granddaughter of Jabez Cartwright, his mother (Penelope Cartwright Root)'s brother. Desdemona's parents were Ephraim Proctor and Mary Cartwright Root. Therefore, James and Desdemona were first cousins once removed. Desdemona's first husband was James Partridge, b. December 10, 1827, d. October 12, 1862. James Partridge enlisted as a private in the 154th Infantry, Company C and it is believed died during the Civil War and was buried in the last row of Wellsville's Woodlawn Cemetery with a marker in evidence. For unknown reasons Desdemona later spelled her first husband's last name as Patridge. The change in spelling was continued by James and Desdemona's two sons, Henry and James. In the 1860 US Census James and Desdemona Procter Partridge had three children: James, Henry, and Ida. Ida was b. a. 1857, but there is no further mention of her. It is assumed she died as a young child and was probably buried in an unmarked grave next to her father James Partridge, but no record for her burial there exists. When Desdemona remarried her two sons moved with her to Bolivar. James and Desdemona Root resided on Main Street in a ten-room house on a ¾ acre next to the Lyman Root residence and blacksmith business. It is possible that this residence survives and is the residence converted into apartments to the right of the current grocery store parking lot and before the Pioneer Oil Museum. Desdemona's sons from her first marriage were sometimes incorrectly listed on New York State and US Census records under the name of Root. James and Desdemona Root had fraternal twins born in 1864, Harlie and Hattie or Harriet.

Truman Bryant Cartwright, a wealthy Alfred/Andover farmer was a first cousin of Desdemona's mother. Mr. Cartwright, a widower without children, took an interest in Desdemona and her family, moved to Bolivar, and bequeathed substantial amounts of money to each member of the James Root family when he died in 1879. Truman Bryant Cartwright was buried in Bolivar's Maple Lawn Cemetery. A marker is in evidence. By 1902, both Mr. and Mrs. Root were in failing health and moved to Olean, New York taking up residence with their daughter, Harriet Root Homer. Desdemona died there from heart disease and was buried in an unmarked grave next to her first husband in Wellsville's Woodlawn Cemetery. James Harlow Root died from paralysis and softening of the brain and was buried with his first wife in an unmarked grave in Bolivar's Maple Lawn Cemetery, probably next to his first wife.

The Root House on Main Street was sold to W. L. Foster by James and Hattie Root Homer in April 1905 for $2,500. Desdemona Proctor Patridge (Partridge) Root left a will dated October 1, 1901, appointing her son James Patridge and her daughter Hattie Root Homer as executors. After her debts were paid daughter Hattie Homer received $450, son Henry P. Patridge was willed $500, grandson Myrl Patridge was given $100, son Harley Root received $400, and husband James H. Root was bequeathed $50 with an additional $100 to cover his funeral expenses when he died. The rest of Desdemona's estate was to be divided among her four children: James and Henry Patridge, Hattie Root Homer, and Harlie Root.

James Patridge, a successful Bolivar businessman, was born in Wellsville, New York November 5, 1852 and died in Olean, New York after kidney surgery August 25, 1918. He moved to Bolivar with his younger brother, Henry in 1864 when his mother remarried. James Patridge was a resident of Bolivar for over fifty years and resided on South Street. He was engaged in the mercantile business of Newton and Patridge in Bolivar with Burr Newton. A second store was owned in Coleville, Pennsylvania. In addition, James Patridge was a successful oil producer and life insurance agent. On May 23, 1879, he married Fannie Cutler, daughter of Bolivar's beloved Dr. J. L. Cutler and Jeanette Mellon. James and Fannie had two children. Their son Jay L. Patridge, born October 1885, died in 1913. Their daughter Alice, b. 1879, married F. J. McMillan by whom she had a son, Cutler McMillan before divorcing by 1920. Alice remarried to James Smith but died from pneumonia in Painesville, Ohio April 1926. Fannie, b. August 25, 1857, died March 6, 1937. James, Fannie, Jay, and Alice are buried in Bolivar's Maple Lawn Cemetery.

Henry P. Patridge was born in Wellsville, New York in 1855. He was listed as Henry P. Root in the 1865 New York State Census. He continued to reside with his mother and step-father at the time of the 1870 US Census and the 1875 New York State Census. Henry married Antoinette; last name not known. Henry Patridge may be mistakenly mentioned in his mother's obituary as her brother. Henry was mentioned in Desdemona Root's will. In 1906 Henry Patridge came to Bolivar to visit his brother James. There was no mention of Henry Patridge in James Patridge's 1918 obituary nor in the obituaries of his half-brother, Harlie Root, and half-sister, Hattie Root Homer. Henry Patridge's death and burial remain undocumented. Henry and Antoinette had a son, Myrl D. Patridge, b. July 5, 1877/78 in New York State, died March 15, 1947 Indianapolis, Indiana where he was employed as a pipeline contractor. Myrl resided with his grandmother, Desdemona Root, and step-grandfather, James Root in the 1900 US Census. When Myrl registered for the draft in 1918, it was noted that his left eye was gone. Myrl married Mamie Cox, and had a son, George Henry Patridge, b. April 10, 1909 and living in Gibson, Indiana according to the 1910 US Census. The 1920 US Census records Myrl and Mamie Patridge residing in Indianapolis with son George age 10 and daughter Naoma Jean age 4 ½ years. Myrl died in 1947 and he was buried along with his son, George H. Patridge, and daughter-in-law, Louise, in Crown Hill Cemetery in Indianapolis, Indiana.

Children (by second marriage)

70. I. ***Hattie Desdemona. Root***, a twin, ***f.***

71. II. ***Harlie James. Root***, a twin, ***f.***

References: US Census: 1830, 1840, 1850, 1860, 1870, 1880, 1900, 1910, 1920; New York State Census: 1855, 1865, 1875, 1892; *Bolivar Breeze 1891-1965*, selected issues; Maple Lawn Cemetery Records, Bolivar, New York; Woodlawn Cemetery Records, Wellsville, New York; Indiana State Board of Health Death Certificates; US World War I Draft Registration Cards, 1917-1918; Indiana Birth Certificates 1907-1940; Beers, F. W., *History of Allegany County, New York, 1806-1879.* New York: F. W. Beers & Co, 1879; New York Wills and Probate Records, 1659-1999, October 1, 1901 (Desdemona Root); New York Wills and Probate Records 1659-1999, July 8, 1876 (Truman Bryant Cartwright); Crown Hill Cemetery Records, Indianapolis, Indiana; Supreme Court of Monroe County, New York Lewis P. Ross vs. Wilber Cook, James H. Root, and Harley J. Root July 16, 1898 and July 25, 1898; Supreme Court of Monroe

County, New York William H. Smith, Isaac, and William Gormly vs. James H. Root, Harley J. Root and Wilber P. Cook July 11, 1898, November 16, 1898; J. H. Wasson June 16, 1898; Harriet H. February 16, 1900; Western Union Telegraph Company May 18, 1899; Wilber P. Cook, James H. Root, Harley J. Root final account, July 27, 1900.

Second Generation Line of Descent from Abel Root, Sr.

40.

Minerva Root, daughter of Abel, Jr. (34), granddaughter of Abel, Sr. (28), b. Bolivar, New York a. 1827, d. place unknown, date unknown; m. (1) Bolivar, New York August 26, 1847 Daniel Holly (Holley, Hawley, Holby), divorced, date unknown, b. New Jersey 1823, d. Olean, New York June 7, 1888; m. (2) date and place not known George Neff, divorced, date unknown, b. Paris, France April 13, 1838, d. McBride, Michigan August 19, 1921.

Minerva Root resided in Bolivar, New York with her parents in the 1830 and 1840 US Census records. Her birth year seems to vary from 1827 to 1829 based on US Census data. In the 1850 US Census she was the wife of Daniel Hawley and they resided in Bolivar. Daniel Hawley's last name has been spelled Holley, Holly, and Holby creating challenges in tracing this line of descent. Minerva was also referred to as Minnie adding a further complication. A son, Elmer Hawley, was born in Bolivar on May 24, 1848, but he was not listed on the 1850 census. I suggest that he died because another son b. a. 1861 was named Elmer D. Hawley. An undocumented family tree on ancestry.com identifies a daughter, Ella Elizabeth Hawley born Bolivar July 23, 1849. This child cannot be documented; therefore, she was not listed as one of the children.

The 1855 New York State Census recorded the Hawley family in Belfast, New York with a son, Judson. Minerva and Daniel Hawley had a daughter, Lydia, b. a. 1856. In the 1860 US Census Daniel and Minerva returned to Bolivar with their two children Judson and Lydia. Daniel worked as a carpenter and joiner. In 1863, when Daniel registered for the draft, he resided in Bolivar and was employed as a joiner. The Hawleys could not be found under any spelling variation of their last name in the 1865 New York State Census. Sometime after 1863, Minerva and Daniel Hawley separated and divorced. No record of divorce has currently been located. At the time of the 1870 US Census, Daniel had remarried to Sarah D., last name not known, b. March 1843 in Michigan, last recorded alive in the 1920 US Census residing in Muskogee, Michigan with daughter Ina. Daniel and Sarah resided in Randolph in Cattaraugus County, New York and with his second wife had three sons: Frank Ellsworth Holly (1868-1933), Barton Kent Holly (1872-1947), and Charles R. Holly (1876-1893), and three daughters: Sarah Holly d. 1871, Ina Edith Holly Terry (1879-1955), and Hannah or Anna Holly Fitzmaurice (1882-1949). Daniel Holly died at 64 years of age after being in ill-health for a year and residing in Olean for almost twenty years. He was buried in Mt. View Cemetery in Olean, New York. Sarah Holly's burial location is not known.

By 1870, Minerva Root Hawley had moved to Detroit, Michigan and remarried to George Neff. It is possible she moved to Michigan at the time her younger sister Mary Jane Root Barber and her brother-in-law, Elmer J. Barber, moved to Detroit. Mr. Neff was employed as a shoe maker. Residing with Minerva and George Neff were two of her Hawley children: Judson and Lydia. Judson and Lydia were recorded twice in the 1870 US Census because they were also listed as residing in Randolph, New York with their father, step-mother, younger brother Elmer, and a half-brother Frank. The New York State Census for 1875 had Lydia and Elmer residing with their father, his wife, and their half-siblings in Olean, New York. In the 1880 US Census Minerva was documented as divorced and was a boarder with a medical doctor along with her sister, Mary Jane Root Barber, and her son, Elmer Hawley. It is believed that George Neff was married a total of three times. Before George Neff married Minerva Root Hawley, he was married to Adelia Greenhoe by whom he had a daughter before divorcing. After divorcing Minerva, George Neff remarried to Catharine Kuntz April 15, 1878 in Muir, Michigan by whom he had two children before being divorced for cruelty and non-support September 25, 1901. George Neff was buried in the McBride Cemetery in McBride, Michigan. Minerva was employed as a dress maker working from her home and was consistently listed in Detroit City Directories from 1880 to 1896 but at different street addresses. In the 1893 Detroit City Directory, Minerva Neff was listed as a widow of George Neff instead of divorced even though Mr. Neff was apparently still alive. Minerva Neff was last mentioned in the 1896 obituary of her brother, Lyman E. Root of Bolivar. Her date and place of death are currently not known and her burial location is unknown.

Children (by first marriage)

72. I. ***Elmer Hawley***, b. Bolivar, May 24, 1848, d. before 1850 US Census. Burial location not known.

73. II. ***Judson L. Hawley**, f.*

74. III. ***Lydia M. Hawley***, b. a. 1856 and was last recorded in the 1877 Detroit City Directory employed as a waitress at Franklin House. It is possible she married making it difficult to trace her since no further documentation about Lydia has been found.

75. IV. ***Elmer D. Hawley**, f.*

References: US Census: 1830, 1840, 1850, 1860, 1870, 1880, 1900, 1910, 1920; New York State Census: 1855, 1865, 1875; Bolivar, New York Marriage Records (marriage of Minerva Root and Daniel Hawley); Bolivar, New York Birth Records: Elmer Hawley; Mt. View Cemetery Records, Olean, New York; *Detroit City Directories:* 1880-1896; *Olean Democrat,* Olean, New York, June 7, 1888; Michigan Death Records 1867-1950 for George Neff; Michigan Marriage and Divorce Records, 1867-1952 for George and Catharine Neff; McBride Cemetery Records, McBride, Michigan; New York Death Index, 1880-1956 Daniel Holly.

41.

Elizabeth Root, daughter of Abel, Jr. (34), granddaughter of Abel, Sr. (28), b. Bolivar, New York November 25, 1830, d. Bolivar, New York December 1, 1859; m. Bolivar, New York July 3, 1851, Charles A. Withey, b. Inavale (near Friendship), New York July 9, 1826, d. Bolivar, New York April 8, 1904.

Elizabeth Root was recorded on the US Census records for 1830, 1840, and 1850 as a member of the Abel Root, Jr. family. Elizabeth and Charles Withey had four children before her death from an inflammation she suffered from for four weeks possibly as a result of a recent childbirth. After Elizabeth's death, widower Charles Withey and his four children resided with his in-laws, Abel and Polly Root of Bolivar. Charles Withey remarried July 19, 1862 to Caroline Stebbins and had two more children. Eldest son, Charles Samuel Withey resided with his father and step-mother. Daughter Emma and son Jesse lived with their maternal grandparents Abel and Polly Root. Ina Withey was raised by her mother's sister, Mary Jane Root Barber, and she was sometimes identified on census records as Ina Barber. Charles Withey was a successful businessman running a lumber business, a wagon shop, and a grocery store in Richburg, New York during the oil boom that swept Allegany County, New York in the 1880s. From March 1869 to December 31, 1878, Charles Withey served as the Justice of the Peace for Wirt Township. He served two terms as both a Wirt town supervisor and deputy sheriff.

The Withey family came from Scotland and settled in Dedham, Massachusetts in the 17th century. The original last name was Macraithe. Upon arrival in the Americas the last name was changed to MacKerwethe and in the early 19th century was again changed to MacWithey. Charles Withey's grandfather changed the name again and this time to Withey. No explanations for the name changes has currently been found. Charles Withey's second wife, Caroline Stebbins Withey, b. February 1, 1861, d. November 8, 1903 was buried in Richburg Cemetery in Richburg, New York. Their son, William Henry Withey, was born February 16, 1865 and died March 23, 1932. He married Lillian Mead and had four children: Grace (March 8, 1890-March 18, 1890), Ward Alva Withey (1891-1958), Clara Withey Ingalls (1892-1959), and Jesse Grant Withey (1895-1958). Ward Withey and his sister Clara Withey Ingalls were prominent residents of Allentown, New York where Ward Withey served as Allentown's postmaster. Grace Withey, Ward Withey and his wife, and Clara Withey Ingalls and her husband were all buried with Caroline Withey in the Richburg Cemetery. Charles and Caroline's daughter, Clara (1866-1943), married twice, first to Benjamin Viger (1862-1918) and later after his death to Wesley Frank Le Vere (1866-1942). The Viger's had one son, Burnett (1892-1981). The 1892 New York State Census does not record Charles Withey, but his wife Caroline resided alone in Richburg.

In the 1900 US Census Charles Withey resided by himself in Eldred, Pennsylvania while Caroline Withey continued to live alone in Richburg. I suggest, based on *Bolivar Breeze* articles regarding Caroline Withey's ill health from 1900 until her death and these census records, that Charles and Caroline Withey had separated sometime prior to 1892. Newspaper articles after 1900 indicate that Charles Withey resided at the home of his son, Jesse Withey, where he eventually died after a five-day illness from pneumonia.

Charles Withey was buried in Maple Lawn Cemetery in Bolivar with his first wife, Elizabeth Root. Markers are in evidence for both.

Children:

76. I. ***Charles Samuel Withey, f.***

77. II. ***Emma Withey, f.***

78. III. ***Ina Withey, f.***

79. IV. ***Jesse Andrew Withey, f.***

References: US Census: 1850, 1860, 1870, 1880, 1900; New York State Census: 1855, 1865, 1875, 1892; Maple Lawn Cemetery Records, Bolivar, New York; Richburg Cemetery Records, Richburg, New York; *Bolivar Breeze 1891-1965*, selected issues; New York Death Index 1880-1956, Caroline Withey and Charles Withey; Beers, F. W. *History of Allegany County, New York, 1806-1879.*

42.

Lyman Eleasure Root, son of Abel, Jr. (34), grandson of Abel, Sr. (28), b. Bolivar, New York December 25, 1832, d. Bolivar, New York October 17, 1896; m. Almyra (Almira) Reed September 2, 1860, b. Skaneateles, New York November 10, 1844, d. Bolivar, New York October 4, 1914.

Lyman Root was a leading citizen of Bolivar. He served in the 189th Regiment, Company B, of the New York Volunteers during the Civil War. He enlisted September 1, 1864 and was honorably discharged May 30, 1865 with a bounty of $600. His discharge papers described him as 5' 4" tall, light complexion, blue eyes, and light hair. Lyman Root served the company as a brigade blacksmith, a profession he continued in Bolivar after the war. His blacksmith shop was located next to his house on the corner of Leather and Main Streets by Root Hollow Creek where, currently a three-story brick house, a grocery store, and parking lot are situated. Lyman Root purchased the property in 1886. Mr. Root served Bolivar as an inspector of elections and overseer of the poor. His death came suddenly from a cold of several days, which developed into acute pneumonia. Lyman Root was a fervent presidential supporter of William McKinley. A few days before his death Mr. Root informed a reporter for the *Bolivar Breeze* that he hoped nothing would interfere with his voting for his favorite presidential candidate. Lyman Root died before he could vote.

Almyra Root was the daughter of Jerome and Ruth Barber Reed of Richburg, New York. She was an active member of the Bolivar Methodist Church, the Women's Christian Temperance Union, the Women's Relief Corps, Trilby Rebekah Lodge, and was a devout church goer. Her obituary described her as a devout Christian, a kindly woman of cheerful disposition, and, above all, a true friend. Almyra joined the Bolivar Methodist Church September 22, 1878 along with her children Lola and Earls. Her husband Lyman was baptized the same day. Daughter Libbie Root joined the church December 1, 1878. Lyman Root joined the church a decade later on June 3, 1888. After Lyman Root's death, Almyra sold the blacksmith tools to Verne Monroe of Bolivar who rented the blacksmith shop beginning November 25, 1897 until Mrs. Root sold the buildings to her son-in-law, Paul Ennis, April 6, 1899 for $125. Mrs. Root was a strong supporter of the Women's Christian Temperance Union, which might have been influenced by the drinking problems of her two youngest sons. Almyra Root had been in ill-health for a year and was a patient at a Friendship, New York sanitarium for several weeks prior to her death. She died from hardening of the arteries and nephritis.

Almyra Reed Root's Will is on file with Belmont County Court House. She named her eldest son, Earls L. Root, as her executor directing her debts be paid. Almyra authorized the placement of headstones in Maple Lawn Cemetery for her deceased son, Ernest J. Root, and one for herself. Her daughter Elizabeth Ennis was given her personal items and $200. To her grandson, Lyman E. Root, she left $10.00 to be kept at interest until his 21st birthday. The rest of the estate was to be divided between her three surviving children: Earls, Elizabeth, and Bernard. Almyra's grandson, Lyman E. Root, remembered his grandmother as a frequent church goer during the years he resided with her. He would accompany his grandmother going early to church in order to pump the organ while she played. Lyman and Almyra Root were buried in Maple Lawn Cemetery next to the graves of Abel and Polly Root. Lyman Root has a second stone commemorating his service in the Civil War.

Children:

80. I. ***Mary Elizabeth Root, f.***

81. II. ***Earls (Earles) Lyman Root, f.***

82. III. ***Lola Root, f.***

83. IV. ***Alla E. Root***, b. Bolivar September 26, 1868, d. Bolivar February 28, 1869 and was buried in Maple Lawn Cemetery with a shared tombstone with two sisters.

84. V. ***Hurba E. Root***, b. Bolivar, date unknown, d. Bolivar, June 10, year unknown and was buried in Maple Lawn Cemetery with a shared tombstone with two sisters.

85. VI. ***Earnest (Ernest) Jerome Root, f.***

86. VII. ***Bernard Abel Root, f.***

References: US Census: 1840, 1850, 1860, 1870, 1880; New York State Census: 1855, 1865, 1875, 1892; *Bolivar Breeze 1891-1965*, selected issues; Beers, F. W., *History of Allegany County, New York, 1806-*

1879. New York: F. W. Beers & Co., 1879; Lyman E. Root's original discharge papers in possession of the author; Will of Almira Reed Root, August 17, 1914, Belmont, New York Court House; Deed and Bill of Sale for the blacksmith's shop, April 6, 1899, Belmont, New York Court House; Maple Lawn Cemetery Records, Bolivar, New York; Bolivar, New York Methodist Church Record Books, Book 1: 1873-1886; New York State Death Index 1880-1956 for Lyman Root and Almyra Root; Interview with the late Lyman E. Root of Bolivar, New York.

43.

Mary Jane Root, daughter of Abel, Jr. (34), granddaughter of Abel, Sr. (28), b. Bolivar, New York April 1837, d. Detroit, Michigan July 22, 1914; m. place and date unknown, but probably Bolivar, New York a. 1859, Elmer J. Barber, b. New York State September 1825/1826, d. Detroit, Michigan March 23, 1905.

Mary Jane Root was recorded on the 1840 US Census, 1850 US Census, and the 1855 New York State Census residing with her parents Abel and Polly Root. Sometime before the 1860 US Census, Mary Jane Root married Elmer J. Barber. Elmer Barber was the son of Moses and Mary Crandall Barber, residents of Portville Township along the New York and Pennsylvania State line in what became Ceres. In the 1860 US Census they resided in Ceres, Pennsylvania just across the state border with New York State on a farm near Barbertown Road, which connects Ceres, Pennsylvania to Eldred, Pennsylvania; and a highway where many Barber family farms were located. The graves in the private Barber Family cemetery were removed in the 20th century and reburied in the East Portville Cemetery in Portville, New York. Elmer Barber was employed as an innkeeper in 1860. Living with Mary Jane and Elmer Barber was Mary Jane's niece, Ina Withey, whose mother, Elizabeth Root Withey, died the previous year. In future US Census records Ina Withey was frequently listed as Ina Barber. Ina Withey never returned to Bolivar or Richburg to live with her father and siblings, but she did visit them. Elmer Barber registered for the draft during the Civil War in McKean County, Pennsylvania July 1, 1863. It does not appear that he saw service.

The reasons or circumstances for the Barbers moving to Michigan are not know, but the move came after the births of their first two children Cora Mary in 1863 and Fred in 1867 in Ceres, Pennsylvania. Elmer Barber was a grocer in Saginaw, Michigan according to the 1870 and 1880 US Census records and with Mary Jane raised her niece, Ina, and their three children Cora, Fred, and Minnie. In the 1900 US Census Elmer Barber's occupation was a builder working in Detroit. Ina Withey had married and left the household as had their son, Fred. Daughters Cora Mary and Minnie were both listed as married but residing with their parents. Minnie was actually divorced as the time of the 1900 US Census and Cora Mary died just after the 1900 US Census was taken. Elmer Barber died from pernicious anemia in Detroit in 1905 and Mary Jane Root Barber died from paralysis in 1914. Both are buried in Detroit's Woodlawn Cemetery, Section 13, and Lot 100. Their individual markers are very overgrown and barely visual above ground. A larger *Barber* marker indicates their general location.

Children:

87. I. ***Cora Mary Barber, f.***

88. II. ***Fred A. Barber, f.***

89. III. ***Minnie Barber, f.***

References: US Census: 1840, 1850, 1860, 1870, 1880, 1900, 1910; New York State Census: 1855; Woodlawn Cemetery Records, Detroit, Michigan; 1869 Beers Map of Portville township; Michigan Death Records, 1897-1920; Interview with the late Ina Withey Burdick McEnroe, Wellsville, New York.

44.

Hiram James Root, son of Abel, Jr. (34), grandson of Abel, Sr. (28), b. Kossuth, Bolivar, New York Township February 27, 1840, d. Bolivar, New York at his home due to heart trouble July 24, 1895; m. place and date not know, Mary Jane White, b. Hebron, Potter County, Pennsylvania April 1842, d. Angelica, New York Allegany County Home January 10, 1913 from organic heart disease where she had been a resident since June 1911.

The date and place of marriage for Hiram Root and Mary Jane White is not currently documented. Because their first child, Flora, was born June 1862, the marriage would have taken place sometime prior to this birth. Hiram Root resided with his parents Abel and Polly Root according to the 1850 US Census, the 1860 US Census, and the 1855 New York State Census. When Hiram registered for the draft on July 1, 1863, he was listed as married. There is no record of his being called to service. Hiram and Mary Jane Root resided next door to Lyman and Almyra Root with their two oldest children as recorded in the 1865 New York State Census later moving to Liberty Street in Bolivar where he owned and operated a produce and butcher shop from the home. He quit this business to work on the oil leases during the 1880s oil boom. Mr. and Mrs. Root joined the Bolivar Methodist Church September 8, 1878 along with their daughter Flora. His grandson, Lewis Richardson, described his grandfather as an expert hunter who went into the hills surrounding Bolivar each fall on hunting trips averaging two weeks. In that era there was no limit on the amount of game one could bag. An early photograph showed Hiram Root surrounded by three deer and three foxes he killed.

Mr. Root was a member of Bolivar's J. B. Bradley Hose Company # 1. In the 1892 New York State Census Hiram, Mary Jane, and Guy Root lived in Burns, New York in Allegany County where Hiram was employed as an oil pumper. His obituary described him as an industrious and honest citizen. Hiram and Mary Jane White Root had three children: Flora, Laphronia, and Elizabeth. They adopted the illegitimate son, Guy, of their eldest daughter, Flora. Records in the Allegany County Court House in Belmont, New York record the adoption but do not identify the name of the father. Guy Root's death certificate names the father as "Fritz Root," but it is unclear who this person could be.

The Bolivar Methodist Church placed Guy Root on probation May 1, 1893.

After Hiram Root's death in 1895, Mary Jane and Guy Root moved to Muncie, Indiana where her son, Laphronia, resided with his family. They still resided in Muncie in 1907 as noted in the Muncie City Directory for that year. By 1910 Mary Jane Root moved back to Bolivar and was living with her daughter, Flora Root Richardson, son-in-law, Edward Richardson, and her Richardson grandchildren. On June 14, 1911, Mary Jane Root was admitted to the Allegany County Almshouse by her daughter, Flora Richardson. Mrs. Root was in poor health, nearly blind, and had no means of financial support. She died there in 1913. Hiram and Mary Jane Root were buried in Maple Lawn Cemetery, Bolivar, in the same row as his parents, Abel and Polly Root, and his brother and sister-in-law, Lyman and Almyra Root.

Children:

90. I. ***Flora M. Root, f.***

91. II. ***Laphronia Hiram Root, f.***

92. III. ***Elizabeth E. Root, f.***

93. IV. ***Guy Arthur Root, f.***

References: US Census: 1840, 1850, 1860, 1870, 1880, 1900, 1910; New York State Census: 1855, 1865, 1875, 1892; Maple Lawn Cemetery Records, Bolivar, New York; 1907 Muncie Indiana City Directory; New York Census of Inmates in Almshouses and Poorhouses, 1830-1920; *Bolivar Breeze, 1891-1965*, selected articles; adoption records Allegany County Court House, Belmont, New York for Guy Root; Pennsylvania Death Certificate, Guy Root; interviews with the late Doris Richardson June, Bolivar, New York; New York State Death Index 1880-1956; Bolivar, New York Methodist Record Books, Book 1 1873-1886 and Book 2.

46.

Huldah Jane Root, daughter of David C. (35), granddaughter of Abel, Sr. (28), b. Bolivar, New York November 21, 1832, d. Bolivar, New York March 30, 1900 from diabetes after a fourteen-year illness at age 67 years, 4 months, and 9 days; m. Bolivar, New York 1852 James Monroe Curtiss, b. Morris, New York December 2, 1823, d. Bolivar, New York October 29, 1901 after being ill for a month with typhoid-malarial fever.

Huldah Root Curtiss was a life-long resident of Bolivar. The eldest of four siblings, Huldah was the last to die. Her obituary described her as a benevolent woman and that all who knew her were Huldah's friends. Huldah spent several summers at Lily Dale, New York, the center of Spiritualism where communication with the dead was deemed possible. She became an ardent spiritualist and contributed to the establishment of the Spiritualist Society in Lily Dale and the First Spiritualist Society in Bolivar. Huldah and James Curtiss never had children. Huldah raised her nephew, George Root, the son of her brother, Albert L. Root, from the age of two years and after the death of George's mother. In Huldah's obituary George's daughter, also named Huldah, was identified as her granddaughter instead of great-niece. The obituary states that little Huldah was given a gold watch by Mrs. Curtiss, but the family said that was an incorrect statement and the little great-niece was given a gold chain, which the family still has. Huldah Curtiss' funeral was conducted at the home with an open casket in the front parlor by noted Buffalo, New York Spiritualist Moses Hull. The casket was white and the mourners wore white as the deceased had requested. Spiritualists did not believe in heavy crepe and somber trappings. Reverend Hull gave a long funeral discourse about the beliefs of Spiritualism as requested by the deceased.

James Monroe Curtiss was born in Morris, Otsego County, New York, the eldest of nine children to Lysander Curtiss, a farmer. By working on the family farm, James Curtiss was able to earn enough money to attend Gilbertville Academy. He then moved to Mt. Upton to read law with Upton and Fenlo and was admitted to the bar in 1847. James Curtiss, Esquire practiced law in the Mt. Upton area until 1849 when he and William Prindle, also a lawyer, went west to Hornellsville where they joined with Hamilton Ward, a future Attorney General and Supreme Court Justice for New York State. The three opened a practice in Angelica, New York, but with too few cases Curtiss and Prindle left Angelica for Bolivar in April 1850. James Curtiss took a position as teacher for the Kossuth school and Mr. Prindle did the same founding a school in Little Genesee. James Curtiss took his earnings from teaching to purchase law books, opened a law office in the upstairs back room of a building on land on Olean Street next to the Clark House. James Curtiss' first law case was about the ownership of a calf. He won the case but was paid in cordwood. Money was scare and barter was the frequent method of payment. It was at the Kossuth School as a teacher that James Curtiss met his future wife, Huldah Root, a pupil.

Described as a shy, young man, James Curtiss fell in love with his pretty pupil. To avoid any appearance of improper behavior, Mr. Curtiss would take detours to get to and return from the David Root residence in Kossuth to court Miss Root. He did not want the residents of Bolivar to know his personal business. However, the town did and found his actions humorous. Over time James Curtiss built a very successful law practice and was Bolivar's first lawyer. Well-liked by Bolivar residents, Mr. Curtiss was elected to the Board of Supervisors and was frequently nominated for county offices. He also served as Justice of the Peace. James Curtiss was a Jefferson-Jackson style Democrat. Being a Democrat kept him from winning more elections in a very Republican Allegany County. The farm land James Curtiss owned contained oil giving Mr. and Mrs. Curtiss a considerable fortune. He stopped practicing law before the courts in 1882 to devote more time to his business interests. Curtiss retained an interest in the law practice but gave the day to day running to law partners, the last one being Walter T. Bliss. At the time of his death, Mr. Curtiss was Allegany County's oldest practicing lawyer.

The Curtiss residence was on Main Street on the right side just past Root Hollow Creek going toward Little Genesee. They also owned a 215-acre farm on Salt Rising Road where oil was discovered. Bolivar's first bank was the Bolivar Banking Company, which opened January 1882 with James Curtiss as a stock holder. That same year Mr. Curtiss organized the State Bank of Bolivar, which merged in 1884 with the Bolivar Banking Company electing James Curtiss its first President. James Curtiss remained the bank's president until his death. As the major stock holder in the bank, Mr. Curtiss dictated strict bank policies, which enabled the bank to weather many a financial panic. It was believed that not one Bolivar resident every lost a single penny with the bank. James Curtiss was perceived as an honest and fair man whose integrity was never criticized. James Curtiss' advice was *Think twice about everything and say nothing.* He was a charter member of Macedonia Lodge No. 258 F. & A. M., a Royal Arch Mason, and a member of St. John's Commandry, No. 24, Knights Templar. Toward the end of his life, James Curtiss was hard of hearing and in the last year, his mind was sometimes clouded. After the death of his brother-in-law, Addison Evans, his sister-in-law, Elosica Root Evans, and her twin daughters Alice and Agnes Evans moved into the Curtiss household. The Evans sisters ran the Curtiss household at the time of both Huldah and James Curtiss' respective deaths. His funeral started at the family home in the dining room where family and friends came to pay their respects and to view the open coffin. The services were moved to the Bolivar Methodist Church with the assistance of the Macedonia Lodge 258, F. & A. M. Burial was in Maple Lawn Cemetery where James Curtiss was buried next to his wife, Huldah, and near the graves of his Root in-laws. To the surprise of Bolivar residents, Mr. Curtiss did not leave a will. His estate was divided among his surviving siblings and the children of his deceased siblings in six equal portions.

Mr. Curtiss' law library was given to his law partner, Walter Bliss. His estate was not as large as was believed amounting to between $40,000 and $50,000, which today would amount to between $1,122,000 to $1,400,00. The Curtiss holdings consisted of real estate, oil property, and bank and mining stock. He did not have a life insurance policy. Not one member of Huldah Root Curtiss' family was given a share of the Curtiss estate. It was long assumed that the nephew, George Root, whom James and Huldah raised as a son and was sometimes identified as George Curtiss, would benefit. Had there been a will, the financial settlements might have been different. Within a decade of James Curtiss' death, all of Huldah's nieces and nephews left Bolivar except Edwin C. Root.

References: US Census: 1850, 1860, 1870, 1880, 1900; New York State Census: 1855, 1865, 1875, 1892; *Bolivar Breeze 1891-1965*, selected issues; Beers, F. W. *History of Allegany County, New York, 1806-1879.* New York: F. W. Beers & Co., 1879; Herrick, John P. *Bolivar, New York Pioneer Oil Town.* Los Angeles: The Ward Ritchie Press, 1952; correspondence with the late Jane Nulsen Bunse, granddaughter of George Root.

47.

Albert Lovace (Lovice/Louis) Root, son of David C. (35), grandson of Abel, Sr. (28), b. Bolivar, New York May 31, 1836, d. Washington, DC November 18, 1898 from vascular disease of the heart complicated by typhoid fever contracted during the Civil War; m. (1) Bolivar, New York December 24, 1865 Armina Kilbury, b. probably Bolivar, New York September 1, 1846, d. Ceres, Pennsylvania June 13, 1872 from complications from childbirth; m (2) Kittery, Maine March 16, 1874 (undocumented source) Anna C. Moore, b. Oxford, Maine March 29,1851 (undocumented source), d. Washington, DC December 2, 1885 due to exhaustion; m. (3) October 6, 1888, place not known, Margaret H. Remick, b. Kittery, Maine July 9, 1850, d. Portsmouth, New Hampshire March 27, 1917.

Albert Root enlisted in Company C, 85th Regiment, New York Volunteers in Bolivar on September 10, 1861. On November 7, 1861 he was promoted to First Sergeant. Mr. Root saw action at the battles of Fair Oaks, Seven Days Campaign of Foster from Suffolk, Virginia to Weldon, North Carolina, Vinton, White Hall and Goldsborough. During the battle of Plymouth Church, North Carolina, Albert was captured along with his brother, Asa Wallace Root, by Confederate forces on April 20, 1864. Albert and Asa Root were imprisoned in Florence, South Carolina, Richmond, Virginia, and Andersonville, Georgia. Asa died at Andersonville in 1864 while Albert survived and was released on February 26, 1865 at N. E. Ferry, North Carolina. Albert reported to Camp Parole March 10, 1865 in Annapolis, Maryland. On March 15 he was sent to the Marine hospital to recover from typhoid. Albert Root served for over three years and was mustered out April 21, 1865 in Elmira, New York. Albert Root resided with his parents as recorded in the US Census for 1840, 1850, and 1860, and the New York State Census for 1855 and 1865 where he worked on the family farm or as a sawyer. After his 1865 marriage to Armina Kilbury, Albert moved to Ceres, Pennsylvania and worked as a lumberman. Born to Albert and Armina Root were five children, sons: Asa Wallace, Edwin Cartwright, Benjamin F., and George Albert and a daughter Bertha Armina. Benjamin F. Root was recorded on the 1870 US Census as one year old, but he cannot be found in any other records.

Armina died from childbirth complications in 1872 after the birth of Bertha Armina and was buried in Maple Lawn Cemetery in Bolivar. The circumstances of Albert Root's meeting and courting of Anna C. Moore from Kittery, Maine are not known. An undocumented source on Ancestry.com provided a marriage date of March 16, 1874. Anna was the daughter of Daniel and Frances Moore of Kittery, Maine. In 1875 Albert and Anna resided in Bolivar where he worked a farm. Residing with them was Anna's mother and younger brother along with Albert's sons Asa and Edwin. Son George was being raised by his sister and brother-in-law Huldah and James Curtiss. His daughter Bertha was under the guardianship of his first wife's parents, the Edwin Kilburys of Bolivar. When Albert and Anna moved to Washington, D. C. by 1880, only his son Asa accompanied them. Edwin Root went to live with his paternal grandparents, David and Marietta Root.

The four surviving children of Albert and Armina were never raised together as a family. The medical circumstances of Anna Root's death from exhaustion are not clear. She was buried at Moshassuck Cemetery in Central Falls, Rhode Island with members of her family. Albert remarried a third time to Margaret Hannah Remick, also, of Kittery, Maine. It is not known if Albert's second and third wives knew each other. Nor is it understood how Albert and Margaret met. Margaret was the daughter of John and Eunice Remick. Before and after her marriage to Albert, she worked as a seamstress. From

November 20, 1884 until February 28, 1894, Albert Root was employed as a watchman at the Bureau of Engraving and Printing in Washington, D. C. He continued to work as a watchman in 1895, but at the Aqueduct Bridge for the Corps of Engineers. His last employment was as a watchman at the Library of Congress starting in 1897. In 1882 Albert Root began receiving a military pension for partial disability from rheumatism contracted in confederate prisons.

Albert Root died in Washington, D. C., but the funeral was conducted in Bolivar from the home of his daughter Bertha Root Cook. His pall bearers included Union soldiers imprisoned along with him at Andersonville, Georgia. Mr. Root was highly regarded by the retired veterans of the Grand Army of the Republic of the District of Columbia who attended his funeral. It was deemed unlikely that he had an enemy in the world. Albert Root's obituary described him as a well-read and congenial man whose passing was deeply regretted. He was buried in Bolivar's Maple Lawn Cemetery beside his first wife, Armina. His will probated in Washington, D. C. left his personal property to his wife, Margaret Root, and his real estate to her for her natural life. Should Margaret Root remarry, her estate share was reduced to 1/3 the estate's value. She never remarried. Upon the death of Margaret Root, the remainder of Albert's estate was to be divided among his four children: Asa, Edwin, George, and Bertha. His will directed that debts owed him by his son George Root be transferred to his son-in-law, Wilbur Cook, for payment. Wilbur Cook was the executor of Albert Root's estate. Margaret Root applied for a widow's pension on November 21, 1898. She returned to New England and resided in Methuen, Massachusetts (1900), Kittery, Maine (1910), and Portsmouth, New Hampshire (1914) where Mrs. Root died March 27, 1917 from mitral regurgitation (a leaking heart value) from which she suffered for years. Margaret Root was buried in Orchard Cemetery in Kittery, Maine.

Children (all from first marriage):

94. I. ***Asa Wallace Root**, f.*

95. II. ***Edwin Cartwright Root**, f.*

96. III. ***Benjamin F. Root***, b. about 1869 Ceres, Pennsylvania. He was listed on the 1870 US Census. There is no further mention of this child of Albert and Armina Root. No burial location has been found.

97. IV. ***George Albert Root**, f.*

98. V. ***Bertha Armina Root**, f.*

References: US Census: 1840, 1850, 1860, 1870, 1880, 1900, 1910; New York State Census: 1855, 1865, 1875; *Bolivar Breeze 1891-1965*, selected issues; letter from the Adjutant General's Office, War Department October 26, 1912 to Mrs. E. F. Root; photocopy of original marriage license of Albert L. Root to Armina Kilbury, December 24, 1865; letter from the Civil Archives Division, General Services

Administration to Mr. W. M. Cook June 7, 1982; biographical information on Albert Root recorded by the late Mrs. Fred Hulbert, Bolivar, New York; Washington, D. C. Wills and Probate Records, 1737-1952 for Albert L. Root; New York Civil War Muster Roll Abstracts, 1861-1900 for Albert Root; New Hampshire Death and Disinterment Records, 1754-1947, Margaret Root; Washington, D. C. City Directories 1882-1898; Maple Lawn Cemetery Records, Bolivar, New York; Orchard Cemetery Records, Kittery, Maine; Moshassuck Cemetery Records, Central Falls, Rhode Island.

48.

Asa Wallace Root, son of David C. (35), grandson of Abel, Sr. (28), b. Bolivar, New York July 13, 1841, d. Andersonville Prison, Georgia August 13, 1864. Asa Root resided with his parents employed as a farmer as recorded on the 1850 and 1860 US Census Records and the 1855 New York State Census. He enlisted September 9, 1861 in the 85th New York Volunteers, Company C along with his brother, Albert L. Root.

Asa W. Root kept a diary in three small volumes about his Civil War experiences. The diaries were donated to the Lily Dale Museum in Lily Dale, New York by his nieces, Alice and Agnes Evans. The diaries describe his duties, travels, war experiences, and his imprisonments. Asa and Albert Root were captured at the Battle of Plymouth Church, North Carolina April 20, 1864. Asa's confinements included stays in Florence, South Carolina, Richmond, Virginia, and Andersonville Georgia. Asa Root contracted malaria and with the rigors of prison life died at the Andersonville prison where he was buried. The official cause of death was *anasarca*, the accumulation of fluid in the intestinal tract contributing to liver, kidney, and heart failure. Originally his name was indented on a board marking his grave. This was replaced by a concrete marker for grave number 5570. Asa W. Root's name and birth and death dates are also on the tombstone of his parents in Maple Lawn Cemetery in Bolivar. Two volumes of Asa Root's diary were mailed home to his parents prior to his capture. The third volume was brought home by his brother Albert Root upon Albert's release from Andersonville prison. Typed copies of Asa Wallace Root's Civil War diary were made by his sister, Elosica Root Evans. Several of the typed copies circulated among branches of the Root family. This author has such a copy.

The original three diaries along with letters Asa wrote to his parents during the Civil War, and a number of family photographs of Asa's parents, siblings, and nieces and nephews were donated to the Lily Dale Museum by the Evans sisters. The diaries are quite small. For each day the weather was indicted and several sentences describe the day's activities. While it cannot be proven, this author believes that the interest in Spiritualism among members of the David Root family may have increased with the early death of Asa Wallace Root. Based on correspondence with the late Wilber (Bill) Cook, which retold the story of Asa W. Root's diary as explained to him by his aunt, Edna Cook Kelly, the United States government decided to put on trial those who were responsible for the inhuman conditions in the Andersonville Prison. As part of the case, the government asked for the diaries of the Union soldiers who were imprisoned there. The Root family sent Asa's diary to the prosecutor.

After the trial either Asa's mother, Marietta Tyler Root, or his sister, Elosica Root Evans, had to petition the government for ten years before they got the diary back.

References: US Census: 1850, 1860; New York State Census: 1855. New York Civil War Muster Roll Abstracts, 1861-1900; New York Town Clerks' Register of Men Who Served in the Civil War; Andersonville Prisoners of War Directory, p. 169; Lily Dale Museum, Lily Dale, New York; U.S. Civil War Soldier Records and Profiles 1861-1865; U.S. National Cemetery Interment Control Forms 1928-1962; U.S. Burial Registers, Military Posts and National Cemeteries 1862-1960; correspondence with the later Wilber (Bill) Cook July 18, 1982 about Asa W. Root's diary.

49.

Elosica (Eloisa) Hannah Root, daughter of David C. (35), granddaughter of Abel, Sr. (28), b. Bolivar, New York October 29, 1845, d. Bolivar, New York October 16, 1897 from Bright's disease; m. Washington, D. C. October 29, 1863 Addison Pliny Evans, b. Richburg, New York February 13, 1837, d. Chicago, Illinois March 3, 1893.

Elosica Root's first name has been spelled a number of different ways. Sometimes the name is spelled Elosica or even listed as Louise. The name's origin is probably *Eloisa*, an old German name meaning famous warrior. Other variations are Eloise and Heloise. Elosica resided with her parents at the time of the 1850 and 1860 US Census records and the 1855 New York State census. Her marriage to Addison Pliny Evans of Richburg, New York was recorded in her brother's (Asa W. Root) diary on page 79. The marriage took place at the Presbyterian Church in Washington, D.C. by Reverend B. Sunderland, the Senate Chaplain, on October 29, 1863. Addison Evans was the son of Pliny L. Evans (1787-1874) and Polly Gilbert Evans (1795-1843) of Richburg, New York. In 1854 Addison moved to nearby Bolivar to clerk for attorney and merchant Stephen W. Thomas with whom he resided as recorded in the 1855 New York State census. Mr. Evans went west to California to conduct some business and returned to Bolivar by November 1860. He enlisted May 1, 1861 at Cuba, New York in Company B of the New York 23rd Infantry Regiment. Private Evans was transferred to Battery B, 4th United States Artillery and saw action at the battles of Rappahannock Station, White Sulphur Springs, the Second Battle of Bull Run, South-Mountain, Antietam, and the Second Battle of Fredericksburg.

At the battle of Antietam Evans was dangerously wounded on the left side by a minnie ball. Addison Evans was mustered out on May 22, 1863. He remained in Washington, D. C. where he kept an eating-saloon until he was appointed *Sutler* for the 189th. A sutler was a civilian merchant who sold provisions to the army in the field, in camp, and in quarters. Sutlers were known to also offer gambling, drinking, and prostitutes, but there is no indication Addison Evans did. Evans was regarded as a man of upright character who conducted a very honest business operation. Mr. and Mrs. Evans returned to Bolivar in 1866 where their daughter Bertha Evans was born. Bertha died in 1869 and Addison and Elosica moved to Hamilton, Missouri where their next four children were born.

In Hamilton Addison ran a stationery store. By 1880 the Evans family had relocated to Quincy, Illinois outside Chicago where Addison Evans was employed as a stockyard's agent. Addison Evans died at the relatively young age of 56 years and was initially buried at Chicago's Mt. Hope Cemetery. His remains were returned to Bolivar and buried with his daughter Bertha Evans and later his wife, Elosica, in Maple Lawn Cemetery. Mrs. Evans filed for the right to administer her husband's estate June 9, 1893 because Addison Evans did not leave a will, and she filed for a widow's military pension October 30, 1893. After Addison's death, Elosica and her two daughters, Alice and Agnes, returned to Bolivar and resided with her sister and brother-in-law, Huldah and James Curtiss. Elosica and her sister Huldah made a number of trips to Lily Dale, the center of Spiritualism. Elosica died at the Curtiss residence from a number of diseases including Bright's disease. She was a member of the Women's Relief corps and Vice-President of the First Spiritualist Society of Bolivar. Elosica was regarded as a bright and cheerful woman who was beloved by all. Huldah Curtiss was named executor of her sister's estate worth $5,000, which today is almost $150,000 in value.

Children:

99. I. ***Bertha Evans***, b. Bolivar July 11, 1866, d. Bolivar July 11, 1869. Buried with her parents in Bolivar's Maple Lawn Cemetery.

100. II. ***Forest G. Evans, f.***

101. III. ***Albert A. Evans, f.***

102. IV. ***Agnes Merittia Evans (twin), f.***

103. V. ***Alice Huldah Evans (twin), f.***

References: US Census: 1850, 1860, 1870, 1880; New York State Census: 1855; *Bolivar, Breeze 1891-1965*, selected issues; Cook County, Illinois Death Index 1878-1922, Addison Evans; Illinois Wills and Probate Records 1772-1999, Addison Evans; New York Wills and Probate Records 1659-1999, Elosica H. Evans; U.S. Civil War Soldier Records and Profiles 1861-1865; District of Columbia Marriage Records 1810-1953; Asa W. Root's Civil War Diary, p. 79; U.S. Civil War Pension Index: General Index to Pension Files 1861-1934; Rogers, William H. *History of the 189th Regiment of the New York Volunteers.* New York: J. A. Gray & Green, 1865; Richburg Cemetery Records, Richburg, New York; Maple Lawn Cemetery Records, Bolivar, New York.

50.

Elizabeth A. Root, daughter of Truman Bishop (36), granddaughter of Abel, Sr. (28), b. Bolivar, New York April 27, 1836, d. Bolivar, New York December 13, 1932 from old age; m. Bolivar, New York November 29, 1857 Christopher Crandall Garthwait, b. Marcellus, New York December 27, 1835, d.

Bolivar, New York July 1, 1918 from infirmities of old age.

Elizabeth Garthwait was affectionately known in the family as *Lib.* She resided in Bolivar all of her life and witnessed many changes in the town that grew from a community of only 200 residents to an oil boom town of several thousand by the beginning of the 20th century. Mrs. Garthwait's sister, Arzulla Root Crandall, resided with the Garthwait family based on the 1865 New York State Census. Mrs. Garthwait was a charter member of the local chapter of the Order of the Eastern Star. Elizabeth Garthwait was a pillar of strength to members of her family providing them a place to stay when necessary and financial support when needed. At the time of her death, Elizabeth Root Garthwait had outlived her five brothers, four sisters, husband, daughter, and a grandson and was Bolivar's oldest living resident. The 1930 US Census records a full-time nurse, Lovina Ingalls, resided with Mrs. Garthwait. Her funeral took place at the family residence at 88 Wellsville Street in Bolivar. Her obituary does not mention the divorce of her parents, Truman Bishop and Polly Mead Root, and the remarriages of both.

Articles on Christopher Garthwait name his birthplace as Alfred, New York. However, this was contradicted by other sources, which named Marcellus, New York as his place of birth. His parents were Benjamin Garthwait (1812-1870) and Phoebe Crandall Garthwait (1813-1878) of Bolivar, New York. The Garthwaits resided for a time on a farm outside Bolivar later owned by A. L. Shaner. The US Census records for 1860, 1870 and 1880 and the New York State Census for 1865 and 1875 listed Christopher Garthwait's occupation as a farmer. Christopher Garthwait owned additional farm property including the former Kenyon and Wixson farms in Bolivar Township. The discovery of oil on Garthwait farm property made the Garthwait's very wealthy. Sometime in the 1880s, they moved to the village of Bolivar residing on Wellsville Street. For many years Christopher Garthwait was engaged in the mercantile business operating stores with his son, Elmer, and with Ira. J. Cooper in buildings later occupied by Cooper and Son and the Ira Dillie store in the Garthwait block, now torn down.

Mr. Garthwait had considerable investments in oil property and he was the Vice-President of Wilson Oil and Gas Company. Christopher Garthwait was a major stockholder and President of the State Bank of Bolivar. The 1900 and 1910 US Census and the 1905 New York Census record his occupation as a banker and later bank president. He was a member of the Bolivar Macedonia Lodge No. 258, F. & A. M. and the Buttrick Chapter of the Order of the Eastern Star. As a young man, Mr. Garthwait worked hard, saved his money, and at the time of his death was one of the wealthiest residents of Bolivar. Their residence on Wellsville Street was valued at $7000 in 1930. Today's value would be closer to $105,000. Elizabeth and Christopher Garthwait were buried in Bolivar's Maple Lawn Cemetery in the cemetery's only mausoleum. On November 29, 1907, Elizabeth and Christopher Garthwait held their 50th wedding anniversary at the residence of Mr. and Mrs. Charles William who were also celebrating their 50th wedding anniversary. The late Helen Ward Hulbert recorded these wedding memories from the 1907 event. Mr. and Mrs. Garthwait were married by Justice Merrill Cowles.

It was a cool, autumn day but the roads were frozen and smooth. When the Garthwaits married Bolivar numbered 150 residents. There was no railroad, no telephone, no telegraph, no cars, and the mail was delivered by a stage coach. When Mr. Garthwait arrived in Bolivar there was only one residence on Wellsville Street, the Frank McDivitt home. The hills were covered with big pine and hemlock trees and game was plentiful. In 1907 only two families living on the road between Bolivar and Allentown were still residing on that highway, the Phillips and Howe families. All the other families had moved away. Christopher Garthwait lived in a board shanty just outside Allentown during the winters of 1841-1842.

In Allentown there was only one log house, which was occupied by the Myron Allen family. Lumbering was the principal industry and some of the best pine and hemlock was in the Allentown area, which sold for $7 per thousand feet. Two sawmills on Knights Creek were where the timber was taken for processing. Mr. Garthwait gave each bride of fifty-years a ten-dollar gold piece. Four generations of the Williams family attended. The day was spent in sharing fifty years of memories and enjoying a splendid meal contributed to by many of the women present.

Children:

104. I. ***Emma Garthwait**, f.*

105. II. ***Elmer Christopher Garthwait**, f.*

References: U.S. Census Records: 1840, 1850, 1860, 1870, 1880, 1900, 1910, 1920, 1930; New York State Census: 1855, 1865, 1875, 1892, 1905, 1915, 1925; *Bolivar Breeze 1891-1965*, selected issues; Maple Lawn Cemetery Records, Bolivar, New York; unpublished Root Family History written by Helen Ward Hulbert.

51.

David Buell Root, son of Truman Bishop (36), grandson of Abel, Sr. (28), b. Bolivar, New York April 11, 1838, d. Bolivar, New York April 29, 1903 from heart disease and an artery rupture at his home on South Street; m. probably Bolivar, New York a. 1870 Emma Morris, b. Friendship, New York March 3, 1846, d. Otsego, Michigan April 28, 1927 from diabetes.

David Buell Root resided with his parents in Bolivar in the US Census for 1840, 1850, and 1860 and the New York State Census for 1855. Mr. Root enlisted in Bolivar on August 21, 1862 as a private in Company A of the 136th Infantry Regiment. Private Root saw military action at Gettysburg and with General Sherman during his March to the Sea. He was honorably discharged July 1, 1865 from the McDougall General Hospital, New York Harbor after three years of service. His discharge papers described him as having blue eyes, brown hair, a light complexion, and 6'1" tall. David Root applied for a disability pension November 11, 1875. He was employed as a farm worker and day laborer at a saw mill. Throughout much of his adult life, David Root suffered ill health probably caused by his military service in the Civil War. His obituary recorded that he returned home from conducting business, sat in his chair talking to Miss Hazel Wasson and her mother, and simply dropped dead.

The 1900 US Census recorded that David and Emma Root had been married for 30 years but never had children. Except for a brief period of residence in Eldred, Pennsylvania based on the 1880 US Census, the Roots spent the majority of their married years in Bolivar. Their property on South Street had the village of Bolivar's only mulberry tree. The tree achieved a height of fourteen feet in ten years' time and was loaded with berries that made excellent pies. The red, white and black berries on the tree were harvested by many a Bolivar family. Emma S. Morris was the daughter of William (1805-1887) and Elizabeth Quay (1808-1880) Morris, a farming family who resided in Wirt and West Clarksville before moving to Larned, Kansas to reside with a son and it was there they died. William Morris saw service in the Civil War with Company l, 85th New York Volunteers.

Mr. and Mrs. Root did not appear on the 1875 New York Census probably because they were living in Eldred, Pennsylvania. Emma Root did not appear in the New York Census for 1905 and 1915. She began collecting a widow's military pension June 8, 1903. In the 1910 US Census she was a widow with her own income in residence on Wellsville Street. In 1920 she resided with her brother-in-law, Erastus Root, and his family on Genesee Road in Bolivar. Around 1922 she moved to Otsego, Michigan to live with a sister and her nephew, Robert L. Wood, where she died. Emma Morris Root's death certificate states she was buried in Otsego; the cemetery not named. David Buell Root was buried in Maple Lawn Cemetery in Bolivar and his tombstone includes his wife's name, but it is unclear if Mrs. Root's remains were returned to Bolivar for burial.

References: US Census: 1840, 1850, 1860, 1870, 1880, 1900, 1910, 1920; New York State Census: 1855, 1865, 1892; *Bolivar Breeze 1891-1965*, selected issues; U.S. Civil War Pension Index: General Index to Pension Files, 1861-1934; New York Veteran Burial Cards 1861-1898; New York Town Clerks' Registers of Men Who Served in the Civil War; New York: Civil War Muster Roll Abstracts 1861-1900; Death Certificate, Michigan Department of Health for Emma S. Root; Maple Lawn Cemetery Records, Bolivar, New York; unpublished history of the Root Family by Helen Ward Hulbert.

52.

Bryant Hebron Root, son of Truman Bishop (36), grandson of Abel, Sr. (28), b. Bolivar, New York January 22, 1840, d. Bolivar, New York February 23, 1927 from apoplexy and heart disease; m. Bolivar, New York June 29, 1864 Martha Ann Crandall, b. Alfred, New York August 16, 1844, d. Bolivar, New York November 6, 1920 of apoplexy and heart disease.

Bryant Hebron Root or *Hebe* as he was known to family and friends resided with his parents in the 1840, 1850, and 1860 US Census records and in the 1855 New York State Census. He registered for the draft July 1, 1863, but Mr. Root was not called for military service. In the 1865 New York State Census Bryant Hebron Root and his wife Martha lived with two of Mr. Root's brothers, David and Erastus Root. The 1870 and 1880 US Census recorded the Roots lived first in Genesee Township and later in Bolivar where he did farm labor or worked as a carpenter. Mr. and Mrs. Root had two children but the 1900 US Census states that three children were born, but only two were living. The identity of the third child is not known. By the time of the 1910 US Census Bryant and Martha Root had moved into the village of Bolivar on South Street where he continued to find work as a carpenter. The 1920 US Census noted that Mr. Root was unemployed and in the 1925 New York State census he was a widower and retired carpenter who continued to reside on South Street. Bryant Hebron Root served the Bolivar community as a member of the Board of Trustees and as the village policeman. Martha Root was the daughter of Stephen (1806-1862) and Almira Odell Crandall (1812-1884). Mrs. Root was a devout Christian and a member of the Bolivar Methodist Church. Bryant Hebron and Martha Crandall Root were buried in Bolivar's Maple Lawn Cemetery.

Children:

106. I. ***Addie Elnora Root**, f.*

107. II. ***Ira Wallace Root**, f.*

References: US Census: 1840, 1850, 1860, 1870, 1880, 1900, 1910, 1920; New York State Census: 1855, 1865, 1875, 1892, 1905, 1915, 1925; *Bolivar Breeze 1891-1965*, selected issues; New York Death Index 1880-1956, Bryant H. Root; Unpublished Root Family History by Helen Ward Hulbert; Maple Lawn Cemetery records, Bolivar, New York.

53.

Arzulla D. Root, daughter of Truman Bishop (36), granddaughter of Abel, Sr. (28), b. Bolivar, New York November 22, 1841, d. Bolivar, New York June 10, 1910 from cancer; m. Bolivar, New York November 5, 1863 Alonzo Crandall while he was on an eleven-day furlough during the Civil War, b. Almond, New York May 6, 1838, d. Willard, New York November 8, 1918 Willard State Hospital from the Spanish Flu and lobar pneumonia.

Arzulla was known to family and friends as *Jule*. She resided with her parents until her 1863 marriage to Alonzo Crandall. While her husband was in military service, Arzulla lived with her married sister, Elizabeth Root Garthwait. Arzulla spent most of her life in Bolivar except for a brief period during the Civil War when she went to Camp Chase in Ohio to nurse her husband. Mr. and Mrs. Crandall resided on a farm two and on-half miles east of Bolivar village on Allentown Road. Arzulla's obituary described her as a woman of strong character and warm sympathies with a long and active life spent in unusual devotion to friends, home, and family. Mrs. Crandall was ill for over seven years and succumbed to recently diagnosed cancer. Her funeral was held at the family home.

Alonzo Crandall was the son of Stephen (1806-1862) and Almira Odell Crandall (1812-1884). His sister, Martha Ann Crandall, married his wife's brother, Bryant Hebron Root. Mr. Crandall resided with his parents on a Bolivar farm until his enlistment August 21 1862 for service in the Civil War. He joined Company A of the 136th Infantry Regiment of the New York Volunteers. Private Alonzo

Crandall saw action at the battles of Lookout Mountain, Resaca Heights, and Gettysburg where he was severely wounded. He was a member of the reserve corps that saw action at Chancellorsville and served with General Sherman on the General's March to the Sea. Alonzo Crandall had gray eyes, light hair, was of dark complexion, and stood 5 feet 9 inches tall. Mr. Crandall farmed his entire married life. He applied for a disability pension December 11, 1891. Alonzo Crandall's funeral took place at the home of his son, Erwin Crandall, in Bolivar. Alonzo and Arzulla Root Crandall were buried together in Bolivar's Maple Lawn Cemetery.

Children:

108. I. ***Ella Annette Crandall, f.***

109. II. ***Viola Vinette Crandall, f.***

110. III. ***Erwin David Crandall, f.***

111. IV. ***Owen Ernest Crandall, f.***

References: US Census: 1850, 1860, 1870, 1880, 1900, 1910, 1920; New York State Census: 1855, 1865, 1875, 1892, 1905, 1915; Maple Lawn Cemetery records, Bolivar, New York; *Bolivar Breeze 1891-1965*, selected issues; Unpublished Root Family History by Helen Ward Hulbert; New York Civil War Muster Roll Abstracts 1861-1900; U.S. Civil War Soldier Records and Profiles 1861-1865; US Civil War Pension Index: General Index to Pension Files 1861-1934; New York Veteran Burial Cards 1861-1898.

54.

Erastus F. Root, son of Truman Bishop (36), grandson of Abel, Sr. (28), b. Bolivar, New York June 7, 1843, d. Bolivar, New York October 4, 1932 from heart disease and hardening of the arteries; m. (1) Bolivar, New York August 17, 1867 Diantha A. Beebe, b. Alfred, New York 1850, d. Bolivar, New York April 27, 1896 from cancer; m. (2) Bolivar, New York December 30, 1907 Louisa Jane Moore Mead, b. Pennsylvania April 18, 1845, d. Bolivar, New York February 13, 1908 from blood poisoning; m. (3) Bolivar, New York August 21, 1909 Cora May Greene Newton, b. Martin's Ferry, West Virginia April 4, 1874, d. Bolivar, New York June 13, 1935 from pulmonary edema.

Erastus Root was a well-known member of the Bolivar community where he farmed and engaged in oil production and the lumber business. He resided with his parents based on the US Census records for 1850, 1860 and the New York State Census for 1855. Mr. Root registered with the draft July 1, 1863, but he did not see service. In the 1865 New York State Census Erastus Root lived with his brother and sister-in-law, Bryant and Martha Root, and an older brother David Root.

By the time of the 1870 US Census Erastus Root had married his first wife, fathered a daughter, and worked as a sawyer in Annin in McKean County Pennsylvania. His youngest brother, Lew Root, resided with them. By the time of the 1875 New York State Census the Root family had returned to Allegany County residing in Genesee Township outside Bolivar. He was employed as a farmer. In the 1880 US Census, Erastus Root's farm, across the highway from Maple Lawn cemetery, consisted of 177 acres of land that was farmed, in pasture, or in woodland. The farm was valued at $3,925. He raised both dairy cows producing 200 lbs. of butter, sheep, and some poultry. His plowed fields produced barley, wheat, Indian corn, oats, buckwheat, and potatoes. His four-acre apple orchard had a harvest of 150 bushels of apples from twenty-two trees. In the 1880 US Census Erastus Root's family had expanded to include a son, Asa Prentice Root, as well as his daughter Myrtie. Mr. Root's father, Truman Bishop Root also lived with them. In later years he was a partner in the Bolivar lumber firm of Parker and Root. Erastus F. Root sued Samuel A. Richardson and Francis Barnes June 15, 1898 for their failure to repay a loan of $159. The outcome of the case is not known. Erastus Root's first wife, Diantha Beebe, was the daughter of Prentice W. (1822-1888) and Mary Ann Hood (1824-1899) Beebe. Her obituary described Mrs. Root as a woman richly endowed with common sense and her death from cancer was a distinct loss to the community. Her funeral service was held at the family home.

In the 1900 US Census Erastus Root lived on the family farm with two servants to assist him. Erastus Root remarried December 30, 1907 in Bolivar to Louisa Jane Moore Mead. Louisa was the widow of William Harvey Mead (1835-1906) and, interestingly, was the daughter of Annie Smith Moore who was believed to be the second wife of Erastus Root's father, Truman Bishop Root. Given the rejection by Annie Moore's descendants of this second marriage for Truman Bishop Root, it was curious that Erastus would marry into the family given the controversy. Mr. Root's second marriage was short lived. In February 1908 Mrs. Root purchased some new undergarments and pressed her hand against a metal price tag, pricking her finger. Within hours her arm began to swell, but even with medical treatment the poisoned blood entered her entire system. She remained conscious until the hour before her death. Louisa Jane Moore Mead Root had five children by her first husband. Her obituary described her as active in all good work for the improvement of the community. She was a loving mother, a good neighbor, and a helpful wife. Louisa Mead Root was buried with her first husband in Bolivar's Maple Lawn Cemetery. Erastus Root married a third time to Cora May Greene Newton. Cora was divorced from her first husband, Burr Newton (1854-1911) in 1909.

Mr. Newton was Bolivar's Postmaster from 1885-1889 when the post office was in the Hoyt and Cowles Building. Burr and Cora Newton had one son, Harry, who was later adopted by Erastus Root. In 1912 Cora gave birth to a daughter, Donna Elizabeth, but the little girl survived only two days. Many contemporaries indicated that Cora Root suffered from periodic bouts of depression. The US Census records for 1910, 1920, and 1930 and the New York State Census records for 1915 and 1925 noted that the Root family consisted of Erastus, Cora, and Harry. By the end of his life Erastus Root was more engaged in lumber than farming. At the time of his death Erastus Root had outlived two wives, two daughters, four brothers, and four sisters. Erastus Root was buried with his first wife, Diantha Root, in Bolivar's Maple Lawn Cemetery. Cora Root was buried in Maple Lawn Cemetery with her son

Harry and daughter-in-law, Marguerite. Erastus Root's granddaughter, Helen Prentice Root Spargur was executor of his estate.

Children (by first marriage):

112. I. ***Myrtie Root, f.***

113. II. ***Asa Prentice Root, f.***

Children (by third marriage):

114. I. ***Harry Newton Root (adopted), f.***

115. II. ***Donna Elizabeth Root***, b. Bolivar November 2, 1912, d. Bolivar November 4, 1912. It is believed but it cannot be confirmed that she was buried in Maple Lawn Cemetery in Bolivar.

References: US Census: 1850, 1860, 1870, 1880, 1900, 1910, 1920, 1930; New York State Census: 1855, 1865, 1875, 1892, 1905, 1915, 1925; *Bolivar Breeze 1891-1965*, selected issues; US Selected Federal Census Non-Population Schedules 1850-1880; New York State Marriage Index 1881-1967; New York State Death Index 1880-1956; Bolivar Town Clerk Birth and Death Records for Donna Elizabeth Root; Maple Lawn Cemetery Records Bolivar, New York; unpublished Root Family History by Helen Ward Hulbert; Supreme Court of Allegany County Erastus F. Root vs. Samuel A. Richardson and Francis Barnes, June 15, 1899.

55.

Charlotte Root, daughter of Truman Bishop (36) and granddaughter of Abel, Sr. (28), b. Bolivar, New York 1846, d. Allen Township in Allegany County, New York November 15, 1896 from complications from multiple diseases; m. Cuba, New York February 22, 1867 (undocumented source) Walter A. Wilcox, b. Wirt, New York November 1848, d. Bolivar, New York May 26, 1913.

Charlotte Root Wilcox was known to family and friends as *Lottie*. In the 1850 and 1860 US Census Charlotte resided with her parents in Bolivar. The 1855 New York State Census had Charlotte staying with her paternal uncle and aunt, Abel and Polly Root. In the 1865 New York State Census, around the time her parents, Truman Bishop and Polly Root, separated and divorced, Charlotte Root was a boarder with the Milton Reed family in Bolivar. Charlotte Root and Walter Wilcox married in Cuba, New York on February 22, 1867. The marital information was undocumented data on Ancestry.com. Walter Wilcox was the son of Lyman (1818-1877) and Asenath Lunn Wilcox (1826-1863) of Wirt, New York.

It is not clear where Walter Wilcox was in 1870 because he cannot be found on the US Census for that year. His wife, Charlotte Root Wilcox, their daughter, Bertha, and his father, Lyman Wilcox, were boarders with the Samuel Allen family in Richburg, New York. Charlotte's sister, Mary Root, was also residing with the Allens. The 1875 New York State Census found the growing Wilcox family living in Friendship, New York where Mr. Wilcox was a grocery store clerk. They moved back to Wirt by 1880 where Walter Wilcox farmed. It was not clear from the 1880 US Census whether or not Walter Wilcox owned the farm, but his frequent job changes and residential moves suggest he rented rather than owned the property.

The 1880 agricultural data had the Wilcox farm consisting of 302 acres with a value on the farm and its equipment at $10,000 and the livestock valued at additional $1,685. The 1879 value of production was $1800. The farm produced 355 lbs. of butter, 100 lbs. of maple sugar, and 700 bushels of apples. Harvested crops included barley, Indian corn, oats, wheat, and potatoes. Ten acres of the farm was in apple orchards with 250 producing apple trees. Livestock included dairy cows and sheep. Walter Wilcox changed his occupation based on the 1892 New York State Census to oil pumper but remained in Wirt. When Charlotte Wilcox died in 1896, they had moved to Allen Township. As a widower, Walter Wilcox resided in Angelica, New York based on the records of the 1900 US Census and 1910 US Census. He was employed as a wheelwright in 1900 and as a laborer in 1910. Three of his children, Donna, Leon, and Carl, resided with him.

The 1900 US Census had Walter Wilcox listed incorrectly as William Wilcox. Walter Wilcox was not recorded on the 1905 New York State Census. Walter Wilcox died in Bolivar, probably at the home of his son Carl, on May 26, 1913. Unfortunately, the *Bolivar Breeze* newspapers for 1912-1915 no longer exist to confirm the death. In the 1990 edition of *The Root Family of Bolivar, New York*, I believed Walter Wilcox had remarried to an Ina Wicks. Documents now indicate that there were three men named Walter A. Wilcox residing in Allegany County. The Walter A. Wilcox who married Ina Wicks was born in 1885 eliminating the Walter A. Wilcox of this narrative as the spouse of Ina Wicks. Charlotte Root Wilcox was buried in Bolivar's Maple Lawn Cemetery. There are three other burials in the Wilcox lot and I suggest they are the graves for Walter Wilcox and Walter and Charlotte's unmarried daughters, Bertha and Donna. Only Charlotte Wilcox has a grave marker but there was space above her name for her husband's name, which was never entered. Maple Lawn Cemetery records did not record a burial for Walter Wilcox.

Children:

116. I. ***Bertha A. Wilcox, f.***

117. II. ***Abijah Lyman Wilcox, f.***

118. III. ***Donna B. Wilcox, f.***

119. IV. ***Leon E. Wilcox, f.***

120. V. ***Carl Stanley Wilcox, f.***

References: US Census: 1850, 1860, 1870, 1880, 1900, 1910; New York State Census: 1855, 1865, 1875, 1892, 1905; *Bolivar Breeze 1891-1965*, selected articles; Maple Lawn Cemetery Records, Bolivar, New York; US Selected Federal Census Non-Population Schedules 1850-1880; New York Death Index 1880-1956 for Walter Wilcox; unpublished Root Family History by Helen Ward Hulbert.

56.

Sidney LeRoy Root, son of Truman Bishop (36), grandson of Abel, Sr. (28), b. Bolivar, New York March 27, 1848, d. Bolivar, New York December 19, 1927 from gastric carcinoma; m. Genesee Township, Allegany County, New York November 8, 1872 Sarah Evans, b. in England February 24, 1854, d. Clarksville or Obi, New York April 6, 1927.

Original US Census records name the fourth son of Truman Bishop and Polly Root as Sidney LeRoy Root. However, as an adult Mr. Root reversed the order of his first and middle names becoming LeRoy Sidney Root. Among family and friends, he was known as *Roy*. Mr. Root's granddaughter, the late Coral Marie Patterson, stated that LeRoy Root met his wife while her family was traveling from England through the United States in 1870. Sarah Evans parents eventually moved on to Wisconsin, but she and a sister remained in Allegany County. LeRoy Root resided with his parents in the US Census for 1850 and 1860 and the 1855 New York State Census. Mr. Root was not recorded in the 1865 New York State Census. This was the time when Truman Bishop and Polly Root separated and divorced and their ten children found places to stay with other family members or as boarders. In the 1870 US Census LeRoy Root resided with his brother and sister-in-law, Bryant Hebron and Martha Root. His brother Erastus Root also resided with them. In the 1875 New York State Census, LeRoy and Sarah were married, living in Genesee Township with his son, Burr LeRoy, and his wife's younger sister, Emma Evans. Mr. Root farmed. The 1880 US Census found the Root family still residing in Genesee Township outside Bolivar on their farm. There were now two children, Burr and Lena, and sister-in-law Emma Evans continued to live with them.

The non-agricultural census for 1880 described the LeRoy Root farm as a property of sixteen acres with the land and buildings valued at $610. Annual produce sales amounted to $150. The Root dairy cows produced 150 lbs. of butter. The plowed fields yielded Indian corn, buckwheat, and oats. They also raised chickens. This farm could not have financially sustained Mr. Root's family. I suggest that the much larger neighboring farm owned by LeRoy's brother, Erastus Root, was where he also worked to support his family. The 1892 New York State census recorded the Root family in Genesee Township farming with three children in residence, Burr, Ernest, and Eva. The 1900 US Census recorded an occupational change for Mr. Root. Still residing in Genesee Township, he was now an oil pumper. Children Burr, Ernest, and Eva continued to reside at home. Daughter Lena had married. The US

Census for 1910 and 1920 and the New York State Census for 1905, 1915, and 1925 recorded the Root family moving from Genesee township into Bolivar village residing on Olean Street. LeRoy Root was listed as both an oil pumper and an oil producer drilling for oil on his own property and buying drilling rights on other farms.

LeRoy Root was extensively involved in many social activities of the Bolivar community. Mr. Root was a prominent Master Mason of the Macedonia Lodge serving as its secretary (1904) and as Past Master (1915, 1916) and was a member of the Buffalo Shrine. An active member of the J. B. Bradley Hose Company # 1, LeRoy Root served as its Treasurer (1908), Vice-President (1909), Acting Chief (1916), and President (1919). Mr. Root was an active member of the I.O.O. F. (Odd Fellows) and was elected Noble Grand (1908). He acted in a number of Odd Fellows productions including *A Happy Pair* (1909), *New Hampshire Folks* (1915), and *Farmer Hawkins Ward* (1918). He wrote poetry for many a Fire Department smoker. LeRoy Root was a life-long Democrat and ran for many an office in Bolivar and Allegany County but usually lost to Republican candidates whose supporters far outnumbered the Democrats.

While working in the oil fields in 1894, LeRoy Root escaped serious injury in a drilling accident when his arm was caught in drilling machinery. The quick efforts of his co-workers got the machine stopped and freed Mr. Root's arm by crushing the left wrist to extricate it. In 1905 Mr. Root purchased the oil rights on the Jordan farm, which led to the successful drilling for oil. In 1924 LeRoy and Sarah Root moved from their Olean Street residence to a smaller house on South Main Street. He was one of the first in 1905 to lay a concrete sidewalk in front of his Olean Street home.

LeRoy and Sarah Root had six children, but three daughters, Mabel, Eva, and Lulu, died young from health issues. Sarah Evans Root was the daughter of Richard and Sarah Evans who came from England seeking better economic opportunities. Mrs. Root was a member of the Eastern Star, a devout Christian, and a kind neighbor and friend who was held in high esteem by the Bolivar community. Her younger sister, Emma (1864-1944), who resided with Sarah and LeRoy Root, married in 1896 Clarence Sylvanus Christman (1870-1953) of Wellsville. Mr. and Mrs. Christman had a son Clarence Richard Christman (1902-1952). Emma Evans Christman raised the only surviving child of Mr. Christman's first marriage to Sarah Hyatt (1867-1896), Kathryn O'Rene Christman (1896-1997) who married Luman Cleveland (1891-1944) of Allentown, New York and was the mother of many prominent Allentown residents. Sarah Root died at her daughter Lena's residence in Obi, New York from a number of ailments she suffered from for many years. LeRoy Root's death came from a number of long-term health issues. LeRoy and Sarah Evans were buried in Bolivar's Maple Lawn Cemetery with their three young daughters, Mabel, Eva, and Lulu.

Children:

121. I. ***Mabel V. Root***, b. Genesee Township February 1874, d. Genesee Township April 2, 1874 from inflammation of the lungs. Mabel was buried in Maple Lawn Cemetery.

122. II. ***Burr LeRoy Root, f.***

123. III. ***Lena E. Root, f.***

124. IV. ***Ernest Stanley Root, f.***

125. V. ***Eva L. Root***, b. Genesee Township February 7, 1888, d. January 21, 1904 from heart trouble. Her obituary described Miss Root as a bright and popular child. She was buried in Maple Lawn Cemetery.

126. VI. ***Lulu or Lula Bell Root***, b. Genesee Township, New York 1893, d. Genesee Township, New York September 2, 1898 from cholera. Her obituary described her as a bright and beloved child. Miss Root was buried in Maple Lawn Cemetery.

References: US Census: 1850, 1860, 1870, 1880, 1900, 1910, 1920; New York State Census: 1855, 1865, 1875, 1892, 1905, 1915, 1925; Bolivar *Breeze 1891-1965*, selected issues; U.S. Selected Federal Census Non-Population Schedules 1850-1880; New York Death Index 1880-1956 for LeRoy and Sarah Root; unpublished Root Family History by Helen Ward Hulbert; Maple Lawn Cemetery Records, Bolivar, New York.

57.

Mary A. Root, daughter of Truman Bishop (36), granddaughter of Abel, Sr. (28), b. Bolivar, New York December 20, 1849, d. Cuba, New York hospital December 31, 1923 from a stroke; m. (1) place and date unknown Justice A. Rew b. Friendship, New York December 1846, d. probably Kansas, date unknown; m. (2) Bolivar, New York May 21, 1897 John H. Richardson, b. place and date unknown, d. place and date not known.

Mary Root resided with her parents as confirmed by the US Census records for 1850 and 1860 and the New York State Census for 1855. She was known among the family as *Mate*. Once her parents, Truman Bishop and Polly Root, separated and divorced, Mary Root resided with the James White family as a boarder in the 1865 New York State Census and with her married sister, Charlotte Root Wilcox based on the 1870 US Census. Sometime between the 1870 US Census and the 1875 New York State Census, Mary A. Root married Justice A. Rew of Friendship, New York.

Justice Rew was the son of Ovid (1816-1900) and Mary Annis Scott Rew (1817-1883). Justice and Mary Rew resided in Wirt, New York based on the 1875 New York State Census where he was employed as a laborer. By the time of the 1880 US Census the Rew family moved to Friendship, New York where Justice Rew was employed as a railroad bridge builder. They had two children, a son Elba and a daughter Lizzie. They moved to Kansas sometime during the 1880s. The reasons and location were never identified. The information about the Rew family becomes vague after the move to Kansas.

Unpublished family histories and Mary Root Rew Richardson's obituary both state that their son Elba Rew died soon after their arrival in Kansas and that Justice Rew also died there.

The 1910 US Census records three children for Mary Richardson, but none were living. The identity of the third child is not known. Information about Mary's second husband was very sketchy. He was referred to as Mr. Richardson and reportedly died shortly after they were married in 1897. Recently released New York marriage documents name him as John H. Richardson and provide the marriage date in Bolivar on May 21, 1897. No connections can currently be found between this John H. Richardson and any other Richardson families then residing in Bolivar. Mary Root Rew Richardson ran a boarding house in West Virginia and later based on the 1900 US Census Mrs. Richardson was living in Eulalia, Potter County, Pennsylvania and ran a boarding house there with her daughter. Her daughter Lizzie died in 1904 and Mary Richardson moved first to Hornellsville (1905), then Friendship (1909), and eventually returned to Bolivar residing with her aunt, Clarissa Mead, as noted in the 1910 New York State Census, working as a housekeeper. The 1915 New York State Census records Mary Richardson residing with the W. Riley Cowles family doing housework. She did not appear on the 1920 US Census.

Mary Richardson suffered a stroke in May 1923 and remained in an Olean, New York hospital until a few weeks before her death when she was moved to the Cuba, New York hospital. During her residence in Bolivar, Mary Richardson was a member of the Buttrick Chapter, Order of the Eastern Star, the Trilby Rebekah Lodge, and the Women's Relief Corps. Her 1924 funeral was held at the home of her nephew, Ernest S. Root. Mary Root Rew Richardson was buried in Bolivar's Maple Lawn Cemetery. Her tombstone was paid for by her sister, Elizabeth Root Garthwait. A further twist to the story of Mary and Justice Rew was documentation on a Justice A. Rew, born in New York and with the same birth year as the husband of Mary Root but alive in 1895 residing in Pratt, Kansas in a boarding house. The 1900 US Census recorded that this Justice A. Rew married in 1895 and was living with his wife Annie in Galena, Kansas. In 1905 this Justice A. Rew and his wife had moved to Cherokee, Kansas. After the 1905 Kansas State Census, the trail goes cold. Therefore, did Justice A. Rew die as recorded by Root family members or did Mary and Justice Rew separate and/or divorce?

Children (by first marriage):

127. I. ***Elba Rew***, b. Friendship, New York a. 1876, d. in Kansas. No further information can be found.

128. II. ***Lizzie Rew***, *f.*

References: US Census: 1850, 1860, 1870, 1880, 1900, 1910; New York State Census: 1855, 1865, 1875, 1915; Kansas State Census Collections: 1895, 1905; New York State Marriage Index 1881-1967; *Bolivar Breeze 1891-1965*, selected issues; Maple Lawn Cemetery Records Bolivar, New York; Unpublished Root Family History by Helen Ward Hulbert.

58.

Olivia Root, daughter of Truman Bishop (36), granddaughter of Abel, Sr. (28), b. Bolivar, New York November 12, 1854, d. Bolivar, New York July 6, 1908 from stomach cancer; m. Friendship, New York September 23, 1874 Orrin Freeman Pire, b. probably Friendship, New York November 12, 1850, d. Bolivar, New York September 25, 1901 from cerebral apoplexy.

Olivia Root resided with her parents, Truman Bishop and Polly Root, based on the 1855 New York State Census and the 1860 US Census. Miss Root cannot be located on the 1865 New York State Census. It was assumed, given her young age, that she was living with her mother and step-father but the location is not known. In the 1870 US Census Olivia Root was incorrectly listed as Olivia Hitchcock and resided in Bolivar with her mother and step-father, Polly and Horace Hitchcock. Orrin Freeman Pire was the son of Russell Pire (1810-1885) and Amanda Miller Pire (1817-1878) of Friendship and later Bolivar, New York. In the 1875 New York State Census Mr. and Mrs. Pire resided in Bolivar where Freeman worked as a laborer. The 1880 US Census records Olivia and Freeman Pire continuing their residence in Bolivar with one son, Floyd, and Mr. Pire employed as a stone mason. They continued to reside in Bolivar based on the 1892 New York State Census with two sons, Floyd and Ward.

Freeman Pire was employed as a tinsmith, an occupation he continued when the Pire family moved to the Coudersport, Pennsylvania area where in 1900 their residence was listed as DeWight Street in Eulalia, Potter County, Pennsylvania. In March of 1900 they moved to East Olean, New York and a few months later in May 1900 they moved back to Pennsylvania to Coudersport where Mr. Pire was briefly employed at the hardware store of Olmstead and Son. The 1900 US Census records that Freeman and Olivia Pire had five children with only two living. The identities of the other three children are not known. In 1901 Freeman Pire returned to Bolivar for employment leaving his wife and children in Coudersport, Pennsylvania. He was a boarder at the residence of Mrs. Louisa Hitchcock where he took cold in late September 1901 and suffered a stroke while sitting in a chair near a warming stove. Mr. Pire was moved to the home of his brother, Addison Pire, and his wife and sons came from Coudersport to take care of him. He died there on September 25, 1901. Olivia Pire worked as a nurse for many years. After her husband's death, she moved back to Bolivar and resided on South Street. Mrs. Pire was able to work until the last year of her life when cancer made further employment impossible. Her obituary described her as a kind and sympathetic woman with many friends. She was buried in Bolivar's Maple Lawn Cemetery next to her husband. Freeman Pire has a grave marker but Olivia Pire does not.

Children:

129 I. ***Floyd Bernard Pire**, f.*

130. II. ***Ward Laurence Pire**, f.*

References: US Census: 1860, 1870, 1880, 1900; New York State Census: 1855, 1875, 1892; *Bolivar Breeze 1891-1965*, selected issues; New York Death Index 1880-1956 for Orrin F. Pire; New York State Census 1875 for wedding date; Maple Lawn Cemetery Records, Bolivar, New York; Unpublished Root Family History by Helen Ward Hulbert.

59.

Arthur Llewellyn Root, son of Truman Bishop (36), grandson of Abel, Sr. (28), b. Bolivar, New York June 6, 1855, d. Independence, Kansas November 18, 1917 from a stroke and a typhoid attack; m. (1) Bolivar, New York, date not known Lydia or Lida Cowles, b. Bolivar, New York a. 1857, d. Bolivar, New York January 2, 1895, divorced; m. (2) a. 1893, place not know, Ida Leora Roberts, b. Potter County, Pennsylvania November 1859, d. Freemont, Ohio November 22, 1916. Lew Root resided with his parents as recorded in the 1855 New York State Census and the 1860 US Census.

He cannot be found on the 1865 New York State Census, which was taken around the time his parents, Truman Bishop and Polly Root, separated and divorced. It is believed, given his age, that he lived with his mother and step-father. The 1870 US Census gave his name as Louell Root residing with his brother Erastus Root in Genesee Township, New York. The 1875 New York State Census records Lew Root living with his mother and step-father, Polly and Horace Hitchcock, in Bolivar employed as a carpenter. Sometime between 1875 and 1880, Lew Root married Lydia Cowles, daughter of Bolivar residents Charles Cowles (1810-1887) and Betsey Jane Davie Cowles (1814-1883).

The Cowles family was one of the earliest families to settle Bolivar. In the 1880 US Census Lew and Lydia Cowles resided with her parents in Bolivar. Mr. Root's first name on the census was listed as Ludlow and he worked as a laborer. Lew and Lydia Root separated and divorced sometime before the 1892 New York State Census. Lydia Cowles Root remarried to Warren J. Rouse, a grocer in Friendship, New York, where she lived in 1892 with her new husband and her daughter from her first marriage, Leona, incorrectly listed as Leona Rouse on the census. Warren Rouse was married a total of three times and was seventeen years older than Lydia was. His marriage to Lydia Root was his second union. Lydia died from cancer on January 2, 1895 and was buried in Bolivar's Maple Lawn Cemetery. Lydia's parents were buried in Maple Lawn Cemetery. There was a third burial in the Cowles lot without a marker and it could be the grave of Lydia Cowles Root Rouse. In 1892 the New York State Census records Lew Root as a single man residing in a boarding house in Bolivar who worked as a laborer.

In 1893 Lew Root remarried to Ida Leora Roberts Stebbins. Ida's first husband was George Stebbins, b. a. 1855 in Wellsville, New York and died June 9, 1891 in Potter County, Pennsylvania. Ida and George Stebbins had four children, Rose Stebbins who died young, Henry Edgar Stebbins, Viva P. Stebbins Willard, and Mary A. Stebbins Beatty. Ida Root was the daughter of John Roberts (1827-1898) and Mary Ann Hoxie Roberts (1829-1893) of Potter County, Pennsylvania. It is not known how Lew and Ida met and became acquainted. The 1900 US Census recorded Lew and Ida Root in Genesee Township with Ida's three surviving children from her first marriage and the two sons from their marriage. They resided on Salt Rising Road. Lew Root worked as an oil pumper.

The 1905 New York State Census noted that the Root family continued to reside in Genesee Township where he worked as an oil pumper. Their two sons, Leon and James Curtiss, resided with them as did one of Ida's daughters from her first marriage. Mr. and Mrs. Root moved to Bolivar village by 1910 with their two sons where they rented a house. Lew Root continued to work as an oil pumper. The 1915 New York State Census recorded Ida Root living alone in Genesee Township. Lew Root and sons Leon and J. Curtiss had already moved to Dewey, Oklahoma in 1915 to work on the Martin O'Connor oil lease. Ida came soon after, but she could not adapt to the climate change and went to Freemont, Ohio where her daughter Vi Willard resided. It was at her daughter's home in Fremont that Mrs. Root died from complications of several unidentified diseases. Lew continued to work in Oklahoma after Ida's death. In the fall of 1917, he accepted a position with an oil company in Peru, Kansas where he became ill from a typhoid attack, suffered a stroke, and died a few months later. The remains of both of Lew and Ida Root were returned to Bolivar for burial in Maple Lawn Cemetery.

Children (by first marriage):

131. I. ***Leona Ruth Root**, f.*

Children (by second marriage):

132. I. ***Leon Erastus Root**, f.*

133. II. ***James Curtiss Root**, f.*

References: US Census: 1860, 1870, 1880, 1900, 1910; New York State Census: 1855, 1875, 1892, 1905, 1915; *Bolivar Breeze 1891-1965*, selected issues; Maple Lawn Cemetery Records, Bolivar, New York; Unpublished Root Family History by Helen Ward Hulbert; Greenlee, Ralph Stebbins and Greenlee Robert Lemuel, *The Stebbins Genealogy*, 2 Volumes. Chicago, Illinois: Privately Printed, 1904.

62.

Francis Albertus Kellogg, son of Huldah Penelope (37), grandson of Abel, Sr. (28), b. Bolivar, New York April 19, 1841, d. Shinglehouse, Pennsylvania September 12, 1910 from uremia and Bright's Disease; m. (1) Wirt, New York February 16, 1862 Abigail Paulina Peterson, b. Wirt, New York August 30, 1840, d. Shinglehouse, Pennsylvania February 11, 1906 from breast cancer; m. (2) Olean, New York August 1, 1906 Fannie Haislip Harlow, b. Charlottesville, Virginia October 11, 1848, d. Shinglehouse, Pennsylvania December 7, 1928.

Francis Albertus Kellogg was sometimes listed on census records as Albertus or Albert Kellogg and on other census documents as Francis A. Kellogg. He was not listed on the US Census records for 1850 and 1860, nor was he listed on the 1855, 1865, and 1875 New York State Census documents. Francis A. Kellogg is recorded in the 1856 Iowa Census when his father, step-mother, and siblings briefly moved there. Mr. Kellogg registered for the draft in June 1863 in Cuba, New York. At the time he registered he was married and employed as a farmer in Friendship, New York. Francis Kellogg did not see military service. Abigail was the daughter of John (1806-?) and Julia Peterson (1814-1858) of Wirt, New York. In 1870 Francis and Abigail Kellogg resided in Cuba, New York with two children, Sarah and Irvin, where Mr. Kellogg farmed. In 1880 Francis Kellogg farmed in Wirt, New York and the Kelloggs had five children, Sarah, Irwin, Willis, Marshall, and Leon. By the time of the 1900 US Census Francis and Abigail Kellogg had moved to Sharon in Potter County Pennsylvania. Their son Leon resided with them on the family farm as did Francis Kellogg's half-brother Abraham. Abigail died in 1906 from breast cancer and Francis Kellogg remarried within six months to Fannie Haislip Harlow. It is not known how they met. Fannie's first husband was Richard Harlow with whom she had five children. Fannie outlived Francis Kellogg by eighteen years dying in 1928 from influenza. Francis and Abigail Kellogg were buried in Shinglehouse's Maple Grove Cemetery in unmarked graves. Fannie Kellogg was also buried in Maple Grove with a headstone marking her grave.

Children (by first marriage):

134. I. ***Sarah Ann Kellogg, f.***

135. II. ***John Irvin Kellogg, f.***

136. III. ***Julia Ann Kellogg***, b. Cuba, New York July 25, 1867, d. Cuba, New York January 25, 1870. Burial location unknown.

137. IV. ***Loring Jesse Kellogg***, b. Cuba, New York July 27, 1869, d. Cuba, New York February 18, 1870. Burial location unknown.

138. V. ***Willis Burr Kellogg, f.***

139. VI. ***Marshall Loring Kellogg, f.***

140. VII. ***Loyal Leon Kellogg, f.***

141. VIII. ***Bertha Dilla Kellogg, f.***

References: US Census: 1870, 1880, 1900, 1910; Iowa State Census: 1856; Hopkins, Timothy. *The Kelloggs in the Old World and the New.* San Francisco, California: Sunset Press, 1903; Maple Grove Cemetery Records, Shinglehouse, Pennsylvania; US Civil War Draft Registration Records 1863-1865; New York State Marriage Index 1881-1967 for F.A. Kellogg second marriage; Pennsylvania Death Certificates 1906-1966 for F. A. Kellogg and Fannie H. Kellogg.

63.

James Fayette Kellogg, son of Huldah Penelope (37), grandson of Abel, Sr. (28), b. Bolivar, New York April 19, 1841; d. Jackson, Mississippi October 22, 1862.

In 1856 he resided with his father, step-mother, and siblings in Iowa. He remained in Iowa with his brother Orlando when most of the family returned to Bolivar, New York. James Fayette Kellogg enlisted in the Union Army on July 1, 1861 in the Fifth Iowa Volunteers, Company C, at the age of 18 years in Columbus City, Iowa. He saw military action at the battles of Pea Ridge, Fort Donelson, and Vicksburg. After the fall of Vicksburg, he was wounded in the right knee at the battle at the junction of the Yazoo and Iuka Railroads in Mississippi. James Kellogg continued firing even when a Confederate Captain rushed him with drawn sword. Kellogg rose on his sound leg, bayoneted his enemy and secured his belt and sword before becoming insensible. James Kellogg was taken from the field to the Jackson, Mississippi hospital where he died from his wounds. Private Kellogg was originally buried near the hospital in an unmarked grave. In 1866 his remains were reburied in the Corinth National Cemetery in Corinth, Mississippi.

References: Iowa State Census: 1856; US Civil War Soldier Records and Profiles, 1861-1865; Corinth National Cemetery Records, Corinth, Mississippi; Hopkins, Timothy. *The Kelloggs in the Old World and the New.* San Francisco, California: Sunset Press, 1903.

64.

Elmedoras or Elmer Doras Cass Kellogg, son of Huldah Penelope (37), grandson of Abel, Sr. (28), b. Bolivar, New York September 2, 1845, d. Florence, North Carolina December 8, 1864 as a prisoner of war.

Elmer Kellogg resided for a brief period in the 1850s in Iowa, but returned to Bolivar and resided with his uncle, James H. Root, based on the 1860 US Census. His occupation at the time of enlistment on September 10, 1861 in Bolivar in Company I, later Company D, of the 85th New York Infantry, was a farmer. The Town of Bolivar paid a $300 bounty for his enlistment. Private Kellogg's Muster Roll describes him as a man standing 5 feet and 8 ½ inches tall with red hair, blue eyes, and a light complexion. He was captured at the Battle of Plymouth, North Carolina April 20, 1864. The Battle of Plymouth was the second largest battle in North Carolina during the Civil War and the last Confederate victory. Mr. Kellogg was transferred to Andersonville Prison in Georgia and lastly to the Florence Stockade in Florence, South Carolina. The Florence Stockade was more brutal to prisoners-of-war than was Andersonville. Probably already weakened by poor care at Andersonville, Elmer Kellogg died at Florence December 8, 1864. He was buried in an unmarked grave, later reinterred, in what became the Florence (South Carolina) National Cemetery. Elmedoras Kellogg's name is on a Civil War Monument in Maple Lawn Cemetery in Bolivar, New York.

References: US Census: 1860; Iowa State Census: 1856; Maple Lawn Cemetery Records, Bolivar, New York; New York Civil War Muster Roll Abstracts 1861-1900; New York Town Clerks' Registers of Men Who Served in the Civil War 1861-1865; Andersonville Prisoners of War; National Park Service Prisoner Details; Hopkins, Timothy. *The Kelloggs in the Old World and in the New.* San Francisco, California: Sunset Press, 1903.

65.

Royal Jasper Kellogg, son of Huldah Penelope (37), grandson of Abel, Sr. (28), b. Bolivar, New York October 15, 1846, d. Galesburg, Illinois August 16, 1917; m. New Milford, Pennsylvania April 20, 1870 Lucy Ellen Beardsley, b. New Milford, Pennsylvania March 9, 1841, d. place and date of death not known. In the 1855 New York State Census and the 1860 US Census Royal or Roy Jasper Kellogg resided with his maternal uncle, James H. Root, of Bolivar. He graduated from Alfred University and began a distinguished career as a clergyman. In 1870 Royal Kellogg resided in New Milford, Pennsylvania with his wife and mother-in-law where he began his clerical career. Mr. and Mrs. Kellogg continued to reside in New Milford in 1880 where he continued his profession as a clergyman. The Kellogg family had grown to include three children, Royal Loren, Mabel Grace, and Mary Ellen.

The 1900 US Census found the Kellogg family living in Dongola, Illinois. By 1900 their daughters Mabel Grace and Mary Ellen had died and son Royal Loren was on his own. A third daughter, Myrtle, born in 1881, lived with them. In 1910 Reverend and Mrs. Kellogg resided in McHenry, North Dakota. Their two surviving children remained in Illinois. Reverend Royal Jasper Kellogg served as a minister of the Methodist Episcopal Church for twenty-eight years. He changed denominations and became a Congregational minister in later life. In 1879 he was principal of the Monrovia Seminary and for two and one-half years was the superintendent of missions on the west coast of Africa returning to America in 1880 with impaired health. In 1897 he was the pastor of a church at Denverside, East St. Louis. The church was too poor to provide a parsonage so Reverend Kellogg took matters into his own hands. With the aid of the congregation and friends, the construction of a parsonage was started. The Carpenter's Union protested and the Union tried to force their own workers onto the project.

Kellogg was assaulted by seven men and driven off the work site but returned with a double-barreled shotgun and a permit to use it. The parsonage was finished without further incident and he took up residence. In 1899 Reverend Kellogg moved on to Alto Pass, Illinois. The February 23, 1911 edition of the *Bolivar Breeze* contains a two-page letter from Reverend Kellogg to the people of Bolivar. Kellogg proudly noted that regardless of where he resided, he continued to regularly receive the Bolivar newspaper. Reverend Kellogg proudly remembered his strict upbringing in the home of his maternal uncle and aunt, James H. and Mary Root. He fondly recalled as a young boy Bolivar's traveling library, which resided in a residence for one year before moving to another house. One year his uncle, Jim Root, was elected librarian and all the books came to the Root house where he greatly enjoyed reading about the settlement of the West.

Reverend Kellogg admitted to drinking as a youth and was glad he had broken that habit. The article discussed his change of ministry to the Congregational Church and his acceptance of positions, which paid from $800 to $1600 per year. By becoming a Congregational minister, he could ordain young men as ministers, which was a privilege denied him as a minister of the Methodist Episcopal Church. In September of 1910, Reverend Kellogg had a serious carriage accident. He suffered two broken ribs and a badly injured hip. The article concluded with descriptions of some of the communities he served and how he would like to get to the area to visit old friends and his older brother in Potter County. It is believed that Reverend Kellogg is buried in Linwood Cemetery in Galesburg, Illinois, where his wife was probably buried, but this cannot be confirmed.

Children:

142. I. ***Loren Royal Kellogg**, f.*

143. II. ***Grace Mabel Kellogg***, b. Damascus, Pennsylvania April 6, 1876, d. Manchester, Connecticut October 12, 1886. Her burial site is not known.

144. III. ***Mary Ellen Kellogg***, b. New Milford, Pennsylvania March 24, 1878, d. Manchester, Connecticut October 19, 1886. Her burial site is not known.

145. IV. ***Myrtle Louise Kellogg**, f.*

References: US Census: 1860, 1870, 1880, 1900, 1910; New York State Census: 1855; *Bolivar Breeze, February 23, 1911;* Hopkins, Timothy. *The Kelloggs in the Old World and the New.* San Francisco, California: Sunset Press, 1903; Illinois Deaths and Stillbirths Index 1916-1947.

68.

Florence A. Root, daughter of Franklin B. (38) and granddaughter of Abel, Sr. (28), b. Angelica, New York June 1854, d. after 1905 place and date not known; m. (1) Angelica, New York, date not known John F. Weir, b. Angelica, New York a. 1845, d. Angelica New York October 17, 1877; m. (2) Ashtabula, Ohio December 25, 1899 John J. Watt, b. Ohio November 1845, d. Jeff Davis Parish, Louisiana January 31, 1913, believed divorced.

Florence Root resided with her parents, Franklin and Jane Root as recorded in the 1855 and 1865 New York State Census and in the 1860 and 1870 US Census. She married John F. Weir of Angelica sometime after 1871 and before the 1875 New York State Census. John Weir was the son of Angelica farmer Andrew Weir (b. a. 1806-1858) and his wife Mercy (b. a. 1805-1868). John Weir was previously married to Hattie, last name not known, who died January 8, 1871 at the age of 19 years, 3 months, and 27 days. John Weir was employed as a farm laborer before his first marriage, made cheese during his first marriage, and was an insurance agent during his marriage to Florence Root. It is not known what caused John Weir's death at age 32. He was buried in Angelica's Until the Dawn of the Day Cemetery with his first wife. John and Florence Weir did not have any children. Florence Root Weir resumed residence with her parents after her husband's death based on the 1880 US Census. She did not appear on the 1892 New York State Census.

Florence remarried in Ashtabula, Ohio on December 25, 1899 to John J. Watt who grew up in Sac City, Iowa but was born in Ohio. Her second marriage application lists her name as Florence A. Root. Florence and John Watt moved to Hickory Flat, Louisiana where they were recorded in residence in the 1900 US Census. John Watt was the son of Samuel Lemon Watt, Sr. (1806-1878) of Sac City, Iowa and probably his first wife, Olive Gilbert Walton (1810-1843?). Florence's second marriage did not last long because the 1910 US Census records John J. Watt, a resident of Jennings, Louisiana, as divorced. Florence Root Weir Watt was last recorded as alive in 1905 living in Madison, Wisconsin based on her father's obituary. It does not appear that she had any children. It is possible she married a third time, which might explain the difficulty in learning what happened to her. It is also unclear when she left Angelica, New York and what Florence did in Iowa before she married John Watt. This leaves a twenty-year gap in her biography. Florence may have stayed with her parents until her mother's death in 1889 and then moved to Iowa where her brother, George H. Root and his family resided.

References: US Census: 1860, 1870, 1880, 1900, 1910; New York State Census: 1855, 1865, 1875; Until the Dawn of the Day Cemetery Records, Angelica, New York; Ohio County Marriage Records 1774-1993; Louisiana Statewide Death Index 1900-1949 for John J. Watt; 1875 Allegany County Business Directory for John F. Weir Insurance.

69.

George Henry Root, son of Franklin B. (38), grandson of Abel, Sr. (28), b. Angelica, New York June 13, 1860, d. Willernie, Minnesota August 24, 1938; m. Benton, Iowa May 22, 1888, Harriet Elizabeth Fentiman, b. Black Hawk County, Iowa October 9, 1867, d. Ramsey County, Minnesota September 9, 1946. George Root resided with his parents based on the 1860 and 1870 US Census and the 1865 and 1875 New York Census records.

It is not known when George Root left Angelica, New York for Iowa or the reasons for this decision. He cannot be located on the 1880 US Census, but George Root did settle in Iowa where Mr. Root met and married Harriet Elizabeth Fentiman in Benton, Iowa in 1888. Mrs. Root was known as Hattie and was the daughter of John Daniel Fentiman (1820-1906) and Christianna Holdiman Fentiman (1834-1910). Hattie had four brothers and two sisters. The 1889 Iowa Census records that George and Hattie Root had a son Arthur, but he died very young as did a daughter named Florence because the 1900 US Census records that George and Hattie had three children, but only one was alive, a daughter Elizabeth. In 1900 the Roots lived in Jefferson, Iowa where Mr. Root was employed as a locomotive engineer. By 1910 George and Hattie Root and their surviving child, Elizabeth, had moved to St. Paul, Minnesota where Mr. Root continued his employment as a railroad engineer. Their St. Paul residency continued through 1920. By 1930 George Henry Root had retired and the family moved to Lincoln, Minnesota where he resided with his wife, divorced daughter Elizabeth, and granddaughter Elizabeth. Mr. Root died in 1938. Hattie Root continued to reside in Lincoln with her daughter and granddaughter until her death in 1946. George and Hattie Root were buried in the Lakeview Cemetery in Mahtomedi, Minnesota.

Children:

146. I. ***Arthur Root***, b. a. 1888 Cherokee, Iowa, d. date and place not know, but before 1900. His burial site is unknown.

147. II. ***Florence E. Root***, b. 1889, d. 1895 was most likely named for George Root's sister. Her burial site is not known. Her birth and death information are undocumented on the Lakeview Cemetery website.

148. III. ***Elizabeth M. Root, f.***

References: US Census: 1860, 1870, 1880, 1900, 1910, 1920, 1930, 1940; New York State Census: 1865, 1875; Lakeview Cemetery Records, Mahtomedi, Minnesota; Iowa Marriage Records, 1880-1937; Iowa State Census Collection 1836-1925 for 1889.

70.

Harriett Desdemona Root, daughter of James Harlow (39), granddaughter of Abel, Sr. (28), b. Bolivar, New York September 26, 1864, d. West Hartford, Connecticut April 2, 1946 from arteriosclerosis; m. Bolivar, New York September 20, 1883 James Madison Homer, b. Olean, New York April 13, 1852, d. Olean, New York December 1, 1921 from injuries suffered in an automobile accident complicated by shock and a ruptured liver.

James Homer's father, Samuel R. Homer, was one of the early settlers of Olean, New York and owned extensive property on what was named *Homer Hill*. Mr. Homer served as President of the Village of Olean and as an Olean Alderman and a Supervisor from the fourth ward. At the time of his death, James Homer was a member of the Board of Water Commissioners, Secretary of the Olean Brewing Company, and owned a private paving contracting business. Mr. Homer was a railroad agent for Shawmut Railroad Company of Bolivar, New York, an agent for the American Express Company at Corry, Pennsylvania, and a telegraph operator for the Union Pipeline Company of Olean. At the time of his death, James Homer was a traveling salesman for Metro Stations, Inc. James Homer was a member of the Olean Lodge, F. and A. M., Olean Chapter R. A. M., and St. John's Commandery, Knights Templar. Harriet or Hattie Root Homer was a fraternal twin with her brother, Harlie J. Root. She had two half-brothers from her mother's first marriage. Hattie took care of both of her parents at her home in Olean at 310 North First Street and later at 229 North Third Street, until their respective deaths. In 1923 she relocated to Connecticut to reside with her daughter, Sarah, where she lived until her death in 1946. Mr. and Mrs. Homer were buried at Mt. View Cemetery in Olean, New York.

Children:

149. I. ***Samuel R. Homer***, b. Olean, New York 1886, d. Olean, New York December 10, 1897 from a fever and ear ulcer. Sammy was described as a bright boy and he was idolized by his parents. He was buried in Mt. View Cemetery in Olean.

150. II. ***Helen Homer**, f.*

151. III. ***Sarah Homer**, f.*

References: US Census: 1870, 1880, 1900, 1910, 1920, 1930, 1940; New York State Census: 1865, 1875, 1892, 1905, 1915; *Bolivar Breeze 1891-1965*, selected issues; Mt. View Cemetery Records, Olean, New York.

71.

Harlie James. Root, son of James Harlow (39), grandson of Abel, Sr. (28), b. Bolivar, New York September 26, 1864, d. Oakfield, New York November 12, 1928 from a heart attack; m. (1) place not known, a. 1887 Rose M. Taylor, b. Pennsylvania March 1869, d. Rochester, New York January 29, 1938 from a heart attack, divorced, date unknown; m. (2) Batavia, New York November 18, 1924 Myrta J. Reed, b. New York State September 1859, d. Buffalo, New York April 1, 1940.

Harlie James Root was the fraternal twin of Hattie Desdemona Root. Based on the US Census for 1870 and 1880 and the New York State Census for 1865 and 1875, Harlie resided with his parents, sister, and with his half-brothers from his mother's first marriage in Bolivar, New York. He married Rose M. Taylor from Cherry Tree, Pennsylvania about 1887. How and where they met is not known. Rose was the daughter of William and Sarah Taylor. Her father was a prominent Baptist minister who preached in Allegany County in the 1870s. They had three children Harlie Taylor Root, Lynn Proctor Root, and Margaret Sarah Root. After their marriage they resided with Harlie's parents on Main Street in Bolivar where he ran the family mercantile store, J. H. Root and Son, until it closed because of financial difficulties in 1898. The building was later occupied by Stimson Bell Hardware. By 1900 Harlie sold his Bolivar residence and a vacant lot and moved his wife and their three children to Rochester, New York. They resided at 36 5th Street where Harlie was employed as a clerk in the dry goods business.

It is not clear when Harlie and Rose Root separated and the circumstances causing the separation are not known, but it was after the 1905 New York State Census and before the 1910 US Census. In July of 1905 Harlie Root spent ten days in Bolivar visiting friends and family before going to Olean to visit his sister. His wife and children were not with him. Perhaps, he was moving to Pennsylvania for employment. Both Harlie J. Root and his eldest son, Harlie T. Root, Jr. cannot be found on the 1910 US Census. In 1910 Rose and daughter Sarah were boarders in the Shipley residence where Rose worked as a servant and son, Lynn Proctor Root, was a boarder at age 13 with the Spencer Sweet family in Walworth, New York. The 1915 New York State Census did not record either Harlie J. Root or his sons Harlie T. Root and Lynn P. Root. However, Lynn P. Root was listed in the 1915 and 1916 Rochester, New York City Directories living as boarder and employed as a clerk.

In 1915 Rose Root resided in a boarding house and was employed as a doll saleslady while daughter Sarah was a companion at age 16 in the household of James and Margaret Rutherford. In 1920 Harlie J. Root was listed as a divorced boarder residing in Punxsutawney, Pennsylvania working as a salesman in a retail store. It must have been very stressful for all three children to leave the financially secure world they were born into in Bolivar to one of an indebted and dispersed family after 1905. Descendants of Harlie J. Root indicated that he failed to support his wife and children after he separated from them. Harlie J. Root remarried to Myrta J. Reed in 1924. She was five years older than Harlie and at the age of sixty-five, this was her first marriage. Myrta was the daughter of Julius W. Reed (died 1881) and Amanda Macomber Reed (1828-1907) from Oakfield, Genesee County, New York. They resided in 1925 in Oakfield where Mr. Root continued to work in retail sales.

Harlie Root suffered from heart trouble for quite some time and he died suddenly from a heart attack in 1928. After his death, his widow, Myrta, lived in Buffalo, New York with relatives from 1930 until her death in 1940. Harlie and Myrta Root were buried in the Reed Cemetery in Oakfield, New York. Harlie's grave does have a tombstone. Rose Taylor Root continued to reside and work in Rochester, New York. Rose died from a heart attack in 1938 and was buried in Riverside Cemetery in Rochester, New York with her two sons, Harlie Jr., and Lynn P. Root, daughter Sarah and Sarah's husband in N Section, lot 122. Rose never remarried. The Rochester, New York City Directory for 1938 gave Rose Root's death date and listed her as the widow of Harlie J. Root instead of as a divorced spouse. No divorce record for Harlie and Rose Root is currently available.

Children (by first marriage):

152. ***Harlie Taylor Root, f.***

153. ***Lynn Proctor Root, f.***

154. ***Margaret Sarah Root, f.***

References: US Census: 1870, 1880, 1900, 1910, 1920, 1930, 1940; New York State Census: 1865, 1875, 1892, 1905, 1915, 1925; *Bolivar Breeze 1891-1965*, selected issues; Reed Cemetery Records, Oakfield, New York; Riverside Cemetery Records, Rochester, New York; New York County Marriages 1907-1936; New York Death Index 1880-1956; Rochester, New York City Directories, including 1938 listing the death date for Rose T. Root.

Third Generation Line of Descent from Abel Root, Sr.

73.

Judson Lloyd Holly (Hawley, Holley, Holby), son of Minerva (40), grandson of Abel, Jr. (34), b. Bolivar, New York September 27, 1852, d. Ypsilanti, Michigan September 1, 1936; m. Ypsilanti, Michigan December 11, 1879 Ida Laura Martin, b. Ypsilanti, Michigan February 3, 1859, d. Ypsilanti, Michigan March 4, 1910.

Researching Judson Holly was challenging given the variety of spellings for his last name in various census records. In the 1855 New York State Census Judson Holly resided with his parents in Belfast, New York. In the 1860 US Census he resided in Bolivar, New York with his parents and sister Lydia. Judson Holly was recorded twice in the US Census for 1870. The first time was with his father and step-mother in Randolph, New York and the second time it was with his mother in Lyons, Michigan. From the time of his marriage to Ida Martin in 1879, Judson resided in Ypsilanti, Michigan until his death in 1936. After the death of his wife in 1910 he continued to reside in the family home with daughters Elizabeth, Florence, and Hazel. In 1920 Judson Holly moved in with his daughter and son-in-law, Hazel and Leo Youngs.

By 1930 he was living alone. Judson Holly was employed as a carpenter during his professional career. In August 1916 he visited Bolivar, New York staying with the Dudley Ennis family. It was his first visit to Bolivar in 44 years. Judson Holly again visited Bolivar in September 1918 staying with the Paul Ennis family. Judson Holly's death was caused by a combination of illnesses affecting both his heart and kidneys. Judson and Ida Holly were buried in Highland Cemetery in Ypsilanti, Michigan in a plot shared with his son Judson E. Holly and his daughter and son-in-law, Hazel and Leo Youngs. Mr. Holly's death certificate has incorrect information on the document regarding his place of birth and the correct first names for both his mother and father. The informant was Hazel Holly Youngs.

Children:

155. I. ***Gladys Leona Holly, f.***

156. II. ***Lloyd Daniel Holly, f.***

157. III. ***Fred Richard Holly, f.***

158. IV. ***Minerva (Minnie)Louise Holly, f.***

159. V. ***Judson E. Holly***, b. Ypsilanti, Michigan March 1891, d. Chelsea, Massachusetts October 3, 1908 from arthritis and heart issues at Chelsea Naval Hospital in Chelsea, Massachusetts. He was a seaman aboard the USS Salem. Judson E. Holly was buried in Highland Cemetery in Ypsilanti, Michigan.

160. VI. ***Elizabeth M. Holly, f.***

161. VII. ***Hazel M. Holly, f.***

162. VIII. ***Florence Adaline Holly, f.***

References: US Census: 1860, 1870, 1880, 1900, 1910, 1920, 1930; New York State Census: 1855; Michigan Death Records 1867-1950; Michigan Marriage Records 1867-1952; *Bolivar Breeze, 1891-1965*, selected issues; Detroit City Directories, selected issues; Ypsilanti City Directories, selected issues; Highland Cemetery records, Ypsilanti, Michigan.

75.

Elmer D. Hawley (Holly), son of Minerva (40), grandson of Abel, Jr. (34), b. Allegany County, New York, a. 1861, d. (?) Chicago, Illinois September 3, 1903. In the 1870 US Census Elmer Hawley resided with his father and step-mother and half-siblings in Cattaraugus County, New York. Given his young age it seemed unusual to this author that he would reside with his father instead of his mother.

Elmer was twice listed in the 1875 New York State Census residing in both Olean, New York with his father and step-mother and in Bolivar, New York at the home of his maternal grandfather, Abel Root, Jr. The *D* middle initial was probably for Daniel, his father's first name. In 1880, Elmer Hawley was employed as a shoe cutter in Detroit residing with his mother. He was listed in the 1881 and 1882 Detroit City Directories working in the shoe industry for Pingree and Smith. It is possible that he was the Elmer D. Halley who died in Chicago, Illinois on September 3, 1903. This Elmer Halley was single at the time of death, resided in the 20th Century Hotel in Chicago, and was employed as a shoe cutter. His remains were interned in the Chic Eclectic Cemetery in Chicago. The cemetery cannot be currently located. The Illinois death certificate listed his birth state as New York but no parents were identified. There was also an Elmer D. Hawley, employed as shoe cutter in Ramsey County, Minnesota; married with one living child of two children born. The 1895 Minnesota State Census offered conflicting information on his birth in Wisconsin contradicting other data giving his birth state as New York. This Elmer D. Hawley was also employed as a shoe cutter. No further information could be found on this Elmer D. Hawley.

References: US Census: 1870, 1880; New York State Census: 1875; Detroit City Directories: 1880, 1881, 1882; Cook County Death Index 1878-1922; Minnesota State Census: 1895.

76.

Charles Samuel Withey, son of Elizabeth (41), grandson of Abel, Jr. (34), b. Richburg, New York a. 1853, d. Richburg, New York May 11, 1876; m. probably Richburg, New York, date not known Mary Eliza Davidson, b. Richburg, New York December 24, 1856, d. place not known, September 6, 1906.

Known in the family as *Sam* he resided with his maternal grandparents in Bolivar after his mother's death in 1859. After his father's remarriage in 1862, he moved to Richburg and resided with them. His niece, the late Ina Withey McEnroe, recalled her father, Jesse Withey, stating that his brother's death occurred shortly after his marriage and followed a nervous breakdown. Ina McEnroe did not remember the name of her uncle's wife. However, the family history, *The Descendants of Andrew Warner*, revealed her identify as Mary Eliza Davidson. Mary Eliza Davidson was the daughter of Titus Beech Davidson (1822-1880) and Eliza Ann Warner Davidson (1821-1867). Her father was a physician and joined the Cortland County Medical Society in 1847. Dr. Davidson practiced in both Richburg and Wellsville, New York. In the 1875 New York State Census Mary Eliza Davidson was unmarried and resided with her parents. The marriage of Charles Samuel Withey and Mary Eliza Davidson, therefore, occurred after the June 1, 1875 New York State Census and before Sam Withey's death in May 1876. On September 13, 1876, Dr. Davidson petitioned the County Court in Angelica for control over the assets of Charles Samuel Withey's estate on behalf of his daughter, Sam's widow. In the 1880 US Census Mary Eliza resumed the use of her maiden name and resided with her father and step-mother in Wellsville. She was listed as widowed. Charles Samuel Withey was buried in Richburg, New York's cemetery. It is not known where Dr. Davidson, his first wife, and daughter Mary Eliza Davidson Withey were buried.

References: US Census: 1860, 1870; New York State Census: 1855, 1865, 1875; Richburg, New York cemetery records; Warner, Lucien C. and Nichols, Josephine Genung, *The Descendants of Andrew Warner*, New Haven, Connecticut: Tuttle, Morehouse, and Taylor Co., 1919; New York Wills and Probate Records 1659-1999.

77.

Emma Elizabeth Withey, daughter of Elizabeth (41), granddaughter of Abel, Jr. (34), b. Richburg, New York November 23, 1854, d. Wellsville, New York October 4, 1923 due to chronic nephritis and heart disease; m. place not known, a. 1873, Rufus Sawyer, b. Wirt, New York October 23, 1850, d. Wellsville, New York July 11, 1926.

Emma Withey was raised by her maternal grandparents, Abel and Polly Scott Root of Bolivar on their Kossuth farm as noted in the 1860 and 1870 US Census records and the 1865 New York State Census after the 1859 death of her mother, Elizabeth Root Withey. The 1900 US Census recorded that Emma Withey married Rufus Sawyer about 1873. In the 1875 New York State Census, the Sawyers resided with Abel and Polly Root. For a brief time, Emma and Rufus Sawyer moved to Barron, Wisconsin where Mr. Sawyer worked in a mill based on 1880 US Census data. The date of their return to New

York State is not known, but in the 1892 New York State Census, the Sawyers resided in Wellsville, New York where he was employed as a hotel keeper. By 1900, they moved to Hornellsville residing at 85 ½ Main Street where Rufus Sawyer found employment as a carpenter. They took in six boarders.

From 1905 until their respective deaths in 1923 and 1926, Emma and Rufus Sawyer lived in Wellsville, New York in rented residences and managed a restaurant first at 128 North Main Street, then at 50 North Main Street with Volney A. Parker, and later at 340 South Main Street. They also took in boarders, some of whom worked in the restaurants they managed. The late Ina Withey McEnroe, Emma's niece, recalled that Rufus Sawyer was seriously burned in a restaurant explosion from his neck down to his waist. Leaders in the Wellsville Baptist Church, Emma and Rufus Sawyer did not have any children. They were buried in Wellsville, New York's Woodlawn Cemetery.

Rufus Sawyer was the son of Isaac D. Sawyer (1816-1912) and Betsey Jane Gillet (1829-1901) who farmed in Bolivar, Wellsville, and Willing, New York. Rufus was one of four sons and three daughters.

References: US Census Records: 1860, 1870, 1880, 1900, 1910, 1920; New York State Census: 1855, 1865, 1875, 1892, 1905, 1915, 1925; New York Death Index 1880-1956 for 1923 and 1926; Woodlawn Cemetery Records, Wellsville, New York; *Bolivar Breeze, 1891-1965,* selected issues.

78.

Ina M. Withey, daughter of Elizabeth (41), granddaughter of Abel, Jr. (34), b. Richburg, New York, b. March 2, 1858/9, d. Detroit, Michigan April 29, 1934 from hardening of the arteries, an intestinal obstruction, and a descending colon; m. Detroit, Michigan January 2, 1881 George James Lockley, b. Ann Arbor, Michigan January 30, 1858, d. Detroit, Michigan March 17, 1940 from senility and a heart condition.

There is confusion over the year of birth for Ina M. Withey. Her death record and the 1900 US Census, which provided the month and year of birth, gave the year as 1859. However, Ina's younger brother, Jesse A. Withey, was born April 27, 1859. Because Ina and her brother, Jesse, were not fraternal twins given their months and days of birth were different, Ina's birth year must be 1858. Ina was raised by her maternal aunt, Mary Jane Root Barber, after her mother's death in December of 1859. In some census records she was identified as Ina Barber. The 1860, 1870, and 1880 US Census recorded her in residence with the Barber family in Ceres, Pennsylvania and later in Detroit, Michigan. George James Lockley resided with his parents George and Amelia Hawkins Lockley in East Saginaw, Michigan until his 1881 marriage with Ina Withey where he was employed as a fire insurance agent. George Lockley's parents were English immigrants to the United States. During his professional career George Lockley was a bookkeeper (1900), a treasurer for an engraving company (1910), a public accountant (1920), and a bank branch manager for Fort National Bank (1930). Except for a brief tenure in 1910 in New York City, the Lockley family resided in Detroit, Michigan on Tuxedo Avenue. Witnesses at their 1881 wedding included Ina's maternal aunt, Minerva Root Neff, and her maternal cousin, Cora Barber, who was raised with her as a sister. Ina and George Lockley were buried in Woodlawn Cemetery in Detroit, Michigan. Their individual markers are barely visual above ground and are on the other side of a tree from the Barber graves.

Children.

163. I. ***Helen Ina Lockley, f.***

References: US Census: 1860, 1870, 1880, 1900, 1910, 1920, 1930; Michigan County Marriage Records 1822-1940; Michigan Death Records 1867-1950; Woodlawn Cemetery Records, Detroit, Michigan

79.

Jesse Andrew Withey, son of Elizabeth (41), grandson of Abel, Jr. (34), b. Richburg, New York April 27, 1859, d. Belmont, New York July 21, 1942 from a stroke; m. Olean, New York September 17, 1899 Sarah A. Doutt, b. Butler, Pennsylvania December 8, 1868, d. Belmont, New York January 10, 1940 from a heart attack.

Jesse was raised by his maternal grandparents, Abel and Polly Root, on their Kossuth, New York farm outside of Bolivar after his mother's death in 1859. His daughter, the late Ina Withey McEnroe, recalled her father reciting a jingle that the family made up to keep track of all the relatives. Unfortunately, most of the identities of the people mentioned are no longer known. The name Polly was probably Jesse's maternal grandmother. The last line of the jingle was: *Sally, Dolly, Eunice, and Polly. John, Jim, Nathan, and Tim.* Jesse Withey and his family lived in a number of different locations based on his successful pursuit of oil production. They resided in Eldred and Haymaker, Pennsylvania (1900), Vosburg or Witheytown (1901-1925), Wellsville (1925-1937), and Belmont, New York (1937-1942). For a time, Jesse Withey owned and operated an oil producing company with his half-brother, William Withey. Jesse purchased the oil interests of both William Withey and those of P. D. Viger, his half-sister's husband. At one time Mr. Withey had 40 wells in production. Mr. Withey invested in the Standard Turbine Corporation in Wellsville, New York in 1924. Unfortunately, the company, established in 1922, folded by 1928. Jesse Withey was a member of Bolivar's Macedonia Lodge # 259, F & M and the Odd Fellows Lodge. He regularly attended the Scott family reunions celebrating the Scott brothers and brothers-in-law participation in the Civil War. Jesse's maternal grandmother was Polly Scott Root. Sarah Withey was a member of the Buttrick Chapter # 109, the O. E. S. of Bolivar, and the Methodist Episcopal Church in Eldred, Pennsylvania. The Withey residence in Vosburg, New York remains as does their home in Wellsville at the corner of Madison Street and Maple Avenue later occupied by the owners of the Texas Hot restaurant, Mr. and Mrs. Gus Rigas. The 1900 US Census indicated that Jesse and Sarah Withey had four children with only three still living. The identity of the deceased child is not known, but two more sons were born to the Witheys after the 1900 Census. In the 1940 US Census Jesse Withey's sister-in-law, Dottie Doutt, resided with him. Jesse and Sarah Withey were buried in Bolivar's Maple Lawn Cemetery.

Children:

164. I. ***Bessie Elizabeth Withey, f.***

165. II. ***Ina Mae Withey, f.***

166. III. ***Harry Ivan Withey, f.***

167. IV. ***Howard Andrew Withey, f.***

168. V. ***Charles David Withey, f.***

References: US Census: 1860, 1870, 1900, 1910, 1920, 1930, 1940; New York State Census: 1865, 1905, 1915, 1925; *Bolivar Breeze1891-1965*, selected issues; Maple Lawn Cemetery Records, Bolivar, New York.

80.

Mary Elizabeth Root, daughter of Lyman (42), granddaughter of Abel, Jr. (34), b. Bolivar, New York July 9, 1861, d. Bolivar, New York January 1, 1924 from pernicious anemia; m. Bolivar, New York, a. 1888, Paul Walter Ennis, b. Cuba, New York March 12, 1857, d. March 22, 1941 at the Jones Memorial Hospital Wellsville, New York after an illness of one day.

Mary Elizabeth was known in the family as *Libbie*. She was a member of the Trilby Rebekah Lodge and the Bolivar Methodist Church. Libbie was baptized and joined the Bolivar Methodist Church on December 1, 1878, was active in the annual Scott family reunions, and was treasurer for the Society of 100 in Bolivar. Her niece the late Mary Elizabeth Root Holland commented that her Aunt Libbie regularly dipped snuff to relieve a variety of maladies. Until the death of her father, Lyman E. Root, Paul and Libbie Ennis resided in Little Genesee, New York. By 1900 they resided on South Main Street in Bolivar. The residence was torn down in the 1970s and replaced with another residential structure.

By profession Paul Ennis was a trained blacksmith. He eventually took over his late father-in-law's blacksmith shop in 1898 on the corner of Leather and Main Streets in Bolivar and operated it until its closure about 1916. The site of the blacksmith shop and Root family residence is where the current Bolivar grocery store stands. For the next ten years Paul Ennis worked with his son, Dudley, as a painter. After the death of his wife and son, Paul Ennis resided with his daughter-in-law, Mattie (Martha) Atkinson Ennis, and his grandson, Paul Ennis, at 557 South Main Street. Paul Ennis' funeral was conducted according to the rites of the Seven Day Adventist Church of Little Genesee, New York. Paul and Libbie Ennis were buried in Wells Cemetery in Little Genesee, New York in the Ennis lot. There are no grave markers for them.

Children:

169. I. ***Dudley Lyman Ennis, f.***

References: US Census: 1870, 1880, 1900, 1910, 1920, 1930, 1940; New York State Census: 1865, 1875, 1892, 1905, 1915, 1925; Bolivar Methodist Church, Book 1: Baptism Records; *Bolivar Breese, 1891-1965,* selected issues; Wells Cemetery Records, Little Genesee, New York.

81.

Earls (Earles) Lyman Root, son of Lyman (42), grandson of Abel, Jr. (34), b. Bolivar, New York March 25, 1863, d. Olean, New York December 3, 1942 from a cerebral embolism and heart disease; m. place not known, a. 1885 Margaret Granger, b. Hornell, New York May 1, 1864, d. Olean, New York May 1, 1931 from carcinoma of the liver.

Earl Root resided with his parents in Bolivar until his marriage. Mr. Root was baptized and joined the Bolivar Methodist Church on September 22, 1878. He was a trained blacksmith and took that skill with him to Olean, New York where he owned and operated a blacksmith shop at 522 North Union Street where the Luther Manufacturing Company later occupied the site. The Root family resided at 44 Orchard Avenue in 1901 but later moved to 714 East State Street where they lived until Maggie Root's death in 1931. A widower, Earl Root moved in with his eldest daughter, Isabelle Root Johnson of Olean where he resided until his death in 1942. Earl L. Root was the executor for his mother's, Almyra Reed Root, estate. Earl Lyman Root was highly regarded by his family and friends and was the longest lived of Lyman and Almyra Root's seven children. Mr. Root was a member of the IOOF Lodge # 471, the Allegany Encampment of the IOOF, and was one of the original organizers of the Bradley Hose Company in Bolivar, New York. Earl and Maggie Root were buried in Allegany Cemetery in Allegany, New York. His grave marker has the birth year of 1864, which is wrong based on surviving documents including the handwritten birth listings in the family Bible.

Children:

170. I. ***Isabelle Lue Root, f.***

171. II. ***Harold William Root, f.***

172. III. ***Lola Blossom Root, f.***

173. IV. ***Selden Jule Root, f.***

References: US Census: 1870, 1880, 1900, 1910, 1920, 1930, 1940; New York State Census: 1865, 1875, 1892, 1905, 1915, 1925; Photocopy of birth records in Earl Root family Bible; *Bolivar Breeze 1891-1965,* selected issues; Allegany Cemetery Records, Allegany, New York; Olean, New York City Directories, selected issues; Bolivar Methodist Church Records, Book 1.

82.

Lola L. Root, daughter of Lyman (42), granddaughter of Abel, Jr. (34), b. Bolivar, New York November 12, 1865, d. Bolivar, New York July 31, 1886 from congestion of the lungs at the age of twenty years, 7 months, and 21 days.

Lola Root was engaged at the time of her death and was soon to be married. The identity of the finance is no longer known. Lola was baptized and joined the Bolivar Methodist Church September 22, 1878. Two funeral bouquet cards were placed in a photograph album belonging to Miss Root's mother, now in the possession of James Wescott, Jr. of Poquoson, Virginia. A silver napkin ring with Lola's name engraved on it belongs to the author. Lola's obituary consisted of flowery tributes. One example follows. Lola Root was buried in Maple Lawn Cemetery in Bolivar, New York with two sisters who died in infancy.

> "…Thus, has passed away one who was young and beautiful; one who was just budding into womanhood and one to whom so much good and noble work and all that makes life enjoyable, lay just within sight. But death spares neither the young nor the aged when searching for victims, and when he laid his icy hand upon Miss Lola, he took from our midst, a true, noble, self-sacrificing and lovable woman…"

References: US Census: 1870, 1880; New York State Census: 1875; Maple Lawn Cemetery Records, Bolivar, New York; Bolivar Methodist Church Records, Book 1; unsourced obituary clippings for Lola Root belonging to the Root family.

83.

Ernest (Earnest) Jerome Root, son of Lyman (42), grandson of Abel, Jr. (34), b. Bolivar, New York July 15, 1873, d. Bolivar, New York July 23, 1904 by suicide drinking carbolic acid; m. Olean, New York February 19, 1898 Belle Fuller, b. Nunda, New York April 16, 1881, d. Binghamton, New York December 14, 1914 from cancer.

Ernest Root's middle name was the first name of his maternal grandfather Jerome Reed. He moved to Olean, New York after the 1892 New York State Census where he, too, worked as a blacksmith, probably with his elder brother, Earl. Belle Fuller moved to Olean in 1896 to attend a female seminary. This was about the time Belle's parents Albert J. Fuller and Edith Carter Fuller separated and Albert Fuller relocated from Nunda, New York to Kalamazoo, Michigan. Belle was about four months' pregnant at the time of her marriage to Ernest Root. Ernest and Belle resided at 306 W. Green Street in Olean.

In the 1900 US Census Ernest was twice listed. He was listed as an Olean resident employed as a blacksmith with his wife, two young children, mother-in-law, sister-in-law, and brother-in-law. Ernest was also listed as a blacksmith working in Smethport, Pennsylvania living in a boarding house. It is possible that the marriage had already broken down as early as 1900. Ernest Root and his family were recorded in the Olean, New York City Directories for 1899, 1900, and 1901. It is possible that Ernest and Belle separated in either 1901 or 1902. Belle and her children moved to Binghamton, New York where her mother and siblings had already settled. Ernest Root was last employed as a blacksmith in Mt. Jewett, Pennsylvania.

Ernest and Belle Root's marriage was not a happy one. Ernest apparently drank too much and was physically and psychologically abusive to his wife and children leading to their separation. Mr. Root's problems were complicated by poor business decisions. Attempts to reconcile with his wife were unsuccessful. Ernest Root returned to his mother's home on Main Street in Bolivar in July 1904, where despondent, he took his own life by drinking carbolic acid on the sidewalk in front of the Root family home. His tombstone in Bolivar's Maple Lawn Cemetery was placed there by direction of his mother's will.

Belle Fuller Root was a direct descendant of *Mayflower* passengers Edward Fuller, his wife, and son Samuel who came to the United States in 1620. Belle was an accomplished seamstress as surviving photographs reveal by the clothes she wore. Mrs. Root operated a dress shop in Binghamton, New York with Jenny J. Cox, a milliner. Belle suffered from cancer from about 1909 until her death in 1914. She had planned to remarry to a William Stone of Binghamton, but the disease's progress prevented the marriage. Mr. Stone's devotion to Belle kept him at her side until her death and he helped her family during Belle's lengthy illness. In conversations with the late Nordica Root Wylie, Ernest and Belle Root's daughter, Mrs. Wylie believed that her mother had a third child who was either born as a stillbirth or died shortly after birth in 1900 or 1901.

No record of a third birth could be found in the Olean, New York City Hall records. Belle Fuller Root was buried in Floral Park Cemetery in Johnson City, New York in a plot jointly owned with her brother, Jesse Fuller, and near the burial site of her mother and younger sister. Custody of the Root children was given to Jesse Fuller but it does not appear that that authority was ever exercised.

Children:

174. I. ***Leo Cassar Root, f.***

175. II. ***Nordica Thelma Root, f.***

References: US Census: 1880, 1900, 1910; New York State Census: 1875, 1892, 1905; *Bolivar Breeze, 1891-1965,* selected issues; Marriage Certificate for Ernest and Belle Root; Death Certificates for Ernest Root and Belle Root; Maple Lawn Cemetery Records, Bolivar, New York; Floral Park Cemetery Records,

Johnson City, New York; Olean, New York City Directory, selected issues.

86.

Bernard Abel Root, son of Lyman (42), grandson of Abel, Jr. (34), b. Bolivar, New York February 1, 1881, d. Sisters Hospital Buffalo, New York October 14, 1927 from complications after surgery for his gall bladder and the removal of his appendix; m. Allentown, New York November 9, 1903 Margaret Snowdon, b. Allentown, New York August 16, 1885, d. Mercy Hospital Buffalo, New York August 29, 1974 after a short illness that began with a fall causing a broken hip.

Bernard Root was a barber by trade. In 1902 he was employed at R. F. Main's barber shop in Bolivar. Mr. Root married Margaret Snowdon three days before Allen John Root was born. The surviving children of Bernard and Maggie Root always believed that their parents were married in 1902 instead of 1903. Margaret Snowdon Root was the daughter of John O. Snowdon (1844-1912) who was born in Scotland and Mary Jane McCariston (1851-1939) who was born in Liverpool, England. John and Mary were married in the United States and settled in Allentown, New York. In 1904 Bernard Root was employed in a new barbershop in the basement of the Bolivar Hotel. The success of the business led to its expansion to a second chair in December 1904. However, this venture did not succeed and Bernard and Maggie and their children moved to Jamestown, New York in March of 1905. They remained in Jamestown until 1908 when they moved to Olean, New York and later back to Bolivar. They left Bolivar in April 1909 for work in Rochester only to return in that same year to Bolivar. In 1910 Bernard Root was employed by the Shawmut Railroad near Angelica, New York.

Bernard and Maggie Root and their young family resided with his mother, Almyra Root, on Main Street until she died in 1914. They later rented a house on Leather Street. In 1923 Mr. Root made another job change working for Pennsylvania Car Shops in Olean, New York. When Bernard Root resided on Leather Street along Root Hollow Creek with his young family, his daughter, the late Mary Root Holland, related the story that her father came home from work after having a few drinks demanding his dinner, which was not yet ready. He and his wife, Maggie, began a loud argument that lasted for a while until Bernard left the house to use the outhouse on a slight incline along Root Hollow Creek. Bernard was so mad that when he entered the outhouse, he slammed the door so hard the outhouse swayed and fell into the creek with Mr. Root afloat in Root Hollow Creek. He survived. Bernard Root was known as *Slive* because he was so thin. The nickname was transferred to two of his sons, Lyman E. Root and Merle F. Root.

The late Kate (Catherine) Snowdon Barnes said her sister; Maggie (Margaret) had twelve children. The identities of only eleven could be found. If there were twelve then 7 died in infancy. They were buried in Maple Lawn Cemetery along with Bernard in unmarked graves behind the graves of Abel Root, Jr. and his wife Polly. The children were buried on top if each other. Maggie Snowdon Root remarried July 15, 1933 to Stephen Weaver in Geneva, New York. They resided in Honeoye, New York. Stephen Delbert Weaver was born in Crawford County Pennsylvania November 17, 1881. His first wife was Marjorie Shaner whose family was in the oil business. Her five brothers, Albert, Paul, Mark, Lester, and Arthur, resided in Bolivar. Mr. Weaver had sixteen children by his first wife, 10 sons (8 living) and 6 daughters (4 living). Marjorie Shaner Weaver died in 1926 at age 41 from pneumonia. Stephen Weaver died August 7, 1945 in Holcomb, New York and was buried with his first wife in the Salem Lutheran Cemetery in Lamartine, Pennsylvania.

Maggie Weaver returned to Bolivar and resided primarily at the residence of her sister, Kate Barnes, at 77 Wellsville Street from whom she rented. The house has since been torn down. I remember Aunt Maggie (my great-great-aunt) as a woman with a ready smile, a keen sense of humor, and an interest and participation in family events. Her ability to put people at ease and to extend a warm welcome made her a special member of the family and the Bolivar community. I can still see her sitting on the front porch watching people drive by and talking to those strolling past her home.

She was a very positive individual given the difficulties of her first marriage, the loss of so many young children, and the financial challenges she faced. Maggie Weaver was buried in Maple Lawn Cemetery in Bolivar and her grave is next to the grave of her son Merle Root.

Children:

176. I. ***Allen John Root, f.***

177. II. ***Limon Dudley Root,*** b. Bolivar, New York September 17, 1904, d. several days later. The exact date is not clear from newspaper accounts. He was buried in an unmarked grave in Maple Lawn Cemetery in Bolivar.

178. III. ***Lyman Erwin Root, f.***

179. IV. ***Jessey Marie Root,*** b. Jamestown, New York March 19, 1907, d. Bolivar, New York July 6, 1908 from a fall while waving to her paternal grandmother from her grandmother's front porch, lost her balance falling two and one-half feet and landing on the top of her head. Jessey Marie was buried in Maple Lawn Cemetery in Bolivar in an unmarked grave.

180. V. ***Mary Elizabeth Root, f.***

181. VI. ***Stanley Eugene Root, f.***

182. VII. ***Harold Lowell Root,*** b. Bolivar, New York September 20, 1913, d. Bolivar, New York October 23, 1913 from an illness lasting seven days. He was buried in Maple Lawn Cemetery in Bolivar in an unmarked grave.

183. VIII. ***Merle Findlay Root, f.***

184. IX. ***Merton Root***, (a twin with Merle Root), b. Bolivar, New York July 18, 1915, d. Bolivar, New York July 19, 1915 from congenital leakage of the heart. He was buried in Maple Lawn Cemetery in Bolivar in an unmarked grave.

185. X. ***Ruth Root,*** b. Bolivar, New York July 31, 1917, d. Bolivar, New York October 7, 1917. She was buried in Maple Lawn Cemetery in an unmarked grave.

186. XI. ***Margaret Geraldine Root***, b. Bolivar, New York August 23, 1918, d. Bolivar, New York October 16, 1918. She was buried in Maple Lawn Cemetery in an unmarked grave.

References: US Census: 1900, 1910, 1920, 1930, 1940; New York State Census: 1892, 1905, 1915, 1925; Maple Lawn Cemetery Records Bolivar, New York; *Bolivar Breeze 1891-1965,* selected issues; New York State Marriage Index 1881-1967 for Margaret Snowdon and Stephen Weaver (1933); New York Death Index 1880-1956 for Merton Root (1915) and Margaret G. Root (1918); Town of Alma marriage record for Margaret Snowdon and Bernard Root; Town of Bolivar birth records of Limon Dudley Root, Harold Lowell Root, Merton Root, Ruth Root, Margaret Geraldine Root; *Jamestown Evening Journal, March 21, 1907* for Jessey Marie Root birth.

87.

Cora Mary Barber, daughter of Mary Jane (43), granddaughter of Abel, Jr. (34), b. Ceres, Pennsylvania December 1863, d. Detroit, Michigan July 18, 1900 from uremia and liver issues lapsing into a coma before dying; m. Detroit, Michigan a. 1891 Edward Ira Rankin, b. Saginaw, Michigan a. 1859, d. Ashtabula, Ohio March 7, 1915. Cora Rankin was buried in Woodlawn Cemetery in Detroit with her parents. Her marker with the name of her son, Carl Rankin, rests against a tree and is visible. Edward Rankin was buried in Mt. Pleasant Cemetery in Ashtabula, Ohio with his mother and sisters.

Children:

187. I. ***Carl B. Rankin***, b. October 1889, d. January 28, 1890 from bronchitis at the age of three months. He was reburied on May 25, 1901 and placed next to his mother's grave in the Barber family lot.

References: US Census: 1870, 1880, 1900; *Detroit Evening News*, selected issues; Woodlawn Cemetery, Detroit, Michigan; Michigan Death Records 1867-1950.

88.

Fred A. Barber, son of Mary Jane (43), grandson of Abel, Jr. (34), b. Ceres, Pennsylvania January 18, 1867, d. St. Louis, Missouri January 2, 1926 from pneumonia; m. Grand Rapids, Michigan September 12, 1899 Elizabeth (Libbie) E. Parker, b. Michigan September 1868, d. Akron, Ohio December 8, 1957 from arteriosclerosis at the home of her daughter.

Fred Barber worked for the railroad industry as a clerk (1900) in Detroit, Michigan and in 1910 as a clerk in St. Louis, Missouri. In 1920 Mr. Barber was the chief accountant for a railroad and resided at 5928A Maple Avenue in St. Louis. At the time of his death, he was an assistant general freight agent for the Wabash Railroad. Fred and Libbie Barber were buried in the Barber family lot in Woodlawn Cemetery in Detroit, Michigan. Their individual markers are barely visual above ground.

Children:

188. I. ***Ellen Miriam Barber, f.***

References: US Census: 1870, 1880, 1900, 1910, 1920, 1930, 1940; Michigan Death Records 1867-1950; Michigan Marriage Records 1822-1940; Woodlawn Cemetery Records, Detroit, Michigan; *Detroit Evening News*, selected issues.

89.

Minnie E. Barber, daughter of Mary Jane (43), granddaughter of Abel, Jr. (34), b. Saginaw, Michigan November 1, 1871, d. Bloomfield Hills, Michigan December 13, 1949; m. (1) Detroit, Michigan March 1, 1892 Theodore Trombley, b. Michigan, date not known, d. Detroit, Michigan April 5, 1936, divorced 1902 for habitual drunkenness; m. (2) Detroit, Michigan January 7, 1903 James V. Bayley, b. Troy, Michigan September 26, 1869, d. Pontiac, Michigan October 6, 1938 from a coronary thrombosis. James Bayley was employed by the tobacco industry as a bookkeeper (1910) and a shipping clerk (1920). At the time of his death Mr. Bayley was the clerk for Bloomfield Township, Michigan. The Bayleys last residence was 430 Park Street in Birmingham, Michigan where Minnie continued to reside until her death. Minnie and James Bayley were buried in the Barber lot in Woodlawn Cemetery Detroit, Michigan. Her marker is no longer visual but James Bayley's marker is. Minnie Barber Trombley Bayley did not have any children by either marriage. She was probably named for her maternal aunt Minerva Root Holly Neff because Minnie is a variation of Minerva.

References: US Census: 1880, 1900, 1910, 1920, 1930, 1940; *Detroit Evening News,* selected issues; Woodlawn Cemetery Records, Detroit, Michigan; Michigan Divorce Records 1897-1952; Michigan Death Records 1867-1950; Michigan Marriage Records 1822-1940; Michigan Birth Records 1867-1911.

90.

Flora M. Root, daughter of Hiram (44), granddaughter of Abel, Jr. (34), b. Bolivar, New York June 11, 1861/June 1862, d. Castile, New York February 6, 1929; m. Bolivar, New York December 31, 1881 Edward Richardson, b. Scio, New York May 26, 1861, d. Silver Springs, New York March 1, 1941 after an illness of two weeks from shock and other medical complications.

There is some confusion over the birth date for Flora Root Richardson. The 1900 US Census gave her birth date as June 1862 but some family records gave her the birth date of June 11, 1861. There is also some confusion over Flora's date of marriage. Flora's obituary gave her marriage date as 1880. The obituary for her husband, Edward Richardson, gave a marriage date of January 1, 1879. The Bolivar Methodist Church recorded the marriage date as December 31, 1881. The confusion over the marriage date may center on the date of birth for their first child, Minnie Richardson, born October 25, 1881. If the marriage was 1880, then Minnie's birth qualified as a legitimate birth. If the church record was accurate and I believe it to be, Minnie's birth made her birth illegitimate. Flora Root gave birth to an illegitimate son, Guy Arthur, January 20, 1880. The identity of the father of that child is not known. Guy Root's obituary listed his father as Fritz Root, but there appears to be no such person. If Flora and Edward were married January 1, 1879, then was Edward Richardson the father?

Conversations with Richardson descendants do not support Edward Richardson being Guy Root's father. Flora Root joined the Bolivar Methodist Church September 8, 1878. All thirteen children of Flora and Edward Richardson were born in Bolivar. Three children died in infancy. Edward Richardson was the son of Almarion and Maryann Clark Richardson. The Richardson family moved from Bolivar to the Portageville area in 1911 where he found employment in the stone quarry. After the death of Flora Richardson in 1929, Edward Richardson moved in with his daughter Mrs. Reinhardt Hinz of Bliss, New York. He died while visiting another daughter Mrs. Dan Baker of Silver Springs, New York. In death, Edward Richardson was remembered as a kind friend and neighbor, devoted family man, and a hard worker. Flora and Edward Richardson were buried in East Coy Cemetery, East Coy, New York.

Children:

189. I. ***Minnie Alice Richardson, f.***

190. II. ***Stanley LaFrone Richardson, f.***

191. III. ***Manley Almarion Richardson, f.***

192. IV. ***Agnes H. Richardson, f.***

193. V. ***Harold Almarion Richardson, f.***

194. VI. ***Mary Elizabeth Richardson, f.***

195. VII. ***Ethel Marion Richardson, f.***

196. VIII. ***Helen Richardson***, b. Bolivar, New York March 11, 1898, d. Bolivar, New York March 13, 1898 and buried in Maple Lawn Cemetery in Bolivar.

197. IX. An unnamed infant son b. and d. March 1899 in Kossuth. His burial site is not known.

198. X. ***Lewis William Richardson, f.***

199. XI. ***Mildred Salome Richardson, f.***

200. XII. ***Loretta A. Richardson,*** b. Bolivar, New York October 22, 1903, d. Bolivar, New York November 6, 1903. She was buried in Maple Lawn Cemetery in Bolivar.

201. XIII. ***Lawrence Erwin Richardson, f.***

References: US Census: 1870, 1880, 1900, 1910, 1920, 1930, 1940; New York State Census: 1865, 1875, 1892, 1905, 1915, 1925; *Bolivar Breeze 1891-1965,* selected issues; Maple Lawn Cemetery Records, Bolivar, New York; Bolivar, New York Methodist Church Records, Book 1 for the marriage of Flora Root to Edward Richardson; *The Castilian*, Castile, New York newspaper March 6, 1941 for Edward Richardson obituary; East Coy Cemetery Records, East Coy, New York.

91.

Laphronia Hiram Root, son of Hiram (44), grandson of Abel, Jr. (34), b. Bolivar, New York December 16, 1863, d. Muncie, Indiana October 30, 1933 from a cerebral thrombosis; m. (1) Peru, Indiana February 27, 1889 Effie Jane Meyers, b. Pennsylvania August 26, 1870, d. Muncie, Indiana November 8, 1922 from cardiac disease and liver congestion; m. (2) Jay County, Indiana January 26, 1924 Stella Curea Hall, b. Miami, Ohio April 20, 1877, d. Muncie, Indiana December 29, 1947 from a coronary occlusion, divorced, Indiana, date not known; m. (3) Delaware County, Indiana October 22, 1929 Carrie Clark Earl, b. Wellsville, New York March 29, 1868, d. Dolgeville, New York July 23, 1938.

There is no clear indication on the origins of Mr. Root's first name, Laphronia. It is not known why his parents gave him that name. The best guess is *Laphronia* means *the wise one*, based on *La* meaning *the*, and *fronia*, a derivation of *phronia*, meaning *wise*. Laphronia Root moved to Muncie, Indiana in the 1880s. He was employed as an oil and gas company driller and probably worked his way from Bolivar through Pennsylvania to Indiana. He married his first wife in 1889. Mr. Root changed careers a number of times. His last employment was with the Ontario Silver Plate Company in Muncie where he rose to the position of foreman. The circumstances of the breakdown of his second marriage are not known.

Laphronia Root's third wife was a childhood sweetheart. They became separated by his frequent job moves. On a trip to New York State after his divorce, he became reacquainted with Carrie Earl, now a widow, and they decided to marry. Laphronia and Effie Root were buried in Beech Grove Cemetery in Muncie, Indiana. Stella Curea Hall Root reverted to her maiden name after the divorce and remained in Muncie, Indiana until her death. Stella Curea was buried in Hillcrest Cemetery in Redkey, Indiana with her daughter and son-in-law, Minnie and Harry Burgess. Carrie Earl Root was buried with her first husband, Howard Earl, in Wellsville, New York's Woodlawn Cemetery in unmarked graves.

Children (by first marriage):

202. I. ***Tina Catherine Root***, b. Muncie, Indiana May 20, 1890, d. Muncie, Indiana April 25, 1909 from tubular meningitis and was buried in Beech Grove Cemetery.

203. II. ***Clifford J. Root***, b. Muncie, Indiana September 13, 1892, d. Muncie, Indiana September 18, 1896 from diphtheria and was buried in Beech Grove Cemetery.

204. III. ***Ruth Irene Root***, b. Muncie, Indiana July 1, 1897, d. Muncie, Indiana April 5, 1898. She was termed a *blue baby* and was buried in Beech Grove Cemetery.

205. IV. ***Claude Paul Root, f.***

206. V. ***Lillie Luella Root, f.***

207. VI. ***Clifton Root, f.***

208. VII. ***Martha Root, f.***

209. VIII. ***Elizabeth Root, f.***

References: US Census: 1870, 1880, 1900, 1910, 1920, 1930; New York State Census: 1865, 1875; Beech Grove Cemetery Records, Muncie, Indiana; Woodlawn Cemetery Records, Wellsville, New York; Hillcrest Cemetery Records, Redkey, Indiana; Indiana Marriages 1810-2001 for Laphronia Root's three marriages; Indiana Death Certificates 1899-2011 for Laphronia Root, Effie Root, and Stella Curea.

92.

Elizabeth E. Root, daughter of Hiram (44), granddaughter of Abel, Jr. (34), b. Bolivar, New York December 28, 1868, d. Huntington, Indiana November 19, 1910 from a cerebral hemorrhage; m. (1) probably Bolivar, New York at least by 1884 Frank Jewett, b. birth date and place of birth not known, d. place of death and death date not known, divorced; m. (2) Anderson, Madison County, Indiana July 30, 1902 Edward A. Fistler, b. Cleveland, Ohio March 1861, d. Colorado Springs, Colorado November 5, 1931.

Elizabeth Root was known in the family as Lizzie. There is little information about her first husband Frank Jewett. It is assumed that he was a Bolivar resident when they met and married by 1884. Both of their sons were born in Bolivar, Forrest Eugene Jewett in 1884 and Harry Frank Jewett in 1886. The family believed that Lizzie and Frank Jewett divorced, but there is currently no record of their divorce. The Jewetts were not listed on the 1892 New York State Census. The 1897 city directory for Muncie, Indiana recorded Lizzie Jewett as the widow of Frank Jewett. However, the 1900 US Census listed Lizzie Jewett as divorced living with her two sons near her brother, Laphronia Root, in Indiana.

It was in Indiana that Lizzie met and married Edward A. Fistler in 1902 and in 1905 they resided in Muncie, Indiana, but later moved to Huntington, Indiana. Mr. Fistler was a printer by profession. He was previously married to Annie Kraus in 1885 in Cleveland. Edward and Annie Fistler divorced by 1900. They had two daughters but his younger daughter, born in 1898, was deceased by 1900. A divorced Annie Kraus Fistler resided in Cleveland with her parents and surviving daughter based on the 1900 US Census data. After Lizzie's death, Edward Fistler remained in Indiana where he continued to work as a printer. In 1924 he retired and moved to Colorado Springs residing in the Printer's Retirement Home. He died there and was buried in Evergreen Cemetery in Colorado Springs.

Lizzie Root Jewett Fistler was buried in Mt. Hope Cemetery in Huntington, Indiana. Lizzie and Edward Fistler did not have any children together.

Children (by first marriage):

210. I. ***Forrest Eugene Jewett, f.***

211. II. ***Harry Frank Jewett, f.***

References: US Census: 1870, 1880, 1900, 1910, 1920, 1930; US Census: 1875; *Bolivar Breeze 1891-1965*, November 24, 1910 obituary; Indiana Death Certificate 1899-2011 for Lizzie Fistler; Indiana Marriage Index 1800-1941 for Lizzie Jewett and Edward Fistler; Mt. Hope Cemetery Records, Huntington, Indiana; Death Record for Edward A. Fistler for the Roman Catholic diocese of Colorado Springs; Evergreen Cemetery Records, Colorado Springs, Colorado; US City Directories for Huntington, Indiana and Colorado Springs, Colorado; Muncie, Indiana City Directory 1897 and 1905.

93.

Guy Arthur Root, adopted son (grandson) of Hiram (44), grandson (great-grandson) of Abel, Jr. (34), b. Bolivar, New York January 20, 1880, d. Erie, Pennsylvania March 21, 1939 from uremia; m. (1) place not known, a. 1902 Jessie Pearl, last name not known, b. Indiana, a. 1883, death place and date of death not known; m. (2) Florence, last name not known, birth place and date of birth not known, death place and date of death not known.

Guy Root was the illegitimate son of Flora M. Root. The identity of his father is not known, but Guy Root's death certificate listed his father as Fritz Root about whom nothing is currently known. Guy was adopted by his maternal grandparents, Hiram and Mary Jane Root, and was consistently identified as their son. The adoption is confirmed by a search of Belmont, New York Allegany County records. He was not mentioned in the obituaries of Hiram and Mary Jane Root or in the obituary for Flora Root Richardson, his mother. Guy Root was recorded in the 1880 US Census and the 1892 New York State Census as the son of Hiram and Mary Jane Root. In the 1900 US Census Guy Root resided with his mother (grandmother) in Center, Indiana. The 1910 US Census noted that Guy Root was married for eight years to Jessie, last name not known, and that they had three children, none living. He was employed as a boiler maker.

In 1911 he moved to Indianapolis but Guy and Jessie returned to Bolivar in 1913 and resided on Liberty Street in Bolivar based on the 1915 New York State Census. When Guy Root registered for the World War I draft, he resided in Cleveland, Ohio with his wife and was employed as a laborer. In 1922-23 Guy Root resided at 307 N. 10th Street in Olean, New York. In 1923 Guy got into legal difficulties when the husband of a woman he was seeing, sued him for alienation of affection. Guy Root had had previous problems with the authorities while growing up. In 1927 Guy Root resided in Silver Springs, New York near Richardson relatives. Guy Root could not be located on the 1930 US Census. It is not known what happened to his first wife. When Guy Root remarried is not known nor is anything known about her background. A wife, Florence Root, was listed on Guy Root's death certificate. It is not known where Guy Root was buried.

References: US Census: 1880, 1900, 1910; New York State Census: 1892. 1915; US World War I Draft Registration Cards, 1817-1919; Pennsylvania Death Certificates 1906-1963; Olean, New York City Directory 1922; *Olean Evening Herald,* selected issues 1920s; *Bolivar Breeze, 1891-1965,* selected issues.

94.

Asa Wallace Root, son of Albert (47), grandson of David C. (35), b. Bolivar, New York September 11, 1866, d. Amarillo, Texas January 30, 1932 from injuries suffered when he was hit by an automobile while walking the evening of January 28, 1932; m. Washington, D.C. June 18, 1890 Emma Frances Toner, b. Washington, D.C. June 21, 1866, d. Washington, D.C. March 28, 1928 from a heart attack complicated by chronic nephritis.

Asa Wallace Root was named for his father's brother who died at Andersonville prison in 1864 during the Civil War. After the death of his mother, Armina Kilbury Root, in 1872, he resided with various relatives, but Asa spent more time with his father in Washington, D.C. than his siblings did. It was in Washington, D.C. that Asa Root met his future wife, Emma Toner. Asa and Emma Root moved to Bolivar in the mid-1890s after the deaths of two infant children in Washington, D.C. In Bolivar Asa was employed as a carpenter and by 1900 owned and operated a carriage and wagon repair shop on lower Main Street, the former Wixson and Mead carriage and blacksmith shop. The business caught fire within two weeks of Asa's ownership on May 2, 1900. The majority of damage was contained to the roof. The fire started from chimney sparks in an adjoining building. The loss was $250 and was insured.

In March 1904, Asa W. Root received a bequest of $2000 from the estate of his maternal grandfather, Edwin Kilbury. In March of 1905 Asa W. Root created and sold the *Allegany Oil Field Buckboard*, which could sustain the weight of 1,500 pounds over rough roads. It was initially a fast seller. During his time in Bolivar, Asa Root was a member of the Bradley Hose Company and sang in the musicals the fire department sponsored. Asa was involved in Republican Party politics and was elected temporary chairman of the McKinley/Roosevelt Club and secretary of the local Republican caucus. Mr. Root was a member of the Bolivar I. O.O. F. Lodge # 515. In June of 1905, Asa W. Root, his brother George A. Root, and Homer Elliott of Wellsville purchased the Doty Wagon Works in Wellsville. The Doty name was retained and the company had an initial stock investment of $10,000. The new location sold the Doty Lumber wagons and the Allegany Oil Field Buckboards. Asa moved his family to Wellsville in August 1905. In January 1907, the Root family moved back to Bolivar residing in the former F. E. Moore home on Liberty Street. The reasons for the return are not known but it was possible that the Wellsville business was starting to experience financial difficulties because on October 8, 1908, Asa Root sold the wagon shop to George P. Bolender.

On October 29, 1908 Asa's wife, son, and daughter returned to Washington, D.C. while Asa moved to St. Louis joining his brother, George Root, and George's family in search of better employment opportunities. Emma suffered from rheumatic heart disease and feared she could not withstand the rigors of travel and the difference in climate. A devout Roman Catholic, Emma Root never considered divorce. Her in-laws provided the funds for Emma, Armina, and Edwin to relocate to Washington, DC where her family still resided. Emma was the daughter of Thomas W. Toner (1843-1908) and Margaret E. Manning Toner (?-1905). Mrs. Root's father was a clerk at the State Department and her unmarried sister, Caroline, was a schoolteacher who taught J. Edgar Hoover, the first head of the F.B.I. Emma jointly owned a house at 1814 Ingleside Terrace with her sister Caroline. For a time, Emma took in laundry and did housework before becoming a clerk with the National Geographic Society in Washington.

Asa W. Root remained in St. Louis until 1918 when his brother, George, died. He moved to Cairo, Illinois and from 1926 until his death resided in Amarillo, Texas. Asa was a retired contractor and architect who designed one of the first *rambler* model homes built in the 1920s. Mr. Root was a member of the Masonic Palo Duro Lodge # 1239 and the Fundamentalist Baptist Church in Amarillo. He resided at the El Blanco tourist camp. Asa Root was struck by a car driven by Ray Armstrong who claimed not to have seen him. Mr. Armstrong stayed with Mr. Root and took Asa to the hospital where he regained consciousness just before he died. Asa Wallace Root was buried in the Llano Cemetery in Amarillo. The lot was part of a settlement with a Mr. W. H. Coble. Emma Root was buried in Washington, D.C.'s Congressional Cemetery with three of her children.

Children:

212. I. ***Unnamed infant***, b. and d. January 1892 in Washington, D. C. and buried in Congressional Cemetery.

213. II. ***Elwood Root***, b. Washington, D. C. November 29, 1893, d. Washington, D.C. December 30, 1893 and buried in Congressional Cemetery.

214. III. ***Armina M. Root***, b. Bolivar, New York December 16, 1898, d. Washington, D.C. January 10, 1919 from the influenza epidemic. She was buried in Congressional Cemetery.

215. IV. ***Edwin (Edward) Albert Root, f.***

References: US Census: 1870, 1889, 1900, 1910, 1920, 1930; New York State Census: 1875, 1905; *Bolivar Breeze 1891-1965*, selected issues; Congressional Cemetery Records, Washington, D.C.; Texas Death Certificates 1903-1982; Llano Cemetery Records, Amarillo, Texas; District of Columbia Select Births and Christenings 1830-1965 for Elwood Root; *Washington Post* January 1890 for wedding record of Asa W. Root and Emma Toner; U.S. City Directories 1822-1965, Washington, D.C., 1915, 1917.

95.

Edwin Cartwright Root, son of Albert (47), grandson of David C. (35), b. Ceres, Pennsylvania October 27, 1867, d. Bolivar, New York December 14, 1931; m. Bolivar, New York March 12, 1895 Harriet (Hattie) J. MacDonald, b. Rouseville, Pennsylvania July 3, 1870, d. Bolivar, New York December 13, 1948. At the age of three years, Edwin Root resided with the Polter Benson family of Ceres, Pennsylvania where his parents also resided. His mother, Armina Root Kilbury, had a baby in 1869 who died soon after the 1870 US Census, so it is probable that neighboring families were helping with the growing Albert Root family. After his mother's 1872 death, Edwin Root moved to Washington, D.C. where he resided with his father until 1880 when he moved to Bolivar and was raised by his paternal grandparents, David C. and Marietta Root of Kossuth. Edwin Root received a bequest of $2000 in the 1904 will of his maternal grandfather, Edwin Kilbury. Mr. Root was a Bolivar oil producer and contractor during the first fifteen years of his married life.

His daughter, the late Gladys Root Nichols, said her father suffered partial paralysis when an oil field co-worker lanced a boil on Edwin Root's neck. On March 20, 1909, Mr. Root purchased a store owned by Joseph Catalinson on Main Street in Bolivar and opened *E. C. Root Confectioners.* He operated this business until his death in 1931. The building was later occupied by Nicholson's Flower Shop and stood next door to the former Dunn's Drug Store. The building has since been torn down. From 1911 until 1931, Edwin Root served as Bolivar's Tax Collector. His obituary described him as a man with an amiable disposition who possessed great patience even though he suffered from his affliction. Mr. Root always had a pleasant word and a ready smile in dealing with the public. He never complained about his physical condition. Hattie MacDonald Root was the daughter of John N. MacDonald (1828-1897) and Jane Adams MacDonald (1841-1903).

She helped her husband operate the family business. Gladys Root Nichols remembered her mother as a very attractive and stately woman who might have been successful in the theater. Mrs. Root was an accomplished elocutionist and made the most impressive bows. Hattie was a skilled seamstress and showed a flair in designing her children's clothes. Edwin's younger brother, George, had already married Hattie's older sister, Lizzie MacDonald in 1889. It is possible that George and Lizzie introduced the two. Edwin and Hattie were married in the home of George and Lizzie Root. Mr. and Mrs. Edwin Root resided at 75 Friendship Street in Bolivar. At the time of her death, Mrs. Root was a member of the Bolivar Methodist Church, the Berean Class, Les Douze Amis Social Club, and the Order of the Eastern Star, Buttrick Chapter. Edwin and Harriet MacDonald Root were buried in Bolivar's Maple Lawn Cemetery.

Children:

216. I. ***Edwin Milford Root, f.***

217. II. ***Gladys Josephine Root, f.***

218. III. ***Bertha Marjory Root, f.***

References: US Census: 1870, 1880, 1900, 1910, 1920, 1930; New York State Census: 1892, 1905, 1915, 1925; New York State Marriage Index 1881-1967; Bolivar Methodist Church Records, Book # 2, Marriages; New York State Death Index 1880-1956 for Edwin Root and Harriet Root; *Bolivar Breeze 1891-1965,* selected issues; Maple Lawn Cemetery Records, Bolivar, New York.

97.

George Albert Root, son of Albert (47), grandson of David C. (35), b. Ceres, Pennsylvania July 4, 1870, d. St. Louis, Missouri February 24, 1918 from cerebral apoplexy; m. Bolivar, New York a. 1889 Elizabeth (Lizzie) May MacDonald, b. Richburg, New York July 8, 1864, d. St. Louis, Missouri April 29, 1945 from heart failure and arteriosclerosis.

George Albert Root was raised by his paternal uncle and aunt, James and Huldah Root Curtiss of Bolivar after the 1872 death of his mother. He worked for his uncle at the State Bank of Bolivar from 1884 until his abrupt resignation without reason on July 1, 1898 and a few months after the death of his aunt, Huldah Root Curtiss. George continued to manage his uncle's extensive farming and oil properties until James Curtiss' death in 1900. However, on February 4, 1899 James M. Curtiss sued his nephew, George Root, and George Van Curen for four loans, two in 1895 and two in 1896, totaling $1,033 plus interest of which only $260 had been repaid. The loans were made to the Rock Glycerin

Company # 2 owned by George Root and George Van Curen. The outcome of the case is not known, but I suggest it interesting that the law suit was made after the death of Mrs. Curtiss (Huldah Root Curtiss) who raised George Root.

Mr. Root later found employment working Bolivar oil leases for the July Oil Company. He was injured on April 4, 1901 in a gas explosion that burned his right hand, eye lashes, and hair. The explosion threw him ten feet back against a nearby fence and caused a large red boil to appear on his knee. George Root also received a $2000 bequest in 1904 from the estate of his maternal grandfather, Edwin Kilbury. For a time, George Root worked with his oldest brother, Asa W. Root in the wagon and carriage business in both Bolivar and Wellsville, New York. George and Lizzie Root resided on Friendship Street. They sold their Bolivar residence in 1905 for $1,250 when they moved to Wellsville. The house had indoor plumbing, gas heat, one indoor bathroom, cement sidewalks and considerable grass frontage. The sale of Doty Wagon Company in 1908 led George Root to move his family to St. Louis, Missouri where he found work as an automobile salesman until his unexpected death in 1918.

Lizzie Root was a daughter of John N. MacDonald (1828-1897) and Jane Adams MacDonald (1841-1903) and the sister of Harriet MacDonald who married George Root's older brother, Edwin Root. George and Lizzie Root had three children. The first child was a stillbirth and the third child died soon after they moved to St. Louis. Mr. and Mrs. Root later adopted a daughter, Alvya. After the death of George Root and the marriage of her surviving biological daughter, Huldah, Lizzie Root moved back to Bolivar where she married Alexander Nicholson on April 18, 1927. Alexander Nicholson had been married twice before. His first wife was Minnie E. McCray by whom he had one daughter before they divorced. Mr. Nicholson remarried to Mary C. Kreiner who died in a tragic automobile accident on October 20, 1921 at a railroad crossing in White House, Pennsylvania. The car was driven by Mary C. Kreiner Nicholson, Alexander Nicholson's second wife, who failed to see the oncoming train. Mrs. Mary Nicholson and two other female passengers died while her daughter, Mary Herrick, survived. Lizzie and Alexander Nicholson resided at 120 Wellsville Street in Bolivar where Mr. Nicholson, an oil and gas producer, died October 14, 1930. Mrs. Root Nicholson was a trained nurse and found work in the Bolivar area in that career. In 1943 and in failing health she returned to St. Louis where she resided with her daughter, Huldah Root Nulsen, until her death in 1945, the victim of several strokes. George Root and Elizabeth MacDonald Root Nicholson were buried in Valhalla Cemetery, St. Louis, Missouri.

Children:

219. I. ***Huldah Jane Root, f.***

220. II. ***Helen Mildred Root***, b. Olean, New York May 13, 1900, d. St. Louis, Missouri January 13, 1910 from scarlet fever and spinal meningitis. She was buried in Bellefontaine Cemetery, St. Louis, Missouri.

221. III. ***Alvya Marie Root (adopted), f.***

References: US Census: 1870, 1880, 1900, 1910; New York State Census: 1875, 1892, 1905; *Bolivar Breeze 1891-1965,* selected issues; New York County Marriage Records 1847-1849 and 1907-1936 for Alexander Nicholson and Elizabeth Root; Missouri State Board of Health Death Certificate for George Albert Root; Valhalla and Bellefontaine Cemetery Records, St. Louis, Missouri; Supreme Court of Allegany County, James M. Curtiss vs George Van Curen and George A. Root, February 4, 1899.

98.

Bertha Armina Root, daughter of Albert (47), granddaughter of David C. (35), b. Ceres, Pennsylvania February 24, 1872, d. San Diego, California April 14, 1912 from heart failure caused by unsupervised dieting; m. Bolivar, New York June 12, 1889 Wilber Porter Cook, b. Ohio July 14, 1865, d. Los Angeles, California April 7, 1957.

Bertha was raised by her maternal grandparents, the Edwin Kilburys of Bolivar, after her mother died giving birth to her. Edwin Kilbury left a $2000 bequest in his will to his granddaughter, Bertha Root. Bertha Root Cook was an accomplished vocalist and for many years was the choir director for the Bolivar Methodist Church. Bertha was baptized at the Bolivar Methodist Church on December 2, 1887 where she and Wilber Cook were married in 1889. Bertha Cook was a member of the Bolivar Eastern Star. In 1898, Mr. and Mrs. Cook moved into their new residence on Boss Street, which was designed by Mrs. Cook's brother, Asa W. Root.

The house was in the Colonial style, stood two stories with an attic, and had an octagon extension on the northeast corner for a conservatory. A veranda extended around the front of the house and half way back on the east side with railing and double columns. The first floor was divided into a hall, parlor, library, sitting room, dining room, and sewing room. A lavatory was on the first floor and entry to the conservatory was through the dining room. The kitchen had hot and cold running water and a refrigerator was built into the wall. Double sliding doors were found throughout the first floor. Two flights of stairs led to the second floor, one from the front hall and a second from the kitchen. The second floor had eight sleeping rooms and a full bathroom. Each bedroom had a closet. The attic was fitted as a play house for the children and had eight dormer windows. A complete basement could be found under the entire house and the residence was heated by a hot air furnace using natural gas and each room had a ventilating register. An internal sewer system ran from the basement to the creek. Wilber Cook had a small machine shop in the basement.

In 1900 Bertha Wilcox, a cousin of Mrs. Cook, worked for the Cook family. The structure was a state-of-the-art residence, which once stood on the left side of the George H. Bradley residence on Boss Street. The residence was later sold to the Acme Milling Company and was converted from a single-family home to four apartments. George Bradley, Wilber Cook's cousin, later purchased the building and in 1944 the structure was razed. In 1906 the Cooks moved to San Diego after a brief stay in Puerto Rico because Mr. Cook suffered from tuberculosis and he needed a healthier climate. Wilber Cook built a beautiful home overlooking the San Diego Bay where Bertha Cook died. Mr. Cook had three years of college education according to the 1940 US Census. He was employed in Bolivar as a bank clerk at the State Bank of Bolivar, a bookkeeper, and later an oil producer. Wilber Cook was the son of William R. Cook (1834-1909) and Lovantia Artemeria Prindle (1834-1871) of Springboro, Pennsylvania. William R. Cook's sister, Naomi Cook, married Justin B. Bradley of Springboro whose son, George H. Bradley, moved to Bolivar and became a very wealthy oil and natural gas producer in Allegany County.

On June 22, 1920 Wilber Cook remarried to Ethel Florence Hicks in Bath, New York. Ethel Hicks Cook, an art student, was born in California August 28, 1890 and died in Los Angeles July 26, 1973. They resided at 2966 Union Street in San Diego. Wilber and Edith Cook did not have any children. Anita Cook Baicher, Wilber and Bertha's daughter, described her father's lifestyle as that of a gentleman farmer and fisherman. He died in a Los Angeles hospital in 1957. Bertha Root Cook's remains were cremated and buried next to her maternal grandparents in Maple Lawn Cemetery in Bolivar. Wilber Cook and his second wife were buried in Santa Barbara Cemetery in Santa Barbara, California.

Children:

222. I. ***Edna Cook, f.***

223. II. ***Homer Cook, f.***

224. III. ***Anita Cook, f.***

References: US Census: 1870, 1880, 1900, 1910, 1930, 1940; New York State Census: 1892, 1905; Maple Lawn Cemetery Records, Bolivar, New York; Santa Barbara Cemetery Records, Santa Barbara, California; New York County Marriage Records 1847-1849, 1907-1936 for Wilber Cook's marriage to Edith Hicks; California Death Index 1940-1997 for Wilber Cook and Edith Cook; *Bolivar Breeze 1891-1965,* selected issues; Bolivar Methodist Church Records, Book 2, Bolivar, New York.

100.

Forrest G. Evans, son of Elosica (49), grandson of David C. (35), b. Hamilton, Missouri November 1870, d. place and date not known; m. (1) St. Joseph, Michigan January 29, 1889 Amelia Grau, b. probably Michigan 1863, d. probably Michigan 1891; m. (2) place not known, a. 1891 Leoda May Underhill, b. Iowa June 1871, d. place and date not known.

Information about Forrest G. Evans is difficult to fine. There are a number of Forrest or Forest G. Evans in residence in Missouri, Illinois, and Michigan where this son of Addison and Elosica Root Evans did reside. The 1870 and 1880 US Census recorded Forrest residing with his parents in Missouri and Illinois. The 1900 and 1910 US Census recorded Forrest G. Evans residing in Chicago, Illinois with his second wife and son. He cannot be traced after the 1910 US Census. His second wife, Leoda

Underhill Evans was recorded in the 1930 US Census residing in Los Angeles, California. At that time, she was unemployed, living in a boarding house, and listed as a widow. No further information can be found for Forrest and Leoda Evans.

Children (by second marriage):

225. I. ***Addison Ross Evans, f.***

References: US Census: 1870, 1880, 1900, 1910, 1930; Michigan Marriage Records 1867-1952 for Forrest G. Evans and Amelia Grau; St. Joseph City Cemetery, St. Joseph, Michigan.

101.

Albert A. Evans, son of Elosica (49), grandson of David C. (35), b. Hamilton, Missouri April 1873, d. place and date of death not known; m. a. 1892 Jessie McPhratride, b. Illinois, March 1874, d. place not known a. 1914. Little is known about this Root descendant. The 1870 and 1880 US Census recorded Albert Evans residing with his parents. In 1900 Albert lived in St. Louis and was married. A photograph survives of Jessie Evans. An Albert A. Evans enlisted in June 1908 in the 17th Infantry, Company G. as a cook. This Albert Evans deserted June 15, 1909. No further documentation or information can be found on either Albert or Jessie Evans. There were no known children from this marriage.

References: US Census: 1880, 1900; US Army Register of Enlistments 1798-1914.

102.

Agnes Merittia Evans, daughter of Elosica (49), granddaughter of David C. (35), b. Hamilton, Missouri June 4, 1877 (a twin), d. Deland, Florida June 15, 1966. Agnes M. Evans was the twin sister of Alice H. Evans. Agnes never married. After her father's death in 1893, Agnes, Alice, and their mother, Elosica Root Evans, returned to Bolivar to reside with Elosica Evans' sister, Huldah Root Curtiss. Agnes worked as a bank clerk at the State Bank of Bolivar where her uncle, James Curtiss, was the President.

Agnes, Alice, their mother, and Aunt Huldah were ardent Spiritualists spending summers at Lily Dale, New York. Agnes was a trained nurse and found employment in Chicago after Mr. Curtiss died in 1900. The US Census records for 1910, 1920, 1930, and 1940 show that the twin sisters were both employed as nurses and roomed together in Chicago boarding houses. It is believed that Agnes and Alice returned to Lily Dale in the early 1940s residing at 20 North Street before moving in 1945 to Deland, Florida where a Spiritualist Community founded as a colony by Lily Dale, New York, existed. Agnes and Alice Evans donated a considerable collection of family photographs, letters, and the Civil War diary of their uncle, Asa W. Root, who died at Andersonville Prison in 1864 to Lily Dale. These items are on display in the Lily Dale Historical Society Museum. Agnes' burial site is not known but it is assumed the burial was in a private cemetery on the grounds of the Spiritualist Society at Lake Helen in Deland, Florida.

References: US Census: 1880, 1900, 1910, 1920, 1930, 1940; Florida Death Records; Lily Dale Historical Society, Lily Dale, New York.

103.

Alice Huldah Evans, daughter of Elosica (49), granddaughter of David C. (35), b. Hamilton, Missouri June 4, 1877 (a twin), d. Deland, Florida April 12, 1960. Alice Huldah Evans was the twin sister of Agnes M. Evans. Alice never married and resided most of her life with her twin sister. After the death of her father in 1893, Alice, her twin sister Agnes, and their mother returned to Bolivar where they resided with their uncle and aunt, James and Huldah Root Curtiss.

Alice ran the Curtiss household as her Aunt Huldah's health declined. Alice, Agnes, their mother, and aunt were actively involved in Spiritualism promoted by Lily Dale, New York. For many summers and for a few years the two sisters resided at Lily Dale in a house on 20 North Street, across the street from the school, which now houses the Lily Dale Historical Society. The sisters dressed alike and were seldom seen separately. Alice was a trained nurse and for at least three decades resided in Chicago where Alice roomed with her sister in boarding houses. By the mid-1940s, the sisters moved to Deland, Florida in retirement and near the Lake Helen Spiritualist Society, a branch of Lily Dale. It is believed that Alice was buried with her twin sister Agnes in a private cemetery at Lake Helen. Alice and Agnes donated a considerable archive of Root memorabilia to Lily Dale Spiritualist Society, which can be seen at the Lily Dale Historical Society Museum.

References: US Census: 1880, 1900, 1910, 1920, 1930, 1940; Florida Death Records; Lily Dale Historical Society, Lily Dale, New York.

104.

Emma Garthwait, daughter of Elizabeth (50), granddaughter of Truman Bishop (36), b. Bolivar, New York January 29, 1859, d. Bolivar, New York December 14, 1931; m. Fred Albert Hulbert Friendship, New York September 23, 1880, b. Bolivar, New York August 15, 1857, d. Bolivar, New York May 24, 1938.

Emma Garthwait resided with her parents until her marriage. Emma and Fred Hulbert resided in Bolivar all of their lives except for a few years in the late 1880s when they lived in Brockport, New York. In 1889, they moved backed to Bolivar where they resided at 97 Wellsville Street. Fred Hulbert was the son of William A. Hulbert (1824-1903) and Amelia Withey Hulbert (1835-1868) of North Spencer, New York. Emma Hulbert was a charter member of the Lady Maccabees, Juanita Hive # 127 where she served as Lady Commander (1896) and Record Keeper (1899). Mrs. Hulbert was also a member of the Eastern Star, Buttrick Chapter # 109 where she was elected Worthy Matron (1903), Assistant Conductor (1905), and Treasurer (1918). Emma and Fred had four children. Emma Garthwait Hulbert's death occurred within thirty minutes after a short walk home from her mother's residence to her own home from heart trouble. Fred Hulbert worked in the grocery business with his father-in-law and brother-in-law, Christopher and Elmer Garthwait, beginning in 1883 until about 1885 when his in-laws purchased his share of the store. For a couple of years Fred was a bookkeeper for the State Bank of Bolivar where the Garthwait family had a financial interest. The brief move to Brockport continued Mr. Hulbert's banking career.

When Emma and Fred Hulbert returned to Bolivar in 1889, Fred resumed working with and for his in-laws in Bolivar and separately ran a grocery store in Wellsville, New York. The purchase of an oil lease on Deer Creek led to greater financial security for the Hulbert family. Mr. Hulbert continued to work as a bookkeeper until he retired in 1923. His last employer was Albert L. Shaner. In 1890 Fred Hulbert was appointed Justice of the Peace for Bolivar and in 1891 served as President of the Bolivar Village Board. Fred Hulbert was appointed Justice of Sessions and Suspensions in 1893. Mr. Hulbert was a member of the Macedonia Lodge # 258, F. and A. M. Bolivar Chapter # 280, R. A. M. Buttrick Chapter # 109, O. E. S., and St. John's Commandery of Olean, New York. Fred was an active member of the Bolivar Methodist Church. He was a trustee of the Bradley Hose Company and served as Chairman of the Bolivar School Board (1921) and as School Board Secretary (1922). Fred Hulbert died at his home from a heart attack. Their son Wayne Hulbert predeceased them dying from a nitroglycerine explosion in 1924. Fred and Emma Garthwait Hulbert were buried in Bolivar's Maple Lawn Cemetery.

Children:

226. I. ***Gerald Fred Hulbert, f.***

227. II. ***Wayne Christopher Hulbert, f.***

228. III. ***Elba William Hulbert, f.***

229. IV. ***Leta Elizabeth Hulbert, f.***

References: US Census: 1860, 1880, 1900, 1910, 1920, 1930; New York State Census: 1865, 1875, 1892, 1905, 1915, 1925; Maple Lawn Cemetery Records, Bolivar, New York; *Bolivar Breeze 1891-1965*, selected issues; New York Death Index 1880-1956 for Emma Hulbert and Fred Hulbert.

105.

Elmer Christopher Garthwait, son of Elizabeth (50), grandson of Truman Bishop (36), b. Bolivar, New York April 8, 1861, d. St. Francis Hospital Olean, New York February 4, 1946 due to complications from an infected left leg; m. place not know June 18, 1884 Millie Rose Hill, b. Eden, New York May 5, 1863, d. St. Francis Hospital Olean, New York November 15, 1952.

Elmer Garthwait was a life-long resident of Bolivar residing with his parents until his marriage in 1884. He started his professional career in the carriage business with his father in a building that later housed Helen's Dress Shop. Elmer and his father also ran a grocery store where Neill's Department Store was later housed. As an oil producer Mr. Garthwait led E. C. Garthwait and Company until its sale in 1942 to the Healey Petroleum Company of Bradford, Pennsylvania. As a young man Elmer Garthwait taught at District # 2 on the Bolivar-Genesee Road and later at the school in Vosburg. Mr. Garthwait was a member of the Bolivar Band and the Fenfield Orchestra playing the bass viola with the latter. A member of the Masons, Elmer Garthwait was on the building committee, active in Macedonia Lodge # 254 F. and A. M., in the Bolivar Chapter, # 250, R. A. M., the Ismailia Temple of Buffalo, and St. John's Commandery in Olean.

He served for twenty-four years as Treasurer of the Maple Lawn Cemetery Association, was a Director of the State Bank of Bolivar, and a member of the Bolivar Fire Department. Millie Rose Hill Garthwait was the daughter of Melvin Hill (1838-1878) and Harriet Webster Hill (1841-?). Mrs. Garthwait's parents were Quakers residing in Erie County, New York. Millie resided in Bolivar for over 75 years where she was a member of the Buttrick Chapter Eastern Star. Elmer and Millie Garthwait resided at 58 Friendship Street, but they also maintained a home in Pinellas, Florida where they resided for part of each year beginning in 1935. The Garthwaits were members of the Allegany/Florida Society. Their only child, Glen, died in 1916 at the age of twenty-six years. For a time, Millie Garthwait spent weekends at Lily Dale, New York noted for Spiritualism and the ability to communicate with the dead, perhaps, seeking to contact her deceased son. Elmer and Millie Garthwait paid for the 1919 construction of the impressive gates and wrought iron fencing at Bolivar's Maple Lawn Cemetery. Mrs. Garthwait later had the circular memorial granite fountain near the Civil War Monument erected in memory of her husband. Elmer and Millie Garthwait were buried in the Garthwait Mausoleum with his parents and their son.

Children:

230. I. ***Glen Christopher Garthwait, f.***

References: US Census: 1870, 1880, 1900, 1910, 1920, 1930, 1940; New York State Census: 1865, 1875, 1892, 1905, 1915, 1925; Maple Lawn Cemetery Records, Bolivar, New York; *Bolivar Breeze 1891-1965,* selected issues; New York Death Index 1880-1956 for Elmer and Millie Garthwait.

106.

Addie Elenora Root, daughter of Bryant Hebron (52), granddaughter of Truman Bishop (36), b. Bolivar, New York January 15, 1867, d. Santa Clara, California September 9, 1956; m. Friendship, New York October 2, 1889 William Allison Mitchell, b. Tarentum, Pennsylvania September 2, 1863, d. Sister's Hospital Buffalo, New York August 25, 1923.

Addie and William Mitchell resided in Oregon, Ohio in 1900 with their two sons, Wade and Dean. Wade was born in Bradford, Pennsylvania in 1895 and Dean was born in Toledo, Ohio in 1898. The Mitchells moved frequently because Mr. Mitchell worked for the oil industry in a variety of occupations. In 1900 he was an oil pumper and in 1903 resided in Lima, Ohio working for the Tidewater Oil Company for over twenty years. The 1910 US Census found the Mitchells living in Wellsville, New York where William worked as a pipe fitter for the local refinery. In 1920 the Mitchell family moved to nearby Scio where Mr. Mitchell was employed as a gauger for an oil pipeline. Their final move was to Bolivar, where they lived on South Street. William Mitchell was the son of William M. Mitchell (1836-1901) and Margaret Jane Lardin Mitchell (1836-1925) of Butler, Pennsylvania. After her husband's 1923 death, Addie Mitchell moved to Chicago, Illinois residing in 1930 with her son Wade and his wife. In the 1940 US Census Addie Root Mitchell resided with both sons and their wives in Chicago. It currently cannot be determined if Addie's two daughters-in-law were sisters. Addie, her son Wade, and his wife moved from Chicago in 1945 to San Mateo, California where she died in 1956. William Mitchell was buried in Bolivar's Maple Lawn Cemetery. It is not known where Addie Root Mitchell was buried.

Children:

231. I. ***Wade Root Mitchell, f.***

232. II. ***Dean McMillan Mitchell, f.***

References: US Census: 1870, 1880, 1900, 1910, 1920, 1930, 1940; New York State census: 1875, 1915; New York Death Index 1880-1956 for William Mitchell; California Death Index 1940-1997 for Addie Mitchell; New York State Marriage Index 1881-1967; Maple Lawn Cemetery Records, Bolivar, New York; *Bolivar Breeze 1891-1965,* selected issues.

107.

Ira Wallace Root, son of Bryant Hebron (52) and grandson of Truman Bishop (36), b. Bolivar, New York May 9, 1868, d. Bolivar, New York May 12, 1945 from cancer; m. Bolivar, New York January 13, 1892 Grace T. Salvage, b. Newark, N. Y. June 3, 1870, d. Olean General Hospital, Olean, New York October 2, 1954.

Ira Wallace Root resided with his parents in Bolivar until his 1892 marriage. He was first employed as a post office clerk under Postmasters J. H. Crandall, George H. Parker, and John P. Herrick. On February 1, 1904 Ira Root purchased his father-in-law's, George Salvage, shoe store on Main Street, a site later occupied by the Kozy Kitchen restaurant. He operated the shoe store until November of 1944 when he retired. For over fifty years, Mr. Root was a member of the Macedonia Lodge, # 258, F. and A. M. Grace Root was the daughter of George Salvage (1829-1914) and Elizabeth Jacques Alcock Salvage (1839-1890) of Bolivar. They were married at the home of Grace's sister, Mrs. R. N. Andrus, on South Street by Reverend Arnold. They had an unnamed male child who was born and died in 1904.

The male child was buried with his maternal grandparents, George and Elizabeth Salvage, with a marker in Maple Lawn Cemetery. Mrs. Root was a member of the Buttrick Chapter # 109 O. E. S, attended the Bolivar Methodist Church, and was a member of the Berean Sunday School Class serving as its treasurer. In the 1920s Mr. and Mrs. Root resided on Friendship Street moving by 1930 to 82 South Street. Ira and Grace Root were buried in Maple Lawn Cemetery in Bolivar next to his parents. A pair of wrought iron candelabra were given in memory of Mrs. Grace Root to the Bolivar Methodist Church by neighbors and friends in November of 1954.

References: US Census: 1870, 1880, 1900, 1910, 1920, 1930, 1940; New York State Census: 1875, 1892, 1905, 1915, 1925; Maple Lawn Cemetery Records, Bolivar, New York; *Bolivar Breeze 1891-1965*, selected issues; New York State Marriage Index 1881-1967; New York Death Index 1880-1956; Bolivar, New York Methodist Church Records, Book 2, Marriage Records.

108.

Ella Annette Crandall, daughter of Arzulla (53), granddaughter of Truman Bishop (26), b. Bolivar, New York October 6, 1866, d. Bolivar, New York January 24, 1954.

Ella Crandall was the eldest child of Alonzo and Arzulla Root Crandall and she lived the longest of her parents' four children. Ella never married. There is some confusion about Ella's middle name. Her gravestone has an "I" for a middle initial and some sources use a "J" for her middle name. I used the middle name of "Annette," which was given by family sources and is the middle name in the lengthy 1949 genealogical history about the descendants of John Crandall of Rhode Island because the information was submitted by Crandall relatives in Bolivar. Ella Crandall was a graduate of the Geneseo Normal School and the University of Chicago. She was a Bolivar school teacher as recorded by the 1892 New York State Census and from 1900-1910 was the Principal of Bolivar High School. In the 1900 US Census Ella resided at a boarding house in Bolivar owned and operated by Burt Stetson.

Three other high school teachers: Nellia Hovey, Sarah Wyman, and Effie Flint, also, resided at the Stetson residence. In 1902, Ella was paid $1000 annually as Principal. The annual salary of a high school teacher was $400. It seems she retired from teaching in 1910, the same year as her mother's death and resided with her father until he died in 1918 on the family farm. The 1915 New York State Census does not provide Ella Crandall with an occupation. The US Census for 1920 and 1930 and the New York State Census for 1925 record that she continued to reside on the family farm in Kossuth raising Jersey cattle until the herd was sold in May 1921 and managing the farm's oil revenues, which were temporarily affected by the collapse of at least one derrick in a severe storm that hit Bolivar in June 1924.

Miss Crandall was an active charter member of the Bolivar Grange, the Bolivar Methodist Church, the Berean Class, the Allegany County Federation of Women's Clubs, and the Sorosis Society. In August of 1921 Ella's home was robbed of fifteen gallons of maple syrup, personal belongings, and other food stuffs when she was in an Olean clinic recovering from burns when her dress caught fire from a gas stove at her home. The culprits were apprehended and most of the missing items recovered. Her family described her as a brilliant woman who in later life became a bit eccentric and odd. During her last years she left the farm in Kossuth and resided at 89 Plum Street until her death. In Ella Crandall's will she gave Alfred University, Alfred, New York $20,000 from which she established a scholarship fund at Alfred University for direct descendants of her parents. The total amount of the scholarship fund was $10,000 and was divided into a $5000 Alonzo Crandall Scholarship and a $5000 Arzulla Root Scholarship. If there were no direct descendants using the scholarship monies, Miss Crandall's Will directed that the scholarship funds could be used by collateral descendants of either the Root or Crandall families. If there were no Root or Crandall descendants using the funds, the monies could be given to a resident of Bolivar who attended Alfred University. Edwin Crandall who predeceased his sister was left $1000 and the children of her brother Owen Crandall were given $1000 but they predeceased Ella as well. The remainder of Ella Crandall's estate was to be divided among Paul M. Crandall, Helma Crandall, Ruth Crandall Quick, Harly Crandall, Clarence Crandall, the estate of Neil Crandall, and her brother-in-law James B. Wakeman. Ella Crandall was buried in Maple Lawn Cemetery in Bolivar, New York next to her parents.

References: US Census: 1870, 1880, 1900, 1920, 1930; New York State Census: 1875, 1892, 1905, 1915, 1925; Unpublished Root family history by Helen Ward Hulbert; New York Death Index 1880-1956; *Bolivar Breeze 1891-1965,* selected issues; Crandall, John Cortland, *Elder John Crandall of Rhode Island and his Descendants*, Woodstock, New York, 1949; Maple Lawn Cemetery Records, Bolivar, New York.

109.

Viola Vinette Crandall, daughter of Arzulla (53), granddaughter of Truman Bishop (36), b. Bolivar, New York May 30, 1868, d. Bolivar, New York July 4, 1915 from cancer; m. probably Bolivar, New York December 11, 1884 (or 1890) James B. Wakeman, b. Walton, New York September 9, 1867, d. Hornell, New York September 13, 1951 at St. James Hospital.

Viola Wakeman was a life-long resident of Bolivar, New York. She resided with her parents until her marriage in 1884 to James Wakeman. There is some confusion on the date of Viola and James Wakeman's marriage. The Crandall genealogy gave the date of 1884 and this information was provided by Viola's sister-in-law, Mrs. Clara Crandall. The 1900 US Census recorded that the Wakemans had been married just ten years, establishing the marriage year as 1890, which is the marriage year stated in Viola Wakeman's obituary. Mrs. Wakeman was a member of the Bolivar Methodist Church, was a devout Christian, and was held in the highest esteem by the Bolivar community. She and her husband resided in Kossuth on a farm with oil producing wells next to her parent's farm. Viola's funeral took place at the home. Viola and James Wakeman did not have any children.

James B. Wakeman was the son of Chester Wakeman (1842-1934) and Margaret Thompson Wakeman (1846-1911). He was an oil producer his entire life. After the death of his wife, Viola, James Wakeman remarried in Buffalo, New York on April 20, 1921 to Edith L. DeVinney Coffin, a widow, from Nunda, New York. It is not known how they met. Mr. Wakeman was a member of Macedonia Lodge # 258, F. and A. M., Bolivar Chapter, the Lodge of Perfection in Olean, New York, the Buffalo Consistory, Ismailia Temple, and the Bolivar Fire Department. Edith DeVinney was born in Mt. Morris, New York November 5, 1870. Her first husband was George Coffin whom she married January 8, 1896. Edith Wakeman had two sons by her first marriage, Leon Coffin (1898-1974) and Howard Coffin (1901-1970). It is not known when George Coffin died. After the death of George Coffin, Edith was employed as a matron in a sanitarium in Hornell, New York. James and Edith Wakeman resided in Bolivar until their respective deaths. James Wakeman died in 1951 and Edith Wakeman died in Bolivar, New York April 12, 1964. Viola and James Wakeman were buried in Maple Lawn Cemetery, Bolivar, New York with her parents. It is not known where Edith Wakeman was buried.

References: US Census: 1870, 1880, 1900, 1910, 1920, 1930, 1940; New York State Census: 1875, 1892, 1905, 1915, 1925; Maple Lawn Cemetery Records, Bolivar, New York; *Bolivar Breeze 1891-1965,* selected issues; New York Death Index 1880-1956 for James B. Wakeman; New York State Death Index 1957-1968 for Edith Wakeman; New York State Marriage Index 1881-1957 for James Wakeman and Edith Coffin; Foote, Abram William *Foote Family: Comprising the Genealogy and History of Nathaniel Foote of Wethersfield, Connecticut,* Rutland, VT: Marble City Press, 1907; Crandall, John Cortland, *Elder John Crandall of Rhode Island and his Descendants,* Woodstock, New York, 1949.

110.

Erwin David Crandall, son of Arzulla (53), grandson of Truman Bishop (36), b. Bolivar, New York April 25, 1870, d. Bolivar, New York December 20, 1950; m. Friendship, New York October 17, 1895 Clarinda (Clara) Edith Georgia, b. Elmira, New York December 3, 1873, d. New York State October 27, 1965.

Erwin Crandall was a lifelong resident of Bolivar, New York. He resided with his parents, Alonzo and Arzulla Root Crandall until his 1895 marriage to Clara Georgia. Mr. Crandall was a Bolivar oil producer residing on a farm in Kossuth, New York next to his parents until 1910 when he moved his family to Olive Street in Bolivar.

In 1898 Erwin Crandall and his brother Owen purchased thirteen oil wells on the Alonzo Crandall farm for $5000. The wells produced five barrels of oil a day. Mr. and Mrs. Crandall later moved to a farm on Foreman Hollow Road in Bolivar Township where he died from heart trouble at age 58 years. The residence has since been torn down. Clara was the daughter of George F. Georgia (1840-1907) and Ann E. Hawley Georgia (1844-1917). Mrs. Crandall was the sole beneficiary of her husband's will and their son Neil was the executor. Erwin and Clara Crandall were buried in Bolivar's Maple Lawn Cemetery with an unnamed infant son who died.

Children:

233. I. ***Neil Alonzo Crandall, f.***

234. II. ***Harley Erwin Crandall, f.***

235. III. ***Roy Stephen Crandall, f.***

236. IV. ***Ralph Merrill Crandall, f.***

237. V. ***Bernice Crandall***, b. Bolivar, New York July 1,1909, d. Bolivar, New York February 17, 1911. Bernice Crandall was buried in Maple Lawn Cemetery, Bolivar, New York.

238. V. ***Clarence Wayne Crandall, f.***

References: US Census: 1870, 1880, 1900, 1910, 1920, 1930, 1940; New York State Census: 1875, 1892, 1905, 1915, 1925; New York State Death Index 1957-1968 for Clara Crandall; New York State Death Index 1880-1956; New York Marriage Index 1881-1967; *Olean Times Herald*, January 30, 1951 for Erwin Crandall's will; Maple Lawn Cemetery Records, Bolivar, New York; *Bolivar Breeze 1891-1965,* selected issues; Crandall, John Cortland, *Elder John Crandall of Rhode Island and His Descendants,* Woodstock, New York, 1949.

111.

Owen Ernest Crandall, son of Arzulla (53), grandson of Truman Bishop (36), b. Bolivar, New York January 2, 1874, d. Bolivar, New York December 14, 1931; m. Hinsdale, New York October 2, 1898 Hattie Elnora Goodrich, b. Bolivar, New York October 13, 1875, d. Rochester, New York June 8, 1959.

Owen Crandall was a lifelong resident of Bolivar, New York. Until his 1898 marriage Owen resided with his parents on their Kossuth, New York farm. Mr. Crandall was a farmer, an oil producer, and a real estate agent. Owen Crandall farmed in Kossuth, drilled and flooded wells he owned on Beers Hollow Road, and sold real estate with W. J. Henderson for the Bolivar Real Estate Agency. Hettie Goodrich Crandall was the daughter of Milton L. Goodrich (1845-1928) and Roba Lucretia Crandall Goodrich (1846-1888). Owen and Hettie Goodrich Crandall were buried in Maple Lawn Cemetery, Bolivar, New York.

Children:

239. I. ***Paul Milton Crandall, f.***

240. II. ***Ruth Crandall, f.***

241. III. ***Lawrence Crandall,*** b. Bolivar, New York July 11, 1906, d. Bolivar, New York 1907. He was buried in Bolivar's Maple Lawn Cemetery.

242. IV. ***Helma Virginia Crandall, f.***

References: US Census: 1880, 1900, 1910, 1920, 1930, 1940; New York State Census: 1875, 1892, 1905, 1915, 1925; Maple Lawn Cemetery Records, Bolivar, New York; *Bolivar Breeze 1891-1965,* selected issues; Crandall, John Cortland, *Elder John Crandall of Rhode Island and His Descendants,* Woodstock, New York, 1949; New York State Death Index 1880-1956; New York State Death Index 1957-1968; New York Marriage Index 1881-1967.

112.

Myrtie (Myrtle) L. Root, daughter of Erastus (54), granddaughter of Truman Bishop (36), b. Bolivar, New York May 1868, d. Bolivar, New York September 21, 1916 from a self-inflicted gunshot wound to the head after suffering from a brain tumor; m. Bolivar, New York April 25, 1894 Edwin M. Strayer, b. Geneva, Pennsylvania March 13, 1868, d. Olean General Hospital, Olean, New York February 2, 1940.

Myrtie Root Strayer was a life-long resident of Bolivar. Her obituary described her as a kindly woman and a devoted wife who was loved by all who knew her. The brain tumor and a recent stay in the Wellsville sanitarium for two weeks led to an increasing sense of melancholy, which ended in Mrs. Strayer taking her own life. Mrs. Strayer was a member of the Bolivar Methodist Church, the Trilby Rebekah Lodge # 169 and the O.T. M. Edwin and Myrtie Strayer did not have any children. Mrs. Strayer was baptized at the Bolivar Methodist Church on February 10, 1888 and joined the Church September 30, 1889. Edwin Strayer was the son of Lorenzo Dow Strayer (1842-1921) and Harriet Lucinda M. Trace Strayer (1841-1932).

Mr. Strayer moved to Bolivar with his parents in 1880 and remained a member of the Bolivar community until his death. He was a tool dresser and driller, an oil producer, and owned and operated a harness shop in Bolivar in part of the building that housed the State Bank of Bolivar. When the State Bank of Bolivar expanded into the entire building on the corner of Main and Boss Streets, Edwin Strayer moved his harness shop to the Main Street building that later housed the Matylas Billiard Room. He retired from the harness business in 1918 due to ill health. Mr. Strayer served as Town Clerk from January 1916 to September 1919 and as Bolivar Supervisor from 1919 until December 31, 1923. Edwin Strayer was a member of the I.O.O.F. and a member and director of the Bolivar Methodist Church. Edwin Strayer remarried in Wayne, New York December 17, 1926 to Irene Rebecca Weed Stebbins.

Irene Weed was born in North Rose, New York April 21, 1885 and had a twin sister, Ruth Sarissa Weed. Irene Weed Stebbins Strayer was the daughter of Addison Weed (1852-1930) and Ida Jessie Cleveland Weed (1855-1940). Irene married Lee Stebbins in Wayne, New York on August 21, 1911. Mr. Stebbins died August 18, 1912. Irene Weed Stebbins attended Oswego Normal School and studied in

1922 for one year at Cornell University. She taught first grade in Bolivar for a number of years. Irene Strayer was a member of the Bolivar Sorosis Society, Buttrick Chapter # 109, Order of the Eastern Star, and the Catherine Schuyler Chapter of the D.A. R. She died in the Wellsville hospital June 25, 1932 from an internal obstruction. Irene Weed Stebbins Strayer was buried in Bolivar's Maple Lawn Cemetery. She and Edwin Strayer did not have any children. Myrtie and Edwin Strayer were buried in Maple Lawn Cemetery in Bolivar, New York.

References: US Census: 1870, 1880, 1900, 1910, 1920, 1930, 1940; New York State Census: 1875, 1892, 1905, 1915, 1925; New York State Marriage Index 1881-1967 for both of Edwin Strayer's marriages; *Bolivar Breeze 1891-1965*, selected issues; New York State Death Index 1880-1956; Maple Lawn Cemetery Records, Bolivar, New York; Bolivar Methodist Church Records, Book # 1; Cleveland, Edmund James, *The Genealogy of the Cleveland and Cleaveland Families,* Hartford, Connecticut: Case, Lockwood, and Brainard Co., 1899.

113.

Asa Prentice Root, son of Erastus (54), grandson of Truman Bishop (36), b. Bolivar, New York June 16, 1875, d. Wellsville, New York hospital February 22, 1943 from pneumonia; m. (1) Wellsville, New York October 22, 1911 Helen M. Morgan Bishop, b. Cuba, New York June 15, 1875, d. Bolivar, New York January 23, 1934 from cancer; m. (2) Pinellas, Florida December 16, 1936 Florence Cooper Metherell b. Union City, Pennsylvania a. 1881, d. Pinellas, Florida March 1962.

Asa P. Root lived his entire life in Bolivar, New York, was one of its leading citizens, and one of Bolivar's wealthiest residents. In 1894 he graduated from Westbrook Commercial Academy in Olean, New York and in 1895 assumed the position of bookkeeper with the State Bank of Bolivar. He resigned from the bank in 1909 where he had been employed as an assistant cashier to devote more time to his oil interests in New York State and Illinois. Although no longer directly employed by the State Bank of Bolivar, his interests in the Bank led to his being appointed as the State Bank of Bolivar's Vice-President and Director. In 1906 Mr. Root purchased an interest in the Van Garden-S. A. Wertman Cigar Factory and an interest in a poolroom in the Crandall building. Asa Root's father, Erastus Root, did not allow his son to frequent pool halls while growing up so Asa later purchased one as an ironic business investment according to his daughter, the late Helen Root Spargur.

In 1922, Asa Root was in a business partnership with S. U. Maxson of Bolivar under the firm name of Maxson and Root, a general garage and auto sales business. Asa P. Root was also financially invested in the following companies; Root, Penman, and Company, Allegany Royalties, Red River Oil Company, Ford Oil Company, and the Empire State Gas Company. Mr. Root's oil properties were located in Allegany County, New York and in Indiana, Oklahoma, West Virginia, and Illinois. Asa Root resided on the corner of Pleasant and Boss Streets in Bolivar. The yellow brick residence still stands. He was the first Bolivar resident to own an automobile, a Cadillac, which he purchased in May 1905. Asa was an avid trap shooter and earned many awards in this sport in both New York and Pennsylvania competitions. Mr. Root was a keen hunter and fisherman and for a time owned a hunting lodge in Pennsylvania. Asa P. Root held memberships in the Elks, the Masons, the Shriners, the Illinois-Indiana Petroleum Association and the Banker's Association.

The late Helen Root Spargur felt her father's greatest asset was his marvelous sense of humor, which always made him good company. Asa was an expert story teller and never lacked good friends or companionship. Asa Prentice Root married Helen Morgan Bishop in 1911. Helen was the daughter of Samuel Huntington Morgan (1845-1919) and Adella A. Freeborn Morgan (1845-1923) of Cuba, New York. Helen Morgan was first married to Gabriel Chamberlayne Bishop (May 12, 1882-May 22, 1906) of Cuba, New York on October 26, 1905. Gabriel Bishop was a mining engineer who died in an automobile accident on Long Island, New York six months after they were married. Gabriel Bishop was buried in Cuba Cemetery in Cuba, New York. Helen battled cancer for almost a year before her death. Cancer surgery at a Sayre, Pennsylvania failed to eliminate the disease. Mrs. Root was a member of the Bolivar Sorosis Club, the Cuba Episcopal Church, and the Berean Club of the Bolivar Methodist Church.

The late Helen Root Spargur remarked that her father's second marriage was not a happy one. Asa Root met his second wife on trips and extended stays in Florida. It seems that the second Mrs. Root was more interested in the financial advantages of the marriage than in her husband. Asa and Florence separated and he returned to Bolivar, New York while she remained in Florida. Florence Cooper Metherell was previously married to an Alfred J. Metherell about whom nothing can currently be found. Florence had a daughter, Dorothy, by Mr. Metherell born in 1906. Florence Root died in Pinellas, Florida in March of 1962. Asa P. Root and his first wife, Helen Morgan Bishop Root, were buried together in Maple Lawn Cemetery in Bolivar. It is not known where Florence Root was buried.

Children (by first marriage):

243. I. ***Helen Prentice Root, f.***

References: US Census: 1880, 1900, 1910, 1920, 1930, 1940; New York State Census: 1892, 1905, 1915, 1925; Maple Lawn Cemetery Records, Bolivar, New York; *Bolivar Breeze 1891-1965*, selected issues; New York Marriage Index 1881-1967 for Helen Morgan's marriage to Gabriel Bishop and to Asa P. Root; New York State Death Index 1880-1956 for Asa P. Root and Helen Root; Cuba Cemetery Records, Cuba, New York; Florida County Marriage Records 1823-1982; Florida Death Index 1877-1998 for Florence Root.

114.

Harry R. (Newton) Root, adopted son of Erastus (54), b. Bolivar, New York September 17, 1902, d. Olean, New York at St. Francis Hospital, m. Franklinville, New York August 20, 1927, Marguerite White b. Bolivar, New York November 11, 1906, d. Wellsville, New York August 23, 1987.

Harry R. Root was born Harry R. Newton, the son of Burr Newton and Cora May Greene. Burr Newton (1854-1911) ran a mercantile business for a time in the same building where previously Hoyt and Cowles, Newton and Patridge, and James H. Root and Son operated businesses. The structure was built by Burr Newton's father. Burr Newton was the Bolivar, New York Postmaster appointed by President Grover Cleveland. From 1901-1903, he ran the Newton House. From 1903-1906 he worked in Buffalo for laundry and soap businesses. Upon his return to Bolivar Burr Newton ran a farm on Miller Hollow Road from 1906-1909. The last two years of his life, Mr. Newton was a bookkeeper for E. J. Wilson and A. L. Shaner. Burr Newton was married twice.

His first wife was Carrie Adell Stout (1855-1897). They had one child who died in infancy. His second wife was Cora May Greene whom he married in 1901. Burr and Cora Newton divorced in 1909. Harry R. Root had the last name of Newton on the New York State Census records for 1905 and 1915 and the US Census for 1910 and 1920. After 1920 he became Harry R. Root. Erastus Root legally adopted his third wife's son but the date of adoption is not known. Harry Root was employed by the Messer Oil Company in Bolivar as an oil field driller for most of his adult life. He served for 52 years as a volunteer with the Bolivar Fire Department. Mr. and Mrs. Root resided on the Bolivar-Genesee Road. Marguerite Root was the daughter of LeRoy and Ola Groshong White. She was a member of the Bolivar Methodist Church, the Trilby Rebekah Lodge, and a charter member of the Bolivar Firemen's Auxiliary. Harry and Marguerite Root were buried in Bolivar's Maple Lawn Cemetery with his mother. They did not have any children.

References: US Census: 1910, 1920, 1930, 1940; New York State Census: 1905, 1915, 1925; Maple Lawn Cemetery Records, Bolivar, New York; *Bolivar Breeze 1891-1965*, selected issues.

116.

Bertha Wilcox, daughter of Charlotte (55), granddaughter of Truman Bishop (36), b. Wirt, New York February 14, 1868, d. Bradford, Pennsylvania hospital October 31, 1909 following surgery for the removal of intestinal tumors. Bertha Wilcox resided with her parents based on US Census records for 1870 and 1880 and New York State Census records for 1875 and 1892. In 1900 she was employed as a domestic servant for the Wilber Cook family. Mrs. Cook was her first cousin. After the Cooks left Bolivar, Miss Wilcox was employed as a domestic for the Alfred McDonnell family of Bolivar based on the 1905 New York State Census.

Bertha Wilcox was described as a faithful worker, a highly estimable woman who was greatly loved by all who knew her. Miss Wilcox was a member of the Trilby Rebekah Lodge of Bolivar and the local Order of the Golden Seal. Her funeral took place at the Bolivar Methodist Church. Bertha Wilcox was buried beside her mother in Bolivar's Maple Lawn Cemetery. There is no grave marker for her nor was her burial recorded in Maple Lawn Cemetery records even though the newspaper indicated her burial was beside her mother's grave. Bertha Wilcox never married.

References: US Census: 1870, 1880, 1900; New York State Census: 1875, 1892, 1905; *Bolivar Breeze 1891-1965*, selected issues; Pennsylvania Death Certificates 1906-1966; Maple Lawn Cemetery Records, Bolivar, New York.

117.

Abijah Lyman Wilcox, son of Charlotte (55), grandson of Truman Bishop (36), b. probably Wirt, New York, a. 1872, d. San Francisco, California October 13, 1923 from heart failure; m. a. 1905 Anna/Anne Harrington Good, b. New Jersey a. 1882, d. place of death and date of death not known. The name *Abijah* is of Biblical Hebrew origin and means *my father is Yah.* One of King David's son was named Abijah and he became the fourth King of Judea. It is not known why Walter and Charlotte Wilcox selected this name for their son.

Abijah Wilcox resided with his parents at least until 1892. He cannot be found on the 1900 US Census but in the 1910 US Census he had married in 1905 to Anne Harrington Good who had been previously married and at age twenty-eight had six children by her first marriage. Mr. Wilcox was employed as an oil driller and in 1910 his mother-in-law and a step-son resided with them in Fresno, California. In the 1920 US Census Abijah and Anne Wilcox resided in San Francisco where he continued to work in the oil industry. They also ran a boarding house. Abijah Wilcox was buried in Holy Cross Cemetery in Colmar, California. He did not have any children.

References: US Census: 1880, 1910, 1920; New York State Census: 1875, 1892; *Bolivar, Breese,* November 15, 1923; California Death Index 1905-1939; Holy Cross Cemetery Records, Colmar, California.

118.

Donna B. Wilcox, daughter of Charlotte (55), granddaughter of Truman Bishop (36), b. Friendship, New York September 1875, d. Angelica, New York January 15/16, 1901. Miss Wilcox resided with her parents until her death in 1901. The cause of death is not known. It is believed that she was buried in Bolivar's Maple Lawn Cemetery with her mother, but no grave marker is in evidence nor was her burial recorded in Maple Lawn Cemetery records. Miss Wilcox never married.

References: US Census: 1880, 1900; New York State Census: 1892; *Bolivar Breeze* January 17, 1901; New York State Death Index 1880-1956.

119.

Leon Erastus Wilcox, son of Charlotte (55), grandson of Truman Bishop (36) b. Wirt, New York October 23, 1883/84, d. Dubois, Pennsylvania Hospital December 13, 1952 from leukemia; m. Jefferson County, Pennsylvania March 25, 1908 Alvira Himes, b. Pennsylvania March 1887, d. Brockway, Pennsylvania 1970.

Leon Wilcox resided with his parents until 1900. There is some confusion about his year of birth. His World War I Draft Registration gave the birth year as 1883 while his death certificate and grave stone gives 1884 as the birth year. Sometime after 1900 he moved to Pennsylvania where he married Alvira Hines, the daughter of Theophilus Himes (1848-1932) and Sarah Nulf Himes (1864-1958) of Brockway, Pennsylvania. Soon after their marriage in 1908, the Wilcox family moved to Blairstown, New Jersey where Mr. Wilcox was employed as a steam shovel operator and where their daughter, Maxime was born in 1909. According to Leon Wilcox's 1917 World War I Registration Card he moved back to Brockway, Pennsylvania where he was employed as a foreman for the Pittsburg, Shawmut, and Northern Railroad.

Mr. and Mrs. Wilcox's two sons, Walter Abijah and Richard T. Wilcox were born in Brockway in 1911 and 1912 respectively. Mr. and Mrs. Wilcox remained in Brockway at 757 Maple Avenue the rest of their lives where Leon Wilcox was employed as a railroad foreman, machinist, and a fireman. Leon and Alvira Wilcox were buried in Wildwood Cemetery in Brockway, Pennsylvania.

Children:

244. I. ***Maxine Sevilla Wilcox, f.***

245. II. ***Walter Abijah Wilcox, f.***

246. III. ***Richard Theophilus Wilcox, f.***

References: US Census Records: 1900, 1910, 1920, 1930, 1940; New York State Census: 1892; Wildwood Cemetery Records, Brockway, Pennsylvania; Pennsylvania Death Certificates 1906-1966 for Leon Wilcox; World War I Draft Registration 1917-1918 for Leon Wilcox.

120.

Carl Stanley Wilcox, son of Charlotte (55) and grandson of Truman Bishop (36), b. Angelica, New York May 20, 1885, d. Bolivar, New York February 21, 1962; m. Bolivar, New York April 16, 1907 Jessie Gail Crandall, b. Genesee, New York September 1884, d. Bolivar, New York September 24, 1959.

Carl Wilcox spent most of his life as a resident of Bolivar, New York. Mrs. Wilcox was the daughter of John H. Crandall (1843-1912) and Laura Finch Crandall (1848-1935). John H. Crandall served in Co. I, 27th New York Volunteers and later Company A, 136th New York Volunteers during the Civil War. Carl Wilcox and Gail Crandall married at her parent's residence on Olean Street.

Gail Wilcox was described a one of Bolivar's bright and popular young women who had a host of friends. She graduated from Bolivar High School in 1902 and worked for four years as a clerk in the Bolivar Post Office. Mrs. Wilcox was involved in Church work and was president of the Bolivar

Chapter of the Epworth League. Carl Wilcox had worked as the bookkeeper for the State Bank of Bolivar for four years at the time of his marriage. Although a bookkeeper by profession for most of his life, Mr. Wilcox did work for the Pittsburg and Shawmut Railroad as a telegraph operator starting in 1917 and into the 1920s. His World War I Draft Registration card described him as tall, of medium build with brown hair and brown eyes. Carl and Gail Wilcox lived with her parents, Mr. and Mrs. John H. Crandall, at 95 Olean Street. In June of 1937, Mr. Wilcox applied for his Social Security pension. Carl and Gail Crandall Wilcox were buried in Maple Lawn Cemetery in Bolivar, New York.

Children:

247. I. ***Carl Crandall Wilcox, f.***

248. II. ***John W. Wilcox, f.***

References: US Census: 1900, 1910, 1920, 1930, 1940; New York State Census: 1892, 1905, 1915, 1925; Social Security Applications 1936-2007; World War I Draft Registration Cards 1917-1918; World War II Draft Registration Cards, 1942; New York State Death Index 1957-1968; *Bolivar Breeze 1891-1965*, selected articles; Maple Lawn Cemetery Records, Bolivar, New York.

122.

Burr LeRoy Root, son of Sidney LeRoy (56), grandson of Truman Bishop (36), b. Genesee Township, Allegany County, New York March 11, 1875, d. Genesee Township, New York June 18, 1956; m. Genesee Township, New York August 22, 1900 Kate (Katherine) Allen Willard, b. Little Genesee, New York September 29, 1879, d. Olean, New York General Hospital April 4, 1953 from cardiovascular problems.

Burr Root was a life-long resident of Genesee Township in Allegany County, New York. He resided with his parents who farmed until his 1900 marriage to Kate Willard. The marriage took place at the home of Mrs. Root's parents, Warren W. Willard (1845-1926) and Lydia Allen Willard (1851-1940) of Little Genesee, New York. As a husband and father Mr. Root was employed as an oil pumper, carpenter, and farmed his own land in Genesee Township. The family farm was on Salt Rising Road. At the time of the 1940 US Census Burr Root had retired. During the first decade of the 20th century, Burr Root was an active member of the Bolivar Socialist Party and in 1911 served as a Socialist Party caucus member. Mr. and Mrs. Root celebrated their 50th wedding anniversary at their home on Salt Rising Road with their five surviving children on August 20, 1950. Burr and Kate Root were buried in the West Genesee Cemetery in Obi, New York.

Children:

249. I. ***Doris Anita Root, f.***

250. II. ***Coral Marie Root, f.***

251. III. ***Raymond W. Root, f.***

252. IV. ***Howard LeRoy Root, f.***

253. V. ***Ruth Louise Root, f.***

254. VI. ***Laurence Allen Root f.***

References: US Census: 1880, 1900, 1910, 1920, 1930, 1940; New York State Census: 1875, 1892, 1905, 1915, 1925; West Genesee Cemetery Records, Obi, New York; New York State Marriage Index 1881-1967; New York Death Index 1880-1956; *Bolivar Breeze 1891-1965,* selected issues.

123.

Lena E. Root, daughter of Sidney LeRoy (56), granddaughter of Truman Bishop (36), b. Genesee Township, Allegany County, New York June 13, 1879, d. Genesee Township September 17, 1945 from cancer; m. Genesee Township, New York July 28, 1897, Otto Williford Perry b. Franklinville, New York May 12, 1874, d. Genesee Township March 30, 1937 from a stroke.

Lena and Otto Perry were life-long residents of Genesee Township, Allegany County, New York. Otto Perry was employed as a carpenter and he also farmed land on Daggett Hollow Road. At the time Otto Perry registered for the draft during World War I he was employed as an oil pumper for Maxson and Sawyer. His draft papers described him as a man of medium height, medium build with blue eyes and gray hair. After Mr. Perry's death, Lena Root Perry's granddaughter, Bernice Perry Sisson, moved in with her as noted in the 1940 US Census. Lena Perry was a member of the United Brethren Church in Obi and was a founding member of The Obi-Clarksville Chapter of the Red Cross. Otto and Lena Perry were buried in the West Genesee Cemetery in Obi, New York.

Children:

255. I./II. ***Walter and Wallis Perry*** (twin boys), b. and d. January 31, 1899. Their burial location is not known.

256. III. ***Orval Laurence Perry, f.***

257. IV. ***Clella Undine Perry, f.***

258. V. ***Keith LeRoy Perry, f.***

References: US Census: 1880, 1900, 1910, 1920, 1930, 1940; New York State Census: 1892, 1905, 1915, 1925; New York State Death Index 1880-1956; New York State Marriage Index (1881-1967); West Genesee Cemetery Records, Obi, New York; US World War I Draft Registration Cards 1917-1918 for Otto Williford Perry; *Bolivar Breeze 1891-1965, selected issues.*

124.

Ernest Stanley Root, son of Sidney LeRoy (56), grandson of Truman Bishop (36), b. Genesee Township, New York May 21, 1882, d. Bolivar, New York November 14, 1946 from a heart attack; m. (1) Bolivar, New York April 6, 1909 Emma Denning, b. Alma, New York August 1892, d. Port Allegany, Pennsylvania hospital November 3, 1918 from pneumonia following an influenza attack; m. Eldred, Pennsylvania February 7, 1920 Fayette J. Arnold, b. Colegrove, Pennsylvania September 1, 1890, d. Farmington Hills, Michigan October 22, 1981.

Ernest S. Root was a successful rig builder, oil producer, and insurance agent for Metropolitan Life Insurance Company. On August 7, 1902, Ernest Root was injured in an accident on the J. B. Gray oil lease on Salt Rising Road. Newspaper accounts indicated that while pulling tubing, the engine started entangling him in the rope which threw him against the rig. His left collar bone was broken and he suffered a deep cut on his cheek. On November 13, 1913 Mr. Root purchased a confectionary store in Olean, New York where he worked for a brief time. Emma Root was the daughter of Richard Denning (1863-1898) and Arabella Eva Stives Denning (1868-1893) of Alma, New York.

Ernest Root met his second wife, Fayette (Faye) when she worked at the Silverman's store in Olean, New York. Ernest came to sell her some life insurance. Twice she refused his offer to go for a ride. The third time, a Sunday, she accepted. They were married three months later. Faye Arnold Root was the daughter of Lewis Arnold (1857-1918) and Ella J. Slagle Arnold (1868-1953). Ernest and Faye Root resided at 546 S. Main Street in Bolivar. After her husband's death Faye Root took care of her mother from 1950 to 1953 at her Bolivar residence. Mrs. Root later moved to Michigan where she resided with her son. Ernest S. Root was buried in Maple Lawn Cemetery, Bolivar, New York with his two wives.

Children (by first marriage):

259. I. ***Alta Irene Root, f.***

Children (second marriage):

260. I. ***Kenneth Ernest Root, f.***

References: US Census: 1900, 1910, 1920, 1930, 1940; New York State Census: 1892, 1905, 1915, 1925; US World War II Draft Registration Cards, 1942; Maple Lawn Cemetery Records, Bolivar, New York; Oak Hill Cemetery Records, Eldred, Pennsylvania; New York State County Marriage Records 1847-9,

1907-1936 for Ernest Root's first marriage; New York State Death Index 1880-1956 for Ernest Root; *Bolivar Breeze 1891-1965,* selected issues.

128.

Lizzie Rew, daughter of Mary (57), granddaughter of Truman Bishop (36), b. probably Wirt, New York a. 1878, d. Richwood, West Virginia November 29, 1904; m. Nicholas, West Virginia, 1903, Howard Small, birth place and birth date not known; d. death place and death date not known.

Lizzie and her mother, Mary Root Rew, moved to West Virginia after the deaths of her father and brother in Kansas where her mother ran a boarding house. Lizzie Rew Small died giving birth to a daughter who was also named Lizzie. Unfortunately, the three-week old daughter died at the home of Mrs. Elizabeth Root Garthwait where the infant girl was brought along with Howard Small to bury Lizzie Rew Small in Bolivar. Mother and daughter, both bearing the same name, were buried in Bolivar's Maple Lawn Cemetery. Their graves are next to the grave of Mary Root Rew Richardson and share a tombstone.

References: US Census: 1880; West Virginia Marriage Index 1785-1971; *Bolivar Breeze 1891-1965*, selected issues; Maple Lawn Cemetery Records, Bolivar, New York.

129.

Floyd Bernard Pire, son of Olivia (58), grandson of Truman Bishop (36), b. Bolivar, New York March 27, 1879, d. Rochester/Irondequoit, New York November 10, 1956; m. Coudersport, Pennsylvania June 3, 1902 Sarah Josephine Teachman, b. Coudersport, Pennsylvania April 30, 1886, d. Rochester General Hospital, Rochester, New York January 4, 1943.

Floyd Pire resided with his parents in Bolivar, New York or Eulalia, Pennsylvania from birth until he married. While single Floyd Pire performed with his cousin, Leona Root, at the Bolivar Opera House in a version of *The Country Girl* November 1898. He also solicited contributions in 1898 for a scholarship to attend the Westbrook Commercial College in Olean, New York. It is not known if Floyd was successful. Floyd and Josephine Pire resided for a short time in Bolivar after their 1902 marriage with his mother, Olivia Root Pire, on Friendship Street. The June 18, 1903 edition of the *Bolivar Breeze* noted that both Mr. and Mrs. Pire and Ward Pire, Floyd's brother, were battling food poisoning from meat purchased from Volney, Scott, and Sons. The article indicated that Ward Pire was not expected to live. Over a dozen people were afflicted and a specialist was called in from Olean, New York to treat the victims. Floyd, Josephine, and Ward all survived. By 1905 the Pires had moved to Coudersport, Pennsylvania residing at 103 Isabelle Street where Floyd worked first as a baggage handler for the railroad and later as a station agent for the CPA Railroad. His World War I Draft Registration Card described Floyd Pire as being of medium height and medium build with gray eyes and brown hair. In 1930 the Pires moved to Rochester, New York where Floyd Pire worked for the Kodak Corporation as a shipping agent. By 1940 they had moved to the Rochester suburb of Irondequoit. Sarah Josephine Teachman Pire was the daughter of George Teachman (1865-1934) and Laura Monroe Teachman (1865-1942) of Potter County, Pennsylvania. Floyd and Josephine Pire were buried in Eulalia Cemetery in Coudersport, Pennsylvania. There is no death date on his tombstone.

Children:

261. I. ***Laura June Pire, f.***

262. II. ***Josephine Virginia Pire***, b. Coudersport, Pennsylvania September 25, 1916, d. Coudersport, Pennsylvania November 8, 1916 from spinal meningitis. She was buried in Eulalia Cemetery in Coudersport, Pennsylvania.

263. III. ***Francis Monroe Pire, f.***

References: US Census: 1880, 1900, 1910, 1920, 1930, 1940; New York State Census: 1892; New York State Death Index 1880-1956 for Floyd Pire, Eulalia Cemetery Records, Coudersport, Pennsylvania; World War I Draft Registration Cards 1917-1918; *Bolivar Breeze 1891-1965,* selected issues; Pennsylvania County Marriages 1845-1963.

130.

Ward Lawrence Pire, son of Olivia (58), grandson of Truman Bishop (36), b. Bolivar, New York May 21, 1884, d. Erie, Pennsylvania September 17, 1962 from congestive heart failure and renal failure; m. place not known, a. 1922 Bertha Riblet, b. Erie, Pennsylvania August 25, 1885, d. Erie, Pennsylvania March 13, 1963 due to a coronary occlusion.

Ward Pire resided with his parents in either Bolivar, New York or Eulalia, Pennsylvania. He lived with his mother, brother, and sister-in-law, Floyd and Josephine Pire, on Friendship Street in Bolivar, New York where he almost died in 1903 from food poisoning. After Floyd and Josephine Pire left Bolivar and moved to Coudersport, Pennsylvania, Ward relocated to Erie, Pennsylvania where he was employed as a clerk in a railroad freight office. In the 1910 US Census he boarded on East 10th Street with the John Strohmenger family. Ward's World War I Draft Registration Card described him as being 5' 7" tall, 162 lbs., with gray eyes and brown hair. In 1917 Ward Pire was employed as an accountant with General Electric, his employer until retirement. In 1920 he was a boarder with the E. L. Birch family at 45 E. 6th Street in Erie. Bertha Pire was the daughter of Winfield Scott Riblet (1848-1908) and Affie Russell Riblet (1849-1921) of Erie, Pennsylvania. Ward and Betha Pire last resided at 1041 West 34th Street in Erie and were buried in Erie Cemetery in Erie, Pennsylvania.

Children:

264. I. ***Mary Lois Pire, f.***

265. II. ***Ward Russell Pire, f.***

References: US Census: 1900, 1910, 1920, 1930, 1940; New York State Census: 1892; US World War I Draft Registration Cards, 1917-1918; US World War II Draft Registration Cards, 1942; Pennsylvania Death Certificates 1906-1964 for Ward Pire; Pennsylvania Death Certificates 1906-1966 for Bertha Pire; Erie Cemetery Records, Erie, Pennsylvania.

131.

Leona Ruth Root, daughter of Arthur (59), granddaughter of Truman Bishop (36), b. Bolivar, New York June 28, 1877, d. Erie, Pennsylvania December 9, 1959 from pneumonia and arteriosclerosis; m. (1) Bolivar, New York December 31, 1902 Raymond Ellis, b. North Hills, Nassau County, New York October 7, 1881, d. Almond, New York June 20, 1913; m. (2) Tampa, Florida July 13, 1916 George B. O'Grady, b. Buffalo, New York June 3, 1879, d. Buffalo, New York September 3, 1940; m. (3) Bolivar, New York December 17, 1941 George A. Wellmon/Wellman, b. Union City, Pennsylvania July 22, 1875, d. Erie, Pennsylvania October 10, 1959.

Leona's niece, Leona Root Gordon, described her aunt as a small, a petite redhead who was spoken of in hushed tones because it was rumored that she had in her youth been *on the stage*. Her aunt was vivacious and friendly and resembled her brother, Leon Root, except she was small. Acting on the stage was considered very risqué at the time Leona was a young woman. Leona did act in *The Country Girl* at the Bolivar, New York Opera House in November 1898 along with her cousin Floyd Pire. In December of 1898 she performed as a member of the female minstrels at the Bolivar Opera House. What additional acting Miss Root did and where is not known.

Leona resided in the 1890s with Dr. Dorr Cutler and his wife, Harriet, in Bolivar. Mrs. Cutler was a Cowles before her marriage and a cousin to Leona. Leona Root was employed as a bookkeeper for the *Hornellsville Tribune* in Hornell, New York. In the 1900 US Census she resided with the James Smith family in Hornell. Leona's first husband, Raymond Ellis, was a jeweler working in Hornell and it is probably that they met in that city as young professionals. Raymond Ellis was the son of William F. Ellis (1851-1933) and Ella Wellington Ellis (1856-1938) of Almond, New York. They were married at the residence of Dr. and Mrs. Cutler in Bolivar. Leona's father and step-mother attended along with Mr. Ellis' parents. The 1905 New York State Census located Mr. and Mrs. Ellis in Angelica, New York where Mr. Ellis was employed as jeweler. In 1906 they moved to Hammondsport, New York. The US Census for 1910 found Mr. and Mrs. Ellis residing with his parents in Almond, New York, but by 1911 they returned to Hornell, New York where they resided at 4 Canisteo Street. Ray Ellis died June 20, 1913 at his parent's home. The cause of death is not known. He was buried in Arkport Heritage Hill Cemetery in Arkport, New York in the Ellis family lot. It is not known if there is a marker for him. Leona Root Ellis remarried July 13, 1916 in Tampa, Florida to George Vincent O'Grady. It is not known how they met or what brought them both to Florida. George O'Grady was originally from Buffalo, New York.

Mr. O'Grady's World War I Draft Registration Card gave his permanent address in 1917 as 15 West 84th Street in New York City. He was employed there as a salesman for the Northam Warren Corporation. George O'Grady was of medium height with a medium build and had blue eyes and dark hair. They lived for a short time in Chicago in 1918, but Leona and her second husband returned to New York City in 1920. Perhaps, Leona did some acting in New York City, which caused her family more concern. By 1930 Leona and George O'Grady had moved to Cliffside Park, New Jersey where he worked as a salesman for a drug company. Ill health brought them to Bolivar about 1938 where he briefly operated an electrical business with Walter Ireland. George O'Grady died unexpectedly at his sister's home in Buffalo, New York in 1940. He was buried in Mt. Olivet Cemetery in Tonawanda, New York. Leona Root Ellis O'Grady probably knew her third husband from her days spent in Bolivar because George Wellmon was employed in Bolivar in the 1900s as a watchmaker and it is where he married his first wife, Lydia Richner, and where the first of this two sons was born.

George Wellman led an orchestra in Bolivar and conducted musical events at a number of Bolivar venues. Mr. Wellmon's first wife died in 1940 from uterine cancer. His two sons from that first marriage were George Richner Wellmon (1907-1996) and Robert Rudolph Wellmon (1910-1985). George Wellmon later moved to Erie, Pennsylvania with his first wife and sons where he owned and operated a jewelry store. Leona and George resided at 903 West 9th Street. Mr. Wellmon died from diabetes, heart disease, and congestive heart failure. George Wellmon was buried with first wife, Lydia, in Laurel Hill Cemetery in Erie, Pennsylvania. Leona Wellmon died soon after on December 9, 1959. She was buried in Laurel Hill Cemetery in Erie but separately from her third husband. Leona Root Ellis O'Grady Wellmon never had any children from any of her three marriages.

References: US Census: 1880, 1900, 1910, 1920, 1930, 1940; New York State Census: 1892, 1905; Arkport Heritage Cemetery Records, Arkport, New York; Mt. Olivet Cemetery Records, Tonawanda, New York; Laurel Hill Cemetery Records, Erie, Pennsylvania; *Bolivar Breeze 1891-1965*, selected issues; Pennsylvania Death Certificates 1906-1964 for George Wellmon and Leona Wellmon; US Social Security Applications and Claims Index 1936-2007 for George O'Grady; US World War I Draft Registration Cards 1917-1918 for George V. O'Grady; New York State Death Index 1880-1956 for Ray Ellis; Florida Marriage Certificate for George and Leona O'Grady; correspondence with the late Leona Root Gordon September 21, 1990.

132.

Leon Erastus Root, son of Arthur (59), grandson of Truman Bishop (36), b. Bolivar, New York January 30, 1897, d. Amarillo, Texas April 10, 1961 from a heart attack; m. (1) Mexico, Missouri May 1, 1919 Beulah Bell Bellamy, b. Hamilton, Missouri May 30, 1904, d. Bartlesville, Oklahoma October 12,

1993, divorced 1939; m. (2) Fort Smith, Arkansas June 7, 1941 Zelma Freeman, b. Jonesboro, Louisiana January 23, 1905, d. Amarillo, Texas September 10, 1995. Leon E. Root resided with his parents in Genesee Township in Allegany County on the old Friar's farm until 1910 when the Root family moved to Bolivar. He enlisted in the Army in Olean, New York during World War I.

His Draft Registration Card described Mr. Root as being tall with blue eyes and light hair. At the time of registration Leon Root worked for the Carter Oil Company in Dewey, Oklahoma as an oil pumper. During enlistment Mr. Root received a bad vaccination, which left him with limited use of his right leg and foot for which Leon Root was awarded a pension of $17 per month and back pay of $70. Leon Root entered as a Private First Class on September 1, 1918 rose to Corporal on September 25, 1918, and was promoted to Sergeant November 2, 1918. His length of service was August 5, 1918 to January 7, 1919. Sergeant Root did not see active duty overseas.

Leon Root married his first wife, Beulah Bellamy in Mexico, Missouri at the residence of the pastor of the local Christian Church. The 1920 and 1930 US Census records found Mr. and Mrs. Root residing in Dewey, Oklahoma where Leon Root first worked as an oil worker and later as the County Under Sheriff. Leon and Beulah Root had three daughters before divorcing in 1939.

When registering for the World War II draft, Leon Root was listed as single and working as a police officer for the Phillips Petroleum Company. He remarried to Zelma Freeman in 1941. Leon Erastus Root was a member of the Bolivar, New York First Methodist Church, the Masonic Lodge of Bartlesville, Oklahoma, and the Khiva Temple Shrine, Amarillo, Texas. He worked as a special agent for the Phillips Petroleum Company until his retirement, just prior to his unexpected death.

Zelma Freeman Root was a graduate of Louisiana Technical University with Bachelor of Arts and a Bachelor of Science degrees. She taught school in both Louisiana and Arkansas before moving to Texas in 1942. She taught for 30 years with the Borger Independent School District, retiring in 1971. From 1971 to 1976 Mrs. Root taught at Frank Phillips College. Zelma Root was active in the American Cancer Society, the United Methodist Church, Professional Business Women's Organization, the Golden Plains Community Hospital as a volunteer, and the Music Club. Leon and Zelma Root did not have any children. Leon and Zelma Root were buried in Westlawn Memorial Park in Borger, Texas. Beulah Bellamy Root was buried in Sunnyside Cemetery in Caney, Kansas with her second husband, Albert Carr (1905-1992).

Children (by first marriage):

266. I. ***Leona Ruth Root, f.***

267. II. ***Betty Louise Root, f.***

268. III. ***Barbara Jean Root, f.***

References: US Census: 1900, 1910, 1920, 1930, 1940; New York State Census: 1905; *Bolivar Breeze 1891-1965,* selected issues; Texas Death Certificate 1903-1982 for Leon E. Root; Sunnyside Cemetery Records, Caney, Kansas; Westlawn Memorial Park Records, Borger, Texas; New York Abstracts of World War I, Military Service 1917-1919; US World War I Draft Registration Cards 1917-1918; Texas Death Index 1903-2000; New York State Birth Index 1881-1942 for Leon E. Root.

133.

James Curtiss Root, son of Arthur (59), grandson of Truman Bishop (36), b. Bolivar, New York September 19, 1899, d. October 7, 1918 in France from lobar pneumonia. Mr. Root was known to his family and friends as *Jay.* He was named for James Curtiss, Bolivar's first lawyer, and the husband of Huldah Root Curtiss, his father's first cousin.

Jay Root attended Bolivar schools but did not graduate. He began working in the local oil fields and followed his father to Peru, Kansas, working in the oil industry there. It was in Kansas on February 8, 1918, that Mr. Root enlisted in the US Army. He was sent to Fort Barrancas, Florida where he was trained. Jay Root was assigned to the 7th Company, Coast Artillery Corps, and was described as a fine soldier. He was raised to the rank of Corporal July 10, 1918. In September 1918 Corporal Root sailed for France where he died a month later from pneumonia. James Curtiss Root was buried at Oise-Aisne American Cemetery and Memorial in Fere-en-Tardenois in Picardie, France. Corporal Root's name and birth and death dates were also listed on his parent's tombstone in Bolivar's Maple Lawn Cemetery. His obituary described him as bright young man and a hard worker who was liked by all who knew him. Mr. Root was honest, had a kindly disposition, and was fair in all his dealings.

References: US Census: 1900, 1910; New York State Census: 1905; *Bolivar Breeze,* November 21, 1918; Find A Grave Index for Burials at Sea and other Select Burial Locations; New York Abstracts of World War I Military Service 1917-1918; Maple Lawn Cemetery Records, Bolivar, New York.

134.

Sarah Ann Kellogg, daughter of Francis (62), granddaughter of Huldah Penelope (37), b. Scio, New York February 16, 1863, d. DuBois, Pennsylvania August 5, 1902; m. Wirt, New York September 4, 1886 John Henry McIntyre, b. Honesdale, Pennsylvania November 19, 1857, d. New Castle, Pennsylvania April 10, 1924.

Sarah Ann Kellogg resided with her parents and siblings in Cuba, New York in 1870 and in Wirt, New York in 1880. In 1900 Sarah McIntyre resided in Washington, Pennsylvania with her husband who was employed as a railroad agent and their two sons. John McIntyre was a Catholic and a Democrat. Sarah Ann Kellogg McIntyre was buried in St. Catherine's Cemetery in DuBois, Pennsylvania in 1902. John McIntyre remarried October 14, 1903 in DuBois, Pennsylvania to Catherine Uhl, b. April 1869 in Pennsylvania, d. January 18, 1929 in New Castle, Pennsylvania. Mr. McIntyre worked as the chief clerk for a railroad company in 1920. He resided with his second wife at 409 Burham Avenue in New Castle. John Henry McIntyre was buried with his second wife, Catherine, in St. Mary's Cemetery in New Castle, Pennsylvania. He did not have any children with his second wife.

Children:

269. I. ***James Irwin McIntyre, f.***

270. II. ***John Edwin McIntyre, f.***

References: US Census: 1870, 1880, 1900, 1910, 1920; St. Catherine's Cemetery Records, DuBois, Pennsylvania; St. Mary's Cemetery, New Castle, Pennsylvania; Hopkins, Timothy. *The Kelloggs in the Old World and the New,* San Francisco: Sunset Press, 1903.

135.

John Irvin/Ervin or Irvin John Kellogg, son of Francis (62), grandson of Huldah Penelope (37), b. Wirt/Friendship/Cuba, New York April 23, 1864, d. Sunnyside, Potter County, Pennsylvania April 27, 1939; m. a. 1890, place not known Helen Stella Reynolds, b. Coudersport, Pennsylvania October 20, 1873, d. Shinglehouse, Pennsylvania June 22, 1948.

Usually known as Irvin Kellogg, Mr. Kellogg resided with his parents in Cuba, New York in 1870 and in 1880 with his parents and siblings in Wirt, New York. After his marriage to Stella Reynolds, Mr. and Mrs. Kellogg resided on Cow Run Road in Sharon, Potter County, Pennsylvania where he owned his own farm and cultivated the land. Irvin Kellogg also found work as a carpenter and oil derrick worker. Stella Reynolds was the daughter of Alonzo Reynolds and Jennie Ellis Reynolds of Potter County. Irvin Kellogg's death was caused by chronic cardiovascular disease. Irvin and Stella Kellogg were buried in Maple Grove Cemetery in Shinglehouse, Pennsylvania.

Children:

271. I. ***Lillian L. Kellogg, f.***

272. II. ***Pearl Ellis Kellogg, f.***

273. III. ***Alonzo Albertus Kellogg, f.***

274. IV. ***Cecil Dell Kellogg, f.***

275. V. ***Kenneth E. Kellogg, f.***

276. VI. ***Heath E. Kellogg, f.***

277. VII. ***Marie Leah Kellogg, f.***

References: US Census: 1870, 1880, 1900, 1910, 1920, 1930; Maple Grove Cemetery Records, Shinglehouse, Pennsylvania. Pennsylvania Death Certificates 1906-1966 for Irvin Kellogg; Hopkins, Timothy. *The Kelloggs in the Old World and the New,* San Francisco: Sunset Press, 1903.

138.

Willis Burr Kellogg, son of Francis (62), grandson of Huldah Penelope (37), b. Wirt, New York March 24, 1872, d. Sharon, Potter County, Pennsylvania December 31, 1906 from syphilis; m. Olean, New York April 2, 1892 Martha or Mattie Kunselman, b. Summerville, Pennsylvania November 14, 1873, d. place not known but before 1906.

Mr. Kellogg was a laborer, a Methodist, and a republican. He resided for a time in Alma, New York. His death certificate gave his occupation as a soldier. It also stated he was a widower. Mattie Kellogg was the daughter of David Frank and Sarah Drayer Kunselman. A newspaper account wrote that he drowned while walking home along the river and implied that alcohol may have played a part in his death as Willis Kellogg was still very much affected by the death of his mother in February of 1906. While this may be true, it is also possible that the doctor who treated him for syphilis provided another reason for his untimely death. Willis Burr Kellogg was buried in Maple Grove Cemetery in Shinglehouse, Pennsylvania. It is not known where his wife was buried.

Children:

278. I. ***Sarah Mabel Kellogg, f.***

279. II. ***Frank Albertus Kellogg, f.***

280. III. ***Loring Grant Kellogg***, b. a. 1901. Listed on the 1910 US Census as residing with his paternal grandparents. There are currently no other documents for Loring Grant Kellogg.

References: US Census: 1880, 1900; Maple Grove Cemetery Records, Shinglehouse, Pennsylvania; Hopkins, Timothy. *The Kelloggs in the Old World and New.* San Francisco: Sunset Press, 1903; Pennsylvania Death Certificate 1906-66.

139.

Marshall Loring Kellogg, son of Francis (62), grandson of Huldah Penelope (37), b. Shinglehouse, Pennsylvania June 25, 1874, d. Ceres, Pennsylvania May 21, 1898. Little is known about this son of Francis Albert and Abigail Kellogg. The 1891 City Directory for Sioux City, Iowa listed his address as 812 Booge Avenue where he was employed as a travel agent. Marshall Kellogg was buried in Maple Grove Cemetery in Shinglehouse, Cemetery with his parents.

References: US Census: 1880, Sioux Falls, Iowa City Directory 1891; Maple Grove Cemetery Records, Shinglehouse, Pennsylvania.

140.

Loyal Leon Kellogg, son of Francis (62), grandson of Huldah Penelope (37), b. Sharon, Pennsylvania June 13, 1878, d. Shinglehouse, Pennsylvania July 10, 1916; m. place and date of marriage not known Cora Smith, b. Pennsylvania December 28, 1887, d. Sharon, Pennsylvania August 12, 1912 from general peritonitis.

Mr. Kellogg went by the name of Leon. Little is known about this son of Francis and Abigail Kellogg. He resided with his parents at least until 1900. He married sometime after the 1900 US Census. The marriage produced three daughters before Cora Kellogg's death in 1912. In the 1910 US Census Mr. Kellogg was employed as a carpenter and a nephew, David F. Kellogg resided with them. They resided on the family farm on Cow Run Road. Leon Kellogg died as the result of injuries from a fall from an oil derrick in 1915. He broke his back and other bones and was bedridden for eight months until his death. Their three daughters were raised separately from each other. Gladys was taken in by Charles and Bertha Nichols Allen of Shinglehouse, Pennsylvania and was sometimes known as Gladys Allen. Pauline was raised by Oscar and Eva Burdick of Little Genesee, New York and sometimes was listed as Pauline Burdick. It is not currently known who raised Winifred Kellogg.

Children:

281. I. ***Gladys Kellogg, f.***

282. II. ***Pauline Kellogg, f.***

283. III. ***Winifred Kellogg, f.***

References: US Census: 1880, 1900, 1910; Maple Grove Cemetery Records, Shinglehouse, Pennsylvania; Pennsylvania Death Certificate 1906-1966 for Cora Kellogg; Hopkins, Timothy. *The Kelloggs in the New World and the Old.* San Francisco: Sunset Press, 1903.

141.

Bertha Dilla Kellogg, daughter of Francis (62), granddaughter of Huldah Penelope (37), b. Wirt, New York August 11, 1880, d. Friendship, New York January 5, 1970; m. Shinglehouse, Pennsylvania August 14, 1899 Ervin/Erwin Eugene Beebe, Cuba, New York June 1854, d. Collins, New York May 27, 1934.

Bertha Kellogg's husband was previously married to Lottie Dayton in 1880. Lottie Beebe died in 1886. Erwin Beebe had a son, Harnie Lamatte Beebe (1881-1958) by his first wife. After Bertha and Erwin married, they resided in Sharon, Pennsylvania where he was employed as an optician. By 1905 they moved to Wellsville, New York where they lived the rest of their married lives at 130 North Highland Avenue. In 1905 Mr. Beebe was employed as a sawmill worker, in 1910 as a stable and gardens keeper, and in 1920 he worked for the McEwen Brothers. For a brief period in 1916, Erwin Beebe was an inmate at the Allegany County home for a rupture with no one to take care of him at home. Bertha Beebe was a trained nurse, an occupation she performed from at least 1925 until sometime after 1940. In the 1940 US Census she moved to Scio, New York residing with her son and his family. Bertha and Erwin Beebe were buried in Wellsville, New York's Woodlawn Cemetery with their son, daughter-in-law, and grandson.

Children:

284. I. ***Marshall Worth Beebe, f.***

References: US Census: 1880, 1900, 1910, 1920, 1930, 1940; New York State Census: 1905, 1915, 1925; Social Security Death Index for Bertha Beebe and Erwin Beebe; New York Census of Inmates in Almshouses and Poorhouses 1830-1920; Woodlawn Cemetery Records, Wellsville, New York; Hopkins, Timothy. *The Kelloggs in the New World and the Old.* San Francisco: Sunset Press, 1903.

142.

Loren Royal Kellogg, son of Royal Jasper (65), grandson of Huldah Penelope (37), b. Waymart, Pennsylvania April 3, 1874, d. place and date of death not known; m. (1) place and date not known Neva/Eva Josephine Hughes, b. Aledo, Illinois April 22, 1885, d. Knox, Illinois December 10, 1921; m. (2) Oklahoma City, Oklahoma January 23, 1926 Jean Sponamore, b. Oklahoma March 13, 1902, d. Sacramento, California August 17, 1949, divorced, Oklahoma September 29, 1938.

Loren Royal Kellogg enlisted in the Spanish-American War on June 24, 1898. He was a private in Troop D, Seventh Regiment, Calvary. Private Kellogg was discharged in Havana, Cuba as a trumpeter on March 10, 1899. In the 1900 US Census Loren Kellogg resided in Alto, Illinois where he was employed as a printer. Sometime before 1906 he married his first wife, Neva or Eva Josephine Hughes, daughter of Thomas J. and Elizabeth Brown Hughes. In the 1910 US Census Loren and Neva Kellogg had two children: Royal Joseph and Elizabeth Kellogg. In 1910 they resided in Galesburg, Illinois where Mr.

Kellogg was a linotype operator. Mr. Kellogg's World War I Draft Registration Card described him as a man of medium height and build with blue eyes and light hair. The Kellogg family resided at 1592 West Broad Street in Galesburg, Illinois. The 1920 US Census recorded that the two children from this marriage were no longer residing with their parents. Royal J. Kellogg lived with his father's sister, Myrtle Kellogg Carrell, and Elizabeth was a ward of Reverend Charles and Mrs. McKinley. Loren Kellogg was not recorded on the 1920 US Census. Neva Kellogg's 1921 death certificate indicates she was buried in Aledo Cemetery, probably with her parents. However, the records for this cemetery do not show a burial for Neva Kellogg.

Loren Royal Kellogg remarried in 1926 to Jean Sponamore, the daughter of Isaac Sponamore (1859-1955) and Emma Franklin Sponamore (1871-1951). In the 1930 US Census Loren and Jean Kellogg resided at 131 ½ East 6th Street in Oklahoma City. He worked as a newspaper printer for the Oklahoma Publishing Company. The Kelloggs had a daughter, Charlene, born in 1928. On April 4, 1939 Loren Kellogg applied for Social Security benefits. The 1940 US Census recorded that Loren and Jean Kellogg had divorced. Jean Kellogg resided at 727 10th Street in Oklahoma City with her daughter and two boarders. Loren Kellogg resided at 71 East 10th Street in Oklahoma City. Jean Sponamore Kellogg remarried to an L. A. Letlow. Jean died in Sacramento, California August 17, 1949. Undocumented sources indicated that Loren Kellogg died in 1958 in Colorado Springs, Colorado. It is not known where Jean and Loren Kellogg were buried.

Children (by first marriage):

285. I. ***Royal Joseph Kellogg, f.***

286. II. ***Elizabeth L. Kellogg, f.***

Children (by second marriage):

287. I. ***Eleanor Charlene Kellogg, f.***

References: US Census: 1880, 1900, 1910, 1920, 1930, 1940; Hopkins, Timothy. *The Kelloggs in the Old World and the New.* San Francisco: Sunset Press, 1903; Aledo Cemetery Records, Aledo, Illinois; US World War I Draft Registration Cars 1917-1918; California Death Index 1940-1997 for Jean Kellogg Letlow; Social Security Applications and Claims Index 1936-2007; Oklahoma County Marriage Records 1890-1995 for Loren and Jean Kellogg marriage; Illinois Deaths and Stillbirths Index 1916-1947 for Neva Josephine Kellogg; US Army Registration of Enlistments 1798-1914; Oklahoma Divorce Records Book 44, page 69.

145.

Myrtle Louise Kellogg, daughter of Royal Jasper (65), granddaughter of Huldah Penelope (37), b.

Troupsburg, New York August 22, 1881, d. El Paso, Texas June 27, 1958; m. Montorville, Minnesota October 18, 1905 Rufus Theodore Carrell/Carroll, b. Reidsville, North Carolina November 25, 1881, d. Galesburg, Illinois March 20, 1955.

Myrtle and Rufus Carrell resided most of their lives in Galesburg, Illinois where Mr. Carrell was employed by the Chicago, Burlington, and Quincy Railroad as a switchman. They resided at 276 West Brooks Street in Galesburg. After Mr. Carrell's death Myrtle Kellogg Carrell moved to Texas where she resided with her daughter until her death. It is assumed that Myrtle and Rufus Carrell were buried in Galesburg, Illinois but there is currently no confirmation from any Galesburg Cemetery. The spelling of the last name from Carrell to Carroll came when Rufus Carrell moved from North Carolina to Illinois at the age of 17 years to seek work with the railroads.

Children:

288. I. ***Glenn Theodore Carrell/Carroll, f.***

289. II. ***Ellen Louise Carrell/Carroll, f.***

References: US Census: 1900, 1910, 1920, 1930, 1940; Minnesota Marriages Index 1849-1950; Texas Death Certificates 1903-1982 for Myrtle Carrell; World War II Draft Registration Cards, 1942 for Rufus Carrell; Social Security Applications and Claims Index 1936-2007.

148.

Elizabeth M. Root, daughter of George H. (69), granddaughter of Franklin (37), b. Blackhawk, Iowa August 13, 1898, d. St. Paul, Minnesota April 1980; m. date and place of marriage not known, a Mr. Turner, divorced, birth place and date of birth not known, death place and date of death not known.

Elizabeth Root married sometime after the 1920 US Census and was divorced before the 1930 US Census. The identity of her husband is not known. Elizabeth Turner had a daughter by this brief marriage. The Humboldt High School Yearbook in St. Paul, Minnesota described Elizabeth as having a beautiful soprano voice that could enchant the stars from their orbits. In the 1930 Census she was employed as a railroad clerk and in the 1940 census Elizabeth Turner was employed as a voice teacher residing with her mother. It is not known where she was buried.

Children:

290. I. ***Elizabeth Harriet "Betty" Turner***, b. Ramsey, Minnesota May 10, 1923. No further information is available on her or on any future descendants of Franklin B. Root.

References: US Census: 1900, 1910, 1920, 1930, 1940; Humboldt High School Yearbook, Minnesota, 1915.

150.

Helen D. Homer, daughter of Harriet (70), granddaughter of James H. (39) b. Olean, New York January 30, 1892, d. Hartford, Connecticut November 22, 1981. Helen resided with her parents, James and Harriet Root Homer in Olean, New York until she graduated from college and accepted a teaching position in Pelham, New York.

Helen Homer's mother, Harriet Root Homer, resided with her beginning in 1925 until her death in 1946. The name of the college Helen attended is not known, but the 1940 US Census recorded that Miss Homer had at least five years of college. She resided in several communities in Westchester County, New York while employed. Upon retirement Helen Homer moved to Simsbury, Connecticut where her younger sister, brother-in-law, and nephew resided. Helen D. Homer never married and was buried in Saint Andrew's Episcopal Church Cemetery in Bloomfield, Connecticut.

References: US Census: 1900, 1910, 1920, 1930, 1940; New York State Census: 1892, 1905, 1915, 1925; Connecticut Death Index 1949-2012; Saint Andrews Episcopal Church Cemetery Record, Bloomfield, Connecticut.

151.

Sarah Homer, daughter of Harriet (70), granddaughter of James H. (39), b. Olean, New York May 17, 1899, d. Hartford, Connecticut May 14, 1984; m. Manhattan, New York June 10, 1922 Blair J. Wormer, b. E. Smethport, Pennsylvania August 4, 1897, d. Farmington, Connecticut February 26, 1980.

Sarah Homer resided with her parents on North Third Street in Olean, New York where in 1920 she was employed as a post office clerk. Blair J. Wormer was the son of Andrew E. Wormer (1862-1946) and Catherine Jones Wormer (1865-1949) of 302 North Clinton Street in Olean, New York. His 1917 World War I Draft Registration Card described Mr. Wormer has being of medium build and height with blue eyes and blonde hair. He was inducted into service at Bellefonte, Pennsylvania on October 19, 1918 and discharged December 5, 1918. Blair Wormer was a student at Penn State College and during his brief military career was in the Officers' Training Program. Mr. Wormer had a law degree and was in general practice in 1930. His employment career until retirement was as an officer of the Travelers Insurance Company of Hartford, Connecticut.
Blair and Sarah Homer Wormer were buried in Saint Andrews Episcopal Church Cemetery in Bloomfield, Connecticut.

Children:

291. I. ***Blair Jones Van Wormer, f.***

References: US Census: 1900, 1910, 1920, 1930; New York State Census: 1905, 1915; Saint Andrews Episcopal Church Cemetery Records, Bloomfield, Connecticut; US World War I Draft Registration Cards 1917-1918; New York Abstracts of World War I Military Service, 1917-1919; New York Marriage Index 1866-1937; Connecticut Death Index 1949-2012; Hartford City Directories, selected issues.

152.

Harlie Taylor Root, Jr., son of Harlie J. (71), grandson of James H. (39), b. Bolivar, New York December 10, 1888, d. Parris Island, South Carolina January 3, 1919 from pneumonia and empyema, an infection of the lung tissue and following an operation to remove an abscess on the right chest.

Harlie Root was a Bolivar resident until 1899 when his parents moved to Rochester, New York following the bankruptcy and closure of J.H. Root and Sons. Mr. Root resided with both parents until his parents separated and the children were dispersed to different homes. In 1915 Harlie T. Root was a resident of Wichita, Kansas residing at 157 North Topeka Avenue where he was employed as a commercial photographer. The City Directory for Wichita in 1915 indicated he was married and his wife's first name was Mabel. There is no further information about a Mabel Root. Mr. Root enlisted in the Marines January 11, 1917 in Missouri. He saw duty in April 1917 at the Marine Barracks in Olongapo, the Philippines and at various Marine bases in South Carolina during two years of duty where he was connected with the chemical and motor divisions. Harlie T. Taylor was a corporal at the time of his death and he was listed as single even though this contradicts the Wichita Directory information. He was buried in Riverside Cemetery, Section N, Lot 122 in Rochester, New York.

References: US Census: 1900; New York State Census: 1892, 1905; Wichita, Kansas City Directory, 1915; New York Abstracts of World War I Military Service 1917-1919; US Marine Corps Muster Rolls, 1798-1958; South Carolina Death Records 1821-1965; *Bolivar Breeze 1891-1965*, January 16, 1919; Riverside Cemetery Records, Rochester, New York.

153.

Lynn Proctor Root, son of Harlie J. (71), grandson of James H. (39), b. Bolivar, New York June 27, 1896, d. Prescott, Arizona April 29, 1949 from a heart attack at the veteran's center. Lynn Root resided with his parents in Bolivar, New York and later Rochester, New York until his parents separated. In the 1910 US Census Lynn was a boarder in Walworth, New York with Mr. and Mrs. Spencer Sweet. On May 10, 1917 he enlisted in the Marines. His World War I Registration Card noted that he supported both his mother and sister.

Lynn Root was described as tall, medium build with blue eyes and brown hair. He was discharged August 20, 1919 for severe arthritis. The 1920 US Census recorded that Lynn Root was a boarder at 80 S. Fitzhugh Street in Rochester where he worked as a bookkeeper for Kodak. The 1930 US Census found Lynn Root as a prisoner in the County Jail in Ordway, Colorado. In 1930 Mr. Root spent a brief time at the Veterans Hospital in Bath, New York. Three times in the 1930s he was in a US National Home for Disabled Volunteer Soldiers in Hot Springs, South Dakota: September 10, 1931, December 21, 1932, and April 1, 1933. Mr. Root was admitted for neurosis and arthritis of the left shoulder. In 1937 he applied for Social Security benefits. His admission documents and his death certificate both indicate he was married to a woman named Jeanette. There is no further information about her. Lynn Root died from tuberculosis and advanced heart disease. He was buried in Riverside Cemetery in Rochester, New York with his mother and brother.

References: US Census: 1900, 1910, 1920, 1930; New York State Census, 1905, 1915; US World War I Draft Registration Cards 1917-1918; US National Homes for Disabled Volunteer Soldiers 1866-1938; World War II Draft Registration Cards, 1942; US Headstone Applications for Military Veterans 1925-1963; Arizona Death Records 1887-1960; Riverside Cemetery Records, Rochester, New York; New York State Birth Index 1881-1942; US Social Security Applications and Claims Index.

154.

Margaret Sarah Root, daughter of Harlie J. (71), granddaughter of James H. (39), b. Bolivar, New York June 30, 1898, d. Rochester, New York September 20, 1983; m. (1) Monroe County, New York August 24, 1918 Fred Elmer Shea, b. DuBois, Pennsylvania August 21, 1897, d. Rochester, New York February 8, 1983, divorced 1943; m. (2) probably Rochester, New York 1962 William Edward Frost, b. LeRoy, New York July 11, 1889, d. Rochester, New York August 5, 1972.

Bolivar birth records list Margaret Root's name as Sarah Mayo Root. She used the name Sarah. Sarah Root resided with her parents from birth until they separated about 1908. In the 1910 US Census she was a boarder in Wolcott, New York with her mother who was employed as a servant with the G. A. Shipley family. In the 1915 New York State Census Miss Root was employed as a companion with the James Rutherford family in Rochester. She resided most of her life in Rochester, New York with brief stays in Benton Harbor, Michigan and a ten-year period from the mid-1920s to the mid-1930s in Ordway, Colorado where she took her daughter, Helen, for a healthier climate. Fred Elmer Shea was the son of Edward Shea (1866-1939) and Anna Margaret Cunningham Shea (1869-1950) of Rochester, New York. Fred Shea was employed as a store clerk both in Colorado and in Rochester. The marriage proved to be an unhappy one and Sarah and Fred Shea were divorced in 1943. It is not known where Fred Shea was buried.

Sarah Root Shea remarried in 1962 to William Edward Frost, the son of Edward Frost and Harriet Seeley Frost of Rochester, New York. William Frost was married three times before his marriage to Sarah Root Shea. Mr. Frost's first wife was Ruth M. Wilcox whom he married September 28, 1910 and who died after their marriage. His second wife was Emma DeMert whom he married September 3, 1919. She died from tuberculosis, but they had a son, Marvin John Frost (1921-1980). William Frost's third wife was Florence M. Carroll whom he married April 16, 1925 and who also predeceased him. Mr. Frost was employed by the Kodak Corporation for forty-two years in the coating department.

Sarah Frost worked for a Rochester, New York Department store. In the last years of her life Sarah resided in a retirement home near her daughter Helen's residence on Culver Road in Rochester. Sarah and William Frost were buried in Riverside Cemetery in Rochester, New York in the Root lot, Section N, lot 122.

Children (by first marriage):

292. I. ***Helen Virginia Shea, f.***

References: US Census: 1900, 1910, 1920, 1930, 1940; New York State Census: 1905, 1915; New York County Marriage Records 1847-1849 and 1907-1936 for Sarah Root and Fred Shea; Social Security Death Index 1925-2014 for Sarah Frost, Fred Shea, and William Frost; Riverside Cemetery Records, Rochester, New York.

Fourth Generation Line of Descent from Abel Root, Sr.

155.

Gladys Leona Holly, daughter of Judson (73), granddaughter of Minerva (40), b. Ypsilanti, Michigan September 14, 1880, d. St. Louis, Missouri June 30, 1953; m. (1) Ypsilanti, Michigan September 14, 1899 Anthony M. Burke, b. Michigan September 20, 1874, d. University of Michigan Hospital October 25, 1916, separated/divorced; m. (2) place of marriage not known, date of marriage not known, John V. Donnelly, b. Massachusetts a. 1895, d. St. Louis, Missouri 1980.

Gladys Holly's last name was also given as Hawley and Holley, thereby, creating some confusion in doing genealogical research. Her first husband was employed as a laborer working for a bakery in Ann Arbor, Michigan. They moved to Cook County, Illinois sometime after the 1910 US Census and before the birth of their son, Thomas Richard Burke in 1911. Anthony Burke's death was caused by both heart problems and cirrhosis of the liver. He was buried in Old St. Patrick's Cemetery in Ann Arbor, Michigan. It appears that Gladys Burke was separated from her first husband and had a child out of wedlock with John V. Donnelly. The son, Donald W. Donnelly, was born in Illinois June 16, 1916, before Anthony Burke's death. Anthony Burke's death certificate indicates that he was married. Currently, no divorce document can be found for Gladys and Anthony Burke nor has a marriage document been located for Gladys and John V. Donnelly. It is not known how they met and exactly when they moved to Missouri from Illinois. Gladys and John Donnelly cannot be found on the US Census records for 1930. In 1920 John Donnelly worked as a truck driver for an artificial ice company and later as a laborer for an engineering company. Gladys and John Donnelly were buried in Resurrection Cemetery in Affton, Missouri.

Children (by first marriage):

293. I. ***Francis Edward Burke, f.***

294. II. ***Richard C. Burke***, b. Ypsilanti, Michigan 1901, d. Ypsilanti, Michigan September 14, 1902 from cholera and was buried in St. John's Cemetery in Ypsilanti, Michigan.

295. III. ***Anthony Burke,*** b. Ypsilanti, Michigan September 8, 1903, d. August 1966; ***nfi***.

296. IV. ***Harold J. Burke, f.***

297. V. ***Howard Thomas Burke, f.***

298. VI. ***Lewis Burke***, b. Ypsilanti, Michigan April 25, 1908, d. Ypsilanti, Michigan August 1, 1908 from immunization issues. He was buried in St. John's Cemetery Ypsilanti, Michigan.

299. VII ***Thomas Richard Burke, f.***

Children (by second marriage):

300. I. ***Donald W. Donnelly, f.***

301. II. ***Marguerite Lane Donnelly, f.***

References: US Census: 1900, 1910, 1920, 1940; Michigan County Marriages 1822-1940 for Gladys Holly and Anthony Burke; Michigan Death Records 1867-1950 for Anthony Burke, Lewis Burke, and Richard C. Burke; St. John's Cemetery Records, Ypsilanti, Michigan; Old St. Patrick's Cemetery Records, Ann Arbor, Michigan; Resurrection Cemetery Records, Affton, Missouri; Missouri Death Certificates 1910-1962 for Gladys Donnelly; Cook County Illinois Birth Certificates Index 1871-1922 for Donald Donnelly.

156.

Lloyd Daniel Holly, son of Judson (73), grandson of Minerva (40), b. Ypsilanti, Michigan September 23, 1881, d. Caro Hospital, Caro, Michigan April 2, 1942 from auricular fibrillation and epilepsy; m. (1) Washtenaw, Michigan January 1, 1901 Grace Vee Cook, b. Bellevue, Michigan May 24, 1883, d. Barryton, Michigan October 13, 1957, divorced Lloyd Holly Genesee, Michigan July 19, 1924 for desertion and non-support; m. (2) Ann Arbor, Michigan March 11, 1925 Effie Grace Browne Kingston, b. Truro, Nova Scotia, Canada September 16, 1897, d. Ypsilanti, Michigan September 24, 1952.

Lloyd Holly was a lifelong resident of Ypsilanti, Michigan. He was an electrician by trade and owned and operated his own company. Lloyd Holly's first wife divorced him before the birth of their daughter Verna who died while an infant. Grace Cook Holly remarried twice more to Frank Wesley Bennett (1870-1943) and Samuel Wesley Hoover (1867-unknown). Grace and Samuel Hoover were married September 18, 1944 and divorced February 28, 1949. Lloyd Holly's second wife, Effie Grace Browne was previously married to Reverend Kenneth Kingston. She divorced Kenneth Kingston March 11, 1925 for extreme cruelty. Effie Grace Browne Kingston had three children by her first husband: Arthur Kingston (1918-1988), Raymond Kingston (1922-2003), and Dorothy Kingston (1923-1997). Lloyd Holly was buried in Highland Cemetery in Ypsilanti, Michigan with his second wife. There is no marker for his grave. The first Mrs. Holly was buried in Flake Cemetery, Barryton, Michigan with her second husband.

Children (by first marriage):

302. I. ***Frederick R. Holly, f.***

303. II. ***William E. Holly, f.***

304. III. ***Lloyd Spencer Holly, f.***

305. IV. ***Verna Francis Holly***, b. Ypsilanti, Michigan April 12, 1924, d. Ypsilanti, Michigan September 8, 1925 and was buried in Highland Cemetery in Ypsilanti.

Children (by second marriage):

306. I. ***Gerald Ralph Holly, f.***

307. II. ***Daniel Holly, f.***

References: US Census: 1900, 1910, 1920, 1930, 1940; Michigan Death Records 1867-1950; US World War I Draft Registration Cards 1917-18 for Lloyd Holly; Michigan Marriage Records 1867-1952; Michigan Divorce Records 1897-1952; US City Directories 1822-1995 for Ypsilanti, Michigan; Highland Cemetery Records, Ypsilanti, Michigan; Flake Cemetery Records, Barryton, Michigan.

157.

Fred Richard Holly, son of Judson (73), grandson of Minerva (40), b. Ypsilanti, Michigan December 18, 1882, d. Verona, New Jersey August 17, 1966; m. Ypsilanti, Michigan December 23, 1903 Grace Blakeslee, b. Ypsilanti, Michigan August 10, 1885, d. Verona, New Jersey August 3, 1972.

Fred and Grace Holly were longtime residents of Ypsilanti, Michigan. Sometime after Fred Holly's registration for the World War II draft, they relocated to New Jersey where they both died. The reason for the move is unclear. Fred Holly was described as being 5' 10" tall, weighing 145 pounds and had blue eyes and gray hair on his World War I Draft Registration Card. For most of his professional career Mr. Holly was employed by the Peninsula Paper Company. Mr. and Mrs. Holly both died in Verona, New Jersey, but they were buried in Highland Cemetery in Ypsilanti, Michigan.

Children:

308. I. ***Lester Martin Holly***, b. Ypsilanti, Michigan September 26, 1905, d. Ypsilanti, Michigan March 31, 1907 from pneumonia, a weak heart, and gastro-intestinal issues. Lester Holly was buried in Highland Cemetery in Ypsilanti, Michigan.

309. II. ***Helen Lauren Holly, f.***

310. III. ***Harold R. Holly, f.***

311. IV. ***Margaret J. Holly, f.***

312. V. ***Lynn Joseph Holly, f.***

313. VI. ***Fred Richard Holly, f.***

314. VII. ***Doris Mae Holly, f.***

References: US Census: 1900, 1910, 1920, 1930, 1940; World War I Draft Registration Records 1917-1918; World War II Draft Registration Records, 1942; Highland Cemetery Records, Ypsilanti, Michigan; Michigan Marriage Records 1867-1952; US City Directories, Ypsilanti, Michigan; US Social Security Death Index 1935-2014.

158.

Minerva Louise Holly, daughter of Judson (73), granddaughter of Minerva (40), b. Ypsilanti, Michigan February 13, 1886, d. Waterford, Michigan April 8, 1953; m. Battle Creek, Michigan April 18, 1915 George Edward Joyce, b. Arenac, Michigan August 29, 1885, d. Waterford, Michigan April 16, 1959.

Minerva or Minnie and George Joyce were lifelong residents of the Ypsilanti area. Mr. Joyce owned and operated Joyce Dry Cleaners on 89 North Saginaw Street in Pontiac, Michigan. For a time, Minerva was employed as a fur trimmer and designer. They first lived in Lansing, Michigan before moving in 1920 to Ingham, Michigan. In 1930 they resided in Raisinville (Michigan) and by 1940 they had moved to Birmingham, Michigan. George Joyce was previously married to Letta Mae Wells whom he married in Flint, Michigan February 12, 1906. George and Letta Joyce divorced in Wayne, Michigan September 29, 1913. George and Letta Joyce did not have any children together but George Joyce fathered two daughters with Minerva Holly before they married: Georgia Louise Joyce and Margaret A. Joyce. Minerva Holly Joyce was described by descendants as a *sort of free spirit* who was also a gifted fortune teller. Minerva and George Joyce were buried in Perry Mount Park Cemetery in Pontiac, Michigan.

Children:

315. I. ***Georgia Louise Joyce, f.***

316. II. ***Margaret A. Joyce, f.***

317. III. ***Judson John Joyce, f.***

318. IV. ***Edward George Joyce, f.***

319. V. ***Minerva Camilla Joyce***, b. Lansing, Michigan September 16, 1919, d. Lansing, Michigan August 6, 1920 from convulsions and intestinal issues. She was buried in Mt. Hope Cemetery Lansing, Michigan.

320. VI. ***Ida Louise Joyce***, b. Lansing, Michigan February 15, 1921, d. Lansing, Michigan October 30, 1921 and was buried in Mt. Hope Cemetery Lansing, Michigan.

321. VII. ***Robert Lloyd Joyce***, b. Ingham, Michigan December 24, 1922, d. Lansing, Michigan October 21, 1923 from pneumonia and was buried in Mt. Hope Cemetery Lansing, Michigan.

322. VIII. ***John "Jack" Joyce, f.***

References: US Census: 1900, 1910, 1920, 1930, 1940; Mt. Hope Cemetery Records, Lansing, Michigan; Perry Mount Park Cemetery, Pontiac, Michigan; Michigan Marriage Records 1867-1952; Michigan Divorce Records 1897-1952 for George Joyce's first marriage; Michigan Department of Health Death Records 1867-1950.

160.

Elizabeth Martin Holly, daughter of Judson (79), granddaughter of Minerva (40), b. Ypsilanti, Michigan June 30, 1894, d. Plymouth, Michigan August 22, 1943 from injuries sustained in an automobile accident; m. Ann Arbor, Michigan September 18, 1913 Frederick Joseph Block, b. Detroit, Michigan May 25, 1895, d. Garden City, Michigan January 14, 1984.

Elizabeth or Bessie and Fred Block resided in the Ypsilanti area during their married lives. Mr. Block was employed as a laborer in area paper mills. After Bessie's death, Fred Block remarried to Ellen F. Hill (1912-2000) in Wayne County Michigan February 20, 1945. The marriage was short lived as they divorced in Ypsilanti on July 29, 1946. Fred Block's last place of residence was Superior, Michigan. Elizabeth and Fred Block were buried in Saint John Cemetery Ypsilanti, Michigan.

Children:

323. I. ***Gladys Leona Block, f.***

324. II. ***Vera Barbara Block, f.***

325. III. ***Donald Frederick Block, f.***

326. IV. ***Frederick J. Block, f.***

327. V. ***Richard M. Block***, b. Ypsilanti, Michigan November 10, 1926, d. Ypsilanti, Michigan December 18, 1930 from pneumonia. He was buried in Highland Cemetery in Ypsilanti.

328. VI. ***Mary Lou Block, f.***

References: US Census: 1900, 1910, 1920, 1930, 1940; Highland Cemetery Records, Ypsilanti, Michigan; Saint John Cemetery Records, Ypsilanti, Michigan; Michigan Marriage Records 1822-1940; Michigan Death Records 1867-1950 for Elizabeth Block; Michigan Divorce Records 1897-1952 for Fred Block's second marriage.

161.

Hazel M. Holly, daughter of Judson (73), granddaughter of Minerva (40), b. Ypsilanti, Michigan May 30, 1896, d. Branch, Michigan April 22, 1962; m. Ann Arbor, Michigan September 16, 1913 Leo Youngs, b. Ypsilanti, Michigan January 22, 1895, d. Ypsilanti, Michigan August 18, 1979.

Hazel resided with her father and two sisters at the time of the 1910 US Census. After her marriage to Leo Youngs, Hazel and Leo spent their entire lives in Ypsilanti, Michigan where Mr. Youngs was employed as a truck driver for a variety of commercial companies. A brief exception was recorded on his World War I Draft Registration Card, which stated that he was a laborer for the Peninsula Paper Company. Leo Youngs was described as being of medium height and build with brown hair and brown eyes. Hazel and Leo Youngs were buried in Highland Cemetery, Ypsilanti, Michigan in the Judson Holly family lot.

Children:

329. I. ***Marion Louise Youngs, f.***

330. II. ***Eugene Edward Youngs, f.***

References: US Census: 1900, 1910, 1920, 1930, 1940; Highland Cemetery Records, Ypsilanti, Michigan; Michigan Death Index 1867-2011; World War I Draft Registration Card 1917-1918; World War II Draft Registration Card, 1942; Michigan Marriage Records 1867-1952.

162.

Florence Adaline Holly, daughter of Judson (73), granddaughter of Minerva (40), b. Ypsilanti, Michigan May 18, 1898, d. date and place not known; m. Ypsilanti, Michigan December 23, 1916 Leo Francis Clerkin, b. Johnsonburg, Pennsylvania December 12, 1896, d. Johnsonburg, Pennsylvania August 2, 1939.

It is possible that Florence Holly met Leo Clerkin when he was employed at a paper mill in Ypsilanti, Michigan. After their marriage Mr. and Mrs. Clerkin moved to Johnsonburg, Pennsylvania where Leo's family resided and where he worked for paper mills there including the Castanea Paper Mill as a machine tender. Leo Clerkin's death was caused by a drinking spree, which lasted for thirty-six hours and acute gastro-enteritis. His World War I Draft Registration Card listed him as tall with brown eyes and dark hair. Florence Holly Clerkin enlisted April 5, 1943 in Newark, New Jersey as a practical nurse serving in the Women's Army Corps during World War II. There are no further records on Florence Holly Clerkin after her military service. Leo Clerkin was buried in Holy Rosary Cemetery Johnsonburg, Pennsylvania. Family trees on Ancestry.Com identify three children born to this marriage but further research indicates a four child, a son, Leo Francis Clerkin, Jr., was also born to them. The Clerkin family cannot be found on the 1930 US Census, which might have clarified this issue. The identify of Leo Francis Clerkin, Jr. came to light via his marriage license, which records his parents as being Leo Clerkin, Sr. and Florence Holly Clerkin. It is not known why this son was not recorded.

Children:

331. I. ***Agnes Clerkin, f.***

332. II. ***Kathryn Margaret Clerkin, f.***

333. III. ***Leo Francis Clerkin, Jr., f.***

334. IV. ***Charles Edward Clerkin, f.***

References: US Census: 1900, 1910, 1920, 1940; World War I Draft Card Registrations 1917-1918; US World War II Army Enlistment Records 1935-1946 for Florence Holly Clerkin; Michigan Marriage Records 1867-1952; Pennsylvania Death Certificates 1906-1966 for Leo F. Clerkin, Sr.; Holy Rosary Cemetery Records, Johnsonburg, Pennsylvania.

163.

Helen Ina Lockley, daughter of Ina (78), granddaughter of Elizabeth (41), b. Detroit, Michigan September 24, 1887, d. Birmingham, Michigan June 8, 1978; m. Detroit, Michigan June 27, 1914 Wayne Williams, b. LaPorte, Indiana September 23, 1884, d. Birmingham, Michigan July 14, 1965.

Helen resided with her parents until her marriage in 1914. During his lifetime Wayne Williams was employed with insurance companies, banks, and underwrote construction bonds. In retirement he worked part-time doing statistical analysis for plastics manufacturers. His World War I Draft Registration Card described him has being 6' ¾ "tall, weighing 205 lbs. with blue eyes and brown hair. During World War I Mr. Williams was the manager for a bonding and security company. Wayne Williams was employed as an office manager for the U.S. Employment Service during World War II. Mr. and Mrs. Williams resided at 2300 Tuxedo Avenue in Birmingham, Michigan. Helen and Wayne Williams were buried in Woodlawn Cemetery in Detroit near the Barber family lots.

Children:

335. I. ***Anne Williams, f.***

336. II. ***Jane Williams, f.***

References: US Census: 1900, 1910, 1920, 1930, 1940; Michigan Births and Christenings 1867-1911 for Helen Lockley; Michigan Marriage Records 1867-1952; Michigan Death Records 1971-1996; World War I Draft Registration Card 1917-1918; World War II Draft Registration Card, 1942; Woodlawn Cemetery Records, Detroit, Michigan; Interview with Richard Biggs.

164.

Bessie Elizabeth Withey, daughter of Jesse (79), granddaughter of Elizabeth (41), b. Haymaker, Pennsylvania June 30, 1891, d. Holly Hill, Florida May 24, 1979; m. Allentown, New York November 28, 1911 Fred Robert Maitland, b. Bolivar, New York June 20, 1889, d. Volusia, Florida May 1, 1963.

Bessie Withey Maitland resided with her parents until her 1911 marriage. The Maitlands resided in Alma/Allentown, New York until they moved to Bolivar, New York by 1920. The 1930 and 1940 US Census records identify their residence as Foster, Pennsylvania. They were members of the Derrick City, Pennsylvania Methodist Church. Fred Maitland's career was in the oil industry as an oil pumper and drilling well contractor for various oil companies including the Empire Gas Company. Mr. Maitland's draft registration card described him as being 5' 8" tall, weighing 145 lbs., and having a ruddy complexion with grey eyes and brown hair. Fred and Bessie Maitland retired to Florida where they resided in Daytona Beach in 1960. Both Fred and Bessie Maitland died in Florida but they were buried in McKean Memorial Park in Mt. Alton, Pennsylvania.

Children:

337. I. ***Jesse Austin Maitland, f.***

338. II. ***Helen Withey Maitland, f.***

339. III. ***Robert Neal Maitland, f.***

340. IV. ***John Bruce Maitland, f.***

341. V. ***Betty Phyllis Maitland, f.***

342. VI. ***Fred Robert Maitland, Jr., f.***

343. VII. ***Kenneth Charles Maitland, f.***

344. VIII. ***Donald Withey Maitland***, b. Derrick City, Pennsylvania December 1, 1925, d. Derrick City, Pennsylvania January 25, 1928 from an intestinal infection and was buried in the Oak Hill Mausoleum, Bradford, Pennsylvania.

345. IX. ***Richard Albert Maitland, f.***

346. X. ***Patricia Sue Maitland, f.***

References: US Census: 1900, 1910, 1920, 1930, 1940; New York State Census: 1915; New York County Marriage Records 1847-9 and 1907-36; World War I Draft Registration Card 1917-1918; World War II Draft Registration Card, 1942; US Social Security Death Index 1935-2014; McKean Memorial Park Cemetery Records, Mt. Alton, Pennsylvania; Oak Hill Mausoleum Records, Bradford, Pennsylvania.

165.

Ina Mae Withey, daughter of Jesse (79), granddaughter of Elizabeth (41), b. Haymaker, Pennsylvania May 18, 1894, d. Palm Beach, Florida April 19, 1988; m. (1) Bolivar, New York April 6, 1918, Earle Leslie Burdick, b. Belmont, New York July 7, 1893, d. Belmont, New York January 21, 1942 from accidental drowning; m. (2) Wellsville, New York May 1951 Walter McEnroe, b. Alma, New York October 15,

1891, d. Wellsville, New York October 11, 1958. The late Ina Withey Burdick McEnroe was a major contributor to the 1990 edition of the Root Genealogy. Ina was a 1916 graduate of Alfred University with a Bachelor's Degree.

She almost died of Spanish Influenza while carrying her first child. Earl Burdick also attended Alfred University. For many summers the Burdicks maintained a summer cottage on Cuba Lake, a tradition continued by all three daughters. Earl Burdick built their residence in Belmont, New York even gathering the rocks for the fireplace from the river where he later died. Ina returned to Alfred University after the death of her first husband and attained a Master's Degree in 1947. Ina McEnroe taught English and Latin in Bolivar and Allentown schools. During World War II, she taught in Belmont schools and for a time was the principal.

Ina Withey Burdick McEnroe was an articulate, elegant, and gracious lady with whom I enjoyed many a pleasant summer afternoon at her home at 37 Oak Street in Wellsville talking about the Root genealogy. Her apple pies were legendary and the secret family recipe remains with the family. Earle Burdick was a Lieutenant in the US Army during World War I. He was wounded in action suffering a foot injury, which caused him considerable pain the rest of his life. Earle was awarded the *Purple Heart* for his military service and received a 25% disability payment from the United States government. He served with the 316th Infantry, American Expeditionary Forces. Earle Burdick was described as being of medium height and weight with light brown hair and blue eyes. Mr. Burdick was employed in Belmont as a life insurance agent, as the Postmaster, and later owned and operated a greenhouse and nursery. Earle and Ina Burdick resided on 5 Genesee Street in Belmont. In her seventies Ina traveled to the Middle East where she rode a camel and swam in the Dead Sea.

Walter McEnroe was previously married to Theresa E. Munkes who died May 27, 1945. Walter and Ina McEnroe resided at 206 West State Street in Wellsville. Mr. McEnroe was a member of the Elks Club, the Holy Name Society of the Immaculate Conception Church, the Wellsville Country Club, New York State Oil Producers Association, the Independent Oil Producers Association, and the Brookland Club. Walter McEnroe was an avid sportsman and was made an Honorary Citizen of Boys town, Nebraska. During his lifetime Walter McEnroe was a prominent oil producer. He had a son, James, from his first marriage. Walter McEnroe was buried in Sacred Heart Cemetery in Wellsville with his first wife. Ina Withey Burdick McEnroe was buried in Forest Hills Cemetery in Belmont with her first husband.

Children (by first marriage):

347. I. ***Jean Elizabeth Burdick, f.***

348. II. ***Sara Ann Burdick, f.***

349. III. ***Laine E. Burdick, f.***

References: US Census: 1900, 1910, 1920, 1930, 1940; New York State Census: 1905, 1915, 1925; Forest Hills Cemetery Records, Belmont, New York; Sacred Heart Cemetery Records, Wellsville, New York; World War I Draft Registration Card 1917-18 for Earle Burdick; New York State County Marriage Records 1847-9 and 1907-36 for Earle Burdick and Ina Withey; *Wellsville Daily Reporter* October 13, 1958 for the obituary of Walter McEnroe; Florida Death Index 1877-1998 for Ina McEnroe.

166.

Harry Ivan Withey, son of Jesse (79), grandson of Elizabeth (41), b. Eldred, Pennsylvania July 10, 1899, d. Derrick City May 16, 1984; m. Bradford, Pennsylvania February 12, 1937 (un- documented source) Dorothy Brown, b. Foster, Pennsylvania May 2, 1906, d. Derrick City, Pennsylvania April 6, 1995.

Harry Withey resided with his parents until he married at the age of 38. He was employed as a farmer and oil driller on oil property owned by his father. His World War II Draft Registration Card described him as being 5' 8" tall and weighing 165 lbs. with brown hair and eyes. Harry and Dorothy Withey did not have any children. Dorothy Withey was buried in Willow Dale Cemetery in Bradford, Pennsylvania, but it is not documented where Harry Withey was buried.

References: US Census: 1900, 1910, 1920, 1930, 1940; New York State Census: 1905, 1915, 1925; World War I Draft Registration Card 1917-18; World War II Draft Registration Card, 1942; Pennsylvania Birth Certificate 1906-1910 for Dorothy Withey; Social Security Death Index 1935-2014 for Harry and Dorothy Withey; Willow Dale Cemetery Records, Bradford, Pennsylvania.

167.

Howard Andrew Withey, son of Jesse (79), grandson of Elizabeth (41), b. Bolivar, New York March 24, 1903, d. Fort Lauderdale September 13, 1975; m. Wellsville, New York November 18, 1928 Kathryn L. Ostrander, b. Wellsville, New York December 28, 1901, d. Fort Lauderdale, Florida October 23, 1987. Howard Withey resided in Bolivar and Wellsville until his marriage in 1928. At the time of the 1930 US Census he and his wife moved to Brooklyn, New York where Mr. Withey was employed as an accountant. The 1940 US Census recorded their move to Yonkers, New York where Howard Withey continued to be employed as an accountant. With retirement Howard and Kathryn Withey moved to Florida where they died. Howard and Kathryn Withey were buried in Lauderdale Memorial Park, Fort Lauderdale, Florida.

Children:

350. I. ***James Vance Withey, f.***

351. II. ***David Jack Withey, f.***

References: US Census: 1910, 1920, 1930, 1940; New York State Census: 1905, 1915, 1925; New York State Birth Index 1881-1942 for Howard Withey; US Social Security Death Index 1935-2014; New York County Marriage Index 1847-49 and 1907-1936; Fort Lauderdale Memorial Park Cemetery Records, Fort Lauderdale, Florida.

168.

Charles David Withey, son of Jesse (79), grandson of Elizabeth (41), b. Bolivar, New York January 9, 1907, d. Kalkaska, Michigan January 28, 1953 from a heart attack; m. Girard, Pennsylvania June 30, 1933 Alice Dorothy Neuman, b. Wellsville, New York May 16, 1909, d. Wellsville, New York June 16, 1974.

Charles Withey resided in Bolivar and Wellsville, New York until his marriage to Alice Neuman in 1933. Mr. Withey attended the University of Michigan, graduating in 1931. After their marriage Mr. and Mrs. Withey moved to Bronx, New York where he was employed as the Assistant Superintendent of a Savings Bank. They moved to Wayne, Michigan in 1942 where Charles Withey was employed at Wayne Wire Cloth Products, Inc. rising to the position of secretary and treasurer of the company. When the company moved to nearby Kalkaska in 1950, the Witheys moved there, too. Charles Withey was a member of the Wayne F. & A. M., Lodge # 112, the Kalkaska Lions Club, and the Kalkaska Chamber of Commerce. He belonged to the Traverse City Episcopal Church and was on the Kalkaska Rural Agricultural School Board.

Charles David Withey's death was a great shock to this family, to the company he worked for, and the community he served. All Kalkaska's businesses were closed on the day of Mr. Withey's funeral. Alice Newman was the daughter of John Newman and Sophia Gallman Newman of Wellsville, New York. It appears she was previously married to Thomas Crofton Phillips of Wellsville. The wedding took place in Wellsville on May 9, 1931. It is assumed that the marriage ended in divorce but no divorce document can currently be found. Alice Withey eventually returned to Wellsville after her children were grown where she died. Charles Withey was buried in Evergreen Cemetery Kalkaska, Michigan while Alice Withey was buried in Woodlawn Cemetery Wellsville, New York.

Children:

352. I. ***Charles David Withey, Jr., nfi.***

353. II. ***Helen Ann Withey***, b. Wayne, Michigan October 10, 1943 d. Ann Arbor, Michigan March 12, 1944. It is not currently known where she was buried.

354. III. ***John Andrew Withey, f.***

355. IV. ***Nancy Withey, f, nfi.***

References: US Census: 1910, 1920, 1930, 1940; New York State Census: 1905, 1915, 1925; New York State Birth Index 1881-1942; Michigan Death Records 1867-1950 for Helen Ann Withey; Pennsylvania County Marriage Index, 1885-1950; *Leader and Kalkasian* January 29, 1953 obituary for Charles Withey; Woodlawn Cemetery Records, Wellsville, New York.

169.

Dudley Lyman Ennis, son of Mary Elizabeth (80), grandson of Lyman (42), b, Bolivar, New York July 4, 1885, d. Higgins Hospital Olean, New York November 11, 1925 from uremic poisoning and pneumonia; m. Olean, New York August 31, 1918 Martha *Mattie* C. Atkinson, b. Oswayo, Pennsylvania September 1, 1889, d. Bolivar, New York October 2, 1978.

Dudley Ennis resided with his parents before and after his 1918 marriage. Mr. Ennis was a self-employed house painter. Mattie worked for the Bell Telephone Company from 1924 until her retirement in 1955. After Dudley Ennis' death, Mattie Ennis continued to reside with her father-in-law on South Main Street. While on a trip to Michigan to visit her sister, Mrs. Hugh Handley of Plainwell, Michigan, Mattie met Thomas Elzy Moore, a recent widower. Mattie Ennis and Thomas Moore were married August 3, 1955 in Plainwell at Mrs. Handley's residence. Thomas Moore was born in Seymour, Michigan on September 1, 1873. Mr. Moore was previously married to Miss Nida Sparks who died in 1949. Thomas Moore had a son and a daughter by his first wife. Thomas Moore died September 20, 1962 in Plainwell and was buried with his first wife at Mt. Ever-Rest Memorial Park in Kalamazoo, Michigan. Mattie Ennis Moore eventually returned to Bolivar residing with her son where she died. Dudley and Mattie Ennis were buried in Wells Cemetery, Little Genesee, New York. There are no markers for either of them.

Children:

356. I. ***Paul J. Ennis, f.***

357. II. ***Beryl A. Ennis***, b. and d. June 11, 1922 in Bolivar, New York and was buried in an unmarked grave in Wells Cemetery, Little Genesee, New York. Beryl was three months premature and lived one hour.

References: US Census: 1900, 1910, 1920, 1930, 1940; New York State Census: 1892, 1905, 1915, 1925; Michigan Death and Burial Index 1867-1955 for Thomas Moore; New York County Marriage Records 1847-9 and 1907-36 for Dudley Ennis marriage; New York State Death Index 1852-1956; *Bolivar Breeze 1891-1965*, August 11, 1955 for wedding of Mattie Ennis and Thomas Moore; *Wellsville Daily Reporter*, August 2, 1978 for death of Mattie Ennis Moore; Wells Cemetery Records, Little Genesee, New York; *Olean Evening Tribune*, November 15, 1925 for the obituary of Dudley Ennis; Schaffner Funeral Home Records, Bolivar, New York for Beryl Ennis.

170.

Isabelle Lue Root, daughter of Earles (81), granddaughter of Lyman (42), b. Olean, New York September 22, 1885, d. Olean, New York September 1, 1946 from cancer; m. Olean, New York May 31, 1904 Theodore Edward Johnson, b. Oil City, Pennsylvania September 6, 1884, d. Olean, New York February 8, 1956 from cancer.

Isabelle was a life-long resident of Olean. For most of her married life Isabelle Root Johnson, her husband, and family resided at 686 Hoop Street in Olean. Mr. Johnson was employed as a machinist working for the Pennsylvania Railroad. Johnson's Draft Registration Card described him as having a ruddy complexion, 5' 5" tall, weighing 148 lbs. with black hair and brown eyes. Isabelle and Theodore Johnson had a total of 9 children, three of whom died in infancy. One of the children who died was named Harold and a second child who died in infancy was named Maria Isabella.

It is not known where these three children were buried. Isabelle's father, Earls Root, resided with the Johnsons the last years of his life, dying at the Johnson home in 1942. Isabelle and Theodore Johnson were buried in Allegany Cemetery in Allegany, New York.

Children:

358. I. ***Jennie Evelyn Johnson, f.***

359. II. ***Theodore Friend Johnson, f.***

360. III. ***Maggie Eloise Johnson, f.***

361. IV. ***Marion B. Johnson, f.***

362. V. ***Beula Marie Johnson, f.***

363. VI. ***Gertrude Lola Johnson, f.***

References: US Census: 1900, 1910, 1920, 1930, 1940; New York State Census: 1905, 1915, 1925; Allegany Cemetery Records, Allegany, New York; New York State Death Index 1852-1956; Bible belonging to Earls L. Root listing births/marriages/deaths; World War I Draft Registration Card 1917-1918; World War II Draft Registration Card, 1942.

171.

Harold William Root, son of Earles (81), grandson of Lyman (42), b. Olean, New York October 29, 1889, d. Salamanca/Great Valley, New York November 3, 1908; m. Olean, New York July 25, 1908 Florence or Flossie Belle Swift, b. Warsaw, New York May 9, 1889, d. Bay, Florida September 28, 1973.

During Harold Root's short life, he was employed as a bell boy at an Olean hotel and later at Robeson Cutlery in Perry, New York where he probably met his wife who was a resident of Perry. Harold Root's family did not learn about his marriage until his death when Flossie Swift Root claimed his body. Mr. Root's death was work-related. He was a switch tender for the B. R. and P. Railroad in East Salamanca, New York. Harold Root held this job for only a month in Salamanca when he was killed. He let an incoming train through the switch, which was worked by means of levers, and when the train backed down onto another track, he was caught and crushed about the middle of his body. Mr. Root was buried in Allegany Cemetery in Allegany, New York. Flossie Swift Root married two more times. Her second marriage was to Charles G. Taylor of Perry, New York in 1911 who also died soon after the marriage. Flossie remarried in 1915 to Alonzo Clyde Keeler in Ohio with whom Flossie had two sons, Robert and Donald.

References: US Census: 1900; New York State Census: 1892, 1905; New York State Death Index 1852-1936 for Harold Root; Florida Death Index 1877-1998 for Flossie Swift Root Taylor, Keeler; Earls Root family bible for marriage date for Harold Root. NY County Marriage Records 1847-48 and 1907-36 for Harold Root's marriage; *The Silver Springs Signal* November 12, 1908 for Harold Root's death; *Bolivar Breeze* November 5, 1908.

172.

Lola Blossom Root, daughter of Earles (81), granddaughter of Lyman (42), b. Olean, New York March 13, 1892, d. Olean, New York January 16, 1975 from a heart attack; m. (1) Olean, New York July 6, 1908 George Weatherell, b. Friendship, New York October 12, 1883, d. Olean, New York October 31, 1950 from Huntington's Disease; m. (2) Olean, New York October 30, 1959, b. Portville, New York December 29, 1886, d. Olean, New York March 31, 1974 from a heart attack.

Lola Root resided with her parents until her marriage in 1908. For many years they resided at 676 Hoop Street in Olean. Toward the end of her life Lola resided at 210 Rowland Avenue in Olean. George Weatherell was a brick layer by trade. His World War I Draft Registration Card described him as being of medium build, medium height with brown hair and eyes. He was a member of St. Stephen's

Episcopal Church and the Brick Masons and Plasterers International Union # 38. Lola Wetherell was a member of St. Stephen's Episcopal Church in Olean, the Olean Senior League, Women of the Moose, and the Woman's Relief Corps. Lola's second husband, Charles Pilon was previously married to Miss Cecil Wheeler who died in 1957. Mr. Pilon was employed by the Niagara Mohawk Power Company until his 1952 retirement. Charles Pilon was a member of the American Legion Post 530, Dads of the VFW, St. Stephen's Club at St. Stephen's Episcopal Church, and the Loyal Order of the Moose # 119. He had three sons by his first wife: Douglas, Neal, and Bernard. Charles Pilon was buried with his first wife in Pleasant Valley Cemetery in Portville, New York. Lola was buried with her first husband in Allegany Cemetery, Allegany, New York.

Children (by first marriage):

364. I. ***Harold Weatherell***, b. Olean, New York September 17, 1909, d. Olean, New York April 20, 1910 from heart problems at the home of his grandfather, Earls Root. Harold was buried in Allegany Cemetery, Allegany, New York.

365. II. ***John Earl Weatherell, f.***

366. III. ***Mary Roberta Weatherell, f.***

367. IV. ***Martha Isabel Weatherell, f.***

368. V. ***Nina Elizabeth Weatherell, f.***

369. VI. ***Anne Belle Weatherell, f.***

370. VII. ***Alice Fern Weatherell, f.***

371. VIII. ***James William Weatherell, f.***

372. IX. ***Ronald Keith Weatherell, f.***

References: US Census: 1900, 1910, 1920, 1930, 1940; New York State Census: 1892, 1905, 1915, 1925; Earls Root family Bible birth records; World War I Draft Registration Card 1917-18 for George Weatherell; Allegany Cemetery Records, Allegany, New York; Pleasant Valley Cemetery Records, Portville, New York; *Olean Times Herald* January 17, 1975, obituary for Lola Root Weatherell Pilon; New York State Marriage Index 1881-1967 for Lola Root's second marriage; New York State Marriage Index 1847-1849 and 1907-1936 for Lola Root's first marriage.

173.

Selden Jule Root, son of Earles (81), grandson of Lyman (42), b. Olean, New York November 28, 1893, d. Olean, New York October 1, 1957 from lymphoblastic lymphoma; m. Olean, New York October 8, 1914 Rosa Mae Ford, b. Allegany, New York October 13, 1894, d. Olean, New York October 20, 1981 following a lengthy illness.

Selden Root was a life-long resident of Olean, New York. He enlisted June 5, 1911 in the New York Guard as a Private in Co. I, 31st Infantry. Seldon's World War I and II Draft Registration Cards described him as being 5' 6" tall, weighing 122 lbs. with a ruddy complexion, and having brown hair and brown eyes. He was an electrician by training working for Herold Electric Shops in 1918 and later for G. Willard Electric in Olean. Selden and Rosa Root were buried in Allegany Cemetery, Allegany, New York.

Children:

373. I. ***Donald Jason Root, f.***

374. II. ***Harold William Root, f.***

375. III. ***Margaret E. Root, f.***

376. IV. ***Demaris Elaine Root, f.***

References: US Census: 1900, 1910, 1920, 1930, 1940; New York State Census: 1905, 1915, 1925; Allegany Cemetery Records, Allegany, New York; Earls Root Bible Birth Records; WW I Draft Registration Card 1917-1918; World War II Draft Registration Card, 1942; New York State County Marriage Index 1847-1849 and 1907-36; New York State Death Index 1957-1968.

174.

Leo Cassar Root, son of Ernest (83), grandson of Lyman (42), b. Olean, New York July 20, 1898, d. Batavia, New York Veterans Hospital, Batavia, New York after suffering several strokes; m. Walden, New York September 25, 1916 Ethel Bernard, b. Gardiner, New York December 20, 1898, d. Wellsville, New York November 21, 1977 after a lengthy illness at the home of her daughter, Dorothy Root Paquette.

Leo Cassar Root was the author's maternal grandfather. Leo Root's middle name was the last name of the doctor who delivered him in Olean, Dr. Cassar. He was born five months after his parent's marriage. Mr. Root's childhood was not a happy one. His father, Ernest J. Root, was physically and emotional abusive to him, his mother, and his sister. Leo's mother, Belle Fuller Root, moved her son and daughter to Binghamton, New York where her family resided sometime after 1902 and before his father's 1904 death.

Leo Root was a challenge for his mother to raise and he was frequently sent to Bolivar, New York to live with his paternal uncle and aunt, Paul and Libbie Root Ennis.

The 1910 US Census recorded twelve-year old Leo Root was a boarder in Bolivar and not living with any relatives. Leo's Uncle Paul was a strict disciplinarian, which might have contributed later to Leo Root's sometimes explosive temper. Leo C. Root's mother was diagnosed with cancer in 1909 and succumbed to the disease in December 1914. The 1915 New York State Census recorded Leo residing with a maternal great-aunt, Alta Carter Palmer, and her family in Binghamton, New York. His sister, Nordica, in 1915 was living with another maternal great-aunt, Nettie Carter Foose, in Buffalo, New York. There were no trust funds in that era. The estate was allegedly overseen by Belle Root's brother, Jesse Fuller. Neither Leo nor his sister benefited from any of the estate. Leo C. Root enlisted in the US Navy in 1915.

He lied about his age in order to enter the navy stating to me that he added two years to his age. His assignment was to be a member of the Mexican Border Campaign. Leo Root was discharged in 1916. On May 20, 1916 Leo Root enlisted in the National Guard at Binghamton, New York. His World War I Draft Registration Card gave his birth year as 1897, which was incorrect. Leo was born in 1898. Leo Root was sent to a Training Camp in Whitman, New York during which time he met and married Ethel Bernard. Leo C. Root was mustered out of service March 10, 1917. After the birth of the first of his eight children in 1917, Leo and Ethel Root moved from Wallkill, New York to Bolivar, New York. According to a July 1919 issue of the *Bolivar Breeze* Leo Root reenlisted in the US Navy going to Bay Bridge, Brooklyn where he was assigned to the *Tanamores*, which embarked for Alaska on August 24, 1919. No military records can be found to support this information.

Newspaper interviews with Leo C. Root recorded his additional World War I service with the Army Reserves as an Infantryman, 27th Division, serving 18 months in France and Germany. In a late 1923 newspaper interview Leo C. Root stated that during his time in the US Navy he sailed along both US coasts and stopped at the island of Cuba. In the early 1920s he disappeared for a month, stating in 1923 that he had gone to Kentucky, but Mr. Root provided no further details about his absence. Leo C. Root returned to Bolivar after his military tour and found employment with the Van Curen High Explosives Company as an oil well shooter and one who transported nitroglycerin via a horse drawn wagon over dirt roads.

On April 13, 1922 the *Bolivar Breeze* recorded that a bottle of nitro fell off the wagon Leo was driving on Main Street in Bolivar. The bottle broke, but there was no explosion. A second nitro bottle fell off Leo's wagon in the spring of 1923 and exploded on Main Street Bolivar leaving a large hole in the road. A third nitro explosion occurred September 6, 1923 at a nitroglycerin shack outside Bolivar. The blast destroyed the magazine and it appeared that Leo C. Root had been blown to bits. The local newspaper reported that he probably died in the explosion although no trace of him could be found at the site. Leo Root did not die, but he claimed the explosion caused him to have amnesia and he eventually returned to Bolivar from Binghamton, New York three weeks after the incident. It appears that Leo C. Root was wanted for bigamy by the authorities in neighboring Cattaraugus County at the time of the September 6, 1923 explosion.

On February 12, 1921 in Olean, New York Leo married Lorena Eiseman of Binghamton, New York, whom he knew from his school years. The second marriage was declared bigamous in 1924 and Mr. Root was fined $200 and sentenced to a six-month suspended sentence. Leo Root had five children and a legal wife in Bolivar to take care of and the court clearly took his legal family's financial interest to heart in the final sentence. Lorena Eiseman born November 16, 1899, died March 28, 1981, and was buried in Chenango Valley Cemetery in New York State. She later married Arthur F. Richards (1902-1972).

Leo and Ethel Root had eight children. His mother-in-law, Jemima Bernard, and his sister-in-law, Eva Bernard (Fisk), moved to Bolivar and resided on Leather Street in the 1920s to help Ethel financially and to assist in raising the Root children. The Root family first resided on South Main Street, the house now torn down, a few doors from the home of Mary *Aunt Mate* Scott, Bolivar's oldest surviving Civil War widow, whom all the Root children fondly remembered. By 1930 they had moved to the former LeSuer farm house outside Bolivar just past Maple Lawn Cemetery, which they rented for a few years. The LeSuer house is now a New York State historic site. Their last Bolivar residence was on Salt Rising Road on a farm past the octagon house on the right side of the highway.

The depression years were a financial challenge for the Root family. There were months when there was no employment even in the oil industry. In 1936 the Root family moved to Clintonville, Pennsylvania where Leo found employment with the Hall Torpedo Company. They resided at 50 Emlenton Street in Clintonville and the family can be found on the 1940 US Census but under the incorrect transcription of their last name as *Rost.* During their time in Clintonville Leo was appointed the Town Constable. With the advent of World War II, Leo Root decided to reenlist in the US Navy leaving a good paying job. He saw active service in the Pacific Theater of the War where he rose to the rank of Machinist Third Class. Leo Root was mustered out October 10, 1944 because of the ill health of his wife. He returned to Clintonville and moved with his wife to Texas to find employment. The heat did not agree with Mrs. Root so they returned to Allegany County in 1945 where Leo found work with the Bradley Oil Producing Company.

They resided just outside Allentown, New York on the Bolivar Road in a duplex on Bradley property from 1945 until 1956. In 1956 they moved into Allentown in a residence across the street from the school owned by Gert Palmer who operated Palmer's Store. In 1957 they moved to a house facing Church Street owned by the Ingalls family. In December 1959 their final move was to the former Allentown Church parsonage on Church Street where they lived until Leo's death in 1961 and where Ethel continued to reside until 1976 when ill health forced her to move to Wellsville, New York where her daughter, Dorothy Paquette, took care of her until her death. On September 23, 1951, Leo Root suffered a severe stroke, which left him paralyzed on the left size. He spent considerable time in the Bath, New York Veterans Hospital. In January 1955, Leo suffered another severe stroke and again stayed at the Bath Veterans Hospital for rehabilitation. Leo Root was an active member of the Kenyon Andrus American Legion Post # 772 in Bolivar, New York. The Post honored him in March 1952 for his World War I service. After his strokes, Leo took an increasing interest in genealogy and it was from him that I learned we were related to a number of families in Allentown, New York even though he did not know how we were related. My own research later confirmed that we were distantly connected to the Woodard, Bartlett, and Storms families of Allentown through Fuller, Adams, Reed, and Root lines of descent. Despite Leo C. Root's difficulties during the first decade of his marriage, his cousins and friends liked and forgave him.

Ethel Bernard Root was descended from French Huguenot families residing along the Hudson River. She was the daughter of James and Jemima Eckert Bernard. Ethel's childhood was a challenging one because she was one of twelve children who, as a teenager, was forced to find work as a young housekeeper and laundress to support the family. I am sure that her courtship and marriage to Leo Root was a whirlwind romance and, perhaps, an escape from the financial challenges of her youth. Unfortunately, raising eight children during the depression years with a husband who could not always find employment or was absent, presented new difficulties. Ethel learned to read and write when her own children went to school. Mrs. Root was a skilled embroiderer, a talented gardener, and her kitchen always smelled of freshly baked bread and delicious desserts. Ethel was a creative canner of fruits and vegetables and her canning recipes survive.

Mrs. Root was a member of the Ladies Auxiliary, Kenyon Andrus American Legion Post in Bolivar, New York and the Clintonville, Pennsylvania Methodist Church. I spent many a weekend at my maternal grandmother's house enjoying her company and finding her a generous and kind person. Some of the best food I ever ate was prepared in her kitchen. In 1975 Mrs. Root suffered a mild heart attack probably brought on by stress she suffered with the republication of the 1923 newspaper articles about her husband's bigamous second marriage, which caused her much embarrassment. Leo and Ethel Root were buried in Floral Park Cemetery in Johnson City, New York next to Leo's mother, Belle Fuller Root.

Children:

377. I. ***Leo Stanley Root, f.***

378. II. ***Nordica Ethel Root, f.***

379. III. ***Eva Jemima Root, f.***

380. IV. ***Ernest Jerome Root, f.***

381. V. ***Fred Root, f.***

382. VI. ***Dorothy Lucille Root, f.***

383. VII. ***Hugh Daniel Root, f.***

384. VIII. ***Lawrence Leonard Root, f.***

References: US Census: 1900, 1910, 1920, 1930, 1940; New York State Census: 1905, 1915, 1925; *Bolivar Breeze 1891-1965,* selected issues; *Oil City Derrick*, selected issues; World War I Draft Registration Card 1917-1918; World War II Draft Registration Card, 1942; NYS Marriage Record Index 1847-9 and 1907-1936 for Leo Root's marriages to Ethel Bernard and Lorena Eiseman; Floral Park Cemetery Records, Johnson City, New York; New York State Birth Certificates for Leo and Ethel Root; New York State Death Certificates for Leo and Ethel Root; Discharge Papers for Leo C. Root, US Navy, filed at the Belmont, New York Court House; Pennsylvania Veteran Compensation Application Files, WW II 1950-1966.

175.

Nordica Thelma Root, daughter of Ernest (83), granddaughter of Lyman (42), b. Olean, New York September 4, 1899, d. Dunedin, Florida June 10, 1996; m. Binghamton, New York January 26, 1922 Hugh Wood Wylie, b. Binghamton, New York November 20, 1898, d. Dunedin, Florida April 20, 1980 from cancer.

Nordica Root was named for the famous 19th century opera singer Lillian Nordica. Her name was suggested by Dr. Cassar who delivered Miss Root. He had just returned from hearing Madame Nordica perform so Dr. Cassar asked Mrs. Root if she would name her first daughter after the opera singer. Belle Root agreed. (Story related in a letter sent by Nordica Root Wylie to her niece Nordica Root Anderson with an article about Madame Nordica from *Yankee* magazine.) Nordica resided in Olean, New York for the first three years of her life until her parents separated. She lived in Binghamton until her mother's death in 1914. For a brief time, Nordica Root lived with her maternal great-aunt, Nettie Carter Foose, in Buffalo. However, that arrangement did not work and she returned to Binghamton probably living with her maternal uncle and aunt, Jesse and Emma Graf Fuller. At the time of the 1920 US Census, Nordica was living with a longtime friend, Gladys Stovall, in Binghamton.

Hugh Wylie's World War I Draft Registration Card described him as having medium height, medium build with brown hair and eyes. In 1917 he was employed as clerk in a drug store. After Nordica's marriage to Hugh Wood Wylie, they continued to reside in the Binghamton area in neighboring Dickinson, New York where he was employed as a salesman for Bristol Myers. Mr. Wylie's career took them to Dearborn, Michigan in 1932, Utica, New York in 1935, and by 1940 to Albany, New York where they resided at 168 Winthrop Avenue and later 35 E. Picotte Drive. Nordica was employed by Walden Books in Albany, New York when they rented rather than sold books. After Hugh's retirement in 1964, they moved first to Clearwater, Florida and later to Dunedin, Florida.

Hugh Wood Wylie was adopted by George and Louise Wylie soon after his birth. Mr. Wylie's middle name was actually his original last name. I met Nordica, Aunt Nord, and Hugh Wylie in 1978 at their home in Dunedin, Florida when I began searching my genealogical roots. My great-aunt Nordica had an amazing memory and could describe the colors of the clothing she and her brother wore in old black and white photographs. However, when she did not want to talk about the past, she claimed she could not remember. It was apparent that her childhood was an unhappy one with secrets she took to her grave. Before my 1978 visit she burned her mother's diary and other materials deciding the contents should never be revealed. While devoted to her brother, Leo, Nordica Root Wylie was not close to his wife or his children with one exception. Nordica was close to her niece and namesake, Nordica Ethel Root Anderson to whom she gave a number of personal mementoes of her mother. Her niece, Nordica Root, bore a striking resemblance to her mother, Belle Fuller Root. Nordica and Hugh Wylie were both cremated and their remains placed in Curlew Hills Memory Garden in Palm Harbor, Florida.

Children;

385. I. ***Jeanne Charis Wylie, f.***

References: US Census: 1900, 1910, 1920, 1940; New York State Census: 1905, 1915, 1925; Florida Death Index 1877-1998; New York County Marriage Records 1847-1849 and 1907-1936; US Presbyterian Church Records 1701-1970 for their marriage; World War I Draft Registration Record 1917-1918; US City Directories for Dearborn, Michigan (1932), Binghamton, New York, and Albany, New York; Curlew Hills Memory Garden Records, Palm Harbor, Florida.

176.

Allen John Root, son of Bernard (84), grandson of Lyman (42), b. Allentown, New York November 12, 1903, d. Bradford, New York December 15, 1967 from cancer; m. Wellsville, New York February 17, 1927 Margaret J. Monroe, b. West Union, New York August 4, 1903, d. Bolivar, New York December 15, 1964 from a heart attack.

Allen Root's middle name, John, honored his maternal grandfather John O. Snowdon. Allen was born in Allentown, New York, not Bolivar, where the Alma, New York township birth was recorded. In 1920 Mr. Root was employed as a clerk in a Bolivar meat market and in 1925 Allen was working as a laborer for a Bolivar ice plant. He resided with his parents on Leather Street until his marriage. Allen served in the US Navy during World War II and was an active member of Bolivar's Kenyon Andrus Post of the American Legion and the Bolivar Fire Department. Allen J. Root retired from the Sinclair Oil Refinery in Wellsville, New York where he was employed as a truck driver for the refinery's pipeline. Margaret Monroe was raised in Willing Township south of Wellsville, New York, graduating from Wellsville High School. She was previously married to a Mr. Sanger of Wellsville. No documentation could be found on this marriage.

Margaret Monroe was single in the 1920 US Census. Margaret J. Monroe Sanger was listed as a widow and a boarder in the 1925 New York State Census residing with the William Van Ness family as a cousin-in-law employed as a nurse. She was a member of the Order of the Eastern Star, Buttrick Chapter in Bolivar and a past president of the Kenyon Andrus and Allegany County American Legion Auxiliaries. Mrs. Root's obituary incorrectly states her marriage date to Allen Root as 1925 when the documentation is 1927. Mr. and Mrs. Root resided at 88 Wellsville Street in Bolivar. The residence was sold in 1966 to Mrs. Helga Root, widow of Hugh D. Root, the son of Allen Root's cousin, Leo C. Root. Allen and Margaret Root were buried in Maple Lawn Cemetery in Bolivar, New York.

Children:

386. I. ***Gale Bernard Root, f.***

References: US Census: 1910, 1920, 1930, 1940; New York State Census: 1905, 1915, 1925; Alma, New York birth record for Allen J. Root; NY County Marriage Records 1847-9 and 1907-1936; NYS Birth Index 1881-1942; New York State Death Index for Allen and Margaret Root; *Bolivar Breeze 1891-1965*, selected issues; Maple Lawn Cemetery Records, Bolivar, New York.

178.

Lyman Erwin Root, son of Bernard (84), grandson of Lyman (42), b. Jamestown, New York August 1, 1905, d. Jones Memorial Hospital, Wellsville, New York August 23, 1981 from cancer; m. Richburg, New York November 9, 1940 Melba Gwendolyn Gladys Norton Drew, b. Windsor, Ontario, Canada January 25, 1915, d. Olean General Hospital, Olean, New York January 3, 1996 after a brief illness.

Lyman Root was named after a brother, Limon Dudley Root, who was born and died in 1904 and for his paternal grandfather, Lyman Eleasure Root, who died in 1896. After his birth in 1905, his parents moved to Bolivar and resided periodically at the residence of his paternal grandmother, Almira Reed Root, until her death in 1914. Lyman Root remembered his grandmother as a deeply religious woman who was involved in a church related activity almost every day. Mr. Root would accompany his grandmother to church and pump the organ so she could play. In 1915 Lyman resided with his parents and siblings on Leather Street. In 1925 he was employed as grocery salesman and in 1930 Lyman operated the picture machine, probably at the Lyric Theater in Bolivar, and boarded with a Josephine Williams.

In 1940 in Richburg, New York Lyman Root married Melba Gwendolyn Gladys Norton Drew. They lived in Richburg until March 1942 when they moved to 57 Olean Street in Bolivar, the former Cady residence, where they resided until their respective deaths. Melba had been previously married in 1934 to Leslie Drew who was killed in an automobile accident April 16, 1939. Leslie and Melba had three children who were adopted by Lyman Root. Tragically, Leslie and Melba's son, Jack Root, was killed in an automobile accident in 1961. Lyman and Melba did not have any children of their own. Lyman was employed by the Sinclair Refining Company in Wellsville, New York and after Sinclair closed in 1958 at the Quaker State Refinery in Farmers Valley, Pennsylvania until he retired in 1966. He also worked for a brief time in 1950 as a sales representative in Olean, New York for Wasson Motors. Mr. Root was an active member of the Bolivar Fire Department serving as the organization's secretary in the 1930s and 1940s and the Bolivar United Methodist Church. He was known in Bolivar by his nickname *Old Slive* because he was so thin. Melba was employed at Bolivar's Dunn's Drug Store from 1949 until her retirement in 1985. After Lyman's death, Melba entrusted the author with the original Civil War discharge papers of Mr. Root's grandfather, Lyman Eleasure Root. Lyman and Melba Root were buried in Maple Lawn Cemetery in Bolivar. Leslie Drew was buried in East Portville Cemetery in Portville, New York.

Children (by adoption):

387. I. ***Audrey Drew Root, f.***

388. II. ***Jack Drew Root, f.***

389. III. ***Kristin Drew Root, f.***

References: US Census: 1910, 1920, 1930, 1940; New York State Census: 1915, 1925; Maple Lawn Cemetery Records, Bolivar, New York; New York State Marriage Index for Lyman and Melba's wedding; *Bolivar Breeze 1891-1965*, selected issues; East Portville Cemetery Records, Portville, New York; 1978 interview with Lyman E. Root.

180.

Mary Elizabeth Root, daughter of Bernard (84), granddaughter of Lyman (42), b. Bolivar, New York August 19, 1909, d. Medina, New York June 7, 2007 after a long illness at the Orchard Manor Nursing Home in Medina; m. Allegany, New York July 15, 1926 Samuel Judson Holland, b. Buffalo, Kentucky August 31, 1901, d. Newport News, Virginia March 30, 1991.

Mary Root resided with her parents at her paternal grandmother's house until 1914 when her grandmother died. From 1915 until her marriage she resided with her parents on Leather Street in Bolivar. After Mary's marriage to Sam Holland they resided first in Bolivar at 142 Main Street later moving to Olean Street. Sam was employed as a pipeline gauger for the Sinclair Oil Refinery in Wellsville, New York. When the refinery closed in 1958 Sam and the other employees lost their pensions. The Hollands moved to Poquoson, Virginia staying with their daughter and son-in-law. In the 1960s they moved to New Port Richey, Florida until 1990 when they moved back to Poquoson, Virginia to be closer to their daughter and grandchildren. A child was born prematurely to Sam and Mary Holland in December 1926 and died unnamed. The Hollands later had two more children.

While residing in Bolivar Mary served as President of the Ladies Bowling League in 1941, was the Captain of the Allegany County March for Polio in 1954 and took adult courses in hair styling and cake decorating at the Bolivar High School. Sam was President of the Allegany County Fireman's Association in 1951 and served for many years as Secretary for the Bolivar Fire Department.

He was a member of the Bolivar Masons, Macedonia Lodge, 258 F and AM and in 1956 was elected President of the Allegany County Masons District. In 1956 Sam was co-chairman for Allegany County's Firemen's Convention in Bolivar and was a Past Secretary of the Southwestern Fireman's Association. Sam served in the US Navy during World War II and was the son of James W. Holland and Alice McDowell Holland. Sam restored antique furniture and caned chairs in retirement. Mary Root Holland bore a striking resemblance to her mother, Maggie Weaver, even down to the smile. She was a very helpful member of the Root family who shared stories about the family. Mary and Sam Holland were buried in Maple Lawn Cemetery in Bolivar, New York.

Children:

390. I. ***Earl Dean Holland, f.***

391. II. ***Barbara Anne Holland, f.***

References: US Census: 1910, 1920, 1930, 1940; New York State Census: 1915, 1925; Maple Lawn Cemetery Records, Bolivar, New York; New York County Marriage Records 1847-9 and 1907-1936; Virginia Death Records 1912-2014 for Sam Holland; New York State Birth Records 1881-1942 for Mary Root Holland; *Bolivar Breeze 1891-1965*, selected issues; *Olean Times Herald*, June 10, 2007 for Mary Root Holland obituary; Schaffner Funeral Home records for death of infant Holland in 1926.

181.

Stanley Eugene Root, son of Bernard (84), grandson of Lyman (42), b. Bolivar, New York April 7, 1912, d. Stuart, Florida May 10, 1990 from Alzheimer's disease; m. Olean, New York March 10, 1934 Mary Bernadine Webber, divorced Wayne County, Michigan July 17, 1947, b. Olean, New York August 15, 1915, d. Wyandotte, Michigan December 18, 1961 from a heart attack. Stanley or Stan Root resided with his parents in Bolivar, New York until his father's death in 1926. In 1930 he continued to reside in Bolivar and stayed with his maternal aunt, Kate Barnes. A member of the Bolivar High School Class of 1931, Stan Root was a star athlete on the Track Team leading Bolivar to a state relay championship in 1931. Before his marriage, Stan participated in a number of plays. He worked for a time in Wellsville, New York before moving to Wyandotte, Michigan in 1937 when he was employed as a chemist for the Penn Salt Company for thirty years.

Mr. Root never remarried and in 1982 moved to Stuart, Florida where he resided with his daughter until his death. Stan Root inherited a number of old Root family photographs but the identities of the people in the photographs were never identified. His remains were cremated and later buried in Maple Lawn Cemetery in Bolivar, New York. Mary Webber Root remarried in Wyandotte, Michigan on November 29, 1947 to William Lufus Ferris. Further information is not available about her place of burial.

Children:

392. I. ***Duane Root, f.***

393. II. ***Dianne Root, f.***

References: US Census: 1920, 1930, 1940; New York State Census: 1915, 1925; New York State Marriage Index 1881-1967; Florida Death Index 1877-1998 for Stanley Root; Michigan Divorce Records 1897-1952; Michigan Marriage Records for Mary Root's second marriage; *Bolivar Breeze 1891-1965*, selected issues.

183.

Merle Findlay Root, son of Bernard (84), grandson of Lyman (42), b. Bolivar, New York July 18, 1915, d. Bath, New York Veterans Hospital November 16, 1982 from cancer. Merle's twin brother, Morton, was also born on July 18, 1915, but died the next day from heart leakage.

Merle spent most of his life in Bolivar, New York residing with his parents on Leather Street. After his mother's remarriage Merle moved to Holcomb, New York living with her and his step-father, Stephen Weaver. On August 1, 1942 Merle Root enlisted in the US Army at Buffalo, New York. PFC Merle Root saw action in 1944 in the Pacific Theater in New Guinea and the Philippines during World War II. He was a member of the Service Battery, 472nd Field Artillery Battalion and was awarded a good conduct medal for his fidelity through faithful and exact performance of duty, efficiency and behavior that deserved emulation. Such a medal was only given to servicemen who were in the military for three years in peacetime or one year in wartime and were recommended by their commanding officer. Merle's battle injuries forced him to have medical treatment at the Hamilton Field Hospital in California and at the Hilton Hospital at Fort Dix, New Jersey.

After the war Merle Root returned to Bolivar and resided with his mother, Maggie Root Weaver, after her husband, Stephen Weaver, died. Merle never married and lived at 77 Wellsville Street until his mother's death and continued to reside there when his aunt, Kate Snowdon Barnes, moved back into her residence until his death. Merle was frequently known as *Young Slive* because he was so thin. His older brother, Lyman Root, was known as *Old Slive* and his father, Bernard Root, was known as *Slive.* After World War II Mr. Root worked for the Bolivar Country Club, the Bolivar Hotel, and the Kenyon Andrus Post of the American Legion in Bolivar as a bartender. He was treasurer of the Bolivar Club, was involved in baseball, and was a Red Cross driver. Merle Root was buried in Maple Lawn Cemetery in Bolivar, New York next to his mother, Maggie Snowdon Root Weaver.

References: US Census: 1920, 1930, 1940; New York State Census: 1925; Maple Lawn Cemetery Records, Bolivar, New York; US Social Security Death Index 1935-2014; New York State Birth Index 1881-1942; *Bolivar Breeze 1891-1965*, selected issues; US Army Enlistment Records 1938-1946.

188.

Ellen Barber, daughter of Fred (88), granddaughter of Mary Jane (43), b. Detroit, Michigan August 17, 1904, d. Flat Rock, North Carolina February 13, 1988; m. place and date not known, Clarence Francis Evans, b. Youngstown, Ohio January 31, 1901; d. d. Henderson, North Carolina July 9, 1981.

It is not known how and where Ellen Barber and Clarence Evans met. Ellen attended Washington University in St. Louis, Missouri. Clarence Francis Evans was the son of David J. and Gwenllian Francis Evans. Ellen resided with her parents until her marriage. Clarence Evans resided in Cleveland, Ohio with his parents in the 1910 US Census and in the 1920 US Census with his parents in Youngstown, Ohio. Ellen Barber and Clarence Evans married before the 1930 Census and lived in Boardman, Ohio with Ellen's mother, Elizabeth Barber, who was a widow.

Clarence Evans was employed as a cement salesman. He had a college degree but further information on the name of the institution is not currently known. In 1940 they moved to Akron, Ohio with Ellen Barber and their two children, Elizabeth and David, where Mr. Evans was employed as a department manager with the rubber industry. Ellen and Clarence Evans retired to North Carolina, but the specific date is not currently known. It is not currently known where Ellen and Clarence Evans were buried. Clarence Evans was cremated and was initially buried in St. John in the Wilderness Cemetery in Flat Rock, North Carolina. However, that memorial has been withdrawn.

Children:

394. I. ***Elizabeth Ellen Evans***, b. Akron, Ohio 1938. Married with at least one daughter and resided in Maryland; ***nfi***.

395. II. ***David B. Evans, f.***

References: US Census: 1910, 1920, 1930, 1940; North Carolina Death Index 1908-2004; Social Security Death Index 1935-2014; Ohio Birth Index 1774-1973.

189.

Minnie Alice Richardson, daughter of Flora (90), granddaughter of Hiram (44), b. Bolivar, New York October 25, 1882, d. Olean, New York June 3, 1920; m. (1) Richburg, New York March 12, 1902 Homer D. Weatherby, b. Bolivar, New York March 30, 1881, d. Bolivar, New York March 19, 1910 from tuberculosis; m. (2) Olean, New York January 4, 1913 Byron "Bert" Barnes, b. Weston Mills, New

York April 1878, d. Olean, New York by suicide April 27, 1917; m. (3) a Mr. Abbott, place and date of marriage not known.

Minnie Alice Richardson resided with her parents until her marriage to Homer Weatherby. The last name of Weatherby has had other spellings including Weatherbee. The Weatherbee spelling was the result of an error made by the teacher who educated Minnie's son, Howard, from her first marriage. Homer Weatherby was a Baptist minister who also worked for the July Oil Company in Bolivar. Reverend Weatherby was previously married to Pearl Cook who died before Homer's marriage to Miss Richardson. Homer Weatherby was well liked by the Bolivar community and his death was a great tragedy for his family and his many friends. Minnie Alice and her two children continued to reside on Richburg Road in Bolivar until 1912 when she moved to Rochester, New York where her daughter, Mercia, was institutionalized because she was a deaf-mute whose special needs were caused by an accident in July 1908.

Minnie Alice then moved to Olean where she did housework and met her second husband, Byron Barnes. Byron or Bert Barnes was the illegitimate son of Wallace W. Barnes. His mother was Elizabeth Hill who was not married to Wallace Barnes. Wallace Barnes was married to Eulalia Hill, Elizabeth Hill's sister, and had children born before and after Byron Barnes' birth by his legal wife. Byron Barnes grew up knowing he was illegitimate and that may have affected his outlook on life. Bert Barnes did a variety of jobs including employment as a bartender, teamster, and cleaning livery stables. It is believed he was not able to adequately support his wife and step-son and assault charges were filed against him by Minnie when they briefly lived in Shinglehouse, Pennsylvania. Minnie continued to do housework and take in boarders to meet the family's financial needs. They resided at 321 South Barry Street in Olean, New York.

Mr. Barnes found work in Cleveland, Ohio and after six weeks went by and Minnie Alice and her son did not follow him, Bert went back to Olean to the family home where he found his mother, wife, step-son, and two boarders in residence on the evening of April 27, 1917. Bert Barnes produced a pistol when Minnie Alice did not agree to move to Cleveland and shot his step-son at point blank range in the lungs. Mr. Barnes then shot his wife four times: twice in the back, once in the neck, and a fourth time in the breast before he went outside to reload. A severely wounded Minnie Alice picked up her critically wounded son and carried him upstairs and barricaded themselves in a bedroom. When Bert Barnes realized he could not break down the bedroom door, he committed suicide. Barnes left behind a suicide note citing his wife's refusal to move to Cleveland as the reason for shooting her and her son, which clearly indicated that the attempted murders were premeditated. Miraculously, both Minnie Alice and her son, Howard Weatherby, survived their wounds. Minnie Alice petitioned the circuit court in Olean on July 14, 1917 to have her last name changed from Barnes back to Weatherby. The court agreed.

In the 1920 US Census Minnie Alice was listed as Alice Abbott. She apparently remarried but the family does not know anything about her third husband and no documentation can currently be found to confirm the third marriage. Minnie Alice died later in 1920 after a six-month illness at her home at 118 West State Street in Olean, but the Richardson family does not know the cause of death. There is no mention of Mr. Abbott in the 1920 US Census or in the obituary for Minnie Alice Richardson Weatherby. Minnie Alice Richardson Weatherby was buried in Bolivar, New York's Maple Lawn Cemetery with her first husband, Homer Weatherby. Byron Barnes was buried in Chestnut Hill Cemetery in Portville, New York.

Children (by first marriage):

396. I. ***Howard Evaland Weatherby, f.***

397. II. ***Mercia (Marsha) Onalee Weatherby, f.***

References: US Census: 1900, 1910, 1920; New York Census: 1892, 1905, 1915; New York State Death Index 1852-1956 for Minnie Weatherby; Maple Lawn Cemetery Records, Bolivar, New York; Chestnut Hill Cemetery Records, Portville, New York; NYS Marriage Index 1881-1967 for marriage of Minnie Alice Richardson and Homer Weatherby; New York County Marriage Index 1847-1849 and 1907-1936 to Byron Barnes; *Olean Evening Herald*, selected issues; *Bolivar Breeze 1891-1965*, selected issues; *Olean Evening Herald,* July 16, 1917 for Minnie Alice Barnes petition to change her name from Barnes to Weatherby.

190.

Stanley Lafrone Richardson, son of Flora (90), grandson of Hiram (44), b. Bolivar, New York March 17, 1884, d. Okmulgee, Oklahoma May 20, 1961; m. Richburg, New York January 1, 1906 Jennie Alice Dealy, b. Coudersport, Pennsylvania August 8, 1887, d. Okmulgee, Oklahoma January 1969.

Stanley Richardson's middle name was the name of his maternal uncle, Lafrone or Laphronia Root. He resided with his parents until his marriage. Stanley Richardson suffered a long illness in 1904 but the cause was not revealed. At the time of his marriage Stanley was an oil pumper on the Phillips farm on Phillips Hill. Stanley Richardson was the first occupant of the tenant house on the Phillips property built next to the much larger Phillips residence. Jennie or Jane Dealy Richardson did house work in Bolivar before her marriage. Stanley and Jennie Richardson were married at the Baptist parsonage in Richburg. In 1910 Mr. and Mrs. Richardson moved to Lawrenceville, Illinois where Stanley found work in the local oil fields. By 1917 the Richardsons had moved to Okmulgee, Oklahoma where Mr. Richardson was employed in the oil fields in a variety of occupations including tool dresser and oil pumper. Stanley Richardson's World War I Draft Registration Card indicated that he worked for the Sequy Oklahoma Oil Refining Company in Collinsville, Oklahoma. Mr. Richardson's World War II Draft Registration Card noted that he was employed in the Bartlett, Oklahoma oil fields. He was 5' 9" tall, weighed 150 pounds and had blue eyes, light hair, and a ruddy complexion. All three sons of Stanley and Jennie Richardson were born in Bolivar, New York. Mr. and Mrs. Richardson were buried in the Okmulgee Cemetery in Okmulgee, Oklahoma.

Children:

398. I. ***Stanley Dale Richardson, f.***

399. II. ***Ralph William Richardson, f.***

400. III. ***Robert Sydney Richardson, f.***

References: US Census: 1900, 1910, 1920, 1930, 1940; New York State Census: 1892, 1905; NYS Marriage Index 1881-1967; World War I Draft Registration Card 1917-18; World War II Draft Registration Card, 1942; Okmulgee Cemetery Records, Okmulgee, Oklahoma; Social Security Death Index 1935-2014; *Bolivar Breeze* December 15, 1904, January 4, 1906, April 9, 1908, November 24, 1910.

191.

Manley Almarion Richardson, son of Flora (90), grandson of Hiram (44), b. Bolivar, New York December 15, 1885, d. Allentown, New York June 8, 1978; m. Richburg, New York August 13, 1905 Margaret *Maggie* Tinsler, b. New York State September 5, 1885, d. Shinglehouse, Pennsylvania October 19, 1977 in a nursing care facility.

Manley Richardson resided with his parents until his marriage in 1905. Manley and Maggie Richardson made their first home with his sister and brother-in-law Minnie Alice and Homer Weatherby, residing in Bolivar until 1910. Maggie and Manley Richardson were residents of Alma, Petrolia, and Allentown, New York where he worked in the local oil fields primarily for the Ebenezer Oil Company. His World War I Draft Registration Card listed his employment as an oil well tool dresser working for George Storms of Allentown, New York. Manley Richardson's World War II Draft Registration Card gave his height as 5' 10, "weighing 184 pounds with brown hair and blue eyes. In 1942 he worked for Ebenezer Oil in Scio, New York. The Richardsons celebrated 60 years of marriage on August 13, 1965. Manley and Maggie Richardson had two daughters, Eloise Belle Richardson and Frances L Richardson. Eloise died at the age of 14 months. Frances married but died at the age of twenty-five years. Three of Frances' children, Roland Durfee and twin daughters Eloise and Eleanor Durfee, and step-son Arthur Durfee were raised by Manley and Maggie Richardson. Mr. and Mrs. Richardson were buried in Maple Lawn Cemetery in Bolivar, New York with their infant daughter Eloise.

Children:

401. I. ***Eloise Belle Richardson***, b. Bolivar, New York October 20, 1907, d. December 11, 1908 from congestion of the lungs. She was buried in Maple Lawn Cemetery.

402. II. ***Frances Louise Richardson, f.***

References: US Census: 1900, 1910, 1920, 1930, 1940; New York State Census: 1892, 1905, 1915, 1925; World War I Draft Registration Card 1917-1918; World War II Draft Registration Card, 1942; NYS Marriage Index 1881-1967; Social Security Death Index 1935-2014; Maple Lawn Cemetery Records, Bolivar, New York; *Bolivar Breeze 1891-1965,* selected issues; *Bolivar Breeze* August 24, 1905 for marriage record; *Bolivar Breeze*, December 17, 1908 for the death of Eloise Bell Richardson.

192.

Agnes H. Richardson, daughter of Flora (90), granddaughter of Hiram (44), b. Bolivar, New York November 29, 1888, d. Largo, Pinellas County, Florida March 4, 1970; m. place not known, May 30, 1907 Daniel T. Baker, b. Andover, New York January 18, 1873, d. East Koy, New York October 25, 1962.

Agnes Richardson resided with her parents until her marriage to Daniel Baker. In 1910 they lived in Pike, New York where Mr. Baker farmed. The census records for 1915, 1920, and 1925 recorded the Baker family lived in Eagle, New York, Pike, New York, and Gainesville, New York, all in Wyoming County where he farmed. The 1930 US Census noted a career change for Mr. Baker who now was employed as a dryer operator for a salt refinery owned by the Morton Salt Company where he worked until his retirement. Mr. and Mrs. Baker had six children including a pair of fraternal twins. Agnes and Daniel Baker were buried in East Koy Cemetery in East Koy, New York.

Children:

403. I. ***Margaret Isabelle Baker, f.***

404. II. ***Raymond Daniel Baker, f.***

405. III. ***Juanita Flora Baker, f.***

406. IV. ***Geraldine Agnes Baker, f.***

407. V. ***Phyllis Orma Baker (a twin), f.***

408. VI. ***Norman James Baker (a twin), f.***

References: US Census: 1900, 1910, 1920, 1930, 1940; New York State Census: 1892, 1905, 1915, 1925; East Koy Cemetery Records, East Koy, New York; Social Security Death Index 1935-2014; Florida Death Index 1877-1998 for Agnes Baker.

193.

Harold Almarion Richardson, son of Flora (90), grandson of Hiram (44), b. Bolivar, New York b. August 22, 1891, d. Chagrin Falls, Ohio February 10, 1964; m. Cuyahoga, Ohio February 16, 1916 Elizabeth Heger or Hager, b. Mentor, Ohio June 20, 1890, d. Cleveland, Ohio July 31, 1969 at St. Luke's Hospital.

Harold Richardson's middle name is the same as his brother Manley's middle name. The family has no explanation for this middle name duplication. Harold resided with his parents until at least 1905. The 1910 US Census found Harold Richardson working as a farm laborer in Castile, New York and living with the Clayton Smith family. Because Harold Richardson was not recorded on the New York State Census for 1915, it is assumed he had already moved to the Cleveland, Ohio area where he married in 1916. Elizabeth's last name can be found spelled as either Heger and Hager in official documents. She was the daughter of Frank Hagar (1841-1930) and Theresa Zeglar (1841-1916). At the time of his marriage Harold worked delivering ice and Elizabeth was employed as a waitress. In Ohio Mr. Richardson worked as a railroad brakeman for the Pennsylvania Railroad based on his World War I Draft Registration Card. His World War II Draft Registration Card described him as 5' 8 ½ "tall, weighing 155 pounds with a light complexion, blue eyes and brown hair. For 19 years he was the custodian for the Philomethian Street School in Chagrin Falls. In retirement Mr. Richardson was employed as a painting contractor and interior decorator. Harold and Elizabeth Richardson were buried in Evergreen Hill Cemetery in Chagrin Falls, Ohio.

Children:

409. I. ***Oliver Thomas Richardson, f.***

410. II. ***Edward Frank Richardson, f.***

411. III. ***Itha Mae Richardson, f.***

412. IV. ***Edna Marie Richardson, f.***

413. V. ***Margaret Elizabeth Richardson, f.***

References: US Census: 1900, 1910, 1920, 1930, 1940; New York State Census: 1892, 1905; World War I Draft Registration Record 1917-1918; World War II Draft Registration Card, 1942; Ohio County Marriage Records 1774-1993; Ohio Death Records 1908-32 and 1938-2007; Evergreen Cemetery Records, Chagrin Falls, Ohio; *Bolivar Breeze* March 5, 1964 for obituary of Harold Richardson.

194.

Mary Elizabeth Richardson, daughter of Flora (90), granddaughter of Hiram (44), b. Bolivar, New York June 1, 1893, d. Olean, New York April 14, 1986; m. Olean, New York November 22, 1913 John Emmett Corcoran, b. Butler, Pennsylvania December 23, 1889, d. Olean, New York February 28, 1958.

Mary Elizabeth Richardson resided with her parents until her marriage and moved to Olean, New York. John Corcoran had relocated to Olean by 1905 living with his mother and two sisters. Mary Elizabeth's mother-in-law, Alice Corcoran, resided with Mary Elizabeth and John Corcoran until her death in 1932. Mr. Corcoran's World War I Draft Registration Card described him as tall and stout with hazel eyes and auburn hair. John Corcoran was employed by the Olean Brewing Company in 1917. In 1920 Mr. Corcoran was employed as a boiler maker, which profession he continued until 1930 when he was employed at a railroad repair shop as a railroad car repairman for Union Tank Company. In 1940 the Corcorans resided at 1305 ½ West State Street. John Corcoran died in 1958 and was cremated. His remains were interred in Pleasant Valley Cemetery in Olean, New York. Mary Elizabeth Corcoran outlived her son, John E. Corcoran, Jr. who died in 1976. Mary Elizabeth resided with her daughter-in-law until declining health forced her to move to a health care facility in Shinglehouse, Pennsylvania. Mary Elizabeth Corcoran was buried with her husband and son at Pleasant Valley Cemetery, Olean, New York.

Children:

414. I. ***John Emmett Corcoran, Jr., f.***

References: US Census: 1910, 1920, 1930, 1940; New York State Census: 1905, 1915, 1925; Pleasant Valley Cemetery Records, Olean, New York; World War I Draft Registration Card 1917-18; New York County Marriage Records 1847-9 and 1907-36; Social Security Death Index 1935-2014; correspondence with the late Mrs. John E. Corcoran, Jr.

195.

Ethel Marion Richardson, daughter of Flora (90), granddaughter of Hiram (44), b. Bolivar, New York December 5, 1895, d. Olean, New York January 24, 1977; m. Portageville, New York June 29, 1920 Albert John Hirliman, b. Olean, New York May 18, 1894, d. Olean, New York November 1, 1964.

Ethel Richardson resided with her parents in Bolivar and later Wyoming County, New York until her marriage. She was known by her middle name Marion. Albert John Hirliman's World War I Draft Registration Card recorded military service from July 25, 1918 to December 21, 1918. Mr. Hirliman served with Company A of the 87th Engineers. His World War II Draft Registration Card described Albert Hirliman as being 6' tall, weighing 152 pounds with blue eyes, gray hair and having a light complexion. Albert Hirliman worked in Olean at Union Cutlery until retirement. In 1930 they resided at 9 Spruce Street in Olean and in 1940 at 313 North 11th Street where they had three boarders. Ethel and Albert Hirliman adopted a daughter. Marion and Albert Hirliman were buried in St. Bonaventure Cemetery in Allegany, New York. No tombstones are in evidence.

Children (by adoption):

415. I. ***Edna Laura or Leora Fedison Hirliman, f.***

References: US Census: 1900, 1910, 1920, 1930, 1940; New York State Census: 1905, 1915, 1925; Social Security Death Index 1935-2014; New York State Death Index 1957-1968; World War I Draft Registration Card 1917-18; World War II Draft Registration Card, 1942; NY County Marriage Records 1847-9 and 1907-1936.

198.

Lewis William Richardson, son of Flora (90), grandson of Hiram (44), b. Bolivar, New York February 21, 1900, d. Bolivar, New York July 8, 1970; m. (1) Portageville, New York September 30, 1918 Lois Mary Cockle, b. Bliss, New York August 23, 1899, d. Bolivar, New York February 15, 1949 from cancer; m. (2) Richburg, New York, June 4, 1949 Marjorie Seamans, b. Bliss, New York August 20, 1913, d. Bolivar, New York March 10, 1954 from a cerebral hemorrhage.

Lewis William Richardson's legal name given him at birth by his parents was Hiram Adolph Richardson. His parents changed his name to Lewis William Richardson without filing the legal papers. This would cause Mr. Richardson considerable difficulties in later life. Lewis Richardson resided with his parents in Bolivar, New York and moved with them to Portageville, New York in 1911. Lewis Richardson's World War I Draft Registration Card described him as tall with medium build and having blue eyes and dark brown hair. He worked as a farm laborer on his father-in-law's farm in Gainesville, New York until he went to Cleveland, Ohio in 1917, where he worked in a powder plant for a year before returning to Wyoming County, New York in 1918. Mr. Richardson did farm work until the late 1920s when he found more highly paid work in the Allentown and the Bolivar, New York oil fields.

In 1932 Lewis Richardson moved his family back to Bliss, New York after his mother-in-law's death. Lewis did farm work in Bliss until 1934 when the decision was made to return to Bolivar, New York again working in the oil fields. In 1951, Lewis Richardson and his second wife and family moved to Metcalf, Texas working in the oil fields there. They returned to Bolivar, New York in 1953 again residing at 103 South Street in Bolivar. Mr. Richardson continued to work in the oil fields until 1960 when emphysema forced him to retire. After the death of his second wife, Lewis Richardson's children by his second marriage were raised by his eldest daughter from his first marriage, Doris Richardson June of Bolivar, New York, and his sister, Marion Hirliman of Olean, New York.

Lois Cockle Richardson was the daughter of William Cockle and Linda Van Luven Cockle of Bliss, New York. Lewis and Lois Richardson were married at the home of Mrs. Daniel Baker, Lewis' sister, in Portageville, New York. Lewis and Lois Richardson were injured in a car accident in August 1930 when a vehicle driven by Alvin Gingrich crashed into the Richardson car on the Norton Summit as they were driving to Wellsville from Allentown. Mr. Gingrich got distracted by a bee who stung him causing him to lose control of his vehicle. Both cars were badly damaged. Mr. Richardson and his niece, Mrs. Harold Durfee suffered serious injuries and Mrs. Lois Richardson and Harold Durfee had minor injuries.

A New York State Marriage Record recorded Lewis Richardson's second marriage in Pike, New York on May 4, 1949, which is in conflict with the marriage document in the possession of the Richardson family. Lewis Richardson was buried with his first wife in Maple Lawn Cemetery in Bolivar, New York. Marjorie Seamans Richardson was buried in Lyonsburg Cemetery, Bliss, New York.

Children (by first marriage):

416. I. ***Doris Linda Richardson, f.***

417. II. ***Blanche Flora Richardson, f.***

418. III. ***Merle William Richardson, f.***

419. IV. ***Theo Agnes Richardson, f.***

420. V. ***Darwin Edward Richardson***, b. and d. Bliss, New York April 19, 1935 from upper respiratory defect and buried in the East Koy, New York Cemetery.

Children (by second marriage):

421. I. ***Terry Lewis Richardson, f.***

422. II. ***James Lawrence Richardson, f.***

423. III. ***Sallie Ann Richardson, f.***

References: US Census: 1900, 1910, 1920, 1930, 1940; New York State Census: 1905, 1915, 1925; Maple Lawn Cemetery Records, Bolivar, New York; Lyonsburg Cemetery Records, Bliss, New York; Social Security Death Index 1935-2014; NYS County Marriage Records 1847-9 and 1907-1935 for first marriage; NYS Marriage Index 1881-1967 for second marriage; NYS Birth Index 1881-1942 for Lewis Richardson under Hiram Adolf Richardson; genealogical information provided by the late Doris Richardson June of Bolivar, New York; World War I Draft Registration Card 1917-1918; *Bolivar Breeze 1891-1965*, selected issues; email correspondence with Rose June Feenaughty, granddaughter of Lewis Richardson.

199.

Mildred Salome Richardson, daughter of Flora (90), granddaughter of Hiram (44), b. Bolivar, New York October 25, 1901, d. Chafee, New York April 24, 1968; m. Portageville, New York February 20, 1918 Rinhart Karl Hinz, b. Gainesville, New York March 5, 1898, d. Hunt, New York June 14, 1977.

Mildred Richardson resided with her parents in Bolivar, New York and in Wyoming County, New York until her 1918 marriage. She lived in the Warsaw, New York area the rest of her life raising a large family of twelve children. Rinhart Hinz was the son of Waldemar Hinz (1873-1949) and Emma Kuhn Hinz (1879-1922). His World War I Draft Registration Card described him as 5'10" tall with blue eyes and brown hair working for the American Car Company in Depew, New York as an ammunition's worker. In 1920 Mr. and Mrs. Hinz lived in Pike, New York where he was employed as farm laborer. The 1930 and 1940 US Census records the family residing in Eagle, New York where in 1930 Rinhart Hinz worked for a novelty company and in 1940 at the Borden Plant until retirement. Mildred and Rinhart Hinz were buried in the East Koy Cemetery in East Koy, New York.

Children:

424. I. ***Edward Waldemar Hinz, f.***

425. II. ***Herman Lafrone Hinz***, b. East Koy, New York May 1, 1920, d. East Koy New York March 5, 1925 and buried in East Koy Cemetery.

426. III. ***Emma Elizabeth "Betty" Hinz, f.***

427. IV. ***Rolland Manley Hinz (a twin), f.***

428. V. ***Robert Stanley Hinz (a twin), f.***

429. VI. ***Arlene Avis Hinz, f.***

430. VII. ***Donald Laverne Hinz, f.***

431. VIII. ***Marion Dolores Hinz, f.***

432. IX. ***Mildred Harriet Hinz, f.***

433. X. ***Edith Elaine Hinz, f.***

434. XI. ***Keith Rinhart Hinz, f.***

435. XII. ***Carol Jane Hinz, f.***

References: US Census: 1900, 1910, 1920, 1930, 1940; US Census: 1905, 1915, 1925; New York County Marriage Records 1847-9 and 1907-1936; World War I Draft Registration Card 1917-1918; East Koy Cemetery Records, East Koy, New York.

201.

Lawrence Edwin Richardson, son of Flora (90), grandson of Hiram (44), b. Bolivar, New York February 7, 1908, d. Portageville, New York December 16, 1929; m. Akron, New York May 25, 1929 Ethel Catherine Mary Chase, b. York, Ontario, Canada August 24, 1907, d. Tonawanda, New York September 1984.

Lawrence Edwin Richardson was also referred to as Ellis or Ellie Richardson in some documents. He resided with his parents in Bolivar, New York and in Wyoming County, New York until his brief marriage. In 1921 *The Bolivar Breeze* reported that Mr. Richardson was confined to his bed for six months but does not identify the cause of the illness. In 1922 Lawrence Richardson was in the Olean Clinic for a fourth surgery. The nature of the illness was not disclosed by the newspaper. Lawrence Richardson was killed from a blow caused by a beam falling while he was repairing a bridge at Letchworth State Park. His only child was born after his death. Ethel Chase Richardson resided with her mother after her husband's death in Newstead, New York. It is currently not known where Lawrence and Ethel Richardson were buried.

Children:

436. I. ***Flora Jeanne Richardson, f.***

References: US Census: 1910, 1920, 1930, 1940; New York State Census: 1915, 1925; New York State Birth Index 1881-1942 for Lawrence Richardson; Ontario, Canada Birth Records 1858-1913 for Ethel Chase; New York State Marriage Index 1881-1967; Social Security Death Index 1935-2014 for Ethel Richardson; *The Bolivar Breeze 1891-1965*, selected issues for 1921 and 1922.

205.

Claude Paul Root, son of Laphronia (91), grandson of Hiram (44). b. Muncie, Indiana February 1, 1899, d. Dade County, Florida April 26, 1958 from a cerebral hemorrhage; m. (1) Muncie, Indiana May 20, 1924 Lilas E. Nokes, b. Cincinnati, Ohio October 29, 1903, d. Coldwater, Ohio August 23, 1993, divorced June 1934; m. (2) Muncie, Indiana August 10, 1935 Leah Marie Isbell b. Ridgeville, Indiana March 14, 1899, d. Miami, Florida December 5, 1973 from a heart attack.

Mr. Root's World War I Draft Registration Card recorded that he worked for the Ontario Silver

Company as a machinist. He was of medium height and weight with black hair and brown eyes. Claude Root lived in Detroit, Michigan during his first marriage where he was employed by a men's clothing store. After his 1934 divorce he returned to Muncie, Indiana where he found employment as a machinist at Pasters Machine Shop. The 1940 US Census listed Claude and Leah residing with his in-laws at 14 Abbot Street in Muncie.

During World War II Mr. and Mrs. Root moved to Florida where he established his profession as a photographer of plants and flowers. Claude hand-colored and hand-tinted each black and white photograph. In 1953 he opened the Camera Art Shop in Coral Gables, Florida. At the time of his unexpected death Claude Root was working on a catalogue for Miami florists. His works were exhibited in the United States and Europe.

One of Mr. Root's works is owned by Queen Elizabeth II and hangs in Buckingham Palace. Lilas Nokes Root remarried to Charles F. Gorsuch and moved to Ohio. Lilas and Charles Gorsuch were buried in North Grove Cemetery in Celina, Ohio. Leah Marie Root was the daughter of Frank and Ethel Dowden Isbell. Claude Root was buried in Woodlawn Park Cemetery in Miami, Florida. Leah Root was cremated and her ashes were buried in Elm Ridge Cemetery in Muncie, Indiana. Claude Root did not have any children by either marriage.

References: US Census: 1900, 1910, 1920, 1930, 1940; World War I Draft Registration Card 1917-1918; Indiana Marriage Records 1810-2001 for both marriages; Florida Death Index 1877-1998 for Claude and Leah Root; Woodlawn Park Cemetery Records, Miami, Florida; Elm Ridge Cemetery Records, Muncie, Indiana; North Grove Cemetery Records, Celina, Ohio.

206.

Lillie Luella Root, daughter of Laphronia (91), granddaughter of Hiram (44), b. Muncie, Indiana April 28, 1901, d. Muncie, Indiana August 20, 1986 from heart disease, a heart attack, and respiratory distress; m. Muncie, Indiana January 20, 1923 George Edward Fox, b. Cincinnati, Ohio July 29, 1897, d. Muncie, Indiana July 29, 1976 from vascular and circulatory ailments.

Lillie Root Fox was a life-long resident of Muncie, Indiana residing with her parents until her marriage. George Fox resided in Dayton, Kentucky in 1900 with his parents who moved to Muncie, Indian by the 1910 US Census. George Fox's World War I Draft Registration Card described him as slender, medium height with blue eyes and light red hair. In 1917 he was employed at Hoosier Auto Parts. Mr. Fox worked for 35 years at the Chevrolet plant in Muncie. He retired in 1961 as a general foreman. George Fox was a member of St. Mary's Parish Church, the Knights of Columbus, and Elks Lodge # 245. Lillie Fox worked for many years for the Collegienne Shops. She was a charter member of St. Mary's Parish and a founding member of the T.K.C. Club with her membership extending 60 years. After Mr. Fox's death, Lillie Fox resided with her son James Fox on Bittersweet Lane. In later years she suffered from Parkinson's Disease. Lillie and George Fox were buried in Elm Ridge Cemetery in Muncie, Indiana.

Children:

437. I. ***George Edward Fox, Jr., f.***

438. II. ***James Edmund Fox, f.***

439. III. ***Jeanne Ann Fox, f.***

References: US Census: 1900, 1910, 1930, 1940; World War I Draft Registration Card 1917-18; Elm Ridge Cemetery Records, Muncie, Indiana; Indiana Death Certificates 1899-2011; Social Security Death Index 1935-2014; Indiana Birth Certificate 1907-1940 for Lillie Root; Indiana Select Marriages Index 1748-1993.

207.

Clifton Laphronia Root, son of Laphronia (91), grandson of Hiram (44), b. Muncie, Indiana November 9, 1903, d. Oklahoma City, Oklahoma June 11, 1968 from a heart attack; m. Muncie, Indiana July 5, 1930 Effie Katherine Smith, b. Missouri August 29, 1902, d. Oklahoma City, Oklahoma March 29, 1993.

Clifton Root was described by his World War II Draft Registration Card as being 5'6" tall with a dark complexion, brown hair and brown eyes and weighed 120 pounds. After Clifton and Effie's marriage they moved to Oklahoma City where her family resided. They stayed in Oklahoma a year and a half before returning to Muncie where Clifton Root found employment as a toolmaker for Warner Gear. In 1936 they returned to Oklahoma City where in 1938 he was employed with Wimbush Market and Grocery. During World War II Clifton Root worked for the post office and later was employed by the Oklahoma Publishing Company. Effie Root was a nursing graduate of the University of Oklahoma working in the nursing field at the American Red Cross before her 1967 retirement. Clifton and Effie Root were buried in Rose Hill Burial Park in Oklahoma City, Oklahoma.

Children:

440. I. ***Edmund Clifton Root, f.***

References: US Census: 1910, 1920, 1940; World War II Draft Registration Card, 1942; Rose Hill Burial Park Records, Oklahoma City, Oklahoma; Social Security Death Index 1935-2014; Oklahoma City Directories, 1938, 1940.

208.

Martha Iona Root, daughter of Laphronia (91), granddaughter of Hiram (44), b. Muncie, Indiana February 1, 1907, d. Muncie, Indiana August 12, 1995 from congestive heart failure, heart disease and renal failure; m. Muncie, Indiana May 31, 1927 Robert James Miller, b. Elwood, Indiana July 1, 1907, d. Muncie, Indiana August 31, 1979 from a heart condition and liver disease.

Robert Miller's biological parents were Fred Carl Diederich (1877-1959) and Emma Greyer Diederich (1882-1910). He was adopted at the age of three years by Dr. Joseph and Alice Brown Miller. Mr. Miller had one year of college and was employed for most of his life by the Delco Battery Division of General Motors in Muncie in quality control. Robert Miller was an accomplished piano player. Martha Root Miller worked as a dental assistant before her marriage. The Millers resided at 4501 North Wheeling Street in Muncie and they were buried in Elm Ridge Cemetery in Muncie, Indiana. The late Martha Root Miller was very helpful in the 1990 publication of the Root family history.

Children:

441. I. ***Donald Miller, f.***

442. II. ***JoAnne Miller, f.***

References: US Census: 1910, 1920, 1930, 1940; Indiana State Department of Health Death Certificates; Indiana Marriage Records 1810-2001; Elm Ridge Memorial Park Records, Muncie, Indiana; Social Security Death Index 1935-2014.

209.

Elizabeth Alberta "Betty" Root, daughter of Laphronia (91), granddaughter of Hiram (44), b. Muncie, Indiana July 31, 1908, d. Muncie, Indiana July 31, 1972 from cancer; m. Muncie, Indiana June 23, 1928 Marvin Lambert, b. Scioto County, Ohio January 11, 1906, d. Muncie, Indiana December 5, 1985 from natural causes.

Betty Root Lambert was active in girl scouts, the Red Cross, and the YMCA. A pianist, she gave piano instruction at her home. In addition to raising 6 children, Betty also boarded 14 other children. Marvin Lambert was a retired tool and die maker at the Warner Gear Division of the Borg Warner Corporation. After his retirement, Marvin continued to do plumbing, remodeling, and some construction work. Mr. Lambert was active in helping the Boy Scouts earn their Silver Beaver Award. Marvin Lambert's other interests included bird watching, gardening, fishing, and taxidermy. He supplied considerable genealogical information for the 1990 edition of the Root family history along with a number of photographs. Betty and Marvin Lambert were buried in Tomlinson Cemetery in Muncie, Indiana.

Children:

443. I. ***David Marvin Lambert, f.***

444. II. ***Jane Ellen Lambert, f.***

445. III. ***James R. Lambert, f.***

446. IV. ***Martha Lambert, f.***

447. V. ***Rebecca Lambert, f.***

448. VI. ***Kathryn Lambert, f.***

References: US Census: 1910, 1920, 1930, 1940; Tomlinson Cemetery Records, Muncie, Indiana; Indiana Marriages 1810-2001; Indiana Death Certificates 1899-2011; Genealogical information supplied by the late Marvin Lambert.

210.

Forrest Eugene Jewett, Sr., son of Elizabeth (92), grandson of Hiram (44), b. Bolivar, New York October 11, 1884, d. Detroit, Michigan August 1, 1947; m. Ashtabula, Ohio October 2, 1912 Pansy Eskew, b. Upshur West Virginia April 1889, d. place and date of death not known.

Forrest or Forest Jewett resided with his mother and brother in Center, Indiana in the 1900 US Census. By 1912 Mr. Jewett had moved to Ashtabula, Ohio where he met and married his wife in 1912 and stayed in Ashtabula until after World War I. His World War I Draft Registration Card described him as having a light complexion, gray eyes and brown hair. Mr. Jewett's World War II Draft Registration Card listed his height as 5'8" and he weighed 135 pounds. Forrest Jewett had a cleft palate and had lost the top of one of his fingers. During World War I, Forrest worked as a hoop puller. In 1920 the Jewett family moved to Detroit where he worked for the Amsworth Manufacturing Company. The 1940 US Census noted the Jewett family resided at 1239 Terminal Avenue in Detroit where he was employed as a machine operator and his wife worked as a clerk. Their eldest son worked as a clerk as well and the second oldest son was a stockroom clerk for an auto factory. Pansy Eskew Jewett was the daughter of Lloyd Clifton Eskew (1850-1900) and Lovelia Mary Stevens Eskew (1850-1892). After her parents' deaths Pansy resided with her siblings at the home of her paternal grandmother in Washington, West Virginia. In 1910 Pansy Eskew lived in Clark, West Virginia boarding with Frank and Minnie Smallwood. It is currently not known where Forrest and Pansy Jewett were buried.

Children:

449. I. ***Forrest Eugene Jewett, Jr., f.***

450. II. ***Edward Lee Jewett, f.***

451. III. ***Harold Lloyd Jewett, f.***

452. IV. ***Richard Jewett***, b. Detroit, Michigan December 10, 1921, d. Detroit, Michigan January 14, 1922 from gastritis and buried in Forest Lawn Cemetery in Detroit.

453. V. ***Charles Kalvin Jewett, f.***

454. VI. ***Margaret "Tiny" Jewett, f.***

455. VII. ***Virginia Lorraine Jewett, f.***

References: US Census: 1900, 1910, 1920, 1930, 1940; World War I Draft Registration Card 1917-18; World War II Draft Registration Card, 1942; Michigan Death Records 1867-1950 for Forrest Jewett, Sr.; Ohio County Marriage Records 1774-1993; Michigan Death Records 1867-1950 for Richard Jewett.

211.

Harry Frank Jewett, son of Elizabeth (92), grandson of Hiram (44), b. Bolivar, New York May 26, 1886/7, d. Calvert City, Kentucky October 25, 1957 from the flu, anemia, and a bad heart; m. (1) Detroit, Michigan April 14, 1919 Mabel Clara Rial or Real, b. Armada, Michigan January 17, 1890, d. Detroit, Michigan March 18, 1941 from uterine cancer; m. (2) Wood, Ohio September 24, 1942 Lela M. McKendree, b. Paducah, Kentucky December 18, 1898, d. Mayfield, Kentucky June 3, 1962 from an upper gastro-intestinal hemorrhage. Harry Frank Jewett resided with his mother and brother in the 1900 US Census in Center, Indiana.

In 1910 Harry Jewett moved to Columbus, Ohio where he worked in a factory and resided with the Garwick family. His World War I Draft Registration Card listed his employment as an electric crane operator for the Continental Motor Company. He resided at 271 Hart Avenue in Detroit. Mr. Jewett's World War II Draft Registration Card described him as being 5'7" tall, weighing 145 pounds with a light complexion, blue eyes and brown hair. In the 1940 US Census Mr. Jewett resided with the Grant Rial family, probably relatives of his first wife, on Hilger Avenue in Detroit. He was employed as a carpenter but listed as divorced. No divorce record has been found for Harry Jewett's first marriage and given he was living with relatives of his first wife, a divorce seems unlikely. Mabel Rial Jewett was the daughter of George Rial (1860-1890) and Eva Sophrona Conger Rial (1867-1897). She was buried in Oakview Cemetery in Oakland County, Michigan. Lela McKendree was previously married twice. She was a widow from her first marriage and divorced her second husband before marrying Harry Jewett. Lela was the daughter of Joseph Lonzo McKendree (1878-1962) and Lillie Van Henson McKendree (1880-1971). Sometime after the end of World War II, Harry and Lela Jewett moved to Kentucky where he operated a grocery store. Harry and Lela Jewett were buried in Birmingham Cemetery in Briensburg, Kentucky. There is a marker for Lela but not for Harry Jewett. Harry Frank Jewett did not have any children by either marriage.

References: US Census: 1900, 1910, 1920, 1930, 1940; World War I Draft Registration Card 1917-1918; World War II Draft Registration Card, 1942; Michigan Marriage Records 1867-1952 for Harry Jewett's first marriage; Ohio County Marriage Records 1774-1993 for Harry Jewett's second marriage; Marshall County, Kentucky Death Records 1852-1964 for Harry Jewett; Michigan Death Records 1867-1950 for Mabel Jewett; Kentucky Death Records 1852-1965 for Lela Jewett; Birmingham Cemetery Records, Briensburg, Kentucky; Oakview Cemetery Records, Oakland County, Michigan.

215.

Edward or Edwin Albert Root, Sr., son of Asa W. (94), grandson of Albert (47), b. Bolivar, New York February 26, 1904, d. Fairfax, Virginia July 22 1962 from heart failure; m. (1) Washington, DC February 22, 1927, Rose Elizabeth Dugan, b. Washington, DC June 17, 1906, d. Washington, DC January 26, 1931 due to complications during childbirth; m. (2) Bolivar, New York March 30, 1932 Margaret Vera Carder, b. Parkersburg, West Virginia July 23, 1910, d. Falls Church, Virginia April 26, 1969 from an acute myocardial infraction brought on by hypertensive cardiovascular disease. Edward has suffered a stroke leaving him paralyzed from the neck down and Margaret nursed him at home from the time of paralysis to his death.

Edward Root was raised by his mother, Emma Toner Root, after his parents separated in 1905 and Edward, his mother, and sister moved to Washington, DC where Emma's family resided. Mr. Root attended Tome Preparatory School in Washington, DC and graduated from George Washington University. Mr. Root went on to attend and graduate from Georgetown University's School of Law. Edward Root entered government service after passing the DC bar exam. His World War II Draft Registration Card described him as having a ruddy complexion, black hair and hazel eyes. Mr. Root stood 5'6" tall and weighed 160 pounds. At the time of his retirement, Edward Root was an Adjudicator Authorizer for the General Accounting Office. Edward Root resided in Washington, DC during his first marriage and until 1941 during his second marriage when the family moved to Falls Church, Virginia. Mr. Root was active in the Kiwanis and introduced Little League into Falls Church. A memorial park for Little League was donated in his memory. Unfortunately, the site is now occupied by an automobile dealership.

Mr. Root met his first wife, Rose Dugan, while attending college. Rose Dugan was the daughter of John Monahan Dugan (1867-1937) and Ellen Stake Cushwa Dugan (1867-1910) and was employed at Riggs Bank in Washington, DC. Rose died giving birth to her second daughter and was buried in Congressional Cemetery in Washington, DC next to her mother-in-law. Mr. Root's second wife, Margaret Vera Carder, was the daughter of George Lawson Carder and Charlotte Lutz of West Virginia. Margaret Root raised her husband's two children from his first marriage along with the two children she had with Edward Root. Margaret played the piano and pump organ by ear in his youth and performed at many weddings and funerals. She had perfect voice pitch and was a star performer in her church choir. Margaret made a striking appearance with her glowing dark red hair and smoky gray eyes. She joined her sisters to sing at community events as the *Carder Sisters.*

Margaret also composed a few songs, of which one came to her in a dream. Mr. Root's aunt, Caroline Toner (1870-1959) was a highly respected educator in Washington, DC public schools. Caroline's love for learning was gained from extensive travel and study, which helped shape Edward Root's intellectual development. Among Caroline Toner's many students was a young J. Edgar Hoover, the first Director of the FBI. Caroline Toner never married and resided with either her sister, Emma Toner, or with her nephew. Caroline Toner was buried with Edward Root and his second wife, Margaret Root, at the Calvary Memorial Park in Fairfax, Virginia.

Children (by first marriage):

456. I. ***Elizabeth Marie Root, f.***

457. II. ***Tracy Rose Root, f.***

Children (by second marriage)

458. I. ***Evelyn Anne Root, f.***

459. II. ***Edward Albert Root, Jr., f.***

References: US Census: 1910, 1920, 1930, 1940; New York State Census: 1905; DC Marriage Record 1810-1953 for Edward Root's first marriage; Virginia Death Records 1912-2014 for Edward and Margaret Root; World War II Draft Registration Card, 1942; Congressional Cemetery Records, Washington, DC for Rose Dugan Root; Calvary Memorial Park Records, Fairfax, Virginia for Edward and Margaret Root and Caroline Toner.

216.

Edwin Milford Root, son of Edwin (95) and grandson of Albert (47), b. Bolivar, New York November 8, 1896, d. Rochester, New York August 5, 1969 from a heart attack; m. (1) Skaneateles, New York July 14, 1924 Ann Betty Bassett, b. Skaneateles, New York May 10, 1898, d. Pittsford, New York September 13, 1989, divorced 1948-49; m. (2) Rochester, New York July 25, 1954 Marian Betty Enos Williams, b. Rochester, New York March 5, 1908, d. Rochester, New York August 9, 1982 from cardiac pulmonary arrest.

Edwin Milford Root was also listed under E. Milford Root and to members of his family was referred to as Milford or Mil. To his business associates he was called Ed. Mr. Root was elected President of his Senior Class at Bolivar, New York High School and in 1965, he was honored during the Class of 1915's 50th anniversary of graduation. In 1920 he was employed with his father in operating the family's grocery store on Main Street in Bolivar next to Dunn's Drug Store. During his residency in Bolivar,

Mr. Root was involved in a variety of community organizations including the Methodist Church, Macedonia Lodge #258 F. and A. M., the Bolivar Mason's Chapter # 280 R. A. M, the Bolivar Chess Club, and the Olean, New York Civic Music Association. He was part owner of the Bolivar Bowling Alley. Milford Root resided in Bolivar with his family until 1936.

During that time Mr. Root was employed as a bank cashier at the State Bank of Bolivar. In September 1936 the Root family moved to Binghamton, New York where Milford Root was employed by IBM. Milford Root's World War II Draft Registration Card described him as being 5' 10 ½ "tall, weighing 170 pounds with black hair and gray eyes. After World War II the Root family moved to Rochester, New York where Milford and Ann divorced and Milford remarried. From 1956 until his retirement in 1967, he was the owner and President of the Rochester Scale Works Company. Milford and Marian Root resided at 143 Branford Road in Brighton, New York. Mr. Root's daughter, JoAnn, related that her father was very interested in astronomy and built his own telescopes and ground his own lenses. Mr. Root was actively involved with the Rochester, New York planetarium and belonged to a number of astronomy clubs. From 1967 until his death, Milford Root sold mutual funds and life insurance. After their divorce Ann Root retired to Pittsford, New York outside Rochester where she resided until her death. Ann Root was buried in Pittsford Cemetery in Pittsford, New York next to a long-time friend Helen S. Price. Milford Root's second wife, Marian Elizabeth Enos Williams was previously married to Warren Williams with whom she had two sons, Warren, Jr. and Brewster.

Warren and Marian Williams were a very socially prominent family in Rochester, New York where Mr. Williams was a very wealthy realtor. Residing with Warren and Marian Williams and their two sons was Marian's younger sister, Eleanor Enos, who was employed as Warren Williams' business secretary. On August 12, 1940 Warren and Eleanor got into an all-day dispute over the young men she was dating. After arriving home, Mr. Williams drew a gun shooting his sister-in-law in the arm with a bullet lodging in her spine. Warren Williams went upstairs in the family home and committed suicide. Eleanor Enos recovered. Warren Williams, Jr. died in 1971 predeceasing his mother. Milford Root was buried in Mt. Hope Cemetery in Rochester, New York in the Enos lot, Section L, lot 71. Marian Enos Root's remains were cremated and her ashes buried in the same lot with Milford Root's remains.

Children: (by first marriage)

460. I. ***JoAnn Root, f.***

References: US Census: 1900, 1910, 1920, 1930, 1940; New York State Census: 1905, 1915, 1925; Mt. Hope Cemetery Records, Rochester, New York; Pittsford Cemetery Records, Pittsford, New York; *Bolivar Breeze 1891-1965, Wellsville Daily Reporter* August 12, 1969 for obituary of Edwin M. Root; NYS Birth Index 1881-1942 for E. Milford Root; Social Security Death Index 1935-2014; World War I Draft Registration Card 1917-18; World War II Draft Registration Card, 1942; NY County Marriage Records 1847-49 and 1907-36 for marriage of E. Milford Root and Ann Basset; *Rochester Democrat and Chronicle* August 13, 1940 for death of Warren Williams.

217.

Gladys Josephine Root, daughter of Edwin (95), granddaughter of Albert (47), b. Bolivar, New York June 11, 1899, d. Bolivar, New York November 6, 1980; m. Bolivar, New York June 26, 1922 William George Nichols, b. Bolivar, New York March 4, 1899, d. Bolivar, New York March 29, 1980.

Gladys Root Nichols was a life-long resident of Bolivar, New York. She resided with her parents on Friendship Street in Bolivar where in 1920 she was employed as a stenographer. After her marriage in 1922, Gladys and William Nichols resided at 153 Wellsville Street in Bolivar. Gladys was a member of the Bolivar United Methodist Church, the Sorosis Club of Bolivar, and the Bolivar Country Club. I met the late Gladys Nichols in the spring of 1979. From then until her death in 1980 Mrs. Nichols and I had many discussions about the Root family. She delighted in sharing stories, memorabilia, and photographs about her family. Gladys had one of the original typed copies of the Civil War diary of her great-uncle, Asa W. Root, who died at Andersonville Prison in Georgia.

I remember Gladys Nichols as elegant, immaculately groomed, stately, and energetic. The meticulous care she gave her home was reflected in the careful display of many precious family heirlooms. Until her illness she took long walks each day and at the age of 80 years could still touch her toes without bending her knees. Her skills at elocution, learned at a young age, remained with Gladys until the end of her life. William G. Nichols was the son of William Leslie Nichols (1860-1924) and Jennie Bell Rosebush (1863-1943) of Bolivar. Mr. Nichols was a graduate of Bolivar High School and Alfred University. During World War I, he briefly served with the US Army from his induction at Alfred University October 1, 1918 until he was mustered out December 10, 1918. William Nichols was an independent oil producer and operated Nichols and Nichols Insurance Agency in Bolivar until he retired in 1965. Mr. Nichols was also a member of the Bolivar Methodist Church, served as Justice of the Peace for the Town of Bolivar for a number of years, and was on the Advisory Board of the First Trust Union Bank. In addition, he was a charter member of the Bolivar Country Club and a member of Macedonia Lodge F & A M of Bolivar. Gladys and William Nichols were buried in Maple Lawn Cemetery in Bolivar, New York.

Children:

461. I. ***William Edwin Nichols, f.***

References: US Census: 1900, 1910, 1920, 1930, 1940; New York State Census: 1905, 1915, 1925; World War I Draft Registration Card 1917-1918; NYS Birth Index 1881-1972; NYS Marriage Record 1847-9 and 1907-1936; Social Security Death Index 1935-2014; *Bolivar Breeze, 1891-1965,* selected issues; Maple Lawn Cemetery Records, Bolivar, New York; *Wellsville Daily Reporter* obituaries March 29, 1980 and November 6, 1980; correspondence with the late Gladys Root Nichols July 19, 1979 and January 15, 1980.

218.

Bertha Marjory Root, daughter of Edwin (95), granddaughter of Albert (47), b. Bolivar, New York December 16, 1901, d. East Aurora, New York November 2, 1964 from a heart attack; m. (1) New Castle, Pennsylvania February 14, 1922 George Edward Osborne, b. Bolivar, New York July 20, 1896, d. Buffalo, New York October 3, 1960 from a heart attack; m. (2) Bolivar, New York August 13, 1964 Baltzar Allendorf, b. Columbus, Ohio May 15, 1902, d Akron, Ohio February 12, 1985.

Bertha Root resided with her parents on Friendship Street in Bolivar until her marriage to George Osborne in 1922. In 1923 they moved to Buffalo, New York where they resided until their respective deaths. George Edward Osborne's original name was George Davie Osborne as written in the July 24, 1896 issue of *The Bolivar Breeze* announcing his birth. George Osborne was born almost three months after his father, George H. Osborne (1865-1896), committed suicide after suffering significant financial losses in oil speculation in Ohio. Mr. Osborne was raised by his mother and maternal grandmother in Bolivar. Mr. Osborne's World War I Draft Registration Card noted that he saw military service from June 14, 1918 until November 11, 1918 as a Seaman Second Class. George was a graduate of the University of Michigan and was employed as a bond salesman for E. H. Rollins Company of Buffalo at the time of marriage. The Osbornes resided briefly in New Castle, Pennsylvania before moving to Buffalo by 1925 as an office manager. His World War II Draft Registration Card described Mr. Osborne as 5'11" tall, weighing 160 pounds and having brown hair and brown eyes.

He was employed by J. A. Webb Belting Company as a business administrator and company treasurer, retiring from that business just prior to his death. Bertha moved back to Bolivar after George Osborne's death and it was in Bolivar where she remarried. Her second marriage was very brief. Bertha and Baltzar had gone to East Aurora so he could vote in the elections and while there she suffered a heart attack and died. Baltazar Allendorf was an insurance adjustor for Michigan Mutual Liability Insurance and later the American Insurance Group. Mr. Allendorf had been previously married to Eleanor M. MacVicker who died in 1953. He had a son, Peter S. Allendorf (1941-2013) by his first marriage. It is not known where Baltzar Allendorf was buried. Bertha and George Osborne were buried in Maple Lawn Cemetery in Bolivar, New York.

Children (by first marriage):

462. I. ***Richard George Osborne, f.***

463. II. ***Robert Charles Osborne, f.***

References: US Census: 1900, 1910, 1920, 1930, 1940; New York State Census: 1905, 1915, 1925; Maple Lawn Cemetery Records, Bolivar, New York; World War I Draft Registration Card, 1917-18. Death Index 1957-1968; NYS Marriage Index 1881-1967 for Bertha Root's second marriage; Ohio Death Records 1908-1932 and 1938-2007 for Baltazar Allendorf; *Bolivar Breeze 1891-1965*, selected issues.

219.

Huldah Jane Root, daughter of George (97), granddaughter of Albert (47), b. Bolivar, New York October 11, 1895, d. St. Louis, Missouri February 25, 1971 from a massive coronary; m. St. Louis, Missouri November 17, 1913 Albert George Nulsen, Jr., b. Hazelwood, Missouri November 2, 1894, d. St. Louis, Missouri March 18, 1972 from emphysema.

Huldah Root was named for her paternal great-aunt, Huldah Jane Root Curtiss, who raised her father, George Root. Just before Huldah Curtiss died, she gave her great-niece a gold necklace or chain. The necklace was in turn given to Mrs. Nulsen's daughter, Jane Nulsen Bunse. At the time of her marriage, Huldah was an accomplished vocalist and a student at the Bathover Institute in St. Louis. Albert Nulsen's parents were Albert George Nulsen, Sr. (1870-1942) and Maude Kreher Nulsen (1870-1936) of St. Louis. Albert's father was the founder and owner of Nulco Paints, which the family sold in 1937 to the National Lead Corporation. Sherwin-Williams became a subsidiary of National Lead. The Nulsen family owned extensive iron ore property in Georgia. Albert Nulsen's World War II Draft Registration Card described him as being 5'10 ½ "tall and weighing 155 pounds with brown hair and blue eyes and a large scar on his left arm. Albert and Huldah Nulsen's remains were cremated and given to their daughter, Jane Bunse. Their present location is not known.

Children:

464. I. ***Albert George Nulsen III, f.***

465. II. ***William Nulsen, f.***

466. III. ***Jane Nulsen, f.***

467. IV. ***Alice Kreher Nulsen***, b. St. Louis, Missouri May 17, 1926, d. Richmond Heights in St. Louis October 19, 1930 in a fire at the family home set by arsonists. Alice's cremated remains were in the possession of the late Jane Nulsen Bunse.

References: US Census: 1900, 1910, 1920, 1930, 1940; New York State Census: 1905; Social Security Death Index 1935-2014 for both Huldah and Albert Nulsen; NYS Birth Index 1881-1942 for Huldah Root Nulsen; World War II Draft Registration Card, 1942; correspondence from the late Jane Nulsen Bunse; Missouri Birth Record 1847-1910 for Albert Nulsen; Missouri Death Certificate 1910-1962 for Alice Bunse.

221.

Alvya Marie Root, adopted daughter of George (97), adopted granddaughter of Albert (47), b. probably Indiana October 2, 1908, d. Olean, New York May 25, 2000; m. (1) Richburg, New York

August 2, 1928 Walter Barton Gridley, b. Duke Center, Pennsylvania October 17, 1905, d. Duke Center, Pennsylvania December 30, 1974, divorced 1945; m. (2) Eldred, Pennsylvania May 29, 1962 Guy E. Richardson b. probably Arcade, New York January 1, 1908, d. Olean, New York November 22, 1989 after an eleven year illness.

Alvya was born Elva or Alva Reuss. Her father was deceased in 1910 when Alvya was two years of age. Her biological mother was Nancie J. Reuss who had borne 8 children, seven of whom were living in 1910 and with whom Alvya resided in Alton, Illinois when she was adopted to replace the recently deceased daughter of George and Elizabeth Root. Alvya remained in touch with her Reuss siblings who claimed they came from Germany and were originally related to the princely family of Reuss. The name Alvya was given her by her adopted sister, Huldah Jane Root. After her adoptive father's death in 1918, Alvya and her adopted mother, Elizabeth Root, moved to Bolivar in 1920. Alvya Root attended St. Elizabeth's Academy in Allegany, New York. Alvya's first husband, Walter Barton Gridley, was a long-time resident of Duke Center, Pennsylvania. He was employed by the Forest Oil Company of Eldred, Pennsylvania. His World War II Draft Registration Card described him as 5'7" tall, weighing 168 pounds with brown hair and brown eyes. During their married years Alvya and Walter Gridley resided in Otto, Pennsylvania. After the breakup of her marriage, Alvya moved back to St. Louis to help take care of her adoptive mother, Elizabeth Root, who had been incapacitated due to crippling strokes. After her mother's death in 1945 Alvya moved from St. Louis to Olean, New York, obtained her divorce, and began work as a beautician. She remarried to Guy Richardson who was employed by the Van DerHorst Corporation in Olean. In 1978 Mr. Richardson suffered a several strokes which left him confined to bed in an Olean nursing home where he died in 1989. Alvya resided at North 13th Street in Olean, New York. In her spare time, she authored over 100 poems of which some were printed in the *Olean Times-Herald*. Presidents Johnson, Carter, and Reagan acknowledged the receipt of her poems written especially for them. During our meetings I found Alvya to be a charming and witty personality. Walter Gridley remarried and was buried with his second wife in the Duke Center Cemetery in Duke Center, Pennsylvania. Guy Richardson was previously married to Dorothy L. Blades from whom he was divorced and with whom he had four sons. Alvya and Guy Richardson were buried in Pleasant Valley Cemetery in Olean, New York.

Children (by first marriage):

468. I. ***Patricia Elizabeth Gridley, f.***

References: US Census: 1910, 1920, 1930, 1940; NYS Marriage Records 1847-9 and 1907-36 for her marriage to Walter Gridley; Social Security Death Index 1935-2014; NYS Marriage Index 1881-1967; World War II Draft Registration Card, 1942 for Walter Gridley; Pleasant Valley Cemetery Records, Olean, New York; Duke Center Cemetery Records, Duke Center, Pennsylvania for Walter Gridley; 1910 US Census for Elva Reuss; correspondence with the late Alvya Root Richardson November 2, 1981, November 9, 1981, September 19, 1982, September 30, 1982, May 4, 1985, December 25, 1985, September 30, 1990, and October 24, 1990.

222.

Edna Cook, daughter of Bertha (98), granddaughter of Albert (47), b. Bolivar, New York July 29, 1890, d. Long Beach, California August 11, 1978; m. Los Angeles, California July 14, 1913 Frank Archibald Kelly, b. Parkers Landing, Pennsylvania August 4, 1880, d. Los Angeles, California July 4, 1947 from acute cardiac failure.

Edna was a professional ceramist. She entered her work in many competitions and won numerous awards. For a time, Edna Kelly maintained her own studio in Long Beach, California where she taught the art of sculpture. Frank Kelly was the son of John Milton Kelly (1837-1911) and Sarah Saddie Balmer Kelly (1854-1940). His World War I Draft Registration Card described him as being slender, of medium height with brown hair and brown eyes. Frank Kelly worked for the Santa Fe Railroad retiring after 50 years of service with the title of Head Claims Agent. The Kellys traveled extensively through the south-western United States exploring ancient Indian sites and collecting artifacts. Frank Kelly was buried in Inglewood Cemetery while Edna was cremated and her remains scattered in the ocean. Edna and Frank Kelly had no children.

References: US Census: 1900, 1910, 1920, 1930, 1940; New York State Census: 1892, 1905; NYS Birth Index 1881-1942 for Edna Cook; California Death Index 1940-1997 for Edna and Frank Kelly; California Marriage Index 1849-1980; World War I Draft Registration Card 1917-18.

223.

Homer Cook, son of Bertha (98), grandson of Albert (47), b. Bolivar, New York March 28, 1893, d. Long Beach, California December 16, 1979 at the Veterans Medical Center in Long Beach from cardiac arrest; m. Los Angeles, California November 3, 1923 Gladys Faith M. Whipple, b. Boston, Massachusetts December 19, 1897, d. Los Angeles, California October 1, 1956.

Homer Cook's World War I Draft Registration Card for 1917 described him as tall and slender with gray eyes and light brown hair working as a timekeeper for the Santa Fe Railroad. During World War I he rose to the rank of sergeant with the US Army's 60th Company. His World War II Draft Registration Card gave Homer Cook's height as 5'10 ½ "and weighing 175 pounds. Homer Cook owned and operated his own electrical wholesale supply business Cook-Nichols Company for over 35 years. Homer Cook's hobbies included hunting and fishing throughout the western United States. Mrs. Cook was employed as a nurse before her marriage. Mr. and Mrs. Cook resided in Hemet, California for many years. After Homer Cook's death, Mrs. Cook moved to Duarte, California for the remainder of her life. Homer and Faith Cook were buried in Forest Lawn Cemetery Park in Glendale, California.

Children:

469. I. ***Wilber Cook, f.***

470. II. ***Ralph Cook, f.***

References: US Census: 1900, 1910, 1920, 1930, 1940; New York State Census: 1905; California Marriage Index 1849-1980; New York Birth Index 1881-1942 for Homer Cook; California Death Index 1940-1997; World War I Draft Registration Card 1917-18; World War II Draft Registration Card, 1942; Forest Lawn Memorial Park Cemetery Records, Glendale, California.

224.

Anita Cook, daughter of Bertha (98), granddaughter of Albert (47), b. Puerto Rico March 24, 1905, d. Los Angeles, California March 11, 1986; m. Chicago, Illinois September 17, 1932 Vladimir or Warren Joseph Baicher (Baicharoff), b. Russia May 28, 1898, d. Pasadena, California May 6, 1971 from bronchopneumonia.

Anita Cook Baicher studied music and piano under Sergio Kanoski at the Bush Conservatory of Music in Chicago and at DePaul University. She later taught piano until her marriage. Warren Joseph Baicher's family were of German origin who lived within the Russian Empire for generations where they were members of the lower nobility. During the Russian Revolution Mr. Baicher fought with the White Armies until their defeat in the early 1920s. He emigrated to the United States entering in 1923. Warren Baicher became an American citizen on February 28, 1929 changing his name from Vladimir Baicharoff to Warren Joseph Baicher. His World War II Draft Registration Card described Warren Baicher as being 5'10" tall, weighing 180 pounds with blue eyes and blonde hair. Mr. Baicher had four years of college education and was employed as an engineer for Manuel Martin Aircraft. Upon his death Mr. Baicher willed his body to the UCLA Medical Center. It is not known where Anita Cook Baicher was buried.

Children:

471. I. ***Vladimir Baicher, f.***

472. II. ***Lida Baicher, f.***

References: US Census: 1910, 1920, 1930, 1940; California Death Index 1940-1997; US Naturalization Records Indexes 1791-1992; World War II Draft Registration Card, 1942; Correspondence with the late Anita Cook Baicher; correspondence with the late Anita Cook Baicher October 14, 1979, October 22, 1979, and August 4, 1980.

225.

Addison Ross Evans, son of Forest (100), grandson of Elosica (49), b. Chicago, Illinois January 17, 1892, d. Los Angeles, California June 4, 1947; m. Chicago, Illinois September 11, 1920 Camilla A.

Mihm, b. Chicago, Illinois June 16, 1897, d. Montrose, California May 10, 1997.

Information about Addison Ross Evans is limited to what can be gleaned from documents. His World War I Draft Registration Card listed him as a resident of Chicago and single who was short with medium build and brown hair and brown eyes. Sometime after the birth of his eldest son David in Chicago in 1923 Addison Evans moved to Glendale, California where his second son Gerald was born in 1927. Mr. Evans resided at 321 Chester Street in Glendale with his wife and sons David and Gerald in 1930 where he owned a wholesale jewelry business. The 1940 US Census recorded the Evans family still residing in Glendale but at 1824 Crestmont Court. A third son, Forrest, was born in 1935.

Addison Evans World War II Draft Registration Card described him as being 5'5 ½ "tall with a ruddy complexion, brown eyes and balding with gray hair. Addison Ross Evans died five years later. The cause is not known. Camilla Evans remarried twice more after Addison's death. On August 13, 1955 Camilla Evans married Archie McWilliams. In Riverside, California on August 22, 1977 she married a third time to Raymond Fulcher. When Camilla Mihm Evans McWilliams Fulcher died in 1997, she was almost 100 years of age. It is not known where Addison and Camilla Evans were buried.

Children:

473. I. ***Addison David Evans, f.***

474. II. ***Gerald Ross Evans,*** b. Los Angeles, California May 26, 1927; ***nfi.***

475. II. ***Forrest Bruce Evans,*** b. Los Angeles, California April 17, 1935, d. Clovis, California August 17, 2019; ***nfi.***

References: US Census: 1900, 1910, 1930, 1940; Cook County Marriage Index 1912-1942; Cook County, Illinois Birth Certificate Index 1871-1922 for Addison Evans and Camilla Mihm; World War I Draft Registration Card 1917-1918; World War II Draft Registration Card, 1942; California Marriage Index 1949-1997 for Camilla Evans' second and third marriages; California Death Index 1940-1997 for Addison and Camilla Evans; Boice Funeral Home, Clovis, California for Forrest Bruce Evans.

226.

Gerald Fred Hulbert, son of Emma (104), grandson of Elizabeth (50), b. Bolivar, New York February 25, 1886, d. Allentown, Pennsylvania June 2, 1939 from a cerebral hemorrhage; m. Angelica, New York April 18, 1906 Viola Maude Blauvelt, b. Angelica, New York November 1, 1882, d. Bethlehem, Pennsylvania June 21, 1959 from breast cancer.

Gerald Hulbert resided with his parents in Bolivar, New York until about 1903 where he was employed by the Pittsburgh, Shawmut, and Northern Railroad. After his marriage Mr. Hulbert moved to St. Mary's,

Pennsylvania residing at 356 Chestnut Street in that community employed as a telegraph operator in 1910. His World War I Draft Registration Card described him as short, stout with blue eyes and dark hair. By 1920 Mr. Hulbert had moved his family to Bethlehem, Pennsylvania where he was employed as a railroad dispatcher for the Leigh and New England Railroad. The family resided at 536 N. Maple Street in Bethlehem. Gerald and Maude Hulbert moved to 652 Lorraine Avenue in Bethlehem by the 1930 US Census where he worked as a train dispatcher until his unexpected death in 1939. Mr. Hulbert was a member of St. Mary's Lodge F. and A. M., Zinzendorf Chapter R. A. M. as Past Commander, Master of the Bethlehem Council No. 36 R. S, Past Commander of Bethlehem Commandery, Knight's Templars advisory council, Wilbur Chapter of the DeMolay, and Chairman of Past Commanders and Line Officers Association. Maude Hulbert died twenty years later from breast cancer. Gerald and Maude Hulbert were buried in Memorial Park Cemetery in Bethlehem, Pennsylvania.

Children:

476. I. ***Yale Malcolm Hulbert, f.***

477. II. ***Geraldine Virginia Hulbert, f.***

478. III. ***Frederick Waldo Hulbert, f.***

References: US Census: 1900, 1910, 1920, 1930, 1940; New York State Census: 1892; NYS Marriage Index 1881-1967; World War I Draft Registration Card 1917-18; Memorial Park Cemetery Records, Bethlehem, Pennsylvania; Pennsylvania Death Certificates 1906-1964.

227.

Wayne Christopher Hulbert, son of Emma (104), grandson of Elizabeth (50), b. Bolivar, New York July 29, 1891, d. Clintonville, Pennsylvania June 12, 1924 from a nitroglycerine explosion; m. (1) Bolivar, New York November 21, 1911 Nettie Williams, b. Millport, Pennsylvania October 1893, death place and date of death not known, divorced Belmont, New York October 23, 1923; m. (2) Little Genesee, New York February 16, 1924 Emily or Emma Elizabeth Bailey, birth place not known, b. a. 1903, death place and death date not known.

Wayne Hulbert resided with his parents in Bolivar working odd jobs as a laborer. Prior to his marriage to Nettie Williams, Wayne Hulbert enlisted June 21, 1911 in Brockport, New York with the New York State National Guard. Nettie Williams was the daughter of Riley Williams and Florence Cook Williams of Bolivar, New York. In 1915 Wayne and Nettie Hulbert resided next door to his parents on Wellsville Street in Bolivar. Mr. Hulbert's World War I Draft Registration Card for 1917 described him as tall and slender with light hair and blue eyes. Wayne worked for American Glycerin. From September 29, 1918 to July 23, 1919 Mr. Hulbert worked with the Supply Company 56 Pioneer Infantry sailing on the

Leviathan for Europe and was reassigned to Company H of the 49th Infantry Division.

By 1920 Mr. and Mrs. Hulbert had moved to Olean, New York where he was employed as a machinist. They resided at 515 Lincoln Avenue. *The Bolivar Breeze* wrote that Wayne Hulbert had moved to Detroit, Michigan in April 1923. However, he returned to Bolivar and filed for a divorce, which was granted October 11, 1923 by Judge Charles H. Brown in Belmont, New York. Mr. Hulbert remarried in Little Genesee at the Seventh Day Baptist Church on February 14, 1924 to Emily Bailey, daughter of Edward and Julia Bailey from Jasper, New York. The newly married couple moved to Clintonville, Pennsylvania where he was employed with the Pease Agency as an oil well shooter. On June 12, 1924, an unexplained nitroglycerin explosion at a magazine at Brandon's Ferry just south of Franklin, Pennsylvania occurred killing Wayne Hulbert. Earlier on May 6, 1924 at the same site a nitroglycerin explosion caused the destruction of a factory and other property. Mr. Hulbert's remains were returned to Bolivar for burial in Maple Lawn Cemetery. Emily Hulbert was employed as a servant for George Bradley of Bolivar in 1930 and after that date there is no further information about her. There is no current information on the burial's sites for either Nettie Williams Hulbert or Emily Bailey Hulbert. There were no children from either marriage.

References: US Census: 1900, 1910, 1920, 1930; New York State Census: 1892, 1905, 1915; *Bolivar Breeze 1891-1965*, selected issues; World War I Draft Registration Card 1917-1918; New York Abstracts of World War I Military Service 1917-1919; NYS County Marriage Records 1847-1949 and 1907-1936; Pennsylvania Death Certificate 1906-1964 for Wayne C. Hulbert; Maple Lawn Cemetery Records, Bolivar, New York.

228.

Elba William Hulbert, son of Emma (104), grandson of Elizabeth (50), b. Bolivar, New York July 27, 1895, d. Bolivar, New York May 7, 1950 from a heart attack; m. Belmont, New York June 30, 1921 Helen Elizabeth Ward, b. Belmont, New York April 1, 1897, d. Wellsville, New York December 3, 1975.

Elba Hulbert was a lifelong resident of Bolivar, New York except for his participation in World War I where he saw action in France. Mr. Hulbert enlisted May 26, 1918 in Belmont, New York and was sent overseas August 24, 1918 until he was mustered out January 21, 1919. He served as a private in Company L, 345th Infantry Division. Elba Hulbert was described as being of medium height and medium build with blue eyes and light hair. After the war Elba Hulbert was employed as an oil well driller in the Bolivar and Richburg, New York oil fields. He resided with his parents at 97 Wellsville Street. The home had been purchased by Christopher Garthwait in 1883 for his daughter, Emma Garthwait Hulbert, and son-in-law Fred Hulbert, Elba's parents. Helen Ward Hulbert was the daughter of Mathias I. Ward (1861-1945) and Margaret Madden Ward (1863-1910) of Belmont, New York.

Helen was employed as a school teacher for the Penfield, Friendship, and Bolivar, New York school systems for a total of eighteen years. Elba and Helen Hulbert later resided at 520 North Main Street until he later purchased his parent's home after their deaths, buying out the interests of his sister and surviving brother. Elba Hulbert's World War II Draft Registration Card noted his height as 5' 5 ½ "tall weighing 200 pounds with blue eyes and blonde hair. In 1942 Mr. Hulbert was employed by Chipman and Holcomb of Bolivar, New York. Elba Hulbert was an active member of the Bolivar, New York Fire Department, a charter member of the Kenyon-Andrus Post of the American Legion in Bolivar, the Olean, New York Lodge of Moose, and the Olean Post of the Veterans of Foreign Wars. Helen Ward Hulbert was engaged in genealogical research on the descendants of Truman Bishop Root, her husband's maternal great-grandfather. Her notes were most helpful in adding more detailed descriptions for descendants of Truman Bishop Root. Elba and Helen Hulbert were buried in St. Mary's Cemetery in Bolivar, New York.

Children:

479. I. ***Gerald Ward Hulbert, f.***

480. II. ***Margaret Elizabeth Hulbert, f.***

481. III. ***James William Hulbert, f.***

482. IV. ***John Matthew Hulbert, f.***

References: US Census: 1900, 1910, 1920, 1930, 1940; New York State Census: 1905, 1915, 1925; World War I Draft Registration Card 1917-18; New York Abstracts Overseas Military Service 1917-1919; World War II Draft Registration Card, 1942; NY County Marriage Index 1847-9 and 1907-36; St. Mary's Cemetery Records, Bolivar, New York; *Bolivar Breeze 1891-1965*, selected issues; Unpublished genealogical history of the Hulbert and Root families by Helen Ward Hulbert.

229.

Leta Elizabeth Hulbert, daughter of Emma (104), and granddaughter of Elizabeth (50), b. Bolivar, New York March 23, 1898, d. St. Francis Hospital Olean, New York February 5, 1975 from pulmonary edema caused by heart disease; m. Bolivar, New York January 20, 1923 Willis Stewart Irvin, b. Angelica, New York February 17, 1899, d, Greenwood, New York September 9, 1956 while returning from the baptism of his grandson in Elmira, New York from a heart attack.

Leta Hulbert resided with her parents in Bolivar until her 1920 marriage. Leta and Willis Irvin's marriage date was also the birth date (January 20, 1923) of their son, Stewart Irvin. Leta was a graduate of the Ithaca Conservatory of Music at Ithaca College in Ithaca, New York. She gave piano lessons at her home in Bolivar and played the organ in the local churches for years. Many a Bolivar wedding reported in the *Bolivar Breeze* listed Leta as the organist. Willis Irvin was the son of Isaac Irvin (1860-1930) and Matilda Umplby (1868-1924) of Angelica, New York. Mr. Irvin enlisted October 13, 1917 with Company A of the 4th Infantry New York Guards. His World War I Draft Registration Card noted that he worked for the Pittsburg, Shawmut, and Northern Railroad as a clerk. Mr. Irvin had blue eyes, black hair and was of medium build and weight. The Irvins lived in Angelica, New York as recorded on the 1925 New York State Census with his father where he worked for a funeral company. In 1930 Leta, Willis, and their two children resided in Belmont, New York where Mr. Irvin was employed as a salesman. They moved to Bolivar after the death of Mr. Irvin's father in 1930 where Willis Irvin was employed in the local oil fields until his unexpected and sudden death while a passenger in a car returning from the baptism of a grandchild in Elmira, New York. Leta and Willis Irvin were buried in Maple Lawn Cemetery in Bolivar, New York.

Children:

483. I. ***Stewart Buffington Irvin, Sr., f.***

484. II. ***Naomi Eileen Irvin, f.***

References: US Census: 1900, 1910, 1930, 1940; New York State Census: 1905, 1915, 1925; NYS County Marriage Index 1847-1849 and 1907-1936; Social Security Death Index 1935-2014; World War I Draft Registration Card 1917-1918; New York Guard Service Cards 1906-1918 and 1940-1948; Maple Lawn Cemetery Records, Bolivar, New York; *The Bolivar Breeze 1891-1965*, selected issues.

230.

Glen Elmer Garthwait, son of Elmer (105), grandson of Elizabeth (50), b. Bolivar, New York February 22, 1890, d. Bolivar, New York October 2, 1916 from a general nervous breakdown after a nine-month illness.

Glen Garthwait was an accomplished vocalist and violinist. His name can be found in many issues of the *Bolivar Breeze* noting his performances for churches, school groups, and community music organizations. Mr. Garthwait was a former choir director for the Bolivar Methodist Church. In 1910 Glen Garthwait was employed as a bookkeeper for the State Bank of Bolivar where his grandfather was the President. He was also a member of the board for the Garthwait Oil Company. Glen held memberships in the Bolivar Macedonia Lodge No. 258 F. & A. M. and the Bolivar Chapter No. 280 R. A. M. In July 1915 Glen Garthwait suffered an episode of blood poisoning from which he seemed to recover and he returned to work at the State Bank of Bolivar. However, his health was never the same. By February of 1916 his parents took Glen to St. Petersburg, Florida for treatment for a general nervous breakdown. The warmer climate did not improve his health and on September 17, 1916, Glen was taken to a sanitarium in Battle Creek, Michigan for additional treatment.

With no improvement Glen Garthwait and his parents returned to Bolivar where his condition grew worse and he died a week later at the family home. Glen Garthwait's obituaries record how popular he was with friends and the Bolivar community. His funeral was the largest in Bolivar's history with forty-five cars following the hearse to Maple Lawn Cemetery for burial. The Garthwait mausoleum was constructed after Glen Garthwait's death to house his remains and eventually the remains of his paternal grandparents, and his parents. The iron fences and concrete archways at each entrance of Maple Lawn Cemetery were installed in his memory by his parents.

References: US Census: 1900, 1910; New York State Census: 1892, 1905, 1915; Maple Lawn Cemetery Records, Bolivar, New York; NYS Death Index 1852-1956; *Bolivar Breeze 1891-1965,* selected issues.

231.

Wade Root Mitchell, son of Addie (106), grandson of Bryant Hebron (52), b. Bradford, Pennsylvania November 24, 1895, d. Sun City, Arizona March 1976; m. Chicago, Illinois June 30, 1925 Ruth L. Swanson, b. Illinois August 22, 1900, d. Tucson, Arizona January 24, 1998.

Wade Mitchell resided with his parents in Bradford, Pennsylvania, Oregon, Ohio, and Wellsville, New York until his move to Chicago, Illinois in the early 1920s. Mr. Mitchell cannot be found on the 1920 US Census. His World War I Draft Registration Card described him as 6' tall, weighing 145 pounds, with blue eyes and light hair. In 1917 Wade Mitchell worked as a timekeeper for the Illinois Steel Company in Gary, Indiana. He served with the US Army during World War I from November 3, 1917 to May 29, 1919. Mr. Mitchell married Ruth L. Swanson of Chicago, Illinois on June 30, 1926. Ruth Swanson was the daughter of Gustave and Lina Swanson. Wade's brother, Dean McMillan, married Viola J. Swanson two days later who was the daughter of Gustave F. Swanson and Alma Sandable Swanson. It is not known if the two women were related. In 1940 Wade, his wife, mother, brother, sister-in-law, and father-in-law all resided together in Chicago at 9201 S. Claremont Street. His employer was Lyon Metal Products of Chicago. Mr. Mitchell's World War II Draft Registration Card noted his weight had increased to 180 pounds and his hair color was listed as brown. After World War II the Mitchell family moved to San Mateo, California based on the San Mateo City Directory for that year. In 1955 the Mitchells had relocated to Redwood City, California. In California he was employed as a field engineer. Upon retirement Wade and Ruth Mitchell moved to Arizona where both died. It is not currently known where they are buried. There were no known children.

References: US Census: 1900, 1910, 1930, 1940; New York State Census: 1905, 1915; World War I Draft Registration Card 1917-18; World War II Draft Registration Card, 1942; Social Security Death Index 1935-2014; San Mateo and Redwood, California City Directories; US Evangelical Lutheran Church in America, Swedish American Church Records 1800-1946 for marriage.

232.

Dean McMillan Mitchell, son of Addie (106), grandson of Bryant Hebron (52), b. Toledo, Ohio December 30, 1898, d. place of death and date of death not known; m. Chicago, Illinois July 2, 1926

Viola Julia Swanson, b. Illinois September 6, 1900, d. Sun City, Arizona November 1987.

Dean Mitchell resided with his parents in Oregon, Ohio and Wellsville, New York. His World War I Draft Registration Card noted that he worked as a clerk for Garwood Shoe Company in Wellsville residing on Maple Avenue. Mr. Mitchell was described as tall and slender with blue eyes and light hair. As a student at Alfred University he joined the student Army Training Program on October 1, 1918. He saw no overseas action and was discharged December 10, 1918. In 1920 Dean Mitchell had moved to Akron, Ohio where he was employed as a clerk for a rubber shop. He moved to Chicago where his older brother, Wade, resided and in 1926 married.

The 1930 US Census recorded that Dean, his wife, Viola, resided in Chicago with his father-in-law and where he worked as an accountant. In the 1940 US Census Dean and his wife lived with his brother, sister-in-law, mother, and his or his brother's father-in-law at 9201 Claremont Street in Chicago. Dean Mitchell was employed as a civil service accountant. In the mid-1950s Dean and Viola Mitchell moved to Redwood City, California where they resided with his brother, sister-in-law, and mother. It is not known when Dean Mitchell died or where he was buried. There is no Social Security Death Index document for him. His death is sometimes incorrectly given as June 3, 1969, but that person was Dean Eugene Mitchell, not Dean McMillan Mitchell. Viola Mitchell died in Arizona but there is no record for a burial location. Dean and Viola Mitchell did not have any children.

References: US Census: 1900, 1910, 1920, 1930, 1940; New York State Census: 1905, 1915; World War I Draft Registration Card 1917-18; New York Abstracts of World War I Military Service 1917-1919; Ohio Birth Records Index 1774-1973 for Dean Mitchell; US Evangelical Lutheran Church in America Swedish American Church Records 1800-1946 for marriage; Redwood City, California City Directories for 1956 and 1957; Social Security Death Index for Viola Mitchell.

233.

Neil Alonzo Crandall, son of Erwin (110), grandson of Arzulla (53), b. Bolivar, New York March 28 1897, d. Oriskany, New York June 23, 1952; m. Bolivar, New York May 10, 1919 Alice Amelia Ingalls, b. New York State August 12, 1901, d. probably New Hampshire December 8, 1987.

Neil Crandall's middle name was the first name of his paternal grandfather Alonzo Crandall. Mr. Crandall's World War I Draft Registration Card noted that he was employed by his father in the oil industry, was slender with medium build and had blue eyes and brown hair. Neil served in the military from July 24, 1918 to November 11, 1918 at the Naval Training Station at Great Lakes, Illinois where he was employed as a landsman machinist. He resided with his parents until his 1919 marriage. In December 1920 Mr. Crandall was involved in an automobile accident in front of the State Bank of Bolivar that resulted in the death of Mrs. A. C. McDonnell. The extreme weather conditions contributed to the car crash. Neil and Alice Crandall lived on South Main Street in Bolivar. Neil was employed as an oil well driller. The 1930 US Census found the Crandalls residing at 120 Main Street, employed as an oil driller with a daughter. Mr. Crandall was a member of Bolivar's Macedonia Lodge # 258 F. and A. M. By 1935 the Crandall family had moved to Camden, New York and in 1940 to Whitestown, New York. In 1948 Oriskany, New York was their place of residence. Alice Ingalls was the daughter of Phyletus Ingalls (1870-1930) and Bertha Richardson Ingalls (1874-1919) of Bolivar, New York. After Neil Crandalls' death Alice moved to New Hampshire residing with her daughter in Swenson, New Hampshire until her death. Neil and Alice Crandall were buried in Maple Lawn Cemetery in Bolivar, New York.

Children:

485. I. ***Marie Mae Crandall, f.***

References: US Census: 1900, 1910, 1920, 1930, 1940; New York State Census: 1905, 1915, 1925; New York County Marriages 1847-9 and 1907-1936; NYS Death Index 1852-1956 for Neil Crandall; New York State Abstracts for World War I Military Service 1917-1919; World War I Draft Registration Card 1917-1918; Maple Lawn Cemetery Records, Bolivar, New York; *Bolivar Breeze 1891-1965*, selected issues.

234.

Harley Erwin Crandall, son of Erwin (110), grandson of Arzulla (53), b. Bolivar, New York May 22, 1899, d. Black Creek, New York January 31, 1993; m. (1) Olean, New York November 10, 1925 Hazel Lavina Wells, b. Ceres, Pennsylvania September 20, 1900, d. McKean County, Pennsylvania April 1, 1990, divorced March 1959; m. (2) Citrus, Florida February 12, 1960 Lillian Anna Wilkinson, b. Odessa, New York January 14, 1911, d. Odessa, New York November 1987.

Harley Crandall resided with his parents on Foreman Hollow Road in Bolivar, New York working for his father as an oil well pumper. He served briefly in the US Army from October 1, 1918 to December 10, 1918. His World War I Draft Registration Card noted that he worked for Al Shaner of Bolivar in the oil fields. He was of medium height and medium build with blue eyes and brown hair. Mr. Crandall was a student at Alfred University and entered military service through Alfred University's student army training program. After Harley's marriage to his first wife, the family resided at 209 Olive Street in Bolivar working as a tool dresser. Harley and Hazel Crandall seem to have gone through periods of separation after their residence in Hammondsport, New York in 1935.

The 1940 US Census recorded Hazel residing with their son Roy at 658 Garden Avenue in Olean, New York. In 1947 Hazel lived in Elyria, Ohio and returned to Olean by 1950. She was the daughter of Ralph B. Wells (1869-1951) and Edith Sikes Wells (1879-1970) of McKean County, Pennsylvania. After their divorce both Harley and Hazel Crandall remarried. Hazel remarried to a Mr. Jonak and Harley to Lillian Wilkinson. In 1960 Harley and Lillian Crandall resided in Brooksville, Florida, but later moved back to Odessa, New York where Lillian Crandall was from. Harley and Lillian Crandall were buried in Highland Cemetery in Odessa, New York. Hazel Wells Crandall Jonak was buried with her parents in Bell Run Cemetery in McKean County, Pennsylvania.

Children (by first marriage):

486. I. ***Roy Stephen Crandall, f.***

487. II. ***Constance or Connie Crandall, f.***

References: US Census: 1900, 1910, 1920, 1930, 1940; New York State Census: 1905, 1915, 1925; Highland Cemetery Records, Odessa, New York; Bell Run Cemetery Records, McKean County, Pennsylvania; Florida Divorce Index, March 1959; Florida Marriage Index 1823-1982 for Harley Crandall's second marriage; World War I Draft Registration Card 1917-18; US Department of Veterans Affairs 1850-2010; Social Security Death Index 1935-2014; Selected City Directories for Olean, New York and Elyria, Ohio.

235.

Roy Stephen Crandall, son of Erwin (110), grandson of Arzulla (53), b. Bolivar, New York April 20, 1902, d. Bolivar, New York March 26, 1918. Roy Crandall resided with his parents in Bolivar until his death in 1918.

Roy Crandall was accidentally killed while at work because a tree cut to fall in an easterly direction by Sherman June struck another tree sending the cut tree in a southerly direction. Roy was working with his brother Neil Crandall on an oil well being drilled on the Shaner lease and was hauling wood to the site. Fearing the tree would fall on his horses, Roy Crandall stepped in front of his horses, failed to hear the shouts to get out of the way of the falling tree, and the tree fell on him breaking his back. Roy Stephen Crandall was buried in Maple Lawn Cemetery in Bolivar.

References: US Census: 1910; New York State Census: 1905, 1915; Maple Lawn Cemetery Records, Bolivar, New York; *Bolivar Breeze*, March 28, 1918; NYS Death Index 1852-1956.

236.

Ralph Merrill Crandall, son of Erwin (110), grandson of Arzulla (53), b. Bolivar, New York December 20, 1906, d. Erie, Pennsylvania January 10, 1954 by suicide; m. Portville, New York May 12, 1928 Ruth Irene Susanna Klein, b. Lincoln, Iowa June 5, 1909, d. Olean, New York September 19, 1987.

Ralph Crandall resided with his parents on Foreman Hollow Road in Bolivar, New York. He was employed as a tool driller until his marriage in 1928. The 1930 US Census recorded his residence in Bolivar at 77 Olive Street with his wife and son, Theodore. He was employed as an oil well driller. In the mid-1930s the Crandall family resided in Penn Yan, New York where their youngest son was born. By 1940 the Crandall family had moved to Galeton, Pennsylvania living at 33 School Street. The Crandalls had three sons: Theodore, Merle, and Neil. Mr. Crandall was a contractor drilling water and oil wells.

His World War II Draft Registration Card described Ralph Crandall as being 5'10" tall, weighing 182 pounds with blue eyes and brown hair. In 1942 the Crandalls returned to Bolivar residing on Daggett Hollow Road near Little Genesee. In 1949 Ralph Crandall and his family moved to Titusville, Pennsylvania where he was employed as an oil producer. Ralph Crandall's death certificate indicated he had committed suicide while his obituary said he died after a short illness. Mr. Crandall was a member of Bolivar's Macedonia Lodge # 258. Ruth Crandall moved to Olean, New York after her husband's death where she was employed as an inspector for Ka-Bar, Inc. Mrs. Crandall died in Olean in 1987. Ralph and Ruth Crandall were buried in Maple Lawn Cemetery in Bolivar, New York.

Children:

488. I. ***Theodore Erwin Crandall, f.***

489. II. ***Merle Ralph Crandall, f.***

490. III. ***Neil R. Crandall, f.***

References: US Census: 1910, 1920, 1930, 1940; New York State Census: 1915, 1925; World War II Draft Registration Card 1940-1947; Pennsylvania Death Certificate 1906-1966 for Ralph M. Crandall; Maple Lawn Cemetery Records, Bolivar, New York; *Bolivar Breeze 1891-1965*, selected issues; Iowa Births and Christenings 1800-1999 for Ruth Klein; NY County Marriage Record 1847-9 and 1907-1936; Olean, New York City Directories, selected issues; Social Security Death Index 1935-2014.

238.

Clarence Wayne Crandall, son of Erwin (110), grandson of Arzulla (53), b. Bolivar, New York June 23, 1914, d. Pine City, New York January 10, 1983; m. Bolivar, New York October 11, 1934 Jennie Marie Hoxie, b. Little Genesee, New York March 28, 1913, d. Pine City, New York January 11, 2016, aged 102 years.

Clarence Crandall resided in Bolivar, New York with his parents until his 1934 marriage. In 1932 Mr. Crandall was elected Steward of the Bolivar Grange. Clarence and Jennie Crandall resided at 63 Foreman Hollow Road until September 1938 when they moved to Rome, New York for employment opportunities. By the 1950s the Crandall family moved to Pine City, New York. Clarence Crandall was employed in nearby Elmira, New York as a salesman selling water heaters and where he owned and operated a water well drilling business. Jennie Hoxie Crandall lived to be 102 years of age. She was an avid reader of books and did daily crossword puzzles. Mrs. Crandall enjoyed needlecrafts and made quilts, hooked rugs, and crochet items. She was famous for her *Jennie Cake*. Jennie's obituary described her as a gentle and optimistic person who had a core of inner strength. She was a member of the Zuleika Temple of the Daughters of the Nile and the Chemung Valley Old Timer's Association. Clarence and Jennie Crandall were buried in Forest Lawn Memorial Park in Pine City, New York.

Children:

491. I. ***Judith A. Crandall,*** b. a. 1940, ***nfi.***

492. II. ***Steven A. Crandall,*** b. New York State December 2, 1946, ***nfi.***

References: US Census: 1920, 1930; New York State Census: 1915, 1925; Social Security Death Index 1935-2014; Forest Lawn Memorial Park Cemetery Records, Pine City, New York; NY County Marriage Records 1847-9 and 1907-1936; Elmira, New York City Directories, selected issues; 2016 Newspaper Obituary for Jennie Crandall.

239.

Paul Milton Crandall, son of Owen (111), grandson of Arzulla (53), b. Bolivar, New York September 14, 1899, d. Bolivar, New York April 17, 1973; m. Bolivar, New York May 12, 1932 Hazel Grace Gadsby, b. Shinglehouse, Pennsylvania 1912, d. Springville, Alabama April 1, 2011.

Paul Crandall resided with his parents until his 1932 marriage. Paul and Hazel Crandall resided on the Bolivar-Little Genesee Road (Route 417) where he was employed as an oil well pumper. His 1917 World War I Draft Registration Card described Paul Crandall as tall and stout with blue eyes and brown hair. In 1917 he worked his father's farm. Hazel Gadsby Crandall was the daughter of John Henry Gadsby (1875-1948) and Myrna Grace Swarthout Gadsby (1877-1963) of Shinglehouse, Pennsylvania. Hazel Crandall was almost 99 years old when she died at the home of her daughter Lois Crandall Turybury in Alabama. Hazel Crandall's obituary described her as a warm, gentle, humorous, and a caring spirit whose memory remained in the hearts of all she touched. Paul and Hazel Crandall were buried in Maple Lawn Cemetery in Bolivar, New York.

Children:

493. I. ***Lois Jean Crandall, f.***

494. II. ***Pauline Ann Crandall, f.***

495. III. ***Charlotte Grace Crandall, f.***

496. IV. ***Erma Crandall, nfi.***

497. V. ***Elaine Crandall, f.***

References: US Census: 1900, 1910, 1920, 1930, 1940; New York State Census: 1905, 1915, 1925; NY County Marriage Index 1847-1849 and 1907-1936; Social Security Death Index 1935-2014; Maple Lawn Cemetery Records, Bolivar, New York; *Bolivar Breeze, 1891-1965*, selected issues.

240.

Ruth Crandall, daughter of Owen (111), granddaughter of Arzulla (53), b. Bolivar, New York December 18, 1903, d. Shinglehouse, Pennsylvania February 1983; m. Angelica, New York January 20, 1926 Adrian Allen Quick, b. Alma/Wellsville, New York October 2, 1889/1890, d. Columbus Hospital, Buffalo, New York June 30, 1963 after a long illness.

Ruth Crandall resided with her parents until her marriage in 1926. No middle name could be found for her. Adrian Quick was employed in the local oil fields for most of his life. In 1917 his World War I Draft Registration Card listed his employer as Frank Miller of Bolivar for whom he worked as an oil rig builder. Mr. Quick's World War II Draft Registration Card stated that he worked for Clarence Busch in the Bradford, Pennsylvania oil fields. Adrian Quick was described as 5'10" tall, weighed 145 pounds, had a ruddy complexion with blue eyes and black hair. In June of 1926 Adrian Quick suffered severe burns when an oil lamp he was lighting in the Bradford, Pennsylvania oil fields exploded. Adrian Quick was the son of Benjamin Quick (1827-1908) and Alice Mesler Quick (1851-1928) of Alma, New York. Mr. Quick was previously married to Hazel Drake on October 15, 1913 of Bolivar.

Hazel Quick died in Bolivar February 29, 1920 from pneumonia. Adrian and Hazel Quick had one daughter, Gertrude (1915-1952) who married Anson L. Knapp (1903-1962). Ruth and Adrian Quick resided at 434 Main Street in Bolivar based on the 1930 US Census. In 1942 Ruth and Adrian lived at 64 Plum Street in Bolivar. They had nine children, two of whom died in infancy. Hazel Drake Quick was buried in Maple Lawn Cemetery in Bolivar, New York as was Adrian Quick.

Ruth Crandall Quick was buried in Shinglehouse, Pennsylvania in Maple Grove Cemetery. Maple Lawn Cemetery records indicate a burial place was planned for Ruth Crandall next to her husband, but the circumstances leading to her burial in Shinglehouse are not known. Ruth Quick's tombstone remembers her as a loving mother and grandmother, but nothing was recorded about her husband.

Children:

498. I. ***Bertha Lois Quick***, b. Bradford, Pennsylvania June 17, 1927, d. Bradford, Pennsylvania December 26, 1927. Her death certificate listed her as a "blue baby." She was buried in Maple Lawn Cemetery in Bolivar, New York.

499. II. ***Jennie Beatrice Quick, f.***

500. III. ***Adrian Allen Quick, Jr., f.***

501. IV. ***Arlene Marie Quick, f.***

502. V. ***Wayne LeRoy Quick, f.***

503. VI. ***Ernest Henry Quick, f.***

504. VII. ***Elnora M. Quick, f.***

505. VIII. ***Rosemary Quick, f.***

506. IX. ***Margaret Ann Quick,*** b. Bolivar, New York March 8, 1945, d. Bolivar, New York December 26, 1945. It is believed she was buried in Maple Lawn Cemetery in Bolivar, New York, but no record can be located for her burial.

References: US Census: 1900, 1910, 1920, 1930, 1940; New York State Census: 1905, 1915, 1925; World War I Draft Registration Card, 1917-18; World War II Draft Registration Card, 1942; NY County Marriage Index 1847-49 and 1907-1936 for both of Adrian Quick's marriages; Social Security Death Index 1935-2014 for Adrian and Ruth Quick; *Bolivar Breeze 1891-1965*, selected issues; Maple Lawn Cemetery Records, Bolivar, New York; Maple Grove Cemetery Records, Shinglehouse, Pennsylvania; NYS Birth Index 1881-1942.

242.

Helma Virginia Crandall, daughter of Owen (111), granddaughter of Arzulla (53), b. Bolivar, New York May 7, 1916, d. Bangor, Maine August 3, 1991; m. (1) Bolivar, New York July 27, 1935 Hollis Earl Crandall, b. Bolivar, New York March 13, 1912, d. Bolivar, New York January 1977; m. (2) Bangor, Maine December 24, 1984 Leonard Arthur D'Amboise, b. Millinocket, Maine July 30, 1913, d. East Millinocket, Maine January 12, 1999.

Helma Crandall resided with her parents in Bolivar until her marriage in 1935. Hollis Crandall was the son of Claude Crandall (1886-1966) and Mary Hardy Crandall (1888-1965) who resided in Shinglehouse, Pennsylvania and later Alma, New York. Helman and Hollis were distant cousins. Upon their marriage Helma and Hollis Crandall resided in Scio, New York where he was employed as a well tester and driller. They had one child, a daughter Marilyn. Upon the death of Hollis, Helma relocated to Maine to be near her daughter and her daughter's family. It was in Maine that Helma met Leonard D'Amboise whom she later married. Upon her death Helma was buried with her first husband in Fairlawn Cemetery in Scio, New York. Leonard D'Amboise was buried in Mt. Pleasant Catholic Cemetery in Bangor, Maine with his first wife, Elizabeth Appleton D'Amboise who died in 1973.

Children (by first marriage):

507. I. ***Marilyn Ann Crandall, f.***

References: US Census: 1920, 1930, 1940; New York State Census: 1925; NY Birth Index 1881-1942; Social Death Index 1935-2014; NYS Marriage Index 1881-1967 for Helma and Hollis Crandall marriage; Maine Marriage Index 1892-1996 for marriage of Helma Crandall and Leonard D'Amboise; Maine Birth Records 1715-1972 for Leonard D'Amboise; Fairlawn Cemetery Records, Scio, New York; Mt. Pleasant Catholic Cemetery Records, Bangor, Maine.

243.

Helen Prentice Root, daughter of Asa P. (113), granddaughter of Erastus (54), b. Wellsville, New York June 17, 1913, d. Wellsville, New York August 25, 1992; m. Wellsville, New York November 21, 1936 William Whitton Spargur, b. Wellsville, New York June 5, 1911, d. Wellsville, New York December 6, 1966 from amyotrophic lateral sclerosis.

Helen or *Peg* Root Spargur resided with her parents in Bolivar until her marriage. Helen was a warm, charming and attractive women with a keen business sense and a special zest for enjoying life. She was a tremendous help in providing photographs, family documents, and correspondence along with her memories of family for the 1990 published history of the Root family. Peg Root attended Bolivar High School, graduated from Olean High School and studied at Penn Hall Junior College in Chambersburg, Pennsylvania, Chevy Chase College in Washington, DC, and Alfred University, Alfred, New York. She was employed by the Allegany Oil Refinery in Bolivar until her 1938 marriage. While married she worked on a part-time basis at Wellsville, New York's Kiddie Corner Shop. One curious family story Peg Spargur related occurred when she was in elementary school. A heavily veiled woman dressed all in black came to the school and requested possession of Peg allegedly at the request of Peg's father. Fortunately, the school refused, called Asa Root, and learned that Mr. Root had not sent this strange woman to the school. The woman disappeared when the school refused to give Peg to her. Later Peg Spargur thought the woman in black might have been her grandfather's third wife, Cora Root who had lost a daughter in 1912 and may have never recovered from the child's loss.

William W. Spargur was the son of William Folwell Spargur, M.D. (1873-1943) and Bertha Mae Sanders Spargur (1883-1960) of Wellsville, New York. He was employed as an accountant at the Sinclair Refining Company until it closed in 1959. Mr. Spargur later took a position with the Air Preheater Corporation in Wellsville. He was both secretary and treasurer for the Congregational Church and the Wellsville Country Club. William Spargur was a Past Master of the Masonic Blue Lodge. In his leisure time he developed special interests in refinishing and upholstering furniture.

Peg was also a member of the Wellsville Country Club, the Friends of the David A. Howe Library, and the Library Art Association. Mrs. Spargur was a member of the First Congregational Church in

Wellsville and Beta Sigma Phi Sorority in Wellsville, Pi Alpha Sorority in Alfred, New York, and in Green Valley, Arizona the Green Valley Presbyterian Church, Green Valley Women's Club, and the Green Valley Lady Elks. After Mr. Spargur's death, Peg worked as a legal secretary for ten years for Wellsville attorney Wayne Feeman. After her retirement in 1977, Peg Spargur resided part of each year in Green Valley, Arizona and the remainder of the year in Wellsville. Helen Spargur battled cancer as did her mother and some of her daughters. Peg and William Spargur were buried in Woodlawn Cemetery in Wellsville, New York. A special friend, Chester Whorton, predeceased her in 1991.

Children:

508. I. ***Helen Joan Spargur, f.***

509. II. ***Judith Anne Spargur, f.***

510. III. ***Mary Jane Spargur, f.***

References: US Census: 1920, 1930, 1940; New York State Census: 1915, 1925; NYS Birth Index 1881-1942; Social Security Death Index 1935-2014; Interviews with Helen Root Spargur; Woodlawn Cemetery Records, Wellsville, New York; *Bolivar Breeze 1891-1965*, selected issues; New York State Marriage Index 1881-1967; *Wellsville Daily Reporter* August 26, 1992 obituary; correspondence with the late Helen Root Spargur March 4, 1980, May 20, 1980, May 23, 1980, February 9, 1981, August 20, 1982, October 15, 1982, August 25, 1990, September 20, 1990, and March 8, 1991.

244.

Maxine Sevilla Wilcox, daughter of Leon (119), granddaughter of Charlotte (55), b. Brockway, Pennsylvania January 26, 1909, d. Bradford, Pennsylvania June 10, 1953; m. place and date of marriage not known Clarence Albert Honadle, b. Brookville, Pennsylvania January 19, 1901, d. Alden, New York July 1979.

Maxine resided with her parents until her marriage. She and her husband resided in Brookville and Brockway, Pennsylvania and later in San Francisco before returning to Pennsylvania and taking up residence in Bradford, Pennsylvania. Maxine Honadle was found unconscious at her home on June 10, 1953 by her husband. She died of cardiac failure. Clarence Honadle was the son of Malcolm C. Honadle (1876-1949) and Lottie E. Himes Honadle (1879-1958) of Brockway, Pennsylvania. From January 7, 1921 to January 6, 1922 Mr. Honadle served in the US Military. He was employed as a barber for most of his professional career. Clarence Honadle's World War II Draft Registration Card described him as being 5'10" tall, weighing 165 pounds with brown hair and brown eyes. He owned his own barber shop in Brockville in 1940 where the family resided at 12 Hiram Street. Maxine and Clarence Honadle were buried in Wildwood Cemetery in Brockway, Pennsylvania.

Children:

511. I. ***Malcolm Leon Honadle, f.***

References: US Census: 1910, 1920, 1930, 1940; Wildwood Cemetery Records, Brockway, Pennsylvania; Pennsylvania Death Certificates 1906-1966 for Maxine Wilcox Honadle; US Department of Veterans Affairs Death File 1850-2010; World War II Draft Registration Card, 1940; October 15, 1953 newspaper obituary for Maxine Honadle of Brockway, Pennsylvania.

245.

Walter Abijah Wilcox, son of Leon (119), grandson of Charlotte (55), b. DuBois, Pennsylvania July 1, 1910, d. Honolulu, Hawaii, MIA with death date listed April 16, 1945; m. place and date not known Elizabeth Stella Williams, b. Carbondale, Pennsylvania March 29, 1913, d. Los Angeles, California/Waymart, Pennsylvania November 2, 1996.

Walter Wilcox was named for his paternal grandfather (Walter Wilcox) and a paternal uncle (Abijah Wilcox). He resided with his parents in Brockway, Pennsylvania until his marriage. Sometime after 1935 he moved to Arcadia, New York where he lived with his wife and son at 609 S. Main Street where he was employed as a hair dresser. Mr. Wilcox served in the US Navy aboard the USS Proteus (March 19, 1944), the USS Zaurak (November 9, 1944), and the USS Cofer (December 10, 1044). Walter A. Wilcox was listed as MIA and officially declared as dead April 16, 1945. His body was never recovered but his name is listed on a memorial at Pearl Harbor. At the time of his death Mr. Wilcox was a Radarman Third Class with the US Navy and was posthumously awarded a Purple Heart. Further information about Elizabeth Williams Wilcox is not known at this time. The California Death Index cites Mrs. Wilcox's death in Los Angeles (where her son had resided) while the Social Security Death Index listed her residence as Waymart, Pennsylvania. Elizabeth Williams Wilcox was the daughter of John R. Williams and Ellen Jones Williams. Her burial place is not known.

Children:

512. I. ***Joe Wilcox***, b. Pennsylvania a. 1937, ***nfi.***

References: US Census: 1910, 1920, 1930, 1940; Pennsylvania Birth Certificates 1906-1910 for Walter A. Wilcox; California Death Index 1940-1997 for Elizabeth Williams Wilcox; WWII Honor Roll List for Walter A. Wilcox; US Navy Military Records; Social Security Death Index 1935-2014.

246.

Richard Theophilus Wilcox, son of Leon (119), grandson of Charlotte (55), b. Brockway, Pennsylvania October 21, 1912, d. Brockway, Pennsylvania May 23, 1989; m. date and place not known, Florence

Evelyn Abrahamson, b. Pennsylvania May 26, 1911, d. Brockway, Pennsylvania April 24, 2006.

Richard Wilcox resided with his parents until his marriage in the late 1930s. In the 1940 US Census he was employed as a laborer in a glass factory in Brockway. His World War II Draft Registration Card described him as 5'10" tall, weighing 170 pounds with brown eyes, brown hair, and a dark complexion. Richard and Florence Wilcox were buried in the Wildwood Cemetery in Brockway, Pennsylvania.

Children:

513. I. ***Linda Wilcox***, b. 1938, ***nfi.***

514. II. ***Richard Leon or Lee Wilcox, f.***

References: US Census: 1920, 1930, 1940; World War II Draft Registration Card, 1940; Wildwood Cemetery Records, Brockway, Pennsylvania.

247.

Carl Crandall Wilcox, son of Carl (120), grandson of Charlotte (55), b. Bolivar, New York June 22/23, 1918, d. Black Mountain, North Carolina, July 3, 2010; m. (1) place and date not known Jacqueline Laura Eastman, b. Ulysses, Pennsylvania August 28, 1918, d. place not known, May 7, 1988, divorced; m. (2) Bolivar, New York October 9, 1965 Lyllia L. Moses, birth place and birth date and death place and death date not known.

Documents refer to Carl Crandall Wilcox as both Carl Wilcox and Crandall Wilcox complicating the search for biographical information. Crandall Wilcox resided with his parents and maternal grandmother at 95 Olean Street in Bolivar, New York. In the 1940 US Census he was employed as a truck driver by Allegany Refiners in Bolivar and still residing with his parents. Sometime after 1940 Crandall Wilcox married Jacqueline Laura Eastman who was identified as his wife in several *Bolivar Breeze* articles during the World War II era. Crandall Wilcox joined the Marine Corps in World War II and served from June 2, 1944 to November 10, 1945 in the Pacific Theater suffering shrapnel wounds on Iwo Jima. Jacqueline Eastman Wilcox was the daughter of Carl A. Eastman (1898-1974) and Lucy Campbell Eastman (1895-1972) of Ulysses, Pennsylvania. Crandall and Jacqueline Wilcox divorced and she returned to Ulysses where her parents and married sister resided. Jacqueline Wilcox died in Ulysses in 1988 and was buried in the Ulysses Cemetery with her parents and sister. Crandall Wilcox remarried in 1965 to Lyllia Moses of Bolivar, New York. Further information on Crandall's second wife is not available at this time. Crandall Wilcox moved to Horseshoe, North Carolina about 1998 where he died in 2010. Crandall Wilcox was buried in the Western Carolina State Veterans Cemetery in Black Mountain, North Carolina. It is not known if there were any children from either marriage. No grandchildren were mentioned in Crandall Wilcox's father's obituary of 1962.

References: US Census: 1920, 1930, 1940; New York State Census: 1925; Ulysses Cemetery Records, Ulysses, Pennsylvania; Western Carolina State Veterans Cemetery Records, Black Mountain, North Carolina; World War II Draft Registration Card, 1942; *Bolivar Breeze*, selected issues during World War II providing information on Crandall Wilcox's military service; Horseshoe, North Carolina City Directories 1998-2002.

248.

John Walter Wilcox, son of Carl (120), grandson of Charlotte (55), b. Olean, New York December 31, 1922, d. Redlands, California September 5, 2013; m. San Pedro, California November 24, 1944 Peggy Jean Whitworth, b. California July 23, 1925, d. California May 6, 2009. John Wilcox resided with his parents in Bolivar through the 1940 US Census. He was employed by McEwen Brothers in Bolivar before entering the service December 1942 with the US Navy Reserves. In April 1943 John Wilcox announced his engagement to former Bolivar, New York resident Irene Margeson. However, the marriage did not take place and in November of 1944 John married Peggy Jean Whitworth of Monticello, California. During his military career John Wilcox was a Seaman Second Class (1943), a Fireman First Class (1943), and left the service as a Motor Machinist Second Class. In June 1945 John Wilcox was a resident of Yucaipa, California. At the time of his father's death in 1962, John lived in El Monte, California. It is currently not known where John and Peggy Wilcox were buried. It is not known if they had any children.

References: US Census: 1930, 1940; New York State Census: 1925; NYS Birth Index 1881-1942 for John W. Wilcox; California County Birth/Marriage/Death Records 1849-1980 for the marriage of John Wilcox; Social Security Death Index 1935-2014 for John and Peggy Wilcox; *Bolivar Breeze, 1891-1965*, issues April 8, 1943 and November 3, 1944.

249.

Doris Anita Root, daughter of Burr LeRoy (122), granddaughter of Sidney LeRoy (56), b. Bolivar, New York August 25, 1901; d. Obi, New York March 6, 1920 from Erysipelas, an acute febrile infection caused by a specific streptococcus which the family believed was transmitted by an insect bite behind the ear. Doris Root graduated from Bolivar High School in 1919 and began teaching at the school on Daggett Hollow Road near the family home. Her obituary described Miss Root as a bright young woman, a devout member of the Obi United Brethren Church and President of the Christian Endeavor Society of Obi. Doris Root was buried in the West Genesee Cemetery in Obi, New York.

References: US Census: 1910, 1920; New York State Census: 1905, 1915. NYS Death Index 1852-1956; West Genesee Cemetery Records, Obi, New York; *Bolivar Breeze, 1891-1965*, selected issues.

250.

Coral Marie Root, daughter of Burr LeRoy (122), granddaughter of Sidney LeRoy (56), b. Bolivar, New York March 16, 1904, d. Bradford, Pennsylvania April 11, 1987 from a myocardial infraction; m. (1) Salamanca, New York February 11, 1924 Milo George Cline, b. Pennsylvania May 3, 1905, d. Bradford, Pennsylvania December 1973, divorced October 1936; m. (2) Kane, Pennsylvania September 12, 1943 Perry Harold Engstrom, b. Bradford, Pennsylvania April 9, 1898, d. Bradford, Pennsylvania March 21, 1952 from a heart attack; m. (3) place not known July 24, 1954 Lewis Patterson, b. Pennsylvania October 29, 1904, d. Bradford, Pennsylvania December 29, 1983 from heart failure.

Coral Root's first husband Milo George Cline, was the son of Willard Cline (1868-1931) and Harriet Mae Thompson Cline (1880-1963). They resided in Bradford. Coral gave birth prematurely to an infant female baby September 24, 1924 who lived only 6 ½ hours. The infant was a seven-month baby. In the 1940 US Census Milo Cline was employed as a fireman and his son resided with him. After the divorce Milo Cline remarried to Vivien Holobilek by whom he had five sons: Martin, Milo III, Richard, Bradley, and Gregory. Milo Cline was buried in Smith Cemetery in Farmers Valley, Pennsylvania. Coral's second husband was employed as a heating engineer.

Perry Engstrom was previously married to Bonnie Bell Morrison (1897-1942) with whom he had two sons: Perry H. Engstrom, Jr. and Carl Morrison Engstrom. In 1917 Perry Engstrom was employed as a car repairman for the Pennsylvania Railroad. He was described as of medium height, medium build with grey eyes and brown hair. Coral Root Cline was employed as a housekeeper by her second husband and his first wife based on the 1940 US Census. Mr. Engstrom was a widower at the time of his marriage to Coral. Perry Engstrom was buried in McKean Memorial Park with his first wife. Lewis Patterson, Coral's third husband, was employed as a carpenter and a building contractor. He was previously married to a Vera Emery. It is not known if they had any children. They were long-time residents of Bradford, Pennsylvania. Coral and Lewis Patterson were buried in McKean Memorial Park in Lafayette, Pennsylvania. There is a marker for Coral Root Patterson but there is no marker for Lewis Patterson.

Children (by first marriage):

515. I. ***Willard Milo Cline, f.***

References: US Census: 1910, 1920, 1930, 1940; New York State Census: 1905, 1915; Pennsylvania Death Certificates 1906-1966 for Infant Cline; Smith Cemetery Records, Farmers Valley, Pennsylvania; McKean Memorial Park Cemetery Records, Lafayette, Pennsylvania; *Bolivar Breeze, 1891-1965,* selected issues; World War I Draft Registration Cards 1917-18 for Perry Engstrom; Pennsylvania Death Certificate 1906-1966 for Perry Engstrom; correspondence with the late Coral Marie Patterson August 13, 1980, September 2, 1980, and January 6, 1983; correspondence with Joyce Cline October 24, 1990.

251.

Raymond Willard Root, son of Burr LeRoy (122), grandson of Sidney LeRoy (56), Bolivar, New York September 21, 1905, d. Summit, New Jersey May 28, 1982/3; m. (1) place not known, April 19, 1928 Carolyn Mary Kay, b. Battle Creek, Michigan October 7, 1908, d. December 31, 1967 from cancer; m. (2) place not known, 1969 Evelyn Spear Duncan, b. Leonia, New Jersey July 3, 1906, d. Summit, New Jersey June 10, 1974 from cancer.

Raymond Root was a graduate of Bolivar High School. He graduated from Milton College in Wisconsin in 1926 where he was elected President of his Class. Mr. Root received his Ph. D. from Duke University in 1931 and was employed by the City College of New York rising to the position of Chairman of the Physiology Department. Dr. Root held that post for thirty years. At the time of his death he was Professor Emeritus in Biology. Dr. Root was an active environmentalist and conservationist. He was particularly concerned about pollution and the problems pollution caused over the long-term on mankind. Dr. Root was a member of Zero Population Growth, Planned Parenthood, and World Population. He was a charter member of the Society of General Physiologists, an annual member of Who's Who in the East, and he was a member of the American Men of Science.

Dr. Root meet his first wife, Carolyn Mary Kay, while teaching at Battle Creek College. She was one of his students. Mrs. Root later attended Duke University where she received a B. A. Degree in 1931. Carolyn Root was the daughter of James Roy Kay (1884-1940) and Bessie Gaffield (1885-1973) of Michigan. Raymond Root's second wife was Evelyn Isham Spear, the daughter of Willard R. Spear (1870-1950) and Mary Isham Spear (1874-1946) of New Jersey. Evelyn was previously married to Gordon Erskine Dunlap (1906-1958). She had three children by her first marriage: daughters Mary and Margaret and a son Duncan. Evelyn Spear Dunlap Root was buried with her first husband in Fairview Cemetery in Fairview, Pennsylvania. Raymond and Carolyn Root were buried in Oak Hill Cemetery in Battle Creek, Michigan. The Social Security Death Index listed Dr. Root's death year as 1983 but other documentation recorded that he died in 1982.

Children (by first marriage):

516. I. ***Richard Kay Root, f.***

517. II. ***(Elizabeth) Carole Root, f.***

References: US Census: 1910, 1920, 1930, 1940; New York State Census: 1905, 1915, 1925; Social Security Death Index 1935-2014; Oak Hill Cemetery Records, Battle Creek, Michigan; Fairview Cemetery Records, Fairview, Pennsylvania; Milton College Yearbook 1925 and 1926; correspondence with the late Dr. Raymond W. Root July 28, 1990 and August 18, 1980; *Bolivar Breeze 1891-1965*, selected issues; correspondence with Carole Root Cole February 28, 1983 and June 10, 1983.

252.

Howard LeRoy Root, Sr., son of Burr LeRoy (122), grandson of Sidney (56), b. Bolivar, New York February 9, 1908, d. Milton, Wisconsin July 6, 2002; m. (1) Albion, Wisconsin July 31, 1930 Anna Mae Sheldon, b. Michigan December 1, 1910, d. Fort Atkinson, Wisconsin June 12, 1986, divorced 1946; m. (2) place and date not known Muriel Arbuckle, place and date of birth not known, place and date of death not known, divorced September 1952.

Howard Root was a graduate of Milton College, the Class of 1931. In 1934 Mr. Root began his employment with the Nunn Bush Shoe Company in Edgerton, Wisconsin. He worked at Nunn Bush until his retirement at age 78 in 1986. Each year Mr. Root was locally renown for maintaining a large vegetable garden from which he took great pleasure and pride. After his second divorce he and Amelia H. Page lived together until her death. Anna Mae Sheldon was the daughter of Carl Maxson Sheldon (1861-1936) and Pearl Crosley Sheldon (1879-1966) of Wisconsin. Howard and Anna Mae were married at the home of her parents in Albion. Howard and Anna Mae Root had five children. Their third child was born and died in November 1936. The infant was not named but was buried in Evergreen Cemetery in Albion, Wisconsin in a lot purchased by Mr. and Mrs. Root. In the 1940 US Census Mrs. Root's brother, his wife, and daughter resided with them.

Anna Mae Sheldon Root remarried to Harold C. Owens (1912-1976) and had two more sons by her second marriage. She was buried with her second husband in Hillside Cemetery in Whitewater, Wisconsin. No information could be found on Howard Root's second wife. Amelia Hudson Page was born July 20, 1907 and died September 3, 1995. She was previously married to Joseph G. Page in 1935. Mr. Page died February 2, 1949 and was buried in Mr. Olivet Cemetery in Janesville, Wisconsin. Amelia and Joseph Page did not have any children. Howard Root was one of the longest-lived Root family members dying at age 94. Mr. Root was buried in Milton Cemetery in Janesville, Wisconsin where Amelia Page was also buried. The Social Security Death Index recorded that Howard Root died July 6, 2002 while Milton Cemetery Records list his death date as January 6, 2002.

Children (by first marriage):

518. I. ***Howard LeRoy Root, Jr., f.***

519. II. ***Carolyne Mae Root, f.***

520. III. ***Duane Root, f.***

521. IV. ***David A. Root, f.***

References: US Census: 1910, 1920, 1930, 1940; New York State Census: 1915, 1925; NYS Birth Index 1881-1942; Milton Cemetery Records, Janesville, Wisconsin; Hillside Cemetery Records, Whitewater,

Wisconsin; Evergreen Cemetery Records, Albion, Wisconsin; Correspondence with the late Howard L. Root, Sr; Social Security Death Index 1935-2014; *Bolivar Breeze 1891-1965,* selected issues.

253.

Ruth Louise Root, son of Burr LeRoy (122), grandson of Sidney (56), b. Genesee Township, Allegany County, New York February 23, 1910, d. Bolivar, New York January 2, 1959 from a heart attack; m. Obi, New York August 3, 1928 Clifford Ernest Foster, b. Clarksville, New York September 10, 1904, d. Bolivar, New York August 1, 1977. Ruth Root resided with her parents until her 1928 marriage to Clifford Foster. Clifford Foster was the son of Frank Elmer Foster (1870-1955) of Portville and Cuba, New York and Mermie Alberta Keller Foster (1878-1929) of Little Genesee, New York. He was an oil field contractor and driller. The Fosters resided in Clarksville (Allegany County), New York where their two sons were born. Ruth and Clifford Foster were buried in Maple Lawn Cemetery, Bolivar, New York.

Children:

522. I. ***Donald Clifford Foster, f.***

523. II. ***James Allen Foster, f.***

References: US Census: 1910, 1920, 1930, 1940; New York State Census: 1905, 1915, 1925; New York State Birth Index 181-1942; New York State Death Index 1957-68 for Ruth Root Foster; Social Security Death Index 1935-2014; *Bolivar Breeze 1891-1965*, selected issues; New York Count Marriage Records 1847-8 and 1907-1936; Maple Lawn Cemetery Records, Bolivar, New York.

254.

Laurence Allen Root, son of Burr LeRoy (122), grandson of Sidney (56), b. Genesee Township, Allegany County, New York May 19, 1917, d. Orlando, Florida April 2, 1974 from a massive coronary; m. Bradford, Pennsylvania October 7, 1939 Rhea Florence Hooker, b. Bradford, Pennsylvania December 1, 1913, d. Orange County, Florida November 2, 1997.

Laurence Root resided with his parents until his move to Bradford, Pennsylvania in 1935. Mr. Root was employed in the Pennsylvania and New York oil fields for many years and later worked as a welder. After his 1939 marriage Laurence and Rhea Root resided in Carrolton, New York where he was employed as an oil well pumper. His World War II Draft Registration Card described Laurence Root as being 6'2" tall, weighing 183 pounds with blue eyes and brown hair. His employers in 1942 were A. and G. C. Stover and G. W. Hooker of Carrollton, New York. Laurence Root served in the US Navy from April 13, 1944 to December 20, 1945 aboard the *USS Clytie*. After his military service Mr. and Mrs. Root moved to Bradford, Pennsylvania. In 1958 Mr. and Mrs. Root retired to Orlando, Florida.

They did not have any children. However, Rhea Hooker had a daughter, Phyllis, born August 24, 1932, before her marriage to Laurence Root. The identity of the father is not known. The daughter was not listed on the 1940 US Census with them. Documentation suggests that Laurence Root adopted Phyllis as she was referred to as Phyllis J. Root on Veterans Compensation Application papers. Phyllis married a Mr. Gertis and resided in Buffalo, New York at the time of Rhea Root's death. Rhea Root was a member of the Ladies Oriental Shrine 86, Order of Amaranth Seminole Court 59, Daughters of the Nile, Bahia Shrine Widows Club, and the Orlando Women's Republican Club. It is not currently known where Laurence and Rhea Root were buried.

References: US Census: 1920, 1930, 1940; New York State Census: 1925; New York State Birth Index 1881-1942; Florida Death Index 1877-1998; Social Security Death Index 1935-2014; US Department of Veterans Affairs 1850-2010; World War II Draft Registration Card 1942; Veterans Compensation Application, 1950; *The Orlando Sentinel* November 5, 1997 for the obituary of Rhea H. Root; correspondence with the late Rhea Root August 22, 1980.

256.

Orval Laurence Perry, son of Lena (123), grandson of Sidney (56), b. Genesee Township, Allegany County, New York January 24, 1900, d. Vestal, New York October 19, 1964; m. Horseheads, New York July 13, 1931 Marjorie Prentice, b. Horseheads, New York October 30, 1905, d. Vestal, New York November 1970.

Orval Perry was a 1922 graduate of Bolivar High School. He studied and graduated from Alfred University, Alfred, New York and later from Cornell University, Ithaca, New York. History was his area of study. He briefly served in the military during World War I being a member of the Alfred University Military Training Program from October 1, 1918 to December 10, 1918. He did not see any overseas actions. Mr. Perry resided with his parents through 1925. In 1927 he was employed at a history teacher in Watkins Glen, New York. Marjorie Prentice Perry was also a teacher. In the 1930 US Census both were single, teaching, and residing in the same lodging house in Watkins Glen. The 1940 US Census found both of them still residing in Watkins Glen with Mrs. Perry's father.

Both were employed as teachers. Later Orval Perry taught at Endicott, New York schools before becoming a history professor at Harpur College in Vestal, New York. Harpur College was later absorbed into the State University System at Binghamton, New York. Orval Perry retired from Harpur College and did substitute teaching at Vestal Central Schools where he was stricken with a heart attack on October 19, 1964 and died. Mrs. Perry died six years later. Orval and Marjorie Perry did not have any children. Mr. and Mrs. Perry were buried in Maple Grove Cemetery in Horseheads, New York.

References: US Census: 1900, 1910, 1920, 1930, 1940; New York State Census: 1905, 1915, 1925; World War I Military Service Records; New York County Marriage Records 1847-9 and 1907-1936; NYS Death Index, 1964; *Bolivar Breeze 1891-1965*, selected issues; Maple Grove Cemetery Records, Horseheads, New York; Social Security Death Index 1935-2014.

257.

Clella Undine Perry, daughter of Lena (123), granddaughter of Sidney (56), b. Genesee Township, Allegany County, New York January 20, 1902, d. Bolivar, New York December 19, 1991; m. Little Genesee, New York April 10, 1920 Mervin Parker Sisson, b. Little Genesee, New York June 4, 1901, d. at the Sweden Valley Manor Nursing Home, Coudersport, Pennsylvania, January 26, 1989.

Clella Undine was given the Indian name by her mother, Lena Root Perry. Mrs. Perry was quite enamored with the name which she found in a book she was reading. Mervin Sisson was the son of John Henry Sisson (1871-1944) and Mary Alice Harris Sisson (1877-1921). Clella and Mervin each resided with their parents until their wedding. They were longtime residents of Clarksville and Bolivar, New York. Mr. Sisson was a self-employed oil well contractor, a lumberman, and a carpenter for over twenty-five years. For a ten-year period, Mervin Sisson operated the Bolivar Home and Auto Hardware Store. Clella and Mervin Sisson were buried in the West Genesee Cemetery in Obi, New York.

Children:

524. I. ***Bernice Virginia Sisson, f.***

525. II. ***Jean M. Sisson, f.***

References: US Census: 1910, 1920, 1930, 1940; New York State Census: 1905, 1915, 1925; New York Marriage Records 1847-1849 and 1907-1936; West Genesee Cemetery Records, Obi, New York; *Bolivar Breeze 1891-1965,* selected issues; Social Security Death Index 1935-2014; correspondence with the late Clella Sisson March 1, 1982, April 12, 1982, and October 2, 1982.

258.

Keith LeRoy Perry, son of Lena (123), grandson of Sidney (56), b. Genesee Township, Allegany County, New York September 19, 1908, d. Port Allegany, Pennsylvania December 14, 1970; m. Clarksville, New York May 18, 1928 Marguerite Pauline Ferrington, b. Cuba, New York December 5, 1908, d. Port Allegany, Pennsylvania June 1987.

Keith Perry resided with his parents until his marriage in 1928. Mr. Perry held a number of jobs while studying for the ministry to become a preacher. The 1930 US Census listed Keith Perry's occupation as a carpenter residing on Daggett Hollow Road in Wirt Township in Allegany County, New York. In 1932 he was employed as a brick layer building a skimming plant in Richburg. The 1940 US Census recorded Keith Perry's occupation as an oil well pumper still residing at Daggett Hollow Road. As a minister Reverend Perry was a graduate of Houghton College in Houghton, New York and was the pastor at the United Brethren Church in Haskell Flats, New York (1940-1942), the Alma, New York United Brethren Church (1942-1946), the United Brethren Church in Degolia and Lewis Run, Pennsylvania (1946-1955), the Grace Evangelical United Brethren Church in Jamestown, New York (1955-1962), and the Evangelical United Brethren in Christ Church in Smethport and the Trinity Church in Port Allegany, Pennsylvania (1962-1970).

He received his license to preach from the Obi, New York United Brethren Church in 1940. He was a member of the United Brethren in Christ Erie Conference becoming an Elder in 1945. In 1952 Reverend Perry was elected President of the Bradford, Pennsylvania Ministerial Group and later became a member of the United Methodist Western Pennsylvania Conference. Marguerite Ferrington Perry was the daughter of George Riley Ferrington (1860-1929) and Florence Foster Ferrington (1879-1969). Keith and Marguerite Perry were buried in West Genesee Cemetery in Obi, New York.

Children:

526. I. ***Joyce Ann Perry,*** b. Olean, New York February 25, 1935; m. Robert L. Terwilliger April 4, 1964; ***nfi.***

527. II. ***Lois M. Perry,*** b. November 5, 1937; m. Jamestown, New York June 20, 1959 Ronald Bowers; ***nfi.***

528. III. ***Jean Perry, nfi.***

References: US Census: 1910, 1920, 1930, 1940; New York State Census: 1915, 1925; *Bolivar Breeze 1891-1965*, selected issues; West Genesee Cemetery Records, Obi, New York; New York County Marriage Records 1847-9 and 1907-1936; Social Security Death Index 1935-2014; New York State Birth Index 1881-1942, including Joyce and Lois Perry; New York State Marriage Index 1881-1967 for Joyce and Lois Perry.

259.

Alta Irene Root, daughter of Ernest (124), granddaughter of Sidney (56), Bolivar, New York March 7, 1910, d. Manatee County, Florida March 29, 2000; m. Hamburg, New York December 12, 1931 Henry Gilbert Schwertfeger/Schwertfager, b. New York State May 10, 1910, d. Bradenton, Florida March 25, 1996. The spelling of Henry's last name has been both presented as Schwertfeger and Schwertfager.

After the death of her mother, Alta Root resided with her father and her Root grandparents in Bolivar. Alta Irene Root left home in 1924 and moved to Bradford where she resided for several years before moving to Hamburg, New York where she found employment as a clerk. Her relationship with her step-mother was strained. Alta returned to Bolivar for weekend visits to her Root grandparents more often than to see her father and step-mother based on *Bolivar Breeze* newspapers articles. The 1930 US Census recorded her occupation as a student nurse for the Mountain Clinic in Olean, New York. She met her future husband through a mutual friend of both while Alta was employed at an ice cream parlor. At the time of her marriage to Henry Gilbert Schwertfeger in 1931 her husband was employed as a railroad worker. In the 1940 US Census the Schwertfeger family resided on Camp Road in Hamburg where he repaired cars at a steel plant. Mr. Schwertfeger retired from Bethlehem Steel as a foreman and in 1986 Henry and Alta Schwertfeger retired to Florida. Henry Schwertfeger was the son of William Schwertfeger who was born in Germany and Elizabeth Volt Schwertfeger from Hamburg, New York. Mr. and Mrs. Schwertfeger were buried in Skyway Memorial Gardens in Palmetto, Florida.

Children:

529. I. ***Richard Ernest Schwertfager, f.***

530. II. ***Larry Dean Schwertfager, f.***

References: US Census: 1910, 1920, 1930, 1940; New York State Census: 1915, 1925; Skyway Memorial Gardens records, Palmetto, Florida; Florida Death Index 1877-1998; Social Security Death Index 1935-2014; New York County Marriages 1847-9 and 1907-1936; *Bolivar Breeze, 1891-1965*, selected issues; correspondence with the late Alta Schwertfeger July 14, 1980 and August 18, 1980.

260.

Kenneth Ernest Root, son of Ernest (124), grandson of Sidney (56), b. Bolivar, New York April 20, 1922, still living; m. Kane, Pennsylvania February 19, 1948 Dorothy Adamkavitz, b. Kane, Pennsylvania February 22, 1927, d. San Diego, California May 16, 2018.

Kenneth Root resided with his parents until his entry into the US Army in 1942. In 1938 Kenneth Root was awarded the highest scouting award at Bolivar High School where he graduated. The March 14, 1940 *Bolivar Breeze* newspaper printed an article about Kenneth Root and how much he had done for Bolivar High School. The article comments on Kenny's sense of humor, his maturity of mind, and caustic wit. Kenny Root was a member of the Bolivar High School band playing the trombone since his freshman year. He played baseball in his sophomore and junior years in high school and football in his senior year. Mr. Root also acted in his junior and senior high school plays. Kenny Root was elected Vice-President of his senior class graduating in 1939. Mr. Root served three years in the US Army from 1942 to 1945 rising to the rank of corporal. He spent one year in England.

After the war Kenneth Root attended and graduated from the University of Buffalo (New York). Mr. Root was employed as the Customer Education Manager for the Burroughs Corporation until his 1981 retirement. Kenneth and Dorothy were married at St. Callixtus Church in Kane, Pennsylvania where she was employed in a beauty salon as an assistant manager. Kenneth Root was in his senior year at the University of Buffalo. Mr. and Mrs. Root resided in Northville, Michigan where they also jointly owned and operated two day-care centers in Livonia called *Livonia Little Tots Day Nursery, Inc.* Dorothy Root was a graduate of Kane, Pennsylvania High School and attended Berwyn Beauty School in Buffalo, New York. She also held a degree in child development. In March of 1983 Kenneth and Dorothy Root moved to San Diego, California where they have resided ever since. The day-care centers were sold when they moved to California.

Children:

531. I. ***Kenneth Ernest Root, Jr., f.***

532. II. ***Terry Edward Root, f.***

533. III. ***Lorrie Ann Root, f.***

References: US Census: 1930, 1940; New York State Census: 1925; New York State Birth Index 1881-1942 for Kenneth Root; *Bolivar Breeze 1891-1965*, selected issues; correspondence with Kenneth E. Root, Sr., July 21, 1980, August 18, 1980, May 5, 1983.

261.

Laura Jane Pire, daughter of Floyd (129), granddaughter of Olivia (58), b. Coudersport, Pennsylvania March 12, 1915, d. Tempe, Arizona April 1978; m. Rochester, New York March 23, 1934 Russell Harris Milford, b. Grove City, Pennsylvania June 1, 1909, d. Rochester, New York February 2, 1963.

Laura Jane Pire was also known by her nickname *Lolly* and Russell Harris Milford was known as Harris Milford. They both resided with their respective parents until their 1934 marriage. The 1940 US Census listed Harris Milford's occupation as a stock clerk in a 5 and 10 cent store. Russell Harris Milford was the son of Charles Milford (1883-1952) and Clorisa Elfleda Limber Milford (1878-1931). The Milfords moved to Rochester, New York in 1910. The Pires moved to Rochester after 1925. It is currently not known where Laura and Russel Harris Milford were buried.

Children:

534. I. ***Robert A. Milford, f.***

535. II. ***Richard J. Milford, f.***

536. III. ***Ward Thomas Milford, f.***

537. IV. ***Dennis Milford, nfi.***

538. V. ***Gary Milford, nfi.***

539. VI. ***Steven Milford, nfi.***

540. VII. ***John Milford, nfi.***

541. VIII. ***Jane Ann Milford Coomber, nfi.***

References: US Census: 1910, 1920, 1930, 1940; New York County Marriage Records 1848-1849 and 1907-1936.

263.

Francis Monroe Pire, son of Floyd (129) and grandson of Olivia (58), b. Coudersport, Pennsylvania May 31, 1919, d. Rochester, New York April 29, 1982; m. Rochester, New York June 18, 1940 Leverne W. DeWells, b. Rochester, New York September 26, 1920, d. Rochester, New York February 20, 1999.

Francis Pire resided with his parents until his enlistment in the US Army. The 1940 US Census recorded that he lived in Irondequoit, Monroe County, New York and was employed as a sales clerk living with his parents. Mr. Pire served with the US Army enlisting in Rochester, New York November 12, 1942 and ending his service July 14, 1945. The Pires had three children, but the identities of two are not currently known. It is not known where Francis and Laverne Pire were buried.

Children:

542. I. ***Floyd M. Pire, f.***

543. II. ***Male Pire, nfi.***

544. III. ***Female Pire, nfi.***

References: US Census: 1920, 1930, 1940; Social Security Death Index 1935-2014; US Army Enlistment Records 1938-1946; NYS Marriage Index 1881-1967; US Veterans Affairs Death File 1850-2010.

264.

Mary Lois Pire, daughter of Ward (130), granddaughter of Olivia (58), b. Erie, Pennsylvania February 27, 1924, d. Staten Island, New York City, New York July 31, 1992. Little is currently known about Mary Pire. She graduated from Academy High School in Erie, Pennsylvania with plans to become a musician. Mary Pire never married and resided most of her adult life on Staten Island in New York

City at 185 Father Capodanno Blvd. She was buried in Erie Cemetery in Erie, Pennsylvania with other Pire family members.

References: US Census: 1930, 1940; US Public Records Index 1950-1993; Erie Cemetery Records, Erie, Pennsylvania; Academy High School Yearbooks, Erie, Pennsylvania.

265.

Ward Russell Pire, son of Ward (130), grandson of Olivia (58), b. Erie, Pennsylvania December 30, 1926, d. Erie, Pennsylvania January 19, 2018; m. (1) probably Erie, Pennsylvania, date not known, Myrna L. Eck, b. Erie, Pennsylvania July 16, 1929, d. Erie, Pennsylvania October 3, 1995 at the St. Vincent Health Center; m. (2) place and date of marriage not known, Judy Dobbs, birth and death places and birth and death dates not known. Ward Pire was known by a nickname *Bud*. He resided with his parents and graduated from Academy High School in Erie, Pennsylvania.

Mr. Pire enlisted in the US Navy where his World War II Draft Registration Card described him as being 5'10" tall, weighing 150 pounds with brown eyes and brown hair. He served from June 12, 1944 until March 2, 1946. After his military service Bud Pire was employed as an assembler for A. O. Smith. He was an active member of the Asbury United Methodist Church and enjoyed the beach and playing chess. Myrna Pire was also an active member of the Ashbury United Methodist Church where she served as Vice-President of the United Methodist Women, was a member of the church choir, and Chairman of the Betty Dalby Circle. Ward Pire was buried at Laurel Hill Cemetery in Millcreek, Pennsylvania with his first wife, Myrna Eck Pire.

Children:

545. I. ***Thomas Lee Pire, f.***

546. II. ***Richard R. Pire, f.***

547. III. ***Nancy Pire,*** b. Erie, Pennsylvania October 21, 1954; m. Jeff Ford; ***nfi.***

References: US Census: 1930, 1940; Laurel Hill Cemetery Records, Millcreek, Pennsylvania; Academy High School, Erie, Pennsylvania Yearbooks; World War II Draft Registration Card, 1940-1947; Pennsylvania Veterans Compensation Files, World War II 1950-1966; Social Security Death Index 1935-2014; *Erie Daily Times* newspaper obituaries for Ward and Myrna Pire.

266.

Leona Ruth Root, daughter of Leon (132), granddaughter of Arthur (59), b. Eldorado But, Kansas June 28, 1921, d. Bartlesville, Oklahoma June 1, 2003; m. (1) Tulsa, Oklahoma April 10, 1943 Eugene

Theodore Hamilton, b. Stillwater, Oklahoma July 7, 1916, d. Caney, Kansas May 4, 1998, divorced April 10, 1954; m. (2) Bartlesville, Oklahoma September 22, 1984 Joseph Kenneth Gordon, b. Nowata, Oklahoma November 7, 1917, d. Bartlesville, Oklahoma June 12, 1992; m. (3) Bexar County, Texas November 22, 1994 Clifton Norman Bellamy, b. Hooker, Oklahoma October 28, 1917, d. Universal City, Texas October 7, 2004.

Leona Root was named for her father's half-sister. She resided with her parents in Bartlesville, Oklahoma until her marriage to Eugene Hamilton. Mr. Hamilton's World War II Draft Registration Card described him as being 5'10" tall, weighing 145 pounds with blue eyes and brown hair. Leon's second husband, Joseph Gordon, served in the US Army in World War II from July 16, 1942 until October 24, 1945 and again in the Korean War from September 1, 1950 to July 9, 1952 rising to the rank of Captain. He also served as an SPI in the United States Coast Guard. Mr. Gordon's World War II Draft Registration Card described him as being 5'11" tall, weighing 158 pounds with blue eyes and brown hair in 1940 when he was employed by the city government as a policeman. Mr. Gordon was previously married to Beulah, last name not known.

Leona and Joe retired from the Phillips Petroleum Company in Bartlesville where she had worked for 29 years and he had worked for 26 years. Mr. and Mrs. Gordon were great geology enthusiasts and spent part of each year exploring the western states of the United States rock hunting. Leon's third husband was Clifton Norman Bellamy, a retired Lieutenant Colonel in the Armed Forces. Mr. Bellamy was also the half-brother of Leona's mother. Clifton Bellamy was previously married to Marjory Louise Miller who died in 1989 and by whom he had one daughter, Edna, who predeceased him in 1991. It is currently not known where Eugene Hamilton was buried. Leona Root Hamilton Gordon Bellamy was buried in Sunnyside Cemetery in Caney, Kansas with her third husband, Clifton Norman Bellamy. Joseph Gordon, Leona's second husband, was also buried in Sunnyside Cemetery.

Children (by first marriage):

548. I. ***Theresa Gay Hamilton, f.***

References: US Census: 1930, 1940; Sunnyside Cemetery Records, Caney, Kansas; Oklahoma County Marriage Licenses 1890-1995 for Leona's first marriage; World War II Draft Registration Card, 1942 for Eugene Theodore Hamilton and Joseph Kenneth Gordon; US Department of Veterans Affairs Death File 1850-2010 for Joseph Kenneth Gordon; Texas Marriage Records for Leona's second marriage; Social Security Death Index 1935-2014; correspondence with the late Leona Root Gordon September 21, 1990.

267.

Betty Louise Root, daughter of Leon (132), granddaughter of Arthur (59), b. Augusta, Kansas November 27, 1922, d. Coffeyville, Kansas June 8, 1994; m. Dearing, Kansas February 11, 1942 Joe

(Joseph) Burton Brown, b. Elgin, Kansas August 28, 1918, d. Coffeyville, Kansas March 2, 2005.

Betty Root resided with her parents until her 1942 marriage. She received her nursing education and training in Coffeyville and was employed as a nurse at the Coffeyville Memorial Hospital. Betty was also a licensed nursing home administrator at Golden Age Lodge until her 1981 retirement. Joe B. Brown was a graduate of Ozark Bible College in Joplin, Missouri and attended Mound Valley, Kansas Seminary. His father was also a minister as would be his son. Mr. Brown's World War II Draft Registration Card described him as being 5'10" tall, weighing 160 pounds with hazel eyes and blonde hair. He was an ordained minister with a church in Coffeyville until his retirement in 1990. Reverend Brown ministered to residents of southeast Kansas for almost 60 years continuing to serve the Lord even after his retirement. Betty Brown assisted her husband in his ministry. In 1987 Mr. and Mrs. Brown celebrated their 45th wedding anniversary with family and friends. Betty and Joe Brown were buried in Robbins Cemetery in Coffeyville, Kansas.

Children:

549. I. ***Donna Brown, f.***

550. II. ***David Bruce Brown, f.***

551. III. ***Jo Lynne Brown, f.***

552. IV. ***Cheryl Brown, f.***

References: US Census: 1930, 1940; World War II Draft Registration Card, 1940; Robbins Cemetery, Coffeyville, Kansas; newspaper obituaries, Coffeyville, Kansas for Betty Louise and Joe Brown; Social Security Death Index 1935-2014.

268.

Barbara Jean Root, daughter of Leon (132), granddaughter of Arthur (59), Bartlesville, Oklahoma, b. July 27, 1928, d. Bozeman, Montana August 25, 2009; m. Bartlesville, Oklahoma March 19, 1948 Joe R. Nelson, b. Spencerville, Ohio October 12, 1921, d. Bartlesville, Oklahoma August 25, 2009.

Barbara Jean Root resided with her parents until her 1948 marriage. Joseph Nelson's Draft Registration Card described him as being 5'9" tall, weighing 170 pounds with gray eyes and brown hair. He served with the Army Air Corps during World War II from January 19, 1942 until September 22, 1945. After the war Mr. Nelson was employed by Phillips Petroleum in Bartlesville until his 1985 retirement. Barbara Nelson moved to Montana after her husband's death. Barbara Jean and Joe Nelson were buried in Sunset Hills Cemetery in Bozeman, Montana.

Children:

553. I. ***Sherri Nelson, f.***

554. II. ***Debra Anne Nelson, f.***

References: US Census: 1930, 1940; Ohio Birth Index 1908-1964 for Joe Nelson; World War II Draft Registration Card, 1942; Social Death Index 1935-2014; Montana Death Index 1907-2015 for Barbara Jean Nelson; Sunset Hills Cemetery, Bozeman, Montana.

269.

James Irvin McIntyre, son of Sarah (134), grandson of Francis (62), b. Carmen, Pennsylvania November 25, 1888, d. New Castle, Pennsylvania July 15, 1961 from heart disease and a coronary occlusion; m. place not known, date not known Margaret Sara Dollinger, b. Pennsylvania April 20, 1886, d. Youngstown, Ohio January 25, 1965. James McIntyre resided with his parents until his marriage. In 1900, they resided in Washington, Pennsylvania.

The 1910 US Census recorded Mr. McIntyre was employed as an electric repairman in Pittsburgh, Pennsylvania where he resided with his wife, Margaret, and two daughters: Katherine aged 3 years and Margret aged 1 year and 9 months. Neither of the two children were recorded on the 1920 US Census when James and Margaret McIntyre lived in New Castle, Pennsylvania. James McIntyre was inducted into the Army May 27, 1918 in New Castle, Pennsylvania.

He served until June 14, 1919. He saw service overseas from August 23, 1918 until May 24, 1919. He was not involved in any military engagements service with the Motor Company. His documents list four children but not the two identified on the 1910 US Census. The 1930 US Census listed their residence in New Castle with four children: Kathryn M. aged 9 years, Ray J. six years of age, and daughters Sara E., age 4, and Mary Ann age 3 years. Mr. McIntyre was employed as a railroad brakeman. The 1940 US Census did not record an occupation for James McIntyre. Daughter Mary Ann was not residing with them but Kathryn or Catherine M., Raymond, and Sara were. James McIntyre's World War II Draft Registration Card described him as being 5'11" tall, weighing 196 pounds with gray hair, blue eyes, and a ruddy complexion. He was employed by J. F. Cable Terminal Company. James and Margaret McIntyre were buried in St. Mary's Cemetery in New Castle, Pennsylvania.

Children:

555. I. ***Katherine McIntyre***, b. a. 1907. Only recorded in the 1910 US Census and may have died by 1920; ***nfi.***

556. II. ***Margret McIntyre***, b. ab. 1908. Only recorded in the 1920 US Census and may have died by 1920; ***nfi.***

557. III. ***Catherine or Kathryn M. McIntyre, f.***

558. IV. ***Raymond J. McIntyre, f.***

559. V. ***Sara E. McIntyre, f.***

560. VI. ***Mary Ann McIntyre, f.***

References: US Census: 1900, 1910, 1920, 1930, 1940; St. Mary's Cemetery Records, New Castle, Pennsylvania; Pennsylvania Death Certificates 1906-1966 for James I McIntyre; Veteran's Compensation Application for Pennsylvania, 1934; World War II Draft Registration Card, 1942.

270.

John Edward McIntyre, son of Sarah (134) and grandson of Francis (62), b. Falls Creek, Pennsylvania March 25, 1891/1892, d. place of death not known, date of death not known.

John Edward McIntyre resided with his parents until his enlistment in the military during World War I. He was inducted into the military in New Castle, Pennsylvania September 19, 1917 and served until his discharge March 31, 1919. Mr. McIntyre saw military action overseas from June 5, 1918 to March 22, 1919 in France. Private McIntyre received unidentified wounds on August 14, 1918 and was at the battle of Chateau Thierry on October 14, 1918. The 1930 US Census recorded Mr. McIntyre residing at a National Military Home. His disabilities included flat feet, deafness, and hemorrhoids. The 1940 US Census listed John McIntyre as a lodger with the Peter Camusso family of New Castle, Pennsylvania. He was employed as a laborer with the Works Progress Administration. It is currently not known what happened to John Edward McIntyre after 1940.

References: US Census: 1900, 1910, 1920, 1930, 1940; Pennsylvania WW I Veterans Service and Compensation Files 1917-1919 and 1934-1948; US National Homes for Disabled Volunteer Soldiers 1866-1938.

271.

Lillian Lenora Kellogg, daughter of John Irvin (135), granddaughter of Francis (62), b. Pennsylvania March 8, 1891, d. Bristol, Virginia August 19, 1986 from cancer; m. (1) Rochester, New York December 23, 1910 John R. Tully, b. New York State a. 1888, d. place of death not known, date of death not known; m. (2) place of marriage not known, date of marriage not known Raymond Leff, b. Russia 1896, place of death not known, date of death not known; m. (3) Niagara Falls, New York November 22, 1947 Henry

J. Vanderwall, place of birth not known, date of birth not known, d. place of death not known, date of death not known.

Lillian Kellogg resided with her parents in Sharon, Potter County, Pennsylvania until her move to Rochester, New York before the 1910 US Census. The 1910 US Census identified her as a lodger with the Way family working as a photopaper maker with the Kodak Corporation. The census notes she was divorced but it is not clear who that husband was. Lillian's sister, Pearl Kellogg, also resided with her as a boarder in the Way household. Lillian married John R. Tully December 23, 1910 but nothing is known about him. They had a daughter together, Onnalee E. Tully, born about 1913. Lillian Kellogg cannot be found on the 1920 US Census but her daughter, Onnalee, was living with maternal uncle and aunt, Cecil and Julia Kellogg, in Ceres, Pennsylvania.

The 1925 New York State Census records Lillian Kellogg Tully as remarried to Raymond Leff with daughter Onnalee residing with them and a second daughter, Marie, born from her marriage to Raymond Leff in Buffalo, New York where Mr. Leff was employed as an electrician. The 1930 US Census found Lillian, Raymond, Onnalee, and Marie living in Buffalo, New York where Raymond Leff continued to be employed as an electrician. The Buffalo, New York City Directories for 1932 and 1933 indicate that she and Raymond Leff lived apart. Raymond Leff's World War II Draft Registration Card described him as being 5'11 ½ "tall, weighing 200 pounds with hazel eyes and brown hair. He was residing with a brother and was unemployed. Lillian Kellogg Tully Leff cannot be found on the 1940 US Census. It is not known how long Lillian's third marriage lasted because the 1957 City Directory for Buffalo, New York indicated she was living alone and worked as a maid. It is not known when and why Lillian moved to Bristol, Virginia where she died. Her death certificate recorded that she was buried in Mountain View Cemetery in Bristol, Virginia.

Children (by first marriage):

561. I. ***Onnalee E. Tully, f.***

Children (by second marriage):

562. I. ***Marie Leff, f.***

References: US Census: 1900, 1910, 1920, 1930; New York State Census: 1925; Virginia Death Index 1986 for Lillian Vanderwall; Social Security Death Index 1935-2014 for Lillian Vanderwall; New York County Marriages 1847-9 and 1907-1936 for the marriage of Lillian Kellogg and John R. Tully; World War II Draft Registration Card, 1942; New York Marriage Index 1881-1967 for the marriage of Lillian Leff to Henry Vanderwall; Buffalo, New York City Directories: 1932, 1933, 1956, 1957.

272.

Pearl Ellis Kellogg, daughter of John Irvin (135), granddaughter of Francis (62), b. probably Sharon, Potter County, Pennsylvania September 22, 1892, d. Olean, New York February 9, 1939; m. Shinglehouse, Pennsylvania April 25, 1908 (unsourced) Harry Hammon McDonald, b. Sharon, Potter County, Pennsylvania August 17, 1886, d. Bradford, Pennsylvania March 10, 1981.

Pearl Kellogg resided with her parents until her move to Rochester, New York where in 1910 she was a lodger with her older sister, Lillian, and was employed at Kodak. This data conflicts with undocumented data giving her wedding date as 1908 in Shinglehouse. Her first child, Weldon McDonald, was born October 22, 1912. A second male child followed but was a premature birth living only 3 hours and 30 minutes on February 6, 1913. Another son was born in 1915 and a daughter in 1923. Harry McDonald was employed as a farmer in the 1920 US Census residing in Sharon, Potter County, Pennsylvania with his family. Of the three children born only Weldon was living in 1920. In the 1930 US Census Mr. and Mrs. McDonald resided at 162 2nd Street in Shinglehouse where he worked as an oil field driller. Mr. McDonald's World War I Draft Registration Card described him as being of medium build and height with dark hair and dark eyes. His occupation in 1917 was that of a farmer. Harry McDonald's World War II Draft Registration Card recorded his employer as Harder and Mitchell of Wellsville, New York working as a drilling contractor. He was 5'7" tall, weighing 152 pounds with brown hair and eyes. Pearl and Harry McDonald were buried in Maple Grove Cemetery in Shinglehouse, Pennsylvania.

Children:

563. I. ***Weldon E. McDonald, f.***

564. II. ***Drexel Dene McDonald***, b. Sharon, Pennsylvania June 3, 1915, d. Shinglehouse, Pennsylvania January 29, 1919 from acute indigestion and convulsions. He wasburied in Maple Grove Cemetery in Shinglehouse.

565. III. ***Joyce M. McDonald, f.***

References: US Census: 1900, 1910, 1920, 1930, 1940; Maple Grove Cemetery Records, Shinglehouse, Pennsylvania; World War I Draft Registration Card 1917-18; World War II Draft Registration Card, 1942; Social Security Death Index 1935-2014; New York State Death Index 1880-1956 for Pearl McDonald.

273.

Alonzo Albertus "Bert" Kellogg, son of John Irvin (135), grandson of Francis (62), b. Inavale/Friendship, New York September 25, 1894, d. Olean, New York October 1, 1962; m. Olean, New York October 10, 1915 Doris Azelle Perry, b. Pennsylvania January 29, 1897, d. Shinglehouse, Pennsylvania

June 11, 1964 from a coronary thrombosis. Bert Kellogg resided with his parents in Sharon, Potter County, Pennsylvania until his 1915 marriage.

Bert and Doris Kellogg and their growing family resided in Shinglehouse, Pennsylvania on Pleasant Street and later at 13 Honeoye Street during the 1920s and 1930s. The 1940 US Census found the Kellogg family living in Sharon in Potter County. Mr. Kellogg was employed as an oil and gas field driller. His World War I Draft Registration Card described him as being of medium build and height with gray eyes and light brown hair. He worked as a laborer for the Potter Gas Company. Mr. Kellogg's World War II Draft Registration Card listed his employer as the John T. Cunningham Drilling Company of Rixford, Pennsylvania. He was described as being 5'8" tall, weighing 230 pounds with black hair, blue eyes, and a ruddy complexion. Bert had a scar on his right hand. Bert and Doris Kellogg were buried in Maple Grove Cemetery in Shinglehouse, Pennsylvania.

Children:

566. I. ***Karl C. Kellogg, f.***

567. II. ***Ervin Glenn Kellogg, f.***

568. III. ***Perry D. Kellogg, f.***

569. IV. ***Gifford C. Kellogg, f.***

570. V. ***Kingdon A. Kellogg, f.***

571. VI. ***Marjorie Dawn Kellogg, f.***

572. VII. ***Laurie Gene Kellogg, f.***

573. VIII. ***Alice E. Kellogg, f.***

574. IX. ***John Richard Kellogg, f.***

References: US Census: 1900, 1910, 1920, 1930, 1940; Maple Grove Cemetery Records, Shinglehouse, Pennsylvania; World War I Draft Registration Cards, 1917-8; World War II Draft Registration Card, 1942; New York County Marriage Records 1848-9 and 1907-1936; Pennsylvania Death Certificates 1906-1966 for Doris Kellogg; Social Security Death Index 1935-2014.

274.

Cecil Dell Kellogg, son of John Irvin (135), grandson of Francis (62), b. Shinglehouse, Pennsylvania

October 17, 1896, d. Olean, New York October 5, 1971; m. place not known July 4, 1918 Julia Wingard, b. McKean County, Pennsylvania, b. McKean County, Pennsylvania September 17, 1895, d. St. Francis Hospital Olean, New York November 17, 1985.

Cecil Kellogg resided with his parents until his 1918 marriage. Mr. Kellogg signed up for student military training with the Army though a Leigh University program from September 19, 1918 to December 7, 1918. He did not see any military action. The 1920 US Census found Cecil and Julia Kellogg residing in Ceres, Pennsylvania with his brother-in-law, Clyde Wingard, and sister-in-law, Marlene Wingard, and his eldest sister's daughter, Onnalee Tully. He was employed as an oil and gas tool dresser. In 1930 Cecil and Julia Kellogg continued to reside with the Wingards with their four children: James, Robert, Muriel, and Donald. Cecil Kellogg was an oil lease driller. The Kellogg family had expanded to include Helen and Thomas. A daughter, Nancy, was born and died in 1937. The Wingards still lived with the Kelloggs in Ceres, Pennsylvania where they resided on Bells Run Road and where Cecil Kellogg was still in the drilling business. Cecil Kellogg's World War I Draft Registration Card listed his employer as the Potter Gas Company in Shinglehouse. His World War II Draft Registration Card described him as of dark complexion with hazel eyes and black hair. He was 5'10" tall and weighed 145 pounds. Mr. Kellogg was employed by Joe Flannagan of Bradford, Pennsylvania. Julia Wingard Kellogg was the daughter of Lorenzo Wingard (1860-1910) and Phebe Karr Wingard (1852-1918). Mrs. Kellogg was an active member of the Bell Run Community Club. Cecil Kellogg was a member of the Veterans of World War I Club of Bradford and the American Legion, Post 530, in Shinglehouse, Pennsylvania. Cecil and Julia Kellogg were buried in Bell Run Cemetery in McKean County, Pennsylvania near Ceres, Pennsylvania.

Children:

575. I. ***James P. Kellogg, f.***

576. II. ***Robert E. Kellogg, f.***

577. III. ***Muriel Kellogg, f.***

578. IV. ***Donald Kellogg, f.***

579. V. ***Helen Kellogg, f.***

580. VI. ***Thomas John Kellogg, f.***

581. VII. ***Nancy Kellogg***, b. and d. Shinglehouse, Pennsylvania November 3, 1937. She was buried in Maple Grove Cemetery, Shinglehouse, Pennsylvania.

References: US Census: 1900, 1910, 1920, 1930, 1940; New York Abstracts of WW I Military Service 1917-1918; World War I Draft Registration Card, 1917-8; World War II Draft Registration Card, 1942; Pennsylvania Death Certificate 1906-1966 for Nancy Kellogg; Social Security Death Index 1935-2014; Maple Grove Cemetery Records, Shinglehouse, Pennsylvania.

275.

Kenneth Erwin Kellogg, son of John Irvin (135), grandson of Francis (62), b. Sharon, Potter County, Pennsylvania December 18, 1899, d. Bellefonte, Pennsylvania April 5, 1985; m. Binghamton, New York August 23, 1919 Leona Price, b. Pennsylvania March 10, 1897, d. Bellefonte, Pennsylvania November 1980.

Kenneth Kellogg resided with his parents until his enlistment in World War I. He was inducted at Fort Slocum, New York December 28, 1917 and was discharged May 2, 1919. Private Kellogg rose to Corporal April 20, 1918 and to Sergeant on September 8, 1918. He saw engagements at St. Michael, Meuse-Argonne, Toulon, and Verdun. Sergeant Kellogg was severely wounded on October 11, 1918. His time overseas was from May10, 1918 to April 20, 1919. At the time of his marriage Kenneth Kellogg was employed as a shoe maker with the Endicott-Johnson Corporation and Leona Kellogg was a shoe assembler. They were married at the First Presbyterian Church in Binghamton, New York. The 1920 US Census found Mr. and Mrs. Kellogg residing with her parents in Union, New York. By the 1930 US Census they had moved to Bellefonte, Pennsylvania where they lived until their respective deaths. Kenneth Kellogg's World War II Draft Registration Card described him as being 5'8" tall, weighing 180 pounds with brown hair and brown eyes. It is believed they had two children, one son and one daughter. Kenneth and Leona Kellogg were buried in Union Cemetery in Bellefonte, Pennsylvania.

Children:

582. I. ***Carl M. Kellogg, f.***

583. II. ***Jean Eileen Kellogg, f.***

References: US Census: 1900, 1910, 1920, 1930, 1940; Pennsylvania WW I Veterans Service 1917-1919; World War II Draft Registration Card; New York County Marriage Records 1848-9 and 1907-1936; Union Cemetery Records, Bellefonte, Pennsylvania.

276.

Heath Everette Kellogg, son of John Irvin (135), grandson of Francis (62), b. Shinglehouse, Pennsylvania April 25, 1908, d. Mountain Clinic Olean, New York after an illness of two years March 23, 1963; m. Coleville, Pennsylvania July 5, 1952 (undocumented) Lyla Swick, b. Detroit, Michigan January 1, 1929, d. Newark, New York July 17, 2005.

Heath Kellogg resided with his parents until his marriage. He was employed as a tool dresser for the oil industry in Sharon, Potter County, Pennsylvania. Mr. Kellogg could not be found on the 1940 US Census. His World War II Draft Registration Card described him as being 6' tall weighing 240 pounds with gray eyes, brown hair, and a ruddy complexion. He worked for eleven years before his ill health and death for the Hooker Oil Company as a pumper in Rixford, Pennsylvania. It is not known how Heath Kellogg and his wife met. Mrs. Kellogg remarried to a Mr. Lawton and resided in Newark, New York before her death in 2005. Kenneth Kellogg was buried in Maple Grove Cemetery in Shinglehouse, Pennsylvania and it is believed that Lyla was also buried with him. There is no death date on her gravestone. There were no children from this marriage.

References: US Census: 1910, 1920, 1930; Pennsylvania Birth Certificates 1906-1910; New York State Death Index 1957-68 for Heath Kellogg; World War II Draft Registration Card, 1942; Maple Grove Cemetery Records, Shinglehouse, Pennsylvania.

277.

Marie Leah Kellogg, daughter of John Irvin (135), granddaughter of Francis (62), b. Shinglehouse, Pennsylvania June 9, 1913, d. Rixford, Pennsylvania August 27, 2006; m. Shinglehouse, Pennsylvania May 10, 1929 (undocumented) James Henry Swift, b. Shinglehouse, Pennsylvania October 2, 1912, d. Rixford, Pennsylvania October 25, 1993.

Marie Leah Kellogg was known to her friends and family as *Leah*. She resided with her parents on Cow Run Road in Sharon, Potter County, Pennsylvania. After her marriage the Swift family resided in Rixford, Pennsylvania where James Swift was employed in the oil industry. Mr. Swift's World War II Draft Registration Card described him as being 5'8" tall, weighing 160 pounds with brown eyes and brown hair. He was described as having a dark complexion. Leah and James Swift were buried in Maple Grove Cemetery in Shinglehouse, Pennsylvania.

Children:

584. I. ***Mildred S. Swift, f.***

585. II. ***Thelma Mae Swift, Jr., f.***

586. III. ***James Henry Swift,*** b. August 21, 1933; ***nfi.***

587. IV. ***Donald J. Swift, f.***

References: US Census: 1920, 1930, 1940; Maple Grove Cemetery Records, Shinglehouse, Pennsylvania; World War II Draft Registration Card 1942; Social Security Death Index 1935-2014.

278.

Sarah Mabel Kellogg, daughter of Willis (138), granddaughter of Francis (62), b. Falls Creek, Pennsylvania March 8, 1893, d. Emporium, Pennsylvania March 8, 1976; m. Force, Elk County, Pennsylvania September 4, 1912, George Ambrose Russell, b. Centreville, Pennsylvania May 29, 1888, d. Buffalo, New York October 28, 1962. Mabel Kellogg resided with her parents until her 1912 marriage. Mabel and George Russell resided in Jay, Pennsylvania where he worked in the coal mines as a mule driver, coal miner, and later as a general foreman. The Russells had eleven children. Mabel and George Russell were buried in St. Mary's Cemetery in St. Mary's, Pennsylvania.

Children:

588. I. ***Willis John Russell***, b. Byrnedale, Pennsylvania April 22, 1913, d. Jay, Pennsylvania May 3, 1921 from streptococci and a sore throat. Buried in Kersey, Pennsylvania.

589. II. ***Gertrude Oletha Russell, f.***

590. III. ***Martha Allene Russell, f.***

591. IV. ***George W. Russell, f.***

592. V. ***Lucille Marie Russell, f.***

593. VI. ***John Russell***, b. DuBois, Pennsylvania March 27, 1922, d. DuBois, Pennsylvania May 30, 1922. John Russell was a premature birth at 7 ½ months and survived four months. Burial location not known.

594. VII. ***Rita Mae Russell, f.***

595. VIII. ***Christine Rosella Russell, f.***

596. IX. ***Eleanor Russell, f.***

597. X. ***David Gerald Russell, f.***

598. XI. ***Anita Russell, f.***

References: US Census: 1900, 1910, 1920, 1930, 1940; St. Mary's Cemetery Records, St. Mary's, Pennsylvania; Pennsylvania Marriage Certificates 1852-1968; New York State Death Index 1957-68 for George Ambrose Russell; Social Security Death Index 1935-2014; Pennsylvania Death Certificates 1906-66 for Willis John Russell and John Russell.

279.

Frank Albertus Kellogg, son of Willis (138), grandson of Francis (62), b. Falls Creek, Pennsylvania July 1894, place of death not known, date of death not known.

Frank Kellogg's middle name was Albertus. A number of documents incorrectly transcribed his middle initial as an *S*, when it was an *A*. Frank Kellogg enlisted in the Army February 13, 1911 at 18 ½ years of age. He was promoted to Corporal First-Class October 1, 1914, as Private July 8, 1916, then Sergeant August 30, 1916, and Sergeant First Class January 23, 1918. Sergeant Kellogg saw overseas action from April 22, 1918 until March 3, 1919. He reenlisted July 8, 1919. From 1934-1948 Frank Kellogg resided in DuBois, Pennsylvania, but there is currently no further information about his life after 1948.

References: US Census: 1900, 1910; Pennsylvania World War I Veterans Service and Compensation Files 1917-1919 and 1934-1938.

281.

Gladys Eleanor Kellogg, daughter of Loyal (140), granddaughter of Francis (62), Shinglehouse, Pennsylvania January 25, 1907, d. Olean, New York April 19, 2000 after a long illness; m. (1) Olean, New York February 4, 1925 Lewis Erwin Torrey, b. Shinglehouse, Pennsylvania January 30, 1900, d. Ettersburg, Potter County, Pennsylvania February 18, 1935 from a gas pipeline explosion; m. (2) West Branch, Potter County, Pennsylvania Burrell Leslie Fox, b. Otto, Pennsylvania April 11, 1908, d. Bradford, Pennsylvania June 12, 1997.

Gladys Kellogg was raised by Charles (1861-1925) and Bertha Nichols Allen (1869-1937) of Shinglehouse, Pennsylvania after her parents' deaths. Charles Allen was a farmer and grocer in Shinglehouse. Mr. and Mrs. Allen had a grown son Eric Allen (1887-1967) who was no longer living at home when they took in Gladys. In some documents Gladys was referred to as Gladys Allen. In the 1930 US Census Gladys and Lewis Torrey resided in Sharon, Potter County, Pennsylvania where he was employed in the oil and gas industry and Gladys worked as a store clerk, probably for her adoptive mother. Gladys and Lewis Torrey had two children before his tragic death at work in 1935. Lewis Torrey had been previously married to Mildred Frances Hanks (1904-1923) and was a widower when he married Gladys. Mr. Torrey had a son, Wayne Torrey (1921-2000) by his first marriage. Gladys Torrey remained a resident of Sharon, Potter County, Pennsylvania in the 1940 US Census with her two children and her maternal grandfather, Henry Smith. Gladys Kellogg Torrey remarried to Burrell Leslie Fox at the Evangelical United Brethren parsonage in West Branch, Pennsylvania in 1947.

Mr. Fox was a widower whose first wife, Martha Elizabeth Stewart (1912-1942) had died from pneumonia and diabetes. Burrell Fox had one daughter Janet (1934-2018) from his first marriage. Gladys Kellogg Torrey Fox was a long-time employee of the Olean, New York Tile Company retiring in

1969. She was a trained beautician. Mrs. Fox was a member of the Christ United Methodist Church in Olean, New York, a twenty-six-year member of the Women of the Moose Lodge 119 in Olean, the Rebekah's of Oswayo, Pennsylvania and Shinglehouse, Pennsylvania, and the Royal Order of Amaranth Court 19 in Olean. Gladys Kellogg Torrey Fox was buried in Sharon Center Cemetery in Sharon Center, Pennsylvania as was Lewis Torrey. Burrell Fox was buried in McKean County Memorial Park in Lafayette, Pennsylvania with his first wife. Gladys' adoptive parents, Charles and Bertha Allen were buried in Maple Grove Cemetery in Shinglehouse, Pennsylvania along with their son and daughter-in-law.

Children (by first marriage):

599. I. ***Helen C. Torrey, f.***

600. II. ***Lewis Laverne Torrey, f.***

References: US Census: 1910, 1920, 1930, 1940; Pennsylvania Birth Certificates 1906-1966 for Gladys Kellogg, Lewis Torrey, and Burrell Fox; McKean County Memorial Park Records, Lafayette, Pennsylvania; Sharon Center Cemetery Records, Sharon Center, Pennsylvania; New York County Marriage Records 1847-9 and 1907-1936 for the marriage of Gladys Kellogg and Lewis Torrey; *Olean Times Herald* April 13, 2000 for Gladys E. Fox obituary.

282.

Pauline M. Kellogg, daughter of Loyal (140), granddaughter of Francis (62), b. Shinglehouse, Pennsylvania May 28, 1908, d. place of death not known, date of death not known but before 2000 based on the obituary of her sister, Gladys Kellogg Torrey Fox; m. (1) Little Genesee, New York February 14, 1925 George Samuel Jandrew, b. Holland, New York July 11, 1905, d. Bolivar, New York February 3, 1960 from a heart attack; m. (2) place of marriage not known, date of marriage not known, a Mr. Hurle.

Pauline Kellogg was raised by Little Genesee, New York school teachers Oscar (1856-1942) and Eva Burdick (1870-1944). In some documents Pauline was identified as Pauline Burdick. This made her difficult to research because after her marriage broke down, she was usually listed as Miss Pauline Burdick in the *Bolivar Breeze* newspaper. At the time of her marriage to George Jandrew Pauline was 16 years of age and a ward of the Coudersport, Pennsylvania courts. Pauline and George Jandrew had two sons, the eldest born and died in 1925. The 1930 US Census recorded Pauline and George as residing on the Bolivar Road in Bolivar. In the birth announcement for their second son, Pauline was listed as Pauline Burdick, not Kellogg. The marriage of Pauline and George Jandrew broke down in the 1930s and they divorced because George Jandrew remarried to Erma Dibble (1911-2001) by whom he had a son, Jack Jandrew. George Jandrew was employed for 33 years by the Bradford Producing Company. In 1958 Mr. Jandrew was appointed Town Superintendent for Highways in Bolivar, New York. He was a member of the F. & A. M. Macedonia Lodge No. 258 of Bolivar, New York, 32nd Degree, the Corning

Consistory, the Bolivar Methodist Church, and the Allegany County Highway Association.

George Jandrew was buried with his second wife, Erma, in Maple Lawn Cemetery in Bolivar. The *Bolivar Breeze* newspaper recorded Pauline's frequent trips from Philadelphia to visit her adoptive mother, Eva Burdick, and in Mrs. Burdick's obituary, Pauline was identified as Eva Burdick's foster daughter. The 1940 US Census indicated that Pauline Burdick had resided in Buffalo, New York in 1935 and in 1940 was a servant at the home of the Sylvester Connolly family of Philadelphia. Public Records indicate that a Pauline Jandrew resided in Allentown, New York in 1986, Richburg, New York in 1992, and Bolivar, New York in 1994-5. In the obituary for Pauline's sister, Gladys Kellogg Torrey Fox, Pauline was identified as Pauline Hurle and noted as deceased. Information about additional marriages and/or children is currently not know. Walter Lee Jandrew's obituary did not identify Pauline as his mother. Instead, his step-mother who likely raised him, was listed as his mother.

Children (by first marriage):

601. I. ***Leon F. Jandrew***, b. and d. in Little Genesee, New York December 1925 and was buried in Wells Cemetery in Little Genesee, New York.

602. II. ***Walter Lee Jandrew, f.***

References: US Census: 1910, 1920, 1930, 1940; New York State Census: 1915; Wells Cemetery Records, Little Genesee, New York; Maple Lawn Cemetery Records, Bolivar, New York; Pennsylvania Birth Certificates 1906-1966 for Pauline Kellogg; New York State County Marriage Records 1847-9 and 1907-36 for Pauline Kellogg's marriage to George Jandrew; Social Security Death Index 1935-2014 for George Jandrew; *Star-Gazette*, March 29, 2010 for the obituary of Walter Lee Jandrew; *Bolivar Breeze 1891-1965*, selected issues.

283.

Winifred Doris Kellogg, daughter of Loyal (140), granddaughter of Francis (62), b. Shinglehouse, Pennsylvania January 18, 1910, d. Yelm, Washington March 31, 2004; m. place not known, date not known Rodney Alex Gilmore, b. Pennsylvania January 3, 1911, d. Yelm, Washington July 26, 2001.

It is currently not known who raised Winifred Kellogg after her parents' deaths. It is currently not known how many marriages she may have had or if she had any children. Her husband, Rodney Gilmore was a bachelor until after World War II. Mr. Gilmore resided in Deptford, New Jersey based on 1920, 1930, and 1940 US Census Records. He served in the US Army from February 4, 1942 until his release September 20, 1945. Winifred and Rodney Gilmore were buried in Yelm Public Cemetery in Yelm, Washington.

References: US Census: 1910, 1920, 1930, 1940; Pennsylvania Birth Certificates 1906-1910 for Winifred Kellogg; Yelm Public Cemetery Records, Yelm, Washington; Washington State Death Index

1940-2014 for Winifred and Rodney Gilmore, Social Security Death Index 1935-2014; World War II Army Enlistment Records 1938-46 for Rodney Gilmore.

284.

Marshall Worth Beebe, son of Bertha (141), grandson of Francis (62), b. Shinglehouse, Pennsylvania June 16, 1900, d. Wellsville, New York June 5, 1985; m. (1) Wellsville, New York March 6, 1919 Della L. Ackerman, b. Scio, New York January 27, 1900, d. Wellsville, New York May 8, 1932; m. (2) Scio, New York December 14, 1933 Virginia Belle Emrick, b. West Milton, Ohio, July 17, 1915, d. Angelica, New York February 1994, divorced.

Marshall Beebe resided with his parents in Wellsville, New York until the 1920 US Census recorded his residence in Scio, New York. He was employed by the Aluminum Works in Wellsville. His World War I Draft Registration Card noted his address as 130 North Highland Avenue working for the Victor Aluminum Company in Wellsville as a welder. He was described as tall with medium build and brown hair and eyes. In the 1930 and 1940 US Census records Marshall Beebe was employed as a welder for the Sinclair Refinery in Wellsville and resided in Scio, New York. Marshall Beebe had three children by his first wife: Barbara, Lewis, and Marjorie. Della Ackerman Beebe was the daughter of Earl Ackerman and Lena Berry Ackerman of Belmont, New York. By his second marriage Marshall Beebe had another son Bruce. Based on Social Security Applications and Claims, it is believed that Marshall and Virginia Beebe were divorced sometime after 1946 because Virginia's Social Security records indicate her name in 1948 was Virginia Ennis, in 1969 Virginia Kiefer, and in 1988 Virginia Palmer. A Virginia Palmer died in Angelica, New York February 1994 and it is assumed that this death was hers. Some undocumented sources suggest that Marshall Beebe remarried a third time, but this information was not included because there was too much conflicting information and no documents to verify such a marriage. Marshall Beebe was buried in Woodlawn Cemetery Wellsville, New York with his first wife, parents, and son Kenneth. It is not currently known where Virginia Beebe was buried.

Children (by first marriage):

603. I. ***Barbara Beebe, f.***

604. II. ***Kenneth Lewis Beebe***, b. Wellsville, New York September 23, 1924, d. Wellsville, New York January 2, 1940 and buried in Woodlawn Cemetery in Wellsville.

605. III. ***Marjorie Beebe, f.***

Children (by second marriage):

606. IV. ***Bruce Marshall Beebe, f.***

References: US Census: 1910, 1920, 1930, 1940; New York State Census: 1905, 1915, 1925; Woodlawn Cemetery Records, Wellsville, New York; New York County Marriage 1847-9 and 1907-1936; Social Security Death Index for Marshall Beebe and Virginia Palmer; World War I Draft Registration Card 1917-8; Social Security Applications and Claims; New York Death Index 1852-1956 for Della Ackerman Beebe.

285.

Royal Joseph Kellogg, son of Loren (142), grandson of Royal Jasper (65), b. Aledo, Illinois February 26, 1906, d. Nevada, California November 3, 1991; m. place not known, date not known, Rose Teresa Swords, b. San Francisco, California February 2, 1911, d. place not known December 9, 1999.

Royal Kellogg resided with his parents as recorded in the 1910 US Census. After his parent's separation, Mr. Kellogg lived with his paternal aunt and uncle, Myrtle and Rufus Carrell in Galesburg, Illinois. The 1930 US Census found Royal Kellogg residing in San Francisco working as a clothing salesman and living with the James Barns family. By 1935 he had moved to San Jose, California and in 1940 to Sacramento, California. His World War II Draft Registration Card noted his employer as the California State Automobile Association. He was 6' tall, weighed 160 pounds with brown hair and brown eyes. Royal and Rose were married before the 1940 US Census. It is not known if they had any children. Royal and Rose Kellogg were buried in St. Patrick's Cemetery in Grass Valley, California.
References: US Census: 1910, 1920, 1930, 1940; City Directories for San Francisco: 1927, 1932, 1933; St. Patrick's Cemetery, Grass Valley, California; California Death Index 1940-1997 for Royal Kellogg; World War II Draft Registration Card, 1940; California Birth Index 1905-1995 for Rose Kellogg; Social Security Death Index 1935-2014.

286.

Elizabeth L. Kellogg, daughter of Loren (142), granddaughter of Royal Jasper (65), b. Illinois 1910, d. Cypress, California June 1, 1948; m. California June 8, 1932 Herbert James Lindstrum, b. Illinois June 3, 1906, d. Orange County, California December 14, 1990.

Elizabeth resided with her parents until their separation. In 1920 she was the ward of Mr. and Mrs. Charles McKinley of Galesburg, Illinois. The 1930 US Census noted her employment and residence as a servant in the household of the Ray Arnold family of Galesburg. It is not known how she met her husband or when she moved to California. In the 1940 US Census Elizabeth and Herbert Lindstrum resided at 7327 Ridge Avenue in Los Angeles. He was an attorney in private practice. They did not have any children in 1940. Herbert Lindstrum served in the US Army during World War II enlisting September 11, 1942 and remaining in active service until August 31, 1961. He was promoted to Captain October 10, 1947. After Elizabeth's death in 1948, Herbert Lindstrum remarried to Stella Mae Steidel. Elizabeth Kellogg Lindstrum was buried in Cypress Lawn Memorial Park in Cypress, California. Herbert Lindstrum was buried with his second wife in Melrose Abbey Memorial Park in

Anaheim, California. It does not appear that Elizabeth and Herbert Lindstrom had any children.

References: US Census: 1910, 1920, 1930, 1940; California County Birth, Marriage, Death Records 1849-1980 for the marriage of Elizabeth Kellogg; Cypress Gardens Memorial Park Cemetery Records, Cypress, California; Melrose Abbey Memorial Park Cemetery Records, Anaheim, California; US Select Military Registers 1862-1985 for Herbert Lindstrum's military records; California Death Index 1940-1997 for Herbert Lindstrum's death.

287.

Eleanor Charlene Kellogg, daughter of Loren (142), granddaughter of Royal Jaspar (65), b. Oklahoma City, California June 7, 1927, d. Edmond, Oklahoma October 29, 2017; m. Oklahoma City, Oklahoma July 23, 1946 William Mitchell Dysart, b. Oklahoma City, Oklahoma October 18, 1922, d. Edmond, Oklahoma December 20, 2014.

Eleanor Charlene Kellogg resided with her parents in the 1930 US Census. After her parents separated, she remained with her mother who took in lodgers based on the 1940 US Census. Eleanor Charlene Kellogg married William Dysart in 1946. Her obituary described her husband as the *love of her life.* William Dysart served in the US Navy during World War II. His World War II Draft Registration Card described him as having a dark complexion, 5'9" tall, weighing 149 pounds with blue eyes and brown hair. After his military service he managed Lindsey Well Service. Eleanor and William Dysart had five children: William Mitchell Dysart, Jr., Ronald Dysart, Patricia Dysart (Palmer), Rebecca Dysart, and Kelly Dysart Garrett who predeceased them. Eleanor's obituary noted twelve grandchildren and eleven great-grandchildren and a grandson, Cliff Blackwood who predeceased her. Further information on Eleanor's descendants is currently unavailable. Eleanor and William Dysart were buried in Fort Sill National Cemetery in Elgin, Oklahoma.

References: US Census: 1930, 1940; Fort Sill National Cemetery Records, Elgin, Oklahoma; World War II Draft Registration Card, 1942; Oklahoma Marriage Records 1890-1995; Duncan, Oklahoma newspaper obituaries courtesy of the Don Grantham Funeral Home.

288.

Glenn Theodore Carrell/Carroll, son of Myrtle (145), grandson of Royal (65), b. North Dakota August 13, 1906, d. Jefferson County, Texas September 14, 1995; m. Warren, Illinois May 28, 1927 Fern Cleon Smith, b. Galesburg, Illinois February 4, 1911, d. probably Texas December 29, 1990.

Glenn Carroll resided with his parents until his marriage in 1927. The 1930 US Census recorded Glenn and Fern Carroll as residents of Galesburg, Illinois with one son, Robert G. Carroll. He was employed as a railroad switchman. In the 1940 US Census the family still resided in Galesburg and there were now six children: Robert, Richard, Marilyn, Mary, David, and Martha. Another daughter

Frances was born in 1951 in Galesburg. It is not known when the Carrolls moved to Texas, nor is it known where there were buried.

Children:

607. I. ***Robert G. Carroll***, b. Illinois July 28, 1928, ***nfi.***

608. II. ***Richard W. Carroll***; m. Alice LaRue Kennon, Norfolk, Virginia June 26, 1953, divorced; ***nfi.***

609. III. ***Marilyn J. Carroll***, b. Illinois April 7, 1933; m. Acie R Winder, ***nfi.***

610. IV. ***Mary P. Carroll***, Illinois August 5, 1936; m. Kenneth Dale Simmons, divorced; ***nfi.***

611. V. ***David L. Carroll,*** b. Galesburg a. 1939; ***nfi.***

612. VI. ***Martha Ann Carroll***, b. Galesburg, Illinois October 2, 1939, d. Galesburg, Illinois June 10, 1940. Burial site is not known.

613. VII. ***Frances Joy Carroll***, b. Galesburg, Illinois September 3, 1951, d. Beaumont, Texas October 23, 1983; ***nfi.***

References: US Census: 1910, 1920, 1930, 1940; Illinois Marriage Records 1800-1940; Social Security Death Index 1935-2014; Social Security Applications and Claims Index for Glenn Carroll.

289.

Ellen Louise Carrell/Carroll, daughter of Myrtle (145), granddaughter of Royal (65), b. North Dakota August 22, 1910, d. El Paso, Texas October 1990; m. place of marriage not known, date of marriage not known Leonard J. Younger, b. Lafayette, Indiana March 2, 1910, d. El Paso, Texas March 28, 1992.

Ellen Louise Carroll resided with her parents as recorded in the 1910, 1920, and 1930 US Census records. However, the 1930 US Census listed Ellen Carroll as divorced and working as a sales lady for a drug store. It is not known who her husband was. Leonard Younger was single in the 1930 US Census working in San Antonio, Texas as an auto mechanic. It is not known how Leonard and Ellen met but they were married by the time of the 1940 US Census. His World War II Draft Registration Card listed their residence as Austin, Texas and described him as having a light complexion, 5'11" tall, weighing 165 pounds with brown hair and eyes. It is not currently known if there were any children, nor is it know where they were buried.

References: US Census: 1910, 1920, 1930, 1940; World War II Draft Registration Card, 1940; Texas

Death Index 1956-2010; Social Security Death Index 1935-2014; Social Security Applications for Louise and Leonard Younger.

291.

Blair Jones Van Wormer, son of Sarah (151), son of Harriet (70), b. Connecticut February 8, 1933, still living; m. (1) Connecticut, 1954 Elizabeth P., maiden name not known, b. 1933, divorced Simsbury, Connecticut 1981; m. (2) Bloomfield, Connecticut April 17, 1982 Anne Marie Hobson Stepler, b. June 15, 1947, still living.

There is little current information available about Blair Wormer. At the time of his first marriage, both he and his wife were college graduates. Mr. Wormer was employed by Connecticut Mutual Life Insurance Company. At the time of the divorce of Blair and Elizabeth Wormer there were no children under 18 years of age. It is believed that they had at least one daughter. Elizabeth Wormer remarried December 18, 1982 to Oliver K. Nelson. Blair Wormer's second wife, Ann Marie Hobson was previously married to Paul S. Stepler with whom she had two children by the time of their 1979 divorce.

Children (by first marriage):

614. I. ***Tobi Sarah Van Wormer***, b. a. 1962, m. Greenwich, Connecticut September 14, 1997 Bruce V. Andrews; ***nfi.***

References: US Census: 1940; Connecticut Divorce Index 1968-91 for Blair and Elizabeth Wormer; Connecticut Marriage Index 1959-2001 for Blair Wormer's second marriage; US Public Records, 1950-1993 for Blair Wormer; Connecticut Marriage Index 1959-2012 for Tobi Sarah Van Wormer.

292.

Helen Virginia Shea, daughter of Margaret (154), granddaughter of Harlie (71), b. Rochester, New York June 1, 1919, d. Rochester, New York March 19, 1995 from natural causes; m. Rochester, New York February 14, 1946 George Conrad Pfromm, Jr., b. January 20, 1920 Herzfeld, Hessen, Germany, d. Rochester, New York December 30, 1977 from lung cancer.

Helen Shea resided with her parents until her marriage in 1946. In the 1940 US Census she was employed as a clerk in a department store. George Conrad Pfromm, Jr. arrived in the United States through New York City from Germany August 8, 1925. He became a naturalized citizen and served in the US Army from January 20, 1938 to November 21, 1945. His World War II Draft Registration Card described him as being 5'7 ½ "tall, weighing 168 pounds with blue eyes and blonde hair. Helen and George Pfromm were buried in Riverside Cemetery, Rochester, New York in Section H6, graves 257 and 258.

Children:

615. I. ***Carol Ann Pfromm, f.***

616. II. ***Bonnie Lee Pfromm, f.***

617. III. ***Susan Lynne Pfromm, f.***

References: US Census: 1920, 1930, 1940; New York State Census: 1925; Social Security Death Index 1935-2014; Riverside Cemetery Records, Rochester, New York; State of Georgia Naturalization Records 1893-1991 for George Pfromm, Jr.; US Veterans Department Affairs Death File 1850-2010 for George Pfromm, Jr.

Fifth Generation Line of Descent from Abel Root, Sr.

293.

Francis Edward Burke, son of Gladys (155), grandson of Judson (73), b. Ypsilanti, Michigan October 4, 1899/1900, d. High Ridge, Missouri June 28, 1978; m. (1) place not known, date not known, Loretta Bell Taylor, b. St. Louis, Missouri November 20, 1902, d. place not known, June 6, 1992, divorced; m. (2) place not known, date not known Gertrude Malcom, b. place not known, April 19, 1923, d. High Ridge, Missouri June 20, 2001.

Francis Burke resided with his parents until World War I. His World War I Draft Registration Card for 1917 listed his residence with an aunt in Chicago, Illinois where he worked for the Ford Motor Company. Mr. Burke was described as being of medium height and weight with gray eyes and light brown hair. He married sometime after registering for the draft because his first child was born in 1918. The 1930 US Census recorded his residence as St. Louis, Missouri with his first wife and three daughters working as a clerk in a grocery store. In 1940 the Burke family continued to reside in St. Louis where Francis Burke was employed as a maintenance man. Mr. Burke's World War II Draft Registration Card listed his employer as a realty company. He was 5'7" tall weighing 150 pounds with blue eyes and brown hair. Francis Burke served in the US military from September 18, 1942 until April 2, 1943. Sometime after World War I Francis and Loretta Burke separated and divorced. Loretta Bell Taylor Burke remarried to John R. Jose. Loretta and her second husband were buried in Jefferson Barracks National Cemetery in St. Louis while Francis and Gertrude Burke were buried in St. John's Cemetery in High Ridge, Missouri.

Children (by first marriage):

618. I. ***Kathleen M. Burke, f.***

619. II. ***Leona F. Burke, f.***

620. III. ***Patricia Virginia Burke, f.***

References: US Census: 1900, 1910, 1930, 1940; World War I Draft Registration Card, 1917-8; World War II Draft Registration Card, 1942; US Veterans Affairs Death File 1850-2010; St. John's Cemetery Records, High Ridge, Missouri; Jefferson Barracks National Cemetery Records, St. Louis, Missouri; Social Security Death Index 1935-2014; Missouri Birth Records 1847-1910 for Loretta Bell Taylor.

296.

Harold J. Burke, son of Gladys (155), grandson of Judson (73), b. Ypsilanti, Michigan November 2, 1904, d. Clearwater, Florida October 29, 1993; m. place not known, date not known Sarah Belle Witherspoon, b. Indiana March 12, 1906, d. Pinellas, Florida October 27 1985.

Harold Burke resided with his parents in the 1910 US Census in Chicago. In 1920 the US Census recorded Harold Burke residing with an aunt and uncle in Ann Arbor, Michigan. At the time of the 1930 US Census Harold Burke had married and had a daughter Lois Elaine. He was employed as a foreman for a lumber company in St. Louis. In 1940 the Burke family resided in Richmond Heights, Missouri with a second daughter, Maxine. Mr. Burke was a salesman for a hardware company. His World War II Draft Registration Card described him as being 5'10" tall, weighing 142 pounds with blue eyes and brown hair. He worked for the Central Hardware Company. It does not appear that he served in the military during World War II. Further information on his later life is not known at this time. Harold and Sarah Burke were buried in the Calvary Catholic Cemetery in Clearwater, Florida.

Children:

621. I. ***Lois Elaine Burke, f.***

622. II. ***Maxine Burke, f.***

References: US Census: 1910, 1920, 1930, 1940; World War II Draft Registration Card; Florida Death Index 1877-1998; Social Security Death Index 1935-2014.

297.

Howard Thomas Burke, son of Gladys (155), grandson of Judson (73), b. Ypsilanti, Michigan April 28, 1906, d. Caseyville, Illinois August 2, 1940; m. place not known, date not known Velma G. Priddy, b, Oklahoma June 27, 1908, d. Illinois September 5, 1958.

Howard Burke resided with his parents in the 1910 US Census. In the 1920 US Census he resided with an aunt and uncle in Chicago. Howard Burke cannot be found on the 1930 US Census but in the 1940 US Census he was married residing in St. Louis where he was employed as an investigator for the Better Business Bureau. His cause of death in 1940 is not currently known but it came a few months after the 1940 Census. It does not appear that he and his wife had any children. Velma Burke had two years of college and was employed as a bookkeeper for a department store in 1940. She remarried to a Mr. Lindhorst and was buried in Valhalla Gardens in Belleville, Illinois. Her grave marker indicates she was a mother but who her children were and by whom is currently not known. Howard Burke was buried in Mt. Hope Cemetery Mausoleum and Crematory in Lemay, Missouri.

References: US Census: 1910, 1920, 1930, 1940; Mt. Hope Cemetery Mausoleum and Crematory Records, Lemay, Missouri; Valhalla Gardens Cemetery Records, Belleville, Illinois; Illinois Death Index 1916-47 for Howard Thomas Burke.

299.

Thomas Richard Burke, son of Gladys (155), grandson of Judson (73), b. Chicago, Illinois January 27, 1911, d. Sunrise, Missouri December 1981; m. place not known, date not known, Mabel B., last name not known, b. a. 1920, death place and date not known.

Thomas Burke resided with his mother and step-father in the 1920 and 1940 US Census records. He cannot be found on the 1930 US Census. In 1940 Mr. Burke was a truck driver for a construction company in St. Louis. His World War II Draft Registration Card for 1940 described him as 5'8" tall, weighing 160 pounds with a ruddy complexion, blue eyes and brown hair. Thomas Burke was single at the time he registered for the draft.

Further information on Thomas Richard Burke and any possible family is currently unavailable. Mr. Burke was buried in Greenmore Memorial Gardens in Barnett, Missouri. It is not known if his wife was buried there as well.

References: US Census: 1920, 1940; World War II Draft Registration Card, 1940; Social Security Death Index 1935-2014 for Thomas R. Burke; Cook County Birth Certificates 1871-1922 for Thomas R. Burke.

300.

Donald P. or Donald Woodburn Donnelly, son of Gladys (155), grandson of Judson (73), b. Illinois June 16, 1915, d. St. Louis, Missouri December 18, 1970; m. place not place, date not known Gertrude Malcom Donnelly, b. Indiana November 23, 1918, d. March 19, 1973.

Little is known at this time about Donald Donnelly. In the 1920 US Census he resided with his parents, but he cannot be found on the 1930 US Census. In the 1940 US Census he was married and was described as 5'11" tall, weighing 147 pounds with a ruddy complexion, blue eyes and brown hair.

He was employed as a truck driver. Donald Donnelly resided with his wife, parents, sister, and a half-brother in St. Louis. A 1960 City Directory for St. Louis identified his employment as a coal dealer. Donald and Gertrude Donnelly were buried in Resurrection Cemetery in Affton, Missouri with a son who died at five years of age. It is not currently known if there were more children.

Children:

623. I. ***Lawrence E. Donnelly***, b. May 1940, d. October 29, 1945. He was buried with his parents in Resurrection Cemetery in Affton, Missouri.

References: US Census: 1920, 1940; World War II Draft Registration Card, 1940; Social Security Death Index 1935-2014; Resurrection Cemetery Records, Affton, Missouri; St. Louis City Directory 1960.

301.

Marguerite Jane Donnelly, daughter of Gladys (155), granddaughter of Judson (73), b. St. Louis, Missouri August 4, 1921, d. St. Louis, Missouri June 24, 2000; m. place not known, date not known Herbert Henry Lohmar, b. Springfield, Illinois May 10, 1916, d. St. Louis, Missouri February 1, 2001 from natural causes. Marguerite Donnelly resided with her parents until her marriage sometime between 1945 and 1950. Her husband, Herbert Lohmar registered with the draft in 1940. He was described as 5'9" tall, weighing 185 pounds with blue eyes and brown hair. He was employed with the Mississippi Glass Company as a cutter, an occupation he returned to after his military service with the US Army from October 24, 1941 to December 9, 1945. Marguerite and Herbert Lohmar were buried in Resurrection Cemetery in Affton, Missouri.

Children:

624. I. ***Michael Herbert Lohmar, f.***

625. II. ***Patrick J. Lohmar, f.***

References: US Census: 1930, 1940; World War II Draft Registration Card, 1940; US Veterans Death File 1850-2010; Social Security Death Index 1935-2014; *St. Louis Post Dispatch*, June 26, 2000 for Marguerite Donnelly Lohmar and February 4, 2001 for Herbert H. Lohmar; St. Louis City Directory, 1960.

302.

Frederick R. Holly, son of Lloyd (156), grandson of Judson (73), b. Ypsilanti, Michigan September 16, 1901, d. Saline, Michigan January 29, 1977; m. place not known, date not known, Ethel Ada Dennis, b. Michigan April 11, 1913, d. Milan, Michigan March 20, 2003.

Frederick Holly resided with his parents in the 1910 US Census. In the 1920 US Census he resided with his paternal aunt and uncle, Minerva and George Joyce in Ingham, Michigan where he worked as a mechanic in an auto factory. Mr. Holly cannot be found on the 1930 US Census but in the 1940 US Census he resided in Monroe, Michigan employed as an automobile factory machinist residing with his wife and three children: Frederick, Margaret, and Mary. Further information about Frederick and Ethel Holly is not currently known. It is not known where they were buried.

Children:

626. I. ***Frederick R. Holly, f.***

627. II. ***Margaret E. Holly, nfi.***

628. III. ***Mary L. Holly,*** b. Detroit, Michigan December 15, 1924/1926, d. Florida June 1, 2007. Resided for a time at 219 Jewell Street, Otsego, Michigan, ***nfi.***

References: US Census: 1910, 1920, 1940; Social Security Death Index 1935-2014; Michigan Death Index 1971-1996 for Frederick Holly.

303.

William E. Holly, son of Lloyd (156), grandson of Judson (73), b. Ypsilanti, Michigan February 3, 1903, d. Flint, Michigan April 3, 1934 from pneumonia and influenza; m. Carson, Michigan September 4, 1922 Helen Isabell Dennis, b. Corunna, Michigan December 12, 1904, d. Los Lunas, New Mexico March 3, 1974.

William Holly resided with his parents until his marriage. At the time of his death he was employed at Chevrolet Factory # 10 as a foreman in Flint, Michigan. He was buried in Sunset Hills Cemetery, Flint, Michigan. Helen Holly remarried to Robert Burch by the time of the 1940 US Census. Mr. Burch was employed as a welder for a furnace company. They resided in Kalamazoo, Michigan. William and Helen Holly had five children, one of whom died at the age of two years. It is not known if Helen and Robert Burch had any children. Helen and Robert Burch were buried in Sunset Memorial Park in Albuquerque, New Mexico.

Children:

629. I. ***William Frank Holly***, b. Ypsilanti, MI July 10, 1923, d. Ypsilanti, MI April 5, 1925 from a fractured skull when hit by a railroad freight train while walking on the railroad tracks. He was buried in Highland Cemetery, Ypsilanti, Michigan.

630. II. ***Wanda Grace Holly, f.***

631. III. ***Lloyd George Holly, f.***

632. IV. ***Wilma E. Holly, f.***

633. V. ***Helen Theresa Holly, f.***

References: US Census: 1910, 1920, 1930, 1940; Michigan Death Records 1867-1950 for William E. Holly and William Frank Holly; Highland Cemetery Records, Ypsilanti, Michigan; Sunset Hills Cemetery, Flint, Michigan; Sunset Memorial Park Records, Albuquerque, New Mexico; Michigan Marriage Records 1867-1952 for the marriage of William E. Holly.

304.

Lloyd Spencer Holly, son of Lloyd (156), grandson of Judson (73), b. Ypsilanti, Michigan October 5, 1904, d. Hayward, California January 19, 1982; m. (1) place not known, date not known, Edyth Adell Tyrell, b. Connecticut December 16, 1901, d. Fresno, California November 10, 1951; m. (2) Fresno, California September 14, 1963 Mildred L. Nichola Baker, divorced Alameda County, August 1966, b. place not known, July 26, 1927, d. San Lorenzo, California June 1987.

Lloyd Holly resided with his parents until he moved to New Haven, Connecticut sometime before the 1930 US Census. The reasons for the move are currently not known. At the time of the 1930 US Census Lloyd Holly was married with a daughter and worked as an operator at a moving picture theater. In the 1940 US Census Mr. Holly still resided in New Haven where he worked as a tire salesman. A son was born in 1931. Lloyd Holly's World War II Draft Registration Card described him as being 5'9" tall, weighing 156 pounds with a ruddy complexion and brown hair and brown eyes.

He worked for Rockbestos Products. Lloyd Holly saw military service in World War II with the US Navy serving from September 10, 1943 to March 30, 1945. The reasons for the Holly family's move to California are not currently known nor is the cause of death for Edyth Holly in 1951. Mr. Holly's second marriage was short lived. It is believed he had a son by his second marriage. Lloyd Holly's second wife was previously married and it is believed remarried after the couple divorced. Further details are not currently available. It is currently not known where Lloyd and Edyth Holly were buried.

Children (by first marriage):

634. I. ***Virginia Dawn Holly, f.***

635. II. ***Lloyd D. Holly, Jr., f.***

Children (by second marriage):

636. I. ***Wayne Holly***, b. California October 21, 1965; ***nfi.***

References: US Census: 1910, 1920, 1930, 1940; California Death Index 1940-1997 for Lloyd and Edyth Holly; California Marriage Index 1960-85 for the marriage of Lloyd Holly and Mildred Baker; California Divorce Index 1940-1997 for Lloyd Holly and Mildred Holly; World War II Draft Registration Card, 1940; US Veterans Death File 1850-2010.

306.

Gerald Ralph Holly, son of Lloyd (156), grandson of Judson (73), b. Ann Arbor, Michigan April 17 1924, d. Ann Arbor, Michigan December 25, 2003; m. Ypsilanti, Michigan April 13, 1946 Leatha M. Townsley, b. Vincennes, Indiana August 10, 1925, d. Ann Arbor, Michigan November 3, 2016. In the 1930 US Census, Gerald Holly resided with his parents and siblings in Ann Arbor, Michigan.

By 1940 Gerald Holly's father had died but he remained in residence with his mother and siblings. Gerald Holly enlisted with the US Army May 13, 1942. His first enlistment period ended July 27, 1943. He reenlisted July 28, 1943 and served until October 6, 1945. Mr. Holly's third enlistment ran from February 1, 1951 to June 30, 1953. Their first child was born and died in Ypsilanti, Michigan. It is believed that reenlistment brought them to Arizona where their second child was born and died. In 1956 they continued to reside in Phoenix, Arizona. At some point they returned to Michigan residing in Ann Arbor. It is not known what career Gerald Holly pursued in Michigan. Gerald and Leatha Holly were buried in Highland Cemetery in Ypsilanti, Michigan but there are no grave markers. It is currently not known if they had additional children, but one undocumented source indicated a second, unnamed daughter was born.

Children:

637. I. ***Donalee Holly***, b. Ypsilanti, Michigan December 9, 1946, d. Ypsilanti, Michigan. She was buried in Highland Cemetery without a marker.

638. II. ***William Daniel Holly***, b. Phoenix, Arizona January 13, 1952, d. Phoenix, Arizona, age 29 days from being a premature birth, fibrocystic disease, and pneumonia. He was buried in Greenwood Memory Lawn Cemetery in Phoenix.

References: US Census: 1930, 1940; Highland Cemetery Records, Ypsilanti, Michigan; Greenwood Memory Lawn Cemetery, Phoenix, Arizona; Arizona Death Record 1887-1960 for William Daniel Holly; Social Security Death Index 1935-2014; Michigan Marriage Records 1867-1952; Indiana Birth Records 1907-1940 for Leatha Townsley Holly; US Veterans Death File 1850-2010; Phoenix City Directory 1956.

307.

Daniel Holly, son of Lloyd (156), grandson of Judson (73), b. Ypsilanti, Michigan January 13, 1930, d. Duval, Florida January 5, 1989; m. Ashtabula, Ohio April 1, 1953 Donna Rhea Erickson, divorced Duval, Florida May 1963.

In the 1930 US Census Daniel Holly resided with his parents and siblings. In 1940 he continued to reside with his mother and siblings in Michigan. The circumstances of his move to Ohio are not currently known. In 1959, Daniel Holly was living in Pensacola, Florida and was a member of the US Navy. Daniel Holly resided in Jacksonville, Florida prior to his death. Further information on additional marriages and/or children are not currently available.

References: US Census: 1930, 1940; Pensacola, Florida City Directory 1959; Ohio County Marriage Record 1774-1993; Florida Divorce Record 1927-2001; Florida Death Index 1877-1998.

309.

Helen Lauren Holly, daughter of Fred (157), granddaughter of Judson (73), b. Ypsilanti, Michigan July 12, 1908, d. Ocala, Florida March 28, 1990; m. (1) Ypsilanti, Michigan August 8, 1925 William Howard Heater, divorced Ypsilanti, Michigan February 7, 1938, b. Ypsilanti, Michigan May 24, 1904, d. Ypsilanti, Michigan August 9, 1954; m. (2) Angola, Indiana June 18, 1938 Daniel Oscar Wilmore, b. Springfield, Tennessee January 17, 1916, d. Ocala, Florida August 3, 1993.

Helen Holly resided with her parents in Ypsilanti, Michigan as recorded in the 1910 and 1920 US Census records. In 1930 Helen resided with her first husband and a son. Mr. Heater was employed as a tinsmith. At the time of the 1940 US Census Helen Holly Heater had remarried and continued to reside in Ypsilanti with her two children from her first marriage. Mr. Wilmore was employed as a painter at a stove works in Ypsilanti. William Heater remarried to a Dorothy Patterson (1918-2004). David Oscar Wilmore was the owner of an electronic company in Thousand Oaks, California, served in the US Air Corps during World War II with the 17th and 82nd Airborne Division Paratroopers. He was the recipient of a Purple Heart. In addition, Mr. Wilmore was a member of the Veterans of Foreign Wars and the Arrow Club of Sioux City, South Dakota before moving to Florida in 1981.

After the death of Helen Holly Wilmore, Mr. Wilmore remarried to Arlene Ann Osbun Smith November 7, 1991. It is currently unclear if Helen and David Wilmore had any children together. David Wilmore's obituary identifies a son, Timothy Stafford, and a daughter, Susan M. Casey, both in Indianapolis, but they could be the children of Mr. Wilmore's second wife. Helen and David Wilmore were buried in Good Shepherd Memorial Gardens in Ocala, Florida.

Children (by first marriage):

639. I. ***William Heater, f.***

640. II. ***Margaret Heater,*** b. Ypsilanti, Michigan a. 1932, ***nfi.***

References: US Census: 1910, 1920, 1930, 1940; Michigan Marriage Records 1867-1952 for Helen Holly's first marriage; Michigan Divorce Records 1897-1952; Good Shepherd Memorial Gardens Records, Ocala, Florida; Florida Death Index 1877-1998; *Ocala Star-Banner*, August 4, 1993 for David Wilmore's Obituary; Indiana Marriage Records 1810-2001 for Helen Holly's marriage to David Wilmore; Florida Marriage Records 1822-1875 and 1927-2001 for David Wilmore's marriage to Arlene Ann Osbun Smith.

310.

Harold Richard Holly, son of Fred (157), grandson of Judson (73), b. Ypsilanti, Michigan September 20, 1910, d. Superior, Michigan August 13, 1988; m. Steuben, Indiana November 9, 1932 and Ypsilanti, Michigan October 28, 1939 Lillian Mary Ann Corbell/Corbeille, b. Menominee, Michigan June 20, 1914, d. Ann Arbor, Michigan June 4, 2004.

There is not much information about Harold Holly and his family. Before his marriage Harold Holly resided with his parents and worked in a paper mill. In the 1940 US Census he is recorded as Richard Holly and even though he married in 1939 was still listed as single and residing with his parents. He was employed as a waiter. It appears that he and his wife married twice, the first time as students. It is not known if the first marriage was dissolved and they later remarried. They had at least two children, a son, and a daughter whose name is not currently known. Harold and Lillian Holly were buried in St. John the Baptist Catholic Cemetery in Ypsilanti, Michigan.

Children:

641. I. ***Frederick Arthur Holly,*** b. Ann Arbor, Michigan April 4, 1949, d. Scio, Michigan September 29, 1995. It is believed that Mr. Holly married and had one Child, but there is no documentation to currently support that.

642. II. ***Female Holly nfi.***

References: US Census: 1920, 1930, 1940; St. John the Baptist Catholic Cemetery Records, Ypsilanti, Michigan; Michigan Death Index 1971-1996 for Harold Holly; Indiana Marriage Records 1810-2001; Marriage Records 1867-1952; Social Security Death Index 1935-2014.

311.

Margaret J. Holly, daughter of Fred (157), granddaughter of Judson (73), b. Ypsilanti, Michigan February 13, 1913, d. place not known, March 2006; m. place not known, date unknown, Charles Gardner, b. Ohio 1911, d. Ypsilanti, Michigan 1964.

There is little information currently available on Margaret Holly and her husband. She did not marry until after the 1930 US Census. Her first child was born in 1934. Charles Gardner was employed at an automobile factory in Ypsilanti. They had two daughters, Betty Jean and Sharon. Charles Gardner was buried in Union-Udell Cemetery in Ypsilanti, Michigan. It is not currently known where Margaret Holly Gardner was buried.

Children:

643. I. ***Betty Jean Gardner,*** b. Michigan, 1934, ***nfi.***

644. II. ***Sharon Lynn Gardner, f.***

References: US Census: 1920, 1930, 1940; Union-Udell Cemetery Records, Ypsilanti, Michigan; Ypsilanti City Directories, selected issues, Social Security Death Index 1935-2014.

312.

Lynn Joseph Holly, son of Fred (157), grandson of Judson (73), b. Ypsilanti, Michigan February 23, 1918, d. Lincoln, Michigan July 28, 2015; m. Williams, Ohio July 3, 1939 Virginia Ruth Rodgers, b. Williams, Ohio October 21, 1918, d. Alpena, Michigan January 23, 2007.

Lynn Holly resided with his parents until his marriage. He was employed by the Ford Motor Company. It is believed that Lynn and Virginia Holly had two sons and one daughter, but currently no information is available to verify the identities of their children. It is not known where Lynn and Virginia Holly were buried.

References: US Census: 1920, 1930, 1940; Social Security Death Index 1935-2014; Ohio County Marriage Records 1774-1993.

313.

Fred Richard Holly, son of Fred (157), grandson of Judson (73), b. Ypsilanti, Michigan March 25, 1920, d. Webster, New York February 15, 2015; m. place and date of marriage not known, Marilyn, last name not know.

It is not known why Fred and his brother Harold both had the same middle names—Richard. Fred resided with his parents as recorded in the 1930 and 1940 US Census records. In 1948 he was a member of the US Naval Reserves. Why he moved to the Rochester, New York area is not known. Further information on his wife and any children is not currently available.

References: US Census: 1930, 1940; Unsourced information on family trees on ancestry.com.

314.

Doris Mae Holly, daughter of Fred (157), granddaughter of Judson (73), b. Ypsilanti, Michigan May 3, 1923, d. Verona, New Jersey November 20, 2002; m. Michigan May 19, 1945 Merle Warden Burdett, b. Newark, New Jersey November 15, 1921, d. Mountainside Hospital Union, New Jersey July 23, 2013. Doris Holly resided with her parents until her marriage. Merle Burdett had three years of college education based on the 1940 US Census. He served with the US Navy in 1945 aboard the USS Pine Island. His occupation in Verona, New Jersey was Chief of the Fire Department. An unsourced obituary indicated Doris and Merle had two sons: Jay and Larry. Further information is not currently available.

References: US Census: 1930, 1940; Social Security Death Index 1935-2014; Michigan Marriage Records 1867-1952; Verona, New Jersey City Directories, selected issues.

315.

Georgia Louise Joyce, daughter of Minerva (158), granddaughter of Judson (73), b. Blue Earth, Mankato County, Minnesota November 14, 1912, d. Metairie, Louisiana July 1987; m. (1) Wood, Ohio December 12, 1931 Carl Ebert, divorced, b. Germany March 10, 1906, d. place and date of death not known; m. (2) place not known, date not known L. Torrey Gomila, b. place not known May 17 1908, d. place not known February 12, 1980, divorced Alabama August 6, 1947; m. (3) Arlington, Virginia June 15, 1962 Carroll Wright, b. Wichita, Kansas a. 1904, d. place and death date not known. Georgia Louise Joyce went by the name of *Jo*.

She was born before her parents were married and resided with them until she married in 1931. At the time of her first marriage Jo was employed as a stenographer. Her first husband was employed as a dry cleaner. Jo and her second husband had one child who died young and remains unnamed. Mr. Gomila served in the US Army from April 15, 1942 to August 28, 1945. They were divorced and L. Torrey Gomila was buried in Metairie Cemetery in New Orleans, Louisiana. Jo's third husband was a real estate consultant. Mr. Wright was previously married. Jo raised the daughter, Judy, of her youngest brother after his death and that of wife in 1952-53. It is not currently known where Jo Joyce Wright was buried.

Children (by second marriage)

645. I. ***Georgia Gomila***, b. and d. New Orleans February 1946, surviving for 36 hours.

646. II. ***Unnamed child.***

647. III. ***Missa Gomila, nfi.***

648. IV. ***L. Torrey Gomila, Jr., nfi.***

References: US Census: 1920, 1930; Minnesota Birth Index 1900-1934 for Georgia Louise Joyce; Social Security Death Index 1935-2014 for Georgia Louise Joyce Wright; Ohio Marriage Records 1774-1993 for Georgia Louise Joyce and Carl Ebert; Virginia Marriage Records 1936-2014 for Georgia Louise Joyce and Carroll Wright; New Orleans Death Records 1804-1949 for Georgia Gomila.

316.

Margaret A. Joyce, daughter of Minerva (158), granddaughter of Judson (73), b. Detroit, Michigan February 22, 1914, d. Sarasota, Florida July 15, 2001; m. (1) Angola, Indiana October 14, 1939 Maxwell Hoots, b. Decatur, Illinois April 17, 1914, d. Wayne County, Michigan December 24, 1961; m. (2) Colin MacFarlane, the widower of Margaret's former sister-in-law, Kathryn Lockmiller Joyce MacFarlane. Margaret Joyce was born before her parents were married. She resided with her parents until her marriage in 1939. Maxwell Hoots was employed as a press operator at the time of their marriage. Mr. Hoots was previously married to LaNora Faehl from December 21, 1935 to July 3, 1939. Maxwell Hoots was buried in White Chapel Memorial Park, Troy, Michigan. It is not currently known where Margaret was buried.

Children (by first marriage):

649. I. ***Joan Irene Hoots, f.***

650. II. ***Richard Maxwell Hoots, f.***

References: US Census: 1920, 1930, 1940; Social Security Death Index 1935-2014 for Margaret MacFarlane; Indiana Marriage Records 1810-2001 for Margaret Joyce and Maxwell Hoots; White Chapel Memorial Park Cemetery Records, Troy, Michigan.

317.

Judson John Joyce, son of Minerva (158), grandson of Judson (73), b. Michigan, February 8, 1915, d. Castro Valley, California November 1, 1968; m. (1) Bowling Green, Ohio September 17, 1932 Kathryn

Elizabeth Lockmiller, divorced May 4, 1938, b. Pemberville, Ohio August 26, 1912, d. Michigan April 2, 1956; m. (2) Hart, Michigan May 4, 1942 Doris May Hurnie, divorced Oceana, Michigan March 16, 1946, b. Hart, Michigan May 19, 1915, d. Florida July 1964; m. (3) Reno, Nevada, April 15, 1946 Helen Lavon Glover, b. Knoxville, Iowa April 29, 1914, d. Knoxville, Iowa December 11, 2002.

Judson John Joyce also went by the name of John Judson Joyce as noted on his tombstone. He resided with his parents until his first marriage in 1932. Mr. Joyce had two years of college and after his first divorce worked for his parents in their dry-cleaning business. He lived in a boarding house in Ypsilanti, Michigan in 1940. From March 31, 1941 until July 1, 1945, Judson Joyce served in the US Navy during World War II. Judson had two children by his first marriage: Judson John Joyce, Jr. and Dixie Lee Joyce. His first wife remarried to Colin MacFarlane of Monroe, Michigan October 14, 1939 in Angola, Indiana. In the 1940 US Census Judson Joyce's two children lived with Colin and Kathryn MacFarlane, her mother, and a boarder. Mr. MacFarlane was employed as a punch presser for an automobile equipment factory. Colin MacFarlane was born in either Scotland or Buffalo, New York, depending on the document, February 27, 1908. He died in Sarasota, Florida February 16, 1978. Kathryn died in Michigan April 2, 1956 and was buried in Roselawn Memorial Park, LaSalle, Michigan. It is not known where Colin MacFarlane was buried.

Colin and Kathryn had one son, *Coke,* who died as a teenager from a football accident. There were no children from Judson Joyce's second marriage. Doris Joyce apparently never remarried and was buried with her parents under her maiden name in the Hart Cemetery, Hart, Michigan. Mr. Joyce had a son and daughter by his third marriage. Helen Joyce, his third wife, was previously married to Cecil Blair (1913-1998) from whom she was divorced when she and John Judson Joyce married. Judson Joyce and Helen Blair met in Oakland, California at the Naval Hospital where Helen worked in the naval exchange and Judson was employed with the laundry and served as Laundry Department Head. Later, Mr. Joyce was employed at Castro Valley Hospital where he managed the laundry and housekeeping departments until his 1968 death. After John Judson Joyce's death Helen remarried to George Edward Thornton February 5, 1969 who was born February 17, 1908 and died November 29, 1994. Helen was buried with John Judson Joyce in Graceland Cemetery Knoxville, Iowa as was Helen's third husband whose remains were cremated and buried at Helen's feet. Helen's family so liked Judson Joyce that Judson and Helen decided to be buried in the same Iowa cemetery as her parents.

Children (by first marriage):

651. I. ***Judson John Joyce, Jr., f.***

652. II. ***Dixie Lee Joyce, f.***

Children (by third marriage):

653. I. ***Charles George Joyce, f.***

654. II. ***Sharon Lynn Joyce, f.***

References: US Census: 1920, 1930, 1940; US WW II Navy Muster Rolls 1938-49; California Death Index 1940-97 for Judson John Joyce; Graceland Cemetery Records, Knoxville, Iowa; Michigan Marriage Records 1867-1952 for Judson Joyce's first and second marriages; Michigan Divorce Records 1897-1952 for Judson Joyce's first and second marriages; Social Security Death Index for Doris Hurnie; Roselawn Memorial Park Cemetery Records, LaSalle, Michigan for Kathryn Joyce MacFarlane; Hart Cemetery Records, Hart, Michigan for Doris Hurnie; unsourced ancestry family tree for Judson Joyce's third marriage.

318.

Edward George Joyce, son of Minerva (158), grandson of Judson (73), b. Battle Creek, Michigan October 30, 1916, d. Pontiac, Michigan April 8, 1982 from coronary thrombosis; m. place not known, date not known, Myrtle Edith Anna Toner, b. Ontario, Canada January 3, 1917, d. Pontiac, Michigan September 13, 1987. Edward Joyce resided with his parents based on the 1920 and 1930 US Census records. He served with the US Army from May 1, 1943 to November 16, 1945. Edward and Myrtle Joyce were longtime residents of Pontiac, Michigan. In 1947 Edward Joyce worked for the family business, Joyce Dry Cleaners. At the time of his death, Mr. Joyce had retired as the custodian for the Walled Lake Schools. Edward and Myrtle Joyce were buried in Crescent Hills Cemetery, Waterford, Michigan. They had two children.

Children:

655. I. ***George Robert Joyce, f.***

656. II ***Ann M. Joyce,*** b. September 8, 1947, ***nfi.***

References: US Census: 1920, 1930, 1940; Michigan Death Certificate 1971-1996 for Edward Joyce; US Veterans Death File 1850-2010; Crescent Hills Cemetery Records, Waterford, Michigan.

322.

John D. "Jack" Joyce, son of Minerva (158), grandson of Judson (73), b. probably Michigan, b. a. 1925, place of death and date of death not known; m. Pontiac, Michigan August 25, 1944 Betty Arlene Ackerson, b. Michigan December 23, 1923, d. Pontiac, Michigan December 22, 1952.

Jack Joyce resided with his parents until his marriage. He enlisted in the US Army Infantry December 4, 1942. At the time of enlistment, he was a hotel and restaurant manager and was 5'7" tall and weighed 152 pounds. Betty Joyce served in the US Naval Reserves from February 18, 1944 until October 14, 1944. After the World War II he worked for the family dry cleaning business from 1947-50. Jack did not remarry but died within a year after Betty died, a purported suicide. Their daughter, Judy, was adopted and raised by his sister, Jo Gomila Wright. The two children were raised by Jo Gomila.

Children:

657. I. ***Ronald Lee Joyce, nfi.***

658. II. ***Gary Joyce, nfi.***

659. III. ***Judy Joyce, nfi.***

References: US Census: 1930, 1940; Michigan Death Index 1867-1950 for Betty Joyce; World War II Draft Registration Card, 1940; Pontiac, Michigan City Directories 1947, 1948, and 1950; Perry Mt. Park Cemetery Records, Pontiac, Michigan; US Headstone Applications for Military Veterans 1925-63 for Betty Joyce; Michigan Marriage Records 1867-1952.

323.

Gladys Leona Block, daughter of Elizabeth (160), granddaughter of Judson (73), b. Ypsilanti, Michigan September 28, 1914, d. Superior, Michigan March 22, 1988; m. Michigan October 21, 1935 Kenneth Root Holcomb, b. Michigan September 6, 1910, d. Milan, Michigan October 19, 1996. Gladys Leona Block went by her middle name of Leona. She resided with her parents until her marriage in 1935. In the 1940 US Census Kenneth Holcomb was a laborer with the Ford Motor Company. The family resided in Pittsfield, Michigan. Leona and Kenneth Holcomb had at least one child. Further information is not available. Leona and Kenneth were buried in Marble Park Cemetery, Milan, Michigan.

Children:

660. I. ***Robert Kenneth Holcomb***, b. Ypsilanti, Michigan August 23, 1936, d. Milan, Michigan November 14, 1995; ***nfi.***

References: US Census: 1920, 1930, 1940; Social Security Death Index 1935-2014; Michigan Death Index 1971-1996; Marble Park Cemetery Records, Milan, Michigan, which included marriage date.

324.

Vera Barbara Block, daughter of Elizabeth (160), granddaughter of Judson (73), b. Ypsilanti, Michigan September 18, 1916, d. Monroe, Michigan March 21, 2004; m. Ypsilanti, Michigan September 28, 1941 George Paul Daschner, b. Rio Grande do Sul, Brazil July 17, 1915, d. Monroe, Michigan November 29, 2006. Vera resided with her parents in Ypsilanti, Michigan until her 1941 marriage. In the 1940 US Census Vera was employed as a sorter in a laundry. Her future husband was employed as a tool and die maker for the automobile industry. George Paul Daschner was born in Brazil where his parents were missionaries. Mr. Daschner was employed with the Ford Motor Company for thirty years retiring in 1980. He was a member of the Emmanuel Lutheran Church, Ypsilanti until they moved in 1979 to Monroe, Michigan where the family joined the Trinity Lutheran Church. George Paul Daschner enjoyed hunting, golfing, fishing, and was a member of the "Clam Diggers." Vera and George Daschner had four children. One child died in infancy. At the time of Mr. Daschner's death in 2006, there were seven grandchildren and seven great-grandchildren whose names and identities are not known at this time. Vera and George Paul Daschner were buried in Highland Cemetery in Ypsilanti, Michigan.

Children:

661. I. ***Paul D. Daschner***, b. and d. Ypsilanti, Michigan August 1942 and buried in Highland Cemetery, Ypsilanti, Michigan.

662. II. ***Paula Kay Daschner, f.***

663. III. ***Theodore Daschner, nfi.***

664. IV. ***Elizabeth "Betsey" Daschner, nfi.***

References: US Census: 1920, 1930, 1940; Highland Cemetery Records, Ypsilanti, Michigan including the obituary for George Paul Daschner; Michigan Marriage Records 1867-1952; Social Security Death Index 1935-2014.

325.

Donald Frederick Block, son of Elizabeth (160), grandson of Judson (73), b. Ypsilanti, Michigan October 14, 1919, d. Ludington, Michigan January 11, 1992 from natural causes; m. Ypsilanti, Michigan February 3, 1940 Juanita F Levell, b. Vincennes, Indiana January 12, 1924, d. Pentwater, Michigan April 7, 1992.

Donald Block resided with his parents until he enlisted in the US Army serving from August 1, 1944 to February 14, 1946. Prior to his enlistment, Mr. Block was employed as a painter in Ypsilanti residing at 34 Jarvis Street. It is believed that Donald and Juanita Block had one son and two daughters but further information on children is not currently available. It is not known where Donald and Juanita Block were buried.

References: US Census: 1920, 1930, 1940; Michigan Marriage Records 1867-1952; Michigan Death Index 1971-1996; US Veterans Death File 1850-2010; Ypsilanti City Directory 1942.

326.

Frederick Lincoln Block, son of Elizabeth (160), grandson of Judson (73), b. Ypsilanti, Michigan February 12, 1924, d. Ypsilanti, Michigan January 19, 1981. Fred Block resided with his parents through 1942 at 615 Voight Street. It is not currently known if Mr. Block married and/or had children. He was buried in St. John the Baptist Catholic Cemetery in Ypsilanti, Michigan.

328.

Mary Lou Block, daughter of Elizabeth (160), granddaughter of Judson (73), b. Ypsilanti, Michigan November 20, 1930, d. North Port, Florida September 7, 2016 from cancer; m. Belleville, Michigan September 18, 1948 Edward William Meyer, b. Ypsilanti, Michigan May 19, 1929, d. Ypsilanti, Michigan December 31, 2007.

Mary Lou Block resided with her parents until her marriage in 1948. She and her husband were life-long residents of Ypsilanti. Mary Lou was a member of the Emanuel Lutheran Church in Ypsilanti and the Ypsilanti Senior Center. She enjoyed gardening, flowers, traveling, and spending time at her Florida residence. Mary Lou and Edward Meyer were buried in Highland Cemetery, Ypsilanti, Michigan.

Children:

665. I. ***James E. Meyer***, b. Ypsilanti, Michigan November 21, 1966, d. 1985 and was buried in Highland Cemetery, Ypsilanti, Michigan; ***nfi.***

666. II. ***Deborah Meyer*** m. Kenneth Walker and had two children: Christopher M. and Rachelle L.; ***nfi.***

References: US Census: 1940; Highland Cemetery Records, which included a newspaper obituary, Ypsilanti, Michigan; Michigan Marriage Records 1867-1952; Social Security Death Index 1935-2014.

329.

Marion Louise Youngs, daughter of Hazel (161), granddaughter of Judson (73), b. Ypsilanti, Michigan November 7, 1914, d. Livonia, Michigan February 14, 1982; m. Ypsilanti, Michigan September 19, 1935 Norman Emmett McCorry, b. Ontonagon, Michigan July 18, 1912, d. Memphis, Tennessee December 27, 2003.

Marion Louise Youngs resided with her parents until marriage in 1935. Norman McCorry had five years of college and in 1939 became a member of the police force in Detroit. The family resided at 13632 Tuller Avenue. From 1995 until his death, Norman McCorry resided in Memphis, Tennessee where he died. It is not known where Marion and Norman McCorry were buried.

Children:

667. I. ***Lynn Norman McCorry, f.***

References: US Census: 1920, 1930, 1940; Michigan Death Index 1974-1996 for Marion Louise McCorry; Social Security Death Index for Marion and Norman McCorry; Michigan Marriage Records 1867-1952; Memphis City Directories.

330.

Eugene Edward Youngs, son of Hazel (161), grandson of Judson (73), b. Ypsilanti, Michigan September 4, 1920, d. Santa Barbara, California July 15, 1991; m. Duval, Florida July 7, 1944 Fredda E. Rapp, b. Adele, Georgia May 17, 1925, d. Panama City, Florida September 4, 1997, divorced Bay, Florida October 19, 1973.

Eugene Youngs resided with his parents until 1941 in Ypsilanti, Michigan at 811 Lowell Street until his enlistment in the US Marine Corps. Mr. Youngs saw action in World War II and the Korean War rising to the rank of Major. US Marine Corps Muster Rolls records his rise from Second Lieutenant beginning in April 1945, Second Lieutenant, July 1946, First Lieutenant, April 1949 Lieutenant, October 1954 Marine Aviation Detective, April 1957 Captain, and 1964 Major. Eugene Youngs was buried in Santa Maria Cemetery in Santa Maria, California. Fredda Youngs was buried with her parents in Woodlawn Cemetery, Adele, Georgia under her maiden name. It is not currently known if there were any children or if Eugene Youngs remarried.

References: US Census: 1930, 1940; California Death Index 1940-97 for Eugene Youngs; Santa Maria Cemetery Records, Santa Maria, California; Woodlawn Cemetery Records, Adele, Georgia; Florida Divorce Records 1927-2001; US Marine Corps Muster Rolls 1798-1958; Social Security Death Index 1935-2014; Florida County Marriage Index 1823-1982.

331.

Agnes Clerkin, daughter of Florence (162), granddaughter of Judson (73), b. Johnsonburg, Pennsylvania October 12, 1917, d. Warren, Pennsylvania February 1989; m. (1) place not known, date not known Harold Edward Danneker, b. Williamsport, Pennsylvania February 9, 1917, d. Warren, Pennsylvania November 12, 1975; m. (2) place not known, date not known Gilbert Thomas Munch, b. Erie, Pennsylvania October 1, 1919, d. Warren, Pennsylvania August 12, 1983.

Agnes Clerkin resided with her parents until her marriage. Little is currently known about Agnes and Harold Danneker. Mr. Danneker served in the US Navy from October 8, 1935 until April 26, 1937. His World War II Draft Registration Card described him as being of dark complexion, 6'4" tall, weighing 176 pounds with blue eyes and brown hair. After the death of Harold Danneker, Agnes remarried to

Gilbert Thomas Munch. Mr. Munch served in the US Army from January 14, 1943 to March 2, 1946. Prior to enlistment he was a clerk for William I. Arbuckle in Erie, Pennsylvania. His World War II Draft Registration Card described him as being 6'1" tall, weighing 163 pounds with blonde hair and blue eyes. Gilbert Much was previously married to Eleanor Kuhn (1919-2001), whom he must have divorced in order to marry Agnes Danneker. Gilbert Much had one son by his prior marriage, Gilbert Munch (1948-2007). Agnes and Harold Danneker were buried in St. Joseph Cemetery in Warren, Pennsylvania as were Gilbert Munch and Eleanor Kuhn Munch. It is not currently known if Agnes and Harold Danneker had any children.

References: US Census: 1920, 1930, 1940; Social Security Death Index 1935-2014; St. Joseph Cemetery Records, Warren, Pennsylvania; World War II Draft Registration Cards for Harold Danneker and Gilbert Munch; US Veterans Death File 1950-2010 for Harold Danneker; US Army Enlistment Records 1938-1946 for Gilbert Munch; Erie, Pennsylvania City Directory 1942.

332.

Kathryn Margaret Clerkin, daughter of Florence (162), granddaughter of Judson (73), b. Johnsonburg, Pennsylvania March 31, 1919, d. Johnsonburg, Pennsylvania August 1990; m. place not known, date not known Stanley Joseph Kissel, b. Medix Run December 13, 1913, d. Johnsonburg, Pennsylvania February 2, 2001.

Kathryn Clerkin resided with her parents until her marriage sometime after 1935 and before the birth of her first child in 1937. Stanley Kissel was employed as a clerk for Louis Notarianni in the 1940 US Census. His World War II Draft Registration Card described him being 6'1" tall, weighing 155 pounds with blue eyes and brown hair. Kathryn and Stanley Kissel had four children, two of whom died prematurely. It is not known where the Kissel family were buried, but it is assumed in Johnsonburg, Pennsylvania where they resided.

Children:

668. I. ***Stanley Joseph Kissel, Jr.,*** b. St. Mary's, Pennsylvania May 20 1937, d. Pennsylvania May 15, 1989. Undocumented sources indicate he was Married and had three children; ***nfi***.

669. II. ***Gerald Thomas Kissel,*** b. Johnsonburg, Pennsylvania July 7, 1939, d. Bel Air, Maryland February 1, 2016. Gerald Kissel married in Ridgeway, Pennsylvania on January 15, 1966. Undocumented sources indicate there were three children; ***nfi.***

670. III. ***Katherine Kissel***, b. St. Mary's, Pennsylvania July 9, 1942, d. Ridgeway, Pennsylvania September 15, 1942 from spina bifida and spinal meningitis. Burial was in Johnsonburg, Pennsylvania.

671. IV. ***Male Kissel***, b. and d. Ridgeway, Pennsylvania May 9, 1945 as a premature birth.

References: US Census: 1920, 1930, 1940; Social Security Death Index 1935-2014; World War II Draft Registration Card, 1942; Pennsylvania Death Certificates 1906-1966 for Katherine Kissel and male Kissel; US Cemetery and Funeral Home Collection 1847 to present.

333.

Leo Francis Clerkin, son of Florence (162), grandson of Judson (73), b. Johnsonburg, Pennsylvania February 28, 1921, d. Burkeville, Virginia March 25, 2018; m. (1) Russell, Alabama August 31, 1942 Georgia Mae Jurena, b. Tobias, Nebraska April 1, 1922, d. Rice, Virginia August 28, 1997; m. (2) place not known, date not know Nadine Flood.

In the 1940 US Census Leo Clerking was a solider serving in Aguadilla, Puerto Rico at the Borinquen Field Base. He served during World War II from February 9, 1942 to December 4, 1945, enlisting at Harrisburg, Pennsylvania. His World War II Draft Registration Card described him as 5'11" tall, weighing 172 pounds with blue eyes and brown hair. His obituary stated that Leo Clerkin was a Paratrooper during World War II serving with the US Army 101 Screaming Eagles. He was a medic and received the Bronze Star along with other medals. It is not known when the Clerkin family moved to Farmville, Virginia, but Leo Francis Clerkin was a member of St. Theresa's Catholic Church and the Old Dominion Beagle Club. Mr. Clerkin's second marriage lasted six months. Leo and Georgia Clerkin had four daughters. Daughter Kathleen Clerkin McGonigal, and grandchildren Tracy Lynn Gilliam and Benjamin Gilliam predeceased Leo Clerkin. He was survived by eight grandchildren and twelve great-grandchildren. Leo and Georgia Clerkin were buried in Trinity Memorial Gardens, Rice, Virginia.

Children:

672. I. ***Geraldine Marie Clerkin, f.***

673. II. ***Kathleen Clerkin, f.***

674. III. ***Diane Lynn Clerkin, f.***

675. IV. ***Mary Lou Clerkin, f.***

References: US Census: 1930, 1940; Social Security Death Index 1935-2014; Alabama Marriage Records 1805-1967 for Leo Clerkin's marriage to Georgia Jurena; Trinity Memorial Gardens Records, Rice, Virginia; World War II Draft Registration Card, 1942; Pennsylvania World War II Compensation Files 1950-1966.

334.

Charles Edward Clerkin, son of Florence (162), grandson of Judson (73), b. Johnsonburg, Pennsylvania August 29, 1927, d. Johnsonburg, Pennsylvania December 9, 2005; m. place not known, date not known July 26, 1947 Mae Steudler, place and date of birth not known, place and date of death not known.

Charles Clerkin resided with his parents in the 1930 US Census. In the 1940 US Census Mr. Clerkin lived with his sister Agnes and her husband. He was single at the time. Charles Clerkin served in the US Navy from January 4, 1945 to March 2, 1946 aboard the USS Joseph P. Kennedy, Jr. Charles and Mae Clerkin had six children, three sons and three daughters. One daughter Paula Kay Clerkin, b. St. Mary's, Pennsylvania March 27, 1956, d. June 4, 1956 from pulmonic stenosis and having only one ventricle. The identities of the other five children are not currently known.

References: US Census: 1930, 1940; Pennsylvania Veterans World War II Files 1950-66; Holy Rosary Cemetery Records, Johnsonburg, Pennsylvania; Pennsylvania Death Certificates 1906-66 for Paula Kay Clerkin.

335.

Anne Williams, daughter of Helen (163), granddaughter of Ina (78), b. Detroit, Michigan September 5, 1917, d. Cheboygan, Michigan May 18, 2009 at Hospice House. Anne Williams worked for forty-five years at J. L. Hudson and Company, later Dayton-Hudson, as an Executive Secretary retiring in 1979. In 1995 Anne moved to Topinabee, Michigan with her sister, Jane Williams Biggs where Anne was active in the Topinabee Community Church, Cheboygan Memorial Hospital Auxiliary, and enjoyed traveling to Scotland, cross-stitch, and bridge. Miss Williams never married.

References: US Census: 1920, 1930, 1940; interview with Richard Biggs, Anne Williams' nephew.

336.

Jane Williams, daughter of Helen (163), granddaughter of Ina (78), b. Detroit, Michigan September 23, 1915, d. Cheboygan, Michigan January 26, 1999 at the Community Memorial Hospital; m. Birmingham, Michigan June 6, 1953 Robert Mitchell Biggs, b. Mio, Michigan August 29, 1915, d. Toledo, Ohio February 18, 1989. Jane Williams graduated from Wayne State University and served as Director of Christian Education in churches in Detroit. From 1944 to 1953 she was the Assistant Director of Young Peoples Work for the Women's Division of the Board of Foreign Missions of the Presbyterian Church in New York City. After her marriage and move to Toledo, Ohio, Jane served as the Treasurer of the University Women's Club and Chairman of the Women's Committee for the Arboretum. She was a member of the Washington Congregational Church and later of Fairgreen Presbyterian where she was ordained an Elder and Stephen Minister.

In 1995 after the death of her husband, Jane moved to Topinabee to reside with her sister. There she became a member of the Topinabee Community Church and the Community Memorial Hospital Auxiliary. Robert Biggs, Ph.D. was a Professor of Economics at the University of Detroit, Jamestown College in North Dakota, and the University of Toledo from 1963 until his retirement in 1982. Dr. Biggs was partially blind and his wife, Jane, was an integral partner, assisting with classroom examinations and with writing and publishing a textbook. Dr. Biggs received his bachelor's degree from Wayne State University and received his Master's Degree and Ph.D. in Economics from the University of Michigan. At the time of his 1982 retirement Dr. Biggs was Chairman of the Economics Department at the University of Toledo. Professor Biggs authored the text *National Income Analysis and Forecasting.* He was a member of Phi Kappa Phi and Phi Beta Kappa fraternities and was listed in *Who's Who in America.*

Children:

676. I. ***Richard Oliver Biggs, f.***

References: US Census: 1920, 1930, 1940; Michigan Birth Record for Robert Biggs; Ohio Death Records 1938-2007 for Robert Biggs; Social Security Death Index 1935-2014; *The Blade*, Toledo, Ohio newspaper obituaries February 1989 for Robert Biggs and January 28, 1999 for Jane Williams Biggs; Interview with Richard Biggs.

337.

Jesse Austin Maitland, son of Bessie (164), grandson of Jesse (79), b. Allentown, New York August 11, 1912, d. Vero Beach, Florida August 25, 1977; m. Bradford, Pennsylvania November 28, 1935 (undocumented) Margaret Ellen Matthews, b. Duke Center, Pennsylvania December 30, 1910, d. Indian River, Florida May 25, 1976.

Jesse Maitland resided with his parents in Alma, New York (1915), Allentown Road, Bolivar (Vosburg) (1920), and Foster, Pennsylvania (1930) until his marriage. His World War I Draft Registration Card recorded that he was self-employed, 6' tall, weighing 210 pounds with blue eyes and brown hair. After their marriage Jesse and Margaret Maitland resided in Bradford, Pennsylvania where he was a self-employed oil producer. Margaret Matthews Maitland was the daughter of James and Katherine Franks Matthews. Jesse and Margaret had three sons. Only the identity of the eldest is currently known. Mr. and Mrs. Maitland were buried in Willowdale Cemetery, Bradford, Pennsylvania.

Children:

677. I. ***Donald Withey Maitland, f.***

678. II. ***Male Maitland, nfi.***

679. III. ***Male Maitland, nfi.***

References: US Census: 1920, 1930, 1940; New York State Census: 1915; World War II Draft Registration Card 1942; New York State Birth Index, 1881-1942; Social Security Death Index 1935-2014; Florida Death Index 1877-1998 for Margaret Maitland; Pennsylvania Birth Certificates 1906-1910 for Margaret Matthews; Willowdale Cemetery Records, Bradford, Pennsylvania.

338.

Helen Withey Maitland, daughter of Bessie (164), granddaughter of Jesse (79), b. Bolivar, New York December 23, 1914, d. Bradford, Pennsylvania April 2, 1979; m. Manhattan, New York City October 12, 1937 Thomas Roy Clark, Jr., b. Bradford, Pennsylvania March 26, 1909, d. Youngstown, Ohio October 25, 1971.

Helen Maitland resided with her parents (Alma, New York-1915; Allentown Road, Bolivar, probably, Vosburg-1920; Foster, Pennsylvania-1930), until her 1937 marriage. Thomas Roy Clark, Jr. was the son of Thomas Roy Clark, Sr. and Nellie Turner Brown Clark of Bradford, Pennsylvania. Tom, Jr.'s World War II Draft Registration Card described him as 5' 11" tall, weighing 190 pounds with blue eyes and brown hair. He resided in Bradford and was employed in the oil industry. It is not known when Helen and Tom moved to Ohio or if they had any children. Helen and Tom were buried in Oak Hill Cemetery, Bradford, Pennsylvania.

References: US Census: 1910, 1920, 1930, 1940; New York State Census: 1915; New York Birth Index 1881-1942 for Helen Maitland; New York Marriage Index 1907-2018; Pennsylvania Birth Certificates 1906-1910 for Tom Clark, Jr.; Ohio Death Records 1908-1932 and 1938-2007 for Tom Clark, Jr.; World War II Draft Registration Card, 1940; Oak Hill Cemetery Records, Bradford, Pennsylvania; Social Security Death Index 1935-2014.

339.

Robert Neal Maitland, Sr., son of Bessie (164), grandson of Jesse (79), b. Allentown, New York July 2, 1917, d. Rochester, New York November 20, 2001; m. Allegany, New York June 9, 1934 Martha Louise Campbell, b. Duke Center, Pennsylvania November 19, 1913, d. Rochester, New York June 27, 2002. Robert Maitland resided with his parents until his marriage in 1934. Mr. Maitland's occupation at the time of his marriage was a rig builder. His World War II Draft Registration Card described him as being 5' 11" tall, weighing 160 pounds with gray eyes and brown hair. He served in Cox US Navy from April 3, 1944 to November 27, 1945. Just prior to his military service Robert Maitland was a tool dresser employed in the oil industry. The Maitland family resided in Derrick City, Pennsylvania in 1950 but by 1987 had moved to Rochester, New York when they lived until their respective deaths. They also lived part of the year in Wilbur by the Sea, Florida. Robert and Martha Maitland were buried in Creekside Cemetery, Churchill, New York.

Children:

680. I. ***Sheila Louise Maitland, f.***

681. II. ***Robert Neal Maitland, Jr., f.***

682. III. ***Karen Elaine Maitland, f.***

References: US Census: 1920, 1930, 1940; New York State Birth Index 1881-1942 for Robert Maitland; World War II Draft Registration Card, 1940; Pennsylvania Veterans File 1950-1966; New York County Marriage Records 1847-9 and 1907-1936; Social Security Death Index 1935-2014; Creekside Cemetery Records, Churchill, New York; US Veterans Death File 1850-2010.

340.

John Bruce Maitland, son of Bessie (164), grandson of Jesse (79), b. Bolivar, New York August 25, 1918, d. Kootenai, Idaho April 14, 1997; m. Bradford, Pennsylvania November 20, 1941 (unsourced) Doris Elizabeth Downing, b. Kane, Pennsylvania September 4, 1922, d. Port Orange, Florida June 28, 1988. Little is known about this member of the Maitland family. He resided in Derrick City in 1940 at the time of his registration with the draft. John Maitland was described as 5' 9" tall, weighing 140 pounds with blue eyes and brown hair. He was probably employed in the oil industry. It is not known when John and Doris Maitland moved to Florida. They had one daughter and two sons whose identities are not currently known. John and Doris Maitland were buried in Greenwood Cemetery, Daytona Beach, Florida.

Children:

683. I. ***Female Maitland, nfi.***

684. II. ***Male Maitland, nfi.***

685. III. ***Male Maitland, nfi.***

References: *US Census: 1920, 1930, 1940; New York Birth Records 1881-1942; World War II* Draft Registration Card, 1940; Social Security Death Index 1935-2014; Florida Death Index 1877-1998 for Doris Maitland; Greenwood Cemetery Records, Daytona Beach, Florida.

341.

Betty Phyliss Maitland, daughter of Bessie (164), granddaughter of Jesse (79), b. Allentown, New York February 4, 1920, d. Matthews, North Carolina March 20, 2001; m. Bradford, Pennsylvania December

18, 1942 (unsourced) Raymond Voil Johnson, b. Corry, Pennsylvania May 3, 1918, d. Mecklenburg County, North Carolina April 25, 1988. Raymond Johnson was the son of Voil Dennis Johnson (1886-1951) and Dora Grace Fletcher Johnson (1888-1977) of northern Pennsylvania. Mr. Johnson resided at home until his marriage to Betty Maitland. His World War II Draft Registration Card said he was 6' 4" tall, weighed 225 pounds and had blue eyes and brown hair. In 1940 he resided with his parents and was employed by Forest Dorn in Bradford, Pennsylvania. It is not known when Betty and Raymond Johnson moved to North Carolina. Some undocumented sources indicate they had a daughter, but this could not be confirmed. The remains of Betty and Raymond Johnson were cremated. It is not known where they currently are.

References: US Census: 1920, 1930, 1940; World War II Draft Registration Card, 1940; North Carolina Death Index 1908-2004 for both; Social Security Death Index 1935-2014.

342.

Fred Robert Maitland, son of Bessie (164), grandson of Jesse (79), b. Derrick City, Pennsylvania, March 22, 1022, d. Olean, New York June 2, 1947 from injuries suffered while working on an oil lease near Eldred, Pennsylvania. Fred Maitland's World War II Draft Registration Card listed his employer as the Quaker State Refining Company. He had blue eyes and brown hair. No height or weight was given. Fred R. Maitland was buried in McKean County Memorial Park, Lafayette, Pennsylvania. It does not appear that he was married or had any children.

References: US Census: 1930, 1940; World War II Draft Registration Card, 1942; New York State Death Index 1852-1956; McKean County Memorial Park Records, Lafayette, Pennsylvania; *The Bradford Era*, obituary June 6, 1947.

343.

Kenneth Charles Maitland, son of Bessie (164), grandson of Jesse (79), b. Bradford, Pennsylvania April 1, 1924, d. Stuart, Florida July 19, 2009; m. Bradford, Pennsylvania January 1948 Betsy Beyeler, b. a. 1923/24, d. place of death not known, date of death not known.

Kenneth Maitland resided with his parents until his enlistment in the US Army. His World War II Draft Registration Card listed his employer as his father, probably working family own oil lease property. Kenneth Maitland was 5' 11" tall, weighed 150 pounds and had gray eyes and brown hair. Mr. Maitland served from March 23, 1943 to February 2, 1946. The exact date of his 1948 wedding is not clear from the Bradford, Pennsylvania newspaper story about the upcoming Maitland/Beyeler nuptials. He was enrolled at Sampson College in Geneseo, New York after the war. The future Mrs. Maitland was employed by the Bell Telephone Company. Kenneth and Betsy Maitland moved from Reynoldsville, Pennsylvania to Stuart, Florida in 1980 where he was employed at the St. Lucie Nuclear Plant. Mr. Maitland was a member of Elks Club, the Veterans of Foreign Wars, and the American Legion.

At the time of his death Kenneth Maitland had eight grandchildren and four great grand-children. It is not currently known where Kenneth and Betsy Maitland were buried.

Children:

686. I. ***David Karl Maitland***, b. Bradford, Pennsylvania March 11, 1950, d. Bradford, Pennsylvania April 13, 1950 from suffocation and was buried in McKean Memorial Park, Lafayette, Pennsylvania.

687. II. ***Sally Anne Maitland, f.***

688. III. ***David Maitland, nfi.***

689. IV. ***Tim Maitland, nfi.***

690. V. ***Molly Maitland (Hoyt), nfi.***

References: US Census: 1930, 1940; Pennsylvania Veterans File WWII 1950-1966; World War II Draft Registration Card, 1942, Social Security Death Index for Kenneth Maitland; *The Bradford Era*, January 5, 1948; Pennsylvania Death Certificate 1906-1966 for David Karl Maitland.

345.

Richard Albert Maitland, son of Bessie (164), grandson of Jesse (79), b. Derrick City, Pennsylvania October 3, 1928, d. Lewis Run, Pennsylvania June 10, 2004; m. Derrick City, Pennsylvania May 27, 1950 Mary Lea Larson, b. Pennsylvania January 2, 1929, d. place of death and date of death not known. Richard Maitland resided with his parents until his 1950 marriage. His World War II Draft Registration Card noted he was a student who was 6' tall, weighed 160 pounds with hazel eyes and brown hair. From February 27, 1952 to March 1, 1954, Mr. Maitland served with the 1209th ASU, US Army in Korea rising to the rank of corporal. He was known as *Moby* to family members and his wife was known as *Mait.* Richard and Mary Maitland had 2 daughters and 1 son, but their identities are not currently known. Richard Maitland was buried in Willowdale Cemetery, Bradford, Pennsylvania where there is a plot for his wife.

Children:

691. I. ***Female Maitland, nfi.***

692. II. ***Richard Albert Maitland, Jr., nfi.***

693. III. ***Female Maitland, nfi.***

References: US Census: 1930, 1940; World War II Draft Registration Card, 1946; Social Security Death Index 1935-2014 for Richard Maitland; Pennsylvania Veterans Burial Cards 1777-2012; Willowdale Cemetery Records, Bradford, Pennsylvania; *The Bradford Era*, June 1, 1950 for wedding article.

346.

Patricia Sue Maitland, daughter of Bessie (164), granddaughter of Jesse (79), Derrick City, Pennsylvania March 31, 1931, d. Northeast, Pennsylvania March 24, 2016; m. place not known May 26, 1951 Richard Elton Cole, b. Erie, Pennsylvania December 2, 1919, d. Northeast, Pennsylvania April 11, 1996.

Pat Maitland Cole attended the Ballard School of Business in New York City. She worked the North East Township as a Wage Tax Collector and from 1973-1996 for North East Fruit Growers, Inc. as the Office Manager. Richard Cole's World War II Draft Registration Card noted that he worked for General Electric, was 6' 2" tall, weighed 178 pounds with brown eyes and black hair. He saw military service from September 19, 1942 to December 6, 1942 with the US Army Air Corps. Mr. Cole was an automobile salesman for a number of dealers in the Erie, Pennsylvania area. Pat and Richard Cole were members of the Park United Methodist Church in North East, Pennsylvania. At the time of Pat Cole's death, there were three children. Burial was in North East Cemetery, North East, Pennsylvania.

Children:

694. I. ***Suzanne Cole***, b. April 4, 1958; m. John P. Bronson. They reside in Ripley, New York and have at least one child, Ashley; ***nfi.***

695. II. ***Sarah Cole***, b. March 15, 1967; m. Robert E. Treveldine; ***nfi.***

696. III. ***Richard Cole***; m. Julia A., last name not known and have a son, Gregory; ***nfi.***

References: US Census: 1930, 1940; World War II Draft Registration Card, 1941; Pennsylvania Veterans World War II Files 1950-1966; Social Security Death Index 1935-2014; North East Cemetery Records, North East, Pennsylvania.

347.

Jean Elizabeth Burdick, daughter of Ina (165), granddaughter of Jesse (79), b. Belmont, New York June 28, 1920, d. Tarpon Springs, Florida February 16, 2000; m. Belmont, New York November 30, 1940 Ralph Wilbur Windus, b. Jamestown, New York June 1, 1920, d. Franklin, Pennsylvania January 26, 1987.

Jean Burdick resident with her parents until her marriage. The 1940 US Census recorded that Jean was a college student. Ralph attended Alfred University. At the time of their marriage Ralph Windus was employed as a clerk in a Belmont retail store. Mr. Windus served in the US Army from May 6, 1942 until November 26, 1945. Jean and Ralph Windus resided in Belmont, New York and later in Franklin, Pennsylvania. Jean enjoyed summers at Cuba Lake and entertaining family and friends. After Ralph's death, Jean moved to Tarpon Springs, Florida where her eldest son, Barry, resided. Jean and Ralph Windus were buried in Forest Hills Cemetery, Belmont, New York.

Children:

697. I. ***Barry Richard Windus, f.***

698. II. ***Bonnie Jean Windus, f.***

699. III. ***John Wilfred Windus, f.***

700. IV. ***Elizabeth Ann Windus, f.***

701. V. ***Beckie Sue Windus, f.***

702. VI. ***Barbara Jane Windus, f.***

References: US Census: 1930, 1940; New York State Census: 1925; New York State Birth Index 1881-1942; New York Marriage Index 1881-1967; US Army Enlistment Records 1938-1946; Social Security Death Index 1935-2014; Forest Hills Cemetery Records, Belmont, New York; *Wellsville Daily Reporter*, February 16, 2000 obituary for Jean Windus.

348.

Sara Ann Burdick, daughter of Ina (165), granddaughter of Jesse (79), b. Wellsville, New York July 9, 1925, d. North Palm Beach, Florida March 13, 2004; m. Wellsville, New York July 23, 1947 Richard R. Sweet, b. Wellsville, New York January 10, 1924, d. Florida March 21, 2013.

Sally Burdick Sweet earned her nursing degree at Buffalo, New York General Hospital, attended Syracuse University, and joined the Cadet Nurses Corps. Twenty years of her professional career was spent in Wellsville, New York where Sally practiced with Dr. Paul Rockwell and served as Maternity Supervisor for the Jones Memorial Hospital. For twenty years she was an occupational health nurse for Bell South. Sally served as president of the Florida State Association of Occupational Health Nurses for five years and served on the board of National Association of Occupational Health Nurses for six years before retiring in 1988. Richard Sweet retired in 1982 after 35 years of service as a Manager at Bell South. Together, Mr. and Mrs. Sweet in retirement traveled and Sally enjoyed painting. Sally Sweet's love and generosity touched many lives and was frequently described as *special.* Sally and Richard Sweet were buried in Riverside Memorial Park, Tequesta, Florida.

Children:

703. I. ***Laine Elizabeth Sweet, f.***

704. II. ***Lisa Ann Sweet, f.***

705. III. ***Lorie Kay Sweet, f.***

References: US Census: 1930, 1940; New York State Census: 1925; New York State Birth Index 1881-1942; New York State Marriage Index 1881-1967; Social Security Death Index; Riverside Memorial Park Cemetery Records, Tequesta, Florida; *Wellsville Daily Reporter*, obituary March 13, 2004 for Sara Ann Sweet; correspondence with Sara Ann Sweet for the 1990 Root Family history.

349.

Laine E. Burdick, daughter of Ina (165), granddaughter of Jesse (79), b. Wellsville, New York April 6, 1930, d. Lake Worth, Florida April 19, 2008; m. Belmont, New York June 13, 1953 Rodney Walter Pike II, b. Belmont, New York August 13, 1928, d. Belmont, New York October 23, 2008.

Laine Burdick graduated from Belmont, New York High School and Montpelier Junior College in Vermont. She was a member of Belmont's St. Phillips Episcopal Church and its Altar Guild, the Herbert DeLong American Legion Auxiliary Post 808, the Jones Memorial Hospital Lilac Twig, and the Southern Tier Girl Scout Council. Laine Pike was active in Belmont, New York and Amity Township government served as Amity Town Clerk. She was also a secretary for William Laidlaw, Inc. Laine was an avid Buffalo Bills fan. Rodney Pile was born in Belmont, New York at 5 Whitney Road where he, his wife Laine, and their children resided. He was the son of Leo W. Pike (1895-1992) and Helen Averill Pike (1894-1940). Rodney Pike served in the US V5 Naval Air Corps. He graduated with a degree in History from the University of Buffalo. Mr. Pike was a bugler in the Belmont Fireman's Drum and Bugle Corps, a member of the Belmont Fire Company, the Conservation Club, the Herbert DeLong American Legion, and the Belmont Sesquicentennial Dirty Old Men. Rodney Pike was active in local politics and served as a trustee for the Village of Belmont. Mr. Pike retired from the Worthington/Dresser Rand as supervisor. In retirement Mr. and Mrs. Pike enjoyed residing at Cuba Lake, New York, Lake Worth, Florida, as well as the Pike residence in Belmont. Rodney Pike was an antiques collector, a furniture restorer, and a vegetable and sunflower gardener. Both were avid Buffalo Bills fans. His obituary described him as the *Captain of his own ship.* Laine and Rodney Pike were buried in Forest Hills Cemetery, Belmont, New York.

Children:

706. I. ***Melissa Burdick Pike, f.***

707. II. ***Melinda Averill Pike, f.***

708. III. ***Molly Withey Pike, f.***

709. IV. ***Rodney Walter Pike II, f.***

References: US Census: 1930, 1940; New York State Birth Index 1881-1942; New York State Marriage Index 1881-1967; Forest Hills Cemetery Records, Belmont, New York; *Wellsville Daily Reporter* obituaries October 27 2008 for Rodney Pike and April 21, 2008 for Laine Pike.

350.

James Vance Withey, son of Howard (167), grandson of Jesse (79), b. Yonkers, New York December 27, 1931, still living; m. (1) place not known, June 23, 1968 Joanne, last name not known, divorced Harris, Texas December 14, 1977; m. (2) Harris, Texas January 30, 1978 Monique Fleury.

James Withey resided with his parents in the 1940 US Census. He joined the US Navy September 1, 1959. In 1961 James Withey was ranked Lieutenant J. G. Mr. Withey had two children by his first marriage. One child was a son, James V. Withey, Jr. who married Anne Burget in Texas April 18, 1982. Further information about James Withey's family is not currently known. It is not currently known where James Vance Withey is buried. There is no further information about either of his wives.

References: US Census: 1940; New York State Birth Index 1881-1942 for James Vance Withey; Texas Divorce Index 1968-2014 for James Withey's first marriage; Texas Marriage Index 1824-2014 for Mr. Withey's second marriage; US Military Registers 1862-1985; Texas Marriage Index 1824-2014 for the marriage of James V. Withey, Jr.

351.

David Jack Withey, son of Howard (167), grandson of Jesse (79), b. Yonkers, New York May 15, 1935, d. Maineville, Ohio May 9, 2018; m. Caldwell, New Jersey September 1, 1956 Joanne Stulen, place of birth not known, date of birth not known, still living.

David Withey graduated from Lehigh University with high honors in Mechanical Engineering. He was a veteran of the Air Force and retired from General Electric after 31 years of service. David and his wife enjoyed traveling the United States. He enjoyed hunting, fishing, camping, and skeet shooting. They resided in Schenectady, New York for a period of years. David Withey was survived by three children, eight grandchildren, and two great-grandchildren. It is not known where David Withey was buried.

Children:

710. I. ***Jack Withey, nfi.***

711. II. ***Robert Withey, nfi.***

712. III. ***Laura Withey, nfi.***

References: US Census: 1940; New York State Birth Index 1881-1942; New York State Marriage Index 1901-2016; Obituary, Maineville, Ohio newspaper.

354.

John Andrew Withey, son of Charles (168), grandson of Jesse (79), b. Ann Arbor, Michigan April 25, 1945, d. Seabrook, Texas January 16, 2015; m. (1) Bexar, Texas April 8, 1967 Sharon Ruth King, b. Alameda, California August 15, 1945, divorced Harris, Texas March 11, 1996; m. (2) Harris, Texas July 12, 1997 Amelia Jackson, b. a. 1952.

John Withey earned a Bachelor of Science degree in Technology Management from American University in Washington, D.C. He served for a time in the United States Air Force seeing service in Vietnam. For thirty-five years John worked as a database engineer for Boeing. His obituary described him as a patient, generous, and loving man. His first wife remarried to John D. Perkins June 9, 1996 in Galveston, Texas. She divorced John Perkins January 6, 2009. Mr. Withey and his first wife had four children: Laura, Lisa, Sarah, and John. He was survived by six grandchildren. John Andrew Withey was buried in Houston National Cemetery, Houston, Texas.

Children (by first marriage):

713. I. ***Laura Withey, nfi.***

714. II. ***Lisa Withey, nfi.***

715. III. ***Sarah Withey, nfi.***

716. IV. ***John Withey, nfi.***

References: California Birth Index 1905-1995 for Sharon King Withey; Texas Marriage Index 1824-2014 for both marriages of John Withey; Texas Divorce Index 1968-2014 for John Withey's first marriage; Houston National Cemetery Records, Houston, Texas; Obituary for John Withey, Houston newspaper.

356.

Paul J. Ennis, son of Dudley (169), grandson of Mary Elizabeth (80), b. Olean, New York May 23, 1920, d. Highland Hospital, Rochester, New York from emphysema; m. Allegany, New York December 7, 1941/January 4, 1942, Coletta Wenke, b. Olean, New York May 17, 1921, d. Teresa House, Geneseo, New York October 17, 2013.

Paul Ennis was named for his paternal grandfather. He resided with his parents until his father's death and then with his paternal grandfather and mother in Bolivar, New York. The *Olean Time Herald* for January 4, 1942 gave Paul and Coletta's marriage date as January 4, 1942. This contradicts what the family has provided for their respective obituaries. Mr. Ennis served in the US Army from October 16, 1942 to October 20, 1945. His World War II Draft Registration Card described him as being 5' 9" tall and weighing 152 pounds. Paul Ennis was a former postmaster for Henrietta, New York and an active member of the Kenyon Andrus Post 772, Bolivar. Because he suffered from emphysema, Paul had to retire early and moved back to Bolivar and the family home at 577 South Main Street. For a short time, his mother resided with him until her death in 1978.

Colette Ennis worked for the New York Telephone Company in Bolivar and later as a packaging supervisor for Pennwalt Pharmaceuticals in Rochester, New York until her retirement in 1983. Coletta commuted to Bolivar on weekends to be with Paul. The Ennis family had an old photograph album with photographs of Root family members, but there were no names on any of the photographs. Paul Ennis was very helpful with suggestions for the 1990 publication on the Root family history. He was well read in history and politics. During my visits to his home we enjoyed many interesting conversations about world affairs.

Colette was the daughter of Charles and Johana Nolder Wenke of Olean, New York. She was a lifelong member of St. Mary's Catholic Church and the Kenyon Andrus Post 772, Bolivar, New York. After Paul Ennis' death, Colette remarried in 1984 to Fenton Lewis Yehl (1917-1993). Fenton Yehl served with the US Army's 4th Armored Division during World War II. Fenton Yehl was previously married to Frances McDermott (1919-1981) with whom he had four children. Mr. Yehl served as mayor of Bolivar, New York. Fenton Yehl was buried with his first wife in St. Mary's Cemetery, Bolivar, New York. Paul and Colette Ennis were also buried in St. Mary's Cemetery, Bolivar, New York.

Children:

717. I. ***Timothy Ennis, f.***

718. II. ***David Ennis, f.***

719. III. ***Marsha Ennis, f.***

References: US Census: 1920, 1930, 1940; New York State Census: 1925; New York State Birth Index 1881-1942 for Paul Ennis; US Veterans Death File 1850-2010; St. Mary's Cemetery Records, Bolivar, New York; *Olean Times Herald* January 14, 1942 for marriage of Paul Ennis and Coletta Wenke and October 20, 2013 for obituary of Coletta Wenke Ennis Yehl; *Wellsville Daily Reporter* September 23, 1979 obituary for Paul Ennis.

358.

Jennie Evelyn Johnson, daughter of Isabelle (170), granddaughter of Earles (81), b. Olean, New York July 4, 1908, d. St. Petersburg/New Port Richey, Florida January 8, 2003; m. White Plains, New York February 11, 1932 James LaFredo (Loffredo), b. Sao Paulo, Brazil June 26, 1905, d. New Port Richey January 5/15, 1985.

Evelyn resided with her parents and was trained as a nurse. In the 1940 US Census Evelyn and James LaFredo resided in New York City where he was employed as a hotel superintendent and Evelyn was employed as a nurse at a New York City hospital. On March 15, 1943 James LaFredo enlisted in Olean, New York in the New York Guard Service, Company I, 74th Regiment. By 1960 the LaFredos moved to Clearwater, Florida where Mr. LaFredo was employed as a custodian for San Jose Elementary School in Clearwater and later in school maintenance in New Port Richey, Florida. Evelyn continued to work as a nurse. James LaFredo came to the United States from Brazil November 22, 1911. His parents were Francesco Loffredo (1879-1956) and Maria Theresa Fracassi (1879-1965). It is not known where Evelyn and James LaFredo were buried.

Children:

720. I. ***James V. LaFredo, Jr., f.***

References: US Census: 1910, 1920, 1930, 1940; New York State Census: 1915, 1925; Social Security Death Index 1935-2014; Florida Death Index 1877-1998; New York Guard Service Cards 1906-1918, 1940-1948; New York Passenger Lists 1820-1957; New York State Marriage Index 1881-1967.

359.

Theodore Friend (Bud) Johnson, son of Isabelle (170), grandson of Earles (81), b. Olean, New York January 27, 1910, d. Olean, New York September 1, 1986; m. Olean, New York June 12, 1938 Ruth Muriel Wilson, b. Portville, New York September 9, 1916, d. Olean, New York April 11, 1993.

Bud Johnson was a lifelong resident of the Olean, New York area. He began his career in the retail grocery business and retired from that career. His last employer was the Highway Market in Portville,

New York where he worked as a meat cutter. Bud resided with his parents until his marriage. His World War II Draft Registration Card described him as 5' 7" tall, weighed 122 pounds with hazel eyes, black hair, and a dark complexion. He served in the US Navy during World War II from March 29, 1944 to October 4, 1945 rising to the rank of CS 3. Bud Johnson adopted Muriel's daughter after their marriage. Bud and Muriel had two children. Bud Johnson was buried in Allegany Cemetery; Allegany New York and it is assumed that Muriel was buried with him.

Children (by adoption):

721. I. ***Joan Louise Johnson, f.***

Children:

722. I. ***Sharron Ann Johnson,*** b. February 15, 1950. She had a son, Michael Anthony Johnson, b. May 19, 1969 and was last known to reside in Olean, New York; ***nfi.***

723. II. ***Thomas Craig Johnson,*** b. June 15, 1958. Last known to reside in Springville,New York; ***nfi.***

References: US Census: 1920, 1930, 1940; New York State Census: 1915, 1925; New York State Birth Index 1910-1965; Social Security Death Index 1935-2014; Allegany Cemetery Records, Allegany, New York; World War II Draft Registration Card, 1940; Department of Veterans Affairs Death File 1850-2010; New York State Marriage Index 1881-1967.

360.

Maggie Eloise Johnson, daughter of Isabelle (170), granddaughter of Earles (81), b. Olean, New York April 29, 1913, d. Dilley, Texas March 23, 2011; m. (1) Olean, New York June 25, 1931 Henry Farnsworth Woodling, b. Phillipsburg, Pennsylvania July 18, 1901, d. Pasco County, Florida August 13, 1971 from kidney disease; m. (2) Pasco County, Florida November 22, 1973, Joseph Charles Leone, b. Boston, Massachusetts December 1, 1899, d. New Port Richey, Florida July 4, 1990.

Eloise Johnson resided with her parents until her marriage. Henry Farnsworth Woodling had two years of college by 1940 and was employed as a laborer. Henry and Eloise and their three children resided at 118 Rowland Avenue in Olean, New York. At the time Mr. Woodling enlisted in the military he was employed as an oil lease worker. Henry Woodling enlisted with the US Marine Corps July 17, 1920. The Woodlings resided in Olean, New York until 1957 when Henry was employed as a machinist. After Henry Woodling's death Eloise remarried to Joseph Leone. Joe Leone's World War I Draft Registration Card recorded that he was employed as a clerk in Lewiston, Maine.

Mr. Leone was 5' 8" tall with medium build, brown eyes and black hair. In Florida Joe was employed with a security service. There is currently no information on Joseph Leone's life before his marriage to Eloise Woodling. Joe Leone was buried in Meadowlawn Memorial Gardens, New Port Richey, Florida with his first wife, Mary W., last name not known (1906-1973). It is not currently known where Eloise and Henry Woodling were buried. Eloise reverted to her maiden name of Johnson as noted on the Social Security Death Index.

Children (by first marriage):

724. I. ***Marcia Sue Woodling, f.***

725. II. ***DeWayne Earls Woodling, f.***

726. III. ***William Farnsworth Woodling, f.***

References: US Census: 1920, 1930, 1940; New York State Census: 1915, 1925; New York State Marriage Records 1847-9 and 1907-36 for Eloise Johnson's first marriage; Social Security Death Index 1935-2014; Florida Death Index 1877-1998 for Henry Woodling and Joseph Leone; US Marine Corps Muster Rolls 1798-1958; Florida Marriage Index 1822-75 and 1927-2001 for Eloise's second marriage; World War I Draft Registration Card 1917-18 for Joseph Leone; Meadowlawn Memorial Gardens Cemetery Records, New Port Richey, Florida.

361.

Marion B. Johnson, daughter of Isabelle (170), granddaughter of Earles (81), b. Olean, New York June 21, 1917, d. Allegany, New York January 7, 2018; m. Olean, New York May 25, 1940 John Bernard Noonan, b. Olean, New York September 28, 1917, d. Olean, New York September 14, 2009. Marion Johnson resided with her parents until her marriage to John Noonan.

She was a member of St. Stephen's Episcopal Church in Olean and was employed for 18 years at Olean High School as a cafeteria service worker. John Noonan was employed at Clark Brothers, later Dresser-Rand, in Olean as a molder. He retired in 1980. Mr. Noonan enlisted with the New York Guard Service on July 19, 1943 serving with Company I, 74th Regiment. Marion and John Noonan were buried in St. Bonaventure Cemetery in Allegany, New York with John Noonan's sister, Mary Zita Noonan.

Children:

727. I. ***Leo John Noonan, f.***

728. II. ***David Michael Noonan, f.***

729. III. ***Edward Allen Noonan, f.***

References: US Census: 1920, 1930, 1940; US Census: 1925; Social Security Death Index 1935-2014; New York Guard Service Card 1906-18 and 1940-48; New York State Birth Index 1881-1942; St. Bonaventure Cemetery Records, Allegany, New York; *Olean Times Herald* January 10, 1918 obituary for Marion Johnson.

362.

Beula Marie Johnson, daughter of Isabelle (170), granddaughter of Earles (81), b. Olean, New York October 3, 1918, d. Bradford, Pennsylvania October 3, 1918 from cancer; m. Olean, New York June 1, 1936 James Paul Haag, b. Grampian, Pennsylvania November 11, 1910, d. Bradford, Pennsylvania December 13, 1963 from hypertension and kidney failure.

Beula Johnson resided with her parents until her marriage. She was employed by the Bradford, Pennsylvania hospital as a cook while James Haag worked in the oil fields and for Bovaird and Seyfang of Bradford. Mr. Haag's World War II Draft Registration Card described him as 5' 4" tall weighing 152 pounds with brown hair and brown eyes. Beula and James Haag were buried in St. Bernard Cemetery, Bradford, Pennsylvania.

Children:

730. I. ***Anita M. Haag, f.***

731. II. ***Theodore M. Haag, f.***

732. III. ***Brenda P. Haag, f.***

733. IV. ***Richard Haag, f.***

734. V. ***James Paul Haag, Jr., f.***

735. VI. ***Janice Haag, f.***

References: US Census: 1920, 1930, 1940; New York State Census: 1925; Pennsylvania Death Certificates 1906-1966 for both Beula and James Haag; Pennsylvania Birth Certificate 1906-11 for James Haag; World War II Draft Registration Card, 1940; St. Bernard Cemetery Records, Bradford, Pennsylvania.

363.

Gertrude Lola Johnson, daughter of Isabelle (170), granddaughter of Earles (81), b. Olean, New York August 7, 1920, d. Clearwater, Florida April 5, 2006; m. Olean, New York Edward Francis Legler, b. Brockway, Pennsylvania September 15, 1915, d. Clearwater, Florida March 25, 1997.

Gertrude and Edward Legler resided in Olean through 1954. They moved to Clearwater, Florida where they spent the rest of their lives. Mr. Legler was employed as an electrician for the Pinellas County Schools until his retirement. The Leglers did not have any children. It is not currently known where Gertrude and Edward Legler were buried.

References: US Census: 1920, 1930, 1940; New York State Census: 1925; Social Security Death Index 1935-2014; Florida Death Index 1877-1998; New York State Birth Index 1881-1942 for Gertrude Johnson.

365.

John Earl Weatherell, son of Lola (172), grandson of Earles (81), b. Olean, New York October 7, 1910, d. Plainfield, New Jersey August 12, 1950 from injuries suffered in an automobile accident; m. Wellsville, New York March 25, 1933 Helen C. Craig, b. Buffalo, New York August 5, 1913, d. San Marino, California September 2, 1996.

John Weatherell resided with his parents at 676 Hoop Street in Olean until his marriage in 1933. John was a child prodigy in music having mastered the piano at the age of 4. During the Silent Film Era, John played the piano at local movie theaters. The family notes that John accompanied actor/singer Al Jolson. In the 1930s John Weatherell conducted the Babcock Theatre Orchestra, in Wellsville and Olean, New York. He played for WHDL Radio in Olean, New York. After his marriage and the birth of his son, John Weatherell took employment during the Depression Era as a brick mason, the profession of his father and uncles to support his family. The 1940 US Census recorded his residence in Olean employed as a bricklayer with his wife and son, John. However, Mr. Weatherell's 1940 World War II Draft Registration card listed his residence as Gadsden, Alabama where he worked for Republic Steele Corporation.

He was 5' 10" tall, weighed 130 pounds with blue eyes and blonde hair. At the time of his death John Weatherell and his family had resided in Plainfield, New Jersey only two months. John had taken a job with Surface Combustion Company as a job Foreman. The Company built blast furnaces and John was working on a project at the Mack Truck plant. Helen Weatherell was injured in the car accident, which took John's life. Mrs. Weatherell moved to Lockport, New York where in 1955 she was employed as a kitchen helper at the Lockport City Hospital. Helen Craig Weatherell later remarried to John Stankiewicz of New Kensington, Pennsylvania around 1973.

There is no further information about her second husband. Helen was the daughter of Howard W. Craig (1883-1965) and Catherine M. Hassey Craig (1889-1962). Her father was employed as a railroad clerk in Wellsville, New York. John and Helen were buried in Woodlawn Cemetery, Wellsville, New York.

Children:

736. I. ***John Weatherell, f.***

References: US Census: 1920, 1930, 1940; New York State Census: 1915, 1925; New York State Birth Index 1881-1942; New York County Marriage Records 1847-9 and 1907-36; World War II Draft Registration Card, 1940; New York State Death Index 1852-1956 for John Weatherell; California Death Index 1940-97 for Helen Craig Weatherell Stankiewicz; *Bradford Era* August 14, 1950 obituary; Woodlawn Cemetery Records, Wellsville, New York; Lockport, New York City Directory 1955.

366.

Mary Roberta Weatherell, daughter of Lola (172), granddaughter of Earles (81), b. Olean, New York March 4, 1914, d. Olean, New York June 9, 1962 from a bleeding ulcer and emphysema; m. Hinsdale, New York August 22, 1934 Leo John Uelbhear, b. Alden, New York January 14, 1907, d. Olean, New York April 1986 from a heart attack. Mary Roberta resided with her parents until her marriage. They resided at in Olean at 314 Main Street, 329 North 6th Street, and 220 W. Forest Avenue. Mr. Uelbhear was employed as a brakeman for the Pennsylvania Railroad and later at Clark Brothers (Dresser Rand) as a molder and as a foreman. Leo Uelbhear later remarried to Ruth Elizabeth Gere who was previously married to Floyd Pilling and with whom she had two sons. Mary Robert and Leo Uelbhear were buried in Allegany Cemetery, Allegany, New York.

Children:

737. I. ***Jan Leslie Uelbhear, f.***

References: US Census: 1920, 1930, 1940; New York State Census: 1915, 1925; New York County Marriage Records 1847-9 and 1907-36; New York Death Index 1957-68 for Mary Roberta Uelbhear; Social Security Death Index 1935-2014 for Leo Uelbhear; Olean City Directories, selected annuals; Allegany Cemetery Records, Allegany, New York.

367.

Martha Isabel Weatherell, daughter of Lola (172), granddaughter of Earles (81), b. Olean, New York January 18, 1917, d. Olean, New York January 11, 2007; m. Richmond, Virginia January 8, 1937 Joseph Edward Matthews, b. Rochester, New York February 20, 1915, d. Clearwater, Florida November 15, 1950 after a long illness. Joseph Matthews was a professional musician employed by the Renaldo Brothers Orchestra. His career necessitated considerable travel. In 1940 they resided in Salamanca, New York and in 1943 at 841 Bishop Street in Olean, New York. Mr. Matthews funeral was held in Rochester, New York. During the 1950s Mrs. Matthews was employed as a saleswoman for A. E. Ewing Company in Olean, New York. Martha Matthews was almost 90 years when she died. It is not currently known where Martha and Joseph Matthews were buried.

Children:

738. I. ***Joseph Matthews, f.***

739. II. ***Judith Carol Matthews, f.***

740. III. ***Robert Stuart Matthews, f.***

References: US Census: 1920, 1930, 1940; New York State Census: 1925; New York Birth Index 1881-1942 for Martha Weatherell; Virginia Marriage Records 1936-2014; Florida Death Index 1877-1998 for Joseph Matthews; Social Security Death Index for Martha Matthews; *Olean Times Herald* November 22, 1950 obituary for Joseph Matthews; Olean City Directories, selected annuals.

368.

Nina Elizabeth Weatherell, daughter of Lola (172), granddaughter of Earles (81), b. Olean, New York February 8, 1920, d. Bradford, Pennsylvania Ecumenical Home April 13, 2018; m. Olean, New York April 4, 1948 Richard James McMullen, b. Olean, New York November 7, 1918, d. Englewood, New Jersey July 26, 1978 from a stroke caused by arteriosclerosis.

Nina resided with her parents until her 1948 marriage at 676 Hoop Street in Olean, New York. Richard McMullen served with the US Army from February 21, 1941 to October 16, 1945 rising to the rank of Corporal. Mr. McMullen was employed by the Olean Lumber Company, which was purchased by his father, Alexander J. McMullen in 1928. Richard McMullen introduced the concept of *Cash and Carry* into the retail business. He served as President of Olean Lumber from 1962 to 1978. Nina McMullen worked as a saleswoman for A. E. Ewing Company in Olean before her marriage. She was a member of the choir, altar guild and a Sunday school teacher at St. Stephen's Episcopal Church in Olean.

Mrs. McMullen was actively involved in the Olean YMCA and its Board of Directors, the Olean Community Theater and its Theater workshops, and danced with Dance Arts. Nina and Richard McMullen were buried in Allegany Cemetery, Allegany, New York.

Children:

741. I. ***Kathleen McMullen, f.***

742. II. ***Jeffrey McMullen,*** b. Olean, New York May 23, 1950 and was President of Olean Lumber Company. He currently resides in Cuba, New York.

743. III. ***Maureen McMullen,*** b. Olean, New York November 27, 1951 and currently resides in Cuba, New York.

744. IV. ***Hollis McMullen, f.***

745. V. ***John McMullen,*** b. Olean, New York August 29, 1955 and served as Vice- President of Olean Lumber Company. He currently resides in Olean, New York.

746. VI. ***Michael McMullen, f.***

747. VII. ***Margaret McMullen, f.***

748. VIII. ***Julie McMullen, f.***

749. IX. ***Daniel McMullen,*** b. Olean, New York May 10, 1963 and currently resides in Cape Charles, Virginia.

References: US Census: 1930, 1940; New York State Census: 1925; New York Birth Index 1881-1942; New York State Marriage Index 1881-1967; US Veterans Death File Index 1850-2010; Social Security Death Index 1935-2014; *Olean Times Herald* April 16/17, 2018 obituary for Nina McMullen; Allegany Cemetery Records, Allegany, New York.

369.

Anne Belle Weatherell, daughter of Lola (172), granddaughter of Earles (81), b. Olean, New York September 23, 1924, d. Corry, Pennsylvania Manor Care October 6, 2014 from Huntington's Disease; m. Olean, New York April 16, 1949 James Howard Judge, b. Olean, New York March 3, 1923, d. Corry, Pennsylvania October 19, 2000.

Anne resided with her parents until her marriage. James and Anne Judge resided in Olean, New York until the early 1960s when the moved to Corry, Pennsylvania where they raised and cared for their family. James Judge was listed in *Who's Who in Finance and Industry 1981-82* and retired as Products Marketing Manager for Cooper Energy Services in Corry. Mr. and Mrs. Judge were members of St. Thomas the Apostle Roman Catholic Church. Anne was a member of the Altar Rosary Society and enjoyed flower gardening, bridge, cooking, and reading. Their last residence was in Columbus, Pennsylvania just outside Corry. Anne and James Judge were buried in Westlawn Cemetery, Columbus, Pennsylvania.

Children:

750. I. ***Molly Judge, f.***

751. II. ***Jill Judge, f.***

752. III. ***Jacquelyn Judge, f.***

References: US Census: 1930, 1940; New York State Census: 1925; New York State Birth Index 1881-1942; New York State Marriage Index 1881-1967; Westlawn Cemetery Records, Columbus, Pennsylvania; *Olean Times Herald* October 8, 2014 obituary for Anne Weatherell Judge.

370.

Alice Fern Weatherell, daughter of Lola (172), granddaughter of Earles (81), b. Olean, New York January 22, 1927, d. Wellsville, New York February 4, 2015; m. Olean, New York May 19, 1945 James D. Moore, b. St. Mary's, Pennsylvania October 24, 1918, d. Olean, New York July 17, 1985 from a massive coronary.

Alice resided with her parents until her 1945 marriage and for a decade after her marriage with her parents at 676 Hoop Street. James Moore was employed as a pipefitter for Clark Brothers, later Dresser Rand, in Olean. Alice was employed for thirty-five years with the Exchange National Bank, Olean, New York retiring in 1989. She served as the bank's Assistant Treasurer and later the manager of the Allegany Branch. She was also employed on a part-time basis at St. Stephen's Episcopal Church for nineteen years as the parish secretary, retiring from that position at the age of 83.

Alice Moore completed numerous courses at the American Institute of Banking and served as President of the local chapter of the Bank Administrative Institute and the National Association of Bank Women. Alice was active in the community serving as chairperson for the local Heart Fund and treasurer of the local March of Dimes chapter. She sang in her church choir for fifty-five years and was a member of the vestry. Alice Weatherell Moore was a tremendous help in detailing the genealogy of the descendants of Earls Root and providing many family photographs for inclusion in the 1990 Root family history. Alice and James Moore were buried in Allegany Cemetery, Allegany, New York.

Children:

753. I. ***Jamie Elizabeth Moore, f.***

754. II. ***Mary Alice Moore, f.***

References: US Census: 1930, 1940; New York State Birth Index 1881-1942; New York State Marriage Index 1881-1967; Social Security Death Index 1935-2014; Olean City Directories, selected annuals; Allegany Cemetery Records, Allegany, New York; *Olean Times Herald* obituary February 6, 2015.

371.

James William Weatherell, Sr., son of Lola (172), grandson of Earles (81), b. Olean, New York April 9, 1930, d. Wellsville, New York February 25, 2018; m. Belmont, New York June 4, 1949 Mary Elizabeth Baker, b. Belmont, New York October 3, 1929, d. Cuba, New York, April 11, 1991.

James Weatherell resided with his parents until his marriage. For a time, he was employed by Clark Brothers (Dresser Rand). He was later President and CEO of Clair Manufacturing, Olean, New York and President and CEO of Olean Finishing Machine. The later business was formed in 1979 and continued in business until 2004. James and Margaret Weatherell resided in Olean until his retirement when they moved to Cuba Lake, New York. Mr. Weatherell was a member of the Bartlett Country Club, Olean, was an avid golfer, and enjoyed his time on his boat on the lake. James Weatherell was buried in St. Bonaventure Cemetery, Allegany, New York and it is assumed his wife is buried there as well.

Children:

755. I. ***James William Weatherell, Jr., f.***

756. II. ***Thomas Martin Weatherell, f.***

757. III. ***Joseph Patrick Weatherell, f.***

References: US Census: 1940; New York State Birth Index 1881-1942; New York State Index 1881-1967; Social Security Death Index 1935-2014; St. Bonaventure Cemetery Records, Allegany, New York; *Olean Times Herald* February 27, 2018 obituary for James Weatherell.

372.

Ronald Keith Weatherell, son of Lola (172), grandson of Earles (81), b. Olean, New York July 28, 1933, d. Montgomery, Alabama March 25, 2001 from Huntington's Disease; m. (1) Olean, New York November 24, 1951 JoAnne M. Taylor, divorced; m. (2) Montgomery, Alabama August 1956 Betty L. Murphy, birth place and date of birth not known, death place and death date not known, divorced. On February 11, 1942 Ronald Weatherell was hit by a car at age 9 when he ran out of a grocery store into an oncoming car.

The injuries were not serious. Ronald and JoAnne divorced soon after their marriage because she remarried August 1, 1953 to Robert King of Olean, New York. Ronald served in the US Air Force from July 29, 1952 to May 26, 1959 seeing time in Korea and Okinawa. After being discharged at Maxwell Air Force Base, Montgomery, Alabama, Mr. Weatherell decided to settle there. He was employed by the Keebler Company as a sales representative and later as a sales representative for the Tropicana and Carnation Companies. Mr. Weatherell was active in the Montgomery Chapter of the Shriners. He was survived by his wife, two children, and five grandchildren. A memorial service was held at Lake Martin, Kowa Liga, Alabama. It is not currently known if a burial took place.

Children (by second marriage):

758. I. ***Ralph Weatherell. f.***

759. II. ***Peggy Weatherell, f.***

References: US Census: 1940; New York State Birth Index 1881-1942; New York State Marriage Index 1881-1967; Montgomery, Alabama Marriage Certificate 1800-1969; US Veterans Affairs Death File 1850-2010; Social Security Death Index 1935-2014; *Olean Times Herald* February 11, 1942 and March 25, 2001.

373.

Donald Jason Root, son of Selden (173), grandson of Earles (81), b. Olean, New York June 5, 1915, d. Olean, New York General Hospital October 20, 1995 after a long illness; m. Olean, New York May 13, 1937 Marian E. Dininny, b. Olean/Buffalo, New York January 22, 1917, d. Rochester, New York Strong Memorial Hospital July 12, 2001 after a short illness.

Donald Root was formerly employed at Thatcher Glass Company and Clark Brothers (Dresser Rand) in Olean, New York where he retired in 1977. He worked part-time for the security service at St. Bonaventure University until his retirement from there in 1995. Mr. Root served in the US Army from March 29, 1944 to December 7, 1945 seeing action in the European Theater. Donald Root was a member of St. Mary of the Angels Church and the American Legion Charles Harbel Post 892. Mrs. Root worked as a waitress for thirty-five years at the Lincoln Diner in Olean. Donald and Marian Root were buried in St. Bonaventure Cemetery, Allegany, New York with her sister, Marie E. Dininny Burgess.

Children:

760. I. ***Donald Timothy Root***, Olean, New York November 16, 1937, d. Olean, New York August 14, 1958 in an automobile accident and was buried in St. Bonaventure Cemetery, Allegany, New York.

761. II. ***Joan Root, f.***

762. III. ***Kathleen Root, f.***

References: US Census: 1920, 1930, 1940; New York State Census: 1925; Social Security Death Index 1935-2014; US Veterans Death File 1850-2010; New York State Marriage Index 1881-1967; St. Bonaventure Cemetery Records, Allegany, New York; *Olean Times Herald* obituaries October 20, 1995 and July 12, 2001.

374.

Harold William Root, son of Selden (173), grandson of Earles (81), b. Olean, New York January 14, 1918, d. Olean, New York General Hospital after a short illness; m. Olean, New York April 23, 1948 Dorothy M. Van Curen, b. Austin, Pennsylvania March 2, 1926, d. Cuba, New York Hospital Palliative Care Program after an extended illness January 20, 2015.

Harold William Root was named for his father's brother who died in 1908. An electrician by trade and a member of the International Brotherhood of Electrical Workers Local 106, Mr. Root was employed by G. Willard Electric Company, the Alcas Cutlery Corporation, and Olean General Hospital from 1962 until his death. During World War II Harold Root served with the First Division of the US Marines in the Pacific Theater from January 8, 1942 to September 19, 1945. Dorothy Root graduated from eighth grade at School Four, East Olean, New York in 1939. She and her School Four classmates started school reunions celebrating annually at Cuba Lake. Dorothy, a 1943 graduate of Olean High School, owned and operated Weston's Crafts Supplies, Weston Mills, New York until the store was sold in 1982 after Mr. Root's death. Mrs. Root was a den mother for Cub Scouts for many years. She enjoyed living at Cuba Lake with her family. Harold and Dorothy Root were buried at Chestnut Hill Cemetery, Portville, New York.

Children:

763. I. ***Richard Root, f.***

764. II. ***Alice Root, f.***

References: US Census: 1920, 1930, 1940; New York State Census: 1925; New York Birth Index 1881-1942; New York State Marriage Index 1881-1967; US Veterans Death File 1850-2010; Chestnut Hill Cemetery Records, Portville, New York; *Olean Times Herald* obituaries February 24, 1981 and January 22, 2015.

375.

Margaret E. Root, daughter of Selden (173), granddaughter of Earles (81), b. Olean, New York April 26, 1920, d. Olean, New York October 6, 2007. Margaret Root was employed as an X-Ray technician at the Olean Medical Group until her retirement by 1990. She resided her entire life at the family home at 653 S. Union Street. Margaret took care of her mother until Rosa Root until she died in 1981. According to family members Margaret Root was cremated and her ashes dispersed.

References: US Census: 1930, 1940; New York State Census: 1925; New York State Birth Index 1881-1942; Social Security Death Index 1935-2014.

376.

DeMaris Elaine Root, daughter of Selden (173), granddaughter of Earles (81), b. Olean, New York September 23, 1928, d. Olean, New York August 12, 2008; m. (1) Olean, New York Basil L. Eaton, b. Allegany, New York March 5, 1925, d. January 6, 1966 from a heart attack; m. (2) Olean, New York July 29, 1972 Michael Lynch, b. a. 1938, still living.

Basil Eaton was a teacher at Archbishop Walsh High School in Olean, New York. Michael Lynch worked for the US Postal Service. DeMaris Root Eaton Lynch worked at the School of Nursing at St. Francis Hospital, Olean, New York. DeMaris was buried with her first husband at St. Bonaventure Cemetery, Allegany, New York.

Children (by first marriage):

765. I. ***Jennifer Eaton, f.***

766. II. ***Michael Eaton, f.***

767. III. ***Christopher Eaton, f.***

768. IV. ***Kevin Eaton, f.***

769. V. ***Lindsey Eaton, f.***

References: US Census: 1930, 1940; New York State Birth Index 1881-1942; New York State Marriage Index 1881-1967 for first marriage; Social Security Death Index 1935-2014; New York State Death Index 1957-1966 for Basil Eaton; St. Bonaventure Cemetery Records, Allegany, New York.

377.

Leo Stanley Root, son of Leo C. (174), grandson of Ernest (83), b. Wallkill, New York May 3, 1917, d. Manchester, New Hampshire Veterans Hospital March 28, 1985 from cancer; m. (1) Grove City, Pennsylvania December 26, 1938 Alberta Wall, b. Grove City, Pennsylvania June 14, 1920, d. Mercer, Pennsylvania December 16, 2009 after an extended illness, divorced Mercer County, Pennsylvania September 23, 1941; m. (2) Windham, New Hampshire February 8, 1942 Barbara Eleanor Lamson,

b. Clinton, Massachusetts June 1, 1921, d. Derry, New Hampshire February 25, 1995 from pancreatic cancer, divorced 1983; m. (3) Place not known, May 20, 1983 Arlene Marie Kardaseski LeBrun, b. Wakefield, Massachusetts March 25, 1935, d. Methuen, Massachusetts February 9, 1999.

Leo Stanley Root was born in Wallkill, New York where his mother and her family resided and where his parents met. By 1919, Leo and his parents had moved to Bolivar, New York where the family resided on South Main Street. Stanley was the name used by his parents and siblings to distinguish him from his father who was also named Leo. Leo Stanley Root attended Bolivar Central School where he completed the first two years of high school. In 1936 when the Root family moved to Clintonville, Pennsylvania, Leo Stanley Root enlisted in the US Army and was stationed with the Madison Barracks, Waterloo, New York. After the completion of two years of service, he returned to Clintonville, Pennsylvania.

Leo Stanley Root married Alberta Wall December 26, 1938 in nearby Grove City, Pennsylvania. The marriage was not a happy one and family members believed that interference by Alberta's widowed mother as well as Stanley's own parents caused a marital rupture that could not be mended. A son was born September 5, 1940 but it is believed that this son, Robert, never learned about his true paternity.

Descendants of Alberta Wall posted on Ancestry.com her marriage to her (second) husband, Jacob Krofcheck, as February 10, 1939 in New Castle, Pennsylvania by a Justice of the Peace. Alberta's obituary gave her marriage date to Mr. Krofcheck as April 1940. Neither could be legally true since Alberta was already married and her divorce from Stanley Root was not filed until May 27, 1940 and a divorce was not granted until September 23, 1941. Stanley and Alberta cannot be found on the 1940 US Census. Stanley Root re-enlisted in the US Army October 16, 1940 in Olean, New York. His registration papers state that he was single and had no dependents. This was obviously incorrect.

Alberta remarried to Jacob J. Krofcheck, Jr. with whom she had nine children. The Krofcheck family did not know that Alberta had a first marriage. Leo Stanley Root served in the US Army from October 16, 1940 to December 4, 1946. He was a member of the 1st Division, Battery A, 5th Field Artillery and was stationed for a time at Fort Devens, Massachusetts. Mr. Root met his second wife while stationed in Massachusetts. He saw action in the Pacific Theatre where he was severely injured during the Okinawa Campaign with the 110th Combat Engineers. He had a long convalescence at Fitzgibbon General Hospital, Denver, Colorado. A lung and ribs on one side were removed. Leo Stanley Root received two Bronze Stars.

After the war he returned to New Hampshire where he resided the rest of his life. Mr. Root was a former Commander and member of the Wilber Tarbell American Legion Post # 109, a member of Disabled Veterans of Derry, New Hampshire, a former Boy Scout Master, and he organized Windham, New Hampshire's first boy scout troop. For over forty years Leo Root was superintendent of the Windham Cemeteries and was employed at a potato chip factory and at the Yours Truly Furniture Store in Nashua, New Hampshire.

Leo Stanley Root and his second wife, Barbara Lamson Root, divorced in 1983 and he remarried. Mr. Root's third wife, Arlene Kardaseski had been previously married and had six children by her first husband. Leo and Arlene had a son together, Lee/Leo Steven, born in 1974 before Leo's second marriage dissolved. Alberta Wall Root Krofcheck was buried in Crestview Memorial Park, Grove City, Pennsylvania with her son Robert, not with her husband. Barbara Lamson Root was a member of the Windham Grange for more than 50 years where she served as Chaplain. She was also a member of the Windham Women's Club, the American Legion Auxiliary, Wilber Tarbell Post # 109 of Windham and the Windham Senior Citizens. At the time of her death Barbara had the longest membership in the Windham Presbyterian Church lasting more than 55 years where she served as an elder, deacon, and as a member and President of the Ladies' Benevolent Society. Barbara Root continued to participate in Root family activities and gatherings after her divorce. She was cremated and buried in the Cemetery on the Plains, Windham, New Hampshire with her parents. Leo Stanley Root was buried with his third wife and her first husband at the Cemetery on the Hill, Windham, New Hampshire.

The day of March 27, 1985, my mother, Dorothy Root Paquette, who resided in Wellsville, New York experienced two events presaging the death of her brother, Leo Stanley Root. The first was a series of knockings at the front door. Each time my mother opened the door, there was no one there. The old superstition is that when one hears door knockings without a person on the other side of the door, someone will die or has died. The second event was a man's voice calling "Dot, Dot," my mother's nickname, from the kitchen. Mom ran downstairs asking her daughter-in-law who was calling her. My mother said the voice was her brother's. Her daughter-in-law heard nothing. My mother and her oldest brother were always close. On the morning of March 29, 1985 at 7:30 a.m., my mother received a phone call informing her of her brother's death on March 28, 1985.

Children (by first marriage):

770. I. ***Robert J. (Root) Krofcheck, f.***

Children (by second marriage):

771. I. ***Leo James Root, f.***

772. II. ***Dennis Alan Root, f.***

773. III. ***Barbara Ellen Root, f.***

774. IV. ***Paul Dana Root, f.***

775. V. ***Marleen Root, f.***

776. VI. ***Deborah Jean Root, f.***

Children (by third marriage):

777. I. ***Leo Steven Root, f.***

References: US Census: 1920, 1930; New York State Census: 1925; New York State Birth Index 1881-1942 for Leo S. Root; Pennsylvania Veterans Compensation Files World War II 1950-66; US Veterans Death Files 1850-2010, Social Security Death Index 1935-2014; Mercer County, Pennsylvania Marriage License # 38807 for the marriage of Leo S. Root and Alberta Wall; Mercer County Divorce Records 1940 and 1941; Massachusetts Birth Index 1860-1970 for Barbara Lamson; New Hampshire Marriage Index 1637-1957 for the marriage of Leo S. Root and Barbara Lamson; Massachusetts Death Index 1970-2003 for Arlene M. Root; US World War II Army Enlistment Records 1938-1946; Crestview Memorial Park Cemetery Records, Grove City, Pennsylvania; Cemetery on the Hill Cemetery Records, Windham, New Hampshire; Cemetery on the Plains Cemetery Records, Windham, New Hampshire; *The Sharon, Pennsylvania Herald* December 17, 2009 obituary for Alberta Wall; *Lawrence Eagle Tribune obituaries* March 29, 1985 and February 25, 1995; *Bolivar Breeze 1891-1965,* selected issues.

378.

Nordica Ethel Root, daughter of Leo C. (174), granddaughter of Ernest (83), b. Bolivar, New York May 11, 1919, d. Wellsville, New York November 5, 1986 at her home from a massive heart attack; m. Wellsville, New York December 14, 1951 Glen Edward Anderson, b. Ridgway, Pennsylvania May 10/15, 1923, d. Wellsville, New York November 11, 2009.

Nordica Ethel Root bore a striking resemblance to her paternal grandmother, Belle Fuller Root, who died five years before she was born. She was named for her paternal aunt, Nordica Root Wylie, and her mother. Nordica resided with her family in Bolivar, New York where she sang in the school choir. She graduated from Clintonville, Pennsylvania High School where she played basketball on the girls' high school team. Nordica was engaged during World War II, but her finance was killed in action. During World War II Nordica was employed as a housekeeper in Oil City, Pennsylvania. After Nordica's parents moved to Allentown, New York, Nordica moved to nearby Wellsville, New York where she was employed as a housekeeper for the Hyslip family until her marriage in 1951.

Nordica and her husband, Glen Anderson, owned and operated a seventy-acre farm on Donovan Road, Wellsville, New York. They first raised rabbits, then pigs, and finally cattle. Nordica was greatly admired and loved by her family and friends, which was reflected in the many donations made in her name after her death to various Wellsville charities. She was a member of the Wellsville United Methodist Church where she taught Sunday School from 1955-1965 and provided nursery care during the Sunday church services. In addition to raising a family and managing a working farm, Nordica was a talented cook, a skilled embroider, and made her daughters' clothes. Nordica's skill with a needle and thread was passed on to her eldest daughter, Diana. Nordy, as she was known in the family, loved flowers and a hillside of lupins graced the side of the hill where atop was a vegetable and flower garden.

Nordica enjoyed the beauty of both peacocks and hummingbirds, the latter clustering around her feeders. She was the family member who kept in regular contact with all branches of her family and gave to this author many historic items associated with the Root family.

Glen's actual birth date was May 10 instead of May 15. The doctor who delivered him failed to get the birth certificate in on time and put the date of May 15 on the document to meet Pennsylvania's statute that birth records be submitted within fifteen days of the birth. Glen Anderson moved to Wellsville in 1941 where he was employed by the Moore Steam Turbine Company (later known as Worthington, Turbodyne, and finally Dresser Rand). He enlisted in the US Navy during World War II serving from 1942 to 1946 aboard the USS Grapple as a salvage diver.

After the war he returned to work at Worthington from which he retired in 1986 after 44 years of service. Glen was a former Supervisor for the Town of Alma, New York and a long-time supporter and past rally chairman and fund-raising chairman of the *Great Wellsville Balloon Rally*. For ten years Glen was a volunteer for Allegany County Literacy. Glen resided with Jean MacMurray from 1998 until her death in 2008. Glen enjoyed hunting, fishing, woodworking, carpentry, and photography. Nordica and Glen Anderson were buried in Maple Lawn Cemetery, Bolivar, New York.

Children:

778. I. ***Diana Kay Anderson, f.***

779. II. ***Sharon Nordica Anderson, f.***

780. III. ***Richard Glen Anderson, f.***

References: US Census: 1920, 1930, 1940; New York State Census: 1925; New York State Marriage Index 1881-1967; Social Security Death Index 1935-2014; *Oil City Derrick* December 29, 1951; *Bolivar Breeze 1891-1965,* selected issues; *Wellsville Daily Reporter* obituaries November 5, 1986 and November 14, 2009; Interviews with Nordica Root Anderson for the 1990 Root family history; Maple Lawn Cemetery, Bolivar, New York; interview Diana Anderson LaFaro April 17, 2019.

379.

Eva Jemima Root, daughter of Leo C. (174), granddaughter of Ernest (83), b. Bolivar, New York Bolivar, New York July 31, 1920, d. Wellsville, New York September 7, 1999 from ovarian cancer.

Eva was named for her maternal aunt, Eva Bernard, and her maternal grandmother, Jemima Bernard. She resided with her parents in Bolivar, New York and Clintonville, Pennsylvania until August 1941 when she found employment as a housekeeper in Sharon, Pennsylvania. From 1942 until the end of World War II, Eva worked in Oil City, Pennsylvania. In the late 1940s she moved to Gloucester,

Massachusetts where Eva was employed as a governess. By 1950 Eva had moved to Wellsville, New York. Her parents and four siblings were living in either Wellsville or nearby Allentown, New York. From 1950 to 1958 Eva was the housekeeper for Wellsville society matron, Mrs. Gertrude Thornton Million. Mrs. Million maintained a residence on Main Street in Wellsville and a summer estate called *Lantern Lodge* in Scio, New York township. After Mrs. Million's death, Eva was the housekeeper for Mrs. Marion Thornton Fisher, Mrs. Million's sister, from 1958 until Mrs. Fisher's death in 1965. After the death of Mrs. Fisher, Eva was last employed by Mrs. Loranah Plants from 1966 to 1974 when Mrs. Plants died.

Eva successfully battled cancer in the 1970s but two decades later succumbed to the disease. Although Eva never married, she had two long term relationships with Lloyd Karr and Chester Whitney. Eva was a particularly talented gardener who could bring almost any plant back to life, had a gift with needle and thread, and loved her chihuahuas. Eva Root was buried in Maple Lawn Cemetery, Bolivar, New York.

References: US Census: 1920, 1930, 1940; New York State Census: 1925; New York State Birth Index 1881-1942; Social Security Death Index 1935-2014; *Oil City Derrick*, selected issues 1941-44; *Wellsville Daily Reporter*, obituary September 8, 1999; Maple Lawn Cemetery Records, Bolivar, New York.

380.

Ernest Jerome Root, son of Leo C. (174), grandson of Ernest (83), b. Bolivar, New York March 7, 1922, d. Youngsville, Pennsylvania June 27, 1992 from a seizure.

Ernest Jerome Root was named for his paternal grandfather, Ernest Jerome Root. In June 1929, Ernest was hit by a passing truck while walking home from school on Root Hollow Creek Bridge. He was knocked to the pavement, rendered unconscious, and suffered a fractured skull. The truck driver was never identified or found. Mr. Root suffered brain damage and experienced seizures the rest of his life as a result of the accident. In April 1937, Ernest Root went missing after their move to Clintonville, Pennsylvania. He was found and it was believed he was trying to find his way back to Bolivar, the only home he had previously known. His World War II Draft Registration Card described him as 5' 11", weighing 155 pounds with brown hair and brown eyes. Ernest resided with his parents in Bolivar, New York and Clintonville, Pennsylvania until he required more medical care. Ernest Root was cared for in medical facilities the rest of his life in North Warren and Youngsville, Pennsylvania. Ernest Jerome Root was buried in Floral Park Cemetery, Johnson City, New York with his parents.

References: US Census: 1930, 1940; New York State Census: 1925; New York Birth Index 1881-1942; Social Security Death Index 1935-2014; World War II Draft Registration Card, 1942; Floral Park Cemetery Records, Johnson City, New York; *Bolivar Breeze*, June 20, 1929; *Oil City Derrick*, April 22, 1937; *Wellsville Daily Reporter*, June 29, 1992.

381.

Fred Root, son of Leo C. (174), grandson of Ernest (83), b. Bolivar, New York May 23, 1923, d. Wellsville, New York March 8, 2001 at the Highland Nursing Home after a lengthy illness. Fred Root was never given a middle name and his first name was Fred, not Frederick. He was named for a maternal uncle, Fred Bernard. He resided with his family in Bolivar, New York and Clintonville, Pennsylvania until he entered military service. His 1942 World War II Draft Registration Card described him as 6' tall, weighing 184 pounds with brown hair and brown eyes.

Fred was employed by Turner Lumber Company, Clintonville, Pennsylvania. Mr. Root served with the US Army from September 14, 1942 until November 11, 1943. He saw action in the Pacific Theatre of World War II and contracted malaria, a disease which plagued him the rest of his life and caused him to seek frequent medical attention. Fred was promoted to Private First Class. After World War II, Fred Root moved to Allentown, New York where he resided the rest of his life until brittle bones and a broken hip forced him to be cared for in a nursing home. Fred Root was a long-time employee of Lunn Lumber Company, Wellsville, New York. On weekends he provided lawn care services for many Allentown residents. Fred Root was briefly engaged to an Allentown girl, but his parents forced him to break off the engagement. Mr. Root never married. Fred's great love was the Allentown Fire Department providing meticulous care to the Fire Department building and the fire trucks. He proudly marched in many an Allegany County parade in his Fireman's uniform, the uniform he was buried in. Fred Root was buried in Maple Lawn Cemetery, Bolivar, New York.

References: US Census: 1930, 1940; New York State Census: 1925; Pennsylvania Veterans Files 1950-66; New York State Birth Index 1881-1942; Social Security Death Index 1935-2014; World War II Draft Registration Card, 1942; Maple Lawn Cemetery Records, Bolivar, New York; *Wellsville Daily Reporter* obituary March 12, 2001.

382.

Dorothy Lucille Root, daughter of Leo C. (174), granddaughter of Ernest (83), b. Bolivar, New York December 24, 1924, d. Fairfax, Virginia December 5, 2003 after a short illness; m. South Lawrence, Massachusetts September 8, 1946 (Joseph) Arthur Conrad Paquette, b. Mexico, Maine August 29, 1921, d. Bath, New York Veterans Hospital June 9, 2006 after a long illness.

Dorothy Root was the first child of Leo and Ethel Root who was not named for family members. She resided in Bolivar, New York where she attended elementary school. Dorothy or Dot, as she was known to family and friends, graduated from Clintonville, Pennsylvania High School. Dot suffered a burst appendix just before graduation. Her senior year she stared in the Senior play and was named Class Poet. Dot wrote poetry under the penname of *Connie Dallas*. Dorothy attended Indiana State Teacher's College, Indiana, Pennsylvania for one year in a nursing program sponsored by the US Army. Deciding she was not suited to the program, Dot moved to Windham, New Hampshire where she stayed with her sister-in-law, Barbara Lamson Root, until the end of World War II. From 1945 until her marriage, Dorothy lived and worked in Andover, Massachusetts at Shawsheen Manor.

She met her future husband the summer of 1946 at Cobbett's Pond, Windham, New Hampshire. They married two months later. Arthur Conrad Paquette's first name was Joseph, a name given all Catholic boys automatically at birth as all Catholic girls were named Marie in honor of the Virgin Mary. French was his first language. Art learned English when he went to elementary school. Arthur's mother died in 1927 at the age of twenty-nine years from tuberculosis leaving a husband and six children from the ages of 7 years to just a few months old. Art's father placed his children in St. Charles Orphanage in Rochester, New Hampshire where the youngest sibling, Oscar, died in 1930 at age three. Two of Arthur's sisters were raised by a paternal aunt and uncle. Art, his brother Leon, and his sister, Irene, remained in the orphanage until each reached the age of sixteen.

Arthur Paquette enlisted in the US Army in Lawrence, Massachusetts January 16, 1941 and served in the US Army's 211th Artillery Unit until the end of the war returning on the *James J. Hill* from Le Havre, France to New York City in 1945. During World War II Arthur served in eastern France and was with one of the first units to enter the concentration camps in southern Germany to free Jewish prisoners. The sights and smells of the concentration camps haunted him the rest of his life. Art found work as a truck driver in Lawrence where he and Dorothy resided on Common Street. In December 1948, Art, Dot, and this author moved from Lawrence, Massachusetts to Allentown, New York. My mother persuaded my father that the culture of rural Allentown was preferable to the industrial world of a textile city. After the move Art became known as *Parky* because the locals could not properly pronounce his last name. From 1949 to 1969, he worked for the Lunn Lumber Company, Wellsville, New York as the Head Sawyer. From 1969 until his retirement in 1992, Art was employed by Don Dillie Industrial Garbage Collection Service, later operating under the name of Busy Bee.

Dorothy worked from 1957 to 1962 at the Olean Tile Company, Olean, New York. Art was a member of the American Legion, Bolivar, New York and the Moose Lodge and the Veterans of Foreign Wars in Wellsville, New York. He played baseball for the team representing Lawrence, Massachusetts in the late 1940s and for Bolivar, New York's American Legion as a second baseman from 1950-1952. In the late 1950s Art Paquette was Vice-Commander for the Wellsville VFW and Dorothy served as Vice-President of the Ladies Auxiliary. Dot wrote an unpublished manuscript *My Walk with God* about the religious and mystical experiences she had during her lifetime.

From a young age Dot loved dogs and had at least one most of her life. Blackie, her last pet, died in 2008. Dorothy was a creative cook and managed to produce balanced meals on a tight budget. As a child we spent many a summer afternoon on the oil leases around Allentown, New York picking blue berries and black berries and maintaining a small garden. Dot taught Sunday School at the Allentown Methodist Church and the Wellsville United Methodist Church. She was also a cub scout Den Mother in Allentown. In Wellsville Dorothy was a volunteer at the David A. Howe Public Library and worked with the nursing staff at the Wellsville Elementary School. My mother loved the color purple and the color choice was reflected in her bedroom and clothing selections. The smell of lilacs in the spring brings back many cherished memories of childhood. Dorothy had some precognitive abilities as noted in the biography of her oldest brother (377) as do the author and the author's sister.

Art was an avid sports fan, deer hunter, and read extensively about World War II often noting that the books did not always reflect what was truly experienced. Art and Dot resided at 345 East Dyke Street in Wellsville, New York, from 1959 until their respective deaths, and where family gatherings were annually held every Memorial Day, 4th of July, Labor Day, Thanksgiving, and Christmas. Arthur and Dorothy Paquette were buried in Maple Lawn Cemetery, Bolivar, New York. The Historic Documents Preservation Room at the Allegany County Historical Society Museum, Andover, New York is named in their honor.

Children:

781. I. ***William Arthur Paquette, f.***

782. II. ***Robert Louis Paquette, f.***

783. III. ***Patricia Adora Paquette, f.***

References: US Census: 1930, 1940; New York State Census: 1925; New York State Birth Index 1881-1942; Virginia Death Record 1912-2014 for Dorothy Paquette; Social Security Death Index 1935-2014; Maine Birth Record 1715-1922 for Arthur Paquette; New York Passenger Lists 1820-1957 for Arthur Paquette's return from Europe; US World War II Army Enlistment Record, 1941; Massachusetts Marriage Index 1901-1955; Maple Lawn Cemetery Records, Bolivar, New York; *Bolivar Breeze 1891-1965*, selected issues.

383.

Hugh Daniel Root, son of Leo C. (174), grandson of Ernest (83), b. Bolivar, New York September 28, 1926, d. Walter Reed Army Hospital Washington, D.C. May 26, 1966 from cancer; m. Berlin, Germany August 7, 1963 Helga Kate Barth, b. Berlin, Germany October 14, 1928, d. Kirk Military Hospital Aberdeen, Maryland January 3, 1974.

Hugh Daniel Root was named for his paternal uncle by marriage, Hugh Wylie, and his maternal uncle, Daniel Bernard. Known to his family as Dan, he graduated from Clintonville High School in Clintonville, Pennsylvania. He enlisted in the US Army after graduation on November 27, 1944 and served until April 23, 1945. Dan reenlisted December 4, 1945 and served until February 17, 1946. Dan's World War II Draft Registration Card described him as 5' 11" tall, weighing 150 pounds with brown hair and brown eyes. He reenlisted a third time and established a military career for himself where in addition to seeing action in World War II, he served in Alaska, Korea, Japan, Germany, and

Italy. At the time of his death Dan Root was a Staff Sergeant First Class, Head Quarters Missile Special Command.

Dan was greatly liked and loved by all who knew him. He met his wife, Helga, in the late 1940s, when he was stationed in Germany. They renewed their relationship in the 1950s and finally were granted permission to marry in 1963. For reasons never clearly established, their earlier requests for marriage permission from the US Government were denied. Helga's family were factory owners in Germany during World War II and the author suggests that the US Government may have considered her a security risk. Daniel adopted Helga's daughter from an earlier relationship. He also adopted Helga's son, Michael, who is believed to have been Dan's natural son. Michael's death certificate listed Daniel Root as his father. Dan Root never communicated to his family prior to his marriage that he had a son until after his 1963 marriage. After Dan's death in 1966 Helga briefly made her home in Allentown, New York with her mother-in-law before purchasing the residence of Allen J. Root in Bolivar on Wellsville Street in 1967.

By 1970 Helga and Michael had moved to Aberdeen, Maryland where her sister resided and where Helga died. Hugh Daniel Root was a member of the George Washington Lodge F. and A. M. of Verona, Italy. Dan and Helga Root were buried in Maple Lawn Cemetery, Bolivar, New York.

Children (by adoption):

784. I. ***Angelika Root***, b. Berlin, Germany; m. Willard Powell April 1966. They had two children and were last known to have resided in San Antonio, Texas. Mr. Powell served in the US Army; ***nfi.***

Children:

785. I. ***Michael Jurgen Klaus Root, f.***

References: US Census: 1930, 1940; New York State Census: 1925; New York State Birth Index 1881-1942; World War II Draft Registration Card, 1944; Pennsylvania Veterans World War II File 1950-1966; Social Security Death Index 1935-2015; Maple Lawn Cemetery Records, Bolivar, New York.

384.

Lawrence Leonard Root, son of Leo C. (174), grandson of Ernest (83), b. Bolivar, New York June 19. 1929, d. Tampa, Florida University Community Hospital March 5, 2003; m. (1) Danville, Virginia December 16, 1948 Margie Ellen Dix, b. Pittsylvania County, Virginia August 11, 1931, d. Danville, Virginia September 15, 2012, divorced 1953; m. (2) Genesee, Pennsylvania February 27, 1954 Betty Mary Orvis Willard, b. Hornell, New York November 17, 1927, d. New Port Richey, Florida October 29, 2017.

Lawrence was known to his family as Larry. His middle name, Leonard, was selected as a variation of his father's name Leo. He resided with his parents in Bolivar, New York, Clintonville, Pennsylvania, and Allentown, New York. Larry graduated from Allentown Union High School in Allentown and joined the US Marine Corps January 1948. After his Marine training in North Carolina, Larry was stationed in Norfolk, Virginia where he met his first wife. Mr. Root transferred from the Marine Corps to the US Navy and when his tour was completed, moved with his wife and son, Larry Wayne, to Allentown, New York. The marriage broke down after the birth of their second son, Ronald Leo in 1951. Margie stayed for a time with her husband's parents until returning to Danville, Virginia with both sons. Margie's mother placed Larry Wayne and Ron in a Danville orphanage because Margie was unable to take care of them.

Larry was never able to obtain custody of his sons and they remained in Danville until each reached the age of eighteen years. Larry was remarried to Betty Orvis who had been previously married to Arthur W. Willard while Larry was married to Margie. Larry's and Betty's divorces took effect in 1953 and they married in 1954. Larry worked for the Air Preheater Corporation, Wellsville, New York and Betty worked as a legal secretary for Wellsville, New York attorney Don Cummings until 1960 when they moved to Orlando, Florida.

From 1960-1967, Betty continued to work as a legal secretary while Larry was employed by the Orange State Casket Company. In 1967 Larry was transferred to Tampa to become the Plant Manager of the Orange Casket Company in that city where he worked until retirement. Betty no longer worked after 1967. Larry was an avid reader of books about World War II, a skilled gardener, and a talented furniture maker. He was a member of the Thomas B. Dobies Funeral Homes and Masonic Lodge # 230, F. and A. M, Wellsville, New York. Larry was cremated and his ashes scattered.

Margie Dix Root remarried September 15, 1956 to Charlie Lee Fuller and resided in Danville until her death. Margie had four children by her second husband. Margie was buried in Oak Grove Christian Church Cemetery, Chatham, Virginia. Arthur W. Willard remarried March 27, 1954 to Shirley Barrett with whom he had five children before his early death in 1969 at age forty-seven. Art Willard was buried in Woodlawn Cemetery, Wellsville, New York. Betty did not have any children by either marriage. Suffering from increasing dementia, Betty was place in a nursing home where she died. Betty was buried in Tucker Cemetery, New Port Richey, Florida.

Children (by first marriage):

786. I. ***Larry Wayne Root, f.***

787. II. ***Ronald Leo Root, f.***

References: US Census: 1930, 1940; New York State Birth Index for Lawrence Root and Betty Orvis; Virginia Marriage Record 1936-2014 for Lawrence Root's first marriage; US Marine Corps Muster Roll

1798-1958; Virginia Birth Record 1912-2014 for Margie Dix; New York State Marriage Index 1881-1967 for Betty Orvis' marriage to Arthur Willard; Virginia Marriage Record 1936-2014 for Margie Dix Root's marriage to Charlie Lee Fuller; Woodlawn Cemetery Records, Wellsville, New York for Arthur Willard; Oak Grove Christian Church Cemetery Records, Chatham, Virginia for Margie Dix Root Fuller; Social Security Death Index 1935-2014; *Tampa Bay Times*, November 1, 2017 obituary for Betty Root.

385.

Jeanne Charis Wylie, daughter of Nordica (175), granddaughter of Ernest (83), b. Binghamton, New York December 2, 1922, still living; m. Albany, New York March 9, 1947 Robert William Crist, b. Albany, New York April 14, 1919, d. Lenox, Massachusetts September 22, 2011.

Jeanne and Robert Crist resided most of their married life in Westport, Connecticut. Mr. Crist was known as *Mike* within the family. Mike Crist attended Albany Business College and served in the US Army Air Force in World War II as a flight navigator flying over forty missions in both war theatres. On his 20th mission Mike's aircraft was downed and later wrote to his mother that he floated merrily around in our *Mae Wests* before being picked up by a patrol. A gentle, humble man, Mike spoke little of his war experience and spent the remainder of his life devoted to forging peace through his work and his international relationships.

Mr. Crist was employed by Caltex Petroleum, a joint venture of Chevron and Texaco and managed the growth of their refining and distribution operation throughout much of Asia for 35 years. He retired in 1982. Jeanne Wylie was Mike Crist's childhood sweetheart and for fifty years resided in Westport, Connecticut until 2010 when they moved to Kimball Farms in Lenox, Massachusetts to be close to their daughter and grandchildren. The Crists had a summer house at Lee's Point on Lake Bomoseen, Vermont. Mike was buried at The Evergreen Cemetery of Saugatuck Congregational Church, Westport, Connecticut beside his two sons.

Children:

788. I. ***Robert Wylie Crist, f.***

789. II. ***Jeffrey H. Crist, f***

790. III. ***Karen Crist, f.***

References: US Census: 1920, 1930, 1940; New York State Census: 1925; New York State Birth Index 1881-1942; New York State Marriage Index 1881-1967; US Presbyterian Records 1701-1970 for Jeanne Wylie; *The Berkshire Eagle* September 24, 2011 obituary for Robert W. Crist; Evergreen Cemetery of Saugatuck Congregational Church Records, Westport, Connecticut.

386.

Gale Bernard Root, son of Allen (176), grandson of Bernard (84), b. Wellsville, New York March 30, 1930, d. Bluffton, South Carolina October 12, 2005 from throat cancer; m. Detroit, Michigan December 1, 1949 Doris Ludlow, b. Toronto, Canada February 14, 1929, d. Bluffton, South Carolina August 24, 2008 from an aneurysm.

Gale Root was known to family and friends as *Rootie*. Mr. Root served in the United States Air Force from August 2, 1946 to November 27, 1946 and from January 2, 1951 to February 7, 1952 seeing action in the Korean War where he rose to the rank of Corporal. After their marriage Gale and Doris Root resided in Bolivar, New York on Plum Street. Gale worked for twenty-five years for Clark Brothers, later Dresser Rand, in Olean, New York. For a number of years Gale was employed by Brown and Root (no relation) Engineering and Construction Company of Houston, Texas. This employment took Mr. and Mrs. Root to Georgia and South Carolina where they retired. During their time in Bolivar, Gale Root was actively involved in the American Legion, Kenyon Andrus Post, Bolivar, New York.

Not only did Gale serve as Commander of the Bolivar branch, but was elected Commander of the Allegany County American Legions in 1956 and from 1964-5, he was Commander of District 8 of the American Legion in New York State. Mr. Root was also a member of the Bolivar Methodist Church, the Bolivar branch of the Masons, the Bolivar Fire Department, and Allegany County Voiture. In retirement Gale was the gold medal winner for two years of the Beaufort County South Carolina Senior Olympics in billiards. Mrs. Root was a member of the Anglican Church of Canada and the American Legion, Post Kenyon Andrus, Bolivar, New York. Gale and Doris Root were buried in Maple Lawn Cemetery, Bolivar, New York.

Children:

791. I. ***Stephen Gale Root, f.***

792. II. ***Douglas Allen Root, f.***

793. III. ***Kimberly Root, f.***

References: US Census: 1930, 1940; New York State Birth Index 1881-1942; Michigan Marriage Record 1867-1952; *Bolivar Breeze 1891-1965*, selected issues; Maple Lawn Cemetery Records, Bolivar, New York; US Department of Veterans Affairs Death File 1952-2010; Social Security Death Index 1935-2014; *The Island Packet*, Hilton Head Island, South Carolina October 14, 2005 and August 24, 2008, newspaper obituaries.

387.

Audrey Drew Root, adopted daughter of Lyman (178), b. Olean, New York February 23, 1936, d. Fairbanks, Alaska September 18, 2006; m. Wirt, New York April 20, 1957 Kenneth Eugene Dunshie, b. Wellsville, New York October 14, 1933, d. Fairbanks, Alaska August 25, 2016.

Audrey was the daughter of Melba Norton and Leslie Drew. Her father was killed in an automobile accident April 16, 1939. In the 1940 US Census Audrey resided with her mother, two siblings, and her maternal grandparents in Wirt, New York. When Melba remarried Lyman Root in November 1940 Audrey, her brother Jack, and sister Kristin were adopted by Lyman Root and their last name changed from Drew to Root. She grew up in Bolivar and married her childhood sweetheart, also from Bolivar, Ken Dunshie in 1957. Ken graduated with a B.A. degree from Buffalo State Teacher College, Buffalo, New York and earned an M. A. in Education from the University of Alaska in 1973.

He began his teaching career at Bolivar High School where he taught juniors history. Mr. Dunshie always felt that Bolivar was a good place to be from. In 1969 Audrey, Ken, and their five children moved to Fairbanks, Alaska where he was employed as a guidance counselor at the newly built Ryan Junior High School. During his long career in education, Mr. Dunshie taught at Ryan Junior High, Lathrop High School, and West Valley High School as a guidance counselor. At North Pole Junior High School, he was vice-principal. Ken coached basketball, wrestling, and hockey. Ken Dunshie retired in in 1994. Audrey and Ken had five children: Kim, Michael, Jack, Kelli, and Jay, six grandchildren, and at the time of Ken's death, three great-grandchildren. Audrey and Ken were cremated and their remains buried in Maple Lawn Cemetery, Bolivar, New York in the plot with Melba and Lyman Root.

References: US Census: 1940; New York State Birth Index 1881-1967; New York State Marriage Index 1881-1942; Social Security Death Index; Maple Lawn Cemetery Records, Bolivar, New York; Fairbanks, Alaska obituary September 17, 2016 for Ken Dunshie.

388.

John "Jack" Norton Drew Root, adopted son of Lyman Root (178), b. Wellsville, New York July 13, 1937, d. Schenectady, New York July 4, 1961 in an automobile accident; m. Oneida, New York August 27, 1960 Donna Doran.

Jack, like his sisters Audrey and Kristin, was adopted by Lyman Root after Lyman married their mother in November 1940. Jack's biological father, Leslie Drew, was killed in an automobile accident in 1939. In the 1940 US Census Jack resided with his mother, two sisters, and maternal grandparents in Wirt, New York. After his adoption, he was known as Jack Root. Jack graduated from Bolivar High School in 1956 where he was an outstanding athlete being a member of the track, football, basketball, and baseball squads. He attended and graduated from Cortland State Teacher's College in 1960 where he participated as a pole vaulter with the track squad, a quarterback with the JV football team, and was a member of the swimming team. During the summers Jack returned to Bolivar where he was the manager of the Moore Swimming Pool from 1958 to 1960.

Jack Root met his wife, Donna Doran, while attending Cortland State. They married in August 1960 and were expecting their first child when Jack was killed in an automobile accident. Mr. Root was a passenger in a car operated by a close friend, Airman Michael Congden, stationed at Griffins Air Force Base, Rome, New York. Airman Congden was staying with Mr. and Mrs. Root and planning to move to Oneida where the Roots resided. Both Jack Root and Michael Congden were killed instantly when their car collided with a tractor trailer. Jack Root was buried in St. Patrick's Cemetery, Oneida, New York. A son was born posthumously to Jack Root in 1961. There is no further information on Jack's widow or son. An Athletic Scholarship was established at Bolivar High School in Jack's name and his mother, Melba Root, gave the award to the winning athlete each year.

References: US Census: 1940; New York State Birth Index 1881-1967; New York State Marriage Index 1881-1942; St. Patrick's Cemetery Records, Oneida, New York; *Bolivar Breeze 1891-1965*, selected issues on Jack Root's athletic career and July 6, 1961 for his obituary.

389.

Kristin Drew Root, adopted daughter of Lyman (178), b. Wellsville, New York March 15, 1939; m. Rochester, New York March 8, 1959 Calage Scalzo.

Kristin was the biological daughter of Leslie Drew and after his death in 1939 and her mother's remarriage in November 1940 to Lyman Root, was adopted by Lyman and her last name was changed to Root. In the 1940 US Census she resided with her mother, brother, and sister with her maternal grandparents in Wirt, New York. Kristin moved to Rochester, New York where she married and had five children. There is no further information on Kristin Drew Root Scalzo and her family.

References: US Census: 1940; New York State Birth Index 1881-1942; New York State Marriage Index 1881-1967.

390.

Earl Dean Holland, son of Mary (180), grandson of Bernard (84), b. Bolivar, New York April 27, 1929, d. Medina, New York January 28, 2001 from cancer; m. (1) Bolivar, New York June 9, 1951 Margaret Suzanne Dunn, b. Bolivar, New York August 28, 1928, d. Medina, New York January 15, 2012, divorced December 22, 1983; m. (2) place not known, January 1, 1988 Susan Beaver, b. Medina, New York May 13, 1942, divorced, date not known.

Known as Dean to family, friends, and colleagues, Mr. Holland was cum laude graduate of Bowling Green University (Ohio) with a B. S. degree in business administration. He was a member of Beta Sigma

Phi and Sigma Nu. For twenty-two years Dean was employed by Orleans County, New York where he developed the Youth at Risk Program. Dean became coordinator of the Youth Diversion Program. Mr. Holland served as Deputy Director of the Probation Department and later served as Director from 1989 to 2000. Dean Holland was a member of the Council of Probation Administrators and served on the State Executive Board. He was co-Chairman of the Planning and Research Committee, a member of the National Association of Probation Executives, and a member of the Criminal Justice Training Committee. Dean Holland was a member of St. Mary's Roman Catholic Church, Bolivar, New York, a former Third-Degree Knight and past President of the Knights of Columbus, Median Council 651, and the Medina Rotary. Mr. Holland co-owned Peddlers' Station and enjoyed fishing and antiquing. Suzanne Dunn was the daughter of Mr. and Mrs. Augustine Dunn of Bolivar, New York. Further information on Dean Holland's wives is not currently available. Earl Dean Holland was buried in St. Mary's Cemetery, Medina, New York.

Children (by first marriage):

794. I. ***Daniel John Holland, f.***

795. II. ***Christine Anne Holland, f.***

796. III. ***Corinne Marie Holland, f.***

797. IV. ***Michael Dean Holland, f.***

798. V. ***Mary Patricia Holland, f.***

799. VI. ***Patrick Joseph Holland***, b. Ohio June 3, 1961. Last known to reside in Medina, New York where he was employed as a carpenter; ***nfi.***

800. VII. ***William Augustine Holland***, b. Ohio January 2, 1965. Mr. Holland graduated from Kent State University, Ohio. He was last known to reside in Medina, New York where he was employed with Ontario Containers, ***nfi.***

References: US Census: 1930, 1940; New York State Birth Index 1881-1967; Social Security Death Index 1935-2014; *Bolivar Breeze 1891-1965*, June 14, 1951 for Holland/Dunn wedding; St. Mary's Cemetery Records, Medina, New York; Medina, New York newspaper obituary January 28, 2001.

391.

Barbara Anne Holland, daughter of Mary (180), granddaughter of Bernard (84), b. Bolivar, New York May 26, 1932, d. Hampton, Virginia July 24, 2000 from cancer; m. Bolivar, New York August 14, 1955 James Ralph Wescott, b. Fort Edward, New York June 24, 1932, d. Fredericksburg, Virginia May 31, 2015.

Barbara was known as *Bobbie* to her friends and family. Jim Wescott grew up in Bolivar as well. The Wescotts moved to Poquoson, Virginia where they raised their children. Jim owned and operated a marina in Hampton, Virginia and Bobbie sold real estate with Goodman/Segar/Hogan. The Wescott family had a red velvet photograph album, which probably was originally owned by Almyra Reed Root, Bobbie's grandmother. Unfortunately, none of the photographs were identified. It is currently not known where Bobbie and Jim Wescott were buried.

Children:

801. I. ***James Robert Wescott, f.***

802. II. ***Mary Elizabeth Wescott, f.***

803. III. ***David Gerald Wescott***, b. August 2, 1961. He was last employed buying and selling cars in the Hampton Roads area of Virginia and resided in Poquoson; ***nfi.***

804. IV. ***William Dean Wescott***, b. November 15, 1962; m. April 23, 1988 Hallie Suzanne McKinley. He was last known to reside in Hampton, Virginia where he owned and operated a car wash business; ***nfi.***

Children:

i. ***Samuel Wescott***, b. January 1989.

References: US Census: 1940; New York State Birth Index 1881-1967; New York State Marriage Index 1881-1942; Social Security Death Index 1935-2014; Virginia Death Records 1912-2014.

392.

Duane Bernard Root, son of Stanley (181), grandson of Bernard (84), b. Olean, New York June 30, 1935, d. Palm Harbor, Florida January 28, 2019; m. (1) Niagara Falls, Ontario, Canada May 7, 1960 Anita Flore, b. August 10, 1938, divorced 1971; m. (2) Miami, Oklahoma January 31, 1972 Linda Higley Lavett, b. Omaha, Nebraska August 17, 1939.

Duane Root was raised in Michigan. He was an outstanding high school athlete in track and field. Duane took these skills to Eastern Michigan State College where he was Captain of the track team. His performances were outstanding in both the high and low hurtles. Mr. Root was the 8th fastest in high hurtle in the world with a 1956 record of 14.2 second for the 120-yard distance. While at college, Duane Root was also treasurer of the Student Council, secretary of the Varsity Club, and a member of Kappa Phi Alpha fraternity. His major was physical education and he received his B. S. Degree in 1958. Duane Root entered military service and retired after thirty years in the US Army in July 1988 rising to the rank of Colonel.

Colonel Root also obtained an M.A. Degree in Education. From 1979-82 he served as Professor of Military Science and Head of the ROTC Program at Bowling Green University (Ohio). For a time, he was stationed at Fort Eustis, Virginia. Since retirement Professor Root taught in the Saudi Arabian International School in Riyadh, Saudi Arabia where he also served as the school's registrar. Linda Root earned both her B.A. and M. A. Degrees from Eastern Michigan State University in Special Education. She completed a second Masters in Administration and taught at Bowling Green University. Mrs. Root also taught at the International School in Saudi Arabia. Colonel and Mrs. Root currently reside in Palm Harbor, Florida. Linda Root has a son, Mark L. Lavett, born August 16, 1961, from her first marriage. It is not known where Duane Root was buried.

Children (from first marriage):

805. I. ***Kevin Root***, b. January 7, 1961. Kevin graduated from Western Washington University and co-owned a packing and shipping company in Bremerton, Washington where he was last known to reside, ***nfi.***

806. II. ***Sean Root***, b. July 14, 1969, resided in Alaska and was last known to reside in Port Orchard, Washington; ***nfi.***

References: US Census: 1940; New York State Birth Index 1881-1942; Niagara Falls, Ontario Register 1949-2001 for Duane Root's first marriage; US Select Military Registers 1862-1985; *Bolivar Breeze*, April 12, 1956; Sunset Point Funeral Home Records, Palm Harbor, Florida.

393.

Dianne Marie Root, daughter of Stanley (181), granddaughter of Bernard (84), b. Olean, New York May 19, 1936; m. place not known, November 19, 1955 John O'Donnell, divorced April 1971. Dianne was a long-time resident of Wyandotte, Michigan where she was employed as an office worker. In 1982, Dianne moved to Stuart, Florida where she later took care of her father, Stanley Root, until he died in 1990. Dianne was employed by the City of Stuart until her retirement. She currently resides in Port St. Lucie, Florida.

Children:

807. I. ***Terrance O'Donnell***, b. February 28, 1956; m. July 31, 1980 Rebecca Frates. They resided in Stuart, Florida where he worked for Stanley Steamer, ***nfi.***

Children:

i. ***Katherine Mary O'Donnell***, b. March 3, 1990.

808. II. ***Patrick O'Donnell***, b. November 19, 1957; m. October 20, 1979 Donna Phelps. They resided in Stuart, Florida where he was employed by Stanley Steamer, ***nfi.***

Children:

i. ***Megan O'Donnell***, b. January 15, 1982.
ii. ***Kyle Patrick O'Donnell***, b. March 14, 1984.

809. III. ***Timothy O'Donnell***, b. February 16, 1959. He was last known to reside in Stuart, Florida where he was employed as a commercial painter.

810. IV. ***Michael O'Donnell***, b. February 26, 1961. He was last known to reside in Stuart, Florida where he was employed with Stanley Steamer.

811. V. ***Kathleen O'Donnell***, b. June 1, 1962; m. April 15, 1982 Mark Filarski. They were last known to reside in Wyandotte, Michigan.

Children:

i. ***Shannon Lynn Filarski***, b. November 22, 1983.

References: US New York State Birth Index 1881-1942; interviews with Dianne Root O'Donnell for the 1990 Root family history.

395.

David Barber Evans, son of Ellen (188), grandson of Fred (88), b. Akron, Ohio July 12, 1939, d. Atlanta, Georgia December 28, 2013. Little is known about this descendant of Abel Root, Sr. He was married and had two daughters and one son. Mr. Evans served in the US Naval Reserve from August 1, 1965 to July 1, 1967. Further information is not currently available.

References: US Census: 1940; US Select Military Registrar Records 1861-1985.

396.

Howard Evaland Weatherby/Weatherbee, son of Minnie (189), grandson of Flora (90), b. Bolivar, New York September 12, 1903, d. Olean, New York October 5, 1967; m. Franklinville, New York September 6, 1924 Hazel E. Woodruff, b. Franklinville, New York August 2, 1899, d. Portville, New York July 6, 1990.

Howard was born into a loving family but tuberculosis caused his father's death in 1910 when Howard was only seven years old. His mother's second marriage to Bryon Barnes was not only an unsuccessful marriage but a brutal one that ended with Mr. Barnes committing suicide after shooting Howard and Howard's mother, Minnie Richardson Weatherby Barnes. Both Howard and his mother survived even though the odds seemed against them. For the rest of his life Howard was both religiously active in the Methodist Church and engaged in community activities. Mr. Weatherbee enjoyed doing magic, a talent he passed on to his son and grandson. He performed around the area, but, particularly at children's events. His show was advertised as *Weatherbee and Son Magic Circus.*

A member of the Masonic Order, Mr. Weatherbee served as Chaplin. Howard Weatherbee was employed as a truck driver and resided in Portville, New York with his wife and son. Hazel Woodruff Weatherbee was the daughter of George Byron Woodruff (1877-1974) and Dora Jean Cleveland (1877-1930). She had two brothers and one sister. Hazel was actively involved in the St. Andrew's Methodist Church in Portville, New York where she served on a variety of committees included the Women's Society of Christian Services. In addition, she was a steward in the Church, a Youth Fellowship Greeter, and a Daughters of Union Veterans. Howard and Hazel Weatherbee were buried in Chestnut Hill Cemetery, Portville, New York.

Children:

812. I. ***Maurice Philip Weatherby/Weatherbee, f.***

References: US Census: 1910, 1920, 1930, 1940; New York State Census: 1915, 1925; New York State Marriage Index 1847-9 and 1907-36; Social Security Death Index 1935-2014; Chestnut Hill Cemetery Records, Portville, New York; New York State Birth Index 1881-1942 for Howard Weatherby; New York State Death Index 1957-68 for Howard Weatherby; *Olean Evening Herald* April 28, 1917.

397.

Mercia Onalee Weatherby, b. Bolivar, New York June 27, 1906, d. Rochester, New York September 24, 1950. Mercia lost her hearing during a childhood illness. She spent most of her teen and adult life in Rochester, New York at an institution for the deaf. She never married. Mercia was buried with her parents in Maple Lawn Cemetery, Bolivar, New York.

References: US Census: 1910, 1920, 1930, 1940; New York State Census: 1915, 1925; Maple Lawn Cemetery Records, Bolivar, New York; New York State Birth Index 1881-1942; New York State Death Index 1852-1956.

398.

Stanley Dale Richardson, son of Stanley (190), grandson of Flora (90), b. Bolivar, New York August 10/13, 1907, d. Okmulgee, Oklahoma February 3, 1983; m. place not known, date not known Edith Thompson, b. McCurtain, Oklahoma May 16, 1912, d. Okmulgee, Oklahoma November 8, 1991.

Stanley Richardson spent most of his life in Oklahoma. He resided with his parents until his marriage, which took place after the 1930 US Census and before the birth of his son in 1935. Mr. Richardson's Draft Registration Card described him as 5' 8" tall, weighing 145 pounds with blue eyes and blonde hair. He was employed as a truck driver with the York Oil Corporation. Further information is not currently available. Stanley and Edith Richardson were buried in Okmulgee Cemetery, Okmulgee, Oklahoma.

Children:

813. I. ***Dale Mac Richardson, f.***

References: US Census: 1910, 1920, 1930, 1940; New York State Birth Index 1881-1942; Social Security Death Index 1935-2014; Okmulgee Cemetery Records, Okmulgee, Oklahoma.

399.

Ralph William Richardson, son of Stanley (190), grandson of Flora (90), b. Bolivar, New York August 18, 1908, d. Mt. Vernon, Missouri June 30, 1968; m. Wewoka, Oklahoma November 28, 1932 Lucille Muriel Garner, b. Tupelo, Mississippi November 22, 1910, d. Mt. Vernon, Missouri June 26, 1992.

Ralph Richardson resided with his parents in Bolivar, New York and Okmulgee, Oklahoma until his marriage in 1932. He was a professional baker and in the 1940 US Census was employed by Eddie's Fine Pastries in Okmulgee. His World War II Draft Registration Card described him as 5' 9" tall, weighing 152 pounds with brown hair and blue eyes. He served in World War II with the US Navy Reserve from October 25, 1942 to September 6, 1945. It is not known when Ralph and Lucille moved to Missouri to Oklahoma where they died. Ralph and Lucille Richardson were buried in Mt. Vernon IOOF Cemetery, Mt. Vernon, Missouri.

Children:

814. I. ***Rex Stanley Richardson, f.***

815. II. ***Michael Gene Richardson, f.***

816. III. ***Richard "Ricky" Dean Richardson, f.***

References: US Census: 1910, 1920, 1930, 1940; New York State Birth Index 1881-1942; Oklahoma Marriage Records 1890-1995; Social Security Death Index; World War II Draft Registration Card; US Naval Reserve Records 1814-1992; Mt. Vernon IOOF Cemetery Records, Mt. Vernon, Missouri.

400.

Robert Sydney Richardson, son of Stanley (190), grandson of Flora (90), b. Bolivar, New York February 19, 1910, d. Okmulgee, Oklahoma May 15, 1985. Little is known about this member of Root/Richardson descent. He resided with his parents through the 1940 US Census. His World War II Draft Registration Card described him as 5' 10" tall, weighing 147 pounds with Blue eyes and brown hair. He was employed as a truck driver for the York Oil Company in Okmulgee.

There is no record of any military service. No records could be found for a marriage or any children. Robert Richardson was buried in Okmulgee Cemetery, Okmulgee, Oklahoma.

References: US census: 1910, 1920, 1930, 1940; World War II Draft Registration Card, 1940; Okmulgee Cemetery Records, Okmulgee, Oklahoma; Social Security Death Index.

402.

Frances Louise Richardson, daughter of Manley (191), granddaughter of Flora (90), b. Bolivar, New York April 13, 1910, d. Warsaw, New York July 13, 1935 as a result of injuries from a fall; m. Genesee Township, Allegany County, New York October 9, 1927 Harold Everett Durfee, b. Warsaw, New York August 29, 1902, d. Silver Springs, New York May 1975.

Frances Richardson resided with her parents until her marriage. Her husband, Harold Durfee, was previously married to Charlotte Ramsey who died in 1925 after childbirth leaving a son, Arthur Ramsey Durfee. The 1930 US Census transcription has misspelled the last name of Durfee. The last name is given as Dorff. Frances and Harold Durfee had three children by 1930, a son Rolland who was being raised with his maternal grandparents, the Manley and Margaret Richardson, and twin daughters, Eloise and Eleanor. Harold's son by his first marriage resided with them as well on Main Street in Allentown next door to the Lewis Richardson family, Frances' uncle.

Mr. Durfee was employed as a tool dresser for an oil company. Sometime after the 1930 US Census the Durfee family moved to Warsaw, New York where Harold was from and where Frances died and was buried. Her cause of death is not known. Manley and Margaret Richardson raised three of Frances' children along with her step-son, Arthur Durfee. Arthur Durfee later legally changed his last time to Ramsey, his mother's maiden name. Harold Durfee remarried to Florence J. Lyons with whom he had two sons: Donald and Richard. Harold Durfee was buried with his third wife in Quaker Settlement Cemetery, Wethersfield Springs, New York. Frances Richardson Durfee was buried in Quaker Settlement Cemetery as well.

Children:

817. I. ***Rolland Everett Durfee, f.***

818. II. ***Eloise Belle Durfee, f.***

819. III. ***Eleanor A. Durfee, f.***

820. IV. ***Elizabeth Durfee, f.***

References: US Census: 1910, 1920, 1930; New York State Census: 1915, 1925; New York State Birth Index 1881-1942; New York State Marriage Record 1847-9 and 1907-1936; New York State Death Index 1852-1956 for Frances Durfee; Quaker Settlement Cemetery, Wethersfield Springs, New York; *Bolivar Breeze* October 13, 1927 for Richardson/Durfee wedding; *Bolivar Breeze* July 13, 1935 obituary for Frances Richardson.

403.

Margaret L. Baker, daughter of Agnes (192), granddaughter of Flora (90), b. New York State August 6, 1908, d. Warsaw, New York January 26, 2000; m. Silver Springs, New York December 31, 1936 Edward W. Mink, b. Troy, New York September 28, 1909, d. Ocala, Florida June 15, 1995.

Margaret Baker resided with her parents until her marriage. Edward Mink was the owner and operator of the Warsaw (New York) Variety Store until his retirement in 1976. Mr. Mink served as Warsaw Village Trustee from 1969-71 and Mayor of Warsaw from 1971 to 1981. He was the former President of the Greater Warsaw Chamber of Commerce. Edward Mink served in the US Army from August 13, 1943 to October 7, 1945. He was a member of the Walter Klein American Legion Post # 532, the Loyal Order of Moose # 560, and a member of the Warsaw Kiwanis. Edward Mink was cremated and buried in Saint Michael's Cemetery, Warsaw, New York. Margaret Mink was buried with him.

Children:

821. I. ***Yvonne Mink, f.***

References: US Census: 1910, 1920, 1930, 1940; New York State Census: 1915, 1925; New York State Birth Index 1881-1942 for Edward Mink; New York State Marriage Index 1881-1967; Social Security Death Index 1935-2014; St. Michael's Cemetery Records, Warsaw, New York.

404.

Raymond Daniel Baker, son of Agnes (192), grandson of Flora (90), b. New York State 1910, d. New York State 1927. Raymond Baker resided with his parents in Pike, New York until 1925 when they moved to Gainesville, New York. It is not known what he died from. Raymond Baker was buried in East Koy Cemetery, East Koy, New York.

References: US Census: 1910, 1920; New York State Census: 1915, 1925; East Koy Cemetery Records, East Koy, New York.

405.

Flora Juanita Baker, daughter of Agnes (192), granddaughter of Flora (90), b. New York State October 7, 1912, d. North Myrtle Beach, South Carolina June 20, 1998; m. Gainesville, New York May 29, 1932 Kenneth W. Cornell, b. Buffalo, New York April 21, 1911, d. Silver Springs, New York April 17, 1986. Flora resided with her parents until her marriage. Juanita and Kenneth Cornell were longtime residents of Silver Springs, New York. Little is known about them. After the death of Kenneth Cornell, Juanita moved to North Myrtle Beach where her daughter resided and remained in North Myrtle Beach after her daughter's death. It is not known where Juanita and Kenneth Cornell were buried.

Children:

822. I. ***Kenneth R. Cornell, f.***

823. II. ***Jacquelin A. Cornell, f.***

References: US Census: 1920, 1930, 1940; New York State Census: 1915, 1925; Social Security Death Index 1935-2014; New York County Marriage Records 1847-9 and 1907-1936.

406.

Geraldine A. Baker, daughter of Agnes (192), granddaughter of Flora (90), b. Portage, New York July 14, 1917, d. Warsaw, New York January 20, 2011; m. New York State October 13, 1962 John Richard *Dick* Brick, b. Rochester, New York December 28, 1923, d. Warsaw, New York February 22, 2017.

Geraldine was known as *Jerry* to family members and friends. She married later than her siblings. Jerry enjoyed being a homemaker who crocheted, made latch hook rugs, and sewed. She was member of the Perry Center Fire Department Ladies Auxiliary, the Perry VFE, Perry Vet's Club, and Dom Polski's and Silver Lake Sportsman Club. Mrs. Baker volunteered for the Perry Emergency Ambulance and served the Board of Elections as an election inspector for many years. Jerry was always remembered for her sense of humor. Dick Brick owned and operated Brickdale Farm in Perry, New York. He served as an elected Assessor and for eight years was a member of the Perry Ambulance Squad and EMT.

Dick was employed for thirty-four years by the Perry Post Office Rural Mail Carriers and served on the Perry Zoning Board and Planning Board. For sixty-eight years Mr. Brick was a member of the

Perry Fire Department serving as President and Secretary/Treasurer. For forty years Dick was an usher at St. Joseph's Church in Perry. He enjoyed his family and playing cards. Dick was previously married and had two children. He and Jerry raised his daughter Mary Anne and son James. They did not have any children. Jerry and Dick Brick were buried in Prospect Hill Cemetery, Perry Center, New York.

References: US Census: 1920, 1930, 1940; New York State Census: 1925; Social Security Death Index 1935-2014; New York Birth Index 1881-1942; Prospect Hill Cemetery Records, Perry, New York.

407.

Phyllis Orma Baker, daughter of Agnes (192), granddaughter of Flora (90), b. Silver Springs, New York May 16, 1928 (a twin), d. Clearwater, Florida March 15, 1997; m. (1) place not known, August 31, 1946 James Stack, divorced; m. (2) William Reynolds *Bill* Lowry, b. Rossburg, New York February 16, 1916, d. Florida October 20, 1998. Little is known about Phyllis and Bill Reynolds. Mr. Reynolds was previously married and divorced. His first wife, Jean, remarried to John J. Sheppard. Both Phyllis and Bill Reynolds were cremated and their ashes scattered in Tampa Bay area.

Children (by first marriage):

824. I. ***Dennis Stack, f.***

825. II. ***Kathleen Stack, f.***

826. III. ***James Stack, f.***

References: US Census: 1920, 1930, 1940; New York State Census: 1925; Florida Death Index 1877-1998; New York State Birth Index 1881-1942; Social Security Death Index 1935-2014.

408.

Norman J. Baker, son of Agnes (192), grandson of Flora (90), b. Silver Springs, New York May 16, 1928 (a twin). Family sources indicate Norman Baker married but did not have any children; ***nfi.***

References: US Census: 1930, 1940; New York State Birth Index 1881-1942.

409.

Oliver Thomas Richardson, son of Harold (193), grandson of Flora (90), b. Cleveland, Ohio December 19, 1915, d. Geauga, Ohio April 1, 2006; m. Cleveland, Ohio January 17, 1939 Violet Margaret Monroe, b. Cleveland, Ohio April 28, 1916, d. Geauga, Ohio January 11, 2004.

Oliver Richardson was an assistant research field worker at the time of his marriage. His wife, Violet Monroe, was a bookkeeper. Little is known about this line of Richardson descent. Oliver and Violet Richardson had six children: four sons and two daughters. Oliver and Violet Richardson were buried in Munn Cemetery, Newbury Center, Ohio.

Children:

827. I. ***Leslie Allen Richardson,*** b. Chagrin Falls, Ohio 1940; m. Constance Joan, last name not known and had at least one child: Kelly Ann Richardson; ***nfi.***

828. II. ***Judith Anna Richardson, nfi.***

829. III. ***Harold Monroe Richardson, nfi.***

830. IV. ***Ronald Ray Richardson, nfi.***

831. V. ***Harry Richardson, nfi.***

832. VI. ***Jack Richardson, nfi.***

References: US Census: 1920, 1930, 1940; Ohio Marriage Records 1810-1973; Social Security Death Index 1935-2014; Ohio Death Records 1908-32, 1938-2007; Munn Cemetery Records, Newbury Center, Ohio.

410.

Edward Frank Richardson, son of Harold (193), grandson of Flora (90), b. Cleveland, Ohio August 27, 1917, d. Cleveland, Ohio October 11, 1981; m. Cuyahoga County, Ohio June 15, 1940 Edna M. Krempin, b. Cuyahoga County, Ohio April 13, 1920, d. Cleveland, Ohio January 23, 2013. No further information is currently known about this Richardson descendant.

References: US Census: 1920, 1930, 1940; Ohio Birth Records 1908-1964; Ohio Marriage Records 1810-1973; Social Security Death Index 1935-2014.

411.

Itha Mae Richardson, daughter of Harold (193), granddaughter of Flora (90), b. Cleveland, Ohio August 28, 1919, d. Cuyahoga Falls, Ohio July 7/8, 2000; m. Cleveland, Ohio December 27, 1939 Deloss Junior Bacon, b. Mahoning, Ohio December 25, 1913, d. Cuyahoga Falls, Ohio June 27, 1993.

Itha Richardson resided with her parents until her 1939 marriage. Deloss Bacon served with the Merchant Marine, US Coast Guard from October 20, 1943 to July 20, 1945. Itha and Deloss resided in Cuyahoga Falls since 1945. Itha was employed by the Cuyahoga Falls General Hospital until her retirement. Itha and Deloss Bacon were buried in Oakwood Cemetery, Cuyahoga Falls, Ohio.

Children:

833. I. ***Elizabeth Luella "Bonnie" Bacon, nfi.***

834. II. ***Doris Jean Bacon, nfi.***

References: US Census: 1920, 1930, 1940; Ohio Marriage Records 1774-1993; Oakwood Cemetery Records, Cuyahoga Falls, Oho; *Akron Beacon Journal*, July 9, 2000 for Itha Bacon obituary; Social Security Death Index 1935-2014.

412.

Edna Marie Richardson, daughter of Harold (193), granddaughter of Flora (90), b. Novelty, Ohio November 25, 1921, d. St. Petersburg, Florida December 5, 2004; m. (1) Ohio February 1942 Lionel George William Morris, b. London, United Kingdom June 22, 1919, d. Newberry, Ohio February 14, 1995, divorced by 1944; m. (2) Cuyahoga Falls, Ohio 1956/57 Lynn Oscar Schnars, b. Philipsburg, Pennsylvania October 20, 1924, d. St. Petersburg, Florida December 7, 1984.

There is not a great deal of information on this Richardson descendant. Edna resided with her parents until her marriage to Lionel Morris. The marriage was short-lived and sometime after the birth of their daughter, Sandra Lee, they divorced. Edna remarried in the mid-1950s. Her second husband, Lynn Oscar Schnars, served in the military during World War II from July 2, 1943 to February 12, 1946. Sometime in 1984 Edna and Oscar moved to St. Petersburg, Florida where he died in December 1984 and she died in there in 2004.

It is not currently known where they were buried. Lionel Morris remarried December 31, 1944 to Jean Davis (1923-2009) and was buried in Markillie Cemetery, Hudson, Ohio.

Children (by first marriage):

835. I. ***Sandra Lee Morris, nfi.***

References: US Census: 1930, 1940; Social Security Death Index 1935-2014; Florida Death Index 1877-1998; Ohio Birth Index 1908-1964 for Edna Richardson; Pennsylvania Veterans Death Files World War II 1950-1966; Markillie Cemetery Records, Hudson, Ohio.

413.

Margaret Elizabeth Richardson, daughter of Harold (193), granddaughter of Flora (90), b. Cuyahoga Falls, Ohio November 25, 1924, d. St. Luke's Hospital Chagrin Falls, Ohio June 4, 1968; m. (1) Cuyahoga Falls, Ohio 1939-41 Robert L. Slupe, b. Geauga, Ohio April 9, 1924, d. Flint, Michigan June 20, 1975, divorced; m. (2) place not known, date not known Stanley O. Hatcher, b. Crawford, Ohio June 24, 1911, d. Chagrin Falls, Ohio November 15, 2001.

Little information is currently available about this Richardson descendant and her two husbands. Stanley O. Hatcher was previously married before his marriage to Margaret Richardson and remarried after her death. Stanley Hatcher was buried in Shadyside Cemetery, Auburn Corners, Ohio, but it is not currently known where Margaret was buried.

Children (by first marriage):

836. I. ***Dennis A. Slupe, f.***

References: US Census: 1930, 1940; Ohio Birth Records 1908-1964; Ohio Death Records 1908-32 and 1938-2007; Shadyside Cemetery Records, Auburn Corners, Ohio; Social Security Death Index 1935-2014; Michigan Death Records 1971-1996 for Robert Slupe.

414.

John Emmett "Pete" Corcoran, Jr., son of Mary Elizabeth (194), grandson of Flora (90), b. Olean, New York June 16, 1918, d. October 28, 1976 from uremic poisoning following gall bladder surgery; m. Olean, New York August 3, 1940 Eileen Jadlowski, b. Olean, New York June 18, 1916, d. Olean, New York October 24, 2005. John briefly served with the US Navy from June 10 1943 to August 27, 1943. He was employed by the Producer Gas Company, later National Fuel Company of Olean, New York. Eileen was a waitress at the Olean House and later at the Alcove restaurant. John and Eileen Corcoran resided on Garden Avenue in Olean.

They did not have any children. Mr. and Mrs. Corcoran were buried in Pleasant Valley Cemetery, Olean, New York.

References: US Census: 1920, 1930, 1940; New York State Census: 1925; Social Security Death Index 1935-2014; US Veterans Death Files 1850-2010; Pleasant Valley Cemetery records, Olean, New York.

415.

Edna Leora Hirliman, adopted daughter of Ethel (195), b. Olean, New York January 6, 1923, d. Machias, New York April 30, 2017. Edna was one of the first women to join the US Marines serving in the Aviation Women's Reserve. She was promoted to the rank of Corporal April 1944 and to Sergeant October 1945. Edna spent most of her military service in El Toro, California. Edna was married several times but family members to not have the documentation for these marriages. Fedison was the last name of her third husband. After she returned to Olean she was employed as a receptionist at Olean General Hospital. She did not have any children. Edna was buried in St. Bonaventure Cemetery, Allegany, New York.

References: US Census: 1930, 1940; New York State Census: 1925; New York State Birth Index 1881-1942; US Marine Corps Muster Rolls 1798-1958; St. Bonaventure Cemetery Records, Allegany, New York; *Olean Times Herald* May 3, 2017 obituary

416.

Doris Linda Richardson, daughter of Lewis (198), granddaughter of Flora (90), b. Bliss, New York July 3, 1920, d. Bolivar, New York September 5, 1997 from cardiac arrest and pulmonary disease; m. Pike, New York July 5, 1937 James Victor June, b. Bolivar, New York November 10, 1908, d. Bolivar, New York April 24, 1972 from cardiac arrest.

Doris Richardson's official birth certificate lists her name as Lois L. Richardson born in Eagle, not Bliss, New York on July 3, 1920. Doris and Victor June resided on Foreman Hollow Road, Bolivar, New York. Not only did Doris raise her own children she also helped raise her half-sister and two half-brothers when their mother, Doris' step-mother, died unexpectedly. Victor June was employed by the former Worthington Corporation in Wellsville, New York, later known as Dresser Rand. Doris was a tremendous help in getting the 1990 edition of the Root Family history updated with genealogical information. She had possession of Flora Root Richardson's red-velvet photograph album and amazingly all the photographs had the identities written on the back of each one.

I found Doris June to be an exceptionally kind, warm, and considerate person whose generosity deeply touched me. During the early 1960s the *Bolivar Breeze* newspaper recorded the many visitations to her home of family and friends as well as her and Victor June's travels to visit relatives on both sides of the family. Doris June was frequently the organizer for the annual June and Richardson family reunions, which continue to this day. During the 1960s Doris was an active member of the Bolivar Grange and served as lecturer and historian. Doris and Victor June are on the 1940 US Census but transcribers misspelled the last name. Instead of June the transcription is *Jene* and there are other misspellings of family names for this census, which may make it a challenge to properly locate. In 1940 Victor June was employed by the New York State Highway Department.

Doris worked at the Bolivar, New York Park and Shop and in the cafeteria at the Bolivar Central School. She was a member of the Bolivar United Methodist Church, the Bolivar VFW Auxiliary, and for many years served as Bolivar historian. Doris and Victor June were buried in Maple Lawn Cemetery, Bolivar, New York.

Children:

837. I. ***Beverly June, f.***

838. II. ***Rose Mary June, f.***

839. III. ***Inez June, f.***

840. IV. ***Dale June, f.***

841. V. ***Dean June, f.***

842. VI. ***Gerald June, f.***

References: US Census: 1910, 1920, 1930, 1940; New York State Census: 1915, 1925; New York State Marriage Index 1881-1967; Social Security Death Index 1935-2014; Maple Lawn Cemetery Records, Bolivar, New York; *Bolivar Breeze 1891-1965*, selected issues; New York State Birth Index 1881-1942.

417.

Blanche Flora Richardson, daughter of Lewis (198), granddaughter of Flora (90), b. Bliss, New York November 3, 1921, d. Elmira, New York March 26, 1978 from cancer; m. (1) Wellsville, New York February 27, 1946 Matthew W. Davis Jr., b. Wellsville, New York July 9, 1921, d. Fairport, New York April 4, 2015, divorced 1955; m. (2) place not known, date not known Alton Henry Donor, b. Glen Falls, New York October 8, 1921, d. Elmira, New York March 20, 1979, divorced after six weeks of marriage.

Blanche resided with her parents in the 1925 New York State Census and the 1930 US Census. The 1940 US Census recorded her residence in Genesee Township in Allegany County New York doing housework for the Kenneth Hunt family of Bolivar, New York. Blanche spent the greater part of her professional career employed by the Acme Markets grocery chain in Elmira, New York. Blanche Richardson David Donor was buried in Maple Lawn Cemetery, Bolivar, New York. Her first husband was buried in Woodlawn Cemetery, Wellsville, New York with his parents. Blanche's second husband was buried in Glen Falls Cemetery, Glen Falls, New York.

Children (by first marriage):

843. I. ***Cheryl Davis, f.***

References: US Census: 1930, 1940; New York State Census: 1925; Social Security Death Index 1935-2014; New York State Birth Index 1881-1942; Maple Lawn Cemetery Records, Bolivar, New York; Woodlawn Cemetery Records, Wellsville, New York; Glen Falls Cemetery Records, Glen Falls, New York.

418.

Merle William Richardson, son of Lewis (198), grandson of Flora (90), b. Bliss, New York May 31, 1925, d. May, Texas Abilene Regional Medical Center after heart surgery February 28, 1995; m. Warsaw, New York November 13, 1943 Beatrice M. Day, b. Bolivar, New York November 1, 1925, d. Big Lake, Texas September 5, 1991 from cancer; m. (2) Brown, Texas January 22, 1994 Joanna A. Hartley Charles.

Merle Richardson resided with his parents in Allentown, New York and later on Christman Hill in Bolivar, New York. He served in the US Army during World War II from March 18, 1944 to April 3, 1946. After World War II Merle and his family moved from Bolivar to Shinglehouse, Pennsylvania and in 1956 to Texas where he was employed by the Union Texas Petroleum Company for thirty-two years. They resided in Big Lake, Texas until 1987 when they relocated to nearby Lake Brownwood. Mr. Richardson was a member of the New Life Assembly of God Church, a life member of the Veterans of Foreign Wars Post 3216, Big Lake, a volunteer for the VNA Hospice of Brownwood, and a fifty-year member of the Bolivar, New York Fire Department. Beatrice Day Richardson was the daughter of Guy O. and Chrystal Taylor Day of Bolivar, New York. Mrs. Richardson was employed by the Reagan County Independent School District, Big Lake, Texas until retirement and their move to Lake Brownwood. Merle and Beatrice Richardson were buried in Glen Rest Cemetery, Big Lake, Texas.

Children:

844. I. ***Margaret Richardson, f.***

845. II. ***Betty Richardson, f.***

846. III. ***Merle William Richardson, Jr., f.***

847. IV. ***Chrystal Richardson, f.***

References: US Census: 1930, 1940; New York State Birth Index 1881-1942; US Veterans Death File 1850-2010; Texas Death Index 1903-2000; Texas Marriage Index 1924-2014 for Merle Richardson's second marriage; Glen Rest Cemetery Records, Big Lake, Texas; New York Marriage Index 1881-1967 for Merle Richardson's marriage to Beatrice Day; Social Security Death Index 1935-2014.

419.

Theo A. Richardson, daughter of Lewis (198), granddaughter of Flora (90), b. Bliss, New York November 30, 1930, still living; m. Bolivar, New York February 13, 1949 William Karl Dickerson, b. Olean, New York March 10, 1929, still living.

Theo and Bill Dickerson owned and operated a dairy farm in Shinglehouse, Pennsylvania until Bill had heart surgery in the mid-1980s. They continue to reside in Shinglehouse. Bill's World War II Draft Registration Card described him as 6' tall, weighing 170 pounds with brown hair and brown eyes. In 1940 he resided in Oswayo Township, Potter County, Pennsylvania and later at 11 Mile Road, Shinglehouse, Pennsylvania.

Children:

848. I. ***Lois Maryette Dickerson, f.***

849. II. ***Lila Dickerson, f.***

850. III. ***Karl Dickerson, f.***

851. IV. ***Carolyn Dickerson, f.***

852. V. ***Earl Dickerson, f.***

853. VI. ***Donald Dickerson, f.***

854. VII. ***Rodney Dickerson, f.***

855. VIII. ***Bradley Dickerson, f.***

References: US Census: 1930, 1940; New York Birth Index 1881-1942; New York State Marriage Index 1881-1967; World War II Draft Registration Card, 1940.

421.

Terry L. Richardson, son of Lewis (198), grandson of Flora (90), b. Wellsville, New York December 20, 1949. Mr. Richardson was previously employed as a security guard with Burns Security at Olean General Hospital. He has a son by Rhonda Miles. Mr. Richardson currently resides in Bolivar, New York.

Children:

856. I. ***David Lee Richardson***, b. December 14, 1989. David is employed in the construction industry with a specialty in carpentry.

422.

James Richardson, son of Lewis (198), grandson of Flora (90), b. Wellsville, New York April 3, 1951; m. place not known, March 1977 Tina Weimer. James and Tina Richardson reside in Bolivar, New York where he is employed as a custodian at the Richburg-Bolivar Schools.

Children:

857. I. ***Shannon Richardson, f.***

858. II. ***Casey Marie Richardson, f.***

References: Interviews with the late Doris Richardson June and Rose June Feenaughty.

423.

Sallie Ann Richardson, daughter of Lewis (198), granddaughter of Flora (90), b. Big Lake, Texas October 10, 1952; m. (1) Olean, New York October 21, 1973 Jeffrey Lynn App, divorced October 1980; m. (2) Olean, New York October 17, 1980 William Reynolds Lowery, Jr., b. Buffalo, New York October 3, 1944.

After her mother's death in 1954, Sallie Richardson was raised by her paternal aunt and uncle, Ethel Marion Richardson Hirliman and Albert Hirliman of Olean, New York. Sallie attended Olean, New York schools graduating in 1970. Bill was raised by his maternal grandparents, Charles Abel Gillespie and Elizabeth Jane Brown Gillespie of Hume, New York after his parents divorced in 1946. He graduated from Fillmore Central School in 1962. Mr. Lowery joined the US Air Force October 5, 1962 and served a tour of duty in Vietnam from 1964 to 1965. He was briefly a prisoner-of-war, but escaped. Bill Reynolds was discharged from the Air Force March 20, 1968. After his discharge he moved to Olean and found employment at Alcas Cutlery as a high-speed buffer. The Lowerys continue to reside in Olean.

Children (by second marriage):

859. I. ***Scott Michael Lowery***, b. Olean, New York January 24, 1983, d. Olean, New York January 29, 1988 from a three-year battle with Non-Hodgkin's Lymphoma.

860. II. ***Lisa Christine Lowery, f.***

861. III. ***Jamie Lyn Lowery, f.***

References: Correspondence from the late Doris Richardson June; Letter from Sallie Richardson Lowery, March 9, 1991.

424.

Edward Waldemar Hinz, son of Mildred (199), grandson of Flora (90), b. Depew, New York December 18, 1918, d. Silver Springs, New York April 22, 2000 from cancer. Mr. Hinz resided with his parents based on the 1920 and 1930 US Census and the New York State Census for 1925. He could not be found on the 1940 US Census. Richardson family members note that Edward Richardson never married or had any children. He was buried in East Koy Cemetery, East Koy, New York.

References: US Census: 1920, 1930; New York State Census: 1925; Social Security Death Index 1935-2014; East Koy Cemetery Records, East Koy, New York; New York State Birth Index 1881-1942; Social Security Death Index 1935-2014.

426.

Elizabeth Emma "Betty" Hinz, daughter of Mildred (199), granddaughter of Flora (90), b. Bliss/ Gainesville, New York January 19, 1922, d. Arcade, New York May 10, 2002 from a heart attack; m. Arcade, New York February 14, 1943 Raymond Toss Cooper, b. New York State January 26, 1919, d. Buffalo, New York September 16, 1992. Raymond T. Cooper enlisted in the US Army in Buffalo, New York September 16, 1943. He was awarded a Purple Heart for his service to the nation. Further information is not currently known about the Cooper family. Raymond and Betty Cooper were buried in Arcade Rural Cemetery, Arcade, New York.

Children:

862. I. ***Glen Cooper***; m. Marlene, last name not known; ***nfi.***

863. II. ***Linda Cooper***; m. Ken Gribble; ***nfi.***

864. III. ***Flora Cooper***; m. John Lyday***; nfi.***

865. IV. ***Katherin Cooper***; m. James Barkowski; ***nfi.***

866. V. ***Lois Marie Cooper, f.***

References: US Census: 1930, 1940; New York State Census: 1925; New York State Birth Index 1881-1942; Social Security Death Index 1925-2014; US World War II Army Enlistment Records 1938-46; Arcade Rural Cemetery Records, Arcade, New York.

427.

Rolland Manley Hinz, son of Mildred (199), grandson of Flora (90), b. Portageville, New York February 6, 1924, d. Arcade, New York April 5, 1991 from cancer; m. Arcade, New York March 5, 1945 Edna M. Bliss, b. Arcade, New York March 7, 1928, d. New York State September 4, 1991 from cancer. Rolland Hinz served in the US Army from July 18, 1945 to November 8, 1946 rising to the rank of Sergeant. Further information on Rolland and Edna Hinz is not currently available. They were buried in Arcade Rural Cemetery, Arcade, New York.

Children:

867. I. ***Ronald Hinz, nfi.***

References: US Census: 1930, 1940; New York State Census: 1925; New York State Birth Index 1881-1942; New York State Marriage Index 1881-1967; Social Security Death Index 1935-2014; Arcade Rural Cemetery Records, Arcade, New York; US Veterans Death File 1850-2010.

428.

Robert Stanley Hinz, son of Mildred (199), grandson of Flora (90), b. Portageville, New York February 6, 1924, d. Yorkshire, New York July 7, 1985; m. Concord, New York November 3, 1945 Violet "Vi" D. Grace, b. Buffalo, New York June 11, 1928, d. Delevan, New York July 18, 2011. Robert served in the US Army as a Tec 5 from June 25, 1946 to May 19, 1947. Further information on Robert Hinz and his family is not currently available. Robert and Vi Hinz were buried in Yorkshire Cemetery, Yorkshire, New York.

Children:

868. I. ***Joan Violet Hinz***, b. March 19, 1948; m. (1) July 31, 1968 Gary William George, b. January 13, 1946, d. April 10, 2011; m. (2) July 19, 1997 David Merton Roberts, b. July 30, 1942, d. January 19, 2006.

Children: (by first marriage)

i. ***Lisa Marie George***, b. May 24, 1967; m. (1) August 3, 1991 Keith Tozier; m. (2) September 29, 2001 Daniel Kemp.

Children: (by first marriage)

a. ***Justin Michael Tozier***, b. October 9, 1992; m. March 18, 2015 Shauna Leigh Giambrone, b. February 21, 1994.

b. ***Patrick David Tozier***, b. March 11, 1995.

ii. ***Michael Gray George***, b. September 19, 1967; m. April 25, 1992 Mary Cecilia Graney, b. October 19, 1967.

Children:

a. ***Mary Margaret George***, b. December 22, 1988; m. September 19, 2015 Deven Penn, b. November 11, 1987.

Children:

1) ***Rowan Sidney Penn***, b. October 27, 2017.

b. ***Mary Caroline George***, b. March 17, 1994; m. October 17, 2015 Brandon Price, b. January 19, 1994.

Children:

1) ***Jackson Salvatore Price***, b. June 1, 2014.
2) ***Finnley Anne Price***, b. January 11, 2017.

c. ***Ryan Michael George***, b. April 3, 1998.

869. II. ***Peggy Lee Hinz***, b. July 3, 1949; m. July 18, 1970 Donald Edward Kehl, b. June 22, 1944. Children:

i. ***Thomas Levi Kehl***, b. June 8, 1972; m. August 14, 1993 Christina Lynn Ross, born December 16, 1971.

Children:

a. ***Jason Michael Kehl***, b. August 13, 1998.
b. ***Nathan Alexander Kehl***, b. October 16, 2001.
c. ***Kimberly Jane Kehl***, b. June 17, 2008.

ii. ***Russell Jacob Kehl***, b. May 15, 1974; m. April 16, 2003 Mediatrix Aline Alejandro, b. November 17, 1970.

Children:

a. ***Austin Jacob Kehl***, b. July 19, 2003.
b. ***Kendra Nicole Kehl***, b. July 16, 2007.
c. ***Brandon Jameson Kehl***, b. August 8, 2009.

870. III. ***Jean Alberta Hinz***, b. July 10, 1950; m. (1) May 27, 1970 David Michael Kay; m. (2) June 16, 1984 Robert Richard Roberts, b. July 15, 1945.

Children: (by second marriage)

i. ***Matthew Jason Roberts***, b. October 9, 1986.

871. IV. ***Robert Byron Hinz***, b. September 8, 1953; m. April 28, 1973 Marcia Ann Trzybinski, b. November 4, 1953.

Children:

i. ***Stephanie Lynn Hinz***, b. April 26, 1975; m. July 29, 1995 Ryan R. Wright, b. November 29, 1970.

Children:

a. ***Brayden Edward Wright***, b. July 26, 2002.
b. ***Mikenna Grace Wright***, b. September 11, 2007

ii. ***Emily Lou Hinz***, b. August 18, 1977; m. May 29, 1998 Joshua Paul Dyer, b. March 22, 1976.

Children:

a. ***Evan Robert Dyer***, b. December 4, 2002.
b. ***Elijah Edward Dyer***, b. October 24, 2004.
c. ***Brandt Thomas Dyer***, b. July 14, 2007.

872. V. ***Richard Clarence Hinz***, b. February 23, 1955; m. June 25, 1993 Iona Ethel Briggs, b. March 1, 1956.

873. VI. ***Pamela Sue Hinz***, b. September 1, 1958; m. August 29, 1981 Michael James Tingue, b. November 17, 1955.

Children:

i. ***James Robert Tingue***, b. October 11, 1979; m. June 25, 2016 Rachael Lynn Tojek, b. September 15, 1990.

Children:

a. ***Dean Michael Tingue***, b. September 21, 2015.
b. ***Charlene Elizabeth Tingue***, b. April 6, 2017.

ii. ***Jared Michael Tingue***, b. December 13, 1981, d. July 18, 2005; m. July 19, 2003 Sara Louise Ellis, b. May 3, 1982.

iii. ***Jeffrey Lee Tingue***, b. June 23, 1983.

874. VII. ***Steven James Hinz***, b. August 25, 1959; m. September 30, 1989 Kimberly Ann Tilton, b. September 25, 1963.

Children:

i. ***Samantha Jane Hinz***, b. January 18, 1988.
ii. ***Dustin Jacob Hinz***, b. June 22, 1991; m. July 16, 2019 Kelly Faith Sikorski, born June 3, 1993.

References: US Census: 1930, 1940; New York State Census: 1925; New York State Birth Index 1881-1942; New York State Marriage Index 1881-1967; US Veterans Death File 1850-2010; Yorkshire Cemetery Records, Yorkshire, New York; Correspondence with Peggy Hinz Kehl.

429.

Avis Arlene Hinz, daughter of Mildred (199), granddaughter of Flora (90), b. Portageville, New York February 15, 1926, d. Buffalo, New York November 8, 1977; m. Eagle, New York February 14, 1948 Elmer George Waite, b. London, Ontario, Canada April 22, 1921, d. Buffalo, New York October 7, 1994. Arlene Hinz resided with her parents until her marriage. Arlene and Elmer Waite were buried in St. John's Cemetery, Cheektowaga, New York.

References: US Census: 1930, 1940; 1921 Census for Canada for Elmer Waite; New York State Birth Index 1881-1942 for Arlene Hinz; New York State Marriage Index 1881-1967; St. John's Cemetery Records, Cheektowaga, New York.

Children:

875. I. ***Susan Gertrude Waite, nfi.***

876. II. ***David Keith Waite, nfi.***

430.

Donald Laverne Hinz, son of Mildred (199), grandson of Flora (90), b. Pike, New York June 13, 1928, d. Eagle, New York March 3, 1954; m. Cheektowaga, New York October 28, 1950 Violet L Phillips, b. October 6, 1929, still living.

Donald Hinz resided with his parents until his marriage. He was employed as a truck driver for a log and lumber company in Eagle, New York. Donald Hinz committed suicide by carbon monoxide poisoning. He was buried in East Koy Cemetery, East Koy, New York. On May 13, 1957 Wyoming County Court appointed Larry L. Brown as guardian over Donald Hinz's three children.

Children:

877. I. ***Edward L. Hinz, nfi.***

878. II. ***Patsy L. Hinz, nfi.***

879. III. ***Dawn Hinz, nfi.***

References: US Census: 1930, 1940; New York State Birth Index 1881-1942; New York State Marriage Index 1881-1967; New York State Death Certificate 1852-1956; Social Security Death Index 1935-2014; Surrogate's Court, Wyoming, New York March 1954 and May 13, 1957.

431.

Marion Delores Hinz, daughter of Mildred (199), granddaughter of Flora (90), b. Eagle/Bliss, New York September 12, 1930, d. Pasadena, Texas August 10, 2015; Buffalo, New York January 4, 1951 Benjamin Herman Miller, Sr., b. DeWitt, Texas October 28, 1920, d. Pasadena, Texas August 5, 1993.

Benjamin Miller served in World War II and Korea with the US Army rising to the rank of Captain. Marion and Benjamin Miller raised their family in Pasadena, Texas. She enjoyed reading, crocheting, and watching her favorite television shows. Marion and Benjamin Miller were buried in Grand View Memorial Park, Pasadena, Texas.

Children:

880. I. ***Diana Karen Miller, nfi.***

881. II. ***Mark B. Miller, nfi.***

882. III. ***Donna Kay Miller, f.***

883. IV. ***Benjamin Herman Miller, Jr., f.***

References: US Census: 1930, 1940; New York Birth Index 1881-1942 for Marion Hinz; Texas Birth Index 1903-1997 for Benjamin Miller; New York Marriage Index 1881-1967; Grand View Memorial Park records, Pasadena, Texas.

432.

Mildred H. Hinz, daughter of Mildred (199), granddaughter of Flora (90), b. Eagle, New York December 5, 1932, still living; m. (1) Rochester, New York September 17, 1955 George Arthur Jacobson, b. place not known, August 19, 1921, d. place not known December 11, 1997, divorced; m. (2) Rochester, New York August 27, 1965 Ralph R. *Bud* Watson, b. Danby, New York June 26, 1928, d. Spencerport, New York July 30, 2002.

Mildred Hinz resided with her parents until her marriage. There is currently little information about her husbands and their careers. George A. Jacobson served in the US Army during World War II earning the Purple Heart and a Bronze Star. He rose to the rank of Sergeant. Mr. Jacobson was buried in Bath National Cemetery, Bath, New York.

Children (by first marriage):

884. I. ***Donald Jacobson, nfi.***

885. II. ***Deborah Sue Jacobson, f.***

References: US Census: 1930, 1940; New York Birth Index 1881-1942; New York State Marriage Index 1881-1967 for both marriages of Mildred Hinz; Bath National Cemetery records, Bath, New York for George Jacobson; Fairfield Cemetery records, Spencerport, New York for Ralph Watson.

433.

Edith Elaine Hinz, daughter of Mildred (199), granddaughter of Flora (90), b. Eagle, New York July 15, 1937 d. Murfreesboro, Tennessee August 6, 2014; m. (1) Cheektowaga New York February 15, 1958

Beverly D. Mowers, divorced; m. (2) New York State January 24, 1960 Jack Femoyne Rush, b. place not known August 18, 1937, d. place not known September 4, 1988. There is currently little information about Edith Hinz and her family. She and her second husband resided in Winter Gardens, Florida. It is not known where Jack Rush was buried. Edith Rush donated her body to science. Edith and Jack Rush adopted a daughter Tresa Joe Rush, born October 20, 1965. The identity of the father of Wesley Hinz is not currently known.

Children:

886. I. ***Wesley Hinz, nfi.***

References: US Census: 1940; New York State Birth Index 1881-1942 for Edith Hinz; New York State Marriage Index 1881-1967 for both marriages; Richardson family reunion notes.

434.

Keith R. Hinz, son of Mildred (199), grandson of Flora (90), b. Warsaw, New York April 22, 1939, d. United Memorial Medical Center, Batavia, New York January 15, 2016; m. Warsaw, New York November 29, 1958 Ruth M. Brown, b. Mt. Pleasant, New York November 31, 1941, still living. Keith Hinz served in the US Marine Corps from December 1, 1956 to November 30, 1959. After his military service Keith was a milk truck driver for Carney and Fugle in Attica, New York. Mr. Hinz was a member of the Immanuel United Church of Christ, Attica, New York. Keith had a great love of horses and for many years he was an active member and served on the Board of the Caravan for Cancer. It is not currently known where Keith Hinz was buried.

Children:

887. I. ***Donald Hinz, nfi.***

888. II. ***Karl Hinz, nfi.***

889. III. ***Marcia Hinz, nfi.***

890. IV. ***Jeffrey Hinz, nfi.***

References: US Census: 1940; New York State Birth Index 1881-1942; US Marine Corps Records 1798-1958.

435.

Carol Hinz, daughter of Mildred (199), granddaughter of Flora (90), b. New York State March 15, 1941; m. Pembroke, New York June 1, 1963 John Slikes, b. Pembroke, New York July 2, 1939.

Children:

891. I. ***Terrie Anne Slikes***, b. May 3, 1965; ***nfi***.

892. II. ***Brenda Marie Slikes***, b. December 5, 1966; ***nfi***.

References: New York State Marriage Index 1881-1967; New York Birth Index 1881-1942 for John Slikes.

436.

Flora Jeanne Richardson, daughter of Laurence (201), granddaughter of Flora (90), b. Akron, New York March 5, 1930, d. Tonawanda, New York April 14, 2001; m. place not known, date not known Harold Ellwood McMaster, b. Peterborough, Ontario, Canada, September 23, 1923, place and date of death not known.

In the 1930 US Census Flora resided with her mother in Newstead, New York. In 1940 she resided with her mother and maternal grandmother at 48 Bloomingdale Avenue, Newstead, New York. Flora was buried in Tonawanda but the cemetery is not currently known. They did not have any children.

References: US Census: 1930, 1940; New York State Birth Index 1881-1942; Social Security Death Index 1935-2014.

437.

George Edward Fox, Jr., son of Lillie (206), grandson of Laphronia (91), b. Muncie, Indiana December 2, 1923, d. St. Petersburg, Florida February 4, 2002; m. Grant, Indiana June 10, 1949 Janice Young, b. Indianapolis, Indiana January 1, 1930, still living.

George Fox, Jr. resided with his parents until his enlistment in the US Navy. He served from February 4, 1943 to February 26, 1946. Mr. Fox's draft registration card described him as 5' 8" tall, weighing 170 pounds with blue eyes and brown hair. Mr. and Mrs. Fox moved from Muncie, Indiana to St. Petersburg, Florida in 1952. George worked for Florida Power Company in Tampa as a Manager. It is not currently known where George Fox was buried.

Children:

893. I. ***Richard K. Fox, f.***

894. II. ***Steven E. Fox, f.***

References: US Census: 1930, 1940; Indian Birth Certificate 1907-1940; Indiana Marriage Index 1831-2008; Social Security Death Index 1935-2014; World War II Draft Registration Card, 1942; US Veterans Death File 1850-2010.

438.

James Edmund Fox, son of Lillie (206), grandson of Laphronia (91), b. Muncie, Indiana August 26, 1929, d. Muncie, Indiana December 14, 2002 by suicide. James Fox resided with his parents until he joined the US Army serving from September 17, 1951 to June 16, 1953. He served as an office manager and Secretary-Treasurer for the Attlin Construction Company until retirement. James Fox took care of his mother until she died in 1986 and resided at the family home until his own death. Mr. Fox never married. James Fox was very helpful with the 1990 Root family history. He was buried in Elm Ridge Memorial Park, Muncie, Indiana with his parents.

References: US Census: 1930, 1940; Indiana Birth Certificates 1907-1940; US Veterans Death File 1850-2010; Indiana Death Certificate 1899-2011; Social Security Death Index 1935-2014.

439.

Jeanne Ann Fox, daughter of Lillie (206), granddaughter of Laphronia (91), b. Muncie, Indiana May 16, 1933, d. Fountain City, Indiana January 4, 2014; m. (1) place not known, date not known Rodney Shafer, divorced; m. (2) Muncie, Indiana August 17, 1957 Carl Max Showalter, birth place and birth date not known, still living.

Jeanne earned both a B. S. and an M. A. from Ball State University in Elementary Education teaching kindergarten until retirement. She taught at Richmond, Delta, and Muncie, Indiana schools during her long career. Jeanne was a member of the National Education Association, the Indiana State Teachers Association, and the Retired Teachers Association. She was an avid reader, enjoyed gardening, and was involved in crafting, Max earned a B.S. in Business Administration and Physical Education and an M. A. in Elementary Education from Ball State University as well. Mr. Showalter taught sixth grade and worked part-time as a tax consultant. It is not currently known where Jeanne Showalter was buried.

Children (by first marriage):

895. I. ***Debra Sue Shafer Showalter, f.***

Children (by second marriage):

896. I. ***Shelley Ann Showalter***, b. and d. July 18, 1959 and buried at Willow Grove Cemetery, Muncie, Indiana.

897. II. ***Sally Lynn Showalter***, b. Muncie, Indiana October 31, 1960. Sally is not married and resides in Muncie; ***nfi.***

898. III. ***Stacey Marie Showalter, f.***

References: US Census: 1940; Indiana Birth Certificate 1907-1940; Social Security Death Index 1935-2014; Willow Grove Cemetery Records, Muncie, Indiana for Shelley Ann Showalter; Muncie, Indiana newspaper obituary for Jeanne Fox Showalter.

440.

Edmund Clifton Root, son of Clifton (207), grandson of Laphronia (91), b. Muncie, Indiana February 8, 1936; m. Oklahoma City August 23, 1958 Mary Ann McCarty, b. Oklahoma City, Oklahoma September 20, 1936, d. Oklahoma City, Oklahoma September 14, 2014.

Edmund Root received a B. S. degree from the University of Oklahoma and his M.B.A. from Oklahoma State University. He was a mechanical engineer at Tinker Air Force Base, Midwest City, Oklahoma. Mary Ann retired in 1992 from Gulfstream Aerospace. She was a member of the Metropolitan Baptist Church. Mrs. Root was buried in Rose Hill Burial Park, Oklahoma City, Oklahoma.

Children:

899. I. ***Kathryn Lee Root, f.***

900. II. ***James Clifton Root, f.***

References: US Census: 1940; Indiana Birth Certificate 1907-1940; Rose Hill Burial Park records, Oklahoma City, Oklahoma.

441.

Donald Keith Miller, son of Martha (208), grandson of Laphronia (91), b. Muncie, Indiana August 1, 1929, d. Noblesville, Indiana October 28, 2016; m. Muncie, Indiana July 31, 1947 Thelma Rae Halteman, b. Muncie, Indiana November 17, 1927, still living.

Donald Miller's World War II Draft Registration Card described him as 5' 8" tall, weighing 125 pounds with blue eyes and blonde hair. In 1946 he was employed at Stecks Clothing Store. Mr. Miller was a graduate of Ball State University. He was employed as an analyst with the Chevrolet Division of General Motors. Donald Miller retired after thirty-one years of employment in the accounting department with General Motors in Muncie. He enjoyed playing golf and working in his yard. Donald Miller's remains were cremated and their current location is not known.

Children:

901. I. ***Michael Scott Miller, f.***

902. II. ***Beth Ellen Miller***, b. July 20, 1954 and last resided in Birmingham, Michigan; ***nfi.***

903. III. ***Meridee Miller***, b. October 3, 1967, graduated from Michigan State University, and last resided in Ann Arbor, Michigan; ***nfi.***

References: US Census: 1930, 1940; Indiana Birth Certificates 1907-1940; Indiana Marriage Records 1810-2001; World War II Draft Registration Card, 1946; Social Security Death Index 1935-2014.

442.

Jo Anne Miller, daughter of Martha (208), granddaughter of Laphronia (91), b. Muncie, Indiana April 22, 1930, d. place not known October 12, 2007; m. Muncie, Indiana October 22, 1950 Buren Eugene Davis, divorced, b. Harford City, Indiana October 22, 1925, place and date of death not known.

Jo Anne Miller resided with her parents until her marriage. She was a graduate of Ball State University where she earned B. A. and an M. Ed. Degrees in special education. Jo Anne taught with the Frankfort, Indiana public school system and resided in Bloomington, Indiana. It is not currently known where Jo Anne Miller Davis was buried. Her death date was found on an ancestry family tree and cannot be confirmed with documentation. Buren Eugene Davis served with the US Navy from 1943 to 1945. His World War II Draft Registration Card described him as being 5' 9" tall, weighed 151 pounds with brown eyes and black hair.

Children:

904. I. ***Robert Buren Davis, f.***

905. II. ***Andrew Allen Davis, f.***

906. III. ***Sharlee Anne Davis, f.***

907. IV. ***Joseph Martin Davis, f.***

References: US Census: 1930, 1940; Indiana Birth Certificates 1907-1940; Indiana Marriage Records 1810-2001; World War II Draft Registration Card, 1943.

443.

David Martin Lambert, son of Elizabeth (209), grandson of Laphronia (91), b. Muncie, Indiana August 27, 1929, d. Muncie, Indiana September 10, 2008 from Alzheimer's; m. Madison, Indiana December 24, 1951 Barbara Ann Wallace, b. Madison, Indiana February 18, 1933, d. Muncie, Indiana October 31, 2011.

David Lambert served with the United States Air Force from December 29, 1950 to December 14, 1954 where he trained as a radar repairman. After his military service, Mr. Lambert was employed as a tool and die maker with Warner Gear in Muncie, Indiana. David was a gourmet cook and served as past president of the Pro Bass Fishing Club. Barbara Wallace Lambert graduated from the Ball State University School of Practical Nursing in 1966. She worked as an LPN at Ball Memorial Hospital and as a private duty nurse. Mrs. Lambert was a member of the Antioch Church of the Brethren and the Alzheimer's Association. David and Barbara Lambert were buried in Beech Grove Cemetery, Muncie, Indiana.

Children:

908. I. ***Christie Lambert, f.***

909. II. ***Judy Lynn Lambert, f.***

910. III. ***David Lambert, f.***

References: US Census: 1930, 1940; Indiana Birth Certificate 1907-1940; Indiana Death Certificate 1899-2011 for David Lambert; US Veterans Death File 1850-2010; Social Security Death Index 1935-2014; Beech Grove Cemetery records, Muncie, Indiana; newspaper obituary for Barbara Wallace Lambert November 1, 2011.

444.

Jane Ellen Lambert, daughter of Elizabeth (209), granddaughter of Laphronia (91), b. Muncie, Indiana March 4, 1931, d. Muncie, Indiana January 24, 1997 from congestive heart failure and breast cancer. Jane Lambert never married. She was employed as an office worker and later secretary for Muncie Public Schools. She resided in the Community Care Center in Muncie prior to her death. Jane was an accomplished craftsman in needlework. Jane Lambert was buried in Tomlinson Cemetery, Muncie, Indiana.

References: US Census: 1940; Indiana Birth Certificates 1907-1940; Indiana Death Certificates 1899-2011, Social Security Death Index 1935-2014; Tomlinson Cemetery records, Muncie, Indiana; Correspondence with the late Barbara Lambert.

445.

James Richard Lambert, son of Elizabeth (209), grandson of Laphronia (91), b. Muncie, Indiana January 5, 1933, d. Muncie, Indiana August 2, 2016; m. Bloomington, Indiana July 1, 1955 Judith Douthitt, b. Indiana January 2, 1933, still living.

James Lambert was a star athlete at Muncie, Indiana High School in Cross Country and Track. Jim was Cross Country champion his junior and senior years. In 1950 he became the Indiana State Mile Champion, which he won again in 1951. In 1951 Jim was selected as a member of the AAU All Scholastic Track and Field Team. Jim Lambert attended Indiana University on an athletic scholarship where he became a member of the NCAA All-American Cross-Country Team in 1952 and 1953. In 1954, Jim was the Big Ten Cross Country Champion and in 1955 he was selected for the All-American College Cross Country Team and received the L.G. Balfour Award for bringing honor and distinction to Indiana University in Track. Jim graduated from Indiana University with a B. S. in Education in 1956 and earned a Master's Degree in Education in 1964 from Ball State University.

He taught at Muncie Community Schools starting in 1959 starting at the Elementary Level. In 1963 he joined the Muncie High School faculty where he taught Physical Education, Health, and Driver's Education for 32 years. Jim coached high school cross country and track. In 1967 his Cross-Country Team won the state championship and he was selected the Indiana State Coach of the Year in Cross Country. In 1974 Jim Lambert was inducted into the Indiana Track and Field Hall of Fame. Certified to become a USA Track and Field Official, Jim would officiate for over 30 years at Big Ten Championships, NCAA Championships, the PAN-AM Games and other international events. For four years, Jim served on the Board of Directors for the Indiana Track and Cross-Country Association.

Jim met his wife, Judy, while attending Indiana University. She became the Director of Education for Delaware County, Indiana Association for Retarded Citizens. Together, they joined the High Street United Methodist Church in 1958. Jim was a member and past President of the Delaware Kiwanis Club (Indiana), served on the Board of the Muncie Mission and Christian Ministry, volunteered for Habitat for Humanity and the Special Olympics. In 2016 Mr. Lambert was named Mentor of the Year in 2016 for 5 ½ years of service. Jim and Judy Lambert had a passion for nature and bird watching. They established their Muncie property as a National Wildlife Backyard Habitat for which they won an award from the National Wildlife Federation in the 1970s. On another property north of Selma, Indiana they would reclaim five acres of farm land as a tall grass prairie, wetlands, and nature pond. Once again, they received an award from the National Wildlife Federation for a Backyard Habitat. It is not currently known where James Lambert was buried.

Children:

911. I. ***Shonet Lambert, f.***

912. II. ***Thomas Lambert, f.***

913. III. ***Mary Beth Lambert, f.***

References: US Census: 1940; Indiana Birth Certificates 1907-1940; *The Muncie Star Press*, August 4, 2016 obituary; Correspondence with the late Barbara Lambert.

446.

Martha Anne Lambert, daughter of Elizabeth (209), granddaughter of Laphronia (91), b. Muncie, Indiana December 9, 1934, still living; m.(1) Muncie, Indiana December 1952 Herman Charles Pearson, b. Middletown, Indiana November 26, 1932, divorced 1957; m. (2) Muncie, Indiana August 18, 1962 Ferol Wayne Girton, b. Terra Haute, Indiana June 20, 1929.

Martha Anne graduated from Muncie Business College. Her second husband was previously married. Wayne Girton worked for Warner Gear in Muncie until he retired. Further information is not currently available.

Children (by first marriage):

914. I. ***Charles Pearson, f.***

915. II. ***Michael Pearson, f.***

916. III. ***Patricia Pearson, f.***

References: US Census: 1940; Indiana Birth Certificate 1907-1940; Indiana Marriage Records 1917-2005 for Martha Anne Lambert's second marriage.

447.

Rebecca Sue Lambert, daughter of Elizabeth (209), granddaughter of Laphronia (91), b. Muncie Indiana December 2, 1940; m. Muncie, Indiana July 6, 1963 Paul Vincent Eiholzer, b. Eaton, New York March 19, 1940.

Rebecca Lambert is a graduate of Ball State University with a B. S. Degree in Education and an M. S. Degree in Counseling and Psychology. Rebecca was employed as a Psychotherapist at Onondaga

Pastoral Counseling Center in Syracuse, New York. Paul is a graduate of Lemoyne College, Syracuse, New York with a major in Physics. He is President and owner of Jade Software Services in Dewitt, which markets the *Veterinarian*, a computer system for veterinarian practices. Rebecca and Paul reside in Jamesville, New York.

Children:

917. I. ***Steven Eiholzer, f.***

918. II. ***Todd Eiholzer***, b. May 22, 1965 graduated from SUNY Potsdam with a B. S. Degree in Mathematics. He is also a songwriter; ***nfi.***

919. III. ***Karl Eiholzer***, b. October 27, 1967 graduated from SUNY Albany with a B.S. Degree in Political Science and an MA in Political Science at SUNY Albany; ***nfi.***

920. IV. ***Joel Eiholzer***, b. November 18, 1969 has an Associate's Degree in Engineering from the University of New York, Canton and B. S. Degree in Electrical Engineering from VPI, Blacksburg, Virginia.

References: Indiana Birth Certificates 1907-1940; New York Birth Index 1881-1942; Indiana Marriage Certificates 1917-2005; Correspondence with the late Barbara Lambert.

448.

Kathryn Louise Lambert, daughter of Elizabeth (209), granddaughter of Laphronia (91), b. Muncie, Indiana November 14, 1942; m. (1) Muncie, Indiana August 22, 1964 James Leighton Tighe, b. Muncie, Indiana March 10, 1942, d. Galion, Ohio April 27, 2012, divorced 1969; m. (2) Muncie, Indiana March 17, 1972 Eugene Victor Vermeulen, b. Canada January 27, 1931.

Kathryn Lambert graduated from Indiana Business College and undertook additional study at Ball State University. Kathryn is an advocate for special education and is active in *Speech is Worth Hearing*. Kathryn serves as both a local and national director for Speech and Hearing Day Camp. She also does volunteer work for Mental Health. Eugene Vermeulen is a welder fitter with Indiana Bridge, part of RTW Industries. He became a naturalized citizen of the United States September 22, 1965. Kathryn's first husband, James Tighe, attended Ball State University, remarried, and died in 2012 and was buried in Calvary Cemetery, Kettering, Ohio.

Children (by first marriage):

921. I. ***Jennifer Marie Tighe, f.***

922. II. ***Margaret Elizabeth Tighe, f.***

Children (by second marriage):

923. I. ***Elizabeth Jeanette Vermeulen***, b. August 19, 1972 graduated from the Burris Laboratory School and Ball State University with a degree in Special Education; ***nfi.***

924. II. ***Rebecca Jean Vermeulen***, b. October 24, 1978; ***nfi.***

References: Indiana Birth Certificates 1907-1940; Indiana Marriage Certificates 1917-2005 for both marriages; Indiana Federal Naturalization Records 1892-1992 for Eugene Vermeulen; Calvary Cemetery records, Kettering, Ohio for James Tighe; correspondence with the late Barbara Lambert; Ohio Marriage Records 1938-2018.

449.

Forrest Eugene Jewett, Jr., son of Forrest (210), grandson of Elizabeth (92), b. Ashtabula, Ohio May 1, 1914, d. place of death not known, date of death not know; m. Detroit, Michigan September 21, 1940 Marie Josephine Jeannette Cousineau, b. Emerum, Ontario, Canada August 29, 1916, place of death not known, date of death not known.

Forrest Jewett resided with his parents through the taking of the 1940 US Census. In 1940 he was employed as a shipping clerk. His future wife arrived from Canada in Detroit November 2, 1938. Further information about Mr. and Mrs. Jewett is not currently available. They had a least one child.

Children:

925. I. ***Marguerite Jewett***, b. Detroit, Michigan 1942; ***nfi.***

References: US Census: 1920, 1930, 1940; Ohio Birth Index 1908-1964 for Forrest Jewett, Jr.; Michigan Marriage Record 1867-1952; Detroit Border Crossings 1905-1963.

450.

Edward Lee Jewett, son of Forrest (210), grandson of Elizabeth (92), b. Schaeuble, Ohio February 5, 1917, d. Port Huron, Michigan February 24, 1994; m. (1) Henry, Ohio March 1, 1942 Doris Marie Coker Fletcher, b. Cleveland, Ohio a. 1916, place of death not known, date of death, not known, divorced Detroit, Michigan September 1, 1951; m. (2) Detroit, Michigan May 3, 1952 Norma Thyra Livingston Irwin, b. Detroit, Michigan September 5, 1921, d. Sanilac, Michigan May 10, 1998.

Edward Jewett resided with his parents and in 1940 he was employed by the Kresge Company. Mr. Jewett served with the US Army from August 24, 1942 to February 3, 1946. His first wife, Doris, was previously married and she married twice more after their 1951 divorce. Norma Jewett was previously married to Joab Lee Irwin. They were divorced April 12, 1951. Norma Jewett enlisted with the Women's Army Corps in Detroit February 13, 1943. Further information about Edward and Norma Jewett's professional careers is not currently known. It is not currently known if Mr. Jewett had any children. Edward Jewett was buried in Elk Township Cemetery, Peck, Michigan. It is not currently known where Norma Jewett was buried.

References: US Census: 1920, 1930, 1940; Ohio Birth Index 1908-1964 for Edward Jewett; Ohio County Marriages 1774-1993 for Edward Jewett's first marriage; Michigan Divorce Records 1897-1952 for the dissolution of Edward Jewett's first marriage; Michigan Marriage Records 1867-1952 for Edward Jewett's second marriage; US Veterans Death File 1950-2010; Elk Township Cemetery records, Peck, Michigan; US World War II Enlistments 1938-1946 for Norma Jewett's military service; Michigan Death Index 1971-1996; Social Security Death Index 1935-2014.

451.

Harold Lloyd Jewett, son of Forrest (210), grandson of Elizabeth (92), b. Detroit, Michigan June 18, 1920, d. Palo Alto, California April 25, 1995. Harold Lloyd served with the US Corps of Engineers and the US Army from December 10, 1941 to December 20, 1945. He was 5' 6" tall and weighed 138 lbs. At the time of his enlistment, Harold Jewett had two years of high school and was employed as a sales clerk. He was buried in Alta Mesa Memorial Park, Palo Alto, California. It is not known if Harold Jewett married or had children.

References: US Census: 1930, 1940; US Veterans Death File 1950-2010; California Death Index 1940-1997; Social Security Death Index 1935-2014; Alta Mesa Memorial Park records, Palo Alto, California.

453.

Charles Kalvin Jewett, son of Forrest (210), grandson of Elizabeth (92), b. Detroit, Michigan June 16, 1923, d. Saginaw, Michigan October 12, 1991; m. Detroit, Michigan October 19, 1946 Ida Mae Leblanc, b. Cheboygan, Michigan January 30, 1928, not known if currently still alive.

Charles Jewett resided in Detroit until 1971 when he and his family moved to Cass City, Michigan. Mr. Jewett was a committeeman for the UAW-CIO Local # 155 and attended the Cass City Church of the Nazarene. Charles Jewett was buried in Elkland Township Cemetery, Cass City, Michigan.

Children:

926. I. ***Linda Jewett, nfi.***

927. II. ***Rita Jewett, nfi.***

928. III. ***Timothy Jewett, nfi.***

References: US Census: 1930, 1940; Michigan Marriage Records 1867-1952; Michigan Death Index 1971-1996; Elkland Township Cemetery records, Cass City, Michigan; *Cass City Chronicle* October 16, 1991 for Charles Jewett's obituary.

454.

Margaret "Tiny" Jewett, daughter of Forrest (210), granddaughter of Elizabeth (92), b. Detroit, Michigan July 2, 1928, d. Ocala, Florida October 25, 2015; m. Detroit, Michigan March 15, 1947 Joseph Omar Wilssens, b. Detroit, Michigan October 27, 1926, no record of a death.

Margaret Jewett Wilssens was employed as an elementary school library technical assistant with Michigan public schools until 1989 when she retired. Margaret started four church libraries in Florida and was a member of Crossroads Church of God in Ocala. Margaret's remains were cremated and given to the care of the family. She was survived by her husband, three children, seven grandchildren, and two great-grandchildren.

Children:

929. I. ***Male Wilssens, nfi.***

930. II. ***Female Wilssens, nfi.***

931. III. ***Female Wilssens nfi.***

References: US Census: 1930, 1940; Michigan Marriage Record 1867-1952; *Ocala Star-Banner*, November 15/16, 2015.

455.

Virginia Lorraine Jewett, daughter of Forrest (210), granddaughter of Elizabeth (92), b. Detroit, Michigan March 28, 1930, d. Cheboygan, Michigan December 6, 2004; m. Detroit, Michigan May 8, 1948 Louis Leblanc, Sr., b. Cheboygan, Michigan December 3, 1925, d. Cheboygan, Michigan December 12, 1997. Little is known about Mr. and Mrs. Leblanc except there must have been at least one child, a son, because Louis Leblanc's grave identifies him as a Sr. Virginia and Louis Leblanc were buried in Pine Hill Cemetery Cheboygan, Michigan.

Children:

932. I. ***Louis Leblanc, Jr., nfi.***

References: US Census: 1930, 1940; Michigan Marriage Records 1867-1952; Social Security Death Index 1935-2014; Pine Hill Cemetery records, Cheboygan, Michigan.

456.

Elizabeth Marie Root, daughter of Edward Albert (215), granddaughter of Asa W. (94), b. Georgetown, Washington, DC April 1, 1929, d. place not known, October 9, 1980 from cardiac-respiratory arrest; m. Falls Church, Virginia April 3, 1948 Raymond Robert Berardi, b. District of Columbia February 4, 1923, d. Ocala, Florida December 7, 2009.

Elizabeth or Betty Root resided with her mother and father in the 1930 US Census at Ingleside Terrace in the District of Columbia. The 1940 US Census found her residing with her father, stepmother and three siblings in Washington, D.C. The family moved to Falls Church, Virginia December 1941 and resided at 416 Brook Drive until she married. Betty was a happy child with an infectious laugh. She had a genuine loving nature and maintained many lifelong friendships. Betty was voted Miss Congeniality by her high school graduating class. After high school Betty was employed as a legal secretary. She was a volunteer with her church with a specialty of cooking meals for the homeless. Betty's and Ray's home was the gathering center for both neighborhood adults and their children's friends. There was always room for one more at the table.

If the menu was Ray's homemade spaghetti, which took days to prepare, the fight for an invite was on. Ray was also renowned for his natural musical ability. Although he did not read music, he not only played anything with a keyboard, but was especially skilled with the accordion and harmonica. Ray had a special place in his heart for purebred crystal-white American Eskimo dogs. Each one was beautiful, always impeccably groomed, well trained, and constantly by his side. Ray was clearly their god. His beloved dogs were cremated and buried with him and Betty. Ray was a salesman for the Sinclair Oil Company. His World War II Draft Registration Card described him as being 5' 6" tall, weighing 144 pounds with blue eyes and brown hair. At the time of his enlistment Mr. Berardi was employed as a Post Office clerk. He served with the US Army from February 1, 1943 to January 10, 1946. Betty and Ray Berardi were buried in the Gate of Heaven Cemetery, Silver Springs, Maryland.

Children:

933. I. ***Willa Jeanne Berardi, f.***

934. II. ***Raymond Michael Berardi, f.***

References: US Census: 1930, 1940; Social Security Claims Index 1936-2007 for Betty Root's birth date; Virginia Marriage Records 1936-2014; World War II Draft Registration Card, 1942; US Veterans Death Files 1850-2010; Social Security Death Index 1935-2014; Gate of Heaven Cemetery records, Silver Springs, Maryland; Correspondence with Anne Root Sale.

457.

Rose Dugan Root, daughter of Edward Albert (215), granddaughter of Asa W. (94), b. Washington, D.C. January 26, 1931, d. Inova Fairfax Hospital, Fairfax, Virginia April 21, 2005 after a stroke; m. (1) Fairfax, Virginia March 1, 1949 Richard Scott Martin, b. Virginia November 20, 1928, d. Virginia March 8, 2001, divorced Fairfax, Virginia September 19, 1972; m. (2) Alexandria, Virginia September 11, 1976 William Edward Summerbell, b. Philadelphia, Pennsylvania December 26, 1916, d. Arlington, Virginia October 6, 2000, annulled Alexandria, Virginia February 16, 1977; m. (3) Washington, D.C. February 14, 1978 William Edward Summerbell, b. Philadelphia, Pennsylvania December 26, 1916, d. Arlington, Virginia October 6, 2000, divorced Virginia April 7, 1982; m. (4) Arlington, Virginia April 24, 1982 Philip Marvin Humphrey, divorced, date not known.

Rose Root legally changed her name to **Tracy Rose Martin** after her last divorce. Tracy was an attractive woman with black hair and blue-gray eyes who seemed to inherit the precognitive ability of her great-great grandmother, Marietta Tyler Root. Tracy Martin was a talented painter, playwright, poet, and author. In 1969 she co-authored with Frances Spatz Leighton, the play *Two Chairs for Three People*, which was based on Tracy's life. Tracy was involved with the Vienna, Virginia Little League, Our Lady of Good Counsel Catholic Church, the Vienna, Virginia Garden Club, and the Ladies Auxiliary for Fairfax Hospital. She was employed with the Department of the Navy as an executive secretary and resided in McLean, Virginia. Tracy was a great help in bringing together information and photographs for the 1990 publication on the Root family history.

Her first husband was buried in National Memorial Park in Falls Church, Virginia with his second wife. Tracy's second and third husband were buried in Arlington National Cemetery. Mr. Summerbell had been previously married and his first wife, Dorothy Selby, died in 1959, and bore him two sons. He was a Lt. Colonel in the US Army serving in World War II.

Tracy Rose Martin's remains were cremated and she was buried in Congressional Cemetery, Washington, D.C. in the Root Toner lot with her mother who died after she was born.

Children (by first marriage):

935. I. ***Paul Malcolm Martin, f.***

936. II. ***Glen Martin, f.***

937. III. ***James Martin, f.***

938. IV. ***Kevin Martin, f.***

References: US Census: 1940; Virginia Marriage Records 1936-2014 for all four marriages; Virginia Divorce Records 1918-2014 for Tracy's first three marriages; Social Security Death Index 1935-2014; Congressional Cemetery records, Washington, DC; National Memorial Park records, Falls Church, Virginia; Arlington National Cemetery records, Arlington, Virginia; correspondence with the late Tracy Rose Root Martin November 12, 1982, January 10, 1983, September 26, 1990, March 18, 1991, April 6, 1991, June 3, 1991, and December 1, 1994.

458.

Evelyn Anne Root, daughter of Edward Albert (215), granddaughter of Asa W. (94), Washington, D.C. August 12, 1934; m. Rockville, Maryland July 30, 1954 Wiley Pendleton Sale, b. Winchester, Frederick County, Virginia June 28, 1931, d. Manassas, Virginia January 7, 2009.

Anne Root Sale is a warm, gracious, and attractive woman who generously arranged meetings with descendants of her grandfather, Asa W. Root, and provided both information and photographs for the 1990 Root family history and for this major revision, enriching both publications. Anne has precognitive powers tracing back to her great-grandmother, Marrietta Tyler Root. A prophetic dream once allowed her to avoid a deadly event. Anne attended Bancroft School, Washington, DC, and Madison Grade School, and Falls Church High School in Falls Church, Virginia. Throughout her life Anne has always had a dog or a pet. Her special connection with animals was recognized from a very early age by both her family and neighbors.

Anne entered employment with the federal government in 1952 with the Surgeon General of the Army at the Main Navy Building, Washington, DC where the Vietnam Memorial is now located. After the birth of their second child, Anne remained home for six years. Two additional children were born during this time and she and Wiley purchased a small farm and had horses, cows, a pig, chickens, wild turkeys, pheasants, dogs, and cats. Each year they raised a garden and "made hay" which they harvested and stored in a large barn they built. In 1981 the family built a large brick colonial home on the property on which they lived. Anne returned to work in 1965. After taking the Federal Service Entrance Examination (FSEE) she obtained a career position. She became the team lead of programmers and systems analysts responsible for implementing the WW Defense Fuels Automated Management System. Anne received many awards during her career and was presented with a Distinguished Career Award at her retirement on September 2, 1989.

After Anne retired a very special dog, *Barney*, a mixed beagle and a special gift from the lord, entered her life. Barney and Anne shared a unique spiritual oneness throughout Barney's life. Anne was always intensively involved in the oversight and care of their youngest son, Roger, whose health declined as he aged. Anne volunteered and served on a local Human Rights Committee, the Community Services Board for Prince William County, the PWC Friends of Horticultural Therapy Board, and many state and local committees. With the exception of church activities, Anne phased out volunteering and now enjoys time with friends, family, gardening, painting, and writing poetry and short stories.

Wiley Sale moved to Prince William County in 1941 where he began his career as a newspaper boy in Occoquan and Woodbridge. His first job was working on the original Occoquan dam. Wiley graduated from Occoquan High School. After two years of service in the US Army in Korea, he returned to Woodbridge and found employment with FGE Railroad where he built specialty rail cars. He moved up to Superintendent and next to his family, the men he worked with were the most important people in this life. Wiley worked for the railroad for thirty-six years. In Prince William County Wiley served as Vice-President of the ARC of Prince William and was instrumental in the establishment and dedication of the Muriel Humphries School for Children. Wiley was a member of the Virginia Wild Turkey Federation, the VFW Post # 1503, and participated in wildlife research projects. Each year Wiley Sale tapped maple sugar trees and made his own maple syrup. He had a garden and made his famous *lime pickles.* Wiley enjoyed going hunting each year taking his son Matt and, later, grandson Kyle along with him.

In 2002 Anne and Wiley Sale moved from their much-loved home in Woodbridge to Nokesville, Virginia due to the encroachment of urban development in what was once a beloved rural home site. Wiley Sale was buried in Quantico National Cemetery, Quantico, Virginia. From March 2011 to December 2016, Anne had a close relationship with Samuel Bradshaw of Broad Run. Virginia. Sam served in the US Air Force in Southeast Asia. When he left the Air Force, Sam made his career with the Department of Defense. After retiring Sam raised and trained pacer horses, which he raced in harness races at Rosecroft Raceway, Maryland. Sam died of kidney failure December 2016.

Children:

939. I. ***Cynthia Anne Sale, f.***

940. II. ***Matthew Alan Sale, f.***

941. III. ***Julie Kathleen Sale, f.***

942. IV. ***Roger Glenn Sale, f.***

References: US Census: 1940; Social Security Death Index 1935-2014; Virginia Death Index 1912-2014; US Veterans Death File 1850-2010; Quantico National Cemetery records, Quantico, Virginia; Interviews with Anne Root Sale; correspondence with Anne Root Sale July 7, 1982, August 31, 1982, January 17, 1983, September 11, 1990, and November 1, 1990.

459.

Edward Albert (Buddy) Root, Jr., son of Edward Albert (215), grandson of Asa W. (94), b. Washington, D. C. September 2, 1938, d. Huntsville, Alabama March 11, 1998 from pancreatic cancer; m. Winterburg, Germany October 13, 1961 Gesa Elke Britta Haase and a second marriage Falls Church, Virginia November 3, 1961, b. Germany, March 19, 1944.

Edward Albert Root, known as *Buddy*, made the Air Force his career. He served from October 1, 1958 to October 31, 1982. Buddy saw service in Vietnam, France, Pferdsfeld in Germany, Thailand, and at the Royal Air Force Base, Chicksands England and rose to the rank of Master Sergeant. Edward continued later worked for the US Army in Wiesbaden as a Training Supervisor. He was a security officer who trained recruits. After his retirement from the Air Force, Buddy, his wife, Gesa, and their children remained in Germany where he was an advisor to Duke Albrecht of Bavaria, the Head of the House of Wittelsbach, which formerly ruled Bavaria in Germany. After his return to the United States, Mr. and Mrs. Root moved to Huntsville, Alabama in 1993 where he accepted a teaching position at Redstone Arsenal in Huntsville, Alabama.

During his military career Edward received numerous medals, awards, and certificates including the German Marksmanship medal. He and his three sons received their German Hunting Licenses from German Partners, which is very difficult to achieve. Edward was fluent in German. Gesa was a stay at home mom until 1974 when she went to work for the US Air Force in Germany until 1976 in the administrative field. In 1978 she took a job with the US Army in Germany as a Budget Analyst, a position, which she held until they returned to the US in 1993. During her employment Gesa received numerous awards including the NCO Academy Achievement Certificates and top honors at military schools. Buddy Root was buried in Arlington National Cemetery, Arlington, Virginia in Section 64, # 2101. Gesa currently resides in Arizona near two of her children.

Children:

943. I. ***Edward Albert Root III, f.***

944. II. ***James Tasso Root, f.***

945. III. ***Enrico Elihu Root, f.***

946. IV. ***Michelle Root, f***

References: US Census: 1940; US Veterans Death Files 1850-2010; Social Security Death Index 1935-2014; US Veterans Gravesites 1775-2006, correspondence with the late Edward Albert Root, Jr. September 24, 1990 and April 8, 1991; Correspondence with Gesa Root.

460.

JoAnn Root, daughter of Edwin Milford (216), granddaughter of Edwin (95), b. Bolivar, New York September 20, 1925, d. Lake Worth, Florida August 7, 2013; m. Rochester, New York November 1, 1947 William Pierson Randall, b. Rochester, New York September 13, 1926, d. Lake Worth, Florida January 14, 2011.

JoAnn Root was a graduate of Bolivar High School and resided with her parents in Bolivar and later Rochester, New York until her marriage. William Pierson served in the US Navy during World War II aboard the USS Ranger as a gunner's mate. He was the son of Rolland Robert Randall (1868-1948) and Gertrude Eugenie Ostrander Randall (1882-1947) of Rochester. By 1992 the Randall family had moved to Lantana, Florida and later to Fort Worth. JoAnn and William Pierson were buried in South Florida National Cemetery in Lake Worth, Florida.

Children:

947. I. ***Elizabeth Ann Randall, f.***

948. II. ***Margaret Jane Randall, f.***

949. III. ***William P. Randall, f.***

950. IV. ***Katherine Jane Randall, f.***

951. V. ***Deborah Jean Randall, f.***

References: US Census: 1930, 1940; New York State Birth Index 1881-1942; New York State Marriage Index 1881-1967; Social Security Death Index 1935-2014; US Navy Muster Rolls 1938-1949; South Florida National Cemetery records, Lake Worth, Florida; correspondence with the later JoAnn Root Randall January 25, 1982, February 7, 1983, February 23, 1983, May 19, 1985, September 14, 1990.

461.

William Edwin Nichols, son of Gladys (217), grandson of Edwin (95), b. Olean, New York February 2, 1924; d. Jones Memorial Hospital Wellsville, New York October 15, 1978 after a brief illness; m. Bolivar, New York July 17, 1948 Cynthia Nan Ford, b. Corning, New York July 10, 1927, d. Arlington, Texas June 23, 2015.

Bill Nichols graduated from Bolivar High School and attended Syracuse University where he met his future wife, Cynthia Ford. He served in the US Army from July 27, 1943 to April 22, 1946 serving with the Third Infantry Division in Germany and attaining the rank of Staff Sergeant. Bill was wounded by a high explosive shell and suffered neck and hand wounds. For almost twenty years Mr. Nichols was employed with his father in the family business *Nichols and Nichols, Agents General Insurance.* They resided at 135 Friendship Street in Bolivar. In 1965 he moved his family to Rochester, New York where he was employed at the A. and R. Photographic Color Lab in nearby Pittsford. For a brief time, they operated a restaurant in Cassadaga, New York. Due to illness, Bill Nichols returned to Bolivar residing with his parents until his 1978 death.

William Nichols was a member of the Macedonia Lodge F. and A. M. of Bolivar, the American Legion in Bolivar, the Bolivar Men's Club, and was a member of Sigma Nu Fraternity at Syracuse University. Cynthia was a strong contributor to the family business, moving and adjusting when they went into the restaurant business where she displayed her cooking skills and talents as a cake decorator and artist. Cynthia created many beautiful renderings in both oils and watercolors. The family enjoyed many family camp-outs as they shared their love of the outdoors. William and Cynthia Nichols were buried in Maple Lawn Cemetery, Bolivar, New York with his parents.

Children:

952. I. ***Barbara Rosier Nichols, f.***

953. II. ***Steven Nichols, f.***

954. III. ***David Ray Nichols, f.***

References: US Census: 1930, 1940; New York State Census: 1925; US Veterans Death File 1850-2010, Social Security Death Index 1935-2014; New York State Birth Index 1881-1942; New York State Marriage Index 1881-1967; Maple Lawn Cemetery records, Bolivar, New York; newspaper obituaries for William E. Nichols and Cynthia Nan Ford Nichols; *Bolivar Breeze 1891-1965.* Selected issues; correspondence with the late Cynthia Ford Nichols October 21, 1981, December 17, 1981, June 25, 1982, January 31, 1983, September 18, 1985.

462.

Richard George Osborne, son of Bertha (218), grandson of Edwin (95), b. Buffalo, New York June 2, 1929, d. Hamburg, New York June 27, 2006; m. Aurora, New York February 26, 1955 Mary Bean, b. Aurora, New York February 27, 1931, d. Hamburg, New York April 20, 2001. There is little information on this Root descendant. He was employed as a sales engineer with the Buffalo Forge Company, Buffalo, New York. Richard's and Mary Osborne's remains were buried in Maple Lawn Cemetery, Bolivar, New York in his parent's lot. Their names are inscribed on the back of the Osborne tombstone.

Children:

955. I. ***Robert Scott Osborne, f.***

956. II. ***William Richard Osborne, f.***

957. III. ***George Edwin Osborne, f.***

References: US Census: 1930, 1940; New York State Birth Index 1881-1942; New York State Marriage Index 1881-1967; Social Security Death Index 1935-2014; Maple Lawn Cemetery records, Bolivar, New York.

463.

Robert Charles Osborne, son of Bertha (218), grandson of Edwin (95), b. Buffalo, New York December 23, 1930, d. Weatherford, Texas February 25, 2017; m. Aurora, New York June 29, 1957 Irene Sylvia Hanninen, b. Westminster, Massachusetts October 14, 1930, d. Austin, Texas December 11, 2005.

Robert or *Oz* made his career with the US Air Force where he spent twenty years of service rising to the rank of Lt. Colonel. He was both a fighter pilot and recon pilot stationed in Japan, Thailand, Turkey, and Alaska during his career. After retirement, Mr. Osborne remained in Austin, Texas until two years before his death when he moved to Weatherford, Texas to be closer to family. Oz was an avid fly fisherman and enjoyed boating, hunting, golf, and travel. Robert's and Irene's remains were buried in the Osborne family lot at Maple Lawn Cemetery, Bolivar, New York. Their names are inscribed on the back of the large family tombstone.

Children:

958. I. ***Patricia Osborne, f.***

References: US Census: 1930, 1940; New York State Birth Index 1881-1942 for Robert Osborne; New York State Marriage Index 1881-1967; Social Security Death Index 1935-2014; Maple Lawn Cemetery records, Bolivar, New York; obituary for Robert Osborne, Galbreaith-Pickard Funeral Home, December 23, 1017 to February 25, 2017; correspondence with the late Robert Osborne August 23, 1980, April 15, 1985, September 11, 1990, and September 28, 1990.

464.

Albert George Nulsen III, son of Huldah (219), grandson of George (97), b. St. Louis, Missouri February 10, 1915, d. Kingman, Arizona August 28, 1984; m. St. Louis, Missouri September 9, 1932 Laveta Isabell *Betty* Sullivan, b. Charleston, Illinois December 30, 1914, d. Arizona November 18, 1991.

Albert Nulsen resided with his parents until his marriage in 1932, first in Richmond Heights, Missouri and later in Joachim, Missouri. His World War II Draft Registration Card described him as 5' 11" tall, weighing 156 pounds with black hair and gray eyes. Mr. Nulsen was employed by La Salco, Incorporated. Over his lifetime, he was involved in many businesses including Dundee Cement. Albert and Betty Nulsen retired to Kingman, Arizona where they died. Their remains were returned to Missouri for burial in Eolia Cemetery, Eolia, Missouri. They had 18 children.

Children:

959. I. ***Albert Garrett Nulsen, f.***

960. II. ***Carolle Deane Nulsen, f.***

961. III. ***Maude Kreher Nulsen, f.***

962. IV. ***Sheila Jane Nulsen, f.***

963. V. ***Betty Nulsen, f.***

964. VI. ***Alice Ann Nulsen, f.***

965. VII. ***David William Nulsen, f.***

966. VIII. ***Vivian Gene Nulsen, f.***

967. IX. ***Pamela Sue Nulsen, f.***

968. X. ***Delores Marie Nulsen, f.***

969. XI. ***Patricia Merle Nulsen, f.***

970. XII. ***Donald Bruce Nulsen, f.***

971. XIII. ***Mary Lou Nulsen, f.***

972. XIV. ***Robert Evans Nulsen, f.***

973. XV. ***Curtis John Nulsen, f.***

974. XVI. ***Sharon Gale Nulsen, f.***

975. XVII. ***Phyllis Ruth Nulsen, f.***

976. XVIII. ***Brian Neal Nulsen, f.***

References: US Census: 1920, 1930, 1940; Social Security Death Index 1935-2014; World War II Draft Registration Card, 1940; Eolia Cemetery records, Eolia, Missouri; correspondence with the late Jane Nulsen Bunce.

465.

William Earl Nulsen, son of Huldah (219), grandson of George (97), b. Cartersville, Georgia September 4, 1917, d. December 31, 1976 from a lung condition; m. (1) place of marriage not known, date of marriage not known Helen Dorothy West, b. Missouri April 27, 1914, d. Missouri April 19, 1944 from tuberculosis; m. (2) Richmond Heights, Missouri October 27, 1945 Merle/Merlen M. Karl, b. Mason, Illinois July 28, 1924, d. place not known, September 25, 2008.

William Nulsen was employed as a paint color matcher and chemist for the H. E. McLeane Company, St. Louis, Missouri. His World War II Draft Registration Card described him as being 5' 8" tall, weighing 140 pounds with brown hair and brown eyes. He served in the US Army from August 19, 1941 to April 3, 1944. Mr. Nulsen's remains were cremated and given to his sister, the late Jane Nulsen Bunse. It is not currently known where they are. William Nulsen's first wife, Helen West Nulsen, was buried in Valhalla Cemetery, Bel-Nor, Missouri.

Children (by second marriage):

977. I. ***Julie Ann Nulsen, f.***

978. II. ***Steven Nulsen, f.***

979. III. ***Gary Nulsen, f.***

References: US Census: 1920, 1930, 1940; Missouri Marriage Records 1805-2002 for William Nulsen's second marriage; World War II Draft Registration Card, 1940; Social Security Death Index 1935-2014; Valhalla Cemetery records, Bel-Nor, Missouri; correspondence with the late Jane Nulsen Bunse.

466.

Jane Elizabeth Nulsen, daughter of Huldah (219), granddaughter of George (97), b. Richmond Heights, Missouri December 26, 1920, d. Marysville, Washington July 26, 2015; m. (1) place not known, May 31, 1945 John David Campbell, b. place and date not known, d. place not known, November 7, 1952 from cancer; m. (2) Webster Groves, Missouri February 27, 1954 Raymond Vincent Bunse, b.

Clover Bottom, Missouri October 23, 1915, d. very suddenly Petoskey, Michigan January 25, 1998.

In October 1930 in Hillsboro, Missouri a terrible explosion rocked the house where Jane Nulsen lived with her parents and siblings. She and her sister, Alice, were asleep. The house was leveled but Jane, her parents, and brothers survived. Her sister, Alice, died in the explosion. Jane had severe burns over 50% of her body. Investigators found gasoline cans around the house and arson was suspected. No arrests were ever made. Jane spent months in a hospital recovering from her burns. Over 40 dolls were given to her and when she left the hospital, her mother told her she could only keep three. The rest were given to charity. Wrapped in bandages and given to some bullying at school, Jane's parents decided to take Jane on a trip around the United States while her body continued to recover from the burns. Eventually the scars faded but her skin was always paper thin.

As an adult Jane became a collector of antiques, dogs, birds, and even wild animals. Her doll collection was worth a fortune as was her wristwatch collection. Jane and Ray Bunse moved to Walloon Lake, Petoskey, Michigan to escape hay fever and remained there until each died. At one time Jane had 23 dogs, a pet raccoon raised from birth and geese and ducks. Jane was a great lover of people, animals, and plants and life, which that terrible explosion did not end in 1930. Jane's first husband, John David Campbell, was a professor at St. Louis University and head of the biology department when she met him as a student at the University. Her second husband, Raymond Vincent Bunse, retired from General Motors where he was a test driver at the automobile plant in St. Louis after twenty-five years of employment. In 1975 Jane and Ray moved to Petoskey, Michigan where they resided until their respective deaths.

Ray's World War II Draft Registration Card described him as being 6' tall, weighing 185 pounds and having gray eyes and brown hair. He enjoyed fishing, hunting, and gardening. Jane was a tremendous help in providing research on the descendants of George Root. In her possession was the sword of Edwin R. Kilbury of Bolivar, New York who fought in the Civil War and who was her maternal great-great grandfather. Jane also possessed the gold chain given to her mother, Huldah Root Nulsen, by her great-aunt, Huldah Root Curtiss, of Bolivar, New York. Ray Bunse was previously married to Margaret Schmidle who died in 1952. Jane raised his two children along with her daughter from her first marriage. Jane and Raymond Bunse were buried in Greenwood Cemetery, Petoskey, Missouri.

At one time Jane had the urns containing the remains of various family members including her parents. It is not currently known where those remains are. Raymond Bunse had a daughter, Jane Gerarda Bunse, b. October 23, 1948 who was married first to Paul Gregory Fry and divorced, and remarried to E. J. Wrolstad. There were no known children and Jane Gerarda resided in Stanwood, Washington with her second husband. Ray's son was also named Raymond. He was born June 30, 1951 and married Deborah Ann Syberg. They resided in St. Louis where he was employed as a chef and they had six children.

Children (by first marriage):

980. I. ***Marianne Cecile Campbell, f.***

References: US Census: 1930, 1940; Missouri Marriage Records 1805-2002 for Jane Nulsen's second marriage; Social Security Death Index 1935-2014; World War II Draft Registration Card, 1940; Greenwood Cemetery records, Petoskey, Michigan; Resurrection Cemetery records, Affton, Missouri; correspondence with the late Jane Nulsen Bunse; *News-Review*, Petoskey, Michigan, Family Section, January 5, 1984; correspondence with the late Jane Nulsen Bunse February 19, 1982, September 3, 1982, October 1, 1982, June 26, 1983, May 22, 1985, October 30, 1990, June 6, 1992, July 9, 1992, July 20, 1992, February 9, 1993, and June 8, 1993.

468.

Patricia Elizabeth Gridley, daughter of Alvya (221), b. Olean, New York April 14, 1936; m. (1) Olean, New York January 24, 1953 Robert A. Morgan, b. place not known, date not known, d. place not known, 1984, divorced; m. (2) place not known, Walter E. Iddings January 23, 1960.

Patricia's mother, Alvya Root, was the adopted daughter of George Root. Patricia had a son by her first marriage, Charles Leon Morgan, born October 26, 1953. He married Kathy Van Gordon August 31, 1974 and they reside in Las Vegas with their two children: Jeremy and Sara. Patricia had three children by her second husband: Joann Marie Iddings, b. September 14, 1958 who resided in Rochester, New York where she was employed as a hairdresser; Walter Allen Iddings, b. July 10, 1960 who married Becky Chabet July 28, 1980 and reside in Horseheads, New York with their son Bret; and Linda Patricia Iddings, b. August 28, 1961 who married Tim Myers August 22, 1981 and reside in Las Vegas with their daughter Erica. Patricia and Walter Iddings were employed in the grocery business in Beaver Dam, New York.

References: US Census: 1940; New York State Birth Index 1881-1942 for Patricia Gridley; New York State Marriage Index 1881-1967 for Patricia Gridley's first marriage; correspondence with the late Alvya Root Gridley Richardson.

469.

Wilber MacNeil Cook, son of Homer (223), grandson of Bertha (98), b. Los Angeles, California October 30, 1924, d. Eagle Rock, California July 6, 2004; m. Los Angeles, California June 10, 1950 Patricia Marie Robinson, b. Los Angeles, California April 22, 1918, d. place not known, date not known.

Wilber Cook resided with his parents in Los Angeles County. His World War II Draft Registration Card described him as 5' 9" tall, weighing 148 pounds with hazel eyes and brown hair. Mr. Cook was a 1950 graduate of the University of Southern California. He was the owner and manager of an electrical wholesale business for twenty years. For eight years he owned and operated the Hayloft restaurant in Torrance, California and for several years the Picnic Box restaurant. In 1991 the Cook family moved from Pasadena to Duarte, California. Wilber Cook was a tremendous help in supplying information and photographs for the 1990 Root family history. Patricia Robinson was previously married. Wilber Cook adopted her two children from her first marriage. Michael John Cook was born September 21, 1942 and married Bronwyn Pierce October 6, `973. Michael graduated from San Jose State University (California) with an MBA. He resided in Pleasanton, California where he owned and operated a chain of fast print shops. Michael and his wife had two children: Jennifer Lynn and Ryan Harrison. Marianne Harrison was born January 1, 1944 and married David Marshall Norcott October 4, 1970. They resided in Los Angeles where David was employed by Coldwell Bankers. They had two children: Bryan Marshall and Kelsey Ann. It is not currently known where Wilber and Patricia Cook were buried.

Children:

981. I. ***Robert Neil Cook, f.***

982. II. ***Kristen Cook, f.***

References: US Census: 1930, 1940; California Birth Index 1905-1995; California Marriage Index 1949-1959; Social Security Death Index 1935-2014 for Wilber Cook; World War II Draft Registration Card, 1942 correspondence with the late Bill Cook April 13, 1982, April 27, 1982, July 2, 1982, July 18, 1982, August 12, 1982, September 26, 1982, November 9, 1982, November 17, 1983, February 4, 1988, and November 21, 1990.

470.

Ralph Homer Cook, son of Homer (223), grandson of Bertha (98), b. Los Angeles, California May 9, 1928, d. California September 23, 2013 from Alzheimer's disease; m. (1) New York City, New York December 21, 1949 Daphne Stafford Clarke, divorced 1960/1961; m. (2) place not known, May 1, 1965 Patricia Branch, separated May 1974; m. (3) place not know, 1996 Patricia Larsen. At the age of 17, Ralph Cook enlisted in the US Navy and at the end of World War II was an officer's driver in Hawaii. He graduated from San Francisco State College (University). Mr. Cook was briefly an actor and was in the John Wayne film *The Flying Leathernecks.* Because acting made him nervous Ralph moved to Connecticut with his first wife and children where he taught high school English.

After his first marriage ended, Mr. Cook moved to New York City where he suffered a nervous breakdown. Ralph went to St. Mark's Church in-the-Bowery where he met the new rector, Reverend J. C. Michael Allen. He convinced Allen to let him establish an acting workshop as part of the Church's youth outreach program. This was the birth of *Theatre Genesis.* For five years Ralph Cook put on shows in a black-box-style theater in a building next to the Church. His first play was written by the 20-

year old *Sam Shepard* and the play was *Cowboys*. Sam Shepard would become one of the United States greatest 20th Century playwrights and actors. *Sam Shepard would later write that "Theater Genesis became my home. It was a place to work, and it was home. I have Ralph to thank for that."*

Other playwrights who Ralph Cook gave their start at Theater Genesis included Leonard Melfi, Murray Mednick, Tony Barsha, and Walter Hadler. Ralph Cook's contributions to *Off Broadway* are detailed in *Playing Underground, A History of Off-Off Broadway* by Stephen J. Bottoms (2004). Ralph Cook left Theatre Genesis in 1969 and moved to Oakland California. Since 1970 Mr. Cook was employed as a jeweler in Berkeley, California, enjoyed fishing, and was a political activist. He met Patricia Larsen in Berkeley shortly after he left Theater Genesis and eventually, they were married in 1996. Ralph and his third wife moved to Perdido Beach, Alabama where he died. Ralph Cook was survived by two sons, Randall and Paul, and four grandchildren.

Children (by first marriage):

983. I. ***Randall Cook,*** b. May 20, 1955 and last known to reside in Toronto, Canada.

984. II. ***Laurel Cook,*** b. California April 27, 1957, deceased by 2013; ***nfi.***

985. III. ***Paul Cook,*** b. April 29, 1958 and last known to reside in Berkeley, California.

References: US Census: 1930, 1940; California Birth Index 1905-1995; Social Security Death Index 1935-2014; *New York Times*, October 21, 2013 obituary; New York, New York Marriage Index 1907-2018 for Ralph Cook's first marriage.

471.

Vladimir Vadim "Ladi" Baicher, son of Anita (224), grandson of Bertha (98), b. Los Angeles, California May 5, 1938, d. Corvallis, Oregon September 28, 2009; m. Palo Alto, California March 10, 1962 Carol Mae Kauffman, b. Alameda, California December 25, 1939, divorced Santa Clara, California August 16, 1984. Mr. Baicher was an aeronautical engineer. Further information is not currently available about him or his family. It is not currently known where he was buried.

Children:

986. I. ***Richard Alexander Baicher***, b. California March 21, 1963, d. California July 23, 1984 and buried at Los Gatos Memorial Park, San Jose, California.

987. II. ***Gregory Marc Baicher,*** b. November 14, 1964; ***nfi.***

988. III. ***Jeffrey Scott Baicher,*** b. November 31, 1968; ***nfi.***

References: US Census: 1940; California Marriage Index 1960-1985; Social Security Death Index 1935-2014; California Birth Index 1905-1995; California Divorce Index 1966-1984; Los Gatos Memorial Park records, San Jose, California.

472.

Lida Armina Baicher, daughter of Anita (224), granddaughter of Bertha (98), b. Pasadena, California May 16, 1940; m. Grafenwöhr, Germany July 16, 1964 William J. Rothman. Lida is a former teacher and her husband is a retired dentist. They resided for many years in Chambersburg, Pennsylvania before moving to Camp Hill, Pennsylvania. There is no further information on this Root descendant.

Children:

989. I. ***Robin Lynn Rothman***, b May 25, 1967, d. June 4, 1967 from acute pulmonary Edema. She was buried in Lincoln Cemetery, Chambersburg, Pennsylvania.

990. II. ***Katherine Carol Rothman,*** b. September 11, 1967 (adopted by the Rothmans October 13, 1968; ***nfi.***

991. III. ***Kristina Lee Rothman,*** b. April 18, 1969; m. May 1989 Rodney Forrester ***nfi.***

References: US Census: 1940; California Birth Index 1905-1995; correspondence with Lida Baicher Rothman October 9, 1979 and June 3, 1982; Lincoln Cemetery Records, Chambersburg, Pennsylvania.

473.

Addison David Evans, son of Addison (225), grandson of Forrest (100), b. Chicago, Illinois September 27, 1923, d. La Crescenta, California June 1, 1989; m. California June 10, 1950 June Lorraine Andersen, b. Muskegon, Michigan June 5, 1926, d. Bullhead City, Arizona August 5, 1998.

Addison David Evans went by *David*. In the 1920 US Census he resided in Chicago and in 1930 resided with his parents in Glendale, California. His World War II Draft Registration Card described him as being 5' 8" tall, weighing 135 pounds with a dark complexion with brown eyes and brown hair. In 1942, he was employed by Vega Aircraft Corporation. After World War II David Evans was employed as a salesman with Air Associates. David and June Evans were buried in Forest Lawn Cemetery, Glendale, California.

Children:

992. I. ***David Bruce Evans,*** b. Glendale, California May 16, 1956, d. Meadview, Arizona May 24, 2015; m. 1979 Cynthia Ballard, divorced 1993. They did not have any children.

993. II. ***Valerie Evans***; m. a Mr. Goslin and had two children: Emily Goslin Clayton and Jeremy Goslin; ***nfi.***

References: US Census: 1930, 1940; Illinois Birth Index 1916-1935; California Marriage Index 1949-1959; World War II Draft Registration Card, 1942; Forest Lawn Memorial Park, Glendale, California; *Mohave Daily News* obituary for David Evans June 7-14, 2015.

476.

Yale Malcolm Hulbert, son of Gerald (226), grandson of Emma (104), b. Angelica, New York November 16, 1907, d. Ocala, Florida March 31, 1977; m. Bethlehem, Pennsylvania June 25, 1938 Lucile Bartholomew, b. Pennsylvania December 9, 1916, d. Reading, Pennsylvania October 28, 2000.

Yale Hulbert resided with his parents in Angelica, New York, St. Mary's, Pennsylvania, and Bethlehem, Pennsylvania until his 1938 marriage. His World War II Draft Registration Card described Mr. Hulbert as being 5' 3" tall, 125 pounds with blue eyes and brown hair. He was employed by the Leigh and New England Railroad. Yale Hulbert made the Railroad his career and received a railroad pension. Yale and Lucille Hulbert had two daughters, but the name of only one daughter can currently be found. Yale Malcolm Hulbert was buried in Fort Lincoln Cemetery, Brentwood, Maryland near the home of one of his daughters. It is not currently known where Lucille Hulbert was buried.

Children:

994. I. ***Joan Hulbert***, b. 1940; ***f.***

995. II. ***Carole Jayne Hulbert***; ***f.***

References: US Census: 1910, 1920, 1930, 1940; New York State Birth Index 1881-1942; World War II Draft Registration Card, 1940; Florida Death Index 1877-1998 for Yale Hulbert; Social Security Death Index 1935-2014; Railroad Pension Records; Fort Lincoln Cemetery records, Brentwood, Maryland.

477.

Geraldine Virginia Hulbert, daughter of Gerald (226), granddaughter of Emma (104), b. St. Mary's, Pennsylvania August 7, 1911, d. Lititz, Pennsylvania July 19, 1998; m. place not known, a. 1941 Ellsworth C. Krueger, b. Bethlehem, Pennsylvania November 19, 1914, d. Bethlehem, Pennsylvania January 21, 1993. Known as Virginia to her family and friends, she resided with her parents until her marriage. Ellsworth Krueger was employed by Bethlehem Steel for 36 years, retiring in 1977. After retirement he worked part-time for Glenn's Car Care Center in Bethlehem, Pennsylvania. Virginia and Ellsworth Krueger were buried in Memorial Park Cemetery, Bethlehem, Pennsylvania.

Children:

996. I. ***Richard Ellsworth Krueger***, b. Bethlehem, Pennsylvania March 8, 1943, d. Bethlehem, Pennsylvania March 16, 1943 from a birth injury and was buried in Memorial Park Cemetery.

997. II. ***Robert Milton Krueger**, f.*

998. III. ***Marilyn V. Krueger**, f.*

References: US Census: 1920, 1930, 1940; Pennsylvania Birth Index 1906-1911 for Virginia Hulbert; Social Security Death Index 1935-2014; Memorial Park Cemetery records, Bethlehem, Pennsylvania; Pennsylvania Death Certificate, 1943 for Richard Krueger.

478.

Frederick Waldo Hulbert, son of Gerald (226), grandson of Emma (104), b. St. Mary's, Pennsylvania May 6, 1917, d. Glendale, Arizona February 18, 2000; m. place not known, a. 1939 Eleanor H. Williams, b. place not known, August 27, 1918, d. Phoenix, Arizona January 2, 2010.

Fred Hulbert resided with his parents until his marriage. His World War II Draft Registration Card described him as being 5' 6" tall, weighed 130 pounds with blue eyes and blonde hair. It is not known if he saw any military service. Mr. Hulbert in 1940 was employed as a driver for Sawyer and Johnson. At some point after retirement Fred and Eleanor Hulbert moved to Arizona where they died. It is not known where they were buried.

Children:

999. I. ***Patricia Louise Hulbert, f.***

1000. II. ***Barbara Jane Hulbert, f.***

1001. III. ***Judith Ann Hulbert, f***

References: US Census: 1920, 1930, 1940; Social Security Death Index 1935-2014; World War II Draft Registration Card 1940.

479.

Gerald Ward Hulbert, son of Elba (228), grandson of Emma (104), b. Bolivar, New York July 29, 1922, d. West Hurley, New York September 18, 1996; m. Bolivar, New York July 10, 1948 Dorothy Jean Goodridge, b. Bolivar, New York April 4, 1926, d. West Hurley, New York December 6, 1996.

Gerald Hulbert was a graduate of Bolivar High School where he participated in Boy Scout Troop # 39 and the Bolivar High School Bank. He graduated *cum laude* from St. Bonaventure University, Allegany, New York where he was elected Secretary of Bon-Nites, a club of night students at St. Bonaventure. In the early 1940s Gerald was employed by the State Bank of Bolivar. He studied at the Rochester Business Institute, Wellsville, New York branch. Mr. Hulbert served with the US Army Air Corps from November 9, 1942 to February 20, 1946 rising to the rank of Corporal. After the war, Gerald Hulbert entered a training program with Sears and Roebuck Company where he eventually rose to the position of comptroller at the Sears Bay Shore store on Long Island. Gerald and Jean Hulbert were buried in St. Mary's Cemetery, Bolivar, New York.

Children:

1002. I. ***Gregory Madden Hulbert, f.***

1003. II. ***Mary Carol Hulbert, f.***

1004. III. ***Jean Elizabeth "Beth" Hulbert, f.***

1005. IV. ***Lois Ann Hulbert, f.***

1006. V. ***Geraldine Marie Hulbert, f.***

1007. VI. ***David Saint John Hulbert, f.***

References: US Census: 1930, 1940; New York State Census: 1925; New York State Birth Index 1881-1942; New York State Marriage Index 1881-1967; Social Security Death Index 1935-2014; US Veterans Death File 1850-2010; *Bolivar Breeze 1891-1965*, selected issues; St. Mary's Cemetery, Bolivar, New York.

480.

Margaret Elizabeth Hulbert, daughter of Elba (228), granddaughter of Emma (104), b. Bolivar, New York January 21, 1924, d. Lake Forest Hospital, Lake Forest, Illinois July 22, 1993; m. Buffalo, New York June 28, 1947 Dr. Joseph Samuel Rangatore, b. Niagara Falls, New York November 22, 1920, d. Downey, Illinois July 1, 1969 from arthritis of the spine.

Margaret was a graduate of Bolivar High School in 1941 as Valedictorian and Cornell University School of Home Economics, Ithaca, New York. She worked at Sisters Hospital, Buffalo, New York as a dietitian until her marriage. From 1967 to 1993, Margaret was employed by the Veterans Administration Medical Center, North Chicago. Mrs. Rangatore was a registered dietician. She was a member of the St. Dismas Church, American Dietetic Association, Kappa Delta Sorority, the Emblem Club Auxiliary of the Waukegan Elks Lodge and Women of the Moose. Dr. Joseph Rangatore was an obstetrician and gynecologist at Niagara Falls until 1958 when they moved to Illinois. In Illinois he was employed as a psychologist. During World War II he served with the US Army rising to rank of Captain. Margaret and Joseph Rangatore were buried in St. Mary's Cemetery, Bolivar, New York.

Children:

1008. I. ***Concetta "Connie" Helen Rangatore, f.***

1009. II. ***Margaret Ann "Peggy" Rangatore, f.***

1010. III. ***Mary Elizabeth Rangatore, f.***

1011. IV. ***Joanne Marie Sarah Rangatore, f.***

1012. V. ***Kathryn "Kathy" Rangatore, f.***

References: US Census: 1930, 1940; New York State Census: 1925; New York State Birth Index 1881-1942; New York State Marriage Index 1881-1967; *Bolivar Breeze 1891-1965*, selected issues; *Wellsville Daily Reporter* obituary July 1993; St. Mary's Cemetery, Bolivar, New York.

481.

James William Hulbert, son of Elba (228), grandson of Emma (104), b. Olean, New York April 17, 1938, d. Ithaca, New York December 19, 2010; m. Wellsville, New York November 27, 1971 Barbara Jo Tarantine, b. Wellsville, New York April 7, 1947.

James Hulbert as a young boy enjoyed horseback riding, scouting, Saturday afternoon movies with his father and brother, and with a paper route purchased a bicycle, which he sold the year before he died. A graduate of Bolivar High School in 1954, Mr. Hulbert graduated from St. Bonaventure University, Allegany, New York with a B. A. in Business Administration in 1960. He worked at Tompkins County Trust Company in the Trust Department while he earned another degree from the National Trust School at Northwestern University in 1972. Mr. Hulbert retired after 38 years of employment from the Tompkins County Trust Company where he was Vice-President, Trust Officer, and Corporate Secretary. He also served as Inspector of Elections each year. James Hulbert was Treasurer for Summer Ithaca, Inc., a member of the Junior Chamber of Commerce in Ithaca, the Auto Salvage Bowling League, the Elks Club for 47 years, and the City Club. Jim was avid golfer and became a licensed pilot. He hangered his plane at the Wellsville, New York airport. Barbara Tarantine Hulbert graduated from Wellsville High School in 1964 and Brockport State. She was employed as a Mathematics teacher in Newfield, New York. James Hulbert was buried in St. Mary's Cemetery, Bolivar, New York.

Children:

1013. I. ***Karen Margaret Hulbert, f.***

References: US Census: 1940; New York State Birth Index 1881-1942; Social Security Death Index 1935-2014; *Wellsville Daily Reporter*, obituary December 21, 2010; St. Mary's Cemetery records, Bolivar, New York.

482.

John Matthew Hulbert, son of Elba (228), grandson of Emma (104), b. Olean, New York September 25, 1939, d. Rochester, New York September 28, 2014; m. Syracuse, New York July 6, 1963 Sue A. Murtagh, b. Malone, New York July 4, 1940.

John Hulbert graduated from Bolivar High School in 1957. He attended St. Bonaventure University, Allegany, New York and graduated from the Rochester Institute of Technology. He served in the US Army for eighteen months in Korea. John worked as an Engineering Technician at Eastman Kodak in Quality Control for twenty-eight years. John and Sue Hulbert had four children. Their first-born daughter died soon after birth January 15, 1964 and was buried in St. Mary's Cemetery, Bolivar, New York. John Hulbert was also buried in St. Mary's.

Children:

1014. I. ***Michael John Hulbert, f.***

1015. II. ***Michele Lynn Hulbert, f.***

1016. III. ***Stephanie Marie Hulbert, f.***

References: US Census: 1940; New York State Birth Index 1881-1942; New York State Marriage Index 1881-1967; St. Mary's Cemetery records, Bolivar, New York; *Wellsville Daily Reporter*, October 1, 2014 obituary; St. Bonaventure Cemetery Records, Allegany, New York; Florida Marriage Index 1927-2001.

483.

Stewart Buffington Irvin, Sr., son of Leta (229), grandson of Emma (104), b. Bolivar, New York January 20, 1923, d. Olean, New York January 16, 2011; m. Wellsville, New York July 27, 1942 Gertrude M. Atkins, b. Wellsville, New York March 13, 1925, d. Olean, New York September 24, 2007.

Stewart Irvin graduated from Bolivar High School in 1940 and from Rochester Business Institute in 1941. During World War II he served with the US Air Corps from January 1943 to February 1946 attending navigation school and as a flight engineer on B-17s. Mr. Irvin worked in the cost accounting department both before his military service and after at the Sinclair Refining Company in Wellsville, New York until it closed in 1958. After the refinery's closure he began a banking career at the State Bank of Bolivar, which later became the Citizens National Bank and Trust Company and finally the Key Bank. Mr. Irvin did additional study about the banking industry at St. Bonaventure University and Mellon Bank in Pittsburgh. For twelve years he was the Vice-President and Manager of the Alfred Office residing in Almond, New York until his 1985 retirement.

Mrs. Irvin was employed by Bausch and Lomb, Wellsville, New York and the Aerovox Corporation in Olean, New York. She was also licensed to make and sell fine chocolate candy. From 1985 until 1999, Stewart and his wife resided in Florida. They moved to Olean, New York in 1999. Mr. Irvin was a member of the Kenyon Andrus Post # 772, Bolivar where he was a member for 58 years. He also served as a Bolivar scoutmaster, and was President of the Allegany County Banker's Association. Mr. and Mrs. Irvin were buried in Maple Lawn Cemetery, Bolivar, New York.

Children:

1017. I. ***Stewart Buffington Irvin, Jr. f.***

1018. II. ***Janet Christine Irvin, f.***

References: US Census: 1930, 1940; New York State Census: 1925; New York State Birth Index 1881-1942; Social Security Death Index 1935-2014; New York State Marriage Index 1881-1967; *Wellsville Daily Reporter*, January 17, 2011 obituary; Maple Lawn Cemetery records, Bolivar, New York.

484.

Naomi Eileen Irvin, daughter of Leta (229), granddaughter of Emma (104), b. Angelica, New York March 29, 1925, d. Hornell, New York May 4, 1978 from cancer; m. Olean, New York August 13, 1955 Herbert Charles Malick, b. Olean, New York April 19, 1930, d. Fairfax, Virginia December 23, 2012.

Naomi worked in the offices of Cornell University, Ithaca, New York and Clark Brothers (later Dresser-Rand), Olean, New York rising to the position of Secretary to the Vice-President at the latter. Herbert Malick was a graduate of the US Naval Academy and held advanced degrees, which enabled him to be employed as a Mathematics Professor at Alfred Agricultural and Technical Institute, Alfred, New York. After Naomi's death in 1978, Professor Malick remarried to Enid Margaret Duffy Johnson at Virginia Beach, Virginia on June 28, 1980. Enid was born in Olean, New York July 3, 1923 and was a widower at the time of her marriage to Herbert Malick. It is not known when she died. Naomi and Herbert Malick were buried at St. Mary's Cemetery, Bolivar, New York.

Children:

1019. I. ***John Cornelius Malick***, b. Elmira, New York August 29, 1956, d. Alfred, New York October 22, 1959 from accidentally getting hold of an open bottle of aspirin and consuming most of the bottle's contents. He was buried in St. Mary's Cemetery.

1020. II. ***Mary Leta Malick, f.***

1021. III. ***William Joseph Malick, f.***

1022. IV. ***Sarah Malick, f.***

1023. V. ***Thomas Malick, f.***

1024. VI. ***Elaine Malick, f.***

References: US Census: 1930, 1940; New York State Census: 1925; New York State Birth Index 1881-1942; New York State Marriage Index 1881-1967; Social Security Death Index 1935-2014; Virginia Marriage Record 1936-2014 for Herbert Malick's second marriage; Virginia Death Record 1912-2014 for Herbert Malick's death; St. Mary's Cemetery records, Bolivar, New York.

485.

Marie Mae Crandall, daughter of Neil (233), granddaughter of Erwin (110), b. Bolivar, New York May 1, 1920, d. Concord, New Hampshire April 5, 2009; m. place not known, 1943 Kneeland Swenson, b. Concord, New Hampshire March 27, 1919, d. New Hampshire March 1979.

Marie Mae Crandall resided with her parents in Bolivar at 120 Main Street until their move to Oriskany, New York in the 1930s. She graduated from Rome Free Academy in Rome, New York and the Central City Business School in Syracuse, New York. Before her marriage Marie was employed as a stenographer for General Cable Corporation in Rome, New York. Kneeland Swenson was a graduate of Dartmouth College and a Lieutenant in the US Navy. His World War II Draft Registration Card described him as 6' 1" tall, weighing 195 pounds with blonde hair and blue eyes. He served from April 27, 1942 to June 20, 1946.

After World War II they moved to Concord, New Hampshire where Kneeland was employed in the family business, Swenson Granite Company. Marie Mae Swenson was active in the Concord community. She was a member of the Concord Hospital Associates and worked as a volunteer at the hospital for over 30 years. She served as a trustee of the Concord Hospital for nine years. Mrs. Swenson was active in the Concord Regional Visiting Nurses Association, the Junior Service League, the Concord Garden Club, and the Concord Flower Mission. In 1998, she received the Rumford

Society Award from the United Way, Merrimack County. In addition, Marie was a 55-year member of the South Congregational Church.

An avid bridge player Marie belonged to three bridge clubs. A strong believer in family, Marie took care of her mother until her death and her husband who suffered from rheumatoid arthritis and died at age 60 years in 1979. Marie Mae Swenson was survived by three children; Kurt, Kevin, and Karen, seven grandchildren: Todd, Jake, and Derek Swenson, Kate Swenson Paterson, Jesse Shue, John Shue, and Holly Shue Duer, and four great-grandchildren: Baden and Kai Paterson and Hadley and Avery Swenson. Marie and Kneeland Swenson were buried in Blossom Hill Cemetery, Concord, New Hampshire.

Children:

1025. I. ***Kurt McFarlen Swenson***, b. Rome, New York February 11, 1945; married with children and resided in Hopkinton, Rhode Island; ***nfi.***

1026. II. ***Kevin Crandall Swenson***, b. September 26, 1949; married with children and resided in Rye, New Hampshire; ***nfi.***

1027. III. ***Karen Swenson***; married to Jay Shue and resided in McMinnville, Oregon; ***nfi.***

References: US Census: 1930, 1940; New York State Census: 1925; New York State Birth Index 1881-1942 for Marie Crandall; Social Security Death Index 1935-2014; World War II Draft Registration Card, 1940; US Veterans Death File 1850-2010; Blossom Hill Cemetery records, Concord, New Hampshire; *Concord Monitor* April 2009 obituary for Marie Swenson; *Bolivar Breeze 1891-1965*, selected issues.

486.

Roy Stephen Crandall, son of Harley (234), grandson of Erwin (110), b. Olean, New York November 14, 1926; Hernando, Florida October 13, 2010; m. (1) Olean, New York September 6, 1947 Jean P. McMullen, b. Olean, New York March 20, 1927, d. Olean, New York February 21, 1984; m. (2) Olean, New York April 5, 1986 Carmelita Peasley Pauly, b. Dansville, New York April 1, 1929, d. Olean, New York September 21, 2012.

Roy Crandall resided with his parents in Olean and graduated from Olean High School. He served with the US Navy Seabees in World War II from November 9, 1944 to May 26, 1946 and saw action in Okinawa. Roy became co-owner and treasurer of Olean Lumber and Supply Corporation. The company was founded by his first wife's parents, Alexander and Leona Curran McMullen. Roy and Jean Crandall were both graduates of Olean High School and attended the St. Mary of the Angels Church. Roy was also a member of Our Lady of Fatima Church in Inverness, Florida, the Olean American Legion Post # 530, the Fraternal Order of the Eagles # 616, the Olean Elks Lodge # 491, and the SPCA of Cattaraugus County. He was an avid bowler, a golfer, and tried out for minor league baseball. Roy Crandall's second wife, Carmelita Peasley Pauly was a long-time Olean resident who was a widow when she married Roy.

Her first husband was Ralph E. Pauly who died in 1983. She had eight children by her first marriage. Carmelita was employed by St. Francis Hospital, Olean, New York Head Start Program and the St. Elizabeth Mission Society until her retirement. Even through life's trials and the deaths of loved ones, Carmelita's positive attitude and unwavering resolve never faltered. Roy was buried in St. Bonaventure Cemetery, Allegany, New York with his first wife, Jean. Carmelita was also buried in St. Bonaventure Cemetery with her first husband and a daughter who died young. Roy and Jean had four children. It is unclear from his obituary how many grandchildren and great-grandchildren were from his first marriage or included his second wife's grandchildren and great-grandchildren.

Children (by first marriage):

1028. I. ***Bonnie Crandall***, m. a Mr. Willard and resided in Olean; ***nfi.***

1029. II. ***Gary S. Crandall***, m. Debbie and resided in Murphy, Texas; ***nfi.***

1030. III. ***Gwen Crandall***, m. Charles Titzer and resided in Newburgh, Indiana; ***nfi.***

1031. IV. ***Kelly Crandall***, m. a Mr. Chaffee and resided in Hinsdale, New York; ***nfi.***

References: US Census: 1930, 1940; New York State Birth Index 1881-1942; New York State Marriage Index 1881-1967 for Roy Crandall's first marriage; Social Security Death Index 1935-2014; US Veterans Death File 1850-2010; St. Bonaventure Cemetery records, Allegany, New York; *Olean Times-Herald*, February 22, 1984 obituary for Jean McMullen Crandall, *Citrus County Chronicle*, October 28-31, 2010 obituary for Roy S. Crandall, *Olean Times Herald*, September 23, 2012 obituary for Carmelita Peasley Pauly Crandall.

487.

Constance "Connie" B. Crandall, daughter of Harley (234), granddaughter of Erwin (110), b. Olean, New York May 4, 1941; m. New York State July 11, 1964 Wayne C. Emerson, b. Cuba, New York April 13, 1937. Further information on this Root descendant is not currently available. In her brother's 2010 obituary, she was living in Hernando, Florida with her husband. It is not currently known how many children were born to the Connie and Wayne Emerson.

References: US Census: 1940 for Wayne Emerson; New York State Birth Index 1881-1942; New York State Marriage Index 1881-1967.

488.

Theodore Erwin Crandall, son of Ralph (236), grandson of Erwin (110), b. Wellsville, New York August 6, 1929, d. Titusville, Pennsylvania November 18, 2004; m. Titusville, Pennsylvania December 27, 1952 Beverly Joan Gustafson, b. Titusville, Pennsylvania, birth date not known.

Ted Crandall resided with his parents in Bolivar in 1930 and in Galeton, Pennsylvania in 1940 before they moved to Titusville, Pennsylvania. He enlisted in the US Army in 1948 and served until June 5, 1952. Three years of service were spent with the European Command in Garmisch Germany where he was the sports editor for the *Garmisch Pass Times.* Ted was promoted to Sergeant April 1952. He returned to Titusville where he married Beverly Joan Gustafson. They had at least one child. Further information about Ted Crandall's career and number of children is not currently available. It is not known where Ted Crandall was buried.

Children:

1032. I. ***Christine Yvonne Crandall, nfi.***

References: US Census: 1930, 1940; New York State Birth Index 1881-1942; Social Security Death Index 1935-2014; *Bolivar Breeze 1891-1965*, selected issues for Ted Crandall's military career, marriage, and the identity of his daughter.

489.

Merle Ralph Crandall, son of Ralph (236), grandson of Erwin (110), b. Bolivar, New York September 15, 1932, d. Allegany, New York September 19, 1959 by suicide. Merle Crandall graduated from Bolivar High School in 1951 and enlisted in the US Marine Corps and saw action in the Korean War. He was stationed for a time aboard the USS Missouri. After his enlistment ended Mr. Crandall found employment as a machinist with Clark Brothers (later Dresser-Rand), Olean, New York. Merle Crandall had been released from the US Veterans Hospital one week before his return home and suicide. He was buried in Maple Lawn Cemetery, Bolivar, New York. Merle Crandall never married or had children.

References: US Census: 1940; Social Security Death Index 1935-2014; Maple Lawn Cemetery records, Bolivar, New York; *Bolivar Breeze 1891-1965*, July 3, 1952 for enlistment and September 24, 1959 for his obituary.

490.

Neil R. Crandall, son of Ralph (236), grandson of Erwin (110), b. Penn Yan, New York May 4, 1937, d. Buffalo, New York March 20, 2016. Neil Crandall never married. He was a long-time resident of the Niagara Lutheran Humboldt House. He enjoyed reading politics and history. Neil Crandall was buried in Maple Lawn Cemetery, Bolivar, New York.

References: US Census: 1940; New York State Birth Index 1881-1942; Maple Lawn Cemetery records, Bolivar, New York; *Olean Times-Herald*, March 29, 2016 for obituary.

493.

Lois Jean Crandall, daughter of Paul (239), granddaughter of Owen (111), b. Bolivar, New York March 19, 1933, d. Springville, Illinois February 2, 2013; m. Millport, Pennsylvania August 26, 1967 Ernest N. Turybury, b. Hartsville, New York June 19, 1923, d. Olean General Hospital, Olean, New York March 15, 1990 after a long illness from cancer.

There is little information currently available on Lois Jean Crandall. However, her husband, Ernest N. Turybury resided in both Greenwood and Almond, New York before entering the US Army and serving in World War II from January 11, 1943 to January 15, 1946. He saw military action in the European Theatre. Mr. Turybury was married twice before his marriage to Lois Crandall. Both marriages ended in divorce. His first marriage was to Winona May Ackerman on December 21, 1946 in Bolivar. He had two sons: Ernest J. and Rodney B. Turybury with his first wife before the divorce. Winona Ackerman Turybury remarried to Robert L. Prince (1921-1993). Ernest Turybury married Marilyn Ferrington May 1951. It does not appear that there were any children from his second marriage or from his marriage to Lois Crandall based on his obituary. Mr. Turybury was a member of the International Union Local 832, Operating Engineers, the Kenyon Andrus American Legion Post 772 in Bolivar, and the Inavale Grange in Wirt Township. Both Lois and Ernest Turybury were buried in Maple Lawn Cemetery, Bolivar, New York.

References: US Census: 1930, 1940; New York State Census: 1925; New York State Birth Index 181-1942; US Veterans Death File 1850-2010; Maple Lawn Cemetery records, Bolivar, New York; obituary for Ernest Turybury posted on Findagrave.com; Social Security Death Index 1935-2014.

494.

Pauline Ann Crandall, daughter of Paul (240), granddaughter of Owen (111), b. Bolivar, New York May 18, 1934, d. Bolivar, New York May 20, 1977; m. Bolivar, New York June 12, 1965 William J. Rapan, b. Wellsville, New York August 6, 1937, d. Wellsville Manor Care, Wellsville, New York December 25, 2012. At the time of Pauline's marriage to William Rapan, she was employed at St. Francis Hospital in Olean, New York and he was employed by Mapes Furniture Company in Wellsville, New York. They had at least one child, Paul R. Rapan (1971-1990). William Rapan remarried to Lucy Kay Jordan (1937-2002) in Wellsville, New York on April 19, 1980. Pauline and William Rapan were buried in St. Mary's Cemetery, Bolivar, New York with their son Paul Rapan. Further information is not currently available.

References: US Census: 1940; New York State Birth Index 1881-1942; New York State Marriage Index 1881-1967; Social Security Death Index 1935-2014; St. Mary's Cemetery records, Bolivar, New York; *Bolivar Breeze* June 17, 1965 for Crandall/Rapan wedding.

495.

Charlotte Grace Crandall, daughter of Paul (239), granddaughter of Owen (111), b. Bolivar, New York January 13, 1940; m. Richmond, Virginia September 12, 1958 Thomas Eugene Payne, b. Wellsville, New York August 11, 1937. Charlotte and Tom Payne resided in both Bolivar, New York and Dansville, New York. Further information about Mr. and Mrs. Payne are not currently available.
References: US Census: 1940; New York State Birth Index 1881-1942; Virginia Marriage Records 1936-2014.

497.

Elaine Marie Crandall, daughter of Paul (239), granddaughter of Owen (111), b. Bolivar, New York 1949; m. (1) Wellsville, New York July 17, 1965 Robert J. Versch, divorced Portage County, Ohio November 3, 1989; m. (2) Portage County, Ohio October 28, 1995 Larry E. Hostetler, b. a. 1938. Elaine and Robert Versch had one child together after twenty-four years of marriage based on the Ohio Divorce Record. Robert Versch remarried in Ohio March 19, 1993 to Sharon A. Karlovec. Further information is not currently available.

References: New York State Marriage Index 1881-1967; Ohio Divorce Records 1973-2007; Ohio Marriage Records 1972-2007 for Elaine Crandall Versch's second marriage; *Bolivar Breeze* July 29, 1965 for Crandall/Versch wedding.

499.

Jennie Beatrice Quick, daughter of Ruth (240), granddaughter of Owen (111), b. Wellsville, New York November 15, 1928, d. King George, Virginia May 21, 2012; m. Bolivar, New York December 11, 1948 Charles Marvin Hosmer, b. Wellsville, New York September 27, 1931, d. Olean, New York August 22, 2004.

Jennie Quick resided with her parents until her marriage. Charles Hosmer founder the Prayer Fellowship Church in Bolivar, New York and was the Church's pastor until his death in 2004. Roy Elliott, husband of Terry L. Hosmer assumed the pastorate in 2004. The Church is no longer in existence. Mrs. Hosmer was described in her obituary as a caring person who deeply loved her family with her love of the Lord, her greatest love. Reverend Hosmer was the son of Ira and Sarah Warner Hosmer of Richburg, New York. Jennie Quick Hosmer was survived by six children, 13 grandchildren, and 20 great-grandchildren. Jennie and Charles Hosmer were buried in Maple Lawn Cemetery, Bolivar, New York.

Children:

1033. I. ***Terry L. Hosmer***; m. Reverend Roy Elliot, resides in Bolivar; ***nfi.***

1034. II. ***Lillian Vanessa Hosmer***; m. David Funk, resides in Stafford, Virginia; ***nfi.***

1035. III. ***Steven M. Hosmer***; married and resides in Silver Creek, New York; ***nfi.***

1036. IV. ***John C. Hosmer***; married and resides in Belmont, New York; ***nfi.***

1037. V. ***Timothy I. Hosmer***; married and resides in Andover, New York; ***nfi.***

1038. VI. ***Paul J. Hosmer***; married and resides in Fredericksburg, Virginia; ***nfi.***

References: US Census: 1930, 1940; New York State Birth Index 1881-1942; New York State Marriage Index 1881-1967; Social Security Death Index 1935-2010; Virginia Death Index 1912-2014 for Jennie Quick Hosmer; *Bolivar Breeze* December 16, 1948 for marriage of Jennie Quick and Charles Hosmer; *Olean Times-Herald* May 22-June 22, 2012 for obituary of Jennie Quick Hosmer.

500.

Adrian Allen Quick, Jr., son of Ruth (240), grandson of Owen (111), b. Bolivar, New York October 13, 1930, d. Vietnam February 7, 1968; m. Wellsville, New York November 10, 1953 Jean D. Brown Reginald.

Adrian Quick enlisted in the US Military February 15, 1951. He was killed during the Vietnam War and his remains returned to the United States for burial at Fort Logan National Cemetery, Denver, Colorado. Adrian Quick was a Specialist 7th Class and was a Master Sergeant at the time of his death. Further information about his wife and if there were any children is not currently known.

References: US Census: 1940; New York State Birth Index 1881-1942; New York State Marriage Index 1881-1967; Fort Logan National Cemetery records, Denver, Colorado; US Vietnam Military Casualties 1956-1998; *Bolivar Breeze 1891-1965*, selected issues.

501.

Arlene/Arlinee M. Quick, daughter of Ruth (240), granddaughter of Owen (111), b. Bolivar, New York June 28, 1932; m. Bolivar, New York August 19, 1948 Gerald Hiram Densmore, b. Oswayo/Coudersport, Pennsylvania November 25, 1924, d. Geneseo, New York April 7, 2015. There is little current information available on Arlene Quick Densmore. Gerald Densmore resided in Independence, New York in 1930 and Ceres, Pennsylvania in 1940. His World War II Draft Registration Card described him as being 5' 6" tall, weighing 135 pounds with blonde hair and blue eyes. Mr. Densmore entered the US Navy November 14, 1944. After the war he was employed by Sweet Briar Farms until his retirement. It is not currently known where Gerald Densmore was buried and there is currently no information about descendants.

References: US Census: 1930, 1940; New York State Birth Index 1881-1942; New York State Marriage Index 1881-1967; World War II Draft Registration Card, 1940; obituary on Findagrave.com.

502.

Wayne Leroy Quick, son of Ruth (240), grandson of Owen (111), b. Bolivar, New York March 9, 1934; m. Scio, New York November 2, 1951 Joyce Hults. Wayne and Joyce Hults resided in Brockport, New York and later Leesburg, Florida. Further information on Mr. and Mrs. Quick is not currently available.

References: US Census: 1940; New York State Birth Index 1881-1942; New York State Marriage Index 1881-1967; Public Records Index for Brockport, New York and Leesburg, Florida.

503.

Ernest Henry Quick, son of Ruth (240), grandson of Owen (111), b. Bolivar, New York April 9, 1937, d. Wellsville, New York June 23, 1951. Ernest Quick fell from a homemade tractor operated by his brother, Wayne Quick, and struck his head on the ground causing a skull fracture. He died at Jones Memorial Hospital in Wellsville, New York. Ernest was a student at Scio Central Schools. Ernest Quick was buried in Maple Lawn Cemetery, Bolivar, New York.

References: US Census: 1940; New York Birth Index 1881-1942; New York State Death Index 1880-1956; Maple Lawn Cemetery records, Bolivar, New York; *Bolivar Breeze*, June 28, 1951 obituary.

504.

Elnora Mae Quick, daughter of Ruth (240), granddaughter of Owen (111), b. Bolivar, New York September 10, 1938, d. place not known, January 19, 2004; m. (1) Bolivar, New York November 10, 1956 James E. Johnson, divorced; m. (2) Place not known January 12, 1974 (undocumented source) William Wilde Snodgrass, b. Mannington, West Virginia April 7, 1940, d. Mannington, West Virginia April 12, 1996. There is currently little information about Elnora Quick Johnson Snodgrass. Undocumented sources indicate she had three daughters by her first marriage. Elnora and William Snodgrass were buried in Mannington Memorial Park, Mannington, West Virginia.

References: US Census: 1940; New York State Birth Index 1881-1942; New York State Marriage Index 1881-1967 for Elnora Quick's first marriage; Social Security Death Index 1935-2014; Mannington Memorial Park records, Mannington, West Virginia.

505.

Rosemary Quick, daughter of Ruth (240), granddaughter of Owen (111), b. Bolivar, New York

January 3, 1941, d. Place not known, August 2, 2015; m. (1) Bolivar, New York June 13, 1959 Donald John Swift, b. Rexford, Pennsylvania November 5, 1935, d. Shinglehouse, Pennsylvania October 25, 2012, divorced; m. (2) Bolivar, New York August 3, 1963 Robert Edward Reynolds, b. Shinglehouse, Pennsylvania January 23, 1940, d. Olean, New York July 23, 2000.

Undocumented sources indicate that Rosemary Quick had two daughters and one son by her first marriage to Donald J. Swift. These same sources indicate that Rosemary had one son and one daughter by her second marriage to Robert Reynolds. The identity of only one child can currently be determined and that was Sherry Rose who is sometimes identified as Sherry Swift and in cemetery records as Sherry Reynolds. Sherry was born April 19, 1963 before Rosemary's marriage to Robert Reynolds. Sherry died October 28, 1995 and was married in August 14, 1992 to a Mr. Hannon. Both Sherry and Robert Reynolds served in the United State Air Force. Donald J. Swift was buried in Maple Grove Cemetery, Shinglehouse, Pennsylvania. Rosemary and Robert Reynolds were also buried in Maple Grove Cemetery as was Sherry Reynolds Hannon.

References: New York State Birth Index 1881-1942; New York State Marriage Index 1881-1967 for both marriages; Maple Grove Cemetery records, Shinglehouse, Pennsylvania.

507.

Marilyn/Marlyn Ann Crandall, daughter of Helma (242), granddaughter of Owen (111), b. Scio, New York October 14, 1939, d. Zephyrhills, Florida October 7, 2004; m. Henriet, New York June 24, 1961 Alvin Whitaker, b. Cuba, New York April 28, 1937. There is currently little information on this Root descendant. Marilyn graduated from Scio Central Schools and SUNY Agricultural and Technical Institute, Morrisville, New York with a degree in Practical Nursing. Information on children and burial location is not currently known.

References: US Census: 1940; New York State Birth Index 1881-1942; New York State Marriage Index 1881-1967; Social Security Death Index 1935-2014 for Marilyn Crandall Whitaker; SUNY Morrisville Agricultural and Technical Institute Yearbooks.

508.

Helen Joan Spargur, daughter of Helen (243), granddaughter of Asa P. (113), b. Wellsville, New York October 10, 1939, d. Benton, Washington July 15, 1999; m. place not known, William Witherell May 1960, b. Gowanda, New York June 21, 1934, d. Kennewick, Washington State March 29, 2014. Joan graduated from Alfred Agricultural Technical Institute, Alfred, New York with a degree in secretarial science. She was employed in the field of journalism and by the National Education Association. Bill Witherell graduated from Alfred University with a B. S. Degree in Ceramic Engineering. He was employed as an engineer with Pratt and Whitney. It is not currently known where they were buried.

Children:

1039. I. ***Steven William Witherell***, b. June 21, 1962; m. Christin C. Rogers, divorced Benton, Washington; divorced October 27, 2003. There were no children. Steven Witherell was last known to resided in Kennewick, Washington; ***nfi.***

1040. II. ***David Scott Witherell***, b. July 15, 1964 and was last known to reside in Kennewick, Washington; ***nfi.***

1041. III. ***Allison March Witherell**, f.*

References: US Census: 1940; New York State Birth Index 1881-1942; Washington Death Index 1940-2004 for Joan Spargur Witherell; Social Security Death Index 1935-2014; Washington Divorce Index 1969-2014 for Steven Witherell; Washington Marriage Index 1969-2014 for Allison Witherell; Interviews with the late Helen Root Spargur; *Tri City Herald*, Kennewick, Washington obituary for Bill Witherell March 30, 2014.

509.

Judith Anne Spargur, daughter of Helen (243), granddaughter of Asa P. (113), b. Wellsville, New York, d. Wellsville, New York September 13, 2009; m. (1) Vernon, Connecticut October 17, 1954 James E. Carroll, b. Newport, Rhode Island May 30, 1939, d. Wheat Ridge, Colorado April 16, 2008, divorced; m. (2) Wellsville, New York November 26, 1975 Robert G. Hardy, b. Allentown, New York May 13, 1935, d. Wellsville, New York October 11, 2006.

Judith Spargur graduated from Wellsville High School in 1961 and the Olean Business Institute in 1962. During her first marriage she was employed by Hartford Insurance Company, General Electric, and Raytheon in New England. She was employed at Air Preheater from 1970 to 1994 in Wellsville, New York. Judith Hardy enjoyed golf, bridge, water aerobics, traveling, hunting, bowling, family life and her pets. She was active in youth sports, the Little League Baseball, youth wrestling, and youth soccer.

Mrs. Hardy was a member of the Women of the Moose, the Wellsville Historical Society, Allegany Royalties, the Red Hat Society, the Wellsville Community Center, and the First Congregational Church, Wellsville. James E. Carroll remarried to Leonor Aguirre in Santa Clara, California May 27, 1965. He served in the US Marine Corps from October 21, 1957 to November 3, 1960. Mr. Carroll was buried in Fort Logan National Cemetery, Denver, Colorado. Bob Hardy was also employed by the Air Preheater Corporation and had retired by 1990. He served in the US Navy during the Korean War. Judith and Robert Hardy were buried in Stannard's Cemetery, Willing, New York.

Children (by first marriage):

1042. I. ***Deborah Anne Carroll, f.***

Children (by second marriage):

1043. II. ***Timothy Michael Hardy, f.***

References: Connecticut Marriage Index 1959-2012 for Judith Spargur's first marriage; Social Security Death Index 1935-2014; Fort Logan National Cemetery records, Denver, Colorado; Stannard's Cemetery records, Willing, New York; *Wellsville Daily Reporter* obituary for Judith Hardy September 15, 2009; Interviews with the late Helen Root Spargur.

510.

Mary Jane Spargur, daughter of Helen (243), granddaughter of Asa P. (113), b. Wellsville, New York November 18, 1946, d. St. Petersburg, Florida December 30, 1988 from cancer; m. (1) Wellsville, New York February 4, 1966 Louis J. Barozzini, divorced Pinellas County, Florida November 16, 1982; m. (2) St. Petersburg, Florida May 15, 1988 Titus Ward Jackson.

Mary Jane was a graduate of Wellsville High School and Olean Business Institute. She was employed as a loan processer in St. Petersburg, Florida at the time of her death. In spite of a devastating illness, which ravaged her body, Mary Jane never lost her enthusiasm for life, never lost her sense of humor, and never complained about what fate had dealt her. Mary Jane's courage and strength and her love for life remain a lasting legacy for those she touched. She was a member of the First Unity Church, St. Petersburg, Florida. A memorial for Mary Jane Spargur Barozzini was placed in Woodlawn Cemetery, Wellsville, New York next to her parent's graves. Louis Barozzini remarried October 16, 1988 to Dawn Eileen Tuohey in St. Petersburg, Florida. He currently resided in Clyde, North Carolina.

Children (by first marriage):

1044. I. ***Tracey Lynn Barozzini, f.***

1045. II. ***Michael Joseph Barozzini, f.***

References: New York State Marriage Index 1881-1967 for Mary Jane Spargur's first marriage; Florida Divorce Index 1927-2001; Florida Marriage Index 1927-2001 for Mary Jane Barozzini's second marriage; Social Security Death Index 1935-2014; *Wellsville Daily Reporter* obituary December 31, 1988 for Mary Jane Spargur Barozzini Jackson; Interviews with the late Helen Root Spargur.

511.

Malcolm Leon Honadle, son of Maxine (244), grandson of Leon (119), b. Brookville, Pennsylvania December 28, 1933, d. Deland, Florida December 10, 2003; m. Bradford, Pennsylvania November 5, 1955 Barbara Ann Bell, b. Bradford, Pennsylvania June 2, 1936. There is currently little information on this Root descendant. Undocumented sources indicated Malcolm and Barbara Ann Honadle had three children: two daughters and one son and moved to Deland Florida in 1994. Currently, only one daughter and the son can be identified. Malcolm Honadle was buried in Deland Memorial Gardens, Deland, Florida.

Children:

1046. I. ***Mark Thomas Honadle***, b. Pennsylvania August 30, 1959; m. Frederick County, Virginia December 16, 1979 Katherine Lee Forbes, b. December 19, 1961; ***nfi.***

1047. II. ***Linda Kay Honadle***, b. New York State, June 25, 1962; m. Springville, Virginia May 28, 1988 Charles Ward Corbin, b. Ohio March 7, 1947. This was Mr. Corbin's fourth marriage; ***nfi.***

1048. III. ***Female Honadle; nfi.***

References: US Census: 1940; Social Security Death Index 1935-2014 for Malcolm Honadle; Virginia Marriage Records 1936-2014 for the marriages of Mark Honadle and Linda Honadle; Deland Memorial Gardens records, Deland, Florida.

514.

Richard Leon/Lee Wilcox, son of Richard (246), grandson of Leon (119), b. Brockway, Pennsylvania November 18, 1947, d. West Sacramento, California, 2008; m. Winchester, Virginia February 15, 1969 Carroll Ann Anderson, b. Pennsylvania July 31, 1947. Richard Wilcox's marriage license recorded that both he and his wife had four years of college education. There is no further information on this Root descendant. It is not currently known where he was buried.

References: Social Security Death Index 1935-2014; Virginia Marriage Records 1936-2014.

515.

Willard Milo Cline, son of Coral (250), grandson of Burr Leroy (122), b. Bradford, Pennsylvania September 26, 1925, still living; m. (1) Olean, New York January 29, 1949, Ruby Jeanne Langfitt, b. Tyler, West Virginia July 30, 1929, d. place not known, December 6, 2007, divorced by 1974; m. (2) place not known, April 27, 1974, Joyce Schiefferle, b. place and date not known, place and date not known.

Milo Cline resided with his parents until he entered the US Navy serving from March 13, 1944 to March 2, 1946. His World War II Draft Registration Card described him as being 5' 11" tall, weighing 154 pounds with blonde hair and blue eyes. Mr. Cline was employed with McCutchen Motors in Olean, New York and with the Cline Oil Company. He eventually became a self-employed oil producer. His first wife, Ruby J. Langfitt was the daughter of Edward Langfitt and Golda G. Knight Langfitt. After their 1974 divorce, Milo Cline was awarded sole custody of their children. Ruby Cline remarried to William Dale Carter of Bradford, Pennsylvania (1932-2007). It is not currently known where Ruby and William Carter were buried.

Children (by first marriage):

1049. I. ***Terrie Anne Cline, f.***

1050. II. ***Cathy Jeanne Cline, f.***

1051. III. ***Willard Lee Cline, f.***

1052. IV. ***Mark Lewis Cline, f.***

1053. V. ***Susan Marie Cline, f.***

1054. VI. ***Mary Jo Cline, f.***

References: US Census: 1930, 1940; World War II Draft Registration Card, 1943; Pennsylvania Veterans World War II Files 1950-1966; West Virginia Birth Index 1804-1938 for Ruby Langfitt; *The Bradford Era*, January 31, 1949 for Cline/Langfitt marriage.

516.

Richard Kay Root, son of Raymond (251), grandson of Burr Leroy (122), b. New York City, New York December 1, 1937, d. from a crocodile attack Kgalagardi, Botswana, Africa March 19, 2006; m. (1) Palisades Park, New Jersey, March 1960, Marilyn Loyola Parletta, b. Union City, New Jersey August 20, 1939, d. Mercer Island, Washington February 6, 2001 from Lou Gehrig's Disease; m. (2) place not known, date not know, but in 2004, Rita O'Boyle.

Richard Root earned his B. A. Degree in Biology from Wesleyan University (1959) and his M.D. Degree from Johns Hopkins University (1963). His postgraduate training and fellowship appointments were at Massachusetts General Hospital, the National Institutes of Health for Allergy and Infectious Diseases, Bethesda, Maryland, and the University of Washington where he specialized in Infectious Diseases. Faculty appointments were held with the National Institutes of Health, The University of Pennsylvania School of Medicine, and the Yale University School of Medicine in the Department for Infectious Diseases.

Dr. Root was Vice-Chairman of the Department of Medicine at the University of Washington and Chief of Medical Services at the Veterans Administration Medical Center in Seattle. September 1985 Dr. Root was appointed Professor and Chairman of Medicine for the University of California at San Francisco. September 1989, Dr. Root was appointed Associate Dean for Clinical Education at the University of California, San Francisco. Dr. Root received numerous professional awards and honorary degrees. He authored and co-authored books, book reviews, journal abstracts, and medical journal articles. He was nationally known as an educator who helped medical schools develop their teaching programs. His research and clinical studies focused on the body's defenses against bacterial infections, particularly the management of sepsis and septic shock, a field he wrote extensively in.

Dr. Richard Root was a mentor to physicians and scientists who moved into leading positions in academic medicine. At the time of his death, Dr. Richard Root was Professor and Vice-Chairman of the Department of Medicine at the University of Washington and Chief of Medical Service at the Medical School in Seattle. Dr. Root held Emeritus Status since December 2002. Dr. Root tragically died while riding a canoe in the Tuli Nature Reserve on the eastern border of Botswana with Zimbabwe when he was attacked by a thirteen-foot crocodile who pulled him into the river. The remains were not recovered. He had been on a two-month assignment to teach and provide medical care for patients, most of them infected with HIV, at the Princess Marina Hospital in Gaborone, Botswana. He was there at the invitation of the University of Pennsylvania and the Botswana Department of Health. The day before the canoe ride, Dr. Root expressed to his wife how happy his was that his career had enabled to come to Botswana to study infectious diseases.

His wife, Rita, was in the canoe behind Dr. Root's and witnessed the attack. At the time of his death, Dr. Root had eight grandchildren. Marilyn Parletta Root was the daughter of Theodore A. Parletta and Carmela M. DiBianco Parletta. She earned an A. B. Degree in Education from Quinnipiac College (1980), Hamden, Connecticut and an M. A. Degree in Marriage, Family, and Child Counseling from the University of San Francisco (1987). She was employed by Epiphany School, San Francisco as a counselor and maintained a private counseling service as well. Mrs. Root was a mental health counselor specializing in the treatment of adolescents and adult survivors of childhood sexual abuse. She pioneered arts therapy for abused women and sexual-abuse survivors in Seattle. Marilyn Root was a skilled photographer of people and scenes, particularly barns, doorways, and ponds, throughout the United States and Europe. She created a diploma program for people in her 21-week group sessions in photography and painting. Mrs. Root was a fine Italian chef, a skill she explored from her Italian heritage.

It is not currently known where Marilyn Root was buried. Rita Simmons O'Boyle was previously married to Patrick J. O'Boyle and had two daughters by her first husband.

Children (by first marriage):

1055. I. ***Richard A. Root,*** b. August 26, 1960; m. Grace, last name not known. Mr. Root earned an A. B. Degree in English from Connecticut College. He was last known to be an English teacher in the Ontario, California area; ***nfi.***

1056. II. ***David L. Root,*** b. February 16, 1963; m. (1) Chris, last name not known; m. (2)King County, Washington July 14, 2012 Gabriell Klisenbaue Meske; ***nfi.***

1057. III. ***Daniel C. Root,*** b. August 7, 1968; m. Amanda, last name not known. He attended Wesleyan University and was last known to reside on Mercer Island, Washington; ***nfi.***

References: US Census: 1940; New York State Birth Index 1881-1942 for Richard K. Root; New Jersey Marriage Index 1901-2016 for Dr. Root's first marriage; Washington State Death Index 1940-2014 for Marilyn Root; Social Security Death Index 1935-2014; *New York Times* obituary for Richard Kay Root March 21, 2006; *Seattle Times* obituary for Richard Kay Root March 26, 2006; *New York Times* February 11, 2001 obituary for Marilyn Root; Correspondence with the late Dr. Richard Kay Root, March 13, 1983, April 15, 1985, and October 17, 1990; Washington State Marriage Index 1969-2017 for David L. Root.

517.

(Elizabeth) Carole Root, daughter of Raymond (251), granddaughter of Burr Leroy (122) b. New York City, New York December 31, 1940, m. (1) Leonia, New Jersey June 1962 Charles J. Cole, b. New Jersey January 5, 1940, divorced; m. (2) Leonia, New Jersey March 15, 1987 Walter J. Neubauer. Carole graduated from the University of Connecticut with a degree in Zoology. She worked for the environmental consulting firm of American NUKEM Corporation. Walter Neubauer worked for the communication's industry.

Children (by first marriage):

1058. I. ***Jeff Cole,*** b. November 25, 1964. He graduated from Louisiana State University with a degree in Biology. He was last known to work for the Navaho Fish and Wildlife Committee in New Mexico; ***nfi.***

1059. II. ***Lisa Marie Cole,*** b. February 4, 1967; m. Fred Fogelman. Lisa and her husband were last known to reside in Mahwah, New Jersey; ***nfi.***

References: New York State Birth Index 1881-1942; New Jersey Marriage Index 1901-10166 for both of Carole Root's marriages; Correspondence with Carole Root Neubauer.

518.

Howard LeRoy Root, Jr., son of Howard L., Sr. (252), grandson of Burr LeRoy (122), b. Edgerton, Wisconsin August 30, 1931, d. Belvidere, Illinois January 9, 1997; m. place not known, September 13, 1960 Janet Hobbs, b. place not known, 1939. Howard Root served with the US Army in Korea. He was a long-time office worker with the Chrysler Corporation. Howard LeRoy Root, Jr. was buried in Belvidere Cemetery, Belvidere, Illinois.

Children:

1060. I. ***Donald James Root, f.***

1061 II. ***Wanda Jean Root, f.***

References: US Census: 1940; US Social Security Claims I 1936-2007; Belvidere Cemetery records, Belvidere, Illinois; correspondence with the late Howard LeRoy Root, Jr. August 12, 1980, October 2, 1990, and October 30, 1990.

519.

Carolyne Mae Root, daughter of Howard LeRoy, Sr. (252), granddaughter of Burr LeRoy (122), b. Edgerton, Wisconsin January 3, 1935, d. Milwaukee, Wisconsin September 22, 2008; m. (1) place and date not known Wallace J. Gaethke, b. Wilkin, Minnesota April 19, 1934, d. Janesville, Wisconsin, August 10, 1981, divorced; m. (2) place and date not known George Williams, divorced.

Carolyne worked for nineteen years at Borg Indak Precision Instrument and Clock Manufacturing Company. She was a founding member of *Octoberfest* for Delavan, Wisconsin. Carolyne Root Williams was survived by three children, five grandchildren, and a special companion Jim Horgan. Wallace Gaethke was previously married to Martha Raatz West and was buried in Oak Hill Cemetery, Delavan, Wisconsin. Carolyne was buried in Spring Grove Cemetery, Delavan, Wisconsin.

Children: (by second marriage):

1062. I. ***Melody Williams, f.***

1063. II. ***Allan Williams,*** b. November 30, 1960 and last resided in Centerline, Michigan where he was employed as an assembly line worker; ***nfi.***

1064. III. ***Matthew Williams,*** b. September 5, 1962 and last resided in Darien, Wisconsin where he was employed as a welder; ***nfi.***

References: US Census: 1940; Social Security Death Index 1935-2014; Spring Grove Cemetery records, Delavan, Wisconsin; Oak Hill Cemetery records, Delavan, Wisconsin for Wallace Gaethke; Delavan newspaper for obituary of Carolyn Mae Root Williams; correspondence with the late Carolyn Root Williams September 5, 1980, July 22, 1985, and September 17, 1990.

520.

Duane Root, son of Howard LeRoy, Sr. (252), grandson of Burr LeRoy (122), b. Edgerton, Wisconsin March 30, 1939; m. (1) Fort Atkinson, Wisconsin May 29, 1958 Judith Peplinski, divorced; (2) Donna, last name not known. Duane Root was employed by the Chrysler Corporation as a factory worker. Further information is not currently available on this Root descendant.

Children: (by first marriage)

1065. I. ***Julie Root, f.***

1066. II. ***Tammy Root, f.***

1067. III. ***Douglas Root, f.***

1068. IV. ***Wade Root, f.***

References: US Census: 1940; Correspondence with Duane Root, September 29, 1980.

521.

David A. Root, son of Howard LeRoy, Sr. (252), grandson of Burr LeRoy (122), b. Edgerton, Wisconsin September 11, 1941; m. Beloit, Illinois August 1, 1959 Marcella E. Williams, b. Wisconsin November 22, 1941. David was employed as an assembler at the General Motors Automobile plant in Janesville, Wisconsin. Further information on this Root descendant is not currently available.

Children:

1069. I. ***David A. Root, Jr., f.***

1070. II. ***Cheryl Root, f.***

1071. III. ***Laurie Root, f.***

References: Correspondence with David A. Root, September 5, 1990.

522.

Donald Clifford Foster, son of Ruth (253), grandson of Burr LeRoy (122), b. Wellsville, New York September 11, 1929, d. Buffalo, New York Veterans Hospital July 17, 1957 from a kidney ailment; m. Bolivar, New York September 30, 1951 Lucille M. Harris, b. Bolivar, New York October 6, 1932, d. Cuba, New York April 28, 2014.

Donald Foster was a graduate of Richburg Central School and served in the Korean War with the US Army rising to the rank of Corporal. He was employed at the Wirthmore Feed Company, Hinsdale, New York for three years prior to his death. Mr. Foster and his family resided in Hinsdale, New York. He was a member of the Veterans of Foreign Wars, Olean, New York. Lucille Harris Foster was the daughter of Lonny Lee Harris and Ruth Waters Harris.

Lucille was a graduate of Bolivar High School and was employed with Market Basket offices, Olean, New York, Tito's Restaurant, the Hinsdale American Legion, and the Olean Answering Service and Home Health Care Center. She was a past president and member of the Olean Eagles Auxiliary. Lucille Harris Foster remarried April 7, 1958 to James Maynard Painter, b. Port Allegany, Pennsylvania February 11, 1937, d. East Baton Rouge, Louisiana August 26, 1988. James Painter adopted Donald Foster's two children and they carry the last name of Painter. Donald Foster and Lucille Harris Foster Painter were buried in Maple Lawn Cemetery, Bolivar, New York. James M. Painter was buried in Mt. View Cemetery, Olean, New York.

Children:

1072. I. ***Thomas A. (Foster) Painter***, b. Brookview, New York September 7, 1953; ***nfi.***

1073. II. ***Karen Ruth (Foster) Painter***; ***nfi.***

References: US Census: 1930, 1940; New York State Birth Index 1881-1942; New York State Marriage Index 1881-1967; New York State Death Index 1957-1968; Social Security Death Index 1035-2014; Maple Lawn Cemetery records, Bolivar, New York; Mt. View Cemetery records, Olean, New York; *Bolivar Breeze 1891-1965*, obituary for Donald Foster July 25, 1957;
Olean Times Herald, April 30, 2014 for Lucille Harris Foster Painter.

523.

James Allen Foster, son of Ruth (253), grandson of Burr LeRoy (122), b. Portville, New York May 29, 1934, d. Olean, New York September 15, 2003; m. place not known, December 22, 1959 Sylvia Lynne Scott. James Foster served in the US Army rising to the rank of Sergeant First Class. He was employed as a clerical worker with Dresser-Rand, formerly Clark Brothers, in Olean, New York. Mr. Foster was buried in Allegany Cemetery, Allegany, New York.

Children:

1074. I. ***David Foster,*** b. June 17, 1959; m. April 9, 1983 Sharon Walters. They were last known to reside in Olean, New York; ***nfi.***

1075. II. ***Stephen Foster,*** b. July 31, 1961 and attended Alfred Ag-Tech, Alfred, NY; ***nfi.***

1076. III. ***Scott Foster,*** b. October 1, 1962 and attended Alfred Ag-Tech, Alfred, NY; ***nfi.***

1077. IV. ***Paul Foster,*** b. June 27, 1966; ***nfi.***

1078. V. ***Douglas Foster,*** b. June 29, 1968; ***nfi.***

References: US Census: 1940; New York State Birth Index 1881-1942; Social Security Death Index 1935-2014; US Veterans Gravesites 1775-2006; Allegany Cemetery records, Allegany, New York.

524.

Bernice Virginia Sisson, daughter of Clella (257), granddaughter of Lena (123), b. Bolivar, New York May 15, 1921, d. Bolivar, New York November 3, 1995; m. Bolivar, New York May 16, 1942 Roy O. Wilder, b. Franklin, Pennsylvania August 30, 1921, d. Bolivar, New York January 13, 2003.

Bernice Sisson and Roy Wilder were married at the home of her uncle, Reverend Keith Perry, Obi, New York. At the time of their marriage Bernice was employed as a book keeper with Keiser Garage in Olean, New York and Roy worked in Arcade, New York in the defense Industry.

Later, Bernice Sisson Wilder was employed as an R and D clerk and Roy was employed as a tool crib operator. They resided on Barber Hollow Road in West Clarksville, New York. Mr. Wilder served in the US Army during World War II from July 9, 1942 to September 29, 1944 rising to the rank of Corporal. Roy Wilder suffered a serious accident in April 1962 when repairing a saw motor, he accidentally placed his left hand on a running saw severing the left thumb and cutting tendons in the first two fingers of the left hand. He was taken to Cuba, New York hospital by his wife for surgery. Roy Wilder served as the representative for Clarksville in Allegany County and was Vice-Chairman of the Bolivar Industrial Planning Committee. Bernice and Roy Wilder were buried in Wells Cemetery, Little Genesee, New York.

Children:

1079. I. ***Joe Roy Wilder, f.***

1080. II. ***Patty Jean Wilder, f.***

References: US Census: 1930, 1940; New York State Census: 1925; New York State Birth Index 1881-1942; Social Security Death Index 1935-2014; US Veterans Death File 1850-2010; Wells Cemetery records, Little Genesee, New York; *Bolivar Breeze 1891-1965*, May 21, 1942 and April 24, 1962.

525.

(Myrtle) Jean Sisson, daughter of Clella (257), granddaughter of Lena (123), b. Clarksville, New York April 18, 1932; m. Clarksville, New York December 24, 1932 Richard Earl Howard, b. Olean, New York June 30, 1953, d. Richburg, New York March 23, 2010.

Jean Sisson resided with her parents until her marriage to Dick Howard in 1953. Jean and Dick Howard lost four children at birth and raised five more to adulthood. Documents indicate the four children were buried in West Genesee Cemetery but current cemetery records do not supply that information. Jean and Dick resided on County Road 8 in Richburg, New York. Jean graduated from Bolivar High School and Dick graduated from Oswayo Valley School.

Dick served two years in the US Army from 1953-1955. He was employed for twenty-five years at the Allegany Highway Department retiring as shop supervisor. Mr. Howard was a town of Wirt assessor for twelve years and town of Wirt Supervisor for 2 ½ years. He was also a past Richburg Fire Chief and was a member of the Friendship Rod and Gun Club. Jean and Dick Howard were active church members of the E.U.B. Obi United Methodist Church and founding members of the Obi Community Church. They also attended the West Clarksville Baptist Church. Jean and Dick Howard were caregivers to many who were family in the Lord. Richard Howard was buried in Dimmick Cemetery, Richburg, New York.

Children:

1081. I. ***Baby Boy Howard***, b. and d. March 3, 1955.

1082. II. ***Judy Elizabeth Howard***, b. and d. November 9, 1955 and buried in West Genesee Cemetery.

1083. III. ***Kathleen Elizabeth Howard, f.***

1084. IV. ***David Lynn Howard, f.***

1085. V. ***Sandra Jean Howard***, b. and d. October 20, 1959 and buried in West Genesee Cemetery.

1086. VI. ***Lori Ann Howard, f.***

1087. VII. ***Harry Earl Howard***, b. and d. August 7, 1963 and buried in West Genesee Cemetery.

1088. VIII. ***Thomas Richard Howard,*** b. July 17, 1964, d. October 28, 1986 from an accidental electrocution at work. Thomas was a graduate of Alfred Ag-Tech and was employed by the Allegany County Department of Public Works. Thomas Howard was buried in Dimmick Cemetery in Wirt Township, New York.

1089. IX. ***Brenda Lee Howard,*** b. January 7, 1966; m. October 1, 1988 Kevin Bruce Brisbee; ***nfi.***

References: US Census: 1940; New York State Birth Index 1881-1942; New York State Marriage Index 1881-1967; Dimmick Cemetery records, Richburg, New York; Social Security Death Index 1935-2014; US Veterans Death File 1850-2010; *Wellsville Daily Reporter*, March 24, 2010 obituary for Richard Howard; correspondence with Jean Howard June 20, 1985 and September 14, 1990.

529.

Richard Ernest Schwertfager, son of Alta (260), grandson of Ernest S. (124), b. Hamburg, New York July 12, 1933, d. Bradenton, Florida June 10, 2011; m. Tonawanda, New York June 20, 1958 Joanne Melissa Moore, b. place and date not known, d. Bradenton, Florida February 28, 2011.

Richard graduated from SUNY Buffalo with a BS Degree and an MS Degree in Education. He served with the US Army. Richard was employed as a Physical Education teacher and coach for the Wilson Central School District, New York. Joanne graduated from SUNY Buffalo with a BS Degree in Education and was a Computer Laboratory Instructor at Lewiston-Porter High School, New York. Richard and Joanne were avid golfers, enjoyed swimming, reading, walking, and socializing with friends. They had five grandchildren, but it is not currently known to which daughter the grandchildren should be assigned. Richard and Joanne were buried in Greenwood Cemetery, Wilson, New York.

Children:

1090. I. ***Richard Ernest Schwertfager, Jr.***, b. North Tonawanda, New York December 27, 1958, d. North Tonawanda, New York May 10, 2004 and was buried in Greenwood Cemetery, Wilson, New York.

1091. II. ***Linda Jayne Schwertfager***, b. May 23, 1961; m. Daniel Kerwin; resided Wilson, New York; ***nfi.***

1092. III. ***Susan Anne Schwertfager***, b. October 19, 1962; m. Mr. Senior; resided Pinehurst, North Carolina; ***nfi.***

References: US Census: 1940; New York State Birth Index 1881-1942; New York State Marriage Index 1881-1967; Social Security Death Index 1935-2014; Green Cemetery records, Wilson, New York.

530.

Larry Dean Schwertfager, son of Alta (259), grandson of Ernest S. (124), b. Buffalo, New York February 16, 1939, d. Rochester, New York October 18, 2001; m. place not known, August 13, 1960 Ramona Walker. Larry Schwertfager was employed and owned *Creative Quality Foods*, which sold food supplies to restaurants. It is not currently known where Larry Schwertfager was buried.

Children:

1093. I. ***Randy Dean Schwertfager***, b. March 31, 1963; ***nfi.***

1094. II. ***Michael Dean Schwertfager***, b. May 8, 1964; ***nfi.***

References: US Census: 1940; New York State Birth Index 1881-1942; Social Security Death Index 1935-2014.

531.

Kenneth Ernest Root, Jr., son of Kenneth, Sr. (260), grandson of Ernest S. (124), b. place not known, June 21, 1949; m. place not known, August 13, 1977 Lynda Austerberry, b. place and date not known.

Kenneth Root was a Doctor of Medicine with a specialty in Neurology. He graduated from John Carroll University, Cleveland, Ohio and the Kansas City College of Osteopathic Medicine. Dr. Root was given a fellowship to the Cleveland Clinic. He has been in practice for more than twenty years in Gilbert, Arizona and is affiliated with Mercy Gilbert Medical Center. Dr. Root has at least one grandchild, Eleanor Root.

Children.

1095. I. ***Brandon Root***, b. January 12, 1984; m. Kristen, last name not known.

1096. II. ***Jason Root,*** b. March 1, 1987; m. Karen, last name not known.

References: Correspondence with Kenneth Ernest Root, Sr., October 10, 1990, October 19, 1990, March 28, 1991, April 1, 1991, April 16, 1991; San Diego, California newspaper obituary for Dorothy Root.

532.

Terry Edward Root, son of Kenneth, Sr. (260), grandson of Ernest S. (124), b. place not known, March 9, 1952; m. Linda, last name not known. Mr. Root graduated from Western Michigan University and attended the University of Colorado, Denver. He is a design engineer. Terry Root is an avid outdoorsman having climbed Mt. McKinley, Alaska and the Matterhorn, France. He heads a mountain climbing club in Denver.

References: Correspondence with Kenneth Ernest Root, Sr., 1990.

533.

Lorrie Ann Root, daughter of Kenneth, Sr. (260), granddaughter of Ernest S. (124), b. place not known August 20, 1956. Lorrie is a graduate of Western Michigan University and was employed as a comptroller for an oil and gas company. She resides in Colorado.

References: Correspondence with Kenneth Ernest Root, Sr., 1990.

534.

Robert Harris Milford, son of Laura (261), grandson of Floyd (129), b. Rochester, New York October 22, 1934, d. Rochester, New York July 26, 2010; m. place not known, a. 1960 June E. Brown, b. place and date not known, d. Rochester, New York February 6, 2013.

Known in the family as *Grumpy*, Robert Milford served in the Korean War with the United States Air Force. Robert and June Milford had four sons and ten grandchildren. They were buried in White Haven Memorial Park, Pittsford, New York.

Children:

1097. I. ***Russell Milford***, married and resided in Summerville, South Carolina; ***nfi.***

1098. II. ***Robert Milford***, resided in Phoenix, Arizona; ***nfi.***

1099. III. ***Wayne Milford***, married and resided in Farmington, New York; ***nfi.***

1100. IV. ***Scott Milford***, married and resided in Atlanta, Georgia; ***nfi.***

References: US Census: 1940; New York State Birth Index 1881-1942; Social Security Death Index 1935-2014; White Haven Memorial Park records, Pittsford, New York; *Rochester Democrat and Chronicle* obituaries July 29, 2010 and February 10, 2013 for Robert and June Milford.

535.

Richard J. Milford, son of Laura (261), grandson of Floyd (129), b. Rochester, New York March 22, 1936, d. Tempe, Arizona February 25, 2004; m. New York State November 26, 1964, Carol A. Hermanet, b. place and date not known. Richard Milford was known for his participation and membership in the Salvation Army, Moose, and Elks Clubs. He was buried in Resthaven Park East Cemetery, Tempe, Arizona. No grandchildren were listed in Mr. Milford's obituary. Further information is not currently available on this Root descendant.

Children:

1101. I. ***Lori Milford***; ***nfi.***

References: US Census: 1940; New York State Birth Index 1881-1942; Social Security Death Index 1935-2014; *The Arizona Republic*, February 27, 2004 obituary; New York State Marriage Index 1881-1967.

536.

Thomas Ward Milford, son of Laura (261), grandson of Floyd (129), b. Rochester, New York October 13, 1945; m. (1) Lynchburg, Virginia October 22, 1966 Nancy Marie Perdieu, b. Lynchburg, Virginia February 4, 1942, d. Phoenix, Arizona October 24, 2008 divorced Lynchburg, Virginia March 30, 1972; m. (2) Scottsdale, Arizona, date not known, spouse's name not known. Thomas Milford was in the military at the time of his first marriage. Divorce documents indicate there was one child from this marriage. Nancy Perdieu Milford remarried James Garland Watts in Lynchburg, Virginia June 8, 1978. Further information on this Root descendant is not currently available.

References: Virginia Birth Records 1912-2016 for Nancy Perdieu; Virginia Marriage Records 1936-2014; Virginia Divorce Records 1936-2014; Arizona Marriage Records 1864-1982.

542.

Floyd M. Pire, son of Francis (263), grandson of Floyd (129), b. place not known, September 1, 1942; m. Rochester, New York August 14, 1965 Dianne M. Humphrey, b. Rochester, New York October 6, 1942, d. Rochester, New York January 12, 2009. US Public Records Indexes 1950-1993 indicated that Floyd and Dianne Pire may have separated as he lived in Bergen, New York and Mrs. Pire resided in Rochester, New York. They had at least one child. Further information on this Root descendant is not currently available.

Children:

1102. I. ***Scott Pire, nfi.***

References: New York State Marriage Index 1881-1967; Social Security Death Index 1935-2014 for Dianne Pire; US Public Records Index 1950-1993, Volume I for Floyd M. Pire birth date and residences for Floyd and Dianne Pire.

545.

Thomas "Tom" Lee Pire, son of Ward (265), grandson of Ward (130), b. Erie, Pennsylvania July 5, 1949, d. Los Angeles, California October 16, 1988. Tom Pire resided in Palm Springs, California until his 1988 death. He was buried in Erie Cemetery, Erie, Pennsylvania. Further information on this Root descendant is not currently available.

References: California Death Index 1940-1947; Erie Cemetery records, Erie, Pennsylvania.

546.

Richard Russell Pire, son of Ward (265), grandson of Ward (130), b. Erie, Pennsylvania February 2, 1949; m. place and date not known, Susan Ring, b. place and date not known. Richard Pire had three children based on the obituary of his son Hunter Karl Pire. Further information on this Root descendant is not currently available.

Children:

1103. I. ***Hunter Karl Pire, f.***

1104. II. ***Scott D. Pire, nfi.***

1105. III. ***Stacy L. Pire Walker***, married and resided in Tacoma, Washington; ***nfi.***

References: Erie Cemetery records, Erie, Pennsylvania including obituary for Hunter Karl Pire.

548.

Theresa Gay Hamilton, daughter of Leona (266), granddaughter of Leon (132), b. Kansas City, Missouri November 22, 1944; m. place not known, December 21, 1965 Talmadge *Tab* Homer Powell, b. Garber, Oklahoma February 23, 1930, d. Tulsa, Oklahoma August 23, 2015. Both Theresa and Tab Powell received B. A. Degrees and M. A. Degrees. Theresa was employed with the Coney, Kansas School System. Tab was employed by Phillips Petroleum and later retired as an elementary school teacher in Coney, Kansas where they resided. Mr. Powell served in the United States Air Force. His remains were cremated and it is not currently known if they were buried.

Children (by adoption):

1106. I. ***Chelsea Collen Powell***, b. New York State, July 3, 1970; ***nfi.***

1107. II. ***Julie JoAnna Powell***, b. Texas, November 10, 1973; ***nfi.***

References: Obituary, August 23, 2015; 1990 correspondence with Sherri Nelson Jack.

549.

Donna Jean Brown, daughter of Betty (267), granddaughter of Leon (132), b. place not known, May 2, 1943; m. (1) place and date not known, Benjamin Kelly, divorced; m. (2) Lynne Millen, divorced. Donna was employed as an administrator for a nursing home in Bell Plain, Kansas. Donna goes by the name of Donna McGlassen.

Children (by first marriage):

1108. I. ***Jeffrey Kelly, nfi.***

1109. II. ***Gregory Kelly, nfi.***

Children (by second marriage):

1110. I. ***Moffitte Millen, nfi.***

References: Correspondence with Sherri Nelson Jack, 1990.

550.

David Bruce Brown, son of Betty (267), grandson of Leon (132), b. Coffeyville, Kansas June 29, 1945, d. Tulsa, Oklahoma September 23, 2014; m. Edna, Kansas June 17, 1965 Marijo Dunn. David Brown was a graduate of Coffeyville Community College and Pittsburg State University. He was a veteran of the Vietnam War serving with the US Air Force.

David and Marijo owned and operator the Fourth Street Laundry, Coffeyville. David Brown also served as Pastor of the Wayside Christian Church, Wayside, Kansas. He was a third-generation minister. Both his father and paternal grandfather were ministers. David enjoyed restoring old cars, hunting, and fishing. He was survived by two sons, five grandchildren: Seth, Zakory, Maggie, Brody, and Ashdyn, and one great-grandchild: Maxten. Reverend Brown was buried in Fawn Creek Cemetery, Tyro, Kansas.

Children:

1111. I. ***Michael Brown***; married Kathleen, last name not known and resided Webb City, Missouri; ***nfi.***

1112. II. ***Mark Brown***, married Melinda, last name not known and resided in Carl Junction, Missouri and is a Doctor; ***nfi.***

References: Obituary for David Bruce Brown September 23, 2014; Correspondence with Sherri Nelson Jack, 1990.

551.

Jo Lynne Brown, daughter of Betty (267), granddaughter of Leon (132), b. place not known, July 3, 1953; m. (1) William Ross, divorced; m. (2) David Abbott. Jo and David Abbott resided in Chetopa, Kansas where he was employed for a motor home company and where she was the office manager for Miner Nursing Home.

Children (by first marriage):

1113. I. ***Melissa Ross, nfi.***

1114. II. ***Robin Ross, nfi.***

References: 1990 correspondence with Sherri Nelson Jack.

552.

Cheryl Elizabeth Brown, daughter of Betty (267), granddaughter of Leon (132), b. place not known, February 29, 1957; m. place and date not known, Rick Valverde. They reside in Cherryvale, Kansas where Rick worked for Parsons Mobil Home. Cheryl was employed by Cherryvale Public Schools. Rick had two additional children by a previous marriage.

Children:

1115. I. ***Nicole Valverde***, b. July 4, 1980; ***nfi.***

1116. II. ***Nicholas Valverde***, b. December 25, 1982; ***nfi.***

References: 1990 correspondence with Sherri Nelson Jack.

553.

Sherri Nelson, daughter of Barbara (268), granddaughter of Leon (132), b. Borger, Texas February 24, 1950; m. (1) 1970, Thomas L. Mayo, divorced 1980; m. (2) 1980 Douglas Jack. Douglas was a chemical engineer with Conoco Oil Company in Ponca City, Oklahoma. Sherri was a tremendous help in providing genealogical information on the descendants of Arthur "Lew" Root for the 1990 edition of the Root family history.

Children (by first marriage and adopted by Douglas Jack):

1117. I. ***Joseph Ryan Mayo Jack***, b. March 15, 1973; ***nfi.***

1118. II. ***Katherine Anne May Jack***, b. November 26, 1976; ***nfi.***

Children (by second marriage):

1119. I. ***Emily Pearson Jack***, b. September 3, 1984; ***nfi.***

References: Correspondence with Sherri Jack 2, 1981, March 21, 1983, March June 10, 1985, July 1, 1987, and October 29, 1990.

554.

Debra Anne Nelson, daughter of Barbara (268), granddaughter of Leon (132), b. place not known, October 19, 1954; m. (1) place not known, June 6, 1974 Dennis Smelser, divorced; m. (2) place not known, February 12, 1983 William Bougher. Debra was employed as a dental hygienist in Tulsa, Oklahoma.

Children (by first marriage):

1120. I. ***Adam Smelser***, b. August 31, 1976; ***nfi.***

Children (by second marriage):

1121. I. ***Christina Noe Bougher***, b. February 26, 1984; ***nfi.***

References: 1990 correspondence from Sherri Nelson Jack.

557.

Catherine/Katherine/Kathryn Mary McIntyre, daughter of James (269), granddaughter of Sarah (134), b. New Castle, Pennsylvania September 23, 1920, d. St. Elizabeth's Hospital, Youngstown, Ohio March 21, 2004; m. place and date not known, Mr. Sandor. There is no further information on this Root descendant.

References: US Census: 1930, 1940; Ohio Death Record 1908-1932, 1938-2007; Social Security Death Index 1935-2014.

558.

Raymond J. McIntyre, son of James (269), grandson of Sarah (134), b. New Castle, Pennsylvania July 30, 1923; d. Ellwood City, Pennsylvania November 5, 2006; m. place not known, June 21, 1952 (undocumented) Elizabeth "Liz" P. Zona, b. Ellwood City, Pennsylvania August 28, 1921, d. Pittsburgh, Pennsylvania July 16, 2010.

Raymond McIntyre resided with his parents until his enlistment in the US Army. His World War II Draft Registration Card described him as being 6' 1" tall weighing 135 pounds with brown eyes and black hair. He served from February 26, 1943 to February 24, 1946. After the War Mr. McIntyre was employed by Johnson Bronze, New Castle, Pennsylvania and Precision Metal Products, Ellwood City, Pennsylvania. Raymond and Elizabeth McIntyre had three children, eight grandchildren, and 4 great-grandchildren at the time of Raymond McIntyre's death in 2006. Raymond J. McIntyre was buried in Holy Redeemer Cemetery, Ellwood City, Pennsylvania. It is believed Mrs. McIntyre was buried with her husband but this cannot be confirmed by current cemetery records. Further information is not currently available.

Children:

1122. I. ***Peggy McIntyre, nfi.***

1123. II. ***Rose McIntyre, nfi.***

1124. III. ***James McIntyre, nfi.***

References: US Census: 1930, 1940; Social Security Death Index 1935-2014; World War II Draft Registration Card, 1942; Pennsylvania Veterans Files 1950-1966; Holy Redeemer Cemetery records, Ellwood City, Pennsylvania.

559.

Sarah "Sally" Elizabeth McIntyre, daughter of James (269), granddaughter of Sarah (134), b. New Castle, Pennsylvania March 3, 1926, d. place not known, September 30, 2005; m. place and date not known, Mr. Maloney. There is currently little information about Sally McIntyre Maloney. Her obituary does not mention a husband; therefore, it was likely they divorced. She was buried in Beaver Cemetery, Beaver, Pennsylvania. Sally McIntyre was a twin with her sister Mary Ann McIntyre.

Children:

1125. I. ***Matthew Maloney***; married and residing in Beaver, Pennsylvania with two children: Devon and Ryan; ***nfi.***

1126. II. ***Karen Maloney***; married Chuck Huskey and resided in Baltimore. No children as of 2005; ***nfi.***

References: US Census: 1930, 1940; Social Security Death Index 1935-2014; Beaver Cemetery records, Beaver, Pennsylvania.

560.

Mary Ann McIntyre, daughter of James (269), granddaughter of Sarah (134), b. New Castle, Pennsylvania March 3, 1926. She was the twin sister of Sarah Elizabeth McIntyre. Mary Ann married Gus Anderson. Further information on this Root descendant is not currently available.

References: US Census: 1930, 1940.

561.

Onalee E. Tully, daughter of Lillian (271), granddaughter of John (135), b. Rochester, New York July 28, 1911, d. Kenmore, Washington November 8, 2005; m. Buffalo, New York October 3, 1934 Norman Lowenstein, b. Buffalo, New York August 10, 1910, d. Kenmore, Washington January 1, 2001.

Onalee Tully resided with her parents in Ceres, Pennsylvania in 1920. Later, she resided with her mother and step-father in Buffalo, New York. Before her marriage Onalee Tully worked for a dry-cleaning business in Buffalo. Norman Lowenstein was a truck driver in auto sales in 1930 and was later a salesman for Standard Brands in Buffalo, New York. They resided at 596 Northland Avenue, Buffalo, New York. It is not known when they moved to Washington State, but it is assumed it was to reside closer to their children and grandchildren. Onalee and Norman Lowenstein had three sons. They were buried in Sunset Hills Memorial Park, Bellevue, Washington.

Children:

1127. I. ***Thomas William Lowenstein***, b. Buffalo, New York July 20, 1935, d. Apex, North Carolina March 6, 2018; m. Washington, DC June 19, 1971 Helen Perun. Helen had a daughter from a previous marriage. Tom graduated from Spring Hill College, Mobile, Alabama. He joined the US Army as an officer. He was employed by the US Labor Department from 1965 to 1994. Tom was buried at Fairfax Memorial Park, Fairfax, Virginia.

Children:

i. ***Christopher Thomas Lowenstein; nfi.***

1128. II. ***James George Lowenstein***, b. Buffalo, New York April 14, 1937; m. (1) Seattle, Washington May 27, 1961 Leilani Nickholm, divorced October 2, 1972; m. (2) Seattle, Washington October 26, 1972 Linda K. Holm; ***nfi.***

1129. III. ***Michael Lowenstein***, b. Buffalo, New York January 28, 1942; d. Kirkland, Washington, January 27, 1997; ***nfi.***

References: US Census: 1920, 1930, 1940; New York State Census: 1915, 1925; New York State Marriage Index 1881-1967; Social Security Death Index 1935-2014; Washington State Death Index 1940-2014; Sunset Hill Memorial Park records, Bellevue, Washington; New York State Birth Index 1881-1942; Washington Marriage Records 1854-2013; Washington Divorce Index 1967-2017; *News and Observer* May 5-6, 2018 obituary for Thomas Lowenstein.

562.

Marie Leff, daughter of Lillian (271), granddaughter of John (135), b. Buffalo, New York July 27, 1921, d. place and date not known; m. (1) place and date not known, William F. Locher; m. (2) North Tonawanda, New York May 18, 1946 John P. Palisano. There is little information on this Root descendant.

In 1942 Marie Locher lived at 19 Halbert Street in Buffalo where her first husband was employed as a machine operator. It is not known she and William Locher divorced or if he died. It is not currently known if there were any children from either marriage.

References: US Census: 1930, 1940; New York State Census: 1925; New York State Birth Index 1881-1942; New York State Marriage Index 1881-1967 for Marie Leff's second marriage; Buffalo, New York City Directory, 1942.

563.

Weldon Ellsworth McDonald, son of Pearl (272), grandson of John (135), b. Shinglehouse, Pennsylvania October 22, 1912, d. Bradford, Pennsylvania January 5, 2000; m. Olean, New York August 31, 1937 (unsourced) Eloise Marguerite Jones, b. Hamburg, New York May 8, 1916, d. Bradford, Pennsylvania June 8, 1997.

Weldon McDonald resided with his parents until his marriage in Sharon, Potter County, Pennsylvania, Shinglehouse, Pennsylvania, and Roulette, Pennsylvania. His World War II Draft Registration Card described him as being 6' 1" tall, weighing 183 pounds with hazel eyes and red hair. He was a school teacher. Weldon and Eloise McDonald were buried in Maple Grove Cemetery, Shinglehouse, Pennsylvania.

Children:

1130. I. ***Wayne E. McDonald***, b. 1939; ***nfi.***

1131. II. ***Karen McDonald***, b. 1940; ***nfi.***

1132. III. ***Male McDonald; nfi.***

1133. IV. ***Male McDonald, nfi.***

1134. V. ***Male McDonald, nfi.***

References: US Census: 1920, 1930, 1940; Social Security Death Index 1935-2014; Maple Grove Cemetery records, Shinglehouse, Pennsylvania; World War II Draft Registration Card, 1940.

565.

Joyce M. McDonald, daughter of Pearl (272), granddaughter of John (135), b. Shinglehouse, Pennsylvania February 24, 1923, d. Richmond, Virginia December 17, 2009; m. place and date not known, Abraham M. Zwirnbaum, b. place not known, May 10, 1916, d. place not known, July 1, 2005. Little is known about this Root descendant. Abraham Zwirnbaum served with the US Army in World War II and in the Korean War rising to the rank of Major. Joyce and Abraham Zwirnbaum were buried in Arlington National Cemetery, Arlington, Virginia. It is not currently known if they had any children.

References: US Census: 1930, 1940, Social Security Death Index 1935-2014; Arlington National Cemetery, Arlington, Virginia.

566.

Karl Calvin Kellogg, son of Bert (273), grandson of John (135), b. Sunnyside, Potter County, Pennsylvania March 5, 1916, d. Shinglehouse, Pennsylvania August 9, 1988; m. Rixford, Pennsylvania May 2, 1939 (unsourced) Gladys M. Pratt, b. Prentisville, Pennsylvania January 15, 1921, d. Olean, New York December 14, 1997.

Karl Kellogg resided in Shinglehouse, Pennsylvania all of his life and with his parents until his marriage. His World War II Draft Registration Card described him as being 5' 9" tall, weighing 170 pounds with brown eyes and brown hair. It does not appear that he was called up to serve in World War II. In the 1940 US Census, Mr. Kellogg was employed as driller. He later worked for the railroads as he retired with a railroad pension. Karl and Gladys Kellogg had at least one child, a son, but it is not currently known if there were more children. Mr. and Mrs. Kellogg were buried in Maple Grove Cemetery, Shinglehouse, Pennsylvania.

Children:

1135. I. ***Calvin J. Kellogg***, b. Sunnyside, Pennsylvania June 6, 1941, d. Sunnyside, Pennsylvania April 1, 1960 and buried in Maple Grove Cemetery.

References: US Census: 1920, 1930, 1940; World War II Draft Registration Card, 1940; Social Security Death Index 1935-2014; Maple Grove Cemetery records, Shinglehouse, Pennsylvania.

567.

Ervin Glenn Kellogg, son of Bert (273), grandson of John (135), b. Shinglehouse, Pennsylvania August 13, 1977, d. Shinglehouse, Pennsylvania January 25, 1977; m. place and date not known, Grace L. Danforth, b. Myrtle, Pennsylvania May 19, 1914, d. Olean, New York March 12, 1968. Glenn resided with his parents until his marriage sometime after the 1940 US Census. His World War II Draft Registration Card described him as being 5' 6" tall, weighing 160 pounds with blue eyes and brown hair. In 1940 he worked for John Cunningham. He resided with his parents until marriage. Glenn and Grace Kellogg had seven children, four sons and three daughters, but the identity of only one daughter is currently known, Nancy Kay Kellogg who was born June 25, 1956 and died October 5, 1956. Mr. and Mrs. Kellogg were buried in Maple Grove Cemetery, Shinglehouse, Pennsylvania as was their daughter, Nancy.

References: US Census: 1920, 1930, 1940; Social Security Death Index 1935-2014; World War II Draft Registration Card, 1940; Maple Grove Cemetery records, Shinglehouse, Pennsylvania.

568

Perry Dene Kellogg, son of Bert (273), grandson of John (135), b. Shinglehouse, Pennsylvania March 31, 1919, d. Coudersport, Pennsylvania October 25, 2000, place and date not known, Gloria J. Danforth, b. Myrtle, Pennsylvania 1923, date and place of death not known. Gloria Danforth and her sister, Grace, married Kellogg brothers.

Perry's World War II Draft Registration Card described him as being 5' 9" tall, weighing 140 pounds with hazel eyes and brown hair. Perry and Gloria had four sons and four daughters but none of their identities are currently known. Perry and Gloria Kellogg were buried in Maple Grove Cemetery, Shinglehouse, Pennsylvania.

References: US Census: 1920, 1930, 1940; World War II Draft Registration Card, 1940; Social Security Death Index 1935-2014 for Perry Kellogg; Maple Grove Cemetery records, Shinglehouse, Pennsylvania.

569.

Gifford Clair Kellogg, son of Bert (273), grandson of John (135), b. Shinglehouse/Sunnyside, Pennsylvania October 25, 1920, d. Buffalo, New York May 27 1981; m. place and date not known, Effie Georgina McLeod, b. Canada September 6, 1921, d. place not known June 24, 2001.

Gifford Kellogg served with the US Army during World War II from January 5, 1943 to November 6, 1945. His World War II Draft Registration Card described him as being 6' tall, weighing 190 pounds with gray eyes and brown hair. After Gifford Kellogg's death, Effie remarried to Arthur Hamelin (1917-1982) and moved back to Canada, her birth place. Mr. Hamelin was a World War II veteran who served with the Royal Canadian Air Force. Arthur Hamelin was buried in Vasey United Cemetery, Vasey, Ontario, Canada. Gifford and Effie were buried in Maple Grove Cemetery, Shinglehouse, Pennsylvania. They have separate headstones, which are next to each other. Gifford and Effie Kellogg had four children: three daughters and one son. The identity of only one daughter is currently known.

Children:

1136. I. ***Male Kellogg, nfi.***

1137. II. ***Female Kellogg, nfi.***

1138. III. ***Female Gifford, nfi.***

1139. IV. ***Kim M. Kellogg***, b. Shinglehouse, Pennsylvania December 22, 1956, d. December 28, 1989; m. Mr. Anders and had children. She is buried in Maple Grove Cemetery, Shinglehouse.

References: US Census: 1930, 1940; World War II Draft Registration Card, 1942; Social Security Death Index 1935-2014; US Veterans Death File 1950-2010; Maple Grove Cemetery records, Shinglehouse, Pennsylvania; Vasey United Cemetery records, Vasey, Canada.

570.

Kingdon Albert Kellogg, son of Bert (273), grandson of John (135), b. Sunnyside, Pennsylvania July 4, 1921, d. Okinawa March 27, 1945/March 28, 1946. Kingdom Kellogg enlisted in the US Navy January 25, 1943. His World War II Draft Registration Card described him as being 5' 8" tall, weighing 160 pounds with blue eyes and blonde hair. At the time of his death in battle at Okinawa he was a Gunner's Mate, Third Class. He was posthumously awarded the Purple Heart. No remains have been found and Mr. Kellogg's name is listed on the *Tablets of the Missing in Action*, Honolulu.

References: US Census: 1930, 1940; World War II Draft Registration Card, 1940, US Navy Casualties 1776-1941; Pennsylvania Veterans Files World War II 1950-1966.

571.

Marjorie Dawn Kellogg, daughter of Bert (273), granddaughter of John (135), b. Shinglehouse, Pennsylvania March 27, 1925, d. Olean, New York April 27, 2011; m. Allegany, New York September 29, 1950 Raymond James Dieteman, b. Olean, New York December 19, 1924, d. Olean, New York July 27, 2013.

Raymond was a 1942 graduate of Allegany High School and served in the US Navy as a seaman during World War II. Mr. Dieteman worked for Dresser Industries for twenty-seven years retiring in 1984. After retirement he worked for McCoy's Hardware for eight years. Raymond Dieteman was a member of the Allegany, New York American Legion Post # 892 and enjoyed carpentry, fishing, and hunting. Raymond and Marjorie Dieteman were buried in St. Bonaventure Cemetery, Allegany, New York. They had grandchildren and great-grandchildren, but their identities are not currently known.

Children:

1140. I. ***Stephen J. Dieteman***; married and resides in Portville, New York; ***nfi.***

1141. II. ***Gregory K. Dieteman***; resides in Denver, Colorado; ***nfi.***

1142. III. ***Anthony A. Dieteman***; married and resides in Olean, New York; ***nfi.***

1143. IV. ***Michelle M. Dieteman***; married Mark Inman, deceased; resides in Olean, New York; ***nfi.***

References: US Census: 1930, 1940; New York State Census: 1925; Social Security Death Index 1935-2014; St. Bonaventure Cemetery records, Allegany, New York; *Olean Times-Herald*, July 30, 2013 obituary.

572.

Laurie Gene Kellogg, daughter of Bert (273), granddaughter of John (135), b. Sunnyside, Pennsylvania February 1928, d. place not known January 22, 1966. Laurie joined the US Armed Forces. Her World War II Draft Registration Card for 1946 described her as being 6' tall, weighing 150 pounds with brown eyes and black hair. She was buried in Maple Grove Cemetery, Shinglehouse, Pennsylvania.

References: US Census: 1930, 1940; World War II Draft Registration Card, 1946; Maple Grove Cemetery records, Shinglehouse, Pennsylvania.

573.

Alice E. Kellogg, daughter of Bert (273), granddaughter of John (135), b. Olean, New York June 19, 1932; m. Hinsdale, New York May 8, 1954 Walter Charles Frost, b. Cuba, New York March 12, 1930, d. Portville, New York April 1994. Little is known about Alice Kellogg. Walter Frost served in the US Army from February 20, 1951 to February 5, 1953. It is not currently known if they had any children. Walter Frost was buried in Cuba Cemetery, Cuba, New York.

References: US Census: 1940; New York State Birth Index 1881-1942; New York State Marriage Index 1881-1967; US Veterans Death Files 1850-2010; Social Security Death Index 1935-2014; Cuba Cemetery records, Cuba, New York.

574.

John Richard Kellogg, son of Bert (273), grandson of John (135), b. Sunnyside, Pennsylvania April 29, 1936, d. Olean, New York May 1, 2000. Known as *Dick* to family and friends, Mr. Kellogg served with the US Army during peacetime. There is no further information about this Root descendant. He was buried in Maple Grove Cemetery, Shinglehouse, Pennsylvania.

References: US Census: 1940; Social Security Death Index 1935-2014; Maple Grove Cemetery records, Shinglehouse, Pennsylvania.

575.

James P. Kellogg, Sr., son of Cecil (274), grandson of John (135), b. Bell Run, Pennsylvania May 24, 1920, d. Olean, New York June 7, 2008; m. Port Allegany, Pennsylvania June 4, 1941, Margaret L. Peterson, b. Burtville, Pennsylvania March 18, 1924, d. Bradford, Pennsylvania April 11, 2013.

James Kellogg resided with his parents in Ceres, Pennsylvania until his 1941 marriage. Mr. Kellogg's World War II Draft Registration Card described him as being 5' 6" tall and weighed 134 pounds. He served in the US Navy during World War II from January 21, 1943 to January 21, 1945 in the Aleutian Islands rising to the rank of Vet Tech 4. Mr. Kellogg resided most of his life in Shinglehouse, Pennsylvania where he owned and operated a well service business. He also worked for Flannigan Brothers Drilling Company as a tool pusher and retired from Air Preheater Corporation in Wellsville, New York in 1983 after nineteen years of employment as a quality control inspector.

James and Margaret Kellogg were members of the Portville Baptist Church, Portville, New York. He enjoyed hunting. Margaret was employed by the former Wilson's Fruit Market, Portville, New York, Viko Furniture Company, Eldred, Pennsylvania, and the Acme Electric Company, Allegany, New York. She was a nurse's aide at St. Elizabeth's Motherhouse, Allegany, New York. At the time of his death James Kellogg was survived by three children, eight grandchildren, and 15 great-grandchildren. When Margaret died, she was survived by eight grand-children, 19 great-grandchildren, and seven great-great grandchildren. James and Margaret Kellogg were buried in Bell Run Cemetery, McKean County, Pennsylvania.

Children:

1144. I. ***James P. Kellogg, Jr.***; married and resided in Shinglehouse, Pennsylvania; ***nfi.***

1145. II. ***Robert Jack Kellogg***, b. Olean, New York August 7, 1945, d. Buffalo, New York March 9, 1961 in a tragic accident and buried in Bell Run Cemetery, McKean County, Pennsylvania.

1146. III. ***Gregory D. Kellogg***; married and resided in Fredonia, New York; ***nfi.***

1147. IV. ***Gale T. Kellogg***; m. and resided in Bradford, Pennsylvania; ***nfi.***

References: US Census: 1930, 1940; Social Security Death Index 1935-2014; Bell Run Cemetery records, McKean County, Pennsylvania; Pennsylvania Veteran Files 1950-1966; World War II Draft Registration Card, 1942; *Olean Times-Herald*, June 8, 2008 obituary for James P. Kellogg; New York State Death Index 1957-68 for Robert Jack Kellogg; *Olean Times-Herald*, April 13, 2013 obituary for Margaret Peterson Kellogg.

576.

Robert Earl Kellogg, son of Cecil (274), grandson of John (135), b. Lewis Run, Pennsylvania, February 5, 1922, d. Olean General Hospital, Olean, New York April 16, 1989 from a heart attack suffered at his home; m. Shinglehouse, Pennsylvania October 22, 1949 Marie Lou Wilson, b. Bolivar, New York January 28, 1930, d. Shinglehouse, Pennsylvania December 18, 1997.

Robert Kellogg resided with his parents until his enlistment in the US Army during World War II. His Draft Registration Card described him as being 5' 8" tall, weighing 155 pounds, with blue eyes and brown hair. He served from November 30, 1942 to December 15, 1945 with the 104th Timber Wolf Division. Mr. Kellogg was a gas well driller for Flannigan Brothers in Bradford, Pennsylvania. He was a member of the American Legion Post # 530, Shinglehouse, Pennsylvania and the Oswayo Rod and Gun Club, Millport, Pennsylvania. He was survived by two children and four grandchildren. Robert and Marie Kellogg were buried in Bell Run Cemetery, McKean County, Pennsylvania.

Children:

1148. I. ***Marlin L. Kellogg***; married and resided in Shinglehouse, Pennsylvania; ***nfi.***

1149. II. ***Dianna L. Kellogg***; married to a Mr. Frost, resided in Shinglehouse, Pennsylvania; ***nfi.***

References: US Census: 1930, 1940; Social Security Death Index 1935-2014; Bell Run Cemetery records, McKean County, Pennsylvania; World War II Draft Registration Card, 1942; US Veterans Death Files 1850-2010; New York State Birth Index 1881-1942 for Marie Lou Wilson; New York State Marriage Index 1881-1967; *Olean Times-Herald* obituary April 18, 1989.

577.

Muriel Estella/Stella Kellogg, daughter of Cecil (274), granddaughter of John (135), b. Bells Run, Pennsylvania January 7, 1924, d. Pennsylvania, June 24, 1994; m. Mr. Montgomery a. 1975. Little is known about this Root descendant. She resided with her parents based on the 1930 and 1940 US Census records. The Social Security Administration notes a last name change to Montgomery in 1975. There is currently no information about her marriage or if there were any children. Muriel Montgomery was buried in Bell Run Cemetery, McKean County, Pennsylvania.

References: US Census: 1930, 1940; Social Security Administration Records 1935-2014; Bell Run Cemetery records, McKean County, Pennsylvania.

578.

Donald Lou Kellogg, son of Cecil (274), grandson of John (135), b. Bells Run, Pennsylvania October 20, 1929, still living; m. place and date not known, Cecile Marie Dick. There is currently little known about this Root descendant other than he resides in East Sparta, Ohio, married and had children. Documented details on his marriage and children are not currently available.

References: US Census: 1930, 1940; obituaries of siblings for residence location.

579.

Helen Jean Kellogg, son of Cecil (274), grandson of John (135), b. Shinglehouse, Pennsylvania July 9, 1931, d. Sunnyside, Potter County, Pennsylvania December 9, 2006; m. Allegany, New York, September 2, 1947 Leo Earl Carpenter, b. Olean, New York September 28, 1926, d. Shinglehouse, Pennsylvania September 16, 1984. Leo Carpenter's World War II Draft Registration Card described him as being 5' 9" tall, weighing 165 pounds with brown eyes and black hair. He served with the US Marines during World War II from December 27, 1944 to July 5, 1946. Mr. Carpenter was wounded in action. Helen and Leo Carpenter lived in Shinglehouse, Pennsylvania most of their lives and were buried in Maple Grove Cemetery, Shinglehouse, Pennsylvania.

Children:

1150. I. ***Christine Carpenter, nfi.***

1151. II. ***Julie Carpenter, nfi.***

1152. III. ***Duane J. "Captain" Carpenter***, b. Shinglehouse, Pennsylvania July 17, 1955, d. Pittsburg, Pennsylvania August 14, 2005; m. Elizabeth A. Long; had children; and was buried in Maple Grove Cemetery, Shinglehouse, Pennsylvania.

1153. IV. ***Dennis E. "Carpy" Carpenter***, a twin with Duane Carpenter, b. Shinglehouse, Pennsylvania July 17, 1955; ***nfi.***

1154. V. ***Randy Carpenter, nfi.***

References: US Census: 1930, 1940; New York State Marriage Index 1881-1967; Social Security Death Index 1935-2014; World War II Draft Registration Card, 1942; US Veterans Death File 1850-2010; Maple Grove Cemetery records, Shinglehouse, Pennsylvania.

580.

Thomas John Kellogg, son of Cecil (274), grandson of John (135), b. Shinglehouse, Pennsylvania August 9, 1936, d. Olean General Hospital, Olean, New York September 28, 2010; m. Pikeville, New York December 24, 1958, Charlotte Maria Dickerson, b. Alma, New York September 22, 1922, d. Allegany, New York June 21, 2013. Thomas and Charlotte Kellogg were longtime residents of Shinglehouse, Pennsylvania. They did not have any children and were buried in Bell Run Cemetery, McKean County, Pennsylvania.

References: US Census: 1930, 1940; Social Security Death Index 1935-2014; Bell Run Cemetery records, McKean County, Pennsylvania; *Potter Leader Enterprise* October 7-13, 2010 for obituary of Thomas Kellogg.

582.

Carl Maynard Kellogg, son of Kenneth (275), grandson of John (135), b. Johnson City, New York June 21, 1921, d. Harrisburg, Pennsylvania December 28, 1965; m. place and date not known, Margaret Rossman, b. Spring, Pennsylvania a. 1926; d. still living in 2017. Mr. Kellogg's World War II Draft Registration Card described him as being 5' 10" tall, weighing 150 pounds with brown eyes and black hair. It does not appear that he served. He died of renal failure. Carl Kellogg was buried in Union Cemetery, Bellefonte, Pennsylvania.

Children:

1155. I. ***Gary Kenneth Kellogg***, b. Bellefonte, Pennsylvania October 31, 1945, d. State College, Pennsylvania September 8, 2017; m. Jerie Schreffler. Gary was employed by and retired from Cerro Metal. He was a life member of the Faith United Methodist Church. Gary served in the US Army Reserves where he was recognized as a M14 Sharpshooter. He was a member of the Pleasant Gap Legion, the 4 X 4 Sportsman Club, and was an avid baseball fan, golfer, hunter, and bowler. In 1958 Gary Kellogg was a member of the Bellefonte Little LeagueTeam that won the State Championship and the Babe Ruth State Championship Team in 1961. Gary Kellogg was buried in Zion Cemetery, Zion, Pennsylvania.

Children:

i. ***Jeffrey Kellogg***; m. Donna, last name not known. They have two daughters: Madison and Mackenzie.

1156. II. ***Susan Kellogg***; m. Robert Kersavage; ***nfi.***

1157. III. ***Michael Kellogg, nfi.***

References: US Census: 1930, 1940; New York State Census: 1925; Social Security Death Index 1935-2014; World War II Draft Registration Card, 1940; Union Cemetery records, Bellefonte, Pennsylvania; Findagrave.com obituary for Garry Kellogg.

583.

Jean Eileen Kellogg, daughter of Kenneth (275), granddaughter of John (135), b. Johnson City, New York January 11, 1924, d. place not known, November 18, 1990; m. a. 1954 Walter F. Burpo, b. Mt. Kiso, New York October 17, 1925, d. Bellefonte, Pennsylvania January 6, 2010. Walter Burpo enlisted in the New York State Guard August 2, 1943. Further information on this Root descendant and her husband is not currently available. It is not known if they had any children or where they are buried.

References: US Census: 1930, 1940; New York State Census: 1925; Social Security Death Index 1935-2014 for Walter Burpo; Social Security Claims Index 1936-2007 for Jean Kellogg's name change to Burpo; New York Guard Service Index 1940-48.

584.

Mildred S. Swift, daughter of Marie (277), granddaughter of John (135), b. Rixford, Pennsylvania February 21, 1931; m. Olean, New York May 12, 1951 Wilbur Russell Hurd, b. place not known, September 13, 1929, d. place not known, February 9, 2001. Little is known about this Root descendant and her husband. It is not currently known if there were any children. Wilbur R. Hurd was buried in Maple Grove Cemetery, Shinglehouse, Pennsylvania.

References: US Census: 1940; New York State Birth Index 1881-1942; New York State Marriage Index 1881-1967; Maple Grove Cemetery records, Shinglehouse, Pennsylvania.

585.

Thelma Mae Swift, daughter of Marie (277), granddaughter of John (135), b. Rixford, Pennsylvania June 7, 1932, d. Rexburg, Idaho June 12, 2005; m. (1) place and date not known Charles David Colley, Jr., b. Allegany, New York June 27, 1926, d. Titusville, Pennsylvania September 23, 1999, divorced April 1953; m. (2) Olean, New York May 9, 1953 Robert Eugene Soules, b. Pennsylvania June 22, 1930, d. place not known, December 10, 1992.

Thelma's first husband served in the US Navy in World War II from November 16, 1943 to April 6, 1946. The circumstances of their marriage are unclear, but they divorced after the birth of a son. Charles Colley was buried in Hinsdale Cemetery, Hinsdale, New York. Robert Eugene Soules also served with the US Navy from June 4, 1948 to March 1, 1951. Thelma's obituary recorded that she was raised by her paternal grandparents although her parents were alive. She was engaged to Robert Soules in 1950 based on a newspaper account in the Portville, New York newspaper. However, their marriage came about in 1953. Thelma had two sons and two daughters with her second husband. Thelma and Robert Soules were buried in Fort Logan National Cemetery, Denver, Colorado.

Children (by first marriage):

1158. I. ***Male Colley, nfi.***

Children (by second marriage):

1159. I. ***John Soules, nfi.***

1160. II. ***Christy Soules, nfi.***

1161. III. ***Pam Soules, nfi.***

1162. IV. ***Sylas William Soules***, b. Arvada, Colorado August 28, 1965, d. Utah April 2, 2013; St. George, Utah April 27, 2007 Michele Sue Naylor. Sylas attended Algonquin College where he earned an Associate's Degree. He briefly served in the US Navy. Sylas was an accomplished machinist and was employed by Zimmer Metals in Colorado and later in Utah Lindon Precision and Star Foundry and Machine. Sylas Soules was a member of the Church of Jesus Christ Latter-Day Saints and served as an Elders Quorum President in Nebraska. He had four children and six grandchildren. Sylas Soules was buried at Camp Williams Cemetery, Bluffdale, Utah.

References: US Census: 1940; Social Security Death Index 1935-2014; US Veterans Death Files 1850-2010 for both Charles Colley and Robert Soules; Fort Logan National Cemetery records, Denver, Colorado; Hinsdale Cemetery Hinsdale, New York; New York Marriage Index 1881-1967 for Thelma's marriage to Robert Soules; Walker Funeral Home obituary April 2013.

587.

Donald J. Swift, son of Marie (277), grandson of John (135), b. Rixford, Pennsylvania November 5, 1935, d. Bradford, Pennsylvania October 25, 2012.

Donald Swift owned and operated Donald Swift Trucking. He enjoyed hunting and fishing. His obituary indicated that he was married, but apparently divorced, lived with Marilyn R. Skillman, and had children and grandchildren, but no names were identified. Donald Swift was buried in Maple Grove Cemetery, Shinglehouse, Pennsylvania.

References: US Census: 1940; Social Security Death Index 1935-2014; *Bradford Era*, October 27-November 5, 2012 obituary for Donald Swift.

589.

Gertrude Oletha Russell, daughter of Sarah (278), granddaughter of Willis (138), b. Byrnedale, Pennsylvania December 13, 1914, d. Tonawanda, New York December 2008; m. Allegany, New York November 10, 1934 Gerald Francis Gardner, b. Elk County, Pennsylvania December 22 1911, d. Tonawanda, New York April 25, 2002.

Gertrude resided with her parents in Jay, Pennsylvania until her marriage and continued to reside in Jay until they moved to Tonawanda in 1943. Gerald Gardner's World War II Draft Registration Card described him as being 5' 7" tall, weighing 140 pounds with gray eyes and brown hair. As a young man Mr. Gardner was a promising amateur boxer, but gave up the sport at the request of his wife. He enjoyed hunting and fishing and was a member of St. Francis of Assisi Parish, the Holy Name Society, and the Forever Young Group. In 1985 Mr. Gardner received the St. Joseph the Worker Award from the Diocese of Buffalo. Gerald Gardner was employed for over thirty years with the Columbus McKinnon Corporation in Tonawanda. It is not currently known where Gertrude and Gerald Gardner were buried. They had eleven grandchildren, at least 19 great-grandchildren, and great-great grandchildren.

Children:

1163. I. ***Allan Gardner***; married and resided in Tonawanda, New York, ***nfi.***

1164. II. ***Gerald E. Gardner***; resided in Pennsylvania; ***nfi.***

1165. III. ***John Gardner***; married and resided in North Tonawanda, New York; ***nfi.***

1166. IV. ***Carol Gardner***; m. Harold Nelson and resided in Lewiston, New York; ***nfi.***

References: US Census: 1920, 1930, 1940; New York State Marriage Index 1881-1967; Social Security Death Index 1935-2014; World War II Draft Registration Card, 1940; *Niagara-Gazette* obituaries for Gerald F. Gardner April 27, 2002 and January 6, 2009 for Gertrude Gardner.

590.

Martha Allene Russell, daughter of Sarah (278), granddaughter of Willis (138), b. Byrnedale, Pennsylvania November 12, 1917, d. St. Mary's, Pennsylvania June 27, 2003; m. place and date not known, Edward Andrew Thompson, b. Emporium, Pennsylvania September 8, 1914, d. St. Mary's January 12, 1995. Known as Allene to family and friends she resided with her parents until her marriage. Edward Thompson's World War II Draft Registration Card described him as being 5' 11" tall, weighing 165 pounds with blue eyes and brown hair. It does not appear that he served in the military in World War II. Allene and Edward Thompson resided most of their lives in St. Mary's, Pennsylvania and were buried in St. Mary's Cemetery.

Children:

1167. I. ***Patricia Thompson, nfi.***

1168. II. ***Edward Thompson***, b. and d. December 12, 1941 and buried in St. Mary's Cemetery, St. Mary's, Pennsylvania. He was a stillbirth.

1169. III. ***Mary Kay Thompson, nfi.***

References: US Census: 1920, 1930, 1940; St. Mary's Cemetery records, St. Mary's, Pennsylvania; World War II Draft Registration Card, 1940; Pennsylvania Death Certificate 1906-1967 for Edward Thompson (son).

591.

George William Russell, son of Sarah (278), grandson of Willis (138), b. Byrnedale, Pennsylvania February 10, 1918, d. Olean, New York June 8, 2012; m. Olean, New York June 14, 1947 Dorothy V. Paugh; b. Kane, Pennsylvania January 20, 1920, d. Olean, New York December 1, 1996.

George Russell's World War II Draft Registration Card described him as being 5' 10" tall, weighing 145 pounds with hazel eyes and brown hair. In the 1950s he was employed as a barber in Olean, New York with Estes Barber Shop. Dorothy Paugh Russell was employed as a winder in a factory prior to her marriage. George and Dorothy Russell were buried in St. Bonaventure Cemetery, Allegany, New York.

Children:

1170. I. ***Kathy/Kathryn Marie Russell, nfi.***

1171. II. ***Jamie/Jannie Russell***; m. Olean, New York May 29, 1965 Ralph E. Gorton; ***nfi.***

References: US Census: 1920, 1930, 1940; Social Security Death Index 1935-2014; World War II Draft Registration Card, 1940; St. Bonaventure Cemetery records, Allegany, New York; US Obituary Collection 1930-present for wedding date; Social Security Claims Index 1936-2007 for birthplace of Dorothy Russell; Olean, New York City Directories 1953, 1954; New York State Marriage Index 1881-1967 for Jamie Russell.

592.

Lucille Marie Russell, daughter of Sarah (278), granddaughter of Willis (138), b. Byrnedale, Pennsylvania July 19, 1920, d. Emporium, Pennsylvania August 23, 1976; m. place and date not known, Kenneth Joseph Miglicio, b. Austin, Pennsylvania December 14, 1915, d. St. Mary's, Pennsylvania May 12, 1997. Little is currently known about this Root descendant. Kenneth Miglicio's World War II Draft Registration Card described him as being 5' 6" tall, weighing 135 pounds with brown eyes and blonde hair. They were buried in St. Mary's Cemetery, St. Mary's, Pennsylvania. It is not currently known if they had any children.

References: US Census: 1920, 1930, 1940; Social Security Death Index 1935-2014; World War II Draft Registration Card, 1940; St. Mary's Cemetery records, St. Mary's, Pennsylvania.

594.

Rita Mae Russell, daughter of Sarah (278), granddaughter of Willis (138), b. Byrnedale, Pennsylvania September 10, 1923, d. Olean, New York January 30, 1987; m. Olean, New York May 27, 1948 Anthony Robert Ross, b. Olean, New York July 30, 1921, d. Olean, New York December 25, 2016.

Little information is currently available about Rita Russell Ross. However, her husband worked for Curtis Aircraft Company, Buffalo, New York until he enlisted in the US Army Air Corps where he served as a pilot in the Pacific Theater and flew B-25 Bombers. He left military service with the rank of Captain. Mr. Ross worked from 1948 to 1986 for Clark Brothers, later Dresser-Rand, in Olean, New York. He was a member of St. Mary of the Angels Church, the American Legion, Veterans of Foreign Wars, and the American Society of Mechanical Engineers, all in Olean, New York. Anthony Ross enjoyed radio-controlled model airplanes and horse racing. After the death of Rita Russell, he remarried to Marilyn F. Teachman who died October 6, 2016. Rita and Anthony Ross were buried in St. Bonaventure Cemetery, Allegany, New York. They had two grandchildren, three great-grandchildren, and five great-great grandchildren.

Children:

1172. I. ***Gary Ross***; married and resided in Napoli, New York; ***nfi.***

1173. II. ***Linda M. Ross***; m. William Foster and resided in Allegany, New York; ***nfi.***

References: US Census: 1930, 1940; St. Bonaventure Cemetery records, Allegany, New York; Social Security Death Index 1935-2014; *Olean Times-Herald*, December 27, 2016 obituary for Anthony Ross.

595.

Christine Rosella Russell, daughter of Sarah (278), granddaughter of Willis (138), b. Weedsville, Pennsylvania March 29, 1925, d. Butler, Pennsylvania June 6, 2006; m. place not known, a. 1958, William Thomas Ayres, b. Melfa, Virginia July 5, 1923, d. Duval, Florida January 1, 1986. Little is known about this Root descendant. Her husband's World War II Draft Registration Card described William Ayres as being 5' 7" tall, weighing 148 pounds with blue eyes and brown hair. He served in the US Air Force from August 9, 1945 to October 2, 1946. Social Security records indicate that Christine Russell's last name was changed to Ayres in 1958. For a time, they resided in Glen Burnie, Maryland and Florida. An undocumented source indicated they had one son. Christine and William Ayres were buried in Fairview Cemetery, Onancock, Virginia.

References: US Census: 1930, 1940; Social Security Death Index 1935-2014; World War II Draft Registration Card, 1942; US Veterans Death File 1850-2010. Fairview Cemetery records, Onancock, Virginia; Social Security Claims Index 1935-2007; Virginia Birth Records 1912-2016 for William Ayres.

596.

Eleanor A. Russell, daughter of Sarah (278), granddaughter of Willis (138), b. Byrnedale, Pennsylvania March 15, 1926, d. Emporium, Pennsylvania August 3, 2012; m. (1) place and date not known, James Clarence Everingham, b. Selinsgrove, Pennsylvania March 9, 1926, d. Mahoning, Pennsylvania March

9, 1958 from congestive heart failure, diabetes, and hypertension; (2) place and date not known John E. Pearson, b. place not known, November 25, 1928, d. place not known, June 2, 1974. James Everingham's World War II Draft Registration Card described him as being 5' 7" tall, weighing 140 pounds with blue eyes and brown hair.

Eleanor was a talented seamstress and worked at the family business, Pearson's Dry Cleaning, Emporium, Pennsylvania. She enjoyed quilting as well. Eleanor Pearson was survived by one child, two grandchildren, and four great-grandchildren. Eleanor and John Pearson were buried in Newton Cemetery, Emporium, Pennsylvania. James Everingham was buried in Witmer's Memorial Cemetery, Fort Trevorton, Pennsylvania.

Children (by first marriage):

1174. I. ***Diane Everingham, nfi.***

References: US Census: 1930, 1940; Newton Cemetery, Emporium, Pennsylvania; Witmer's Memorial Cemetery, Fort Trevorton, Pennsylvania; World War II Draft Registration Card, 1944 for James Everingham; Pennsylvania Death Records 1906-1967 for James Everingham; Barnett Funeral Home records, Emporium, Pennsylvania for Eleanor Pearson.

597.

David Gerald Russell, son of Sarah (278), grandson of Willis (138), b. Byrnedale, Pennsylvania September 16, 1927, d. South Dayton, New York November 21, 1978. David Russell served in the US Military from February 15, 1946 to August 14, 1947. He last resided in Angola, New York. It is believed he was married and had at least one child because his tombstone has *Beloved Father* written on it. The identities of his wife and any children are not currently known. Mr. Russell was buried in Villenouva Cemetery, Balcom Corners, New York.

References: US Census: 1930, 1940; Social Security Death Index 1935-2014; US Veterans Death Files 1850-2010; Villenouva Cemetery records, Balcom Corners, New York.

598.

Anita Catherine Russell, daughter of Sarah (278), granddaughter of Willis (138), b. probably Byrnedale, Pennsylvania January 28, 1930, still living; m. Olean, New York June 4, 1950 Howard Alvine Bowersox, b. Olean, New York August 25, 1927, d. Rochester, New York October 11, 2001. Al was employed as a former warehouse manager for Curtis Burns in Leicester, New York. He also operated a lawn service and resided with his wife, Anita, and family in York, New York. Mr. Bowersox was a member of the Geneseo Masonic Lodge # 214, the Order of the Eastern Star, Geneseo Chapter, and the Mt. Morris Rotary Club. He served with the US Army during World War II. Al Bowersox was buried in Pleasant Valley Cemetery, Piffard, New York. At the time of Al's death, he and Anita had seven grandchildren.

Children;

1175. I. ***Roger Bowersox***; resided Athens, Georgia; ***nfi.***

1176. II. ***Nita Rae Bowersox***; married William Hawkins, resided Piffard, New York; ***nfi.***

1177. III. ***Howard G. Bowersox***, b. New York State July 15, 1955, d. Rochester, New York August 16, 1975 and buried Pleasant Valley Cemetery with his father.

1178. IV. ***Deborah Kae Bowersox***; m. Charles Kruger, resided Conesus, New York; ***nfi.***

1179. V. ***Rebecca Bowersox***; m. Timothy Minnich, resided York, New York; ***nfi.***

1180. VI. ***Cathy Bowersox***; m. Dean Olsowsky, resided Leicester, New York; ***nfi.***

References: US Census: 1930, 1940; New York State Birth Index 1881-1942 for Howard A. Bowersox; New York State Marriage Index 1881-1967; Pleasant Valley Cemetery records, Piffard, New York; *Clarion Publications*, Geneseo, New York for October 18, 2001 obituary of Howard Bowersox.

599.

Helen C. Torrey, daughter of Gladys (281), granddaughter of Loyal (140), b. Millport, Pennsylvania September 29, 1929, d. Portville, New York June 5, 2017; m Eldred, Pennsylvania November 18, 1951 William R. Miller, b. Shinglehouse, Pennsylvania April 8, 1930, d. Portville, New York May 27, 1997.

Helen was employed at Fibercell Corporation, Brand Names, and BJs. She attended Portville Baptist Church, was a member of the Ladies Auxiliary of the Portville Fire Department, and a volunteer for Meals on Wheels. In 2010 she was chosen Volunteer of the Year by the Retired Senior Volunteer Program. William Miller served in the US Army from January 31, 1952 to January 8, 1954 during the Korean War rising to the rank of Corporal. Helen and William Miller were buried in Chestnut Hill Cemetery, Portville, New York. At the time of Helen's death, she had five grandchildren and five great-grandchildren.

Children:

1181. I. ***Linda Miller***; married a Mr. Cook, is a Doctor, and resides in Pasadena, Maryland; ***nfi.***

1182. II. ***Kathy Miller***; resided in Portville, New York; ***nfi.***

1183. III. ***Robert Miller***; resided Rixford, Pennsylvania; ***nfi.***

1184. IV. ***Thomas Miller***; married and resided in Portville, New York; ***nfi.***

1185. V. ***Larry Miller***; resided Portville, New York; ***nfi.***

References: US Census: 1930, 1940; Social Security Death Index 1935-2014; US Veterans Death Files 1850-2010; Chestnut Hill Cemetery records, Portville, New York; *Olean Times-Herald* June 7, 2017 obituary.

600.

Lewis LaVerne Torrey, son of Gladys (281), grandson of Loyal (140), b. McLean, New York July 23, 1935, d. Tonawanda, New York February 18, 2008 from lung cancer; m. place not known, a. 1958, JoAnn Parmeter, b. Olean, New York February 4, 1936, d. Tonawanda, New York November 20, 2006.

Mr. Torrey was the co-founder and lifetime member of PAC, Tonawanda Moose Lodge # 2163, and the Antique Boat Club. He enjoyed woodworking and restoring his wooden boat and rowboat. Lewis Torrey was a welder and retired from Bell Aerospace. At the time of his death, his son, Jeffrey had died, and he was survived by three children and three grandchildren. Lewis and JoAnn Torrey were buried in Acacia Park Cemetery, North Tonawanda, New York.

Children:

1186. I. ***Cathy Jo Torrey***; married Terry Miller, two children: Trevor and Keith, and resided Albion, New York; ***nfi.***

1187. II. ***Cindy Ann Torrey***; resided St. Petersburg, Florida; ***nfi.***

1188. III. ***Gerald Torrey***; resided St. Petersburg, Florida; ***nfi.***

1189. IV. ***Jeffrey Torrey***, b. 1962, d. 2005; married, deceased, resided Tonawanda, New York, one son, Steven. Mr. Torrey was buried in Acacia Park Cemetery; ***nfi.***

References: US Census: 1940; Social Security Death Index 1935-2014; New York State Birth Index 1881-1942; *Niagara Gazette*, February 19, 2008 obituary of Lewis Torrey; Social Security Claims Index 1936-2007 for JoAnn Parmeter's name change; Acacia Park Cemetery records, North Tonawanda, New York.

602.

Walter Lee Jandrew, son of Pauline (282), grandson of Loyal (140), b. Bolivar, New York May 10,1930, d. Ocala, Florida March 27, 2010; m. Duke Center, Pennsylvania August 28, 1951, Rosenia M. Sprague, b. Pennsylvania November 16, 1932, still living.

Walter Jandrew served in the US Army during the Korean War rising to the rank of Sergeant. For a time, Mr. Jandrew resided in the communities of Bolivar, Allentown, Shinglehouse, and Olean, all in New York State before moving to Horseheads, New York where he was employed with the New York State Department of Transportation. He retired as Highway Superintendent. Mr. and Mrs. Jandrew spent part of each year in Horseheads and in Ocala, Florida. Mr. Jandrew was a member of the Masonic Lodge, Olean, New York, the United Methodist Church, Ocala, Florida and the Chemung United Methodist Church, Chemung, New York. Walter Lee Jandrew was buried in Woodlawn Cemetery, Elmira, New York. In addition to his children Walt Jandrew was survived by twelve grandchildren and eleven great-grandchildren.

Children:

1190. I. ***Robert Jandrew***; married and resided in Shenandoah, Iowa; ***nfi.***

1191. II. ***Ricky Jandrew***; resided in Millerton, Pennsylvania; ***nfi.***

1192. III. ***Dixie Jandrew***; married Jerry Disney, resided Millerton, Pennsylvania; ***nfi.***

1193. IV. ***Penny Jandrew***; married Vince Taylor, resided Chesapeake, Virginia; ***nfi.***

References: US Census: 1930, 1940; New York State Birth Index 1881-1942; Social Security Death Index 1935-2014; *Bolivar Breeze 1891-1965*, August 30, 1951 for wedding; *Star Gazette* March 29, 2010 obituary for Walter Jandrew; Olean, New York City Directories, selected issues; Woodlawn Cemetery records, Elmira, New York.

603.

Barbara L. Beebe, daughter of Marshall (284), granddaughter of Bertha (141), b. Scio, New York January 31, 1920, d. Olean, New York May 25, 1994; m. Olean, New York September 2, 1939 Carl C. Veno, b. Olean, New York January 21, 1917, d. Olean, New York February 2, 2007. Barbara and Carl Veno were buried in St. Bonaventure Cemetery, Allegany, New York.

Children:

1194. I. ***Salvatore Veno***; married and resided in Olean, New York; ***nfi.***

1195. II. ***Kathleen M. Veno***, b. Olean, New York September 29, 1943, d. Allegany, New York March 19, 2018; m. February 10, 1962 Wilbur L. Frost. She was a member of the Jesus Christ Church of Latter-Day Saints. Kathleen enjoyed going fishing and camping, playing cards, and worshipping the Lord. She was survived by three children: Richard Frost of Olean, New York; Sharon Frost Simon of Gadsden, Alabama, and Carla Frost Budaj of Olean, thirteen grandchildren, 19 great-grandchildren.

1196. III. ***David Veno***; married, resided Weston Mills, New York; ***nfi.***

1197. IV. ***Carl Veno***; married, resided Olean, New York; ***nfi.***

References: US Census: 1920, 1930, 1940; New York State Census: 1925; New York State Birth Index 1881-1942; New York State Marriage Index 1881-1967; Social Security Death Index 1935-2014; St. Bonaventure Cemetery records, Allegany, New York; Letro / McIntosh / Spink Funeral Home obituary, March 2018.

605.

Marjorie C. Beebe, daughter of Marshall (284), granddaughter of Bertha (141), b. Wellsville, New York December 25, 1925, d. place of death and date of death not known; m. (1) Belmont, New York March 23, 1945 Thomas Frank Baker, b. Angelica, New York September 15, 1920, d. Greenwich, Ohio December 16, 1992, divorced; m. (2) Alfred, New York March 23, 1957 Lawrence A. Weinhauer. There is currently no further information on this Root descendant. Thomas Baker moved to Ohio in the early 1950s. It is not known if he and Marjorie had divorced by the time of his move. Mr. Baker remarried and had five children. He was buried in Greenwich Greenlawn Cemetery, Greenwich, Ohio.

References: US Census: 1930, 1940; New York State Birth Index 1881-1942 for Marjorie Beebe and Thomas Baker; New York State Marriage Index 1881-1967 for both marriages; *Olean Times-Herald* March 26, 1945 for Beebe/Baker marriage; Greenwich Greenlawn Cemetery records, Greenwich, Ohio; Greenwich newspaper obituary for Thomas F. Baker.

606.

Bruce Marshall Beebe, son of Marshall (284), grandson of Bertha (141), b. Wellsville, New York June 1, 1935, d. Friendship, New York August 30, 1998; m. Miami, Ohio December 8, 1956 Beverly Kay Gladman, b. Ohio, 1938, d. Ohio 1974.

Marshall Beebe served with the US Army in Korea rising to the rank of SP 2. He was buried in Fairview Cemetery, Scio, New York. Further information on this Root descendant is not currently available.

References: US Census: 1940; New York State Birth Index 1881-1942; Ohio County Marriage Records 1774-1993; Fairview Cemetery records, Scio, New York; Riverdale Cemetery records, Troy, Ohio for Beverly Gladman.

615.

Carol Ann Pfromm, daughter of Helen (292), granddaughter of Margaret (154), b. Rochester, New York August 26, 1952; m. Arthur Salie. They resided in Webster, New York where Carol was employed with the Better Business Bureau. Her husband is a professional photographer. They have five children. There is currently no further information on these Root descendants.

References: Correspondence with the late Helen Shea Pfromm.

616.

Bonnie Lee Pfromm, daughter of Helen (292), granddaughter of Margaret (154), b. Rochester, New York March 24, 1956; m. Steve MacDonald. They reside in Tampa, Florida where both are employed in the nursing profession. They have one child, Lindsey Lee. There is no further information on these Root descendants.

References: Correspondence with the late Helen Shea Pfromm.

617.

Susan Lynne Pfromm, daughter of Helen (292), granddaughter of Margaret (154), b. Rochester, New York August 12, 1957; m. Wayne Lampi. They reside in Rochester, New York where he worked as a manager for Star Markets and Susan is an office worker. There is currently no further information on this Root descendant.

References: Correspondence with the late Helen Shea Pfromm.

Sixth, Seventh, and Eighth Generations of Descent from Abel Root, Sr.

618.

Kathleen M. Burke, daughter of Francis (293), granddaughter of Gladys (155), b. St. Louis, Missouri, May 2, 1919, d. St. Louis, Missouri May 15, 2013; m. St. Louis, Missouri June 10, 1937 Charles George Frank, b. St. Louis, Missouri September 1, 1917, d. St. Louis, Missouri March 7, 1986.

Kathleen Burke resided with her parents until her 1937 marriage when she and her husband moved to Kansas City, Missouri where Mr. Frank was employed as a merchandise packer for a wholesale drug company. Charles Frank's World War II Draft Registration Card described him as weighing 133 pounds with a height of 5' 6" tall and having gray eyes and brown hair. He was employed by Abbott Laboratories. Kathleen Burke Frank's 2013 obituary recorded three children: Linda (Bill) Weckback, David Frank, and Charleen (Ron) Franklin and five grandchildren: Cheryl (Bob) Stevens, Christine (Mark) White, Ron (Jessica) Franklain, Deanna Frank, and Brandon Frank. Kathleen and Charles Frank were buried in Sacred Heart Cemetery, Florissant, Missouri.

Children:

1198. I. ***Linda Frank***; m. Bob Stevens; ***nfi.***

1199. II. ***David Frank***; ***nfi.***

1200. III. ***Charleen Frank***; m. Ron Franklin; ***nfi.***

References: US Census: 1920, 1930, 1940; Social Security Death Index 1935-2014; Sacred Heart Cemetery Records, Florissant, Missouri; *St. Louis Dispatch*, obituary for Kathleen Burke Frank, May 19, 2013; WW II Draft Registration Card, 1940-1947.

619.

Leona F. Burke, daughter of Francis (293), granddaughter of Gladys (155), b. St. Louis, Missouri December 27, 1923, d. Foley, Missouri June 22, 2014 from cancer; m. St. Louis, Missouri October 18, 1941 Albert A. Jose, b. St. Louis, Missouri April 27, 1919, d. Missouri December 4, 1985.

Leona Burke resided with her parents until her 1941 marriage. Albert Jose served in the US Army from June 16, 1941 until November 19, 1945 rising to the rank of corporal. He was described as being 5' 11" tall, weighing 175 pounds with a ruddy complexion, brown hair, and brown eyes. Mr. Jose served with the Army Corps of Engineers. Further information on these descendants of Abel Root, Sr. is not currently available.

It is believed that they had three children, but the identify of only one child is currently known. Albert was buried in the Jefferson Barracks National Cemetery in Lemay, Missouri. It is not currently known where Leona Burke was buried.

Children:

1201. I. ***Albert A. Jose, Jr.***, b. St. Louis September 8, 1942, d. St. Louis April 30, 1943 From pneumonia and buried in Mt. Hope Cemetery, St. Louis, Missouri.

References: US Census: 1920, 1930, 1940; World War II Draft Registration Cards 1940-1947; Missouri Marriage Records 1805-present; Jefferson Barrack National Cemetery Records, Lemay, Missouri; Social Security Death Index 1935-2014; Missouri Death Certificate for Albert A. Jose, Jr., May 7, 1943.

620.

Patricia Virginia Burke, daughter of Francis (293), granddaughter of Gladys (155), b. St. Louis, Missouri June 6, 1926, d. Cottonwood, Arizona March 6, 2008; m. St. Louis, Missouri June 22, 1942 Charles Alexander Rennie, b. Orange County, California June 5, 1920, d. Santa Anna, California March 6, 2018.

Patricia Virginia Burke resided with her parents until her marriage. Charles Rennie served in the US Air Force during World War II from 1941 to 1945. At the time of his World War II Draft Registration he was employed with Booth and Company and was described as being 5' 9" tall, weighing 150 pounds with blue eyes and brown hair. During World War II, Mr. Rennie saw combat action in China, Burma, and India.

He received an Air Medal for over twenty-five combat flights in transport planes through combat zones. In 1959, the Rennie family moved to Clarksdale, Arizona where Charles Rennie was employed with the Phoenix Cement Plant rising to the position of production supervisor when he retired in 1983. He served on the Clarksdale, Arizona Town Council in the 1970s and was a volunteer EMT with Verde Valley REACT. At the time of his death, Mr. Rennie was survived by four children, 10 grandchildren, 14 great-grandchildren, and 3 great-great grandchildren. Patricia and Charles Rennie were buried in All Souls Cemetery, Cottonwood, Arizona.

Children:

1202. I. ***Charles Alexander Rennie, Jr.***, b. Missouri 1945; m. place and date not known, Shirley J. Hubbs, b. 1945, d. Clarksdale, Arizona May 26, 2017. Mrs. Rennie was a skilled crafts and quilting artisan and enjoyed raising a family. She was buried in All Souls Cemetery, Cottonwood, Arizona; ***nfi.***

1203. II. ***Maurice Rennie***; married and resided in Metropolis, Illinois; ***nfi.***

1204. III. ***Michelle Rennie***; m. Mike Morrison and resided in Clarksdale, Arizona; ***nfi.***

1205. IV. ***La Dean Rennie***; m. Gregg St. Clair and resided in Clarksdale, Arizona; ***nfi.***

References: US Census: 1930, 1940; World War II Draft Registration Cards 1940-1947; All Souls Cemetery Records, Cottonwood, Arizona; newspaper obituaries for Charles Alexander Rennie and Shirley J. Rennie on Findagrave.com.

621.

Lois Elaine Burke, daughter of Harold (296), granddaughter of Gladys (155), b. St. Louis, Missouri December 13, 1926, d. place not known January 21, 2003.

Lois Burke resided in St. Louis with her parents until she entered the Cadet Nursing Corps in 1942. She served until 1948 graduating St. John's Hospital, Springfield, Missouri. It is not known if Lois Burke married or had children. She is listed under her maiden name in the Social Security Death Index. A burial location is not currently known.

References: US Census: 1930, 1940; World War II Cadet Nursing Corps 1942-1948; Social Security Death Index 1935-2014.

622.

Maxine Margaret Burke, daughter of Harold (296), granddaughter of Gladys (155), b. St. Louis a. 1930, d. Redstone, Alabama September 7, 1968; m. Arkansas August 25, 1949 James Hugh Varner, b. Ty, Georgia March 10, 1923, d. Huntsville, Alabama March 7, 2014. Little is known about these descendants of Abel Root, Sr. James Varner served in the US Army for twenty years and owned Auto Center Upholstery for forty years in Huntsville. Mr. Varner's obituary indicates that he remarried after the 1968 death of Maxine and had children by his first wife, but his obituary does not provide any details. Maxine and James Varner were buried in Huntsville Memory Gardens in Huntsville, Alabama.

References: US Census: 1930, 1940; Alabama Death and Burial Index 1881-1974 for Maxine Varner; Huntsville Memory Gardens Records, Huntsville, Alabama; obituary on Findagrave.com.

624.

Michael Herbert Lohmar, son of Marguerite (301), grandson of Gladys (155), b. St. Louis, Missouri October 25, 1950, d. St. Louis, Missouri February 6, 1992; m. Brenda Maupin, place and date not known. Michael Lohmar had two children, Kelly and Ryan, but further information on these descendants is not currently available. Michael Lohmar was buried in Resurrection Cemetery, Affton, Missouri.

References: Obituary *St. Louis Post-Dispatch* February 8, 1992; Resurrection Cemetery Records, Affton, Missouri; Social Security Death Index 1935-2014.

625.

Patrick J. Lohmar, son of Marguerite (301), grandson of Gladys (155), b. St. Louis May 14, 1954; m. Janice, last name not known. It is believed he had at least one child, Brian. Further information on this family is not currently available.

References: Obituary of Marguerite J. Lohmar, *St. Louis Post-Dispatch*, June 26, 2000.

626.

Fred R. Holly, son of Fred (302), grandson of Lloyd (156), b. Ypsilanti, Michigan May 25, 1920, d. place not known, February 15, 2015; m. place and date not known, Marilyn, last name not known.

Mr. Holly resided with his parents in the 1920, 1930, and 1940 US Census records. His World War II Draft Registration Card indicated he registered for the draft July 1, 1941, but it is not clear if he served in World War II. Fred Holly was described as being 5' 11" tall, weighed 138 pounds with blue eyes and brown hair. He did serve in the US Naval Reserve. Further information about children and occupation is not currently known.
References: US Census: 1920, 1930, 1940; World War II Draft Registration Card 1940-1947; Social Security Death Index 1935-2014; US Military Registers 1862-1985.

630.

Wanda Grace Holly, daughter of William (303), granddaughter of Lloyd (156), b. Ypsilanti, Michigan a. 1924, d. possibly Albuquerque, New Mexico, date not known; m. Kalamazoo, Michigan August 4, 1945 James Frank Nelson, b. For Morgan, Colorado December 19, 1924/1925, d. Kalamazoo, Michigan April 28, 2007. Little is known about Wanda Holly Nelson. She is not mentioned in her husband's obituary and it is believed they were divorced, but there is no document to confirm this.

James Nelson served in the US Navy during World War II enlisting April 29, 1944. He was a long-time resident of Kalamazoo and worked for the City of Kalamazoo for twenty-four years. Mr. Nelson was a collector of John Deere memorabilia, enjoyed country western music, and was a member of the American Legion and the Carpenter's Union. James Nelson was survived by his long-term partner Lucille Lang. At time of his death, Mr. Nelson was survived by three children, nine grandchildren, and two great-grandchildren. He was buried in Fort Custer National Cemetery, Augusta, Michigan. It is not known where Wanda Holly Nelson was buried and if she remarried.

Children:

1206. I. ***Dale Nelson***, died young, ***nfi.***

1207. II. ***Robert Nelson***; married and resided in Dana Point, California, ***nfi.***

1208. III. ***Deborah Nelson***; m. Thomas Smaller and resided in Otsego, Michigan, ***nfi.***

1209. IV. ***Victoria Nelson***; m. David Chenelle and resided in Saratoga, New York, ***nfi.***

References: US Census: 1930, 1940; Michigan Marriage Records 1867-1952; US Veterans Death Files 1850-2010; obituary posted on Findagrave.com.

631.

Lloyd George Holly, son of William (303), grandson of Lloyd (156), b. Ypsilanti, Michigan August 18, 1926, d. Albuquerque, New Mexico May 26, 1993; m. Battle Greek, Michigan November 16, 1946 Elaine B. Bera, b. Nashville, Michigan, 1928, d. place and date not known. Lloyd Holly registered for the draft and served in the US Navy from October 4, 1943 to April 12, 1946. He was described as being 5' 10" tall, weighed 152 pounds with blue eyes and brown hair.

In 1947 Mr. Holly was employed as welder in Battle Creek, Michigan and later as an auto mechanic in the same city. In 1959 the Holly family had moved to Albuquerque, New Mexico where Lloyd Holly was employed as an electrician. Mr. Holly was known as Pete to his family and friends. Lloyd Holly is buried in Sunset Memorial Park in Albuquerque, New Mexico. Elaine Bera Holly remarried October 17, 2010 to Robert Patrick Dowling. Further information on her second marriage is not currently available. Undocumented sources indicate there were three children born to Pete and Elaine Holly, but currently no material can prove this.

References: US Census: 1930, 1940; War II Draft Registration Card 1940-1947; Michigan Marriage Records 1867-1952; US Veterans Death Files 1950-2010; Kalamazoo City Directories 1947 and 1948; Albuquerque, New Mexico City Directory 1959; Sunset Memorial Park, Albuquerque, New Mexico; Social Security Death Index 1935-2014; New Mexico Marriage Index 1888-2017; Sunset Memorial Park Cemetery Records, Albuquerque, New Mexico.

632.

Wilma E. Holly, daughter of William (303), granddaughter of Lloyd (156), b. Owosso, Michigan September 28, 1928, d. Mesa, Arizona August 15, 1998; m. Parchment, Michigan December 14, 1946 Harold William Vander Roest, b. Muncie, Indiana June 16, 1926, d. October 1, 1997. Little is known about Wilma and Harold Vander Roest. Harold served with the US Navy during World War II. He was previously married to Robbie Lee Johnson on December 3, 1943 in Kalamazoo, Michigan. They divorced March 10, 1945 in Kalamazoo. By 1959 Wilma and Harold had moved to El Paso, Texas where he was employed as a merchandise manager. They resided in Mesa, Arizona by 1994. Wilma and Harold Vander Roest were buried in the City of Mesa Cemetery, Mesa, Arizona. It is not known if they had children.

References: US Census: 1930, 1940; City of Mesa Cemetery Records, Mesa, Arizona; Michigan Marriage Records 1867-1952; Michigan Divorce Records 1897-1952; Social Security Death Index 1935-2010; US Navy Muster Rolls 1938-1949; 1959 El Paso City Directory.

633.

Helen Theresa Holly, daughter of William (303), granddaughter of Lloyd (156), b. Owosso, Michigan August 2, 1930, d. Dexter, Michigan April 13, 2002; m. (1) Kalamazoo, Michigan March 18, 1950 Gordon Dale Stickney, b. Kalamazoo, Michigan May 9, 1929, d. Hot Springs, Arkansas February 15, 2013, divorced by 1960; m. (2) place not known August 26, 1960 Russell M. Morgan, b. Howell, Michigan September 14, 1928, d. Jackson, Michigan November 16, 2013.

Little is known about Helen Holly. Her first husband was employed as a salesman with Stanley Home Products. They had no children. Gordon Stickney married twice more after his divorce. He was cremated and what was done with his ashes is not currently known. Russell Morgan was an active outdoorsman who enjoyed fishing, hunting, snowmobiling, golf, and NASCAR.

He worked for Chelsea Chrysler Proving Grounds for thirty-five years, retiring in 1988. During World War II Mr. Morgan served with the US Army and was stationed in Occupied Japan. Helen and Russell Morgan had two sons and at the time of his death, five grandchildren and two great-grandchildren. They were buried in Oak Grove East Cemetery, Chelsea, Michigan.

Children:

1210. I. ***Dennis Morgan***; married with children residing in New Era, Michigan, ***nfi.***

1211. II. ***Gordan Morgan***; married with children residing in Munith, Michigan, ***nfi.***

References: US Census 1930, 1940; Social Security Death Index 1935-2014; Michigan Marriage Record 1867-1952 for Helen Holly's first marriage; Obituary for Russell Morgan on Findagrave.com; Oak Grove East Cemetery Records, Chelsea, Michigan.

634.

Virginia "Ginny" Dawn Holly, daughter of Lloyd (304), granddaughter of Lloyd (156), b. New Haven, Connecticut May 8, 1924, d. Figarden, California March 29, 2009; m. New Haven, Connecticut March 20, 1946 Kenneth Frank Lane, b. West Sacramento, California February 7, 1918, d. Madera County, California March 26, 1999.

Ginny Holly was a singer and dancer with the Glenn Miller Band. She was also employed with the Fresno Bank of America as a Branch Manager. When Kenneth Frank Lane registered for the draft during World War II he was described as being 5' 9" tall, weighted 175 pounds and had hazel eyes and brown hair. He was employed with the Railway Express Agency. It is not clear if he actually served in World War II. They moved to California in 1948. Mr. and Mrs. Lane had three daughters and five grandchildren. They were buried in Arbor Vitae Cemetery, Madera, California.

Children:

1212. I. ***Julie Dawn Lane, nfi.***

1213. II. ***Jeri Lane, nfi.***

1214. III. ***Doreen Lane, nfi.***

References: US Census: 1920, 1930, 1940; World War II Draft Registration Card 1940-1947; Social Security Death Index 1935-2014; Arbor Vitae Cemetery Records, Madera, California; Connecticut Marriage Records 1897-1968; obituary for Ginny Holly Lane posted on Findagrave.com.

635.

Lloyd Daniel Holly, son of Lloyd (304), grandson of Lloyd (156), b. Waterbury, Connecticut January 25, 1931, d. Mariposa, California September 18, 1998; m. (1) Alameda City, California August 2, 1970 Phyllis C. Amouroux Chesley, divorced March 1973; m. (2) Alameda City, California September 22, 1973 Constance Parker Scott, b. Logan, Utah May 16, 1944, d. Modesto, California May 15, 2011, divorced September 1977; m. (3) Alameda City, California December 3, 1978 Clara Louise Orlando, place and date of birth not known, place and date of death not known.

Little is known about this descendant of Abel Root, Sr. He had two children, a son Mark and a daughter Chris, probably by his third wife. Lloyd Holly was buried in Arbor Vitae Cemetery, Madera, California. There is a place for his third wife with him at the cemetery, but vital statistics information is not currently known.

References: US Census: 1940; Social Security Death Index 1935-2014; Arbor Vitae Records, Madera, California; California Marriage Index 1960-1985; California Divorce Index 1966-1984.

639.

William F. Heater, son of Helen (309), grandson of Fred (157), b. Ypsilanti, Michigan June 15, 1929, d. place and date of death not known; m. (1) Ypsilanti, Michigan October 18, 1952 Betty M. Watling, b. a. 1932, believed divorced; m. (2) Multnomah, Oregon July 27, 1968 Betty McClaren. Further information on this Root descendant is not currently available.

References: US Census: 1930, 1940; Michigan Marriage Records 1867-1952; Oregon Marriage Index 1906-2009; US Public Records 1950-1993, Volume I.

643.

Sharron/Sharon Lynn Gardner, daughter of Margaret (311), granddaughter of Fred (157), b. Michigan March 30, 1940, d. San Bernardino, California, March 10,2001; m. (1) place and date not known Robert Leroy Houghtalin, Jr., b. Ann Arbor, Michigan June 30, 1938, d. Lincoln, Illinois October 31, 2008, divorced Los Angeles, California October 1966; m. (2). place and date not known, Mr. Sigler.

Sharron's last name was changed on Social Security Records to Sharon Lynn Sigler September 22, 1980. The identity of her second husband is not known. In 1974 she was employed as a bank teller in San Diego, California. Undocumented sources indicated that Sharron and her first husband had two children, but this cannot currently be confirmed by documentation. It is not known where she was buried.

References: US Census: 1940; California Divorce Index 1966-1984; Social Security Death Index 1935-2014; 1974 City Directory for San Diego, California; Social Security Claims Index 1936-2007.

649.

Joan Irene Hoots, daughter of Margaret (316), granddaughter of Minerva (158), b. Detroit, Michigan September 24, 1940, d. Leon, Florida April 12, 1998; m. (1) Bexar, Texas February 20, 1959 Jacques Turner, divorced Palm Beach, Florida February 25, 1970; m. (2) Sarasota, Florida August 28, 1989, Mr. Nilsen.

Social Security Claims Index records that Joan Hoots had two additional name changes between her first and second listed marriages. January 15, 1976 she was listed as Joan Irene Smith and on March 6, 1984 she was listed as Joan Irene Ellard before becoming Joan Irene Nilsen on December 4, 1989. The identify of her last husband is not currently known. Joan joined the US Air Force enlisting October 13, 1958. Joan Hoots Nilsen was buried in Florida National Cemetery, Bushnell, Florida. It is not currently known is she had any children.

References: Florida National Cemetery Records, Bushnell, Florida; Social Security Death Index 1935-2014; Texas Marriage Records 1837-2015; Florida Divorce Index 1970; Florida Marriage Index 1927-2001; US Social Security Claims Index 1936-2007.

650.

Richard Maxwell Hoots, son of Margaret (316), grandson of Minerva (158), b. Detroit, Michigan December 11, 1947, d. Quang Nam, Vietnam November 9, 1967.

Richard Hoots joined the US Marine Corps serving in Company K, 1st Marine Division. He was killed by snipers while on a combat mission. His body was recovered and Corporal Hoots was buried in Gulf Pines Memorial Park, Englewood, Florida. Corporal Hoots' name is on the Vietnam Memorial Wall, number 29E059.

References: Gulf Pines Memorial Park Records, Englewood, Florida; US/Vietnam Military Casualties 1956-1998.

651.

Judson John Joyce, Jr., son of Judson (317), grandson of Minerva (158), b. Michigan, November 23, 1933, still living; m. (1) Monroe, Michigan January 28, 1955 Lyne E. Stoner, divorced San Diego, California December 30, 1980; m. (2) spouse identity not known; (3) Anne, last name not known, d. 2012; m. (4) Patty, last name not known.

In the 1940 US Census Judson resided with his sister, Dixie, in the MacFarlane residence. Mr. Joyce currently resides in Wesley Chapel, Florida. He had five children by his first wife: Judson John Joyce III, James Joyce, Joanne Joyce, Jerry Joyce, and William Joyce.

References: US Census: 1940; US Presbyterian Church Records 1701-1970 for Judson Joyce's first marriage; California Divorce Index 1966-1984; correspondence with Sharon Lynn Joyce Cardwell in 2019.

652.

Dixie Lee Joyce, daughter of Judson (317), granddaughter of Minerva (158), b. Monroe, Michigan, September 21, 1935; m. Monroe, Michigan, September 4, 1954, Russell Andrew Mahan, b. Monroe, Michigan November 21, 1934, d. Sarasota, Florida November 7, 2010.

Dixie Joyce resided with her brother Judson in the 1940 US Census in the McFarlane household. After her marriage Dixie and Russ resided in Ames, Iowa in 1959, Brooklyn, New York in 1983, and in 2002 moved to Sarasota, Florida. They had four children: Mark, Kathy, Sara, and Laura.

References: US Census: 1940; US Presbyterian Church Records 1701-1970; Social Security Death Index 1935-2014; 2019 correspondence with Sharon Lynn Joyce Cardwell.

653.

Charles George Joyce, son of Judson (317), grandson of Minerva (158), b. Michigan October 31, 1946; m. (1) Jeanette, last name not known, divorced; m. (2) Dani, last name not known. Charles and Dani Joyce had had one daughter who died at birth in 2001. They currently reside in Livermore, California.

References: 2019 correspondence with Sharon Lynn Joyce Cardwell.

654.

Sharon Lynn Joyce, daughter of Judson (317), granddaughter of Minerva (158), b. August 19, 1946; m. April 6, 1968 Robert Shurman Cardwell. They currently reside in St. Louis County, Missouri where they raised two children. They have five grandchildren.

Children:

1215. I. ***Kristy Joyce Cardwell***, b. July 27, 1972; m. June 22, 2002 Jason Mitchell. They have two daughters.

1216. II. ***Kelly Shurman Cardwell***, b. December 21, 1974; m. June 24, 2000, Sarah Anderson. They have two sons and one daughter.

References: 2019 correspondence with Sharon Joyce Cardwell.

655.

George Robert Joyce, son of Edward (318), grandson of Minerva (158), b. Caro, Michigan January 6, 1941, d. Waterford, Michigan July 26, 2005; m. place and date not known, Anne Kathleen Crebassa, b. Pontiac, Michigan March 28, 1943, d. Southfield, Michigan July 29, 2009 from Alzheimer's. Anne Kathleen Joyce taught at a private school. Mr. and Mrs. Joyce had two sons, but further information is not currently known. They were buried in Perry Mount Park Cemetery, Pontiac, Michigan.

Children:

1217. I. ***David Alan Joyce***, b. Erie, Pennsylvania June 12, 1970, d. Jennings, Michigan February 22, 2009; m. Terri Chilton. David and Terri did not have any children but he raised her daughter, Lauren, from an earlier marriage. Dave was a ten-year veteran of the Jennings Police Department, a driving force with the JPD-ATF Violent Crime Task Force and the St. Louis Metropolitan Major Case Squad. He was buried in Memorial Park Cemetery, Jennings, Michigan. He was a Detective Sergeant at the time of his death.

1218. II. ***Peter Joyce***; m. Jennifer, last name not known. They had three sons: Ian, Jack and Benjamin David.

References: Social Security Death Index 1935-2014; Michigan Death Record, August 2, 2007 for Anne Joyce; Social Security Claims Index 1936-2007; Perry Mount Park Cemetery Records, Pontiac, Michigan; *St. Louis Post-Dispatch* February 24, 2009 for David Joyce.

662.

Paula Kay Daschner, daughter of Vera (324), granddaughter of Elizabeth (160), b. Rio Grande de Sol, Brazil May 19, 1947, d. Ann Arbor, Michigan August 11, 2006; m. place and date not known, Frank Moore, b. place not known, 1947. They had at least one child. Further information is not currently available. Paula was buried in Woodland Cemetery in Monroe, Michigan.

Children:

1219. I. ***David Moore***, b. Ypsilanti, Michigan February 27, 1970, d. Monroe, Michigan July 1, 1991 and buried Woodland Cemetery, Monroe, Michigan.

References: Social Security Death Index for Paula Daschner Moore; Woodland Cemetery Records, Monroe, Michigan.

667.

Lynn Norman McCorry, son of Marie Louise (329), grandson of Hazel (161), b. Michigan October 13, 1937; m. (1) Identify of first wife not known, divorced September 3, 1983; m. (2) McLean, Virginia June 18, 1983 Sandra Aileen Coon Hesler, b. Illinois November 19, 1937, d. Cleveland, Ohio June 2, 1985.

Lynn McCorry graduated from Eastern Michigan College. Sandra Coon Hesler divorced her previous husband March 15, 1982. Undocumented sources suggest that there were three children, but the identities of the mothers are not clear. The eldest daughter was a Sherri S. McCorry born in Cordova, Tennessee, but this was before Mr. McCorry's marriage to Sherri's mother Sandra Coon Hesler McCorry. Further information is not currently available.

References: US Census: 1940; Virginia Marriage Records 1936-2014.

672.

Geraldine Marie Clerkin, daughter of Leo (333), granddaughter of Florence (162), b. Cumberland County, North Carolina May 7, 1944, believed still living; m. (1) place and date not known, Mr., first name not known, Rippy, died July 20, 1975; m. (2) Cumberland County, Virginia June 3, 1978 John Dale Woodson, b. Virginia April 20, 1948, d. Richmond, Virginia April 11, 1984.

Information about Geraldine Clerkin's first husband cannot currently be located. Her marriage certificate to John Woodson indicated she was a widow. John Dale Woodson served in the US Military from January 16, 1969 until August 18, 1969. He died from heart disease and a heart attack and was buried in Trinity Memorial Gardens, Prince Edward County, Virginia. Mr. Woodson owned and operated Woody's Machine Shop. Mr. and Mrs. Woodson resided in Farmville, Virginia. John Woodson was previously married to Paulette Sewell Franchi on July 28, 1973 in Farmville. John and Paulette divorced August 25, 1976 in Cumberland County, Virginia. Information on children born to Geraldine Clerkin, Rippy Woodson is not currently available.

References: Virginia Marriage Records 1936-2014; Virginia Divorce Records 1918-2014; Trinity Memorial Gardens Records, Prince Edward County, Virginia; North Carolina Birth Index 1800-2000 for Geraldine Clerkin; Virginia Death Record 1912-2014 for John Woodson; US Military Claims Index for John Woodson.

673.

Kathleen/Cathleen Rose Clerkin, daughter of Leo (333), granddaughter of Florence (162), b. Johnsonburg, Pennsylvania September 1948, d. Tampa, Florida September 21, 2011; m. place and date not known, Mr., first name not known, McGonigal. She had three sons: Brian, Scott, and Chris. Kathleen McGonigal resided in Johnsonburg and Greencastle, Pennsylvania. Where she was buried is not currently known.

References: Social Security Death Index 1935-2014; Obituary for Leo Francis Clerkin, March 25, 2018.

674.

Diane Lynn Clerkin, daughter of Leo (333), granddaughter of Florence (162), b. Johnsonburg, Pennsylvania January 18, 1951; m. Farmville, Virginia June 20, 1970 Donald Brent Gilliam, b. Lynchburg, Virginia September 2, 1950.

It is known that Diane and Donald Gilliam had three children. Donald Benjamin Gilliam was born in Lynchburg, Virginia May 24, 1978 and died in Pamplin, Virginia July 9, 1978 from SIDS. A daughter Tracy Lynn Gilliam, b. Prince Edward County, Virginia February 22, 1975, d. Lynchburg, Virginia June 9, 1993 from spinal meningitis, and Allison Jurene Gilliam Hunter. Ben and Tracy Gilliam were buried in Olive Branch Cemetery, Prospect, Virginia. Further information on this Root descendant is not currently available.

References: Virginia Marriage Records 1936-2014; Virginia Death Records 1912-2014; Obituary for Leo Francis Clerkin, March 25, 2018; Olive Branch Cemetery Records, Prospect, Virginia.

675.

Mary Lou Clerkin, daughter of Leo (333), granddaughter of Florence (162), b. Johnsonburg, Pennsylvania, a. 1953; m. Los Angeles, California James Stephen Cornwell, b. Cleveland County, North Carolina September 28, 1949. They had at least one child; James. Further information is not currently available.

References: California Marriage Index 1960-1985; Obituary for Leo Clerkin March 25, 2018.

676.

Richard Oliver Biggs, son of Jane (336), grandson of Helen (163), b. Detroit, Michigan March 22, 1956. Rich received a B. S. in Mathematics at the University of Toledo.

He worked for Pilkington, N.A. (formerly LOF) in Toledo, Ohio from 1977-1991. From 1993 to the present he has worked for Owens Corning, Toledo in the Information Technology Division. His interests are swimming and reading non-fiction. Rich is unmarried. He has been a great help in documenting his line of descent from Ina Withey Lockley.

References: Correspondence with Rich Biggs in 2019.

677.

Donald Withey Maitland, son of Jesse (337), grandson of Bessie (164), b. Derrick City, Pennsylvania December 1/3, 1925, d. Foster, Pennsylvania January 23/25, 1928, age two years, one month, and 24 days. Donald Maitland was originally buried in the Allentown, New York Cemetery, but his remains were disinterred on November 14, 1977 and reinterred in McKean Memorial Cemetery, Mt. Alton, Pennsylvania.

References: Pennsylvania Death Certificates 1906-1967; *Bradford Evening Star*, January 25, 1928; Allentown Cemetery Records, Allentown, New York.

680.

Sheila Louise Maitland, daughter of Robert (339), granddaughter of Bessie (164), b. Olean, New York February 13, 1927, d. Chili, New York January 4, 1993; m. Derrick City, Pennsylvania October 26, 1957, Donald James Maas, b. Northeast, Pennsylvania October 10, 1930, d. Rochester, New York January 24, 2009. Sheila and Donald Maas resided in Pueblo, Colorado in 1962, Corpus Christi, Texas by 1992, and in 1993 where they resided in Rochester, New York.

Donald Maas served in the US Army during the Korean War rising to the rank of Corporal by the time of discharge. Mr. and Mrs. Maas were buried in Creekside Cemetery, Churchville, New York.

Children:

1220. I. ***Martin Maas***; married to Holly, last name not known; ***nfi.***

1221. II. ***Martha Maas***; m. Tim Daley; ***nfi.***

1222. III. ***Matthew David Maas***, b. place not known October 22, 1964, d. place not known November 9, 2014; m. place not known, a. 1985 Annette Jorolemon. Matt was a Veteran of the United States Army and worked as a foreman in the commercial roofing industry. His obituary described him as a kind, compassionate person and would be missed by everyone with whom he was a friend. Mr. Maas last resided in Rochester, New York and had two children: Ashley June Maas and Austin David Maas. It is not currently known where his cremated remains were placed.

References: US Census: 1940; Social Security Death Index 1935-2014; Creekside Cemetery Records, Churchville, New York; 1962 City Directory for Pueblo, Colorado; 1992 City Directory for Corpus Christi, Texas; 1993 City Directory for Rochester, New York; Obituary for Matthew David Maas on Findagrave.com.

681.

Robert Neal Maitland Jr., son of Robert (339), grandson of Bessie (164), b. Olean, New York November 4, 1940; d. Corpus Christi, Texas February 15, 1992; m. place not known June18, 1960 Sheila Ann O'Connor, b. Bradford, Pennsylvania August 27, 1940, d. Beckley, West Virginia May 10, 2017.

Robert Maitland served with the US Army in Vietnam. He enlisted March 31, 1961 and was mustered out August 31, 1981 rising to the rank of Master Sergeant. Robert and Sheila Maitland were buried in Salisbury National Cemetery, Salisbury, North Carolina.

Children:

1223. I. ***Jay William Maitland***, b. Pennsylvania July 16, 1961; m. Bluefield, Virginia December 19, 1980 Annette Kay Finley, b. Nebraska December 13, 1962, ***nfi.***

1224. II. ***Andrew Withey Maitland***, b. place not known, November 7, 1963, ***nfi.***

References: US Veterans Grave Sites, 1775-2006; Salisbury National Cemetery Records, Salisbury, North Carolina; US Veterans Death Files 1850-2010; Social Security Death Index 1935-2014; Virginia Marriage Records 1936-2014 for Jay Maitland.

682.

Karen Elaine Maitland, daughter of Robert (339), granddaughter of Bessie (164), b. Olean, New York November 22, 1941, d. Rochester, New York July 28, 2001; m. place not known, April 14, 1962 Brian M. O'Connor, b. Derrick City, Pennsylvania August 15, 1936, d. Rochester, New York September 8, 2017. Karen and Brian O'Connor were buried in Creekside Cemetery, Churchville, New York. They had four children. The identity of only one child is currently known.

Children:

1225. I. ***Kevin Michael O'Connor***, b. Brockport, New York November 22, 1965, d. Rochester, New York January 2, 2016; was married and has one child, Avonelle Contrell residing in Virginia.

1226. II. ***Karen O'Connor, nfi.***

1227. III. ***Shelly O'Connor***; m. George Borrelli; ***nfi.***

1228. IV. ***Michael O'Connor***; m. April, last name not known and a son, Kyle, ***nfi***.

References: New York State Birth Index 1881-1942; Social Security Death Index 1935-2014; Creekside Cemetery Records, Churchville, New York; *Rochester Democrat and Chronicle*, obituaries January 7, 2016 and September 10, 2017.

687.

Sally Anne Maitland, daughter of Kenneth (343), granddaughter of Bessie (164), b. Bradford, Pennsylvania March 5, 1957, d. Stuart, Florida August 21, 1996; m. Reynoldsville, Pennsylvania February 26, 1977 Nicholas Kovalscik, b. place not known, March 16, 1954. During their marriage they resided in the Youngstown, Ohio area. Sally Kovalscik was buried in Belmont Park Cemetery, Liberty, Ohio. They had four sons: Joshua, Stephen, Nicholas, and Timothy. Further information is not currently available.

References: Florida Death Index 1877-1998; Belmont Park Cemetery Records, Liberty, Ohio; Obituary for Sally Kovalscik on Findagrave.com; Social Security Death Index 1935-2014; Ohio Death Record 1938-2007.

697.

Barry Richard Windus, son of Jean (347), grandson of Ina (165), b. place not known, December 12, 1944; m. (1) New York State October 3, 1964, Ruth L. Baker, b. place not known, October 1950, divorced; m. (2) place not known, April 1978, Mitzi Gould, b. June 23, 1949.

Children: (by first marriage)

1229. I. ***Ina Jean Windus***, b. April 29, 1965; m. (1) Thomas LeBlanc, divorced; (2) George Curtis Wise, Jr., divorced; m. (3) Darin McCormick, now deceased.

Children: (by second marriage)

i. ***Genevieve Leigh Wise***, b. January 28, 1984; m. Michael James DeGraeve.

Children:

a. ***Haleigh Maree DeGraeve***, b. July 29, 2005.
b. ***Caralyn Grace DeGraeve***, June 21, 2007.
c. ***James Austin DeGraeve***, December 15, 2009.

ii. ***Seth Patrick Wise***, b. March 17, 1985.
iii. ***Alyson Michelle Wise***, b. October 4, 1989; m. Brandon Phillip Rowe, b. March 5, 1986.

Children: (by second marriage)

1230. II. ***Richard Barry Windus***. b. February 24, 1965; m. Lisa Samuel, divorced.

Children:

i. ***Jeremy Windus***, b. December 27, 1985.
ii. ***Justin Windus***, b. December 27, 1985.

1231. III. ***Christopher Windus***, b. January 4, 1970.

References: New York State Marriage Index 1881-1967 for Barry Windus' first marriage; interviews and correspondence with the late Ina Withey Burdick McEnroe; Correspondence with Elizabeth Windus Dinger.

698.

Bonnie Jean Windus, daughter of Jean (347), granddaughter of Ina (165), b. Wellsville, New York October 24, 1946, d. place not known, December 18, 1969, brain cancer; m. New York State May 15, 1965 James R. Jones. Bonnie Jean was buried in Woodlawn Cemetery, Wellsville, New York. The cause of death is not currently known.

Children:

1232. I. ***Terri Lynn Jones***, b. Wellsville, New York December 13, 1965, d. Portville, New York August 30, 1992; m. place not known, May 17, 1986 Stephan Sisson. Terri and her family resided in Shinglehouse, Pennsylvania and Olean and Portville, New York. She was buried next to her mother in Woodlawn Cemetery, Wellsville, New York. Terri was killed in a car accident.

Children:

i. ***Shawna Marie Sisson***, b. February 1986.

Children:

a. ***Abigayle Sunshine Taylor***, b. February 25, 2011.
b. ***Aurora Jayde Taylor***, b. March 29, 2013.
c. ***Amelia Iris Wardner***, b. January 27, 2019.

ii. ***Steffan James Sisson***, b. March 29, 1990.

Children:

a. ***Reznor Xzavier Sisson***, b. July 1, 2013.
b. ***Rayden Xzander Sisson***, b. August 25, 2015.

iii. ***Bonnie-lee Louise Sisson***, b. March 12, 1991; m. August 25, 2014 Tyler William Salada, b. August 12, 1965. Bonnie-lee and her husband Tyler adopted the two sons of her brother, Steffan.

Children:

a. ***Daivony Audrna Salada*** (step-daughter), b. March 1, 2011.
b. ***Teri-lynne Louise Latten***, b. December 13, 2011.
c. ***Tessa-jean Kathleen Salada***, b. September 23, 2013.

d. ***Talyah-mae Joyce Salada***, b. March 4, 2015.

References: New York State Marriage Index 1881-1967 for Bonnie Windus; Social Security Death Index 1935-2014; Woodlawn Cemetery Records, Wellsville, New York; Interviews and correspondence with the late Ina Withey Burdick McEnroe; Correspondence with Elizabeth Windus Dinger.

699.

John Wilfred Windus, son of Jean (347), grandson of Ina (165), b. Grand Gorge, New York March 7, 1950; m. place not known, May 31, 1969 Patricia Tucker, divorced Harris, b. November 26, 1948; m. (2) Texas April 27, 1995 Elise Ruth Benjamin, b. September 13, 1960.

Children: (by first marriage)

1233. I. ***Jennifer Ann Windus***, b. February 4, 1972; m. Kristopher Monte John, b. March 9, 1974.

Children:

i. ***Cecilia Helene John***, b. June 2, 2011.

1234. II. ***Carolyn Lee Windus***, b. November 4, 1981; m. Charles Allen Patrick, b. September 8, 1981.

Children:

i. ***Hayden Marie Patrick***, b. November 28, 2014.
ii. ***Quinn Honorah Patrick***, b. June 14, 2018.

References: New York Episcopal Diocese of Rochester, New York Records 1800-1970 for John Windus' birth record; Texas Divorce Index 1968-2014; Interviews and correspondence with the late Ina Withey Burdick McEnroe; Correspondence with Elizabeth Windus Dinger.

700.

Elizabeth Ann Windus, daughter of Jean (347), granddaughter of Ina (165), b. place not known, July 18, 1956; m. place not known September 3, 1978 Bruce Dinger, b. November 11, 1955. They reside in South Carolina.

In the tradition of her grandmother, Ina Withey Burdick McEnroe, Betsey also traveled to the Middle East and with her husband and swam in the Dead Sea and rode camels in memory of Ina. Betsey is a long arm quilter. People bring their pieced tops and she quilts them on a big machine.

Children:

1235. I. ***Lori Beth Dinger***, b. September 16, 1979; m. John Bernard Crooks III. Lori runs her own consulting business traveling India, China, Australia, and South Africa for both work and pleasure.

1236. II. ***Steven Charles Dinger***, b. April 1, 1983. Steve is a college professor and Teaches Analytics at Elon University, North Carolina.

1237. III. ***Michael Richard Dinger***, b. April 24, 1985; m. Erin Bailey, divorced. Mike is an Economics and Marketing Professor at the University of South Carolina Upstate, Spartanburg, South Carolina.

Children:

i. ***Wynne Larue Dinger***, b. October 4, 2010.
ii. ***Lachlen Violet Dinger***, b. February 7, 2012.

References: Interviews and correspondence with the late Ina Withey Burdick McEnroe; Correspondence with Elizabeth Windus Dinger 2020.

701.

Beckie Sue Windus, daughter of Jean (347), granddaughter of Ina (165), b. Wellsville, New York May 8, 1958; m. May 1977 Matthew Morris.

Children:

1238. I. ***Nicholas Stirling Norris***, b. November 1, 1980; m. August 1, 2015 Brittany Renee Short (Savannah Norris' mother), b. May 28, 1986. Children:

i. ***Katrina Ann Norris***, b. October 29, 2002.

Children: (by marriage)

i. ***Savannah Jolie Norris***, b. August 8, 2007.

1239. II. ***Jesse Todd Norris***, b. February 19, 1986; married and divorced. Named for his great-great grandfather, Jesse A. Withey.

1240. I. ***Kiefer Lee Jay Norris***, b. August 25, 1994; m. September 28, 2019 Rachel Lynn Morgan, b. May 22, 1996.

References: Interviews and correspondence with the late Ina Withey Burdick McEnroe; Correspondence with Beckie Sue Windus Norris, 2020.

702.

Barbara Jane Windus, daughter of Jean (347), granddaughter of Ina (165), b. May 24, 1962; m. August 31, 1987 John William Fretts, b. February 12, 1958, divorced 2020. Barbara is an artist.

Children:

1241. I. ***Duranna Elaine Fretts***, b. March 2, 1989; m. June 15, 2019 Travis Duran, b. December 25, 1992. Duranna is an occupational therapist for children from Birth to three-years old in Pittsburgh, Pennsylvania. Travis, a geophysicist, who graduated from Cornell University. The Durans run a one-hundred acre farm. Upon her marriage Duranna became Duranna Duran. The band *Duran Duran* sent her a message and video congratulating them for their wedding.

1242. II. ***John William Fretts III***, b. June 7, 1994. John served in the US Army and was deployed with NATO to Germany. He continued service with the National Guard. John is now using his GI Bill to attend Slippery Rock State University to become a history teacher. He and his daughter reside in Grove City, Pennsylvania.

Children:

i. ***Gwenivere Bowie Fretts***, b. April 14, 2016.

1243. III. ***Noelle Cortenay Fretts***, b. December 19, 1995. Noelle is a Special Education teacher and reading specialist residing in Clarion, Pennsylvania.

1244. IV. ***Greta Jane Fretts***, b. March 31, 1997. Greta graduated from Chatham University, Pittsburgh in 2020 with degrees in Biology, Chemistry, and Psychology. She resides in Pittsburgh, Pennsylvania.

References: Interviews and correspondence with the late Ina Withey Burdick McEnroe; Correspondence with Barbara Windus Fretts.

703.

Laine Elizabeth Sweet, daughter of Sara (348), granddaughter of Ina (165), b. Wellsville, New York, May 21, 1952; m. (1) place not known, April 2, 1977, Mark Golden, divorced January 2001, b. place not known March 8, 1948; m. (2) place not known, June 19,2018 Flynn (mononym), b. September 4, 1961.

Laine graduated from the University of Florida, Gainesville with a B. A. in Education. She was an Elementary Teacher and English Middle School Teacher in the Palm Beach County School System and retired after forty years of service. Mark owned the South Florida Systems Corporation. Flynn is employed with Wall Street, Real Estate, and is a Musician.

Children:

1245. I. ***Sarah Withey Golden***, b. place not known, December 18, 1980 and is an Elementary and Middle School Science Teacher.

References: Interviews and correspondence with the late Ina Withey Burdick McEnroe; Correspondence with the late Sally Sweet. Correspondence with Laine Sweet.

704.

Lisa Ann Sweet, daughter of Sara (348), granddaughter of Ina (165), b. Wellsville, New York, August 3, 1954; m. place not known, February 4, 1972 Harry Tuthill Fountain, b. Riverhead, New York, February 13, 1952. Lisa is a retired Cafeteria Manager for the Palm Beach County School System. Harry was employed by Southern Bell and retired as a fiber optic cable splicer. They reside in Hobe Sound, Florida.

Children:

1246. I. ***Shannon Earl Fountain***, b. Palm Beach Gardens, Florida, July 7, 1972; m. October 17, 1994 Kelli Ann Widd, b. Detroit, Michigan December 13, 1967. Shannon is a boat captain on the Miss Blue Heron, Key West, Florida. Kell is the Director of Market Research for Monroe County Tourist Development Council, Key West, Florida. They reside in Bay Point, Florida in Key West.

Children:

i. ***Reagan Riley Fountain,*** b. Jupiter, Florida December 25, 2000 and is a Freshman at the University of Florida.

ii. ***Kelsy Reese Fountain***, b. Key West, Florida January 23, 2003 and is currently a dual enrollment student at Key West High School and Key West State College.

1247. II. ***Shawn Merle Fountain***, b. Palm Beach Gardens, March 4, 1975; m. Daryle Lynn Digiacinto, b. Allentown, Pennsylvania July 26, 1976. Shawn is retired from the Coast Guard and currently works for the city of Jupiter, Florida Parks and Recreation Department. His wife is an art teacher with William T. Dwyer High School and is a Tatoo Artist. They reside in Jupiter, Florida.

Children:

i. ***Cooper Tuthill Fountain***, b. San Francisco, California October 24, 2006 and is currently in the seventh grade.

ii. ***Sailor Wray Fountain***, b. Key West, Florida December 7, 2010 and is currently in the third grade.

1248. III. ***Shelby Ann Fountain***, West Palm Beach, Florida, October 12, 1977; m. April 26, 2014, Branson Daniel Montgomery, b. Palm Beach Gardens, Florida, February 16, 1980. Shelby is a veterinary technician in Jupiter, Florida while her husband is an Electrician with North Atlantic in Jupiter where they reside.
Children:

i. ***Reef Branson Montgomery***, b. Jupiter, Florida February 11, 2016.

References: Interviews and correspondence with the late Ina Withey Burdick McEnroe; Correspondence with the late Sally Sweet; Correspondence with Lisa Sweet Fountain.

705.

Lorie Kay Sweet, daughter of Sara (348), granddaughter of Ina (165), b. Wellsville, New York July 16, 1961; m. August 28, 1993 John William Biederwolf III, b. April 27, 1962. Lorie graduated from the Art Institute of Fort Lauderdale with an Associate's Degree. Lorie and her husband own and operate a West Palm Beach Restaurant called *This Is It Café*. Lorie is also a physical therapist.

Children:

1249. I. ***Delaney Averill Biederwolf***, b. May 15, 1997. She graduated from FGC U in 2019 and is currently a spa manager for Naples Grande, Naples, Florida.

1250. II. ***Jesse Withey Biederwolf***, b. June 15, 1999 and is currently a junior at FGC U.

1251. III. ***Marley Burdick Biederwolf***, b. February 13, 2001, is a freshman at UCF and is a twin.

1252. IV. ***Avery Richard Biederwolf***, b. February 13, 2001, is a twin and is a freshman at Valencia College.

References: Interviews and correspondence with the late Ina Withey Burdick McEnroe; Correspondence with the late Sally Sweet; Correspondence with Lorie Biederwolf.

706.

Melissa Burdick Pike, daughter of Laine (349), granddaughter of Ina (165), b. place not known, January 20, 1954; m. place not known October 14, 1987 Jeffery Staub, divorced. Melissa resides in Reisterstown, Maryland and is the owner of Liquid Amber Landscaping.

Children:

1253. I. ***Rhiannon Averill Staub***, b. December 22, 1984; graduated from Elon University in North Carolina. She resides in Baltimore, Maryland.

References: Interviews and correspondence with the late Ina Withey Burdick McEnroe; correspondence with Molly Pike Riccardi.

707.

Melinda Averill Pike, daughter of Laine (349), granddaughter of Ina (165), b. place not known, October 23, 1959; m. (1) place not known June 7, 1986 John Thomas Hansen, divorced; m. (2) place not known, April 18, 2016 Kenneth Senick. Melinda and Kenneth enjoy retirement in North Palm Beach, Florida.

Children: (by first marriage)

1254. I. ***Tayler Laine Hansen***, b. July 29, 1989. Tayler received her Master's Degree from the University of Kentucky and her Ph. D. in Animal Science from the University of Florida. She is completing her post-doctoral study at Cornell Veterinary School, Ithaca, New York.

1255. II. ***Rodney Thomas Hansen***, b. October 22, 1992. Rod pursues his passion for music as a keyboarder for *Guavatron*. He resides in Lake Worth, Florida.

References: Interviews and correspondence with the late Ina Withey Burdick McEnroe; Correspondence with Molly Pike Riccardi.

708.

Molly Withey Pike, daughter of Laine (349), granddaughter of Ina (165), b. place not known, April 12, 1965; m. place not known, February 24, 1990 David W. Riccardi, divorced.

Molly is a freelance Graphic Artist and resides in the Pike family home in Belmont, New York. She has been a tremendous help in providing genealogical information and photographs on the descendants of her maternal grandmother, Ina Withey Burdick McEnroe.

Children:

1256. I. ***Adrian Averill Riccardi***, b. October 15, 1997. Adrian is a transgender female who identities as non-binary. She is a talented freelance artist and resides in Kutztown, Pennsylvania.

1257. II. ***Elaina Micaela Riccardi***, b. August 18, 2000. She is an art student at Alfred University, Alfred, New York.

1258. III. ***Jillian Frances Riccardi***, b. February 13, 2002. Jillian graduated from Central Bucks West High School, Doylestown, Pennsylvania and plans to study Physics and Astrophysics.

References: Interviews and correspondence with the late Ina Withey Burdick McEnroe; Correspondence with Molly Pike Riccardi.

709.

Rodney Walter Pike II, son of Laine (349), grandson of Ina (165), b. January 14, 1971, d. Belmont, New York July 9, 1987. Rod was accidentally electrocuted at the family summer home in Cuba, New York. He was buried in Forest Hills Cemetery, Belmont, New York.

References: Interviews and correspondence with the late Ina Withey Burdick McEnroe; Correspondence with Molly Pike Riccardi; Forest Hills Cemetery Records, Belmont, New York.

717.

Timothy Paul Ennis, son of Paul (356), grandson of Dudley (169), b. Olean, New York August 17, 1942; m. Williamson, New York August 30, 1969 Gladys A. Strong, b. Syracuse, New York February 21, 1943. Gladys worked as a dental assistant before her marriage.

Tim Ennis was employed as a steam fitter working in North Dakota, Dansville, New York for twenty years, and lastly in Florida. Tim and Gladys Ennis currently reside in St. Cloud, Florida moving there in 2004.

Children:

1259. I. ***David Lee Ennis***, b. Newark, New York October 1, 1969. David received a Bachelor's Degree from the University of Buffalo. He currently is employed with security for Buffalo International Airport.

1260. II. ***Andrea Caroline Ennis***, b. Newark, New York October 20, 1973; m. Rochester, New York April 29, 1969 Daniel Robert Monahan, b. May 11, 1969. Andrea graduated from St. John Fisher College in Rochester, New York. She is the Coordinator for the Nature Reserve for Irondequoit Public Schools. Daniel is employed as a computer programmer. They reside in Irondequoit.

Children:

i. ***Carina Marie Monahan***, b. August 11, 2003.
ii. ***Connor Evan Monahan***, b. March 21, 2006.

References: Telephone conversations with Timothy Paul Ennis, February 2020.

718.

David Charles Ennis, son of Paul (356), grandson of Dudley (169), b. Olean, New York September 17, 1944; m. Henrietta, New York June 29, 1972 Suzanne L. Katz, b. August 25, 1950, divorced 1996. David and his family resided for many years in West Clarksville, New York where he was employed as a general contractor. His wife was employed with Western New York Home Health Care. David currently resides in the Ennis family home on South Main Street in Bolivar, New York.

Children:

1261. I. ***Joseph Ennis***, b. Rochester, New York March 20, 1972; m. place and date not known, Jennifer, last name not known. Joseph works for an electric utility company.

Children:

i. ***Logan Ennis***, b. May 7, 1994. She has a daughter, Liv, born April 15, 2016.
ii. ***Bryce Ennis***, b. October 26, 1999.

1262. II. ***Charles Ennis***, b. May 16, 1973. Charles Ennis' current whereabouts are not known by the family.

Children:

i. ***Kasey Ennis.***

1263. III. ***Patricia Ennis***, b. July 23, 1977; m. Casey Linderman, Sr., divorced. They resided in Cuba, New York.

Children:

i. ***Casey Linderman, Jr.***, b. April 12, 2004.
ii. ***Jacob Linderman***, b. September 4, 2005.

References: Telephone conversations with David Ennis October 2019.

719.

Marsha Ennis, daughter of Paul (356), granddaughter of Dudley (169), b. Olean, New York November 14, 1947; m. (1) Rochester, New York October 10, 1967 Vincent D. Burroughs, divorced; m. (2) Rochester, New York June 30, 1983, Robert Majors, divorced 2014. Marsha was employed as a dental hygienist until her retirement.

Children: (by first marriage)

1264. I. ***Michelle Burroughs***, b. Rochester, New York May 28, 1968; m. York, New York David Calogero, b. Syracuse, New York May 5, 1965. Michelle earned a Bachelor's Degree from Fredonia State University, New York and a Master's Degree from Nazareth College, New York. She is a special education teacher with the Rochester Public Schools.

David earned a Bachelor's Degree from Plattsburgh State and a Master's Degree from Brockport State, both in New York. He is a contract specialist with the New York State's Teachers Union. They reside in Rochester, New York.

Children:

i. ***Madeline Calogero***, b. Rochester, New York June 15, 1997.
ii. ***Katheryn Calogero***, b. Rochester, New York Mary 25, 2002.
iii. ***Michael Calogero***, b. Rochester, New York January 11, 2007.

1265. II. ***Kimberly Burroughs***, b. Rochester, New York December 7, 1970; m. Rochester, New York May 22, 1999 Douglas Rivers, b. November 16, 1968. Kimberly Earned a Bachelor's Degree in Speech Pathology from Fredonia State University, New York and a Master's

Degree from Nazareth College in Rochester, New York. Douglas earned his Bachelor's Degree from Oswego State University and his Master's Degree from Brockport State University, New York. He teaches auto mechanics at Monroe Community College in Rochester, New York.

Children:

i. ***Lucas Rivers*** (adopted), b. Guatemala February 2, 2004.

References: Telephone conversations February 2020 with Marsha Ennis Majors.

720.

James V. LaFredo, Jr., son of Evelyn (358), grandson of Isabelle (170), b. place not known, June 21, 1935; m. London, July 10, 1957 Hilda Grace Baker. Buddy was a legal supervisor and Senior Master Sergeant in the US Air Force and retired after thirty years of active service. He has a Bachelor's Degree and a Master's Degree from Texas Universities. He was working on a Ph.D. and was last employed in a civilian capacity at Kelly Air Force Base in San Antonio. There is not further information on this Root descendant.

Children:

1266. I. ***Steve Paul LaFredo***, b. place not known, May 5, 1958. Steve has a B. A. Degree from the University of Texas and an M.A. Degree from New York University. He has resided in Live Oak, Texas, Boca Raton, Florida, and Singapore; ***nfi.***

1267. II. ***Evelyn Margaret LaFredo***, b. place not known, October 10, 1960; m. Bexar, Texas April 27, 1984, Joseph G. Grelle, divorced Bexar, Texas March 6, 2001. Joseph Grelle who was an Air Traffic Controller with the US Air Force at Homestead Air Force Base, San Antonio, Texas; ***nfi.***

Children:

i. ***Derrick Grelle***, b. 1984.
ii. ***Michael Grelle***, b. 1985.

1268. III. ***James Alan LaFredo***, b. place not known, October 10, 1960; m. (1) Tarrant, Texas August 2, 1983 Tara L. Newlin, divorced Bexar, Texas May 9, 1990; m. (2) Bexar, Texas May 13, 1991, Susie A. Garcia, b. a. 1967. James was last known to be employed at the Kelly Air Force Base in Texas in a civilian capacity.

Children: (by first marriage)

i. *Kaeli LaFredo*, b. 1984.
ii. *Dani LaFredo*, b. 1985.
iii. *Andraya LaFredo*, b. 1988.

References: Correspondence with the late Evelyn Johnson LaFredo; Texas Marriage Index 1824-2014; Texas Divorce Index 1968-2014.

721.

Joan Johnson, adopted daughter of Theodore (359), b. Olean, New York January 10, 1934, d. Olean, New York December 21, 2014; m. Olean, New York January 14, 1950 Joseph Lewis Maurouard, b. Olean, New York June 14, 1928, d. Olean, New York April 3, 1994. Joseph Maurouard served in the US Army from September 20, 1946 to March 6, 1948. After his military service, Mr. Maurouard was employed as a machine operator for the Van Der Horst Corporation in Salamanca, New York. Joan and Joseph Maurouard were buried in Chestnut Hill Cemetery, Portville, New York.

Children:

1269. I. ***Pamela Maurouard***, b. Olean, New York June 8, 1950, d. Olean, New York June 8, 1950. Burial location not known.

1270. II. ***Linda Sue Maurouard***, b. Kaufman, Texas November 18, 1952, d. Volusia, Florida December 29, 1995; m. place not known, December 8, 1971 Robert F. Stritof. They had two children; ***nfi***.

1271. III. ***Laurie Ann Maurouard***, b. place not known, December 17, 1954; m. place not known, October 11, 1971 Gerard L. Robbins. Last know residence in Florida; ***nfi***.

1272. IV. ***Lisa Kay Maurouard***, place not known, November 24, 1955; m. (1) place not known, July 22. 1978 Randy H. Buckley; m. (2) Rick Muchler and last known to reside in Plattsburg, New York; ***nfi***.

1273. V. ***Timothy Joseph Maurouard***, b. place not known June 16, 1959; m. May 31, 1980 Sandra L. Liquari and resided in Olean, New York; ***nfi***.

1274. VI. ***Tamara Lee Maurouard***, b. Salamanca, New York, August 2, 1960, d. Cuba, New York February 17, 2015 from lung cancer; m. place not known, June 21, 1980 Alan K. Haight, divorced. Tamara collected elephants and enjoyed camping and riding her unicycle. It is not known where she was buried.

She had two children: Alan Haight, Jr. and Kristy who married Fran Skiver and nine grandchildren.

1275. VII. ***Ronald Louis Maurouard***, b. place not known, January 24, 1963; m. September 4, 1982 Katherine Gould and resided in Olean, New York; ***nfi***.

1276. VIII. ***Jody Lyn Maurouard***, b. place not known, February 15, 1950; m. Mr. Murphy and resided in Olean, New York; ***nfi***.

References: US Census: 1940; Interviews and correspondence with the late Alice Weatherell Moore; Social Security Death Index 1935-2014; New York State Marriage Index 1881-1967 for Joan Johnson; US Veterans Death File 1850-2010 for Joseph Maurouard; Chestnut Hill Cemetery Records, Portville, New York; Texas Birth Index 1903-1997 for Linda Sue Maurouard; *Olean Times Herald* February 18, 2015 for Tamara Lee Haight.

724.

Marcia Sue Woodling, daughter of Maggie (360), granddaughter of Isabelle (170), b. Olean, New York May 9, 1932, Little Genesee, New York October 10, 2011; m. (1) Portville, New York October 1, 1951 Philip Edwin Johnson, b. Olean, New York April 25, 1930, d. Eldred, Pennsylvania April 27, 2008, divorced; m. (2) Clark County, Nevada July 1, 1961 Richard Edward Ripley, b. Smethport, Pennsylvania November 28, 1929, d. New Port Richey, Florida, July 17, 1999.

In the 1930 US Census Marcia resided with her parents in Keating, Pennsylvania and in 1940 in Otto, Pennsylvania. Marcia's first husband served with the US Army from March 22, 1951 to January 17, 1953. He was buried in Mt. View Cemetery in Olean, New York. Richard Ripley was previously married to Madelyn Karpin and was divorced. Mr. Ripley had two children by his first wife. Marcia did not have any children from either marriage.
Marcia and Richard Ripley were buried in Bowler Memorial Cemetery, Little Genesee, New York.

References: US Census: 1930, 1940; New York Birth Index 1881-1942; New York State Marriage Index 1881-1967 for Marcia's first marriage; Nevada Marriage Index 1956-2005 for Marcia's second marriage; Social Security Death Index 1935-2014; Mt. View Cemetery Records, Olean, New York; Bowler Cemetery Records, Little Genesee, New York; US Veterans Death File 1850-2010; Correspondence with the Maggie Leone.

725.

DeWayne Earles Woodling, son of Maggie (360), grandson of Isabelle (170), b. Olean, New York February 26, 1934/35; m. Olean, New York February 23, 1954 Dorothy Karroach. He was last known to reside in the Orlando, Florida area and was employed as an electrician by Disneyworld.

Children:

1277. I. ***Robert Woodling, nfi.***

1278. II. ***Cathy Woodling*** who had a daughter Tonya Marie Woodling, ***nfi.***

References: US Census: 1940; Correspondence with the late Maggie Leone; New York State Birth Index 1881-1942; New York State Marriage Index 1881-1967.

726.

William Farnsworth Woodling, son of Maggie (360), granddaughter of Isabelle (170), b. Olean, New York May 7, 1939; m. (1) place and date not known, Betty Ann Brown, divorced Bay, Florida March 1968; m. (2) Pinellas County, Florida June 1, 1973 Gaye Elaine Crandall. Mr. and Mrs. Woodling last resided in Clearwater, Florida where he was employed with the City of Clearwater. William Woodling served with the US Air Force.

Children: (by first marriage)

1279. I. ***Frieda Ann Woodling***; m. (1) Mr. Masters; m. (2) William Caster. She adopted three children: Victoria, Angelique, and Christina; ***nfi.***

1280. II. ***Timothy Woodling***; m. and resided in Panama City, Florida where he owned a roofing business; ***nfi.***

References: New York State Birth Index 1881-1942; Florida Divorce Index 1927-2001; Florida Marriage Index 1927-2001; Correspondence with the late Maggie Leone.

727.

Leo John Noonan, son of Marion (361), grandson of Isabelle (170), b. Olean, New York August 9, 1941; m. Olean, New York October 29, 1966 Susan Cashimere. The Noonan family resides in Olean, New York where Leo Noonan owned Business Interiors; ***nfi.***

Children:

1281. I. ***Megan Ann Noonan***, b. Olean, New York February 16, 1968; ***nfi.***

1282. II. ***Michael Cashimere Noonan***, b. Olean, New York October 6, 1969; ***nfi.***

References: Correspondence with the late Marion Noonan; New York State Birth Index 1881-1942;

New York State Marriage Index 1881-1967; *Olean Times Herald* obituary for Marion Noonan January 10, 2018.

728.

David Michael Noonan, son of Marion (361), grandson of Isabelle (170), b. Olean, New York September 9, 1948 and was last known to reside in Taylor, Michigan.

Children:

1283. I. ***David John Noonan***, b. September 29, 1984.

References: Correspondence with the late Marion Noonan; *Olean Times Herald* obituary for Marion Noonan January 10, 2018.

729.

Edward Allen Noonan, son of Marion (361), grandson of Isabelle (170), b. Olean, New York July 7, 1950; m. (1) place not known, October 4, 1971 Nicki Nicks, divorced; m. (2) place not known, April 1988 Kristie Butts. Edward Noonan was a Master Sergeant with the US Air Force and was stationed in Honolulu, Hawaii.

Children: (by first marriage)

1284. I. ***Sean Mckele Noonan***, b. November 16, 1973.

1285. II. ***Staci Michele Noonan***, b. September 13, 1975.

References: Correspondence with the late Marion Noonan; *Olean Times Herald* for Marion Noonan, January 10, 2018.

730.

Anita Marie Haag, daughter of Beula (362), granddaughter of Isabel (170), b. Olean, New York January 1, 1937, d. Punxsutawney, Pennsylvania May 29, 2003; m. (1) place not known, July 11, 1953 John L. Taylor, divorced; m. (2) place not known, June 24, 1964 Samuel M. Shaffer, b. DuBois, Pennsylvania 1929, d. place not known February 3, 1980. It is believed that Anita's second husband was previously married. It is not currently known where either husband of Anita Haag Taylor Shaffer was buried. Anita was buried in Circle Hill Cemetery, Punxsutawney, Pennsylvania.

Children: (by first marriage)

1286. I. ***Lu Ann Taylor***, b. Bradford, Pennsylvania January 10, 1954, d. Curwensville, Pennsylvania April 16, 1954 from cardiac asthma and congenital heart disease and was buried in St. Bernard's Cemetery.

1287. II. ***Stephen M. Taylor***, b. March 12, 1955, ***nfi.***

Children: (by second marriage)

1288. I. ***Mindy L. Shaffer***, b. June 10, 1956, ***nfi.***

1289. II. ***Mary Beth Shaffer***, b. February 18, 1972, ***nfi.***

References: US Census: 1940; Circle Hill Cemetery Records, Punxsutawney, Pennsylvania; Pennsylvania Death Certificates 1906-1967 for Lu Ann Taylor; Correspondence with the late Brenda Haag Skaggs.

731.

Theodore M. Haag, son of Beula (362), grandson of Isabelle (170), b. place not known, January 27, 1938; m. place not known, April 2, 1965 Mabel L. Keller. Mr. Haag was self-employed and they resided in Bradford, Pennsylvania. They currently reside in DuBois, Pennsylvania; ***nfi.***

Children:

1290. I. ***Beulah M. Haag***, b. April 1, 1966; m. December 20, 1989 Richard A. Hurd.

Children:

i. ***Joshua Hurd***, b. July 3, 1990.

1291. II. ***Theodore M. Haag, Jr.***, b. February 10, 1969.

References: US Census: 1940; Correspondence with the late Brenda Haag Skaggs.

732.

Brenda Pauline Haag, daughter of Beula (362), granddaughter of Isabelle (170), b. Olean, New York September 22, 1939, d. Erie, Pennsylvania hospital November 30, 2014; m. Bradford, Pennsylvania December 8, 1958 Floyd Eugene Skaggs, b. Bradford, Pennsylvania February 23, 1937.

Brenda worked for W. R. Case and Sons Cutlery in Bradford as a buffer and held other positions on the factory floor retiring in 1998 from the customer service repair department. In addition to raising a family of seven children, Brenda as a den mother for the Cub Scouts and a member of St. Francis of Assisi Church. Floyd Skaggs was part owner of Pure Sil, Inc. of Bradford where silicon wafers were made. Brenda Haag Skaggs was buried in St. Bernard Cemetery in Bradford, Pennsylvania.

Children:

1292. I. ***Dennis B. Skaggs***, b. February 22, 1956; m. (1) September 28, 1985 Brenda Johnson; m. (2) Carita, last name not known; ***nfi.***

1293. II. ***Floyd Eugene Skaggs, Jr.***, b. Bradford, Pennsylvania December 22, 1957, d. Bradford, Pennsylvania December 28, 2002; m. December 4, 1981 Theresa Baker. Mr. Skaggs was buried in St. Bernard Cemetery, Bradford, Pennsylvania.

Children:

i. ***Jemery S. Skaggs***, b. April 5, 1982.
ii. ***Annette M. Skaggs***, b. March 6, 1988.

1294. III. ***Larry Skaggs***, b. August 31, 1959; m. (1) June 2, 1979 Christine Bisker, divorced; (2) July 2, 1988 Diane Dennis, divorced. Last know residence was Pittsburgh, Pennsylvania.

Children: (by second marriage)

i. ***Jonathon Skaggs***, b. October 24, 1988.

1295. IV. ***Steven Skaggs***, b. August 27, 1960; m. Kimberly, last name not known and last known to reside in Bradford, Pennsylvania.

1296. V. ***Janet Skaggs***, b. November 16, 1962; m. July 5, 1980 Jeffrey Morris and last resided in Bradford, Pennsylvania.

Children:

i. ***Michael Morris***, b. October 23, 1980.

1297. VI. ***David Skaggs***, b. April 9, 1964 and last resided in Bradford, Pennsylvania.

1298. VII. ***Susan Skaggs***, b. February 16, 1967; m. Mr. Coder, divorced and last resided in Philadelphia, Pennsylvania.

References: US Census: 1940; Correspondence with the last Brenda Haag Skaggs; *The Bradford Era* obituary December 2-9, 2014 for Brenda Haag Skaggs; St. Bernard Cemetery Records, Bradford, Pennsylvania.

733.

Richard Elliott Haag, son of Beula (362), grandson of Isabelle (170), b. Bradford, Pennsylvania April 30, 1944, d. Erie, Pennsylvania June 25, 1996; m. place and date not known, Helen Peterson. Richard Haag served in the US Army during the Vietnam War from November 29, 1963 to September 8, 1966 with the rank of Private. He was buried in Wintergreen Gorge Cemetery, Erie, Pennsylvania.

Children:

1299. I. ***Richard Elliott Haag, Jr.***, (twin), b. Bradford, Pennsylvania July 31, 1971, d. Harbor Creek, Pennsylvania January 20, 2017; m. place and date not known Valerie L. Shaffer and had two children and three granddaughters at the time of his death. Richard Haag, Jr. was buried in Wintergreen Gorge Cemetery, Erie, Pennsylvania.

Children:

i. ***Chad Haag***; m. Leanna Roberts
ii. ***Christopher Haag***; m. Kimberly, last name not known.

1300. II. ***Paul Haag***, b. Bradford, Pennsylvania July 31, 1971; m. Paulette, last name not known.

1301. III. ***Kay Haag***; m. Mr. Bizzarro.

1302. IV. ***Kathleen Haag***; m. Mr. Rathmell.

References: Correspondence with the late Brenda Haag Skaggs; Social Security Death Index 1935-2014; Wintergreen Gorge Cemetery Records, Erie, Pennsylvania; US Veterans Death File 1850-2010; obituary on findagrave.com.

734.

James Paul Haag, Jr., son of Beula (362), grandson of Isabelle (170), b. Bradford, Pennsylvania August 26, 1946, d. Bradford, Pennsylvania March 15, 1992; m. Bradford, Pennsylvania May 1, 1965 Linda Marlene Burkett, b. Kane, Pennsylvania November 5, 1949. James Haag was employed with the Corning Glass Company, Bradford, Pennsylvania. Lina Haag remarried May 12, 2004 to Stephen Krol. It is not currently known where James Haag, Jr. was buried.

Children:

1303. I. ***Kelley Sue Haag***, b. October 4, 1965.

1304. II. ***Amy Beth Haag***, b. June 28, 1968.

References: Correspondence with the late Brenda Haag Skaggs; Social Security Death Index 1935-2014.

735.

Janice Haag, daughter of Beula (362), granddaughter of Isabelle (170), b. December 6, 1950; m. (1) December 14, 1968 James Covell, divorced; m. (2) September 11, 1976 James Barnoff and last known to reside in Florida.

Children: (by first marriage)

1305. I. ***Jay Paul Covell***, b. June 18, 1968.

1306. II. ***Christina Covell***, b. July 31, 1969.

References: Correspondence with the late Brenda Haag Skaggs.

736.

John Weatherell, son of John (365), grandson of Lola (172), b. Olean, New York January 8, 1935; m. (1) Joanne Sanberg, divorced; m. (2) 1957 Marjorie Carroll, divorced 1965; m. (3) 1965 Bonnie Jo Whitman, divorced 1979; m. (4) St. Petersburg, Florida November 15, 1980 Diane Hopkins Lake. Mr. Weatherell is retired and resides in St. Petersburg, Florida.

Children: (by second marriage)

1307. I. ***Helen Mary Weatherell***, b. January 28, 1960; m. Stephen L. Bay, divorced.

Children: (by marriage)

i. ***Maxwell Markus Bay***, b. April 17, 1987; m. March 4, 2017 Aline Madikian.

Children:

a. ***Nikolai Madikian Bay***, b. August 14, 2019.

ii. ***Olivia Kathryn Bay***, b. February 22, 2019.

Children:

a. ***Maya Christina Long***, b. March 4, 2002.

1308. II. ***John Howard (Jack) Weatherell***, b. April 15, 1961; m. August 1, 1990 Joanne DiTonmaso, divorced; m. (2) January 1, 1999 Holly Chester. Jack Resides in Vancouver, British Columbia, Canada.

Children: (by first marriage)

i. ***Jesse Alexander Weatherell***, b. April 9, 1991; m. January 22, 2018 Sawa Takeuchi.

Children: (by second marriage)

i. ***Aiden Delaney Weatherell***, b. March 27, 2001.

1309. III. ***Kathryn Anne Weatherell***, March 13, 1962 Adam R. Whittaker, b. September 15, 1955. They reside in the United Kingdom.

Children:

i. ***Josephine Kelly Whittaker***, b. March 28, 1994.
ii. ***Francis Emile Whittaker***, b. April 7, 1997.

1310. IV. ***Thomas Dennis Weatherell***, October 18, 1963; m. August 18, 1996 Debra Denise Steele, b. November 20, 1966. Tom works as a high school biology teacher and resides in Upland, California.

Children:

i. ***Thomas James Weatherell***, b. February 6, 1997.
ii. ***Michael Denis Weatherell***, b. May 18, 2000.
iii. ***Isabella Renee Weatherell***, b. May 6, 2004.

Children: (by third marriage)

1311. I. ***Colleen Marie Weatherell***, b. January 23, 1966; m. November 3, 1991 Gerald James (Jay) Cavalieri. Jay is a retired Navy Commander. He and Colleen own and operate a

Vom Foss Shop in San Diego, California.

Children:

i. ***Alexa Jaye Cavalieri***, b. November 17, 1992.
ii. ***Troy Michael Cavalieri,*** b. July 2, 1998.

Children: (by fourth marriage)

1312. I. ***Ian Lake Weatherell***, b. June 27, 1991.

References: Interviews and correspondence with the late Alice Weatherell Moore; Correspondence with Reverend Joseph Weatherell.

737.

Jan Leslie Ueblhear, daughter of Mary Roberta (366), b. Olean, New York February 11, 1952; m. place not known, April 18, 1975 Nick Cucciarella. Jan and Nick reside in Putnam Garrison, New York where there were employed as teachers.

Children:

1313. I. ***Emily Francine Cucciarella***, b. November 15, 1981; m. August 15, 2009 Dave Warburton. Emily and her family reside in Rensselaerville, New York.

Children:

i. ***Rose Huxford Warburton***, b. July 3, 2012.
ii. ***Caris Francine Warburton***, b. May 7, 2015.

1314. II. ***Alex Michael Cucciarella***, b. September 8, 1984; m. July 30, 2016 Katie Giachinta. Alex and Katie reside in Garrison, New York.

Children:

i. ***Grant Luciano Cucciarella***, b. April 27, 2017.

References: Interviews and correspondence with the late Alice Weatherell Moore; Correspondence with Reverend Joseph Weatherell.

738.

Joseph Edward Matthews, son of Martha (367), grandson of Lola (172), b. Olean, New York January 29, 1938, d. Olean, New York April 24, 2016; m. Olean, New York December 9, 1972 Elaine Carass, b. Olean, New York May 6, 1946, d. Olean, New York January 24, 2000. Joseph Matthews served in the US Army from 1962 to 1964 and remained in the Army Reserves until 1967.

He graduated from St. Bonaventure University and received a post-graduate degree in business science from the University of Buffalo. Mr. Matthews had a successful career in Arcade, New York as a banker and Senior Vice-President for the Central Trust Company of Rochester, New York. Joseph Matthews was employed as the chief financial officer for the Wyoming County Community Hospital in Warsaw, New York until his retirement. He was an avid golfer and a member of the Springville Country Club. Joseph enjoyed performing magic shows for children and making balloon figures to the delight of children. Joseph and Elaine were buried in the Arcade Rural Cemetery, Arcade, New York.

Children:

1315. I. ***Lorraine Mathews***, b. October 29, 1965; m. March 4, 1989 Bradley Cagwin, Divorced and last resided in Dansville, Virginia.

Children:

i. ***Callie Cagwin***; m. Patrick Ragland.
ii. ***Caleb Cagwin***.

1316. II. ***Jason Matthews***, b. June 27, 1973; m. name of spouse not known and last known to reside in Olean, New York.

Children:

i. ***Iann Matthews, nfi.***
ii. ***Kayden Matthews, nfi.***

References: US Census: 1940; New York Episcopal Diocese of Rochester, New York 1800-1970 for birth record; Arcade Rural Cemetery Records, Arcade, New York; *Olean Times-Herald* obituary April 27, 2016; Interviews and correspondence with the late Alice Weatherell Moore; Correspondence with Reverend Joseph Weatherell.

739.

Judith Carol Matthews, daughter of Martha (367), granddaughter of Lola (172), b. Olean, New York November 26, 1939; m. (1) Olean, New York November 26, 1960 Donald E. Farleo, Sr., b. Olean, New York June 11, 1937, d. Binghamton, New York June 8, 2009, divorced; m. (2) Olean, New York July 2, 1994 Robert J. Bell. Judith's first husband served in the US Army from June 3, 1957 to June 2, 1960 and continued in the Army Reserves until 1962. He was a police officer for the City of Olean for six years, graduated from St. Bonaventure University in 1972 with a B. S. Degree, and worked with the mentally disabled.

For a time, he was the Executive Director of the Allegany County ARC, worked as a social worker for Cattaraugus County, and served on the Cattaraugus County Council on Alcoholism and Substance Abuse. Donald Farleo never remarried. He was buried in St. Bonaventure Cemetery, Allegany, New York. Mr. Bell retired from National Grid. They reside in Olean, New York.

Children:

1317. I. ***Donald E. Farleo, Jr.***, b. Olean, New York November 30, 1961; m. Olean, New York August 8, 1987 Diane Koska and last resided in St. Cloud, Minnesota.

Children:

i. ***Matthew Farleo***, b. November 24, 1987. Matthew is a successful commercial artist and resides in Denver, Colorado.

ii. ***Franklin Farleo***, b. May 27, 1992. Frank is a nurse and resides in Minneapolis, Minnesota.

iii. ***Charlotte Farleo***, b. May 27, 1992; m. October 14, 2017 Cullen Klimek. Charlotte works in the culinary field with preschoolers in a Montessori School. Charlotte and Cullen reside in Minneapolis.
Children:

a. ***Arlo Klimek***, b. July 4, 2018.

1318. II. ***Thomas Farleo***, b. Olean, New York October 26, 1964; m. Gina Salero. They reside in New Port Richey, Florida.

Children:

i. ***Andrew Farleo***, b. July 13, 1990.

ii. ***Nicholas Farleo***, b. July 29, 1992.

1319. III. ***Jon Farleo***, b. Olean, New York May 9, 1967; m. July 27, 2019 Kelly Button. They reside in Olean, New York.

Children:

i. ***Nicholas Farleo,*** b. May 9, 1987 and resides in Newport, California.

1320. IV. ***James Farleo***, b. Olean, New York November 3, 1968; m. June 26, 1998 Kirsten Shields. They reside in Williamsville, New York.

Children:

i. ***Benjamin Farleo***, b. September 8, 2001.
ii. ***Emily Farleo***, b. July 26, 2011.

References: US Census: 1940; New York State Birth Index 1881-1942; New York State Marriage Index 1881-1967; US Veterans Death Files 1850-2010 for Donald Farleo, Sr.; Obituary posted on findagrave.com; St. Bonaventure Cemetery Records, Allegany, New York; Interviews and correspondence with the late Alice Weatherell Moore; Correspondence with Reverend Joseph Weatherell.

740.

Robert Stuart Matthews, son of Martha (367), grandson of Lola (172), b. Salamanca, New York January 1, 1942, d. Olean, New York February 2, 2003; b. Olean, New York December 30, 1967 Gail Salvan, b. Olean, New York June 24, 1947.

Mr. Matthews served in the US Army from February 19, 1964 to February 12, 1966 seeing action in Vietnam. He organized and managed the Ambassadors Drum and Bugle Corps representing Olean, New York. Robert Matthews owned and operated Cuba Storage, Inc. and Blueberry Meadows in Weston Mills, New York. He was buried in Pleasant Valley Cemetery, Olean, New York.

Children:

1321. I. ***Leslie Matthews***, b. October 4, 1968; m. May 25, 1991 Jeff Szymanski.

Children:

i. ***Lydia Szymanski.***
ii. ***Simon Szymanski.***

1322. II. ***Scott Matthews***, b. April 28, 1970; m. Nancy Carruth, divorced.

Children:

i. ***Hannah Matthews.***

References: Social Security Death Index 1935-2014; New York State Birth Index 1881-1942; US Veterans Death File 1850-2010; Obituary posted on findagrave.com; Pleasant Valley Cemetery Records, Olean, New York; Interviews and correspondence with the late Alice Weatherell Moore; Correspondence with Reverend Joseph Weatherell.

741.

Kathleen A. McMullen, daughter of Nina (368), granddaughter of Lola (362), b. Olean, New York December 18, 1948, d. Buffalo, New York General Hospital September 25, 2018; m. Olean, New York March 20, 1971 Jon L. Champlin. Jon Champlin worked for Dresser-Rand, Olean, New York.

Kathleen was a live long resident of the Olean-Portville, New York area. She earned an Associate's Degree in lab technology from SUNY School of Technology, Alfred, New York. She worked at Strong Memorial Hospital for one year, and the MDS in Olean, New York for fifteen years. Kathleen worked at the Olean Medical Group until her 2013 retirement. She was a member of St. Stephen's Episcopal Church, Concerned Citizens of Cattaraugus County, and the Citizens Action Network, all in Olean. Kathleen enjoyed flower gardening, bird watching, vacationing in Maine, and the New York Yankees. She and her husband did not have any children. Kathleen McMullen Champlin was buried in Chestnut Hill Cemetery, Portville, New York.

References: Interviews and correspondence with the late Alice Weatherell Moore; Chestnut Hill Cemetery Records, Portville, New York; *Olean Times Herald* obituary September 28, 2018.

744.

Hollis (Holly) McMullen, daughter of Nina (368), granddaughter of Lola (172), b. Olean, New York November 26, 1953; m. 1978 Stephen Johnson, divorced.

Holly graduated from Portville Central School in 1971 and Alfred State College in 1973. She was employed by the accounting firm of Weinaug and Irwin, Hills Department Store, both in Olean, New York, Newport News Shipbuilding and Dry Dock Company, Newport News, Virginia, Maida Development, Hampton, Virginia and the law firm of Wattenburg and Isaac, Olean, New York. Holly resides in Portville, New York.

Children:

1323. I. ***Erik Johnson***, b. August 4, 1978; m. October 5, 2002 Hillary Kenney.

Children:

i. ***Gavin Everett Johnson***, b. December 9, 2002.
ii. ***Brekin Richard Johnson***, b. April 16, 2007.

1324. II. ***Jeannie Johnson,*** b. December 11, 1981; m. July 28, 2017 Richie Ortiz.

Children:

i. ***Kiera Marie Johnson,*** b. February 13, 1998.
ii. ***Avianna Alane Johnson Howell***, b. December 9, 2000.
iii. ***Tahjae Marshaun Johnson***, b. September 1, 2002.

References: Interviews and correspondence with the late Alice Weatherell Moore; Correspondence with Reverend Joseph Weatherell.

746.

Michael McMullen, son of Nina (368), grandson of Lola (172), b. Olean, New York January 12, 1958; m. Olean, New York September 12, 1986 Krislyn Conner. Michael was previously employed at Olean Lumber Company. He currently resides with his family in Elizabethtown, Pennsylvania.

Children:

1325. I. ***Alyssa Kristine McMullen***, b. July 12, 1989.

Children:

i. ***Sophie Redcay***, b. May 12, 2013.
ii. ***Gabrielle Redcay***, b. December 27, 2017.

1326. II. ***Rachel Erin McMullen***, b. September 15, 1993; m. October 7, 2018 Jacob Koscil.

References: Interviews with the late Alice Weatherell Moore; Correspondence with Reverend Joseph Weatherell.

747.

Margaret McMullen, daughter of Nina (362), granddaughter of Lola (172), b. Olean, New York May 31, 1960; m. Olean, New York June 27, 1987 Bradley Cradduck, divorced. Peggy resides in Olean, New York.

Children:

1327. I. ***Joshua Cradduck***, b. March 7, 1986.

1328. II. ***Emily Cradduck***, b. June 30, 1989,

References: Interviews and Correspondence with the late Alice Weatherell Moore; Correspondence with Reverend Joseph Weatherell.

748.

Julie McMullen, daughter of Nina (368), granddaughter of Lola (172), b. Olean, New York May 20, 1961; m. Terry Bellamy. Julie resides in Olean, New York.

Children;

1329. I. ***Casey Bellamy***, b. December 19, 1987.

1330. II. ***Keriann N. Bellamy***, b. November 1, 1991.

1331. III. ***Jacob R. Bellamy***, b. September 1, 1995.

References: Correspondence with the late Alice Weatherell Moore; Correspondence with Reverend Joseph Weatherell.

750.

Molly Judge, daughter of Anne (369), granddaughter of Lola (172), b. July 14, 1952; m. July 1978 Michael Erickson. Michael was employed as a compressor serviceman for Tidewater Oil Company. Last known residence was Columbus, Pennsylvania.

Children:

1332. I. ***Stephanie Lynn Erickson***, b. May 26, 1981; m. March 21, 2009 Derrick Wu. Stephanie and Derrick reside in Western Springs, Illinois.

Children:

i. ***Alexander Richard Wu***, b. October 30, 2009.
ii. ***Orla Allen Wu***, b. August 23, 2011.

1333. II. ***Daniel Patrick Erickson***, b. July 20, 1983. Daniel resides in Philadelphia, Pennsylvania.

References: Interviews and correspondence with the late Alice Weatherell Moore; Correspondence with Reverend Joseph Weatherell.

751.

Jill Judge, daughter of Anne (369), granddaughter of Lola (172), b. August 5, 1953; m. May 1975 Robert Scherer. Robert was a commander in the US Navy and were last known to reside in Fort Orange, Florida.

Children:

1334. I. ***Sarah Anne Scherer***, b. September 5, 1976; June 2001 John Nightingale, divorced. Sara and her children reside in Port Orange, Florida.

Children:

i. ***James Nightingale***, b. December 10, 2002.
ii. ***Nathaniel Nightingale,*** b. September 13, 2004.

1335. II. ***Andrew Robert Scherer***, b. March 26, 1983; m. June 5, 2010 Danielle Conaway. Andrew and Danielle reside in Lansdale, Pennsylvania.

Children:

i. ***Bryce Andrew Scherer***, b. July 11, 2012.
ii. ***Finn Patrick Scherer***, b. February 27, 2014.
iii. ***Emmett Eugene Scherer***, b. November 2, 1015.
iv. ***Casey James Scherer***, b. September 29, 2017.

1336. III. ***Julian Scherer***, b. November 1, 1994 and resides in Riverside, California.

References: Interviews and correspondence with the late Alice Weatherell Moore; Correspondence with Reverend Joseph Weatherell.

752.

Jacquelyn Judge, daughter of Anne (369), granddaughter of Lola (172), b. January 15, 1961; m. Craig Eleftherion. Jacquelyn was a graduate of Bryn Mawr College in Pennsylvania. She resides in Harleysville, Pennsylvania.

Children:

1337. I. ***Megan Elizabeth Eleftherion***, b. April 6, 1986; m. September 25, 2011 Dan Hagey. They reside in Harleysville, Pennsylvania.

Children:

i. ***Dominique Hagey***, b. March 23, 2002.
ii. ***Landon Daniel Hagey***, b. April 8, 2011.
iii. ***Blake Michael Hagey***, b. July 2, 2012.
iv. ***Dylan Donahue Hagey***, b. August 11, 2014.
v. ***Mason James Hagey***, b. August 5, 2019.

1338. II. ***Michele Anne Eleftherion***, b. June 18, 1989. She resides in Harleysville, Pennsylvania.

References: Interviews and correspondence with the late Alice Weatherell Moore; Correspondence with Reverend Joseph Weatherell.

753.

Jamie Elizabeth Moore, daughter of Alice (370), granddaughter of Lola (172), b. Olean, New York June 23, 1946; m. (1) 1965 Alfred Kroenhe, divorced; m. (2) June 15, 1974 Willard Hutcheon, b. October 8, 1922, d. August 28, 1999. Jamie's husband was a retired lecturer in philosophy at CCNY, New York City. At the time of his death, they resided in Albuquerque, New Mexico

Children: (by first marriage)

1339. I. ***Karin Roberts Kroenhe***, b. August 13, 1966. Karin earned a Ph.D. from UC Berkley and resides in Alexandria, Virginia.

References: Correspondence with the late Alice Weatherell Moore; Correspondence with Reverend Joseph Weatherell.

754.

Mary Alice Moore, daughter of Alice (370), granddaughter of Lola (172), b. Olean, New York September 15, 1947; m. (1) January 4, 1967 Terry Staff, divorced; m. (2) June 22, 1974 William Baxter, divorced. Mary Alice is retired and resides in Tucson, Arizona.

Children: (by first marriage)

1340. I. ***Jamie Eugene Staff***, b. December 10, 1967; m. name of spouse not known. Jamie served with the 101st Airborne Division with the US Army in Saudi Arabia.

Children;

i. ***Dawn Staff.***

Children:

a. ***Emily.***

Children: (by second marriage)

1341. II. ***Matthew William Baxter***, b. June 1, 1977.

References: Interviews and correspondence with the late Alice Weatherell Moore. *Olean Times Herald* obituary February 6, 2015 for Alice Weatherell Moore; Correspondence with Reverend Joseph Weatherell.

755.

James William Bill Weatherell, Jr., son of James (371), grandson of Lola (172), b. Olean, New York April 18, 1950; m. (1) July 15, 1969 Peggy Brenneman, divorced; (2) September 1, 1973 Karen Keisee, divorced; m. (3) August 2, 1980 Karen Chesner.

Bill retired after working for several years as a computer systems consultant. Bill and Karen Weatherell reside in Olean, New York.

Children: (by first marriage)

1342. I. ***Wendy Weatherell***, b. Olean, New York September 20, 1969; Rochester, New York Dan Feldman. Wendy and her husband reside in Chesterfield, Virginia where she works at Swift Creek Family YMCA.

Children:

i. ***Jacob Kyle Feldman***, b. Folsom, California July 7, 2000.
ii. ***Tanner Patrick Feldman***, b. Folsom, California April 5, 2002.
iii. ***Joseph Connor Feldman***, b. Folsom, California March 31, 2006.

1343. II. ***Amy Weatherell***, b. September 13, 1971; m. Makena Maui, Hawaii May 4, 2006 Robert Jerry Bolden, b. July 10, 1965. Jerry was a firefighter for the City of Sacramento, California, now retired. Amy works as a financial analyst. They reside in Rancho Cordova, California. Jerry has a daughter from an earlier marriage: Danielle Rose Bolden, born Sacramento, California August 4, 1997.

Children: (by another relationship)

1344. I. ***Brent Scott Cygan***, b. Olean, New York March 11, 1972; m. June 16, 2001 Thanhnhan Thi Do.

Children:

i. ***Courtney Mai-Ahn Cygan***, b. November 15, 2002.
ii. ***Megan Minh-Ahn Cygan***, b. June 9, 2004.

Children: (by second marriage)

1345. I. ***Aledia Marie Weatherell***, b. February 14, 1973, d. Erie, Pennsylvania May 9, 1994 from injuries sustained in an automobile accident.

1346. II. ***Aubrey Ann Weatherell***, b. Clearwater, Florida September 5, 1974. She resides in Meadville, Pennsylvania.

Children:

i. ***Amber Nichole Weatherell***, b. Meadville, Pennsylvania December 4, 1993.
ii. ***Rusty Alan Dougherty***, b. Meadville, Pennsylvania November 7, 1995.
iii. ***Cheyanne Marie Coulter***, b. Meadville, Pennsylvania July 21, 2001.

Children:

a. ***Everly Nichole Brown***, b. Meadville, Pennsylvania August 6, 2018.

1347. III. ***Tennille Lynn Weatherell***, b. April 30, 1977; m. April 17, 1999 James Ruhl. Tennille and James reside in Bessemer City, North Carolina where Tennille is employed as a cook for Webb Custom Kitchen.

Children:

i. ***Ashleigh Elizabeth Ruhl***, b. July 26, 2000.
ii. ***Tory May Ruhl***, b. February 22, 2002.

Children: (by third marriage)

1348. I. ***Marissa Jean Weatherell***, b. Olean, New York December 24, 1982; m. Cuba, New York September 10, 2011 Eric Glad. Eric and Marissa reside in Walworth, New York. Children:

i. ***Riley Jean Glad***, b. January 7, 2013.
ii. ***Ryder Francis Glad***, b. October 29, 2014.

1349. II. ***James William Weatherell III***, b. April 18, 1986. James is the lead Information Technology Solutions Architect at Harvard Medical School, Boston, Massachusetts. He resides in New Hampshire.

References: Interviews and correspondence with the late Alice Weatherell Moore; *Olean Times Herald* obituary February 26/27, 2018 for James William Weatherell, Sr.; Correspondence with Reverend Joseph Weatherell.

756.

Thomas Martin Weatherell, son of James (371), grandson of Lola (172), b. Olean, New York January 8, 1954; m. May31, 1980 Debbie Shembeda. Thomas owned a sub shop in Olean while Debbie was a nurse at the Bradford, Pennsylvania hospital. They reside at Cuba Lake, New York.

Children:

1350. I. ***Adam Thomas Weatherell***, b. September 8, 1985.

1351. II. ***Eric Anthony Weatherell***, b. June 21, 1988.

References: Interviews and correspondence with the late Alice Weatherell Moore; *Olean Times Herald* obituary February 26/27, 2018 for James William Weatherell, Sr.

757.

Rev. Joseph Patrick Weatherell, son of James (371), grandson of Lola (172), b. Olean, New York March 22, 1962; m. (1) Hinsdale, New York June 4, 1983 Debrah Matteson; m. (2) Bound Brook, New Jersey October 15, 201 Jennifer Janeway Cumins.

Joseph attended Concordia Seminary in St. Louis, Missouri, graduating in 2004. He was ordained as a pastor in the Lutheran Church-Missouri Synod. Joseph and Jennifer reside in Wellsboro, Pennsylvania where he serves as pastor for Trinity Lutheran Church. Jennifer has two children from her first marriage: Alexander Benton Cumins b. Hemet, California July 3, 1997 who resides in Edison, New Jersey and Bethany Aleise Cumins, b. Hemet, California January 22, 2001 who resides in Wellsboro, Pennsylvania and is expecting her first child.

Children: (by first marriage)

1352. I. ***Randy Lee Weatherell***, b. December 31, 1981; m. St. Charles, Missouri May 6, 2002 Melissa Gray, divorced. Randy is a well-known musician in the western and central New York State area.

Children:

i. ***Jayden Nicholas Serra***, b. St. Louis, Missouri July 4, 2001. He serves in the US Army Reserves, St. Louis, Missouri.

Children: (by marriage)

i. ***Lillien Victoria Weatherell***, b. St. Louis, Missouri November 21, 2002.

Children:

i. ***Liam James Weatherell***, b. New Brunswick, New Jersey June 14, 2010.

1353. II. ***Brandi Lynn Weatherell***, b. June 11, 1984; m. (1) Allegany, New York Cody Hatch, divorced; m. (2) Franklinville, New York July 28, 2018 Daniel Johnston. Brandi works as a CAN at The Pines Nursing Home, Olean, New York. Brandi and Danny reside in Cuba, New York. Daniel Johnston has a daughter from an earlier marriage: Chloey Johnston, born August 13, 2008.

Children: (by first marriage)

i. ***Codi Elizabeth Hatch***, b. October 10, 2004.

ii. ***Aryanna Marie Hatch***, b. August 27, 2006.

Children:

i. ***Aaron Lynn Stearns***, b. September 7, 2010.

1354. III. ***Joseph Michael Weatherell***, b. February 27, 1986; m. Bismarck, Arizona September 17, 2009 Mellissa Babb, divorced. Michael resides in Cuba, New York.

Children:

i. ***Brandon Eugene Weatherell***, Hayden, Colorado May 14, 2007.
ii. ***Jacob Michael Weatherell***, b. Bismarck, Arizona April 13, 2009.
iii. ***Savannah Jolene Weatherell,*** b. Bismarck, Arizona September 13, 2011.
iv. ***William Isaac Weatherell***, b. Bismarck, Arizona September 6, 2013.

References: Interviews and correspondence with the late Alice Weatherell Moore; *Olean Times Herald* February 26/27, 2018 for James William Weatherell, Sr.; Correspondence with Reverend Joseph Weatherell.

758.

Ralph Alan Weatherell, son of Ronald (372), grandson of Lola (172), b. Montgomery, Alabama August 15, 1958; m. October 31, 1987 Starla Watterson. Ralph works for Xerox and resides in Nashville, Tennessee.

Children:

1355. I. ***Austin Alexander Weatherell***, b. October 14, 1991.

1356. II. ***Adam Carrington Weatherell***, b. May 14, 1993.

1357. III. ***Savannah Catherine Weatherell***, b. July 2, 1994.

1358. IV. ***Margaret Joan Weatherell***, December 14, 2001.

References: Correspondence with Reverend Joseph Weatherell.

759.

Peggy Ann Weatherell, daughter of Ronald (372), grandson of Lola (172), b. Montgomery, Alabama June 12, 1963; m. December 15, 1985 Charles Scott Robertson. Peggy is a registered nurse at Northside Hospital Healthcare System and resides in Johns Creek, Georgia.

Children:

1359. I. ***Elisabeth Diane Robertson***, b. December 23, 1988; m. December 23, 2019 Scott Diego Palomino. Elisabeth kept her maiden name and resides in New York City.

1360. II. ***Lauren Nicole Robertson***, b. November 11, 19991; m. June 25, 2016 Dustin Spenser Knickrehm. Lauren and her husband reside in Birmingham, Alabama.

761.

Joan Root, daughter of Donald (373), granddaughter of Selden (173), b. Olean, New York March 7, 1939; m. Olean, New York May 26, 1962 Joseph John May, b. Olean, New York September 6, 1938, d. Buffalo General Hospital, Buffalo, New York April 17, 2017 from a heart attack.

Joan retired from the Bon Ton department store in 2001. Joseph was employed with F. H. Oakleaf Company in Olean and James B. Schwab Co. as a service technician retiring in 2007. After retirement Mr. May worked at NAPA and Auto Parts Plus until his death. Joseph May was buried in St. Bonaventure Cemetery, Allegany, New York.

Children:

1361. I. ***Debra May***, b. March 26, 1963; m. Olean, New York March 26, 1985 Steven McPherson. Debra works in Customer Service at the Ashely Home Store, Weston Mills, New York.

Children:

i. ***Steven McPherson***, b. August 31, 1985; m. June 26, 2010 Hillary Jo Freeman. Steven is a Police Officer in the Bolivar Resource Office at the Bolivar/Richburg Central School, Bolivar, New York. Hillary is a Teacher's Aide at Wellsville Central School.

Children:

a. ***Noah McPherson***, b. July 24, 2012.
b. ***Natalie McPherson***, b. January 4, 2015.

ii. ***Christopher McPherson***, b. February 3, 1987; m. September 28, 2013 Lisa Knipple. Christopher is the General Manager at Ashley Homestore, Weston Mills, New York. Lisa is a Registered Nurse at Olean General.

Children:

a. ***Hayden McPherson***, b. May 29, 2011.
b. ***Thomas McPherson***, b. August 29, 2015.

iii. ***Rebecca McPherson***, b. June 27, 1988; m. September 10, 2011 Staff Sargent Timothy Bush. Rebecca is a military spouse and a stay at home Mom. Tim is serving in the United States Air Force with the Civil Engineer Squadron.

Children:

a. ***Ava Bush***, b. November 21, 2013.
b. ***Lia Bush***, b. March 23, 2017.

1362. II. ***Michelle May***, b. Olean, New York January 18, 1969; m. October 12, 1996 Brian Rohrabacher. Michelle is a Receptionist at Orthodontist Associates of Western New York. Brian is a Social Studies Teacher at Allegany/Limestone Central School, Allegany, New York.

Children:

i. ***Hannah Rohrabacher***, b. July 31, 2001.
ii. ***Matthew Rohrabacher***, b. June 30, 2005.

References: Correspondence with Joan Root May; *Olean Times Herald* April 20, 2017 obituary for Joseph May.

762.

Kathleen Root, daughter of Donald (373), granddaughter of Selden (173), b. Olean, New York July 2, 1942; m. Olean, New York September 30, 1961 Albert Abdo, Jr. Kathleen is now retired having worked been manager of Austin's Gift World. Albert Abdo retired January 1986 with the rank of Captain from the Olean Fire Department. He retired as Director of Security from St. Bonaventure University June 1995 and from Cutco Cutler Corporation, Olean, New York October 2010.

Children:

1363. I. ***Valerie Abdo***, b. Olean New York July 23, 1962; m. August 21, 1982 Paul Belleisle. Valerie is an Office Manager at Advance Circuit Technology, Inc. Paul is an Engineering Manager at Pfaudler, Inc.

Children:

i. ***Katelyn Belleisle***, b. September 13, 1986; m. August 17, 2014 Paul Shoe. Katelyn is a family physician and Paul is a nurse manager.

Children:

a. ***Amaris Grace Shoe***, b. December 6, 2015.
b. ***Elijah Jacob Shoe***, b. January 18, 2019.

ii. ***Kristine Belleisle***, b. January 13, 1988; m. August 6, 2011 Louis Horton. Kristine is a teacher and Louis is a Performance Engineer.

Children:

a. ***Simon Stewart Horton***, b. April 2017.
b. ***Baby Horton***, b. November 2019.

1364. II. ***Kimberly Abdo***, b. Olean, New York November 30, 1968; married and divorced. Kathleen works at the Winery in Ellicottville, New York.

Children:

i. ***Tyler Jason Wirth***, b. March 16, 1996 and graduated from Fredonia State University, May 19, 2018 Cum Laude Bachelor of Science Degree.

ii. ***Nathan Jacob Wirth***, b. December 2, 1999 and is a student at Fredonia State University, New York.

iii. ***Chandler Joseph Wirth***, b. February 13, 2004 is a student at Cuba-Rushford Central School.

1365. III. ***Annette Abdo***, b. Olean New York November 4, 1971; m. (1) Mr. McGraw, divorced; (2) October 6, 2012 Sean Donavon. Annette is a Book Store Manager at St. Bonaventure University and Sean works at Bimbo Bakeries, USA. Sean has two children from a previous marriage: Kaleigh Donavon, b. March 21, 2002 and Noah Donavon, b. August 16, 2004.

Children: (by first marriage)

i. ***Kyle Christopher McGraw***, b. February 4, 1997 and graduated from St. Bonaventure University.
ii. ***Joshua Michael McGraw***, b. February 4, 1997, a twin with Kyle and also graduated from St. Bonaventure University.

1366. IV. ***Timothy Abdo***, b. Olean, New York January 21, 1974; married and divorced. Timothy is a CNC Operator at Cutco Cutlery Corporation, Olean, New York.

References: Correspondence with Kathleen Root Abdo.

763.

Richard F. Root, son of Harold (374), grandson of Selden (173), b. December 10, 1950; m. May 3, 1975 Carolyn Dodge, b. November 12, 1953. Rick retired from St. Bonaventure University Maintenance Department January 2, 2013. Carolyn retired as an accountant with the Cuba-Rushford Business Office December 30, 1015. They reside in Cuba, New York.

Children:

1367. I. ***Kelly Jean Root***, b. April 18, 1978; m. Christopher Filkins, divorced. Kelly resides in Dunkirk, New York.

Children:

i. ***Gabriel C. Filkins***, b. September 8, 2009.
ii. ***Oliver M. Filkins***, b. April 22, 2013.

1368. I. ***Timothy Richard Root***, b. February 3, 1982; m. (1) July 17, 2004 Stacy Preston, divorced; m. (2) Amanda Burrows, b. September 3, 1982. Tim is a technician for Spectrum TV Cable and Amanda is a Dealer Support Specialist at Community Bank, Olean, New York.

Children: (by first marriage)

i. ***Nathan Preston Root***, b. January 31, 2001.
ii. ***Trey M. Root***, b. October 27, 2003.

iii. ***Caleb J. Root***, b. December 10, 2004.

Children: (by second marriage)

i. ***Kallie R. Root***, b. March 18, 2010.

References: Correspondence with Richard Root.

764.

Alice (Ginger) Root, daughter of Harold (374), granddaughter of Selden (173), b. Olean, New York September 2, 1954; m. Olean, New York August 1976 Thomas Moser, b. Bradford, Pennsylvania. Ginger worked as an aide at BOCES, East View School and retired from the Village of Portville in 2013. Tom taught Biology at Olean High School retiring in 2008.

Children:

1369. I. ***Mark Thomas Moser***, b. Olean, New York January 15, 1983; m. February 3, 2017 Ashley Sheil, b. Charlotte, North Carolina February 3, 2017, b. Waukegan, Illinois February 21, 1985 Mark has a Bachelor's Degree and an MBA Degree from St. Bonaventure University, Allegany, New York. Mark is a Senior Project Manager for JELD-WEN Windows and Doors. Ashley received a Bachelor's Degree from the University of Illinois and a Master's Degree from Northwestern University. Ashley is the Director of the Renfrew Center for Eating Disorders. Mark and Ashley reside in Fort Mill, South Carolina and work in Charlotte, North Carolina.

Children:

i. ***Ace Kaeden Moser***, b. July 18, 2017.
ii. ***Baby Moser***, November 2020.

References: Correspondence with Ginger Root Moser.

765.

Jennifer L. Eaton, daughter of DeMaris (376), granddaughter of Selden (173), b. Olean, New York September 30, 1949, d. Hemet, California June 23, 2012; m. Orange, California September 17, 2005 John C. Hart.

Jennifer attended St. Bonaventure University. She was employed for almost thirty years at St. Francis Hospital where she worked in registration and billing. In 1988 Jennifer moved to California to be near her daughter, Sarah and her granddaughters and was an active member of the Fun Club. Jennifer was buried in St. Bonaventure Cemetery, Allegany, New York.

Children:

1370. I. ***Sarah Beth Eaton***, b. February 26, 1977; m. Brandon Hargreaves and resides in Tustin, California.

Children:

i. ***Isabelle Rose Hargreaves.***
ii. ***Gwen Maris Hargreaves.***

References: Correspondence with the late Demaris Root Eaton Lynch; *Olean Times Herald* obituary for Jennifer Easton Hart July 22-August 20, 2012.

766.

Michael Eaton, son of DeMaris (376), grandson of Selden (173), b. April 24, 1953; m. Phyllis, last name not known. Michael worked for a time at St. Francis Hospital, Olean, New York as a Psychiatric Technician. He currently resides in Chesapeake, Virginia; nfi.

References: Correspondence with the late DeMaris Root Eaton Lynch; *Olean Times Herald* obituary for Jennifer Eaton Hart July 22-August 20, 2012.

767.

Christopher Eaton, son of DeMaris (376), grandson of Selden (173), b. February 11, 1955; m. January 15, 1983 Tina Lynn Youngblood. Christopher is employed with Air Express, Dallas, Texas and resides in Grapevine, Texas; nfi.

References: Correspondence with the late DeMaris Root Eaton Lynch; *Olean Times Herald* obituary for Jennifer Eaton Hart July 22-August 20, 2012.

768.

Kevin Eaton, son of DeMaris (376), grandson of Selden (173), b. February 22, 1956; m. (1) July 5, 1980 Loretta Newark; m. (2) Carla, last name not known. Kevin graduated from St. Bonaventure University, Allegany, New York. He is employed as a certified public accountant in Dallas, Texas; nfi.

Children: (by first marriage)

1371. I. ***Kevin Paul Eaton***, b. July 3, 1987; ***nfi.***

References: Correspondence with the late DeMaris Root Eaton Lynch; *Olean Times Herald* obituary for Jennifer Eaton Hart July 22-August 20, 2012.

769.

Lindsey Eaton, daughter of DeMaris (376), granddaughter of Selden (173), b. May 28, 1958; m. (1) September 23, 1982 Richard Mansfield, divorced; m. (2) Bryan Dodson. Lindsay worked at the former Olean Tile Company in Olean, New York where they reside; ***nfi.***

Children: (by first marriage)

1372. I. ***Jessica Mansfield***, b. April 6, 1983; m. David Straub.

References: Correspondence with the late DeMaris Root Eaton Lynch; *Olean Times Herald* obituary for Jennifer Eaton July 22-August 20, 2012.

770.

Robert Jack (Root) Krofcheck/Krafcheck, son of Leo Stanley (377), grandson of Leo C. (174), b. Grove City, Pennsylvania September 5, 1940, d. San Bernardino, California July 9, 1989; m. (1) Las Vegas, Nevada January 10, 1971 Mary L. Speas, b. Mississippi August 7, 1929, d. Los Angeles, California March 4, 1994, divorced; m. (2) Bobbi, last name not known, divorced.

The author has never seen a birth certificate for Robert (Root) Krofcheck. He was born when his mother, Alberta Wall Root, was still married to Leo Stanley Root. Alberta and Leo Stanley separated before Robert's birth. Alberta's request for a divorce was dated September 3, 1940, two days before Robert's birth, and included desertion among the reasons. Leo Stanley Root enlisted in the US Army in Olean, New York October 16, 1940, and he claimed he was single. Alberta's divorce was not final until September 23, 1941. Therefore, the Krofcheck marriage date of April 1940 for Alberta and her second husband cannot be correct.

It is assumed by the author that Robert may never have known that Leo Stanley Root was his father. Recent contact with the Krofcheck family resulted in their shock and surprise that Alberta had had an earlier marriage and that Robert might not be the son of Jacob Krofcheck, Jr. Robert (Root) Krofcheck served several years in the US Army and was stationed in France. He was discharged July 9, 1960. Robert spent most of his life after leaving the military in California residing in Big Bear. At the time of his death, his remains were cremated and buried in the Catholic section of Crestview Memorial Park in Grove City, Pennsylvania. Robert's mother, Alberta, was later buried with him. He did not have any children from either marriage.

References: California Death Index 1940-1997; Nevada Marriage Index 1956-2005; Correspondence with Joanne Krafcheck Ellis; Crestview Memorial Park Records, Grove City, Pennsylvania; US Veterans Gravesites 1777-2012.

771.

Leo James Root, son of Leo Stanley (377), grandson of Leo C. (174), b. Grove City, Pennsylvania July 23, 1943; m. Hof, Germany May 10, 1968 Ilse Muehlbauer, b. Germany November 14, 1946. Leo served in the US Air Force from 1964 to 1968 rising to the rank of Sergeant. He served in the Air Force Intelligence Division with a specialty in Russian.

Mr. Root attended Salem State University, Salem, Massachusetts and Southern New Hampshire University where he earned a Bachelor's Degree in Business Management. From 1973 to 1999 Leo Root was employed as a postal clerk in New Hampshire and served as Shop Steward and State Steward with the Rural Carriers Postal Union. Mr. Root was made Director of Labor Relations within the Union and later served as Vice-President of the Rural Carriers Union residing in Alexandria, Virginia. With retirement in 1999, Leo and Ilse moved to Las Vegas, Nevada where he was employed for fourteen years as a postal carrier advisor. Ilse attended Secretarial School and while residing in New Hampshire was employed by a number of retail grocery chains. Leo and Ilse Root continue to reside in Las Vegas. They do not have any children.

References: Interview with Leo James Root 2019.

772.

Dennis Alan Root, son of Leo Stanley (377), grandson of Leo C. (174), b. Lawrence, Massachusetts October 14, 1944; m. Melrose, Massachusetts July 1, 1967 Janice Hughes, b. Massachusetts November 5, 1944.

Dennis served with the US Army from September 8, 1964 to September 7, 1967 serving in Vietnam for 110 days where he was a Specialist E4 Heavy Equipment Operator. After his military service Dennis was employed as a care taker of Windham, New Hampshire cemeteries working with his father and also working with C. J. Miers Roofing. From 1969-1995, Dennis was employed with the US Postal Service. Mr. Root was Windham, New Hampshire Constable from 1969-1970. Dennis has a gift with anything mechanical and after retiring from the Post Office repaired and sold used cars. He currently works as a volunteer driver taking the elderly to retail establishments to purchase their groceries and other needed items. Janice Hughes Root graduated from Salem State University, Salem, Massachusetts in 1966 with a Bachelor's Degree in Elementary Education.

From 1966 to 1968 she was employed as a teacher with Lynnfield, Massachusetts schools. For the next ten years she raised four children before returning to teach as a Substitute Teacher in 1978 and full-time with Windham, New Hampshire Schools from 1980-2006 as a first-grade teacher. Since retirement, Jan teaches ESL at the New England Bible Church and the Presbyterian Church in Windham. Dennis and Jan Root reside on Cobbett's Pond, Windham, New Hampshire where their home has become a center for New Hampshire Root reunions and holiday gatherings. Dennis collects antique cars.

Children:

1373. I. ***Kimberly Ann Root***, b. Lawrence, Massachusetts July 29, 1968; m. Windham, New Hampshire August 19, 1995 Chris Monterio, b. Methuen, Massachusetts July 10, 1971. Kim received a Bachelor's Degree in History from the University of New Hampshire, Durham, New Hampshire and a Master's Degree in History from Duquesne University, Pittsburgh, Pennsylvania. From 1995 to 2001, Kim was employed with the American Textile History Museum, Lowell, Massachusetts. She has home schooled both of her sons. Chris graduated from the University of New Hampshire's Whittemore School of Business with a B.S. in Business Administration. He is a CPA and is currently employed as a Comptroller with AgaMatrix in New Hampshire. Chris is active in coaching community sports. Kim and Chris reside in Windham, New Hampshire.

Children:

i. ***Henry Jon Monterio***, b. February 4, 2001.
ii. ***Mason Carl Monterio***, b. April 8, 2005.

1374. II. ***Jlene Amy Root***, b. Lawrence, Massachusetts September 10, 1969; m. (1) Windham, New Hampshire August 14, 1988 Daniel Blackwood, divorced; m. (2) Las Vegas, Nevada 2000 Tom Rogers, divorced 2005; m. (3) August 2010 Matthew Plummer, divorced 2018. Jlene graduated in 1990 from Plymouth State University, Plymouth, New Hampshire in 1990. When not raising her own children, Jlene works with adults with special needs. She resides in Windham, New Hampshire.

Children: (by first marriage)

i. ***Hannah Elizabeth Blackwood***, b. Laconia, New Hampshire January 28, 1991; m. May 3, 2014 Shadane "Dane" Davis, b. Jamaica September 18, 1989. Hannah earned a degree in Business from Nashua Community College, Nashua, New Hampshire. She is currently Assistant Town Clerk for Windham, New Hampshire. Dane completed a degree in Nursing at St. Joseph's Hospital, Nashua, New Hampshire in 2020 where he is employed.

Children:

a. ***Chelsea Davis***, b. August 10, 2017.

ii. ***Zachary Daniel Blackwood***, b. Methuen, Massachusetts October 24, 1994. Zachary is employed with Temco Tool in Manchester, New Hampshire and resides in the family home in Windham.

iii. ***Abigail Grace Blackwood***, b. Methuen, Massachusetts April 9, 1996. She develops programs for mentally challenged children and adults and resides in the family home in Windham, New Hampshire.

1375. III. ***Daniel Dennis Root***, b. Methuen, Massachusetts September 24, 1971; m. Rochester, New York July 18, 1998 Melissa Coffey, b. Rochester, New York September 22, 1971. Daniel graduated from the University of New Hampshire, Durham, New Hampshire with a Bachelor's Degree in English. He earned a Master's Degree in Business from Northeastern University, Boston. Daniel Root is a partner in the firm Open Systems Resources, Manchester, New Hampshire. Melissa has a Bachelor's Degree from St. Bonaventure University, Allegany, New York and a Master's Degree from Boston College in Social Work. She is a representative for Scholastic Books. Dan and Melissa and their daughters reside in Londonderry, New Hampshire.

Children:

i. ***Delaney Margaret Root***, b. January 6, 2003.
ii. ***Bridget Coffey Root***, b. August 4, 2005.

1376. IV. ***Christa Joy Root***, b. Methuen, Massachusetts June 30, 1974; m. Windham, New Hampshire January 29, 1995 Jamie M. Corson, b. New Hampshire October 19, 1973. Christa attended Castle College, Windham, New Hampshire and Hesser College, Manchester, New Hampshire earning an Associate's Degree in Business Science. In addition to raising a family, Christa worked as a hotel manager at the Grand Olde Oprey Hotel, Nashville, Tennessee. Jamie earned a Bachelor's Degree in Professional Aeronautics from Embry-Riddle University, Daytona Beach, Florida and a Master's Degree in Divinity from Liberty University, Lynchburg, Virginia. He is a Chaplain in the US Army Reserve and is employed with a Defense Contractor Management Agency. Christa and Jamie currently reside outside Olympia, Washington with their youngest son.

Children:

i. ***Nathaniel Alan Corson***, b. Albuquerque, New Mexico June 2, 1995; m. Warner Robbins, Georgia August 3, 2017 Sabrina Cox, b. Atlanta, Georgia August 28, 1995. Nate is a certified Audio Engineer and Sabrina is employed by Chick-fil-A and attends Athens State University, Alabama. They currently reside in Windham, New Hampshire on Cobbett's Pond.

ii. ***Samuel James Corson***, b. Methuen, Massachusetts January 5, 1999; m. Perry, Georgia July 7, 2018 Emily Rene Edge. Sam is in the US Army, rank E4 and stationed at Fort Campbell, Kentucky. Emily is a Dance Force Instructor and a student at Liberty University, Lynchburg, Virginia. They reside at Fort Campbell.

iii. ***Isaac Reed Corson***, b. Elgin, Florida April 2, 2004.

References: Interviews with Mrs. Janice Hughes Root.

773.

Barbara E. "Bunny" Root, daughter of Leo Stanley (377), granddaughter of Leo C. (174), b. Lawrence, Massachusetts November 9, 1947, d. St. Joseph's Hospital, Nashua, New Hampshire January 17, 2004 from a cerebral infarction following surgery; m. Windham, New Hampshire March 1, 1968 Joseph L. Martin V, b. July 15, 1938, d. February 25, 1994, divorced 1973.

Bunny was employed with the Market Basket grocery chain and was a member of the Windham Presbyterian Church and the Ladies Benevolent Society, Windham, New Hampshire. She faced many challenges raising three children as a single parent but her strong faith and kind nature helped her through many crises. Bunny knitted baby blankets for anyone she knew was having a baby and annually sent all members of her extended family birthday cards. Her unexpected death was a great shock to all of her friends and family. Joseph Martin V was buried in Forest Hill Cemetery, East Derry, New Hampshire. Bunny's remains were cremated and buried with her mother and maternal grandparents in the Cemetery on the Plain, Windham, New Hampshire.

Children: (by marriage)

1377 I. ***Joseph Martin VI***, b. Derry, New Hampshire October 4, 1969; m. Derry, New Hampshire October 9, 2004 Lynne Marie Hackbert, b. Chicago, Illinois December 24, 1961, d. Derry, New Hampshire September 3, 2019 from a heart attack. Joey is a licensed Tractor-Trailer driver. He resides in Derry, New Hampshire. Lynne was previously married and had three children and four grandchildren. She was cremated. Joey Martin does not have any children of his own.

Children: (by Robert Callison)

1378. I. ***Sheila Martin***, b. Manchester, New Hampshire May 17, 1978; m. place not known, June 17, 1996 Richard Gollop, divorced. After residing a number of years in Arizona, Sheila returned to New Hampshire in November 2018.

1379. II. ***David Martin***, b. Manchester, New Hampshire August 2, 1979; m. place and date not known, Amy, last name not known, divorced. David resides in Concord, New Hampshire.

Children:

i. ***Talia Martin.***
ii. ***Calvin Martin.***

References: Interviews and correspondence with Mrs. Janice Hughes Root; New Hampshire Death Certificate for Barbara E. Martin January 19, 2004; Cemetery on the Plain Records, Windham, New Hampshire; Forest Hill Cemetery Records, East Derry, New Hampshire.

774.

Paul Dana Root, son of Leo Stanley (377), grandson of Leo C. (174) b. Derry, New Hampshire October 26, 1948; m. Salem, New Hampshire March 24, 1973 Barbara Ann Bogannam, b. Lawrence, Massachusetts March 30, 1949.

Paul served with the US Army from 1968 to 1971 stationed in Italy and Germany. After leaving military service, Paul was employed as a machinist with a number of different companies in New Hampshire. He retired March 2020 from Temco Tool Company, Manchester, New Hampshire where he worked in quality control. Barbara was employed with Osram Sylvania in Manchester, New Hampshire where she worked for seventeen years. Paul and Barbara's home in Goffstown, New Hampshire was a gathering place for many family reunions. In March 2020 they sold their ten-acre property with residence and moved to Clarksville, Tennessee, but will maintain a summer home in northern New Hampshire. Both Paul and Barbara are motorcycle enthusiasts.

Children:

1380. I. ***Daneille Root***, b. Derry, New Hampshire October 20, 1973. Daneille was not given a middle name and her first name is spelled Daneille. She received a Bachelor's Degree, cum laude. in criminal justice from Franklin Pierce College in 2002. In 2007 Daneille earned a Law Degree from the New England School of Law, Boston. She worked for five years with Comcast in Customer Service.

In 2019, Daneille moved to Clarksville, Tennessee where she is employed with 911. Daneille is single.

1381. II. ***Cheryl Ann Root***, b. Manchester, New Hampshire August 2, 1979; m. Nashua, New Hampshire May 16, 2020 Phillip Richard Graham. Cheryl is employed with the Bedford, New Hampshire Women's Care, coding medical billing. Cheryl and her husband lived together for twelve years before getting married. Mr. Graham works construction. Phillip Graham was previously married and has a son, Phillip Graham II, b. July 22, 2002 whom Cheryl has helped raised. Phillip II is nicknamed *Deuce.*

References: Interviews with Paul and Barbara Root.

775.

Marleen Ann Root, daughter of Leo Stanley (377), granddaughter of Leo C. (174), b. Lawrence, Massachusetts January 20, 1953; m. (1) Windham, New Hampshire December 1, 1973, b. September 22, 1952 Robert Deshaies, divorced March 1979; m. (2) place not known, August 27, 1983 Daniel Armand Benoit, b. Manchester, New Hampshire July 12, 1952, d. New Ipswich, New Hampshire August 25, 2019 from lung cancer. Marleen worked at a variety of jobs while raising a family. Dan worked as a communications specialist with Interactive Data in Massachusetts. Dan was previously married and had three children by his first marriage. His remains were cremated and buried at the Cemetery on the Plains, Windham, New Hampshire. Marlene resides in New Ipswich.

Children: (by first marriage)

1382. I. ***Aaron Lee Deshaies***, b. May 13, 1974; m. Nashua, New Hampshire 2007 Karen, last name not known, divorced. Aaron currently resides in Jaffrey, New Hampshire and works for the *Keene Sentinel.* Aaron does not have any children.

Children: (by Robert Taylor)

1383. I. ***Jennifer Lynn Deshaies***, b. Derry, New Hampshire October 5, 1980. Jennifer resides in Concord, New Hampshire.

Children:

i. ***Corey Deshaies***, b. Lebanon, New Hampshire December 1, 2002.

Children: (by second marriage)

1384. I. ***Sara Jane Benoit***, b. Derry, New Hampshire January 28, 1984; m. Nashua, New

Hampshire July 14, 2012, Ronnie Wilson, divorced. Sara resides in New Ipswich, New Hampshire.

Children:

i. ***Ashley Benoit***, b. Peterborough, New Hampshire March 7, 2004.
ii. ***Tyler Benoit***, b. Peterborough, New Hampshire June 21, 2005.

Children: (by marriage to Ronnie Wilson)

i. ***Matthew Wilson***, b. Peterborough, New Hampshire June 9, 2010.
ii. ***Dylan Wilson***, b. Peterborough, New Hampshire June 7, 2013.

Children: (by Mitchell Beausoleil)

i. ***Caleb Beausoleil***, b. Peterborough, New Hampshire January 1, 2017.

Children:

i. ***Logan Daniel Wilson***, b. March 1, 2020.

1385. II. ***Sherri Ann Benoit***, b. Derry, New Hampshire August 16, 1985; m. Greenville, New Hampshire August 23, 2014 David Lamb, divorced December 19, 2018. Sherri resides in Jaffrey, New Hampshire.

Children:

i. ***Braelynn Lamb***, b. Peterborough, New Hampshire February 16, 2018.

References: Interviews with Marleen Root Deshaies Benoit; *Monadnock Ledger-Transcript* obituary August 29, 2019.

776.

Deborah J. Root, daughter of Leo Stanley (377), granddaughter of Leo C. (174), b. Lawrence, Massachusetts April 6, 1956, d. New Ipswich, New Hampshire April 22, 2019 from esophageal cancer; m. (1) Windham, New Hampshire June 30, 1973 Donald J. Mancini, b. New Hampshire July 21, 1948, d. New Hampshire August 26, 2005, divorced; m. (2) place and date not known, Allen Gagne.

Debbie and Don were married twice and divorced twice according to family members. The only date that can be confirmed is their first date of marriage. Debbie worked for many years in the hospitality field and home daycare. Don Mancini served in the US Navy from September 1, 1965 to June 1, 1968 and saw action in Vietnam. He was buried in the New Hampshire State Cemetery, Boscawen, New Hampshire. Debbie's remains were cremated and are in the possession of her family.

Children: (by first marriage)

1386. I. ***Tracy Lee Mancini***, b. New Hampshire May 17, 1974; m. (1) place and date not known Paul Presley Waller, Sr., b. New Hampshire December 16, 1966, divorced; m. (2) Todd Renshaw. Tracy and Todd reside in New Ipswich, New Hampshire.

Children: (by first marriage)

i. ***Paul Presley Waller, Jr.***, b. October 23, 1990.
ii. ***Anthony Raymond Waller***, b. September 13, 1993.
iii. ***Brittni Alece Waller***, b. February 18, 1998.

Children: (by second marriage)

i. ***Cordell Renshaw.***

1387. II. ***Donald J. Mancini, Jr.***, b. April 22, 1976; m. Lisa, last name not known. They reside in Concord, New Hampshire.

Children:

i. ***Megan Mancini.***

Children:

a. ***James Mancini.***

ii. ***Emily Mancini.***

1388. III. ***Timothy Mancini***, b. November 29, 1977; m. (1) first wife died from cancer leaving two small children; m. (2) married and divorced. Tim served in the US Air Force for twenty years and lived in North Dakota until his move back to New Hampshire in 2019. He currently resides in Nashua, New Hampshire with his two sons.

Children: (by first marriage)

i. ***Orian Mancini.***
ii. ***Alec Mancini.***

1389. IV. ***Jason Allen Mancini***, b. August 20, 1982; married and divorced. Jason resides in Nashua, New Hampshire.

Children:

i. ***Catlynne Mancini.***
ii. ***Aaliyah Mancini.***

Children: (by second marriage)

1390. I. ***Brenda Nicole Gagne***, b. August 26, 1994.

Children:

i. ***Aiden Gagne.***
ii. ***Michael Gagne.***
iii. ***Trinity Scott.***

References: Interviews with Mrs. Janice Hughes Root; obituary Cournoyer Funeral Home, Jaffrey, New Hampshire for Deborah Gagne; US Veterans Gravesites 1775-2006 for Donald Mancini, Sr.; US Veterans Death File 1850-2010.

777.

Leo Steven Root, son of Leo Stanley (377), grandson of Leo C. (174), b. Nashua, New Hampshire July 13, 1974. Leo or Lee is unmarried, resides in Derry, New Hampshire, and works for a tree cutting service.

References: Interview with Dennis Root.

778.

Diana Kay Anderson, daughter of Nordica (378), granddaughter of Leo C. (174), b. Wellsville, New York July 22, 1953; m. Hornell, New York July 23, 1994 James LaFaro, b. Hornell, New York October 18, 1949.

Diana graduated from Brockport State University, New York with a B. S. Degree in Mathematics. For thirty-two and one-half years she was employed with the Allegany County, New York Department of Social Services where she served as a Child Support Investigator retiring in 2008. Until her marriage in 1994, Diana resided in Belmont, New York. Diana inherited skills with a needle that both her mother and maternal grandmother had and is a talented sewer, quilter, and knitter. Jim served with the US Navy and saw ten months of active service in Vietnam. His military service spanned four years. He was stationed in Ben Loc in the Mekong Delta during the Vietnam War and later in New London, Connecticut aboard the USS Felton. He trained in firefighting and survival skills.

Jim worked at the Hornell Railroad yards for many years, first when it was the Erie Railroad, later the Erie-Lackawanna Railroad, then Conrail, and lastly the Morrison-Knutson Company. His last job was with the Allegany County, New York Department of Social Services as a Welfare to Work Supervisor for twenty-one years until his retirement in 2010. Jim was previously married and has three daughters. Maria, born December 28, 1971 holds a Doctor of Nursing Degree and is a Professor with the University of Rochester. Michelle was born November 13, 1973 and currently works for Alstom in Hornell, New York. Alstom manufactures subway and high-speed railroad cars at the Hornell Rail yards. This makes Michelle the fourth generation LaFaro member to work at the Hornell yards.

Sarah was born August 3, 1988 and earned a Bachelor's Degree from Alfred University and a Master's Degree from the University of Rochester. She is employed as a Mental Health Counselor and resides in New London, Connecticut. Diana helped Jim raise Sarah. Diana and Jim reside in a "painted lady," a Victorian Queen Anne style residence in Hornell, New York.

References: Interviews with Diana and Jim LaFaro.

779.

Sharon Nordica Anderson, daughter of Nordica (378), granddaughter of Leo C. (174), b. Wellsville, New York May 23, 1955; m. Wellsville, New York August 4, 1979 David L Wallace, b. Hornell, New York May 27, 1957, d. Andover, New York December 8, 2015 from a heart attack.

Sharon attended Alfred Agricultural and Technical and Jamestown Community College earning an Associate's Degree in May 1990. She earned a Bachelor's Degree from Empire State College, New York in Human Services in October 1995. Sharon was employed for almost forty years with the Allegany County, New York Department of Social Services as a Child Support Coordinator retiring in 2016. She was a member of the Andover Central Schools School Board from 1988 to 1992. In addition, Sharon not only was the Treasurer for the Andover Methodist Church, but a Sunday School Teacher there from 1987-2000 and from 1996 to 2006, the Church's Treasurer.

From 2016 to 2019 Sharon was the Treasurer for the Allegany County Historical Society and Museum, Andover, New York. Mrs. Wallace served the American Red Cross, Allegany County, New York's

Disaster Relief Agency from 2016 to 2019. Sharon enjoys reading and walking.

Dave Wallace worked for Hetzel Buick and Garage, Wellsville, New York from 1976 to 1980. From 1980 to 1987 for the Village of Andover and from 1988 until his death was Andover Highway Superintendent. He was scheduled to retire at the time of his unexpected death. From 1984 until his death, Dave was a substitute school bus driver for Andover and worked part-time as the caretaker of the Country Estates, Andover. Dave was a dedicated member of the Andover Volunteer Fire Department and Andover Rescue Squad since 1978 where he served as Fire Chief, Treasurer, and Emergency Medical Technician. He was named Fireman of the Year in 1986 and 1999. Dave served as a member of the Allegany County Town Highway Superintendents since 1988 and was its President 1999-2000. He was a long-standing member of the New York State Highway Superintendents Association.

From 2004 Dave was the Allegany County District Fire Coordinator for District IV. In 2008 Dave and Sharon purchased a summer home on Lamoka Lake where Dave served as a board member of the Lamoka Waneta Lakes' Association starting in 2010. Dave enjoyed boating, jet skiing, his family and dogs, Shea and Nelli and his black Trans Am and red Stingray automobiles. Dave Wallace was given a fireman's funeral. Every township in Allegany County sent a Fire Department truck and contingent as did several townships in Steuben and Cattaraugus Counties. Dave was buried in Valley Brook Cemetery, Andover, New York. In 2019 Sharon sold the family residence on Baker Street and moved permanently to Lamoka Lake. The Wallace Family established the David L. Wallace Memorial Scholarship in 2018. Annually three scholarships are awarded each year in the County for graduating seniors who intend to go to a college, university, or vocational school and have at least one parent or guardian who is an active member of a Volunteer Fire Department in Allegany County. The digital LED sign outside the Andover Volunteer Fire Department was donated in Dave Wallace's memory.

Children:

1391. I. ***Andrew John Wallace***, b. Wellsville, New York August 8, 1982. Andy attended the University of Buffalo, New York and graduated from Erie Community College in May 2010 with an Associate's Degree in Medical Lab Technology. He is employed by Target's Online Sales Division and resides in Tonawanda, New York.

References: Interviews with Sharon Anderson Wallace; *Wellsville Daily Reporter* obituary for Dave Wallace, December 8, 2015.

780.

Richard Glen Anderson, son of Nordica (378), grandson of Leo C. (174), b. Wellsville, New York June 10, 1958; m. (1) Wellsville, New York June 30, 1979 Vickie Walker, divorced 1981; m. (2) June 7, 2003 Laurel, last name not provided, b. Long Island, New York June 5, 1948.

Rich worked for Bell Equipment as a mechanic until it closed. For the last twenty years Rich has been employed in highway construction with the New York State Labors Union. From a previous marriage Laurel has a daughter, Bethany, and grandchildren.

Children: (by first marriage)

1392. I. ***Dillon Anderson***, b. Wellsville, New York October 16, 1978. Dillon's long term partner is Howie Hinckle. Dillon purchased the house of her paternal grandparents, Glen and Nordica Root Anderson, along with twenty acres on Donovan Road.

Children:

i. ***Gage Wyatt Hinckle***, b. Wellsville, New York July 15, 1996. Gage is Employed with J.S.S. Vapor Shop, Wellsville, New York.

References: Interviews with Sharon Anderson Wallace.

781.

William Arthur Paquette, son of Dorothy (382), grandson of Leo C. (174), b. Lawrence, Massachusetts August 6, 1947; m. (1) Wexford, Pennsylvania June 14, 1969 Sylvia Lois Kreps, b. Butler, Pennsylvania June 30 1946, divorced 1987; m. (2) Portsmouth, Virginia January 2, 1988 Rebecca Owen Barclay, b. Portsmouth, Virginia March 22, 1951, divorced 1999.

Dr. Paquette's first wife was the daughter of a Pittsburgh Steel Executive. They both attended Grove City College in Grove City, Pennsylvania as undergraduates. Professor Paquette's second wife was a member of the Scottish Banking Family, Barclays. Neither marriage produced any children. In 1983 Dr. Paquette separated from his first wife and moved to Atlanta, Georgia to enroll in a doctoral program at Emory University. There he met a former Ralph Lauren model whom he planned to marry as soon as his divorce from his first wife was final. Unfortunately, Anne was diagnosed with cancer during the pregnancy and died in 1984, three months after delivering baby Edward. Edward's health was fragile and he was cared for by his maternal grandparents until his death May 18, 1989. Mother and son were buried together on Staten Island, New York City.

Dr. William Paquette was a Professor of History at Tidewater Community College in Portsmouth, Virginia where he taught Latin American History, World Civilization, U. S. History, and Western Civilization. Professor Paquette received a Bachelor's Degree from Grove City College, Pennsylvania, a Master's Degree from Duquesne University (Pittsburgh) and a Ph. D. from Emory University (Atlanta). During his academic career, Dr. Paquette was awarded 14 National Endowment for the Humanities Grants for professional study and Institutional grants that enabled him to study and conduct research in China and Japan.

He traveled to southern Mexico over a ten-year period examining the archaeology at Maya and Aztec sites and studied the Maya language at Duke University (Durham, NC). Professor Paquette presented research at international conferences at the University of Louvain (Belgium), the Sorbonne (Paris), the University of Acala de Henares (Spain), the University of Copenhagen (Denmark), Lorand Eotvos University (Budapest), and San Pablo University (Madrid). He has published over 165 articles and thirteen books and served as a consultant to the U.S. Department of Education, the United States Institute of Peace, the National Endowment for the Humanities, and all major history textbook publishers. For a decade, he was the History Editor for the international MERLOT (Multimedia Education Resources for Learning and Online Teaching) Project instructing college and university faculty on how to teach online courses.

In 2016, Dr. Paquette went to Eastern Europe to study firsthand the legacy of World War II and Communism on the people and nations of Bulgaria, Romania, Serbia, Hungary, Slovakia, Austria, and the Czech Republic. During his professional career Dr. Paquette met the late King Michael I and the late Queen Anne of Romania, King Simeon II of Bulgaria, the late Pope John Paul II, the Dalai Lama, members of the British Royal Family, and numerous Heads of Government from European States. In 1997, Professor Paquette received a National Humanities Award and in 2009 was given an International Award for Online Course Development and Instruction. Dr. Paquette has been annually listed in *Who's Who in America* and *Who's Who in the World.* He currently resides in Northern Virginia.

References: The author.

782.

Robert Louis Paquette, son of Dorothy (382), grandson of Leo C. (174), b. Wellsville, New York April 17, 1951; m. (1) North Canton, Ohio August 18, 1973 Susan L. Bowers, divorced 1974; m. (2) Rochester, New York August 8, 1981 Zoya Berlin.

Robert Paquette received his B. A. Cum Laude in 1973 from Bowling Green University, Ohio. His Ph.D. was received with Honors in 1982 from the University of Rochester, New York. He has published extensively on the history of slavery. *Sugar Is Made with Blood*, 1988 was awarded the Elsa Goveia Prize by the Association of Caribbean Historians. Bob's essay "Of Facts and Fables: New Light on the Denmark Vesey Affair" won the Malcolm C. Clark Award given by the South Carolina Historical Society. Other works Dr. Paquette has either authored or co-authored include: *The Lesser Antilles in the Age of European Expansion; Slavery, Secession, and Southern History; Slavery; The Oxford Handbook of Slavery in the Americas; Unbought Grace; The Denmark Vesey Affair: A Documentary History.*

In 2005, Dr. Paquette was given the Mary Young Award for distinguished achievement by the University of Rochester. He received a number of grants from the American Historical Association, the American Council of Learned Societies, the National Endowment for the Humanities, the Thomas W. Smith Foundation, the Watson-Brown Foundation, the Armstrong and Apgar Foundations, the Jack

Miller Center, and Charles G. Koch Foundation. In 2008 he was nominated by President George W. Bush for a seat on the National Council of the National Endowment for the Humanities. Other awards included the Heroes of Conscience Award (2012), the Lynde and Harry Bradley Foundation Award (2014), and the Jeanne Jordan Kirkpatrick Prize for Academic Freedom (2014). Professor Paquette taught at Hamilton College for thirty-seven years, 1981-2018. He held the Publius Virgilius Rogers Chair in American History for seventeen years. In 2007 Dr. Robert Paquette co-founded the Alexander Hamilton Institute for the Study of Western Civilization with Douglas Ambrose and James Bradfield. He currently serves as its Executive Director.

Zoya Borisovna Berlin emigrated to the United States from Minsk, the capital of Belarus, with her mother and father, Rachel and Boris Berlin, in 1978. She attended Belarusian State University in the former Soviet Union, where she majored in Geology, and upon arrival in Rochester, New York, entered the University of Rochester. There she majored in math and computer science, receiving her Bachelor of Science Degree in 1981. She married Robert Paquette, a graduate student in history at the University of Rochester, that same year. Zoya worked as a systems analyst, designed computer software, for almost twenty years. She dotes on her two children, Alexander and Natalie, and enjoys opera, classical music, reding, long walks in the outdoors, and meditation. Zoya's father, Boris Berlin, was a highly talented engineer with a number of patents to his name at the time he emigrated to the United States. He brought those same talents to several US companies and was awarded additional patents in the United States. Rachel Berlin, Zoya's mother, was medical doctor who specialized in sports medicine. Dr. Berlin was the medical doctor for the Women's Gymnastics Team at the 1972 Olympic Games.

Children: (by second marriage)

1393. I. ***Alexander Loren Paquette***, b. Syracuse, New York January 22, 1985. Called an *old soul* by those that know him and some that meet him, Alexander was a curious, inquisitive child. As he grew through grade school, sports, girls, art and a rebellious nature guided his spirit. The height of his athletic accomplishments include being elected as an All-Conference D-III collegiate baseball player. After graduating Clinton High School in 2003, Alexander attended Hampden-Sydney College, Virginia for two years and majored in English, then worked as a salesman for over a year before attending MVCC, New York for one semester, and subsequently graduating from Keuka College, New York with a B. S. Degree in 2010. After graduating college and coaching baseball at his high school alma mater for one season, Alexander did his best to become a nomad and traveled by car down the west coast from Portland to Southern California, yet, eventually found himself in Ithaca, New York. In college, Alexander had his first live music performance. It was after this performance in 2009 that he began teaching himself the art of music production in the digital age. A love for comedy, counter-culture, old-time radio detectives, Salvador Dali, and spiritual growth serves as the foundation of his changing creative sensibilities. He has taught himself how to play the piano, guitar, and ukulele. In 2020 Alexander founded a musical co-op production company named

ProDuckshin Creations, which helps up-and-coming artists of all mediums grow their art and grow themselves, especially if they feel a love for channeling their passion into a source of income. Inspired by an eclectic mix of humans and characters such as Dr. Joe Dispenza, Shel Silverstein, Eckhart Tolle, Marcus Aurelius, Arya Tark, Dali, Tariq Trotter, Dr. Seuss, and Peter Parker, Alexander is currently recording, producing, and mastering his first studio album with his band, Koodge & Mr. Bones while taking online classes from Berklee School of Music, which range from The Technology of Music Production to Music Theory. He believes the process of gaining musical knowledge and applying it is a never-ending, lifelong endeavor and joy.

1394. II. ***Natalie Marie Paquette***, b. Syracuse, New York October 16, 1990. Natalie was Raised in Clinton, New York and attended Clinton Central Schools as a Varsity athlete in volleyball and tennis. During high school she was a Docent and later employee at the Education Department of the Utica Zoo driven by an abiding love of animals and conservation. She graduated from Clinton High School as Valedictorian in 2008 and then attended Cornell University, Ithaca, New York from which she graduated *summa cum laude* in 2012 with Honors in Research. Her degrees were in Applied and Engineering Physics and Applied Mathematics. She then earned her Ph.D. in theoretical physics from Sanford University in 2017, where she was an NSF Graduate Research Fellow and a Stanford Humanities and Science Fellow. Her research interests are in string theory, quantum field theory, and mathematical physics, and she is best known for studying questions at the interface between modern mathematics and theoretical physics. Natalie was a Sherman Fairchild Postdoctoral Fellow at Caltech from 2017-2020, a Member at the Institute for Advanced Study in Princeton, New Jersey 2020-21, and takes up a tenure appointment as Assistant Professor of Physics at the University of Seattle, Washington State in 2021. Outside of her academic life, Natalie is a martial arts enthusiast and combat sports fan who trains in Muay Thai and boxing. She enjoys hiking (in moderation), wine-tasting (in-excess), traveling, reading, and watching movies. She has particular penchants for economics texts and horror movies.

References: Biography of Dr. Robert L. Paquette on the Alexander Hamilton Institute website; Biography for Dr. Natalie M. Paquette on the California Institute of Technology website; Correspondence with Dr. Robert Paquette; Correspondence with Alexander Paquette, Correspondence with Dr. Natalie Paquette.

783.

Patricia Adora Paquette, daughter of Dorothy (382), granddaughter of Leo C. (174), b. Hornell, New York September 26, 1964; m. Fairfax, Virginia July 23, 1988 John Porasky, divorced 2006.

Patti graduated summa cum laude from Northern Virginia Community College and has a Bachelor's Degree in Accounting from George Mason University, Fairfax, Virginia. In 2003 she passed the CPA exam with one of the highest scores in the State of Virginia. For a decade Patti was employed with the Brown's Automotive Group in Fairfax, Virginia as Controller. In 2004 she joined the Penske Automotive Group as Area Financial Controller for the Washington, DC Metro Region overseeing four automotive franchises. In 2006 Patti accepted the position of Western Region Internal Audit Manager for the Penske Automotive Group; relocating to Los Angeles, California. In February 2015 she joined Penske Power Systems in Sydney, Australia as Financial Operations and Planning Manager.

During her four years in Australia Patti was appointed Chief Financial Officer of Penske Transportation Group International. In late 2018 Patti was promoted to Director of Internal Audit for Penske Automotive Group headquartered in Bloomfield Hills, Michigan, overseeing operations in the United Kingdom, Europe, Australia, New Zealand, and the United States. In addition to a residence in Birmingham, Michigan, Patti maintains her Los Angeles condo in a downtown 1930s green Art Deco high rise frequently featured in movies including *Transformers.* Patti has long been an enthusiastic fan of the original *Star Trek* television series. She and the author attended a number of annual science fiction conventions in Atlanta, Georgia where we were able to meet the original cast. In addition, Patti is an avid reader of *Sherlock Holmes* and she and the author visited the Holmes Museum on Baker Street in London. Patti is an avid dog lover and has competed in many Los Angeles and Sydney marathons.

Her partner is actor Dean Haglund who was born in Oakbank, Manitoba, Canada on July 29 1965. Dean is probably best known for his role on *X-Files* as Richard *Ringo* Langly, the Lone Gunman. Haglund is also a stand-up comedian specializing in improvisational comedy and was formerly with the Vancouver TheatreSports League. He has done comedy in Los Angeles, across the United States, Australia, and the Edinburgh, Scotland Fringe Festival. Dean played the voice of Sid in *Tom Sawyer* and starred for thirteen episodes in the 2001 series *The Lone Gunman.* He invented the *Chill Pak*, a commercial external product for laptop computers. Dean was awarded a *Silver Medal* in 2006 for the *Chill Pak* at the International Exhibition of Inventions, Geneva, Switzerland. *Dean* Haglund can claim direct descent from Swedish King, Eric XIV, but through an illegitimate son of that monarch. His family was close friends with the late Swedish playwright August Strindberg and the family in Stockholm still has the author's desk. In addition, Dean is an accomplished artist and has done a number of art shows from New York to Los Angeles. In 2016 Dean published *Broadway* an illustrated history of the movie palaces on Broadway in Los Angeles. Dean did all the illustrations of these once great movie palaces. The author has several of his paintings.

References: Correspondence with Patti Paquette and Dean Haglund.

785.

Michael Jurgen Klaus Root, son of Hugh Daniel (383), grandson of Leo C. (174), b. Berlin, Germany April 4, 1957, d. San Antonio, Texas January 15, 1981 from congenital heart disease and cardiac tamponade due to the rupture of a dilated pulmonary artery at the residence of his sister; m. Bexar, Texas March 18, 1978 Lisa J. Turner, b. 1958, divorced January 25, 1980. Michael was buried in Chapel Hill Memorial Gardens, Converse, Texas.

References: Texas Death Index 1968-2014; Texas Marriage Certificate 1966-2011; Texas Divorce Certificate 1903-1982; Social Security Death Index 1935-2014; Chapel Hill Memorial Gardens Records, Converse, Texas.

786.

Larry Wayne Root, son of Lawrence (384), grandson of Leo C. (174), b. Norfolk, Virginia June 4, 1950, d. Landrum, South Carolina March 31, 2016 from a heart attack caused by hypertension and heart disease; m. (1) Puerto Rico, date not known Gianna Marie Rodriquez, b. Santurce, Puerto, Rico February 9, 1948, d. San Juan, Puerto Rico April 19, 1999 from an intercranial hematoma, divorced; m. (2) Maxine Young May 1986, divorced 1989; m. (3) place not known, December 15, 2000 Pamela Denise Hardin, divorced.

Larry Wayne served in the US Marine Corps from 1968 to 1972. According to some family sources, Larry Wayne and Gianna were married twice and divorced twice. The Social Security Claims Index 1936-2007 record that Gianna changed her last name from Rodriquez to Root in October 1969. Gabriel was born while Larry Wayne was still legally married to his second wife. At the time of his death was a self-employed software engineer. Larry Wayne's remains were cremated and are in the possession of his son, Alexander. Gianna's remains were cremated and buried in Carolina, Puerto Rico.

Children: (by first marriage)

1395. I. ***Gabriel Root***, b. Puerto Rico January 4, 1989; m. San Juan, Puerto Rico June 2, 2016 Jessenia Attishia Matos Ortiz. Gaby is a Sergeant in the US Army National Guard stationed at Fort Greely, Alaska with the Military Police.

Children:

i. ***Alexander Gabriel Root Matos***, b. November 22, 2013.
ii. ***Gianna Gabriela Root Matos***, b. May 29, 2017.

Children: (by second marriage)

1396. I. ***Alexander Paten Root***, b. South Carolina August 14, 2001. Alexander is Serving with the US Army National Guard and is stationed in Campobello, South Carolina.

References: Virginia Birth Records 1912-2015; *Spartanburg Herald-Journal* obituary April 4, 2016 for Larry Wayne Root; Puerto Rico Death Records 1885-2001 for Gianna Rodriquez Root; Interviews with Ronald L. Root; Social Security Claims Index 1936-2007.

787.

Ronald Leo Root, son of Lawrence (384), grandson of Leo C. (174), b. Wellsville, New York May 16, 1951; m. Danville, Virginia January 11, 1975 Nannie Hardy, b. Danville, Virginia July 27, 1950, divorced January 14, 1999 Orange County, Florida.

Ron attended Averett College, Danville, Virginia where he attained a B. S. Degree in Business Administration. He earned a Master's in Business Administration from the Florida Institute of Technology. Ron served in the US Marine Corps from 1970-1977 where he was employed as an air traffic controller. From 1978 to 1979 Ron was employed with the FAA as a Control Representative working with the New Jersey Air Traffic Control. Since 1980 he was employed with the Department of the Navy, Naval Air Warfare Training Systems Center. Ron retired December 31, 2011 and currently resides in Orlando, Florida.

References: Virginia Marriage Record 1936-2014; Florida Divorce Index 1927-2001; Interviews with Ronald Root.

788.

Robert Wylie Crist, son of Jeanne (385), grandson of Nordica (175), b. New York City, New York January 15, 1950, d. South Kingstown, Rhode Island December 9, 1983 from brain cancer; m. Westport, Connecticut August 27, 1977 Darleen J. Trew, b. Rhode Island, a. 1954.

Lee was a graduate of Syracuse University and held a graduate degree from American University. He was employed as a marine biologist with the US Government Agency, NOAA. Lee, as he was known to family and friends, served in the US military from July 26, 1972 to July 25, 1974. Darleen Crist was employed as a staff member for a Rhode Island State Representative and resided in South Kingstown, Rhode Island. Lee was buried Evergreen Cemetery, Westport, Connecticut.

References: New York State Birth Index 1910-1996; Connecticut Marriage Index 1959-2012; Social Security Death Index 1935-2014; US Veterans Death Files 1850-2010; Evergreen Cemetery Records, Westport, Connecticut.

789.

Jeffrey Hugh Wylie, son of Jeanne (385), grandson of Nordica (175), b. New York City December 14, 1951; d. San Francisco 2017; m. Jefferson, Washington March 20, 1972 Robin A. Anderson. Jeffrey Wylie resided in San Francisco since at least 1988 until his death. He was diagnosed with cerebral palsy as a young boy. Nothing further is known about his wife or what career he pursued. Jeffrey was buried with his father and brother in Evergreen Cemetery, Westport, Connecticut.

References: Washington State Marriage Index 1969-2017; Evergreen Cemetery Records, Westport, Connecticut; Correspondence with Jeanne Wylie Crist.

790.

Karen Crist, daughter of Jeanne (385), granddaughter of Nordica (175), b. place not known January 24, 1956; m. Westport, Connecticut May 26, 1979 Matthew J. Miller.

Karen graduated from Russell Sage College with a degree in special education and worked for a time with a computer firm. Matthew Miller graduated from Rensselaer Polytechnic Institute and was employed as a Materials Engineer for A. M. F. They reside in Cheshire, Connecticut.

Children:

1397. I. ***Matthew Charles Miller***, b. August 21, 1984.

1398. II. ***Geoffrey Robert Miller***, b. February 7, 1986.

References: Connecticut Marriage Index 1959-2012; Correspondence with Jeanne Wylie Crist.

791.

Stephen Gale Root, son of Gale (386), grandson of Allen (176), b. April 18, 1950; m. (1) June 15, 1974 Gail Lockwood, divorced; m. (2) April 22, 1978 Gloria Jones Norton, divorced; m. (3) July 15, 1984 Karen Freels; m. (4) May 23, 1999 Donna, last name not known.

Stephen Root was Chief of Mail Operations for Delta Airlines, Atlanta, until his retirement and move to Hilton Head, South Carolina. He was active in both the Shriners and the Masons.

Children: (by first marriage)

1399. I. ***Blair Root***, b. September 3, 1975, resides in Stuart, Florida where he is employed with a contracting business. He is single.

References: Interviews with Douglas Root, 2019.

792.

Douglas Allen Root, don of Gale (386), grandson of Allen (176), b. June 22, 1951; m. May 4, 1975 Cecelia Cawley.

Doug served the Bolivar, New York Community in a number of positions. He was Assistant Chief of Police, served with the Bolivar Fire Department and worked for 32 years in public works, Bolivar, New York retiring as Superintendent. Mrs. Root was a long-time employee of the Steuben Trust Bank, Bolivar, New York. Their youngest daughter is the last Root in residence in Bolivar, New York. They currently reside in Lake Placid, Florida.

Children:

1400. I. ***Anne Christina Root***, b. September 12, 1980; m. September 23, 2009 Ronald MacNeal. Anne is a social worker graduating from St. Bonaventure University, Allegany, New York and is currently working on a Master's Degree. Ron is a Medical Coder with an online university. They reside in Lake Placid, Florida.

Children:

i. ***Jayden Cecilia MacNeal***, b. Sebring, Florida November 14, 2010.
ii. ***Abigail Michele MacNeal***, b. Sebring, Florida November 8, 2013.

1401. II. ***Catherine Suzanne Root***, b. September 25, 1983; m. July 27, 2019 Jedediah Ingalls. Catherine works with Century Link, a telecommunications company and her husband is employed with Clein Cutlery. They reside in Bolivar, New York.

References: Interviews with Douglas Root, 2019.

793.

Kimberly Ann Root, daughter of Gale (386), granddaughter of Allen (176), b. September 27, 1954; m. (1) July 31, 1972 Van Rickicki, divorced; m. (2) February 14, 1987 Kenneth Skodack. Ken was the Golf Course Architect and Planner in Hilton Head, South Carolina. Kim was his business partner in the enterprise. They do not have any children and currently reside in Lake Placid, Florida.

References: Interviews with Douglas Root, 2019.

794.

Daniel John Holland, son of Dean (390), grandson of Mary (180), b. Ohio, March 31, 1952; m. July 28, 1979 Victoria Lazzar. Daniel was the District Sales Manager for the Fairfield American Corporation. Vicki was employed as a branch manager for Crawford Rehabilitation Services. They resided in Campbell Hall, New York. Further information on these Root descendants is not currently available.

References: Ohio Birth Index 1908-1998; Interviews with the late Mary Root Holland, 1990.

795.

Christine Anne Holland, daughter of Dean (390), granddaughter of Mary (180), b. Ohio March 15, 1953; m. August 24, 1974 Thomas Zappala. They were last known to reside in Amesbury, Massachusetts where Tom was employed as a buyer for the Eaton Corporation. Further information is not currently available.

Children:

1402. I. ***Nicole Christina Zappala***, b. July 1, 1976.

1403. II. ***Jessica Anne Zappala***, b. March 18, 1980.

1404. III. ***Thomas Augustine Zappala***, b. October 20, 1981, a twin.

1405. IV. ***Jacqueline Suzanne Zappala***, b. October 20, 1981, a twin.

References: Ohio Birth Index 1908-1998; Interviews with the late Mary Root Holland, 1990.

796.

Corinne Marie Holland, daughter of Dean (390), granddaughter of Mary (180), b. Ohio June 12, 1954; m. (1) August 18, 1973 Timothy Pollard, divorced 1983; m. (2) 1989 Bryan Walker. Corrine was employed with Cable Vision while her husband was a Vice-President for Citibank in Buffalo, New York. Further information on these Root descendants is not currently available.

Children: (by first marriage)

1406. I. ***Katherine Elizabeth Pollard***, b. July 27, 1975.

1407. II. ***Maggie Mathews Pollard***, b. January 30, 1979.

1408. III. ***Patrick Timothy Pollard***, b. March 8, 1982.

References: Ohio Birth Index 1908-1998; Interviews with the late Mary Root Holland, 1990.

797.

Michael Dean Holland, son of Dean (390), grandson of Mary (180), b. Ohio July 7, 1955; m. Summit, Ohio October 29, 1988 Janice L. Kerchelich, divorced Ohio, March 21, 2002.

Michael was employed with Berman Moving and Storage while in residence in Ohio. After his divorce, public records indicate he resided in Long Beach, California and Mississippi. Further information is not currently available.

Children:

1409. I. ***Jordan Patricia Holland***, b. Ohio October 4, 1989.

1410. II. ***Rian Grace Holland***, b. Ohio February 23, 1991.

1411. III. A third child based on divorce records; identity not known.

References: Ohio Birth Index 1908-1998; Ohio Divorce Abstracts 1973-2007; Ohio Marriage Abstracts 1972-2007; Interviews with the late Mary Root Holland, 1990.

798.

Mary Patricia Holland, daughter of Dean (390), granddaughter of Mary (180), b. Ohio February 28, 1959; m. January 21, 1985 Mario Martinez.

Mary graduated from the Defense Language Institute with Honors in 1984 with a specialty in the Czech language. Her husband was a sergeant in the US Marine Corps and after leaving the service was employed in the construction industry. Mary later worked in advertising. These Root descendants were last known to reside in Sanford, Florida.

Children:

1412. I. ***Eleana Martinez***, b. August 19, 1985.

1413. II. ***Mario Dean Martinez***, b. November 20, 1987.

References: Ohio Birth Index 1908-1998; Interviews with the late Mary Root Holland, 1990.

801.

James Robert Wescott, son of Barbara (391), grandson of Mary (180), b. May 19, 1956; m. June 26, 1975 Regina Leigh Bunting, divorced; m. (2) September 5, 1987 Sherri Ryan, b. August 1, 1958. These Root descendants were last known to reside in Hampton, Virginia where Jimmy owned his own service station. He inherited an old photo album once owned by Almyra Reed Root, his maternal grandmother's, paternal grandmother. Unfortunately, none of the images were ever identified. Further information on these Root descendants is not currently available.

Children: (by first marriage).

1414. I. ***James Brian Wescott***, b. March 6, 1978.

1415. II. ***Gerald Taylor Wescott***, b. June 18, 1979.

1416. III. ***Steven Robert Wescott***, b. February 28, 1982.

References: Interviews with the late Mary Root Holland.

802.

Mary Elizabeth Wescott, daughter of Barbara (391), granddaughter of Mary (180), b. April 23, 1959; m. March 23, 1985 Naval Lieutenant Commander Mark Winston Bock, Jr. They were last known to reside in Washington, D.C. Mary Elizabeth was named for her maternal grandmother, Mary Elizabeth Root Holland. Further information on these Root descendants is not currently available.

Children:

1417. I. ***Mark Winston Bock III***, b. October 29, 1985.

1418. II. ***Robert Bock***, b. April 3, 1987.

1419. III. ***James Andrew Bock***, b. December 28, 1989.

References: Interviews with the late Mary Root Holland, 1990.

812.

Maurice Philip Weatherby/Weatherbee, son of Howard (396), grandson of Minnie (189), b. Portville, New York, d. Cuba Hospital, Cuba, New York September 7, 2018; m. Olean, New York June 17, 1950 Edith M. Critchlow, b. Olean, New York June 22, 1925, d. Cuba, New York April 25, 2010.

Maurice served in the US Army December 22, 1944 and was stationed in Shinagawa, Japan as a 33rd Quartermaster. At the time of his enlistment Maury was described as being 5' 6" talk with hazel eyes and brown hair. In 1944 he was employed with the Hydrox Dairy. For twenty-five years he was employed at Cutco and worked for BOCES until his 1984 retirement. Maury was a member of the Olean Community Evangelical Church. During his free time, Maury continued the magic traditions of his father and was known as *Magical Maurice*. He performed in shows around the area. Both Maury and Edith operated cotton candy, snow cone, and popcorn concessions at Olean events. Edith was a Sunday School Teacher and was employed as both a private secretary and a financial secretary. She was a member of the Eastern Star, collected antiques including cut-glass, salt dips, dolls, and glass baskets while Maury collected music boxes, Edison machines, and white metal soldiers. Maurice and Edith Weatherby were buried in Chestnut Hill Cemetery, Portville, New York with their infant daughter Maureen.

Children:

1420. I. ***Maureen Rose Weatherbee***, b. and d. December 9, 1963 and was buried in Chestnut Hill Cemetery.

1421. II. ***Paul Elton Weatherbee***, b. Olean, New York January 17, 1965; m. Polk City, Florida November 30, 1996 Karen Suzanne Horne. They reside in Lakeland, Florida and do not have any children.

References: US Census: 1930, 1940; New York State Census: 1925; World War II Draft Registration Card; New York State Marriage Index 1881-1967; Social Security Death Index 1935-2014; Chestnut Hill Cemetery Records, Portville, New York; World War II Army Records 1938-1946; *Olean Times Herald* obituary for Maurice Weatherby/Weatherbee September 8, 2018; Florida Marriage Index 1927-2001 for Paul Weatherbee.

813.

Dale Mac Richardson, son of Stanley (398), grandson of Stanley (190), b. Oklahoma October 3, 1935, d. Oklahoma January 28, 2010. Mr. Richardson was buried in Okmulgee Cemetery in Okmulgee, Oklahoma. There is no mention of his being married or having children.

References: US Census: 1940; Social Security Death Index 1935-2014; Okmulgee Cemetery Records, Okmulgee, Oklahoma.

814.

Rex Stanley Richardson, son of Ralph (399), grandson of Stanley (190), b. Oklahoma City, Oklahoma May 6, 1939, d. Mt. Vernon, Missouri March 13, 2013; m. (1) Mt. Vernon, Missouri December 24, 1958 Onisko Kaye Mason, b. Lawrence County, Kansas August 15, 1942, d. Joplin, Missouri February 7, 2009, divorced; m. (2) Miami, Oklahoma December 17, 1970 Mary Bryson, b. place not known, September 23, 1950. He was survived by eight grandchildren and four great-grandchildren. Two sons predeceased him. Mr. Richardson was buried in Mt. Vernon IOOF Cemetery, Mt. Vernon, Missouri. Onisko Kaye Mason Baker was buried in Miller Memorial Gardens, Miller, Missouri.

Children: (by first marriage)

1422. I. ***Donald Richardson***; last known to reside in Mt. Vernon, Missouri; ***nfi.***

1423. II. ***Scott Richardson***; m. Lynne and last resided in Mt. Vernon, Missouri; ***nfi.***

1424. III. ***Robert William Richardson***, b. May 18, 1968, d. January 10, 1977 and buried in Mt. Vernon IOOF Cemetery.

Children: (by second marriage)

1425. I. ***Brian Keith Richardson***, b. April 6, 1970, d. January 10, 1977 and buried in Mt. Vernon IOOF Cemetery.

1426. II. ***Jane Richardson***; m. Lowell Phillips and last reside Mt. Vernon, Missouri; ***nfi.***

1427. III. ***Susie Richardson***; m. Brad Dorris and last resided Ozark, Missouri; ***nfi.***

References: US Census: 1940; Social Security Death Index 1935-2014 for Rex Richardson and his first wife; Missouri Marriage Records 1805-2008 for Rex Richardson's first marriage; obituaries posted on findagrave.com for Rex Stanley Richardson and Onisko Kaye Mason Baker; Mt. Vernon IOOF Cemetery Records, Mt. Vernon, Missouri; Miller Memorial Gardens Records, Miller, Missouri.

815.

Michael Gene Richardson, son of Ralph (399), grandson of Stanley (190), b. place not known, January 6, 1944; m. Miller, Missouri June 6, 1964 Linda Suzanne Ruark. They were last known to reside in Joplin, Missouri. Further information on this Root descendant is not currently available.

Reference: Missouri Marriage Record 1805-2002.

816.

Richard "Ricky" Dean Richardson, son of Ralph (393), grandson of Stanley (190), b. place not known, a. 1946; m. (1) Mt. Vernon, Missouri February 29, 1964 Gloria Jean Dame, b. Placer, California March 24, 1947, d. Kentucky, a. 2013, divorced; m. (2) Mt. Vernon, Missouri November 24, 1978 Sharon Elaine Gotway. They were last known to reside in Mt. Vernon, Missouri. There is currently no further information on this Root descendant.

References: Missouri Marriage Records 1805-2002.

817.

Rolland Everett Durfee, son of Frances (402), grandson of Manley (191), b. Alma, New York March 26, 1928, d. Macedon, New York July 16, 1963 from a motorcycle accident; m. Olean, New York January 15, 1949 Patricia Weaver.

Mr. Durfee was known as *Uncle Ronny* to family members. He enlisted in the US Military February 26, 1946 with the Panama Canal Division. After his military service Rolland Durfee was employed with the Pennsylvania Railroad and resided in Olean, New York. It is not currently known where Mr. Durfee was buried.

References: US Census: 1930, 1940; New York State Birth Index 1881-1942; New York State Death Index 1957-1968; New York State Marriage Index 1881-1967; World War II Army Enlistment Records 1938-1946; Olean, New York City Directory, 1950.

818.

Eloise Belle Durfee (a twin), daughter of Frances (402), granddaughter of Manley (191), b. Wellsville, New York May 24, 1929; d. Wellsville, New York January 13, 2016; m. Wellsville, New York August 29, 1947 Warren Richard Vossler, b. Wellsville, New York November 27, 1927, d. Wellsville, New York September 14, 1995.

Eloise, her twin sister, Eleanor, and her brother, Rolland, were raised by their maternal grandparents, Mr. and Mrs. Manley Richardson, after their mother's early death. Eloise was a former employee of the Olean Tile Company, Olean, New York where she was employed for twelve years. For twenty-five years she was employed as a beautician. In addition to being a member of the Wellsville Business and Professional Women's Club, she taught Sunday School at the Obi, New York church, and was a life member of the Petrolia Hose Company No. 2.

Warren Vossler's World War II Draft Registration Card described him as being 6' 1" tall, weighed 140 pounds, had ruddy complexion with blue eyes and brown hair. Warren Vossler purchased in 1948, the former one-room school in Petrolia, New York, Scio District School #8, and converted it into a two-story residence. Mr. Vossler was employed as a truck driver, logger, mechanic, welder, and for many years at the Air Preheater Corporation, Wellsville, New York. Eloise and Warren enjoyed traveling, camping, boating, and fishing. Eloise did crossword puzzles, needlepoint, and crochet. Eloise and Warren Vossler were buried in Woodlawn Cemetery, Wellsville, New York.

Children:

1428. I. ***Patricia A. Vossler***, b. Wellsville, New York February 23, 1948; m. (1) Neil K. Clarke, b. February 5, 1947, d. November 22, 1994; m. (2) Douglas Pobgee. Neil Clarke served with the US Army in Vietnam rising to the rank of SP 4. Kay was employed by several lawyers and later the Air Preheater Corporation in Wellsville, New York. Neil Clarke was employed with the US Post Office in Wellsville. Doug was also employed at Air Preheater. When Pat and Doug moved to York, Pennsylvania, they were both employed by Metso. Neil Clark was buried in Woodlawn Cemetery, Wellsville, New York.

Children: (by first marriage)

i. ***Jay Kenyon Clarke***, b. Wellsville, New York April 12, 1972, d. York, Pennsylvania December 12, 2010 after a long illness. Jay attended York Suburban High School, York, Pennsylvania and Shippensburg University, Pennsylvania where he was an avid runner. He was twice York County, Pennsylvania champion and was awarded many state medals. Jay Clarke was buried in Woodlawn Cemetery, Wellsville, New York.

ii. ***Amanda K. Clarke***, b. Wellsville, New York November 10, 1975; James Howell.

Children:

a. ***Kayla Howell.***
b. ***Tyler Howell.***

iii. ***Nathan Clarke***, b. Wellsville, New York December 23, 1977; m. Apple, last name not known.

Children:

a. ***Karaked Clarke.***

1429. II. ***Kay F. Vossler***, b. Wellsville, New York February 3, 1950; m. (1) Hank Schekell, Deceased; m. (2) Tom Lauzee. Kay worked as a beautician and later for Dresser-Rank where her second husband was also employed.

Children: (by second marriage)

i. ***Bradley Lauzee***; m. Keira, last name not known.

Children:

a. ***Mila Lauzee.***

1430. III. ***James R. Vossler***, b. Wellsville, New York August 28, 1952; m. Wellsville, New York April 21, 1972 Dale Clayson. Jim attended college for truck and Diesel mechanics and worked for forty-two years at a machine shop in Scio, New York. Dale was employed for a number of years at a beautician and a waitress and lastly at Wellsville Schools.

Children:

i. ***Craig R. Vossler***, b. Wellsville, New York November 1, 1972; m. (1) Susan Baker, divorced; m. (2) Scio, New York February 20, 2010 Jill Culberson. Craig resides in the former school house in Petrolia his paternal grandfather converted into a two-story residence. Craig was employed in mining in Tennessee as a mechanic, later at the Air Preheater as a welder, at Lufkin as a machinist, and currently at Corning Glass, Corning, New York as a programmer.

Children: (by first marriage)

a. ***Jacob H. Vossler***, b. October 20, 1998.

Children: (by second marriage)

a. ***Rowen K. Vossler***, b. June 5, 2000.
b. ***Max W. Vossler,*** b. January 1, 2014.

ii. ***Kevin M. Vossler***, b. Wellsville, New York September 5, 1974, d. Wellsville, New York October 15, 1990 and was buried in Woodlawn Cemetery, Wellsville, New York.

References: US Census: 1930,1940; New York State Birth Index 1881-1942; Social Security Death Index 1935-2014; New York State Marriage Index 1881-1967; Woodlawn Cemetery Records, Wellsville, New York; World War II Draft Registration Card; Obituary on findagrave.com; Interviews with James Vossler, 2020.

819.

Eleanor Ann Durfee (a twin), daughter of Frances (402), granddaughter of Manley (191), b. Wellsville, New York May 24, 1929, still living; m. (1) Wellsville, New York August 29, 1947 Chester E. Wood, b. Pennsylvania May 19, 1926, d. Wellsville, New York November 7, 1982; m. (2) place and date not known, Basil C. Shutt, b. a. 1934, d. place and date not known.

Eleanor, her twin sister Eloise, and her brother Rolland were raised by their maternal grandparents, Mr. and Mrs. Manley Richardson. Eleanor was a life-long resident of Allentown, New York where she raised two daughters. Like her sister, Eloise, Eleanor also worked for the Olean Tile Company, Olean, New York. During World War II Chester Wood served with the US Army from July 24, 1944 to August 9, 1946 rising to the rank of Tech 4. Chester Wood was buried in Maple Lawn Cemetery, Bolivar, New York. Eleanor has been living in a Wellsville, New York nursing home since 2016.

Children: (by first marriage)

1431. I. ***Marilyn Wood, nfi.***

1432. II. ***Linda Wood; nfi.***

References: US Census: 1930, 1940; New York State Birth Index 1881-1942; New York State Marriage Index 1881-1967 for Eleanor's first marriage; US Veterans Death File 1850-2010; Maple Lawn Cemetery Records, Bolivar, New York.

820.

Elizabeth Durfee, daughter of Frances (402), granddaughter of Manley (191), b. New York State, a. 1932, still living.

In the 1940 US Census Elizabeth resided with Charles Henry Powell (1887-1969) and Anna Grace Eisenhart (1890-1970) in Rochester, New York. Grace's mother was a Durfee and, therefore related to Elizabeth's father Harold Durfee. Over time Elizabeth was referred to as Elizabeth Powell. It is not currently known if she was adopted, or simply used the Powell last name, or, perhaps, married someone with the last name of Powell. In the 2016 obituary of her sister, Eloise, Elizabeth Powell resided in Texas. Further information is not currently available. Charles and Grace Powell were buried in Oak Hill Burial Park, Lakeland, Florida.

References: US Census: 1940; Oak Hill Burial Park Records, Lakeland, Florida; 2016 obituary of Eloise Durfee Vossler.

821.

Yvonne Mink, daughter of Margaret (403), granddaughter of Agnes (192), b. place not known, July 24, 1951; m. (1) place not known October 3, 1969 Dean Habberfield, divorced; m. (2) place not known, 1984, Mr. Krupper. Her last known address was Topeka, Kansas.

Children: (by first marriage)

1433. I. ***Beezy James Habberfield***, b. November 27, 1969; ***nfi.***

1434. II. ***Danielle Ann Habberfield***, b. July 4, 1973; ***nfi.***

References: Correspondence with Rose June Feenaughty.

822.

Kenneth Richard Cornell, Jr., son of Flora (405), grandson of Agnes (192), b. Silver Springs, New York February 7, 1933, d. Rochester, New York March 9, 2005; married and divorced but the identity of his spouse is not known. Mr. Cornell served in the US Army in Korea and rose to the rank of Corporal. He had a daughter, Juanita Cornell, a grandson, and a great-grandson according to an obituary on findagrave.com. He resided in LeRoy, New York and was buried in East Koy Cemetery, East Koy, New York.

References: Social Security Death Index 1935-2014; US Veterans Gravesites 1775-2006; New York State Birth Index 1881-1942; obituary on findagrave.com.

823.

Jacquelin Ann Cornell, daughter of Flora (405), granddaughter of Agnes (192), b. Silver Springs, New York November 19, 1934, d. North Myrtle Beach November 1993; m. five times but the identities of her husband are not currently known.

The Social Security Claims Index notes that Jacquelin Cornell's last name changed to Yencer in 1951, to Perkins in 1957, to Diggins in 1962, to Perry in 1966, and to Wright in 1976. Mrs. Wright retired from the Morton Salt Company in Western New York. In addition to four children surviving her, Jacquelin Wright was survived by seven grandchildren and one-great-grandchild.

Children: (by Mr. Perry)

1435. I. ***Kenneth Perry***, last known to reside in Rochester, New York; ***nfi.***

Children: (by Mr. Diggins)

1436. I. ***Martin Diggins***, last known to reside in Perry, New York; ***nfi.***

Children: (Identify of father not known)

1437. I. ***Sharon Sanfertillo***, last known to reside in Fairport, New York; ***nfi.***

1438. II. ***Alexandria Carl***, last known to reside in Silver Springs, New York; ***nfi.***

References: New York State Birth Index 1881-1941; Social Security Death Index 1935-2014; Social Security Claims I 1936-2007; November 21, 1993 obituary *The State*, Richland, South Carolina.

824.

Dennis Stack, son of Phyllis (407), grandson of Agnes (192, b. place not known, April 12, 1947; m. identity of spouse not known. Last known residing in Florida; ***nfi.***

Children:

1439. I. ***Male Stack***, b. 1974; ***nfi.***

References: Correspondence with Rose June Feenaughty.

825.

Kathleen Stack, daughter of Phyllis (407), granddaughter of Agnes (192), b. place not known, August 8, 1948; m. place not known, 1968 Michael Dodge; ***nfi.***

Children:

1440. I. ***David Dodge***, b. April 8, 1970; ***nfi.***

1441. II. ***Jason Dodge***, August 28, 1971; ***nfi.***

1442. III. ***John Dodge***, b. October 31, 1973; ***nfi.***

References: Correspondence with Rose June Feenaughty.

826.

James Stack, son of Phyllis (407), grandson of Agnes (192), b. place not known June 14, 1949; m. February 1963 Carol Wilyol; ***nfi.***

Children:

1443. I. ***James Stack***, b. September 1, 1963; ***nfi.***

1444. II. ***Hillary Stack***, b. September 1, 1963; ***nfi.***

References: Correspondence with Rose June Feenaughty.

835.

Dennis Alan Slupe, son of Margaret (413), grandson of Harold (193), b. Cleveland, Ohio June 15, 1943, d. Medina, Ohio September 18, 1979. Mr. Slupe served in the US Army in Vietnam from January 8, 1965 to January 6, 1967 rising to the rank of SP 4. According to death record information, he had never married. Dennis Slupe was buried in Oakwood Cemetery, Cuyahoga Falls, Ohio.

References: US Veterans Death File 1850-2010; Social Security Death Index 1935-2014; Oakwood Cemetery Records, Cuyahoga Falls, Ohio; Ohio Death Index 1938-2007.

837.

Beverly Doris June, daughter of Doris (416), granddaughter of Lewis (198), b. Bolivar, New York March 10, 1938; m. Warsaw, New York May 3, 1958 Gifford H. *Giff* Van Allen, b. Warsaw, New York March 30, 1930, d. Warsaw, New York January 31, 2019.

Mr. Van Allen was a life-long resident of Warsaw, New York. After serving in the US Army from 1951-1953, he received his High School diploma from Warsaw, New York High School. He drove truck for the road paint crew with the New York State Department of Transportation for thirty-five years retiring in 1992. Giff was a volunteer fireman for over twenty-five years with the Warsaw Fire Department. In addition, he was member of Exempts, the Valley Chapel Free Methodist Church, Warsaw, New York and an avid bowler.

Mr. Van Allen served in the US Army during the Korean War. Giff and Beverly toured all fifty states, Canada, and Mexico during their sixty-year marriage. Beverly Van Allen is a graduate of Geneseo State College, New York. She was the first female deputy sheriff for Wyoming County, New York. In addition, she was employed as a mental health social worker for Wyoming County. Mr. Van Allen was previously married and had a son, Gregory (July 12, 1955-March 9, 1975), by his first wife. Gregory Van Allen was killed in an automobile accident in 1975. Gifford Van Allen was buried in Elmwood Cemetery, Silver Springs, New York.

Children:

1445. I. ***Stephen Shayne Van Allen***, b. Warsaw, New York February 19, 1960; m. September 24, 1988 Hanna Granger, divorced December 3, 1997. Stephen resides in Warsaw, New York where he is employed in the nursing care profession.

1446. II. ***Tawnee Veronica Van Allen***, b. August 17, 1963; m. June 19, 1982 Terry Dean Conley, b. Warsaw, New York September 9, 1957, d. April 19, 2018. Terry was a lifelong resident of Warsaw and worked for Unidex, Warsaw as an industrial painter. Terry graduated from Warsaw High School as did Tawnee who also graduated from Genesee

Community College, Batavia, New York. She is a Registered Nurse at Warsaw Central Schools. Terry previously owned a carpentry business, Conley's Home Improvements. Mr. Conley was a devoted family man, a faithful man of God, an avid fisherman, hunger, and outdoorsman. He was a member of the New Testament Church in Perry, New York. Mr. Conley was buried in Elmwood Cemetery, Silver Springs, New York. He died from cancer.

Children:

i. ***Luke Gregory Conley***, b. March 13, 1993. Luke earned a Bachelor's Degree from Brockport College and a Master's Degree in Library Science from the University of Buffalo.

ii. ***Markie Grace Conley***, b. and d. February 7, 1995 and buried in Elmwood Cemetery.

iii. ***Taryn Elizabeth Conley***, b. July 23, 1996. She graduated from Genesee Valley Education Partnership in 2019 as a Certified Nursing Assistant. She is employed at CAN Eastside Rehabilitation Center, Warsaw, New York.

1447. III. ***Heather Faith Van Allen***, b. May 27, 1967; m. (1) October 17, 1993 Jason Pierce, divorced September 17, 1996; m. (2) July 5, 2010 Alejandro Cruz, b. June 30, 1954. Mr. Cruz has a daughter from an earlier marriage. Heather earned an Associate's Degree in Hospitality Management at Genesee Community College, New York in 1987. Heather moved with her eldest daughter to Galveston County, Texas where she was employed at Landry's restaurant, Kemah, Texas. Later Heather worked as caseworker and then as Assistant Supervisor at the Texas Department of Human Resources. Because her eldest daughter was hit by a truck and suffered significant injuries, Heather took a leave of absence from work and completed a Bachelor's Degree in the Social Sciences from San Jacinto College and later an additional degree from the University of Houston Clear Lake in the Humanities. Alex Cruz attended the School for the Performing Arts for trombone. He graduated with Freddy Prince and later played with the Duke Ellington Band. Alex got his Teacher's Certification in music and was employed for the Houston Independent School District until he retired. Heather and Alex reside in Perry, New York.

Children: (by Steven N. Soto)

i. ***Taeler Capri Van Allen***, b. July 19, 1988; m. December 26, 2015 Ernesto Kimori, b. August 8, 1952. Taeler retains the Van Allen last name. Taeler obtained her high school diploma from Warsaw, New York Central School residing with her maternal grandparents. Taeler graduated from Deamon College with a Bachelor's Degree in Nursing and received her registered nursing license. They reside in Getsville, New York.

Children:

a. ***Eva Jade Caronbo Kimori,*** b. May 19, 2017.
b. ***Jocelyn Elizabeth June Nyrosa Kimori,*** b. May 27, 2019.

Children:

i. Christa ***Rae Van Allen***, b. December 23, 1994. Christa participated in two Student Ambassador trips to Europe during High School. She graduated from San Jacinto College in 2015 with an Associate's Degree in Social Sciences and received a Bachelor's Degree in Literature in 2018 from the University of Houston, Texas.

Children: (by second marriage)

i. ***Christopher Medina Cruz***, b. March 9, 2007.

References: US Census: 1930, 1940; New York State Birth Index 1881-1942; New York State Marriage Index 1881-1967; Correspondence with the late Doris June; Correspondence with Beverly Van Allen; Elmwood Cemetery Records, Silver Springs, New York; *The Daily News* April 11, 2018 obituary for Terry Conley; *The Daily News* January 31, 2019 for Gifford Van Allen; Richardson Family Reunion Annual Minutes.

838.

Rose Mary June, daughter of Doris (416), granddaughter of Lewis (198), b. Bolivar, New York February 16, 1939; m. Bolivar, New York September 3, 1960 LeDale J. Feenaughty, b. Canisteo, New York March 13, 1938. Rose graduated from the St. James Hospital's Nursing Program, Hornell, New York where she received the St. Bernard Obstetric Award and Phoenix College, Arizona. She was employed for a number of years at Mountain Clinic, Olean, New York, Jones Memorial Hospital, Wellsville, New York and later worked for Dr. John Scott, also in Wellsville until 1996. LeDale Feenaughty served with the US Navy, Naval Support Activity in Dan Ang, Vietnam with the 7th Fleet during the Vietnam War, and as part of the US Ceremonial Guard, Washington, D.C. He was also an Enlisted Captain of the Presidential Yacht U.S.S. Sequoia, Washington, DC during the Presidencies of Richard Nixon and Gerald Ford. On June 6, 1977 he was awarded the Navy and Marine Corps' Achievement Medal for Meritorious Action. Mr. Feenaughty served twenty-two and one-half years with the US Navy and retired with a rank of Chief Boatswains Mate E-7. He was last employed with the Bolivar Central

School as a refrigerator/heat custodian until 1996. Rose is currently Historian for the Township of Bolivar. Mr. and Mrs. Feenaughty reside in Bolivar, New York.

Children:

1448. I. ***Darryl James Feenaughty***, b. Wellsville, New York February 22, 1961, d. March 13, 1966 from a post-tonsillectomy hemorrhage. Darryl was buried in Maple Lawn Cemetery, Bolivar, New York.

1449. II. ***Shannon Feenaughty***, b. Key West, Florida April 22, 1963; m. Bolivar, New York July 19, 1986 Vicki Davis; divorced 1999. Shannon is employed as a Shop Foreman and resides in Albion, New York.

Children:

i. ***Lee Ann Feenaughty***, b. Warsaw, New York February 27, 1985; m. Marilla, New York August 6, 2011 Randy Goodenow, divorced 2019. She resides in Warsaw, New York where she is a Financial Money Transfer Specialist for Five Star Bank, Warsaw, New York.

Children:

a. ***Hailey Starr Goodenow***, b. Warsaw, New York July 28, 2012. ***Dakota Moon Goodenow***, b. Warsaw, New York August 16, 2015.

ii. ***Ashley Feenaughty***, b. Warsaw, New York December 29, 1986. She resides in Middleport, New York where she is employed as a Secretary/Financial Advisor of a Family business.

iii. ***Amber Shae Feenaughty***, b. Warsaw, New York April 29, 1988; m. 2012 Robert Sheffield, divorced 2012. She is a Practical Nurse at East Side Nursing and Rehabilitation Center, Warsaw, New York and resides in Silver Springs, New York.

Children: (by Jason Tagg)

a. ***Shae Marie Feenaughty***, b. Lockport, New York December 25, 2009.

References: US Census: 1940; New York State Birth Index 1881-1942; New York State Marriage Index 1881-1967; US Navy and Marine Awards 1942-1994; New York State Death Index 1957-1968 for Darryl Feenaughty; Maple Lawn Cemetery Records, Bolivar, New York; Richardson Annual Family Reunions Notes; Correspondence with the late Doris Richardson June; Correspondence with Rose June Feenaughty.

839.

Inez Lorraine June, daughter of Doris (416), granddaughter of Lewis (198), b. Bolivar, New York July 18, 1940; m. Warsaw, New York August 5, 1961, Richard Elmore Pervorse, Sr., b. Batavia, New York March 2, 1939, d. Buffalo, New York June 20, 2008 from Leukemia.

Inez worked as an LPN in Danville, Kentucky. Richard Pervorse served with the US Army from November 13, 1961 to November 12, 1964. Richard was a design engineer who worked in Kentucky until April 1987 when the family moved to Bolivar, New York. Until his retirement he was employed with Emporium Industries, Austin, Pennsylvania. From 1994-2005 Mr. Pervorse served as pastor for the Yorkshire United Methodist church. He was buried in Maple Lawn Cemetery, Bolivar, New York.

Children:

1450. I. ***Richard Elmore Pervorse, Jr.***, b. Fort Devens, Massachusetts July 4, 1962. Richard resides in Wellsville, New York.

1451. II. ***Alan Tracey Pervorse***, b. Mineral Springs, Texas July 21, 1964. Alan worked for thirty-two years with ARC transportation retiring February 2019. He currently resides in Bolivar, New York.

References: US Census: 1940; New York State Birth Index 1881-1942; New York State Marriage Index 1881-1967; Social Security Death Index 1935-2014; US Veterans Death File 1850-2010; Maple Lawn Cemetery Records, Bolivar, New York; Correspondence with the later Doris Richardson June; Correspondence with Rose June Feenaughty.

840.

Dale Lewis June, son of Doris (416), grandson of Lewis (198), b. Bolivar, New York February 25, 1942; m. (1) Shasta, California August 27, 1966 Judith A. Weir, b. California October 16, 1945, divorced June 1995; m. Los Angeles 2000, Muslima Fazal Dossa, b. Tanzania, Africa October 1, 1962.

Dale June graduated from Mt. Shasta College with a degree in Police Science and from Sacramento State University, California with a degree in Criminal Justice and Public Administration. He obtained a Master's Degree from George Washington University, Washington, D.C. in Special Studies and Criminal Justice. From 1965 to 1968 Mr. June was employed by the Shasta County Sheriff's Department, the Redding Police Department, and the Sacramento Police Department. For eleven years he was employed with the US Treasury Department as a member of the Secret Service serving Presidents Johnson, Nixon, Ford, Carter, and Reagan with service at the White House from 1971-1976. He also served in the Sacramento and San Diego Field Offices during the same period.

Dale June was employed with the US Customs Intelligence Research Specialist for Terrorism and Organized Crime. He has been on the staff of the National University San Diego and Los Angeles from 1981, the National Polytech College, Lakeview, California since 2017, and Compton College, California from 2017. He is the original Co-Founder and teacher of Henley-Putnam University from 2001 to 2010.Until 1984 Dale June owned and operated his own security business in San Diego called *Patriot Protection Investigative Corporation.* Since its sale, Dale June continued to work in the security and protective fields with the US Customs Department.

Judith June was a high school physical education teacher in Vestabula, California. Muslima June is a widow with a son: Mohammed Ali-Mehdi Dossa, born Los Angeles, California May 15, 1991. His last name was changed to June in 1996. Muslima was employed as the manager and ticket sales representative for three major airlines and is the owner and operator of M and M Travel. She is an Instructor with Wing Chun Kung Fu for children.

Children:

1452. I. ***Kelleen Andrea (Kelly) June***, b. March 14, 1970; m. June 22, 1997 Christopher Nolin. She graduated from Redland University, California and enlisted in the US Army June 27, 1992. She obtained a Master's Degree from Old Dominion University in 1997 and a Ph.D. from the University of Denver in 2002. Kelly and Chris reside in Fort Collins, Colorado.

1453. II. ***Kason Andrew (Casey) June***, b. November 9, 1971; m. Orange, California November 14, 1998 Michelle Diane Paulus. He graduated from California State University, Long Beach in 1995. Casey and Michelle currently reside in Mission Vejo, California.

Children:

i. ***Jake June***, b. October 24, 2001.
ii. ***Michelle June***, b. September 7, 2004.

1454. III. ***Victoria Nicole (Tori) June***, b. June 26, 1975; m. September 21, 2010 Jeffrey Hudson. Tori graduated from California State University, Chico in 1999. Tori and Jeff currently reside in Maui, Hawaii.

Children:

i. ***Alaia Mahama Hudson***, b. June 20, 2018.

1455. IV. ***Katherine Denise (Katy) June***, b. July 20, 1978; m. June 21, 2018 Rick Ellis. Katy graduated from the University of Santa Cruz in 2001. Katy and Rick currently reside in

Santa Cruz with Rick's three children Reed, Bailey, and Wade.

References: New York State Birth Index 1881-1942; California Marriage Index 1960-1985; Correspondence with the late Doris Richardson June; Correspondence with Rose June Feenaughty; Richardson Annual Family Reunions Minutes; Correspondence with Dale June.

841.

Dean Victor June, son of Doris (416), grandson of Lewis (198), b. Bolivar, New York January 26, 1945; m. (1) Glen Cove, New York, March 25, 1967, Deidre Nagel b. February 4, 1945, d. Olean, New York July 20, 1969 from a car accident; m. (2) place not known March 23, 1970 Sally Dean.

Dean June graduated from Geneseo State University, New York and taught seventh and grade Social Studies. Dean's first wife was eight months pregnant at the time of her death. Sally June attended Geneseo State University and was employed as a substitute teacher. They resided in Attica, New York. Deidre June was buried in Maple Lawn Cemetery, Bolivar, New York.

Children: (by second marriage)

1456. I. ***Amy June***, b. Batavia, New York November 22, 1970; m. Attica, New York July 26, 1997 Thomas Rowcliff, divorced 2020. Amy attended SUNY Fredonia and graduated from the University of Dayton, Ohio with a major in French and International Relations. Amy works for York Tech and works with the Sports Boaster Club. Tom works for Dick's Sporting Goods. They reside in Attica, New York.

Children:

i. ***Samuel George Rowcliff***, b. October 5, 2000. He works for an IT Company after graduating from York Tech.

ii. ***Grace Rowcliff***, b. June 19, 2002 and is active in a variety of high school activities and plans to attend Millersville Colle, Pennsylvania in the Fall of 2020.

1457. II. ***Kara June***, b. March 10, 1973; m. (1) May 13, 2000 Robert Baker, divorced 2008. She resides in Attica, New York.

Children: (by first marriage)

i. ***Noble Robert Baker***, b. May 3, 2003.

Children: (by Zeke Palan)

i. *Ryder Dean Palan*, b. June 10, 2009.

1458. III. ***Rebecca June***, b. May 29, 1977; m. Oswego, New York June 26, 2004 Paul Andrew George, b. August 17, 1976. Becky and Paul reside in Vermont. Paul is employed as an arborist and Kara is a stay-at-home Mom after working in banking for ten years.

Children:

i. ***Andrew David George***, b. April 19, 2015.
ii. ***Alyse Dean George***, b. November 17, 2017.

References: Correspondence with the late Doris Richardson June; Correspondence with Rose June Feenaughty; Richardson Annual Family Reunion Minutes.

842.

Gerald Melvyn June, son of Doris (416), grandson of Lewis (198), b. Bolivar, New York October 24, 1946; m. November 2, 1968 Diane Kruger. Gerald served with the US Military during the Vietnam War from 1966 to 1968. They reside in Holbrook, New York where he was employed with telephone company and Diane was employed as a librarian.

Children:

1459. I. ***David Christopher June***, b. March 12, 1972; (1) m. Holbrook, New York October 15, 2000 Jennifer Ann War, b. January 30, 1975, divorced 2003; m. (2) Farmingville, New York February 21, 2009 Heather Volkle, b. January 1982.

Children: (by second marriage)

i. ***Carl Joseph June***, b. June 22, 2009.
ii. ***Mackenzie Grace June***, b. December 30, 2010.

1460. II. ***Scott Michael June***, b. November 3, 1973; m. Blue Point, New York August 6, 2005 Karen Michele Salinas.

Children:

i. ***Jake Salinas June***, b. August 30, 2006.

References: Correspondence with the late Doris June Richardson; Correspondence with Rose June Feenaughty; Richardson Annual Family Reunion Minutes.

843.

Cheryl Davis, daughter of Blanche (417), granddaughter of Lewis (198), b. place not known, January 12, 1951; m. (1) place and date not known, William "Bill" Rychel, divorced 1976; m. (2) place not known, February 26, 1977 Michael Irish; m. (3) Midland, Texas May 15, 1999 Russell Lee Quarella, b. Greene, New York March 12, 1953; d. Midland, Texas August 7, 2018. Little information is currently available on Cheryl's first two husbands. Russell Quarella served in the US Army for six years and was employed for thirty years at Midland Memorial Hospital. He enjoyed motorcycle riding, fishing, hunting, and camping. Russell Quarella was buried at Serenity Memorial Garden, Midland, Texas.

Children: (by first marriage)

1461. I. ***Kevin Michael Rychel***, b. September 24, 1971; m. December 23, 1996 Misty Chapman. Kevin who is 5' 9" tall and weighed 176 pounds was drafted by the Pittsburgh Pirates in 1989 and played Minor League Baseball for the Pirates from 1989 to 1996.

Children:

i. ***Hannah Alyse Rychel***, b. April 1999.
ii. ***Kevin Michael Rychel, Jr.***, b. date not known.
iii. ***Hayden Austin Rychel***, b. June 28, 2007.

Children: (by second marriage)

1462. I. ***Tiffany Irish***, b. September 10, 1977; m. May 3, 2003 Christopher Lawson.

Children:

i. ***Kaitlen Nicole Irish***, b. August 13, 1998.

Children: (by marriage)

i. ***Caleb William Lawson***, b. August 21, 2006.

References: Texas Marriage Index 1824-2014 for Cheryl Davis' third marriage; Midland, Texas obituary for Russell Lee Quarella; Baseball Reference.com for Kevin Rychel, Sr.; Correspondence with the late Doris Richardson June; Richardson Annual Family Reunion Minutes.

844.

Margaret Louise Richardson, daughter of Merle (418), granddaughter of Lewis (198), b. Texas, August 8, 1925; m. Texas October 1960 Dickie Lee Flanagan, b. Qumatta Valley, Texas October 11, 1940; d. Midland, Texas May 28, 2007. Mr. Flanagan was employed in the Midland, Texas oil fields. He was buried at Glenn Rest Cemetery, Big Lake, Texas.

Children:

1463. I. ***Garry Wayne Flanagan***, b. January 19, 1962, d. January 20, 1962 and buried Cedar Hill Cemetery, Ozona, Texas with his twin brother.

1464. II. ***Glenn Ross Flanagan***, b. January 19, 1962, d. January 20, 1962 and buried Cedar Hill Cemetery, Ozona, Texas with his twin brother.

1465. III. ***Eric Lee Flanagan***, b. and d. November 30, 1963 and buried Cedar Hill Cemetery, Ozona, Texas.

1466. IV. ***Dickie Lee Flanagan, Jr.***, b. November 19, 1967; m. November 21, 1987 Adrian Thornton. Dickie's twin brother died before birth. Dickie works in the Texas oil fields.

Children:

i. ***Eric Flanagan***, b. October 19, 1989.

References: Correspondence with the late Doris Richardson June; Cedar Hill Cemetery Records, Ozona, Texas; Glenn Rest Cemetery, Big Lake, Texas.

845.

Betty Richardson, daughter of Merle (418), granddaughter of Lewis (198), b. September 2, 1947; m. (1) June 4, 1965 Ronald Quick, divorced Polk County, Florida November 3, 1977; m. (2) Polk County, Florida June 10, 1978 Franklin Ross Roderus, b. September 21, 1942, d. Spring Hill, Florida December 17, 2015, divorced Sarasota, Florida November 29, 1993; m. (3) Florida, December 17, 1997 James Charles Boyd, b. December 23, 1944.

Frank Roderus was previously married before his marriage to Betty and would remarry after their divorce. Mr. Roderus was a prolific writer of western novels. For a time, he wrote for the now defunct *Rocky Mountain News*, Denver, Colorado. It is estimated that Frank wrote between 300-400 novels. In 1980 he was awarded the Sweepstakes Award for best news story by the Colorado Press Association.

Twice he was awarded the Spur Award by the Western Writers of America and he received a Lifetime Achievement Award by Western Fictioneers. His best-known novel might be *Jason Evers: His Own Story.* Frank Roderus adopted Betty Richardson's two children from her first marriage.

Children: (by first marriage and adopted by second)

1467. I. ***Stephen (Quick) Roderus***, b. August 15, 1967; m. September 23, 1989 Michelle Walker, b. Orlando, Florida January 10, 1964.

1468. II. ***Amanda (Quick) Roderus***, b. August 23, 1974; m. (1) May 1995 Michael Bush, divorced 2001; m. (2) July 16, 2004 John Schlabach, b. February 23. 1974. She is the owner of Elegant Rides Airport Shuttle and More. Amanda resides in Sarasota, Florida.

Children (by first marriage)

i. ***Alana Marie Bush,*** b. December 15, 1996.
ii. ***Michael Ray Bush***, b. September 7,1999.

Children: (by second marriage)

i. ***Kailey Lynn Schlabach***, b. July 9, 2005.
ii. ***Kendra Joy Schlabach***, b. February 29, 2008.

References: Florida Divorce Index 1927-2001; Florida Marriage Index 1927-2001; *Hernando Sun* 2011 article on Frank Roderus; Correspondence with the late Doris Richardson June; Richardson Annual Family Reunion Minutes.

846.

Merle William Richardson, Jr., son of Merle (418), grandson of Lewis (198), b. Texas December 5, 1953; m. (1) Reagan County, Texas March 30, 1975 Lea Chapman; m. (2) Texas January 22, 1994 Joanna Charles. Merle worked in the Midland, Texas oil fields.

Children: (by first marriage)

1469. I. ***Ryan Curt Richardson***, b. February 25, 1976; m. Texas April 8, 2000 Amber Nicole McClellan, b. October 24, 1980.

Children:

i. ***Dorian Nicole Richardson***, b. August 16, 2000.

ii. ***Brayden James Richardson***, b. March 6, 2003.
iii. ***Rylan Richardson***, b. April 2015.

1470. II. ***Tina Richardson***, b. November 27, 1977; m. Texas July 1, 2000 Jerald Daniel Benton, b. February 6, 1971.

Children: (by James Dowling)

i. ***Madison Lea Dowling***, b. October 4, 1998.

References: Texas Marriage Index 1824-2014 for Merle Richardson's first marriage; Correspondence with the late Doris Richardson June; Richardson Annual Family Reunion Minutes.

847.

Chrystal Marie Richardson, daughter of Merle (418), granddaughter of Lewis (198), b. Texas February 12, 1956; m. (1) August 12, 1973 Joe Ralph Collins, b. Midland, Texas October 12, 1953, d. Big Lake Texas May 12, 1974 while an operator trainee at a gas processing plant; m. (2) April 6, 1975 David Swanner. They reside in Monahan, Texas where David was employed as a truck driver. Joe Collins was buried in Glen Rest Cemetery, Big Lake, Texas.

Children: (by second marriage)

1471. I. ***Kevin Swanner***, b. December 13, 1977; m. Texas August 9, 2003 Shannon Lynn McDonald.

1472. II. ***Kellie Swanner***, b. September 8, 1981.

References: Texas Marriage Index 1824-2014 for Chrystal's first marriage; Texas Death Index 19093-1982 for Joe Collins; Correspondence with the late Doris Richardson June; Richardson Annual Family Reunion Minutes.

848.

Lois Maryette Dickerson, daughter of Theo (419), granddaughter of Lewis (198), b. Olean, New York August 12, 1949. d. Coudersport, Pennsylvania June 17, 2019; m. Shinglehouse, Pennsylvania September 26, 1970 Chester "Chet" "Bill" Duell, b. Wellsville, New York June 15, 1946, d. Sweden Valley, Pennsylvania September 9, 2013 from cancer.

Bill served with the US Air Force from 1964-66 and continue with the Reserves until 1995. He retired as an Electrician after thirty-nine years with the former Air Preheater Corporation, Wellsville,

New York. Lois was employed as a Friendly Home Toy Party representative, an Avon representative, McDonald's in Wellsville, New York, Olean Tile Company, Olean, New York, and in the kitchens at Oswayo Valley Elementary and High Schools. She also did catering. Mrs. Duell was a member of the Millport United Methodist Church where she served as a treasurer and was a member of the Mission Circle. In addition, Lois was a former member of the Shinglehouse Fireman's Ladies Auxiliary, the Tri-County Fireman's Ladies Auxiliary, the Allegany County, New York Ladies Firemen's Auxiliary, and the Oswayo Valley Senior Center in Shinglehouse. Chester and Lois Duell were buried in Maple Grove Cemetery, Shinglehouse, Pennsylvania.

Children:

1473. I. ***Sheilla Duell***, b. and d. February 20, 1972 and buried in Maple Grove Cemetery.

1474. II. ***Neil Chester Duell***, b. March 15, 1978; m. Millport, Pennsylvania April 27, 2002 Sharon Marie Pettinger, b. August 13, 1971. They reside in Coudersport, Pennsylvania.

Children:

i. ***Joshua Neil Duell***, b. September 7, 2002.
ii. ***Shawn Michael Duell***, b. February 6, 2004.

References: Correspondence with the late Doris Richardson June; Maple Grove Cemetery, Shinglehouse, Pennsylvania; Richardson Annual Family Reunion Minutes; *Olean Times-Herald*, obituary June 19, 2019.

849.

Lila Dickerson, daughter of Theo (419), granddaughter of Lewis (198), b. November 23, 1950; m. (1) April 11, 1970 Gary L. Nelson, b. Smethport, Pennsylvania November 23, 1949 d. September 15, 1974 in an automobile accident; m. (2) October 24, 1975 Edward D. Curry, b. Wellsville, New York August 18, 1943, d. Coudersport, Pennsylvania hospital September 14, 2011. Ed retired early with a work-related disability. He was buried in Woodlawn Cemetery, Wellsville, New York. Lila continues to reside in Genesee, Pennsylvania in the family home. Gary Nelson was buried in Rose Hill Cemetery, Smethport, Pennsylvania.

Children: (by first marriage)

1475. I. ***Andrew R. Nelson***, b. and d. June 11, 1971 and buried Rose Hill Cemetery.

1476. II. ***Robert Nelson***, b. September 25, 1972; Ulysses, Pennsylvania October 17, 1998 Tracey Knowles.

Children:

i. ***Emma Grace Nelson***, b. December 2, 2004.
ii. ***Dylon Andrew Nelson***, b. September 7, 2012.

Children: (by second marriage)

1477. I. ***Jo Ann Curry***, b. August 22, 1976; m. (1) June 1, 1996 Jeremy Slawson, divorced, February 25, 2001; m. (2) Genesee, Pennsylvania May 20, 2006, Todd Phillips, b. November 24, 1972. Todd has a son, Devon Phillips, born June 23, 1996, from a previous marriage.

Children: (by first marriage)

i. ***Miranda Lynne Slawson***, b. September 18, 1997; m. Shadi Tawil.

Children:

a. ***Adam Thomas Tawil***, b. March 3, 2017.
b. ***Anna Marie Tawil***, b. October 9, 2018.

ii. ***Ryan Michael Slawson***, b. July 22, 1999; m. June 2017 Sierra Smith, b. March 1, 1998. Ryan joined the Marines and reported to Camp Lejeune, South Carolina June 2007. He was injured in service and discharged September 29, 2017.

Children: (by second marriage)

i. ***Conner Edward Phillips***, b. February 11, 2004.

1478. II, ***Scott Curry***, b. September 22, 1977; m. Augusta, Georgia December 12, 2005 Christina Jordan, b. July 19, 1977. Scott entered military service February 25, 1997 with the US Army. He spent a year in Korea and six months in Guatemala. Scott was discharged January 25, 2001 and enlisted in the National Guard February 25, 2001. He saw service in Baghdad, Iraq from April 27, 2004 to April 26, 2005.

Children:

i. ***Cameron Scott Curry***, b. November 18, 2010.

References: Correspondence with the late Doris Richardson June; Richardson Annual Family Reunion Minutes; Social Security Death Index for Edward Curry; Rose Hill Cemetery Records, Smethport, Pennsylvania; Woodlawn Cemetery Records, Wellsville, New York.

850.

Karl J. Dickerson, son of Theo (419), grandson of Lewis (198), b. February 8,1952; m. (1) August 1, 1970 Jill Davison, divorced December 20, 1978; m. (2) October 22, 1980 Bonnie Allen Foster; m. (3) Delavan, New York May 2, 1998 Susan Barr Argauer, b. Springville, New York April 1, 1944, d. Warsaw, New York October 6, 2018 from cancer.

Karl Dickerson previously resided in Arcade, New York. His third wife was employed for twenty-five years by Motorola in Arcade and Elma, New York as an accounting manager. Susan Dickerson owned and operated Dickerson's Tax and Accounting Services. Karl Dickerson's second wife had two children from a previous marriage. Susan Dickerson had five children before her marriage to Karl.

Children: (by first marriage)

1479. I. ***Valerie Dickerson***, b. March 29, 1973; m. April 11, 1992 James Cline. They reside in Cuba, New York.

Children:

i. ***Tara Cline***, b. October 3, 1992; m. November 29, 2014 Jeffrey Paul McElhany.

Children:

a. ***Judah Benjamin McElhany***, b. June 10, 2018.

ii. ***Tyler James Cline***, b. August 1, 1996.

iii. ***Tevin Morgan William Cline***, b. February 26, 1998.

1480. II. ***Jeannette Dickerson***, b. February 28, 1974; m. Cuba, New York September 27, 1997 Chris Smith. They reside in Eldred, Pennsylvania.

Children:

i. ***Emily Jean Smith***, b. September 28, 1999.
ii. ***Autumn Elizabeth Smith***, b. March 18, 2001.
iii. ***Ethan Christopher Smith***, b. October 24, 2002.

1481. III. ***Brenda Sue Dickerson***, b. May 19, 1974; m. (1) August 26, 1995 Arthur Inannie (2) Rushford, New York September 21, 1996, Jason Pastorias, divorced 1998; m. (3) Rushford, New York September 4, 1999 Sam Austin. Brenda and Sam reside in Rushford, New York.

Children: (by second marriage)

i. ***Leah Jean Pastorias***, b. September 22, 1995; m. Olean, New York December 31, 2016 Alex Dick.

Children: (by third marriage)

i. ***Breanna Karen Austin***, b. November 22, 2000.
ii. ***Brooklyn Rae Austin***, b. November 22, 2000.
iii. ***Wyatt Matthew Austin***, b. June 19, 2004.

References: Correspondence with the late Doris Richardson June; Richardson Annual Family Reunion Minutes; *Olean Times Herald* obituary October 10, 2018 for Susan Dickerson.

851.

Carolyn JoAnn Dickerson, daughter of Theo (419), granddaughter of Lewis (198), b. October 20, 1953; m. (1) July 15, 1972 Buckley Drake, b. Olean, New York January 24, 1944, d. Shinglehouse, Pennsylvania October 23, 1998 from a heart attack; m. (2) Hawaii February 25, 2003 David Gustin, b. Shinglehouse, Pennsylvania October 13, 1955.

Carolyn previously worked for Olean Tile Company, Olean, New York. Buckley Drake was buried in Maple Grove Cemetery, Shinglehouse, Pennsylvania. David Gustin has two sons from an earlier marriage.

Children: (by first marriage)

1482. I. ***Melissa Drake***, b. May 13, 1973, d. June 1, 1994 in an automobile accident. She was buried in Maple Grove Cemetery, Shinglehouse, Pennsylvania.

1483. II. ***Brian Drake***, b. May 24, 1974; m. Bristol, Indiana July 26, 2003 Jessica Packer, divorced. Jessica had a child, Reilly Gene Howard, by a previous marriage. Brian and his partner Megan have three children.

Children: (by first marriage)

i. ***Caleb Joshua Drake***, b. May 10, 2003.
ii. ***Collin James Drake***, b. November 19, 2009.

Children: (by Megan Willets)

i. ***Paxton Ezra Drake***, b. April 10, 2018.
ii. ***Hadley Rainne Drake***, b. August 7, 2019.
iii. ***Brinley Lainne Drake***, b. August 7, 2019.

References: Correspondence with the late Doris Richardson June; Maple Grove Cemetery Records, Shinglehouse, Pennsylvania; Richardson Annual Reunion Minutes; Indian Marriage Certificates 1960-2005 for Brian Drake's first marriage.

852.

Earl William Dickerson, son of Theo (419), grandson of Lewis (198), b. March 2, 1956; m. (1) March 3, 1979 Luanne A. Higgins, b. July 26, 1960, divorced September 6, 1979; m. (2) September 8, 1998 Sharon D. Goss, b. October 7, 1948, d. March 1, 2013; m. (3) 2015 Sharon Minderler. Earl resides in Shinglehouse, Pennsylvania and worked for a scissors plant in Bolivar, New York and is now retired.

Children: (by Cheryl Layfield Reed)

1484. I. ***Miranda Dickerson Reed***; m. Allentown, New York June 14, 1997 Mike Mesler.

Children:

i. ***Adrianna Mesler***, b. August 22, 1998; m. Port Allegany, Pennsylvania October 11, 2018 Jake Wise.

Children:

a. ***Lynn Wise***, b. November 27, 2018.

ii. ***Dawson Jacob Mesler***, b. March 4, 2002, d. May 28, 2016 by drowning in the Oswayo River, Shinglehouse. Buried in East Sharon Cemetery, Pennsylvania.

iii. ***Ashley Bentley Mesler***, b. October 24, 2010.

1485. II. ***Jody Dickerson***; m. Iowa, 2003 Christ Foust.

Children:

i. ***Taylor Foust***, b. 2003.

References: Correspondence with the late Doris Richardson June; Richardson Annual Reunion Minutes.

853.

Donald Dickerson, son of Theo (419), grandson of Lewis (198), b. April 18, 1957; m. December 1, 1979 Judith Straight. Donald worked for Combustion Engineering Air Preheater, Wellsville, New York. They reside in Shinglehouse, Pennsylvania.

Children:

1486. I. ***Amy Dickerson***, b. May 15, 1981; m. Farmington, Pennsylvania June 28, 2003 Brian Murray, b. January 18, 1979.

Children:

i. ***Chase Lucas Murray***, b. October 15, 2004.
ii. ***Xavier Alex Murray***, b. September 14, 2006.
iii. ***Cassandra Elizabeth Murray***, b. November 27, 2007.

1487. II. ***Jennifer Dickerson***, b. October 27, 1983; m. Port Allegany, Pennsylvania October 8, 2016 Edward Jackson, b. November 2, 1981. Edward has a daughter, Damon, by a previous marriage.

1488. III. ***William Dickerson***, b. June 11, 1986.

References: Correspondence with the late Doris Richardson June; Richardson Annual Reunion Minutes.

854.

Rodney Richardson, son of Theo (419), grandson of Lewis (198), b. August 9, 1959; m. May 22, 1982 Kimberly Wheeler. Rodney worked for Agway. They reside in Shinglehouse, Pennsylvania. They own and operate Riverside Sales in Wellsville, New York.

Children:

1489. I. ***Erin Dickerson***, b. October 15, 1987; m. October 6, 2012 Bradley Cornell.

Children:

i. ***Marshall Richard Cornell***, b. August 11, 2014.
ii. ***Jolene Grace Cornell***, b. January 2, 2018.

1490. II. ***Jessica Dickerson***, b. November 25, 1989, d. November 29, 1989.

1491. III. ***Hilary Marie Dickerson***, b. May 30, 1991; m. Millport, Pennsylvania May 20, 2017 Kyle Mullen.

References: Correspondence with the late Doris Richardson June; Richardson Annual Reunion Minutes.

855.

Bradley Dickerson, son of Theo (419), grandson of Lewis (198), b. March 2, 1964; m. Obi, New York July 14, 1990 Carla Blanche Otto, b. June 17, 1970. They reside in McConnellsburg, Pennsylvania. Bradley has a Master's Degree in Education and taught Art for grades Kindergarten to 12th grade at Central Fulton School District, McConnellsburg.

Children:

1492. I. ***A'Lesse Dickerson***, b. August 25, 1992 has a Master's Degree in Reading with a focus on Secondary Education. She is an English Teacher in Charles County Public Schools, Maryland. She resides in Waldorf, Maryland.

1493. II. ***DeAnne Mallory Dickerson***, b. October 14, 1997; m. September 10, 2016 Ryan Patrick Drewry, b. May 8, 1978. Ryan has a B.S. Degree in Photography from Penn State. DeAnne is a certified CNA. They reside in Breezewood, Pennsylvania.

Children:

i. ***Larkin Grant Drewry***, b. August 10, 2016.
ii. ***Joleah Rae Drewry***, b. January 14, 2019.
iii. ***Third Child due June 25, 2020.***

1494. III. ***Evan Michael Dickerson***, b. August 6, 2002 has been accepted to Shippensburg State University, Pennsylvania where he plans to major in Secondary English Education.

1495. IV. ***Faith Meredith Dickerson***, b. June 12, 2005 and currently attends McConnellsburg High School.

References: Correspondence with the late Doris Richardson June; Richardson Annual Reunion Minutes.

857.

Shannon Richardson, daughter of James (422), granddaughter of Lewis (198), b. August 8, 1977; m. Wellsville, New York July 14, 2012 Jarrod Billings.

References: Correspondence with the late Doris Richardson June; Richardson Annual Reunion Minutes.

858.

Casey Richardson, daughter of James (422), granddaughter of Lewis (198) b. September 4, 1980; m. Wellsville, New York May 15, 1999 Richard A. Chind, Jr. Casey is a health care worker. Richard served in the US Army from 1996 to 2002 and is currently employed as a carpenter. They reside in Friendship, New York.

Children:

1496. I. ***Kennedy Chyna Chind***, b. July 1, 2000. He is a trained horticulturist and organic gardener. He is also working for Sidelines Restaurant, Bolivar, New York.

1497. II. ***Jason Lawrence Chind***, b. March 16, 2004.

References: Correspondence with the late Doris Richardson June; Richardson Annual Reunion Minutes.

860.

Lisa Christine Lowrey, daughter of Sallie (423), granddaughter of Lewis (198), b. November 4, 1985.

Children: (by Richie Thompson)

1498. I. ***Mia Jade Lowrey***, b. Erie, Pennsylvania October 16, 2019.

861.

Jamie Lyn Reynolds Lowery, daughter of Sallie (423), granddaughter of Lewis (198), b. June 6, 1988; m. Justin Harris.

Children:

1499. I. ***Tucker Jaxson Harris***, b. May 22, 2013.
1500. II. ***Austin Jacob Harris***, b. April 7, 2016.

References: Correspondence with the late Doris Richardson June; Correspondence with Sallie Richardson Lowery; Richardson Annual Reunion Minutes.

866.

Lois Marie Cooper, daughter of Elizabeth (426), granddaughter of Mildred (199), b. March 11, 1961, d. Riverview, Florida July 18, 2009 from cancer; m. David Egloff. It is not currently known where Lois Egloff was buried.

Children:

1501. I. ***Zachary Egloff, nfi.***

1502. II. ***Benjamin Egloff, nfi.***

References: Serenity Meadows Funeral Home obituary.

882.

Donna Kay Miller, daughter of Marion (431), granddaughter of Mildred (199), b. Indiana, a. 1956; m. Harris, Texas May 14, 1999 David J. Lacombe, divorced Harris, Texas June 9, 2009; ***nfi.***

References: Texas Marriage Index 1824-2014; Texas Divorce Index 1968-2014.

883.

Benjamin H. Miller, Jr., son of Marion (431), grandson of Mildred (199), b. Indiana; m. Harris, Texas July 18, 1987 Kathryn L. Knepper, divorced Bexar, Texas August 23, 1990; ***nfi.***

References: Texas Marriage Index 1824-2014; Texas Divorce Index 1968-2014.

885.

Deborah Sue Jacobson, daughter of Mildred (432), granddaughter of Mildred (199), b. Springville, New York, 1957; m. Fort Benjamin, Indiana February 28, 1976 Gary Michael Baty, divorced Bell, Teas November 17, 1977; ***nfi.***

References: Indiana Marriage Certificates 1960-2005; Texas Divorce Index 1968-2014.

893.

Richard Kenneth Fox, son of George (437), grandson of Lillie (206), b. Florida January 13, 1950; m. Pinellas County, Florida June 14, 1974 Jean M. Warmkessel. Mr. and Mrs. Fox reside in St. Petersburg, Florida where he was a partner in a public accounting firm.

Children:

1503. I. ***Jennifer Fox***, b. February 2, 1971; ***nfi.***

1504. II. ***Jason Fox***, b. January 25, 1983; ***nfi.***

References: Correspondence with the late James Fox; Florida Marriage Index 1927-2001.

894.

Steven Edward Fox, son of George (437), grandson of Lillie (206), b. Richmond, Virginia August 20, 1953; m. Pinellas County, Florida February 25, 1977 Billie Elaine Ballew, divorced Pinellas County, Florida March 24, 1992. Mr. Fox resides in St. Petersburg, Florida where he is employed as a technician with General Telephone Electronics.

Children:

1505. I. ***Stephanie Fox***, b. March 24, 1978; ***nfi.***

References: Correspondence with the late James Fox; Virginia Birth Records 1912-2015; Florida Marriage Index 1927-2001; Florida Divorce Index 1927-2001.

895.

Debra Sue Showalter, daughter of Jeanne (439), granddaughter of Lillie (206), b. Richmond, Virginia October 31, 1952; m. August 17, 1974 Dennis Martin Duermit. Debra Sue was adopted by her step-father.

Children:

1506. I. ***Kathrun Leigh Duermit***, b. July 4, 1980; ***nfi.***

1507. II. ***Christopher Lee Duermit***, b. April 14, 1987; ***nfi.***

898.

Stacey Marie Showalter, daughter of Jeanne (439), granddaughter of Lillie (206), b. Muncie, Indiana March 28, 1965, d. Gaithersburg, Maryland November 23, 1997.

Stacey graduated from Purdue University with a B. A. degree and earned a Master's Degree from the University of Indianapolis. At the time of her death she was employed as an occupational therapist with Montgomery County Schools, Gaithersburg, Maryland. Stacey Showalter was buried in Willow Grove Cemetery, Fountain City, Indiana.

References: Correspondence with the late James Fox; Social Security Death Index 1935-2014; Willow Grove Cemetery Records, Fountain City, Indian.

899.

Kathryn Lee Root, daughter of Edmund (440), granddaughter of Clifton (207), b. July 1, 1959; m. (1) Craig Allen Crawford, divorced; m. (2) July 23, 1983 John Howard Lineback. They reside in Tulsa, Oklahoma where Kathi worked for the Amoco Oil Company and John was employed by Anadarko Production; ***nfi.***

Children: (by second marriage)

1508. I. ***Matthew Kyle Lineback***, b. January 4, 1985.

1509. II. ***Nicholas Carter Lineback***, b. October 24, 1988.

References: Correspondence with the late Edmund Root.

900.

James Clifton Root, son of Edmund (440), grandson of Clifton (207), b. June 1, 1963; m. Wichita, Kansas July 16, 1988 Connie Sue Green. Jimmy worked for Perfection Equipment Company and Connie was employed by *Friday*, a weekly magazine. They resided in Oklahoma City, Oklahoma; ***nfi.***

References: Correspondence with the late Edmund Root.

901.

Michael Scott Miller, son of Donald (441), grandson of Martha (208), b. November 9, 1949; m. August 26, 1969 Gaylin Green. The Millers resided in Birmingham, Michigan where Michael attended Western Michigan University; ***nfi.***

Children:

1510. I. ***Amy Jo Miller***, b. December 23, 1968.

References: Correspondence with the late Martha Miller.

904.

Robert Buren Davis, son of Jo Anne (442), grandson of Martha (208), b. October 17, 1951; m. Bloomington, Indiana October 27, 1982 Barbara Rothbauer Doris. Robert was the founder and former owner of a Tofu plant in Bloomington; ***nfi.***

References: Correspondence with the late Martha Miller; Indian Marriage Certificates 1960-2005.

905.

Andrew Allen Davis, son of Jo Anne (442), grandson of Martha (208), b. September 26, 1953; m. (1) Frankfort, Indiana December 31, 1977 Bonita Lewell Craver, divorced; m. (2) May 28, 1989 Rebecca Dee; ***nfi.***

Children: (by second marriage)

1511. I. ***Kasey Davis***, b. September 26, 1990.

References: Correspondence with the late Martha Miller; Indiana Marriage Certificates 1960-2005.

906.

Sharlee Anne Davis, daughter of Jo Anne (442), granddaughter of Martha (208); b. January 23, 1956; m. (1) Frankfort, Indiana January 3, 1976 David Verner Mahn, divorced; m. (2) Jeff Hutchens. Jeff is a Professor of Chemistry at Indian University; ***nfi.***

References: Correspondence with the late Martha Miller; Indiana Marriage Certificates 1960-2005.

907.

Joseph Martin Davis, son of Jo Anne (442), grandson of Martha (208), b. January 7, 1960; m. Indianapolis, Indiana July 28, 1989 Wendy Ann Pattison; ***nfi.***

Children:

1512. I. ***Chelsea Davis***, b. January 14, 1990.

References: Correspondence with the late Martha Miller; Indiana Marriage Certificates 1960-2005.

908.

Christie Lambert, daughter of David (443), granddaughter of Elizabeth (209), b. Washington State October 4, 1932; m. (1) Indiana December 29, 1973 Steven Lee Cox, divorced 1984; m. (2) Muncie, Indiana December 4, 1986 Robert D. Horvath, b. Indiana February 11, 1946, d. June 19, 2002.

Mr. Cox was an Executive with the Boy Scouts. Robert Horvath served in the US Army in Vietnam and West Germany. He was employed as a mechanic at an automobile dealership and also worked at Prairie Creek Pawn as a clerk and jeweler. Robert Horvath was a member of the Delaware County, Indiana Masonic Lodge. Mr. Horvath had two children by a previous marriage and is buried in Beech Grove Cemetery, Muncie, Indiana. Christie was a graduate of Ball State University, Muncie and was the Director of Applied Gerontology, Muncie, Indiana.

Children: (by first marriage)

1513. I. ***Laura Cox***, b. February 18, 1976; m. Philip Couch; ***nfi.***

Children:

i. ***Alexis Couch.***
ii. ***Ashley Couch.***

1514. II. ***Malina Kathryn (Katie) Cox***, b. June 4, 1982; m. (1) Mr. Maxwell, divorced July 8, 2002; m. (2) Muncie, Indiana March 26, 2004 Kyle A. Campbell. Mr. Campbell is a restaurant manager.

Children: (by first marriage)

i. ***Bailey Maxwell.***

References: Correspondence with the late Barbara Lambert; Indiana Marriage Certificates 1960-2005; Findagrave.com obituary for Robert D. Horvath June 2002.

909.

Judy Lynn Lambert, daughter of David (443), granddaughter of Elizabeth (209), b. March 26, 1955; m. (1) Muncie, Indiana February 1, 1973 Richard Alan Wilson, divorced 1980; m. (2) Muncie, Indiana July 16, 1994 Charles R. Bartlett. Judy attended Ball State University and was employed as a clerical worker; ***nfi.***

Children: (by first marriage)

1515. I. ***Shannon Wilson***; b. August 28, 1973; m. (1) Muncie, Indiana June 19, 1993 Christopher L. Duncan, divorced 1994; m. (2) Mt. Pleasant, Indiana December 12, 1998 Larry J. Moran. Mr. Moran is a machine operator with two previous marriages and Shannon is an Insurance Claims Representative; ***nfi.***

1516. II. ***Michael Wilson*** b. May 12, 1979; m. Cyndee, last name not known; ***nfi.***

References: Correspondence with the late Barbara Lambert; Indiana Marriage Certificates 1960-2005; Findagrave.com obituary for Barbara Lambert.

910.

David Lambert, son of David (443), grandson of Elizabeth (209), b. January 4, 1954; m. (1) Yorktown, Indiana July 23, 1983 Kelli Lynn Stouder, divorced 1986; m. (2) Yorktown, Indiana January 1, 1989 Lydia Gibbs, divorced 1994; m. (3) Muncie Indiana August 8, 1997 Irene E. Wilt, divorced 2011. David Lambert was active in high school and college athletics participating in wrestling, swimming, and baseball. He was employed as a book binder/printer with A. E. Boyce; ***nfi.***

Children: (by first marriage)

1517. I. ***Patrick Adam Lambert***, b. February 29, 1984.

Children: (by second marriage)

1518. I. ***Brooklyn Lambert.***

References: Correspondence with the late Barbara Lambert; Indiana Marriage Certificates 1960-2005; Findagrave.com obituary for Barbara Lambert.

911.

Shonet Lambert, daughter of James (445), granddaughter of Elizabeth (209), b. July 26, 1957; m. Muncie, Indiana February 28, 1981 Douglas Jay Martin.

Both Shonet and her husband are graduates of Ball State University. During her college years, Shonet won the one, the two, and the three-mile runs. Previously an art teacher and girl's track coach, Shonet has since earned an M.A. in Fine Arts at Ball State. Doug was employed at the Miller's Woodmill. They reside in Muncie, Indiana.

Children:

1519. I. ***Jesse Louise Martin***, b. December 9, 1982; m. Muncie, Indiana June 19,2004 Christopher Daniel.

Children:

i. ***Caitlyn Daniel.***
ii. ***Carter Daniel.***

1520. II. ***James Bert Martin***, b. April 27, 1984; ***nfi.***

1521. III. ***Emily Ann Martin***, b. November 3, 1986; m. Trey Scott; ***nfi.***

References: Correspondence with the late Barbara Lambert; Indiana Marriage Certificates 1960-2005; *The Muncie Star Press* August 4, 2016 obituary for James Lambert.

912.

Thomas Lambert, son of James (445), grandson of Elizabeth (209), b. January 16, 1961; m. December 29, 1989 Sue Shikaze.

Thom has a B. S. Degree in Environmental Studies in 1984 from Ball State University. He is employed at Bach Lake Provincial Leadership Center, Ontario, Canada. Sue graduated from Lakehead University, Ontario, Canada and completed an M.A. Degree at Queen's University, Kingston, Ontario. The continue to reside in Canada and do not have any children.

References: Correspondence with the late Barbara Lambert; *The Muncie Star Press* August 4, 2016 obituary for James Lambert.

913.

Mary Beth Lambert, daughter of James (445), granddaughter of Elizabeth (209), b. December 31, 1964. Mary Beth graduated from Indiana University with a B. S. Degree in Recreation Therapy. She worked for the Bloomington, Indian Parks and Recreation Department. She resides with her partner, Cecil Slayton. They do not have any children.

References: Correspondence with the late Barbara Lambert; *The Muncie Star Press* August 4, 2016 obituary for James Lambert.

914.

Charles Pearson, son of Martha (446), grandson of Elizabeth (209), b. August 16, 1953. He was a local band promoter; ***nfi.***

References: Correspondence with the late Barbara Lambert.

915.

Michael Pearson, son of Martha (446), grandson of Elizabeth (209), b. March 31, 1956; m. Muncie, Indiana June 14, 1975 Barbara Lawrence. They reside in Muncie where Michael is employed with the Ball Corporation Experimental Laboratory and Barbara is employed with the Industrial Trust Bank.

Children:

1522. I. ***Darren Matthew Pearson***, b. April 16, 1977; m. Noblesville, Indiana August 10, 2002, Claire Andrea Schowe. Darren is a water planner and Claire is an Environmental Analyst; ***nfi.***

1523. II. ***Robin Pearson***, b. April 17, 1980; ***nfi.***

1524. III. ***Michael Adam Pearson***, b. November 23, 1983; ***nfi.***

References: Correspondence with the late Barbara Lambert; Indiana Marriage Certificates 1960-2005.

916.

Patricia Pearson, daughter of Martha (446), granddaughter of Elizabeth (209), b. October 17, 1957; m. Muncie, Indiana June 24, 1980 Joseph P. Cardaci, b. Colorado, a. 1958. Mr. and Mrs. Cardaci reside in Muncie, Indiana where she is a beautician and her husband does advertising sales for the school newspaper at Ball State University, Muncie. Joe is also a lay preacher; ***nfi.***

Children:

1525. I. ***Leah Cardaci***, b. March 27, 1981.

References: Correspondence with the late Barbara Lambert; Indian Marriage Certificates 1960-2005.

917.

Steven Eiholzer, son of Rebecca (447), grandson of Elizabeth (209), b. June 27, 1964; m. September 13, 1986 Denise Ann Eddinger. Steven worked as a general merchandise manager for a New York grocery chain; ***nfi.***

Children:

1526. I. ***Megan Denise Eiholzer***, b. December 2, 1987.

1527. II. ***Sean Steven Eiholzer***, b. September 6, 1989.

References: Correspondence with the late Barbara Lambert.

921.

Jennifer Marie Tighe, daughter of Kathryn (448), granddaughter of Elizabeth (209), b. Dayton, Ohio September 3, 1965; m. Muncie, Indiana December 28, 1988 Paul Joseph Orchard. Jennifer graduated Magna Cum Laude from Ball State University, Indiana with a B. S. Degree in Speech/Language Pathology and Audiology.

She completed a M. A. Degree in 1989 in Speech and Language Pathology at Ball State. Jennifer works as a speech/language pathologist for Muncie, Indian Public Schools. Paul as a B. S. Degree in Criminal Justice from Ball State. He teaches high school Social Studies, Health, and Physical Education and coaches' football in Muncie. Paul completed an MA Degree in Sports Administration; ***nfi.***

922.

Margaret Elizabeth Tighe, daughter of Kathryn (448), granddaughter of Elizabeth (209), b. Dayton, Ohio December 24, 1966; m May 25, 1989 Nathan Orchard, b. Medina, Ohio January 28, 1961, d. Ohio January 6, 2012 (brother of Paul Orchard). Kate is a Ball State graduate with a B. S. Degree in Psychology. Nathan did not complete a degree in surveying, but he opened a land surveying business in the Cleveland, Ohio area; ***nfi.***

Children:

1528. I. ***Isaiah Nathan Orchard***, b. Ohio September 13, 1989.

1529. II. ***Hannah Shiloh Orchard***, b. Ohio, February 22, 1992.

1530. III. ***Sarah Orchard***, b. Ohio.

References: Correspondence with the late Barbara Lambert; Indiana Marriage Certificate 1960-2005; Ohio Birth Index 1908-1998; Ohio Death Records 1938-2018.

933.

Willa Jeanne Berardi, daughter of Elizabeth (456), grandson of Edward Albert (215), b. Washington, DC September 7, 1952, d. Florida March 6, 2007 from complications associated with diabetes; m. (1) August 1986 Rex Moyer, divorced; m. (2) 2003 Robert Keeley.

Willa was a talented beautician who resided in Orlando, Florida. Her husband is a truck driver. Willa was involved in national van gatherings where owners of vans from the 1970 to the 1990s gathered to tell stories.

Children: (by first husband)

1531. I. ***Brianna Moyer***, b. December 26, 1992; m. Mike Arcilla. Brianna and her husband reside in Dallas, Texas where Briana is both a college student and the Assistant Manager of a Bed/Bath/and Beyond.

References: Social Security Death Index 1935-2014; Interview with Mickey Berardi; Correspondence with the late Raymond Berardi.

934.

Raymond Michael "Mickey" Berardi, son of Elizabeth (456), grandson of Edward Albert (215), b. Washington, DC December 12, 1955; m. May 16, 1986 Sherry Clements, b. May 16, 1986. Mickey studied drafting and design and for seventeen years was employed as a plumber before moving to Ocala, Florida. He has worked for Campaign Graphics for seven years before changing to Lighted Signage. Mickey continues to do consulting work in the field. He volunteered in sports his children were involved with during their school years. Mickey umpires for youth, High School, Junior College, Amateur Athletic Union (AAU), and Babe Ruth Baseball. He umpired professional minor league baseball at the Minnesota Twins Hammond Stadium Complex, Fort Meyers, Florida. Mickey and Sherry reside in Ocala, Florida.

Children:

1532. I. ***Carolyn McGuire Berardi***, b. February 24, 1973.

Children:

i. ***Tristyn I. Burnham***, b. March 22, 1993; m. Cheyenne Burnham. They reside in Ocala, Florida.

Children:

a. ***Kavry Rizzo***, b. July 13, 2010.
b. ***Joel Rizzo***, b. May 29, 2012.
c. ***Camdyn Burnham***, September 7, 2011.
d. ***Margaret (Marcie) Hazel Burnham***, b. November 17, 2014.
e. ***Olivar Michael Burnham***, b. June 22, 2016.

1533. II. ***Jason S. McGuire Berardi***, b. December 31, 1980.

Children:

i. ***Jason S. Berardi II***, b. May 27, 2003.

References: Interview with Mickey Berardi.

935.

Paul Malcolm Martin, son of Rose (457), grandson of Edward Albert (215), b. July 29, 1950; m. (1) January 25, 1973 Gayla Umholz, divorced 1979; m. (2) October 1983 Monika Darragh.

Paul is a graduate of George Mason University, Fairfax, Virginia with a degree in Business Management. He learned the electrical trade from his father. Paul is the Senior Special Projects Manager for VSC Fire and Security's Washington, DC District. Paul and Monika bred bench and field champion long haired standard dachshunds since 1983. Paul has served on the Board of Directors for the Dachshunds Club of America since 2007. Paul and Monika reside in Middleburg, Virginia.

Children: (by second marriage)

1534. I. ***Alexander Hart Martin***, b. June 24, 1988. Alex graduated from Penn State in 2010 with a BS Degree in Meteorology and obtained his Master's Degree from the University of Maryland, Baltimore Campus in 2015. He resides in Baltimore, Maryland.

References: Correspondence with Paul Martin.

936.

Glen Martin, son of Rose (457), grandson of Edward Albert (215), b. December 27, 1951; m. (1) 1971 Cynthia DePriest, divorced; m. (2) Missoula, Montana September 1982 Dawn Ackerman. Glen is a member of the *Robin Banks Band* which tours the west and mid-west. He resides in Missoula, Montana.

Children: (by first marriage)

1535. I. ***Jon Christian Martin***, b. December 29, 1971.

Children:

i. ***Christian Jon Martin***, b. June 2, 1990.

Children: (by second marriage)

1536. I. ***Destiny Rose Martin***, b. June 2, 1990.

References: Correspondence with the late Tracy Rose Root Martin.

937.

James Martin, son of Rose (457), grandson of Edward Albert (215), b. July 17, 1953; m. September 1975 Patricia Nakamura. Jim and his family reside in Reston, Virginia where he is the owner and construction manager of M. S. and C. Building Contractors, Inc.

Children:

1537. I. ***Garrett Nakamura Martin***, b. October 9, 1977.

1538. II. ***Jenna Elise Martin***, b. December 16, 1985.

References: Correspondence with the late Tracy Rose Root Martin.

938.

Kevin Martin, son of Rose (457), grandson of Edward Albert (215), b. October 11, 1958; m. May 9, 1981 Michelle Bovee. They reside in Vienna, Virginia where Kevin is a carpenter restoring old homes. Michelle works for the Department of the Navy.

Children:

1539. I. ***Carson Samuel Martin***, b. July 16, 1984.

1540. II. ***Louise Tavey Martin***, b. December 23, 1988.

References: Correspondence with the late Tracy Rose Root Martin.

939.

Cynthia Anne Sale, daughter of Anne (458), granddaughter of Edwin Albert (215), b. February 6, 1956.

Cindy graduated from VPI, Virginia with a BS Degree in Biology. She retired from Virginia State Government where she was a water resources manager with the State Water Control Board. Cindy is an accomplished artist and has won awards for her paintings, stained glass, and paper cuttings in local crafts fairs. She resides in Nokesville, Virginia.

References: Correspondence with Anne Root Sale.

940.

Matthew Alan Sale, son of Anne (458), grandson of Edward Albert (215), b. Washington, DC December 8, 1958; m. 1994 Sandra Bender, divorced 2019.

Matt owned and operated the Minnieville Masonry business for many years. Prior to his marriage, Matt resided in a stone and brick ranch house in Nokesville, Virginia that he designed and built. He and Sandra lived there until 2006 when they relocated to Gainesville, Virginia. Matt is employed with the Prince William County Division of Parks, Recreation, and Tourism and teaches Science in the Park during the school year. Matt keeps the family mountain hunting camp near McDowell, Virginia in repair and enjoys hunting and the outdoors as his father did. He currently resides in Nokesville, Virginia.

Children: (from wife's first marriage)

1541. I. ***Kim Bender***; m. Jim Logan. They reside in North Carolina and have three children: Amanda, Britton, and James.

1542. II. ***Tish Bender***; m. Josh Weinstein. They reside in Bull Run, Virginia with twins Ethan Matthew and Hailey Ann., b. February 5, 2007.

References: Correspondence with Anne Root Sale.

941.

Julie Kathleen Sale, daughter of Anne (458), granddaughter of Edward Albert (215), b. July 8, 1960; m. May 17, 1980 Edward Buck Waters.

Julie designed their home in Nokesville, Virginia. Buck graduated from Mary Washington College, Virginia with a BS Degree in Economics and History. He was President of *The Waters Corporation*, a consulting firm handling retirement plans. Buck is currently Chairman of Burroughs and Chapin Company, a large privately owned experiential real estate trust. Julie worked for the Government's Defense Logistics Agency in her early years and has since been running her non-profit *The Waters Foundation* for the past seventeen years helping to place emergency equipment with schools and first responders along with charitable funding in the community. Both Julie and Buck continue to support the Arts and various charities. They welcome being empty nesters while continuing to live in a rural section of Nokesville, Virginia next to Julie's mother, Anne Sale.

Children:

1543. I. ***Calandra Anne Waters***, b. October 15, 1981; m. August 8, 2008 Samuel Lake. A stubborn redhead from birth, Cali demonstrates a passion for all things environmental. She received a BS Degree from Virginia Tech and a Master's Degree of Art in Education from the College of William and Mary. Cali taught secondary Earth Science and Environmental Science before becoming the first Sustainability Director for the College of William and Mary.

Children:

i. ***Naia Calandra Waters Lake***, b. December 20, 2012. Naia is a Polynesian name for dolphin or sea nymph. Naia enjoys dancing, art, rock-climbing, and mountain biking.

ii. ***Kai Alan Buck Lake***, b. November 20, 2014. Kai's name is Polynesian for ocean or sea and his middle name is for his uncle and grandfather. A redhead like his mother, Kai enjoys cooking, rock-climbing, and bothering his sister.

1544. II. ***Heather Kathleen Waters***, b. March 26, 1983; m. June 27, 2015 Jonathan Tyler Parks. Heather is a Personal Trainer and Group Fitness Instructor in San Francisco, California. She obtained a BS Degree in Parks and Recreation from UNC Greensboro, North Carolina.

Children:

i. ***Calvin George Emerson Parks*** b. San Leandro, California November 24, 2016.

1545. III. ***Kyle Edward Buck Waters***, b. September 10, 1983; m. Jacqueline Marie Lamouroux, b. July 21, 1993. Kyle is a graduate of VPI with a BS Degree in Wildlife Science. He is a Wildlife Biologist with the US Department of Agriculture. Jacqueline owns and operates a photography business that specializes in weddings and family portraiture. They reside in Farmville, Virginia.

1546. IV. ***George Matthew Riley Waters***, b. January 18, 2000. George attends Virginia Tech where he is developing his writing skills for a Journalism Major. He enjoys photography and loves to travel.

References: Correspondence with Julie Sale Waters.

942.

Roger Glenn Sale, son of Anne (458), grandson of Edward Albert (215), b. Fairfax, Virginia August 4, 1962, d. Prince William County September 12, 2015.

Roger suffered brain damage at birth. He was extremely medically fragile and sometimes had over a hundred seizures a day. For the first ten years of his life, Roger resided at home with his parents who provided both extensive care and love for him. He was included as *one of the gang* in the neighborhood and enjoyed the support and love of his sisters, brother, and extended family. From 1974 to June 2015 Roger lived at the Northern Virginia Training Center (NVTC) and spent alternate weekends with his family. In 2015 the State closed NVTC where Roger received the intensive medical care he required. He died, surrounded by his loving family, less than three months after being discharged to a group home in the community. Roger is buried with his father, Wiley Sale, in the Quantico National Cemetery, Quantico, Virginia.

References: Correspondence with Anne Root Sale.

943.

Edward Albert Root III, son of Edward Albert (459), grandson of Edward Albert (215), b. Grand Forks, North Dakota May 22, 1962; m. Wiesbaden, Germany June 29, 1985 Racine Frances Rosch, b. Marysville, California February 20, 1965.

Ed graduated from General H. H. Arnold High School, Wiesbaden, Germany in 1980. He and Racine were married in the chapel on Lindsay Air Station, Wiesbaden. Ed joined Motorola Taunusstein, Germany as a computer/business analyst in October 1980. In 2004 Ed was a member of Motorola's Semiconductor Division, which became Freescale Semiconductor. He currently works for NXP Semiconductors, which acquired Freescale in 2015. From 1992-2000, Ed flew hang gliders as both a pilot and as a basic instructor in northern Arizona. From 2000-2008 Ed spent most of his time flying a trike, a powered hang glider) and towing up tandem and single hang gliders from the airports at Coolidge, Arizona and Maricopa, Arizona for Sky Masters School of Hang Gliding.

Children:

1547. I. ***Edward Albert Root IV***, b. Mesa, Arizona June 18, 1990. Ted enjoys online posting of his video game adventures and writing fantasy stories.

1548. II. ***Randall Philip Root***, b. Mesa, Arizona May 2, 1994. Andy participated in the marching band all four years at Corona del Sol High School playing the flute, piccolo, and mellophone (French horn). Andy's main interests are music and welding. Andy attended Mesa Community College, Mesa, Arizona for welding and is certified in several welding techniques. He currently works at UCT (Ultra Clean Technologies).

References: Correspondence with Edward Albert Root III.

944.

James Tasso Root, son of Edward Albert (459), grandson of Edward Albert (215), b. January 15, 1964; m. Svenborg, Denmark March 10, 1983 Sandra Kay Nance.

Jim and Sandy were high school sweethearts while attending General H. H. Arnold High School, Wiesbaden, Germany. Jim stayed in Wiesbaden until 1987 working locally for the Air Force Air Station attending classes at the University of Maryland and City College of Chicago studying Electronics. Sandy worked at the base library. In 1987 Jim was hired by the Army Recreation Machine Program (ARMP) and relocated his family to Wurzburg, Germany where he repaired slot machines on Army installations. Sandy worked at the Middle School on Leighton Barracks.

In 1994 Jim was promoted to Office Manager for ARMP. The family moved to Barstow, California where Jim opened an office on Fort Irwin and Sandy worked for DRMO at the Barstow Marine Corp Logistic Base. In 1996 Jim was promoted to the Eastern Regional Manager for ARMP and moved his family to Columbus, Georgia outside Ft. Benning. This was a blessing as the family was much closer to Jim's parents living in Huntsville, Alabama. In 2005 Jim was promoted to US District Director and relocated to Colorado Springs, Colorado where he worked on Fort Carson and Sandy worked for Pike's Peak Community College and received her AAS Degree in Photography. Jim and Sandy love spending time with their children and grandchildren and Jim is an avid fly fisher and can often be found on the golf course improving his game.

Children:

1549. I. ***James Christopher Root***, b. Wiesbaden, Germany March 24, 1983; m. (1) 2007 Misti Ray, divorced 2012; m. (2) December 6, 2014 Kristina Sorg. James was employed with Best Buy managing the automotive Installation department while attending Columbus State University, Georgia where he earned his AAS Degree in Criminal Justice. James Joined the Columbus, Georgia Police Department and graduated from the Police Academy in June 2014. In 2018 James and his family moved to Colorado Springs, Colorado where James works for the Aurora Police Department. James enjoys spending time with family, hiking, camping, and working on cars.

Children: (by first marriage)

i. ***Masen James Root***, b. Columbus, Georgia January 7, 2010.

Children: (by second marriage)

i. ***Kristopher Edward Root***, b. Columbus, Georgia March 7, 2015.
ii. ***Axl Root***, b. Columbus Georgia April 28, 2017.

1550. II. ***Jonathan Daniel Root***, b. Wiesbaden, Germany December 11, 1985; m. June 12, 2006 Shannon Ley Rumps. Jon is a firefighter with the Colorado Springs Fire Department. Shannon earned an Associate's Degree in Science, Magna Cum Laude

Children: (by adoption)

i. ***Zane Quentin Root***, b. December 4, 2002 to Shannon and adopted by Jon August 17, 2018.

Children:
i. ***Staci Lynn Root***, b. September 2, 2008.

References: Correspondence with James Tasso Root and Gesa Root.

945.

Enrico Elihu Root, son of Edward Albert (459), grandson of Edward Albert (215) b. Chanute AF Hospital Rantoul, Illinois February 11, 1966.

Enrico attended school in Wiesbaden, Germany during his childhood and teen years graduating in 1984 from General H. H. Arnold High School. He worked in Frankfurt and Wiesbaden in Germany from 1985 to 1992 as a civilian in support of the US Military. Since 1992 Enrico has lived and worked in Alabama for ten years and in Arizona for the last fourteen years where he is employed as a sales representative for the largest merchandising company that services major convenience store chains. Enrico is unmarried and has no children.

References: Correspondence with Gesa Root.

946.

Michelle Gerda Margaret Root, daughter of Edward Albert (459), granddaughter of Edward Albert (215), b. Sumter, South Carolina September 16, 1969; m. Huntsville, Alabama January 2, 1998 David William Jenkins.

Michelle graduated from General H. H. Arnold High School, Wiesbaden, Germany. She met her future husband in Wiesbaden in 1995. Michelle earned an Associate's Degree in Computer Information Systems and has worked in that field in Germany and later as a teacher's assistant in Maryland and in Wiesbaden to this date. David graduated from Archbishop Curley High School, Baltimore and graduated from the Citadel in Columbia, South Carolina. He received his Master's Degree from the University of Maryland, Bowie State in 1999. David is currently working on his doctorate at Northeastern University, Boston. Michelle and family expect to return to the US in 2019.

Children:

1551. I. ***Maria Jenkins***, b. Wiesbaden, Germany January 20, 1999. Maria Attended St. Joan of Arc School, Aberdeen, Maryland, North Hartford High School Animal Science Magnet Program, and graduated from Wiesbaden High School in 2017. She is currently attending Salisbury University, Maryland studying pre-med. During her high school career Maria played softball, wrestling, and was a football manager. In addition to being a member of the Honor Society, she was a Student Ambassador, on the Debate team, and a member of both the JROTC and culinary club.

1552. II. ***William Jenkins***, b. Baltimore, Maryland March 25, 2001. He Attended St. Joan of Arc School, Aberdeen, Maryland and Graduated from high school in Wiesbaden, Germany in 2019. William participated in cross country, wrestling, track and field, band, robotics, and was a member of the JROTC and the National Honor Society. He has enrolled in Salisbury University, Maryland to study both computer science and history.

1553. III. ***Alexandra Jenkins***, Baltimore, Maryland August 22, 2008. She attended St. Joan of Arc School, Aberdeen, Maryland and Wiesbaden Elementary School, Germany. Alexandra enjoys both chorus and drama.

References: Correspondence with Gesa Root.

947.

Elizabeth Ann Randall, daughter of JoAnn (460), granddaughter of Edwin Milford (216), b. May 17, 1948; m. Palm Beach, Florida June 16, 1996 Mark Edward Johnson; ***nfi.***

References: Correspondence with the late JoAnn Randall; Florida Marriage Index 1927-2001.

948.

Margaret Jane Randall, daughter of JoAnn (460), granddaughter of Edwin Milford (216), b. March 25, 1950; m. Broward County, Florida January 9, 1982 Joern John Curtiss. They were last known to reside in Hollywood, Florida where Joern owned and operated a boat making and boat repair shop while Margaret was employed as a physical therapist; ***nfi.***

References: Correspondence with the late JoAnn Randall; Florida Marriage Index 1927-2001.

949.

William Peirson Randall, Jr., son of JoAnn (460), grandson of Edwin Milford (216), b. December 19, 1951; m. Broward County February 15, 1975 Maria Magdalena Gomez, divorced. Mr. Randall was the manager of a United Parcel Service Office; ***nfi.***

Children:

1554. I. ***Chrystie Michelle Randall***, b. November 16, 1976.

1555. II. ***William Alton Randall***, b. November 24, 1978.

References: Correspondence with the late JoAnn Root Randall; Florida Marriage Index 1927-2001.

950.

Katherine Jane Randall, daughter of JoAnn (460), granddaughter of Edwin Milford (216), b. September 7, 1954; Mitchell Greenberg. They were last known to reside in West Palm Beach where Katherine was employed as a registered nurse and her husband was employed as a paramedic and fireman; ***nfi.***

Children:

1556. I. ***Melissa Greenberg***, b. August 1981.

1557. II. ***Amie Heather Greenberg***, b. November 20, 1984.

1558. III. ***Matthew Hayden Greenberg***, b. January 25, 1989.

References: Correspondence with the late JoAnn Root Randall.

951.

Deborah Jean Randall, daughter of JoAnn (460), granddaughter of Edwin Milford (216), b. February 23, 1961; m. (1) February 25, 1979 Donald Allen Kania, divorced Palm Beach, Florida June 18, 1982; m. (2) Palm Beach, Florida September 10, 1983 Michael Kevin Corcoran. Deborah was head cashier for Home Depot in Boynton Beach, Florida while Mike managed the service department for an Isuzu car dealership; ***nfi.***

References: Correspondence with the late JoAnn Root Randall; Florida Marriage Index 1927-2001; Florida Divorce Index 1927-2001.

952.

Barbara Rosier Nichols, daughter of William (461), granddaughter of Gladys (217), b. November 11, 1954; m. June 24, 1978 Michael Frazer, b. May 20, 1953. The Frazers were last known to reside in Arlington, Texas where Michael was employed with the Agfa Geveart Photographic Company; ***nfi.***

Children:

1559. I. ***John Michael Frazer***, b. July 2, 1982.

1560. II. ***Mark William Frazer***, b. January 14, 1985.

References: Correspondence with the late Cynthia Nicholas.

953.

Steven Nicholas, son of William (461), grandson of Gladys (217), b. February 11, 1957; m. Mary Louise Sullivan, b. March 12, 1965. Steven was involved in both farming and the operation of a sawmill in Texas; ***nfi.***

Children:

1561. I. ***William Lee Nichols***, b. August 19, 1985.

References: Correspondence with the late Cynthia Nichols.

954.

David Ray Nichols, son of William (461), grandson of Gladys (217), b. August 21, 1965. He attended Alfred University, Alfred, New York; ***nfi.***

References: Correspondence with the late Cynthia Nichols.

955.

Robert Scott Osborne, son of Richard (462), grandson of Bertha (218), b. July 22, 1956; m. (1) June 11, 1977, Janet Page, divorced; m. (2) February 14, 1986, name of spouse not known. Last known to reside in Olean, New York; ***nfi.***

Children: (by first marriage)

1562. I. ***Tonya Marie Osborne***, b. November 29, 1977.

1563. II. ***Robert Scott Osborne, Jr.***, b. February 15, 1979.

References: Correspondence with the late Richard Osborne.

956.

William Richard Osborne, son of Richard (462), grandson of Bertha (218), b. North Tarrytown, New York November 9, 1959, d. Rochester, New York December 6, 2004; m. September 22, 1990 Anne Harris. Bill worked as a surveyor and resided in Lancaster, New York with his family. It is believed that Bill Osborne's remains were cremated and the ashes placed in the Osborne plot in Maple Lawn Cemetery because his name is on the backside of the monument; ***nfi.***

Children:

1564. I. ***Sarah Osborne, nfi.***

References: Correspondence with the late Richard Osborne; Social Security Death Index 1935-20014; US Obituary Collection 1930-present; Maple Lawn Cemetery Records, Bolivar, New York.

957.

George Edwin Osborne, son of Richard (462), grandson of Bertha (218), b. August 9, 1961; m. February 17, 1990 Patrice Anderson. They were last known to reside in San Diego, California; ***nfi.***

Children:

1565. I. ***Michael Ryan Osborne***, b. May 15, 1990.

References: Correspondence with the late Richard Osborne.

958.

Patricia Lynn Osborne, daughter of Robert (463), granddaughter of Bertha (218), b. Austin, Texas August 29, 1962; m. August 7, 1982 Charles David Allen, b. Travis City, Texas March 31, 1958. Mr. Allen was previously married and had two children by his first wife. They were last known to reside in Plano, Texas; ***nfi.***

Children:

1566. I. ***Tracy Marie Allen***, b. October 29, 1985.

References: Correspondence with the late Richard Osborne; Texas Birth Index 1903-1997.

959.

Albert Garret Nulsen, son of Albert (464), grandson of Huldah (219), b. April 27, 1933, d. Arizona April 27, 1933; m. Dolan Springs, Arizona October 28, 1967 Judy Bradshaw.

Albert Nulsen served three tours of duty with the US Army: December 6, 1951 to December 11, 1954, October 10, 1956 to October 6, 1959, and December 12, 1961 to December 11 1964. He saw military service in Korea and rose to the rank of Sergeant. Since 1993 he was a resident of Dolan Springs, Arizona and he was buried in Chloride Cemetery, Chloride Arizona; ***nfi.***

Children:

1567. I. ***Eugene Nulsen***, b. 1971.

1568. II. ***Albert Nulsen***, b. 1975.

1569. III. ***Tertius Nulsen***, b. 1981.

References: US Census: 1940; Correspondence with the late Jane Nulsen Bunse; Chloride Cemetery Records, Chloride Arizona; US VA Death Files 1859-2010; Social Security Death Index 1935-2014.

960.

Carolle Deane Nulsen, daughter of Albert (464), granddaughter of Huldah (219), b. Hazelwood, Missouri April 2, 1935, d. Eolia, Missouri March 6, 2005; m. Louisiana, Missouri November 21, 1953 Nelson F. Harrison, Sr., b. March 6, 1928, d. March 17, 2013. They adopted one son and have three sons and one daughter of their own; ***nfi.***

Children:

1570. I. ***Nelson F. Harrison, Jr.***, (adopted son), b. August 1946. Last resided in Providence, Rhode Island.

Children:

i. ***Melissa Anne Harrison***, b. March 29, 1971.
ii. ***Shelly Jean Harrison***, August 1972.

1571. II. ***Terry Russell Harrison***, b. Louisiana, Missouri June 1, 1954, d. Columbia, Missouri May 14, 2017; m. Centertown, Missouri October 26, 1979 Wanda Allbritton. He was employed as a truck driver for over thirty years. He served with the US Army from January 25, 1972 to June 6, 1974. He was survived by five children, fourteen grandchildren, and two great-grandchildren. He was buried in Laddonia Cemetery, Laddonia, Missouri.

Children:

i. ***Terry Shawn Harrison*** of Laddonia, Missouri.
ii. ***Kevin Harrison*** of Laddonia, Missouri.
iii. ***William Russell Harrison*** of Mexico.
iv. ***Heather Harrison Vaughn***, b. September 14, 1972, of Ponotoc, Mississippi.

v. ***Theresa Harrison Tadlock***, b. October 26, 1974, of Mexico.

1572. III. ***Ronald Gene Harrison***, last resided Troy, Missouri.

Children:

i. ***Rick Lee Harrison***, b. April 21, 1974.
ii. ***Jennifer Harrison***, b. June 1975.

1573. IV. ***Steven Michael Harrison***, last known residence Elsberry, Missouri.

Children:

i. ***Stacy Jean Harrison***, b. December 26, 1974.

1574. V. ***Susan Carolle Harrison DeCamp***, last known residence Louisiana, Missouri.

References: US Census: 1940; Correspondence with the late Jane Nulsen Bunse; Laddonia Cemetery Records, Laddonia, Missouri; Findagrave obituary for Terry Russell Harrison.

961.

Maude Kreher Nulsen, daughter of Albert (464), granddaughter of Huldah (219), b. August 28, 1936; m. (1) Pike, Missouri July 6, 1953 Lee Roy Stewart, Jr., b. 1932, divorced Butte, Montana August 8, 1967; m. (2) San Diego, California August 24, 1967 Philip J. Finstuen, divorced Clark, Nevada October 7, 1969; m. (3) San Diego, California December 19, 1969 Stanley E. Mair, divorced San Diego, California May 1971; m. (4) Clark County, Arizona September 11, 1980 Thayer Elijah Ver Schoor, deceased; m. (5) a Mr. Bright. Last known residence was Safford, Arizona; ***nfi.***

Children: (by first marriage)

1575. I. ***Rose Lee Stewart***, b. December 7, 1953; m. a Mr. Westmoreland.

Children:

i. ***Paul Westmoreland***, b. March 7, 1992.

1576. II. ***Kathleen Diane Stewart***; m. a Mr. Danley. Had a son Caine Andrew Michael, b. August 8, 1974; ***nfi.***

1577. III. ***Lee Roy Steward, Jr.***, b. Louisiana, Montana October 28, 1955; d. Miami, Arizona February 26, 2012; married but name of spouse not known.

Children:

i. ***Jason Lee Stewart.***
ii. ***Valerie Anne Stewart.***
iii. ***Lee Roy Stewart.***

1578. IV. ***Laura Marie Stewart***, b. June 18, 1957; m. (1) Pike, Missouri August 17, 1974 Charles Mark Henley; m. (2) a Mr. Rea.

Children: (by first marriage)

i. ***Jon Henley***, b. October 1975.

1579. V. ***Linda Sue Stewart***, b. October 16, 1960; m. a Mr. Arquette.

1580. VI. ***Glen Edward Stewart***, b. June 12, 1963.

References: US Census: 1940; Correspondence with the late Jane Nulsen Bunse; Montana Divorce Records 1943-1988; Nevada Marriage Index 1956-2005; California Marriage Index 1960-1985; California Divorce Index 1966-1984; US Obituary Collections 1930-present; Nevada Divorce Index 1968-20215.

962.

Sheila Jane Nulsen, daughter of Albert (464), granddaughter of Huldah (219), b. October 12, 1938; m. (1) February 13, 1954 Edwin E. Michael, Jr.; m. (2) Mr. Ray. They had at least one child. Her last known residence was Newton, Illinois; ***nfi.***

Children:

1581. I. ***Wendy Jane Michael***, b. January 2, 1955; m. William B. McCallister.

References: US Census: 1940; Correspondence with the late Jane Nulsen Bunse.

963.

Betty Isabelle Nulsen, daughter of Albert (464), granddaughter of Huldah (219), b. August 3, 1940; m. (1) Louisiana, Missouri April 29, 1957 Donald James Irvin; m. (2) February 14, 1973 George Segress.

Last known residence was Elsberry, Missouri; ***nfi.***

Children: (by first marriage)

1582. I. ***Susan Denise Irvin***, b. December 22, 1958.

1583. II. ***Donald James Irvin, Jr.***, b. December 11, 1959.

1584. III. ***Barbara Louise Irvin***, b. April 9 1961.

1585. IV. ***Christine Gale Irvin***, b. April 9 1963.

1586. V. ***Jan Ellen Irvin***, b. July 17, 1969.

Children: (by second marriage)

1587. I. ***Anne Marie Segress***, b. October 1975.

References: US Census: 1940; Correspondence with the late Jane Nulsen Bunse.

964.

Alice Ann Nulsen, daughter of Albert (464), granddaughter of Huldah (219), b. December 18, 1942; m. (1) a Mr. Wolcott, divorced; (2) Imperial, California July 22, 1965 Victor Melvin Nicholson; divorced San Diego, California March 1972. Last known residence was Kingman, Arizona; ***nfi.***

References: Correspondence with the late Jane Nulsen Bunse; California Marriage Index 1960-1985; California Divorce Index 1966-1984.

965.

David William Nulsen, son of Albert (464), grandson of Huldah (219), b. November 5, 1944; m. January 9, 1965, divorced; remarried, name of second spouse not known. Last known residence was Eolia, Missouri; ***nfi.***

Children: (by first marriage)

1588. I. ***David Scott Nulsen***, b. January 4, 1967.

1589. II. ***Rebecca Diane Nulsen***, b. July 8, 1969.

References: Correspondence with the late Jane Nulsen Bunse.

966.

Vivian Gene Nulsen, daughter of Albert (464), granddaughter of Huldah (219), b. February 2, 1946; m. August 7, 1965 Kenneth Barnet Lee. Last known residence was Bowling Green, Missouri; ***nfi.***

Children:

1590. I. ***Kenna Gene Lee*** (adopted), b. August 20, 1972.

1591. II. ***Chad Barnet Lee***, b. September 9, 1974, d. September 19, 1974.

References: Correspondence with the late Jane Nulsen Bunse.

967.

Pamela Sue Nulsen, daughter of Albert (464), granddaughter of Huldah (219), b. March 28, 1947; m. August 12, 1964 Arnold Guthrie. Last known address was Pleasant Hill, Illinois; ***nfi.***

Children:

1592. I. ***Leah Sue Guthrie***, b. September 25, 1966.

1593. II. ***Melissa Dawn Guthrie***, b. March 3, 1970.

1594. III. ***William Arnold Guthrie***, b. January 21, 1974.

References: Correspondence with the late Jane Nulsen Bunse.

968.

Delores Marie Nulsen, daughter of Albert (464), granddaughter of Huldah (219), b. March 7, 1949; m. December 11, 1968 Robert Eugene Martin. They have three daughters but their names are not currently known. Last known address was Blue Springs, Missouri; ***nfi.***

References: Correspondence with the late Jane Nulsen Bunse.

969.

Patricia Marie Nulsen, daughter of Albert (464), granddaughter of Huldah (219), b. March 17, 1950;

m. (1) October 19 1968 Gary Ray Harrison; m. (2) a Mr. Williams. They have six children but the identities of only two are currently known. Last known address was Bowling Green, Missouri; ***nfi.***

Children:

1595. I. ***Angela Marie Harrison***, b. August 15, 1970.

1596. II. ***Faith Michelle Harrison***, b. March 17, 1974.

References: Correspondence with the late Jane Nulsen Bunse.

970.

Donald Bruce Nulsen, son of Albert (464), grandson of Huldah (219), b. Eolia, Missouri April 15, 1951, d. Bowling Green, Missouri June 12, 2011; m. February 19, 1972. They have a son and a daughter but their identities are not currently known; ***nfi.***

References: Correspondence with the late Jane Nulsen Bunse; Social Security Death Index 1935-2014.

971.

Mary Lou Nulsen, daughter of Albert (464), granddaughter of Huldah (219), b. August 25, 1952; (1) m. February 19, 1972 Duane Roed; m. (2) a Mr. Flores. Last known residence was Louisiana; ***nfi.***

Children:

1597. I. ***Timothy Lee Roed***, b. March 18, 1970.

1598. II. ***Tracey Lynn Roed***, b. April 9, 1972.

1599. III. ***Misty Dawn Roed***, b. May 23, 1975.

References: Correspondence with the late Jane Nulsen Bunse.

972.

Robert "Bob" Evan Nulsen, son of Albert (464), grandson of Huldah (219), b. Louisiana, Missouri, d. Curryville, Missouri December 8, 2013; m. (1) February 12, 1972 Rosemary Neese, divorced; m. (2) June 1975 Patricia Crowe, divorced; m. (3) Rosemary Autery, deceased.

Robert lived in Curryville most of his life. He served in the US Army as a mechanic. In civilian life,

Bob was employed as a truck driver; his last employer was Sisbro. Bob enjoyed working as a mechanic, a farmer, gardening, and was a *jack-of-all-trades.* His obituary did not identify a burial location. He had seven grandchildren.

Children: (by first marriage)

1600. I. ***Christopher DeWayne Nulsen***, b. July 2, 1973; m. Karen, last name not known and resided in Hudson, Colorado.

Children: (by other marriages)

1601. I. ***Tiffany Nulsen***; m. Ryland Coffer and resided in Mexico.

1602. II. ***Nicole Nulsen***, predeceased her father.

References: Correspondence with the late Jane Nulsen Bunse; Obituary posted on Findagrave.com.

973.

Curtis John Nulsen, son of Albert (464), grandson of Huldah (219), b. October 17, 1955; m. July 14, 1974 Linda Elgin. Last known address Pleasant Hill, Illinois; ***nfi.***

References: Correspondence with the late Jane Nulsen Bunse.

974.

Sharon Gale Nulsen, daughter of Albert (464), granddaughter of Huldah (219), b. January 6, 1957; m. (1) November 16, 1974 William Light, divorced; m. (2) a Mr. McAllister. Last know residence was Blue Springs, Missouri; ***nfi.***

References: Correspondence with the late Jane Nulsen Bunse.

975.

Phyllis Ruth Nulsen, daughter of Albert (464), granddaughter of Huldah (219), b. February 3, 1959; m. a Mr. Preston. She had a daughter before her marriage, but the identity of the daughter is not known. She was last known to reside in Bowling Green, Missouri; ***nfi.***

976.

Brian Neal Nulsen, son of Albert (464), grandson of Huldah (219), b. July 15, 1960; m. Shelley, last name not known. Last known address was Sedalia, Kansas; ***nfi.***

Children:

1603. I. ***Shelly Nulsen.***

1604. II. ***Rodney David Nulsen.***

1605. III. ***Brandon Keith Nulsen.***

References: Correspondence with the late Jane Nulsen Bunse.

977.

Julie Ann Nulsen, daughter of William (465), granddaughter of Huldah (219), b. Missouri November 13, 1946, d. Cincinnati, Ohio February 22, 1987 from cancer; m. (1) a Mr. Ostrander, divorced; m. (2) Cael Michael Elsbernd, b. Ohio September 24, 1946, d. Madeira, Ohio August 19, 2006, divorced, Hamilton, Ohio July 19, 1974; m. (3) Hamilton, Ohio June 27, 1975 Charles A. Russell. It is not known where Julie Nulsen Russell was buried. Her second husband was buried in Gate of Heaven Cemetery, Montgomery, Ohio.

Children: (by first marriage)

1606. I. ***Lynn Marie Ostrander***, b. Ohio August 8, 1965; m. (1) Butler, Ohio March 27, 1993, divorced Clermont, Ohio March 13, 1997; m. (2) Denton, Texas April 1, 2006 Mark R. Dunn.

Children: (by second marriage)

1607. I. ***Stephen Andrew Elsbernd***, b. Ohio December 28, 1969; m. (1) Hamilton, Ohio January 25, 1992 Laurie A. Oliver, divorced Butler, Ohio November 7, 1997; m. (2) Patricia L., last name not known, divorced Hamilton, Ohio May 30, 2003; m. (3) Hamilton, Ohio August 7, 2004 Bridget A. Bell.

References: Correspondence with the late Jane Nulsen Bunse; Ohio Death Records 1938-2018; Ohio Birth Index 1908-1998; Ohio Divorce Records 1973-2007; Ohio Marriage Records 1972-2007; Gate of Heaven Cemetery Records, Montgomery, Ohio.

978.

Steven J. Nulsen, son of William (465), grandson of Huldah (219), b. January 27, 1948; m. (1) Carole, last name not known, divorced; m. (2) Glenda, last name not known. Last known to reside in Granite City, Illinois; ***nfi.***

Children: (by first marriage)

1608. I. ***Keith Nulsen***, b. January 22, 1970.

References: Correspondence with the late Jane Nulsen Bunse.

979.

Gary P. Nulsen, son of William (465), grandson of Huldah (219), b. March 13, 1951; m. Nancy, last name not known and were last known to reside in St. Louis, Missouri; ***nfi.***

Children:

1609. I. ***Candice Nulsen***, b. 1971.

1610. II. ***Jennifer Nulsen***, b. October 23, 1979.

1611. III. ***Sidney Nulsen***, b. April 1989.

References: Correspondence with the last Jane Nulsen Bunse.

980.

Marianne Cecile Campbell, daughter of Jane (466), granddaughter of Huldah (219), b. May 14, 1949; m. (1) William Beshore, divorced; m. (2) January 8, 1985 John Turner. They were last living in Texas where Marianne was employed as a nurse; ***nfi.***

Children: (by second marriage)

1612. I. ***Mickey Stewart Turner***, b. November 17, 1987.

References: Correspondence with the late Jane Nulsen Bunse.

981.

Robert Neil Cook, son of Wilber (469), grandson of Homer (223), b. June 16, 1959; m. Becky Brown September 26, 1987. Last known to reside in Los Angeles County, California; ***nfi.***

Children:

1613. I. ***Megan Cook***, b. May 27, 1989.

References: Correspondence with the late Wilber Cook.

982.

Kristen Cook, daughter of Wilber (469), granddaughter of Homer (223), b. December 24, 1960. She graduated from El Camino College and was employed as an account executive with B. D. S. Marketing in Costa Mesa, California; ***nfi.***

994.

Joan Marie Hulbert, daughter of Yale (476), granddaughter of Gerald (226). b. Bethlehem, Pennsylvania February 18, 1940; m. Bethlehem, Pennsylvania December 30, 1961 Charles Franklin Wentz. Joan is employed by the Pentagon while Charles is the Chief of Military Police, Fort Myer, Virginia. They reside in Bowie, Maryland.

References: Correspondence with Barbara Tarantine Hulbert.

995.

Carole Jayne Hulbert, daughter of Yale (476), granddaughter of Gerald (226), b. Bethlehem, Pennsylvania October 12, 1946; m. Bethlehem, Pennsylvania September 9, 1967 Timothy Kraus.

Carole is employed as a teacher with Baltimore City Schools. Timothy works as with Catonsville Plumbing and Heating where he is both Vice-President and Project Manager. His father is President and his grandfather founded the company. They have two children but the name of only one is currently known.

Children:

1614. I. ***Kimberly Kraus***, b. Baltimore, Maryland October 6, 1969.

1615. II. ***Male Kraus***, b. 1974; ***nfi.***

References: Correspondence with Barbara Tarantine Hulbert.

997.

Robert Milton Krueger, son of Geraldine (477), granddaughter of Gerald (226), b. Bethlehem, Pennsylvania December 28, 1944, d. August 1985 from a massive heart attack after being the seventh heart transplant at Temple University Hospital; m. Bethlehem, Pennsylvania June 17, 1967 Karen Jay White, b. place not known, December 12, 1947.

Robert graduated from Alfred University. He owned and operated Krueger's Sunoco, Bethlehem, Pennsylvania for the last ten years of his life. Karen graduated from the Lancaster (Pennsylvania) Hospital Nurses' Training School and is employed as a nurse. Robert Krueger was buried in Memorial Park Cemetery, Bethlehem, Pennsylvania.

Children:

1616. I. ***Robin Joy Krueger***, b. Bethlehem, Pennsylvania April 1, 1968.

1617. II. ***Kevin Charles Krueger***, b. Bethlehem, Pennsylvania December 22, 1971.

1618. III. ***Mark Brian Krueger***, b. Bethlehem, Pennsylvania September 26, 1976.

References: Correspondence with Barbara Tarantine Hulbert; Memorial Park Cemetery Records, Bethlehem, Pennsylvania.

998.

Marilyn Virginia Krueger, daughter of Geraldine (477), granddaughter of Gerald (226), b. Bethlehem, Pennsylvania March 16, 1947, d. January 18, 1990; m. June 12, 1971 Dennis Rae Jones, divorced April 11, 1973, Hale County, Texas. Marilyn was employed as an Administrative Assistant by Dr. L. H. Sweterlitsch. She was buried in Memorial Park Cemetery, Bethlehem, Pennsylvania.

References: Correspondence with Barbara Tarantine Hulbert; Memorial Park Cemetery Records, Bethlehem, Pennsylvania; Obituary on Findagrave.com; Texas Marriage Index 1824-2014; Texas Divorce Index 1968-2014.

999.

Patricia Louise Hulbert, daughter of Frederick (478), granddaughter of Gerald (226), b. Baltimore, Maryland November 24, 1944; m. Phoenix Pope, Arkansas March 26, 1966 Glenn Connor. Patricia is employed as a secretary with Pioneer Bank and Glenn works at Hughes Air West Air Lines, Scottsdale, Arizona.

References: Correspondence with Barbara Tarantine Hulbert.

1000.

Barbara Jane Hulbert, daughter of Frederick (478), granddaughter of Gerald (226), b. Bethlehem, Pennsylvania August 1, 1950; m. place not known June 6, 1970 Dio McElrath, Jr. Barbara is employed as a legal secretary while Dio works at Talley Industries, Mesa, Arizona.

Children:

1619. I. ***Mark Wayne McElrath***, b. Phoenix, Arizona October 1974.

References: Correspondence with Barbara Tarantine Hulbert.

1001.

Judith Ann Hulbert, daughter of Frederick (478), granddaughter of Gerald (226), b. Bethlehem, Pennsylvania January 11, 1952; m. place not known July 3, 1971 Boyd Sonewald, Jr. Judith worked as a bookkeeper for a Chevrolet dealership until 1971. Boyd is in the Air Force at Travis Air Force Base, Fairfield, California.

References: Correspondence with Barbara Tarantine Hulbert.

1002.

Gregory Madden Hulbert, son of Gerald (479), grandson of Elba (228), b. Olean, New York December 24, 1949; m. Saugerties, New York May 16, 1971 Darilyn Ann Daley, b. Saugerties, New York March 11, 1950.

Mr. Hulbert was employed by the Kingston, New York Sears Department Store as the Manager for toys and garden center from 1969 to 1977. From 1969 to 1998 he was in the military with the US Army Reserves 854th Engineer Battalion. He retired as a First Sergeant. From 1976 to 2008 he was both a police officer and Chief of Police for the Saugerties Police Department. Darilyn graduated from New Paltz College with a BSN and a Masters in Health Administration from Capella University. She worked for the Health Alliance of the Hudson Valley for over forty years in various positions, retiring in 2020 as the Director of Nursing Informatics at Health Alliance.

Children:

1620. I. ***Christopher John Hulbert***, b. Kingston, New York February 18, 1974; m. (1) Saugerties, New York October 16, 1998 Tanya Turck, divorced May 2008; m. (2) place not known,

April 16, 2011 Lindsay Hartman, b. September 25, 1977. Chris works as a Detective Specialist with the Kingston Police Department stationed at the Kingston High School as a School Resource Officer. Lindsay is employed as a School Counselor with Kingston High School.

Children: (by first marriage)

i. ***Jordan Christopher Hulbert.***

Children; (by second marriage)

i. ***Hadley Madden Hulbert.***
ii. ***Grady Reid Hulbert.***

1621. II. ***Jeffrey Madden Hulbert***, b. January 18, 1981; m. Valley Stream, New York November 9, 2007 Pamela Ann Toscano, b. September 25, 1981. Jeffrey has a marketing degree, Summa Cum Laue from SUNY Albany, an MBA from the College of St. Rose; and a JC Degree from Albany Law / Union College. Pamela works as a Marketing Manager at Carson Optical, Long Island.

Children:

i. ***Avery Grace Hulbert.***
ii. ***Shea Noel Hulbert.***

References: Correspondence with the late Helen Root Spargur; Correspondence with Barbara Tarantine Hulbert.

1003.

Mary Carol Cronan, daughter of Gerald (479), granddaughter of Elba (228), b. Olean, New York December 24, 1949; m. Kingston, New York February 16, 1969 James Anthony Cronan, b. Mount Tremper, New York June 7, 1949, divorced Chittenden, Vermont August 12, 1995. James Cronan remarried to Bonnie W. Blondin on August 23, 2002. They resided in West Battleboro, Vermont.

Mary was employed as a bookkeeper by the Holiday Inn, Brattleboro, Vermont, Bilodeau Wells and Company, Essex Junction, Vermont and was the Office Manager for Wallkill Valley Publications, Newburgh, New York. She currently resides in Newburgh with her partner, an old high school sweetheart, Edward Ted L Corney. James Cronan was a State Trooper in Vermont from 1972 to 1999 retiring with the rank of Captain.

Children:

1622. I. ***James Robert Cronan***, b. Kingston, New York July 2, 1969; m. Essex Junction, Vermont February 18, 1995 Andrea Jackson, b. Farmington, Maine February 19, 1971. James is an administrator for Public Safety Answering Point, Williston, Vermont.

Children:

i. ***Julia Carolyn Cronan.***

1623. II. ***Michael John Cronan***, b. Kingston, New York August 25, 1971; m. Grand Isle, Vermont July 16, 2005 Jennifer Leslie Ball, b. Springfield, Massachusetts March 28, 1975. Michael has a BS Degree from the University of Vermont and is employed as a Project Manager with Haley and Aldrich, Boston, Massachusetts.

Children:

i. ***Alden James Cronan.***
ii. ***Serafina Rose Cronan.***

References: Correspondence with the late Helen Root Spargur; Vermont Divorce Records 1925-2003; Vermont Marriage Records 1909-2008; Correspondence with Barbara Tarantine Hulbert.

1004.

Jean Elizabeth (Beth) Hulbert, daughter of Gerald (479), granddaughter of Elba (228), b. Olean, New York April 6, 1951; m. Huntington Station, New York September 16, 1972 Walter A. Schreiber, b. Queens, New York May 25, 1948, divorced September 10, 1999. Beth graduated from Farmingdale State University, New York and was employed as a medical secretary. She resides in Levittown, New York.

Children:

1624. I. ***Janet Marie Schreiber***, b. Johnson City, New York January 27, 1974; m. Hopewell Junction, New York July 5, 2002 Paul Andrew Sokol, b. Poughkeepsie, New York December 9, 1971. Janet is employed as a Respiratory Therapist/Speech Language Pathologist. Paul is a carpenter. They reside in Fishkill, New York.

Children:

i. ***Sarah Jane Sokol.***

ii. ***Michael Andrew Sokol.***
iii. ***Kaylee Jane Sokol.***

1625. II. ***Jennifer Jean Schreiber***, b. Johnson City, New York January 27, 1974; m. Hopewell Junction, New York September 6, 2002 Joseph John Matta, b. Poughkeepsie, New York June 26, 1972. Jennifer is a Pharmaceutical presentative and Joseph is a Mechanical Engineer. They reside in Fishkill, New York.

Children:

i. ***Miranda Jean Matta.***
ii. ***Patrick Joseph Matta.***
iii. ***Thomas James Matta.***

1626. III. ***Heather Lynn Schreiber***, b. West Islip, New York November 5, 1976; m. Hicksville, New York June 10, 2002 Mark Wolters., b. Rockville Centre, New York December 4, 1978.

1627. IV. ***Walter Michael Schreiber***, b. Plainview, New York February 20, 1983.

References: Correspondence with the late Helen Root Spargur; Correspondence with Barbara Tarantine Hulbert.

1005.

Lois Anne Hulbert, daughter of Gerald (479), granddaughter of Elba (228), b. Mineola, New York April 2, 1952; m. Huntington Station, New York October 11, 1980 Robert Daniel McKeown, b. New York, New York July 18, 1952. Lois graduated from SUNY Farmingdale and was employed as a Dental Hygienist from 1974 to 1980, an Administrative Assistant for AeroVironment, Inc. from 1981 to 1991 and at San Marino High School from 2006 to 2010. Robert was a Professor Physics at California Institute of Technology from 1980 to 2010. He last worked as a Deputy Director for Science at the Thomas Jefferson National Accelerator Facility, Newport News, Virginia. They reside in Williamsburg, Virginia.

Children:

1628. I. ***Kaitlyn Aileen McKeown***, b. Hollywood, California April 18, 1988. She is employed as a Biomedical Engineer, Genetech, San Francisco, California.

1629. II. ***Michael Patrick McKeown***, b. Hollywood, California June 6, 1990. He graduated from the University of California, Santa Barbara and earned a Ph. D. from Princeton University in 2020.

References: Correspondence with Barbara Tarantine Hulbert.

1006.

Geraldine Marie Hulbert, daughter of Gerald (479), granddaughter of Elba (228), b. Teaneck, New Jersey April 23, 1955; m. Huntington Station, New York October 16, 1976 Gary Richard Parker, b. Utica, New York December 22, 1951.

Geraldine graduated from SUNY Brockport. Gary also graduated from SUNY Brockport. He works as a Technical Assistant at Mohawk Valley Community College coaching the Men's and Women's Cross Country, Indoor in Outdoor Track and Field. The Mohawk Valley Community College Cross Country team he coached from 1990 to 1999 was named the *Team of the Decade.* They reside in Whitesboro, New York.

Children:

1630. I. ***Gregory Richard Parker***, b. New Hartford, New York February 23, 1982; m. Rebecca Dodge, b. February 19, 1980. Gregory has an RN Degree from St. Elizabeth's School of Nursing, Utica, New York where he is currently employed.

1631. II. ***Genny Marie Parker***, b. New Hartford, New York February 2, 1984. She has a Bachelor's Degree from Boston University, a Master's Degree from the University of Pittsburgh and is employed at the University of Tulsa.

1632. III. ***Garrett Richard Parker***, b. New Hartford, New York November 18, 1989; m. Poughkeepsie, New York June 15, 2019 Dayna Eikeseth, b. May 2, 1992. Garrett graduated from SUNY Cortland and is employed with Aerotek in New Jersey.

References: Correspondence with Barbara Tarantine Hulbert.

1007.

David Saint John Hulbert, son of Gerald (479), grandson of Elba (228), b. Newburgh, New York January 3, 1961; m. Brookville, New York September 4, 1988 Randi Martin, b. June 30, 1964.

David graduated from SUNY Binghamton Cum Laude and from Hershey in 1987. He is an Ob-Gyn. Randi graduated from the Penn State University School of Nursing and is employed as a nurse. They reside in Moorestown, New Jersey.

Children:

1633. I. ***Kevin Ward Hulbert***, b. Newark, Delaware April 15, 1991.

1634. II. ***William Martin Hulbert***, b. Willingboro, New Jersey September 23, 1993.

1635. III. ***Emily Jayne Hulbert***, b. Willingboro, New Jersey October 16, 1997.

References: Correspondence with Barbara Tarantine Hulbert.

1008.

Concetta (Connie) Helen Rangatore, daughter of Margaret (480), granddaughter of Elba (228), b. Detroit, Michigan May 21, 1951; m. (1) June 9, 1979 Mark Ryan, divorced December 30, 1988; m. (2) June 19, 1999 Stuart J. Crawshaw.

Connie graduated from Carroll College, Waukesha, Wisconsin and was employed as a physical education teacher in Calhan, Colorado until 1974. She is employed with the University of Colorado's police department. On June 8, 2000 Stuart Crawshaw was ordained to the Sacred Order of Deacon in the Holy Catholic Church (Anglican Rite). They reside in Douglas, Wyoming.

References: Correspondence with the late Helen Root Spargur; Correspondence with Barbara Tartine Hulbert.

1009.

Margaret (Peggy) Ann Rangatore, daughter of Margaret (480), granddaughter of Elba (228), b. Niagara Falls, New York August 14, 1952; m. North Chicago, Illinois August 19, 1972 Joseph W. Rygiel, divorced. Peggy was a graduate of the Columbia Business College and was employed as a secretary until the birth of her first child. Peggy is now employed as a Senior Regulatory Manager. Joseph Rygiel is a carpenter.

Children:

1636. I. ***Joseph Walter Rygiel***, b. Lake Forest, Illinois June 21, 1974. He was educated at the Wyoming Technical Trade School.

1637. II. ***Brian David Rygiel***, b. Lake Forest, Illinois November 29, 1975; m. (1) September 2004 Alison Burke, divorced; m. (2) November1, 2018 Shalundar Williams. They reside in Santa Rosa, California.

Children: (by first marriage)

i. ***Elouise Ann Rygiel.***

1638. III. ***Kristine Margaret Rygiel***, b. Lake Forest, Illinois November 12, 1982; m. October 23, 2015 Thomas James Bequette. Kristine graduated from Illinois Wesleyan University.

Children:

i. ***Felicity Marie Bequette.***

References: Correspondence with the late Helen Root Spargur; Correspondence with Barbara Tarantine Hulbert.

1010.

Mary Elizabeth Rangatore, daughter of Margaret (480), granddaughter of Elba (228), b. Niagara Falls, New York August 27, 1955; m. (1) North Chicago, Illinois June 2, 1974 Terry Raber, divorced November 21, 1985; m. (2) Terrell, Texas November 27, 1998 Darren Yarborough. Mary Elizabeth graduated from Loyola University with a Bachelor's Degree and from the University of Texas with a Master's Degree. They reside in Keller, Texas.

Children: (by first marriage)

1639. I. ***Joseph Ivan Raber***, b. August 24, 1980.

1640. II. ***Scott Morrison Raber***, b. Dallas, Texas February 11, 1985.

References: Correspondence with the late Helen Root Spargur; Correspondence with Barbara Tarantine Hulbert.

1011.

Joanne Marie Sarah Rangatore, daughter of Margaret (480), granddaughter of Elba (228), b. Niagara Falls, New York February 2, 1957; m. Lake Zurich, Illinois June 10, 1988 Michael L. Anderson, b. Chicago, Illinois August 1, 1955; d. Libertyville, Illinois August 30, 2013.

Mike enjoyed playing golf, baseball, and skiing. He was a fan of the Chicago Blackhawks, Chicago Cubs, and the Chicago White Sox as well as the Green Bay Packers. His burial location is not currently known. Michael Anderson was survived by three children but no grandchildren. Joanne graduated from Marquette University with a Bachelor's Degree and from Illinois Northeastern University with a Master's Degree.

Children:

1641. I. ***Martin Joseph Anderson***, b. Lake Forest, Illinois January 18, 1992.

1642. II. ***Daniel Steven Anderson***, b. Lake Forest, Illinois July 21, 1993.

References: *Chicago Suburban Daily Herald* September 1-2, 2013 obituary for Michael L. Anderson; Correspondence with Barbara Tarantine Hulbert.

1012.

Kathryn (Kathy) Hulbert Rangatore, daughter of Margaret (480), granddaughter of Elba (228), b. Lake Forest, Illinois September 14, 1958; m. August 12,1978 Ken Roden, b. December 14, 1955.

Children:

1643. I. ***Ken Roden***, b. January 9, 1980.

References: Correspondence with the late Helen Root Spargur; Correspondence with Barbara Tarantine Hulbert.

1013.

Karen Margaret Hulbert, daughter of James (481), granddaughter of Elba (228), b. Ithaca, New York May 2, 1974; m. Ithaca, New York June 14, 2003 Matthew Paul Schindler, b. February 16, 1974. Both Karen and Matthew are employed as teachers.

Children:

1644. I. ***Jacob James Schindler***, b. Rochester, New York May 20, 2005.

1645. II. ***Luke Joseph Schindler***, b. Rochester, New York July 23, 2006.

1646. III. ***David Matthew Schindler***, b. Rochester, New York October 11, 2009.

References: Correspondence with Barbara Tarantine Hulbert.

1014.

Michael John Hulbert, son of John (482), grandson of Elba (228), b. Rochester, New York December 10, 1006; m. Wellington, Florida November 11, 1994 Jennifer Jude Fitzpatrick, b. July 12, 1969. They reside in Naples, Florida where Michael is employed as a USGA Certified Golf Pro and a Certified Podiatrist.

Children:

1647. I. ***Michaela Erin Hulbert***, b. Naples, Florida October 2, 1996.

1648. II. ***Liam Fitzpatrick Hulbert***, b. Naples, Florida June 3, 2001.

References: Correspondence with Barbara Tarantine Hulbert.

1015.

Michele Lynn Hulbert, daughter of John (482), granddaughter of Elba (228), b. Rochester, New York February 7, 1969; m. Greece, New York July 23, 1993 Wayne Edward Balch. Michele graduated from SUNY Geneseo and is employed as a teacher. Wayne served with the US Army from 1987 to 1991 and is employed with Kodak.

Children:

1649. I. ***Jessica Lynn Balch***, b. North Carolina July 9, 1996.

1650. II. ***Andrew John Balch***, b. August 13, 2002.

References: Correspondence with Barbara Tarantine Hulbert.

1016.

Stephanie Marie Hulbert, daughter of John (482), granddaughter of Elba (228), b. Rochester, New York June 16, 1971; m Rochester, New York July 3, 1998 Del Lewis Allen, divorced. Stephanie attended Genesee Community College and is employed with Kodak.

Children:

1651. I. ***Ryan Allen***, b. January 3, 2003.

References: Correspondence with Barbara Tarantine Hulbert.

1017.

Stewart Buffington Irvin, Jr., son of Stewart (483), grandson of Leta (229), b. Wellsville, New York

June 21, 1943, d. Utica, New York February 18, 2017 from cancer; m. Bolivar, New York June 6, 1944 Elaine R. Button.

Mr. Irvin graduated from Syracuse Mortician School and Alfred Agricultural and Technical Institute. He served his apprenticeship with Robertson's Funeral Home, Hornell, New York. Stew was Director of Computing and Telecommunications at SUNY It and SUNY Delhi, New York. He was an outdoorsman who enjoyed the Adirondacks with friends and members of the Mohawk Valley Motorcade Car Club. He enjoyed the car shows and won many trophies.

He was survived by his daughter and three granddaughters: Haley Marie and Hunter Rose of New Hartford and Crystal Witter of Portville and great-grandchildren Shane and Kara Witter of Portville. Stewart Irvin was buried in Maple Lawn Cemetery, Bolivar, New York. Elaine graduated from SUNY Geneseo and taught elementary grades for several years in Hornell, New York.

Children:

1652. I. ***Duane Curtis Irvin*** b. Hornell, New York January 7, 1968, d. February 22. 1990 in a car accident while in college in Arizona, and he was buried in Maple Lawn Cemetery.

1653. II. ***Christine Jacqueline Irvin***, b. Hornell, New York January 2, 1970; m. Mr. Wagner, divorced.

Children:

i. ***Haley Marie Wagner.***
ii. ***Hunter Rose Wagner.***
iii. ***Crystal Wagner Witter*** and resides in Portville, New York with two children: Shane and Kara Witter.

References: New York State Marriage Index 1881-1967; Social Security Death Index 1935-2014; *Olean Times Herald* February 20, 2017 obituary for Stewart B. Irvin, Jr.; Maple Lawn Cemetery Records, Bolivar, New York; Correspondence with Barbara Tarantine Hulbert.

1018.

Janet Christine Irvin, daughter of Stewart (483), granddaughter of Leta (229), b. Wellsville, New York May 24, 1952; m. (1) September 18, 1976 Kirk Johnson, divorced; m. (2) Mr. Haggerty. Janet resides in Olean, New York and is employed by Aerovox.

References: Correspondence with Barbara Tarantine Hulbert.

1019.

John Cornelius Malick, son of Naomi (484), grandson of Emma (104), b. Elmira, New York August 29, 1956, d. Hornell, New York October 22, 1959 from accidentally getting hold of an open bottle of aspirin and consuming most of the bottle's contents. He was buried in Saint Mary's Cemetery, Bolivar, New York.

References: Maple Lawn Cemetery Records, Bolivar, New York; *Bolivar Breeze*, selected issues; Correspondence with Barbara Tarantine Hulbert.

1020.

Mary Leta Malick, daughter of Naomi (484), granddaughter of Emma (104), b. Wellsville, New York January 6, 1958; m. Annapolis, Maryland October 3, 1981 William Richard Burke, b. Hornell, New York November 4, 1956. They reside in Gorton, Connecticut.

References: Correspondence with Barbara Tarantine Hulbert.

1021.

William Joseph Malick, son of Naomi (484), grandson of Emma (104), b. Hornell, New York April 21, 1959; m. Catherine Collier. They last resided in Annandale, Virginia.

Children:

1654. I. ***John Malick.***

References: Correspondence with Barbara Tarantine Hulbert.

1022.

Sarah Malick, daughter of Naomi (484), granddaughter of Emma (104), b. Hornell, New York August 9, 1960 and was last known to reside in Ann Arbor, Michigan.

References: Correspondence with Barbara Tarantine Hulbert.

1023.

Thomas Malick, son of Naomi (484), grandson of Emma (104), b. Hornell, New York December 12, 1961; m. Allyson Scott Russell, b. May 13, 1962. They were last known to reside in Mount Pleasant, South Carolina.

Children:

1655. I. ***Mikayla Kiersten Consalvo Malick***, b. December 30, 1989.

Children: (by marriage)

1656. I. ***Sarah Elizabeth Malick***, b. December 26, 1993.

References: Correspondence with Barbara Tarantine Hulbert.

1024.

Elaine Malick, daughter of Naomi (484), granddaughter of Emma (104), b. Hornell, New York October 1, 1963 in a car on the way to the hospital; m. Joseph Andrew Coen. They were last known to reside in Mount Pleasant, South Carolina.

References: Correspondence with Barbara Tarantine Hulbert.

1041.

Allison March Witherell, daughter of Helen Joan (508), granddaughter of Helen (243), b. April 6, 1969, d. Bellevue, Washington September 1, 2011 from amyotrophic lateral sclerosis; Skagit, Washington July 20, 1997 David A. Turner.

Allison and David Turner resided in Jacksonville, Florida and New Orleans, Louisiana before returning to Washington State. It is currently not known where Allison Turner was buried. They had two children.

Children:

1657. I. ***Alexander Turner***, b. a. 2003.

1658. II. ***Katharine Turner***, b. a. 2005.

References: Findagrave.com obituary for Allison Witherell Turner; Washington Marriage Index 1969-2014.

1042.

Deborah Anne (Carroll) Hardy, daughter of Judith (509), granddaughter of Helen (243), b. February 18, 1965 and adopted by Robert Hardy; m. Deltona, Florida Jay Clark. Deborah attended Olean Business Institute. Jay is employed making pipe fittings. They reside in Deltona, Florida.

Children:

1659. I. ***Drew Huston Clark***, b. September 9, 1986; m. Carrie.

Children:

i. ***Jaxon Clark.***
ii. ***Mila Clark.***

1660. II. ***Kayla Suzette Clark***, b. March 14, 1990.

1661. III. ***Brice Clark***, b. March 14, 1900.

References: Correspondence with the late Helen Root Spargur; Interview with Timothy Hardy.

1043.

Timothy Michael Hardy, son of Judith (509), grandson of Helen (243), b. Wellsville June 28, 1976; m. Trumansburg, New York July 11, 2009 Amber Scott, b. December 15, 1983.

Tim graduated from Alfred University with a degree in mathematics. He currently works for the Developmentally Disabled in Wellsville, New York. Amber attended Cortland State University, New York and has a Master's Degree from Alfred University. She currently is a counselor at Scio Central School, Scio, New York.

Children:

1662. I. ***Michaela Ann Hardy***, b. Wellsville, New York December 28, 2010.

References: Interview with Timothy Hardy.

1044.

Tracey Lynn Barozzini, daughter of Mary Jane (510), granddaughter of Helen (243), b. August 8, 1966; m. St. Petersburg, Florida April 29, 1989 Raymond Surdyk, divorced 2002.

Tracey took care of her brother, Michael, until he died from ALS in 2018. She is currently completing a Bachelor of Science Degree at Walden University with a graduation date of 2020. Tracey is employed as a Human Resources Consultant for nursing homes throughout Florida. She has been in the Health Care Industry for thirty years in the administrative part of it. Tracey resides in Tampa, Florida.

Children:

1663. I. ***Taylor C. Surdyk***, b. July 12, 1991. Taylor is a pre-K teacher and is expecting her first child. Taylor resides with her boyfriend, Aaron Delage in St. Petersburg, Florida.

1664. II. ***Brett J. Surdyk***, b. August 24, 1994 works in construction.

References: Correspondence with Tracey Surdyk.

1045.

Michael Joseph Barozzini, son of Mary Jane (510), grandson of Helen (243), b. June 29, 1971, d. Tampa, Florida December 7, 2018 from ALS (Lou Gehrig's Disease) as did his maternal grandfather and a maternal cousin.

Michael obtained a Master's Degree from Walden University in 2015. At the time of his death he was working on a Ph.D. He was employed as Vice-President of Patient Safety and Quality Outcomes for Moffitt Cancer Center in Tampa, Florida.

References: Correspondence with Tracey Surdyk.

1049.

Terri Anne Cline, daughter of Willard (515), granddaughter of Coral (250), b. February 14, 1950; m. (1) September 3, 1971 William Doyle III, divorced; m. (2) November 28, 1980 Donald Cothard. Terri Anne was last known to reside in Bradford, Pennsylvania; ***nfi.***

Children: (by first marriage)

1665. I. ***Julianne Doyle***, b. March 16, 1973.

References: Correspondence with the late Willard Cline.

1050.

Cathy Jeanne Cline, daughter of Willard (515), granddaughter of Coral (250), b. Bradford, Pennsylvania October 1952, d. Auburn, New York March 21, 2011; m. (1) October 19, 1974 Christopher Farrar, divorced; m. (2) October 26, 1985 Brian Walsh, divorced.

Cathy worked at Powell's Drug Store on Main Street, Bradford and was one of the first volunteers at the Penn-Brad Oil Museum in Custer City. For over twenty-five years, she was employed as a store manager with Shehadi Oriental Rugs, Syracuse, New York and was still employed there at the time of her death. Cathy was a former member of the Church of Christ and was active with theater groups after moving to Auburn. She had a special fondness for the Kinzua Bridge that started in high school and continued through her adult life. Cathy Jean Cline Walsh was buried in Bridge View Cemetery, Mt. Jewett, Pennsylvania.

Children:

1666. I. ***Alissa Jeanne Cline***, b. November 1, 1983. She was engaged to Charles Marks at the time of her mother's death.

Children: (by second marriage)

1667. I. ***Jessica Walsh***, b. June 21, 1986. Jessie resided with a partner, Kevin Schafer at the time of her mother's death.

References: Correspondence with the late Willard Cline; March 22, 2011 newspaper obituary.

1051.

Willard Lee Cline, son of Willard (515), grandson of Coral (250), b. October 10, 1954; m. (1) April 7, 1973 Linda Fiebelkorn, divorced 1985; m. (2) September 7, 1985 Deborah Lee Torrey; m. (3) Brenda, last name not known. Mr. Cline was employed by his father in the Bradford oil fields; ***nfi.***

Children: (by first marriage)

1668. I. ***Carrie Ann Cline***, b. September 15, 1974.

1669. II. ***Jamie Lee Cline***, b. October 20, 1977.

1670. III. ***Lisa Pearl Cline***, b. September 23, 1980.

1671. IV. ***Kimberly Sue Cline***, b. September 2, 1982.
Children: (by second marriage)

1672. I. ***Whitney Lee Cline***, b. April 4, 1989.

References: Correspondence with the late Willard Cline.

1052.

Mark Lewis Cline, son of Willard (515), grandson of Coral (250), b. July 13, 1956; m. (1) August 29, 1987 Tammy Rimer; m. (2) Amber, last name not known. Mark resided in Bradford and was employed in his father's oil fields; ***nfi***.

Children: (by first marriage)

1673. I. ***Mark Lewis Cline, Jr.***, b. April 29, 1988.

References: Correspondence with the late Willard Cline.

1053.

Susan Marie Cline, daughter of Willard (515), granddaughter of Coral (250), b October 11, 1957; m. Paul Krathas; ***nfi.***

References: Correspondence with the late Willard Cline.

1054.

Mary Jo Cline, daughter of Willard (515), granddaughter of Coral (250), b. September 29, 1961; m. May 6, 1989 Edward Szewczyk.

Mary Jo graduated from Mercyhurst College in Pennsylvania and obtained an M.S. Degree from Gannon University, Pennsylvania. She was employed by the Erie County Pennsylvania Office of Children and Youth Services. Ed was a self-employed member of Szewczyk and Sons Plumbing and Heating in Harborcreek, Pennsylvania; ***nfi.***

References: Correspondence with the late Willard Cline.

1060.

Donald James Root, son of Howard (518), grandson of Howard (252), b. November 7, 1964; m. December 1, 1984 Dena Sheppard; and last known to reside in Belvidere, Illinois; ***nfi.***

Children:

1674. I. ***Leah Louise Root***, b. May 12, 1984.

1675. II. ***Kathern Ellen Root***, b. July 6, 1988, a twin.

1676. III. ***Kristen Marie Root***, b. July 6, 1988, a twin.

References: Correspondence with the late Carolyne Williams.

1061.

Wanda Jean Root, daughter of Howard (518), granddaughter of Howard (252), b. September 21, 1967; m. February 27, 1987 Perry Stuaffacher; and last known to reside in Belvidere, Illinois; ***nfi.***

Children:

1677. I. ***Brandie Nichole Stauffacher***, b. March 14, 1990.

References: Correspondence with the late Carolyne Williams.

1062.

Melody Williams, daughter of Carolyne (519), granddaughter of Howard (252), b. February 4, 1959; m. June 2, 1990 Robert Kolodzie. Melody's husband had two children from a previous marriage. They were last known to reside in Peoria, Illinois; ***nfi.***

Children:

1678. I. ***Jeremy Paul Kolodzie***, b. March 14, 1990.

References: Correspondence with the late Carolyne Williams.

1065.

Julie Root, daughter of Duane (520), granddaughter of Howard (252), b. May 26, 1958; m. Peter Urdahl and last known to reside in Fort Atkinson, Wisconsin; ***nfi.***

Children: (before marriage)

1679. I. ***Shawn Root***, b. November 19, 1972.
1680. II. ***Amy Root***, b. February 24, 1974.

References: Correspondence with the late Carolyne Williams; 2016 Obituary of Judith Peplinski Root Beck.

1066.

Tammy Root, daughter of Duane (520), granddaughter of Howard (252), b. March 30, 1960;

m. Walworth, Wisconsin February 23, 1980 Scott Wiedenhoef. They were last known to reside in Whitewater, Wisconsin; ***nfi.***

Children:

1681. I. ***Jason Wiedenhoef***, b. July 6, 1979.

1682. II. ***Matthew Wiedenhoef***, b. 1982.

References: Correspondence with the late Carolyne Williams; 2016 Obituary of Judith Peplinski Root Beck.

1067.

Douglas D. Root, son of Duane (520), grandson of Howard (252); b. April 16, 1961; m. (1) Jefferson, Wisconsin August 23, 1980 Debra L. Grischow; m. (2) Amy, last name not known. They were last known to reside in Fort Atkinson, Wisconsin; ***nfi.***

References: Correspondence with the late Carolyne Williams; 2016 Obituary of Judith Peplinski Root Beck; Wisconsin Marriage Index 1973-1977.

1068.

Wade Vincent Root, son of Duane (520), grandson of Howard (252), b. June 26, 1963; m. Jefferson, Wisconsin May 18, 1988 Lisa Loreen Goss. They were last known to reside in Fort Atkinson, Wisconsin; ***nfi.***

References: Correspondence with the late Carolyne Williams; 2016 Obituary of Judith Peplinski Root Beck; Wisconsin Marriage Index 1973-1997.

1069.

David Alan Root, Jr., son of David (521), grandson of Howard (252), b. March 17, 1960; m. Janesville, Wisconsin May 18, 1985 Debra Joan Bogg. They had one daughter and were last known to reside in Janesville, Wisconsin; ***nfi.***

References: Correspondence with the late Carolyne Williams; Wisconsin Marriage Index 1973-1997.

1070.

Cheryl Lynn Root, daughter of David (521), granddaughter of Howard (252), b. January 27, 1962; m. (1) Rock County, Wisconsin November 22, 1982 Brian Dwayne Rose, divorced April 29, 1999; m. (2) Indianapolis, Indiana December 10, 1999 Mark Robert Runyon; ***nfi.***

References: Correspondence with the late Carolyne Williams; Wisconsin Marriage Index 1973-1997; Indiana Marriage Certificates 1960-2005.

1071.

Laurie Ann Root, daughter of David (521), granddaughter of Howard (252), b. May 23, 1963; m. (1) Rock County, Wisconsin February 18, 1984 Matthew Stephen Gardner; m. (2) Rock County, Wisconsin January 24, 1989 James Charles Lewis; ***nfi.***

References: Correspondence with the late Carolyne Williams; Wisconsin Marriage Index 1973-1997.

1079.

Joe Roy Wilder, son of Bernice (524), grandson of Clella (257), b. June 26, 1950; m. August 4, 1973 Deborah Ann Benedict; ***nfi.***

Children:

1683. I. ***Jeffre Scott Wilder***, b. February 11, 1977.

1684. II. ***Jodie Marie Wilder***, b. October 5, 1979.

1685. III. ***Jonelle Marie Wilder***, b. October 13, 1980.

References: Correspondence with the late Jean Howard.

1080.

Patty Jean Wilder, daughter of Bernice (524), granddaughter of Clella (257), b. Hornell, New York August 24, 1956, d. Paul's Valley, Oklahoma August 3, 2013; m. September 2, 1978 David Mosher. Before settling in Oklahoma, Patty Jean resided in Torrance, California and Richmond, Texas. She was buried in Memphis Memorial Gardens, Bartlett, Tennessee.

Children:

1686. I. ***Michelle Marie Mosher***, b. November 18, 1983; m. a Mr. Sanders and had two children; ***nfi.***

Children:

i. ***Haley Sanders.***
ii. ***Toby Sanders.***

1687. II. ***Stephanie Marie Mosher***, b. December 10, 1987; m. a Mr. Barrom; ***nfi.***

1688. III. ***Nathan Thomas Mosher***, b. September 1, 1989.

1689. IV. ***Justin Mosher.***

References: Correspondence with the late Jean Howard; US Cemetery and Funeral Home Collection 1947-present.

1083.

Kathleen Elizabeth Howard, daughter of Jean (525), granddaughter of Clella (257), b. August 24, 1956; m. March 18, 1979 Willie Earl Jones, divorced 1989; ***nfi.***

Children:

1690. I. ***Amber Jenelle Jones***, b. November 14, 1980.

1691. II. ***Derrick Marshall Jones***, b. February 20, 1985.

References: Correspondence with the late Jean Howard.

1084.

David Lynn Howard, son of Jean (525), grandson of Clella (257), b. April 1, 1958; m. March 17, 1978 Phyllis Ann Rathaack; ***nfi.***

Children:

1692. I. ***Jennifer Lynn Howard***, b. June 9, 1979.

1693. II. ***Nathaniel Philip Howard***, b. April 20, 1981.

References: Correspondence with the late Jean Howard.

1086.

Lori Ann Howard, daughter of Jean (525), granddaughter of Clella (257), b. July 31, 1961; m. August 18, 1979 Edward Childs; ***nfi.***

Children:

1694. I. ***Erin Dawn Childs***, b. December 1, 1980.

1695. II. ***Justin Edward Childs***, b. May 30, 1985.

1696. III. ***Corey Thomas Childs***, b. August 24, 1987.

References: Correspondence with the late Jean Howard.

1103.

Hunter Karl Pire, son of Richard (546), grandson of Ward (265), b. Erie, Pennsylvania January 3, 1968, d. Ranson, West Virginia October 9, 1994; m. Winchester, Virginia September 6, 1991 Kimberly Dawn Biggs, b. Inwood, West Virginia November 28, 1971.

Hunter Pire was an electrician with the National Park Service, a member of the Freedom Baptist Church in Charles Town, West Virginia, and served in the US Marine Corps. Mr. Pire was first buried in Edge Hill Cemetery, Charles Town, West Virginia and later reburied July 26, 1995 in Erie Cemetery, Erie Pennsylvania.

Children:

1697. I. ***Ethan Mitchel Pire.***

1698. II. ***Gage Mackenzie Pire.***

References: US Public Records Index 1950-93, Vol. 2; *Erie Times-News* October 12, 1994 obituary; Erie Cemetery Records, Erie, Pennsylvania; Edge Hill Cemetery Records, Charles Town, West Virginia.

Part II | The Photographs

List of Photographs

A special thank you to my long-time friend, colleague and photographer, *Mike C. Beaty,* for the hundreds of hours he spent in scanning and restoring the photographs for this book.

1. Bolivar, New York, 1875, looking north up Main Street towards Richburg. This is the earliest known photograph of Bolivar. (Collection of Dr. William Paquette).
2. De Beers Insurance Map, 1879, Bolivar, New York. (Collection of Dr. William Paquette).
3. Bolivar, New York, Main Street looking west, 1900. (Collection of Dr. William Paquette).
4. Bolivar, New York, Main Street looking north, 1900. (Collection of Dr. William Paquette).
5. Bolivar Methodist Church, Root family church. (Collection of Dr. William Paquette).
6. Abel Root, Sr. farm across from Maple Lawn Cemetery, Bolivar, New York. (Collection of Dr. William Paquette).
7. Abel Root, Jr. (Collection of the late Doris Richardson June).
8. Polly Scott Root, Mrs. Abel Root, Jr. (Collection of the late Doris Richardson June).
9. Maple Lawn Cemetery graves of Abel Root, Jr. and wife, Polly. (Collection of Dr. William Paquette).
10. Union Cemetery, Fort Edward, New York grave of Frances E. Bancroft Root. (Collection of Dr. William Paquette).
11. David Cartwright Root. (Collection of the late Doris Richardson June).
12. Alceba Tyler Youngs and Marrietta Tyler Root (Mrs. David C. Root). Collection of the late Doris Richardson June).

13. Maple Lawn Cemetery graves of David C. Root and wife Marietta. (Collection of Dr. William Paquette).

14. Truman Bishop Root. (Collection of the late Doris Richardson June).

15. Polly Mead Root, Mrs. Truman Bishop Root. (Collection of Dr. William Paquette).

16. Maples Lawn Cemetery graves of Bishop and Polly Root. (Collection of Dr. William Paquette).

17. Maple Lawn Cemetery grave of Huldah Penelope Root Kellogg. (Collection of Dr. William Paquette).

18. Maple Lawn Cemetery grave of Loring Grant Kellogg. (Collection of Dr. William Paquette).

19. Until the Day Dawn Cemetery grave of Jane Voakes Root (and possibly of her husband, Franklin Root), Angelica, New York. (Collection of Dr. William Paquette).

20. John F. Weir, Insurance Agent, Angelica, NY, son-in-law of Franklin Root. (Collection of Dr. William Paquette).

21. Until the Day Dawn Cemetery, Angelica, NY grave of John Weir, first husband of Florence Root. (Collection of Dr. William Paquette).

22. Desdemona Proctor Partridge Root, second wife of James H. Root. (Collection of Dr. William Paquette).

23. Maple Lawn Cemetery grave of Mary W. Root, first wife of James H. Root (Collection of Dr. William Paquette).

24. Charles A. Withey, second wife, Caroline Stebbins, and their son, William, 1865. (Collection of the late Doris Richardson June).

25. Maple Lawn Cemetery grave of Elizabeth Root Withey. (Collection of Dr. William Paquette).

26. Richburg, New York Cemetery grave of Samuel Charles Withey, eldest son of Charles and Elizabeth Root Withey. (Collection of Dr. William Paquette).

27. The children of Charles A. Withey, L to R: William, Ina, Emma, Jesse, and Clara. (Collection of the late Ina Withey Burdick McEnroe).

28. The Jesse A. Withey family, Witheytown (Vosburg), July 10, 1910. L to R: Rufus Sawyer, Bessie, Harry, Ina, Charles, Sarah, Howard, Emma Withey Sawyer, and Jesse. (Collection of the late Ina Withey Burdick McEnroe).

29. 1865 Civil War Discharge Papers of Lyman E. Root. (Collection of Dr. William Paquette).

30. Almyra and Lyman E. Root. (Collection of the late Doris Richardson June)

31. Jerome B. Reed and wife, Ruth Barber Reed. (Collection of the late Doris Richardson June)

32. Earles, Lola, and Libbie Root, Children of Lyman and Almyra Root. (Collection of the late Doris Richardson June).

33. Lyman E. Root in later years. (Collection of the late Doris Richardson June).

34. Lyman Root Blacksmith Shop and residence, Main Street, Bolivar, New York. (Collection of the late Alice Weatherell Moore).

35. Almyra Root in front of the family home, Main Street, Bolivar, 1910. (Collection of Dr. William Paquette).

36. Almyra Reed Root and Maggie Granger Root. (Collection of Dr. William Paquette).

37. The Paul Ennis, formerly Lyman Root, Blacksmith shop, Main and Leather Streets, Bolivar. L to R: Ward Rice, Bill Coon, Ted Macavanie, Leo Root with his dog Spot, and Lester George, 1910. (Collection of Dr. William Paquette).

38. The Paul Ennis residence, South Main Street, Bolivar. L to R: Maggie Granger Root and Libbie Root Ennis. The house was demolished in 1983. (Collection of Dr. William Paquette)..

39. Maggie Granger Root and her husband Earles Root. (Collection of the late Mary Root Holland).

40. Lola, Isabelle, and Harold Root with their uncle Bernard Root and cousin Dudley Root, 1893. (Collection of the late Alice Weatherell Moore).

41. Isabelle Root, Dudley Ennis with their uncle Bernard Root. (Collection of the late Doris Richardson June).

42. Lola Root, daughter of Almyra and Lyman Root. (Collection of the late Alice Weatherell Moore).

43. Ernest Jerome Root. (Collection of Dr. William Paquette).

44. Belle Fuller Root, Mrs. Ernest J. Root. (Collection of Dr. William Paquette).

45. Leo C. Root. (Collection of Dr. William Paquette).

46. Leo C. Root and sister Nordica Root Wylie, 1910. (Collection of Dr. William Paquette).

47. L to R: Jenny Cox and Belle Fuller Root, owners of a millinery and dress shop in Binghamton, New York. (Collection of Dr. William Paquette).

48. Mary Jane Root Barber, Mrs. Elmer Barber. (Collection of the late Doris Richardson June).

49. Hiram and Mary Jane White Root with Flora, Laphronia, and Elizabeth. (Collection of the late Doris Richardson June).

50. Hiram Root standing in front of his residence and store, the Bee Hive, on Liberty Street after a hunting trip. (Collection of Rose June Feenaughty).

51. Flora Root Richardson. (Collection of the later Doris Richardson June).

52. Edward A. Richardson (Collection of the late Doris Richardson June).

53. Laphronia and Effie Meyers Root. (Collection of the late Doris Richardson June).

54. Laphronia and Effie Meyers Root with Clifford and Tina. (Collection of the late James Fox).

55. Laphronia Root and his second wife, Carrie Earl Root. (Collection of the late James Fox).

56. Elizabeth Root Jewett Fistler. (Collection of the late Doris Richardson June).

57. David Root. (Courtesy of the Lily Dale Museum, Lily Dale, New York).

58. Marietta Tyler Root. (Courtesy of the Lily Dale Museum, Lily Dale, New York).

59. Huldah Root Curtiss as a young girl. (Collection of the late Jane Nulsen Bunse).

60. Back L to R: Albert Root and 2nd or 3rd wife, Addison Evans. Front L to R: Huldah Root Curtiss, James Curtiss, Elosica Root Evans. (Collection of the late Jane Nulsen Bunse).

61. Jane Huldah Root Curtiss. (Courtesy of the Lily Dale Museum, Lily Dale, New York).

62. Elosica Root Evans, as a young girl. (Courtesy of the Lily Dale Museum, Lily Dale, New York).

63. Elosica Root Evans. (Courtesy of the Lily Dale Museum, Lily Dale, New York).

64. Albert Louis Root. (Courtesy of the Lily Dale Museum, Lily Dale, New York).

65. Asa W. Root, died Andersonville Prison, Georgia. (Collection of Lily Dale Museum, Lily Dale, New York).

66. Grave of Asa W. Root, Andersonville, Georgia. (Collection of Dr. William Paquette).

67. Asa W. Root, son of Albert Root, as a young man. (Collection of Lily Dale Museum, Lily Dale, New York).

68. Asa W. Root, son of Albert Root, in later years. (Collection of Lily Dale Museum, Lily Dale, New York).

69. Amina Root, daughter of Asa W. and Emma Toner Root. (Collection of Lily Dale Museum, Lily Dale, New York).

70. Alice, Albert, and Agnes Evans at Lily Dale. (Collection of Lily Dale Museum, Lily Dale, New York).

71. Alice and Agnes Evans as young girls. (Collection of Lily Dale Museum, Lily Dale, New York).

72. Alice and Agnes Evans as teenagers. (Collection of Lily Dale Museum, Lily Dale, New York).

73. Agnes Evans, 1895. (Collection of Lily Dale Museum, Lily Dale, New York).

74. Alice and Agnes Evans. (Collection of Lily Dale Museum, Lily Dale, New York).

75. Alice Evans. (Collection of Lily Dale Museum, Lily Dale, New York).

76. Alice Evans in later years. (Collection of Lily Dale Museum, Lily Dale, New York).

77. Jessie Evans, wife of Albert Evans. (Collection of Lily Dale Museum, Lily Dale, New York).

78. Gladys, Bertha, and Milford Root, children of Edwin C. Root. (Collection of Lily Dale Museum, Lily Dale, New York).

79. Milford Root as a young man. (Collection of Lily Dale Museum, Lily Dale, New York).

80. Albert George Nulsen, son of Huldah and Albert Nulsen. (Collection of Lily Dale Museum, Lily Dale, New York).

81. Albert L. Root with beard. (Collection of the late Bill Cook).

82. Armina Kilbury Root, Mrs. Albert Root. (Collection of the late Bill Cook).

83. Anna C. Moore, second wife of Albert Root. (Collection of Dr. William Paquette).

84. Civil War sword and photograph of Colonel Edwin Kilbury of Bolivar. (Collection of the late Jane Nulsen Bunse).

85. Root/MacDonald Photo: L to R, Back Row: George Root, ?, Della MacDonald, Edwin C. Root; Center: L to R: Jane MacDonald, Elizabeth MacDonald Root, Charlie MacDonald, Harriet MacDonald Root; Front: Sadie MacDonald Hall. (Collection of the late Gladys Root Nichols).

86. L to R: Elizabeth MacDonald Root and Harriet MacDonald Root. (Collection of the late Jane Nulsen Bunse).

87. L to R: Gladys Root Nichols, Edwin C. Root; Edwin Milford Root, Bertha Root Osborne, Hattie Root. (Collection of the late Gladys Root Nichols..

88. Asa W. Root in formal attire. (Collection of Anne Root Sale).

89. Emma Toner Root, Mrs. Asa W. Root. (Collection of Anne Root Sale).

90. Edward A. Root and his sister, Armina. (Photo courtesy of Anne Root Sale).

91. Edward Albert Root as a boy. (Collection of Anne Root Sale).

92. Wilber P. Cook. (Collection of the late Bill Cook).

93. Bertha Root Cook. (Collection of the late Bill Cook).

94. Boss Street residence of Wilber and Bertha Cook, designed by Asa W. Root. (Courtesy of Jean Milliman).

95. George and Elizabeth MacDonald Root. (Collection of Dr. William Paquette).

96. Maple Lawn Cemetery Civil War Memorial listing E. C. Kellogg among the Civil War dead. (Collection of Dr. William Paquette).

97. Christopher and Elizabeth Root Garthwait, 1907. (Courtesy of BRAG).

98. Emma Garthwait Hulbert. (Collection of Barbara Tarantine Hulbert).

99. Fred and Emma Garthwait Hulbert. (Courtesy of BRAG).

100. Emma, Gerry, Elba Hulbert, Elizabeth Root Garthwait, Margaret Hulbert. (Collection of Barbara Tarantine Hulbert).

101. Fred Hulbert family: Back L to R: Wayne and Gerald; Front L to R: Fred, Leta, Emma, Elba, Maude. (Collection of Barbara Tarantine Hulbert).

102. Hulbert family: L to R: Leta and Naomi Irvin, Emma Garthwait Hulbert, Elizabeth Root Garthwait, Helen and Margaret Hulbert, Maude and Virginia Hulbert. (Collection of Barbara Tarantine Hulbert).

103. Maple Lawn Cemetery gates and fence erected by Mr. and Mrs. Elmer Garthwait in memory of their son, Glen. (Collection of Dr. William Paquette).

104. Maple Lawn Cemetery, Garthwait Mausoleum. (Collection of Dr. William Paquette).

105. Erastus Root as a young man. (Collection of the late Doris Richardson June).

106. Erastus Root holding his granddaughter, Helen Root. (Collection of the late Helen Root Spargur).

107. Asa P. Root. (Collection of the late Helen Root Spargur).

108. Erastus Root family: Cora Root, Erastus Root holding Helen Root Spargur, Myrtie Root Strayer, Helen Prentice Root and Asa P. Root in chair. (Collection of the late Helen Root Spargur).

109. Myrtie Root Strayer holding her niece Helen Root. (Collection of the late Helen Root Spargur).

110. Helen Morgan Root, wife of Asa P. Root. (Collection of the late Helen Root Spargur).

111. Arthur Lew Root and his second wife, Ida Roberts Root. (Collection of Sherri Nelsen Jack).

112. Leona Root Ellis with her father, Lew Root, Salt Rising Road, Bolivar, 1900. (Courtesy of the later Leona Root Gordon).

113. Leona Root Ellis with her first husband Ray Ellis, Deer Creek, NY. (Collection of the late Leona Root Gordon).

114. Ray Ellis with his father-in-law, Lew Root, Titusville, Pennsylvania. (Collection of the late Leona Root Gordon).

115. Leon Erastus Root. (Photo courtesy of the late Leona Root Gordon).

116. James Curtis Root. (Bolivar Breeze obituary photograph).

117. Seated: L to R: Burr LeRoy and Kate Root; Standing, L to R: their children: Howard Leroy, Coral Marie, Laurence, Ruth, and Dr. Raymond Root. (Collection of the late Dr. Raymond Root).

118. Mattie Ennis with her son Paul J. Ennis. (Collection of the late Merle Root).

119. Paul Ennis with nephew, Leo C. Root, daughter-in-law Mattie Ennis and grandson Paul. (Collection of Dr. William Paquette).

120. Bernard and Maggie Snowdon Root at their home on Leather Street. (Collection of Dr. William Paquette).

121. Leo C. Root, US Navy, 1916. (Collection of Dr. William Paquette).

122. 1916 Wedding picture of Leo C. Root and Ethel Bernard Root. (Collection of Dr. William Paquette).

123. Van Curen High Explosives stock certificate in the name of Leo C. Root. (Collection of Dr William Paquette).

124. Leo C. Root driving the Van Curen nitroglycerine wagon, Bolivar, 1920. (Collection of the late Dorothy Root Paquette).

125. LeSuer House, State Historic Site, where the Leo C. Root family resided from 1930 to 1933. (Collection of Dr. William Paquette).

126. Leo C. Root children, Clintonville, Pennsylvania: Top L to R: Ernest and Fred; Seated: L to R: Eva, Lawrence, Dan, Nordica, and Dorothy. (Collection of Dr. William Paquette).

127. L to R: Ethel, Dorothy, Eva, and Nordica Root, 1940, Clintonville, Pennsylvania. (Collection of Dr. William Paquette).

128. Former Allentown, New York parsonage, residence of Leo and Ethel Root from1959 to 1976. (Collection of Dr. William Paquette).

129. Leo Stanley Root and his wife, Barbara Lamson, 1942. (Collection of Dr. William Paquette).

130. Children of Leo S. and Barbara Root: L to R: Jimmy, Bunny, Marleen, Debbie, Paul, and Dennis. (Collection of Dr. William Paquette).

131. 1999 wedding of Melissa Coffey to Dan Root; L to R: Jamie Corson, Krista Root Corson, Nate Corson, Dennis and Janice Root, bride and groom, Jlene Root and daughter Hannah, Kim Root Monterio and Chris Monterio. (Courtesy of Dennis Root).

132. Paul, Barbara and daughters Daneille and Cheryl Root. (Courtesy of Paul Root).

133. Nordica Root, high school graduation. (Collection of Dr. William Paquette).

134. 1951 Wedding photograph of Nordica Root to Glen Anderson. (Collection of Dr. William Paquette).

135. Diana Anderson LaFaro and her husband Jim. (Courtesy of Diana LaFaro).

136. Sharon Anderson Wallace with husband Dave and son Andy. (Courtesy of Sharon Wallace).

137. Richard Anderson and daughter Dillon. (Courtesy of Sharon Wallace).

138. Eva J. Root, 1939. (Collection of Dr. William Paquette).

139. Eva J. Root, 1960. (Collection of Dr. William Paquette).

140. Lantern Lodge, Scio, New York, residence of Eva Root. (Collection of Dr. William Paquette).

141. Fred Root, 1943. (Collection of Dr. William Paquette).

142. Fred Root in Allentown Fire Department's Uniform. (Collection of Dr. William Paquette).

143. Arthur C. and Dorothy Root Paquette, 1946. (Collection of Dr. William Paquette).

144. Robert, Dorothy, Arthur, and William Paquette, 1951. (Collection of Dr. William Paquette).

145. Hugh Daniel Root during military service. (Collection of Dr. William Paquette).

146. Helga, Dan, Michael, and Angelika Root, 1963, Berlin, Germany. (Collection of Dr. William Paquette).

147. Lawrence Leonard Root in Marine uniform. (Collection of Dr. William Paquette).

148. Lawrence Root and his first wife, Margie, with sons Larry Wayne and Ronnie, 1951, Allentown, New York. (Collection of Dr. William Paquette).

149. Betty Orvis Root, second wife of Lawrence Root. (Collection of Dr. William Paquette).

150. Seated L to R: Mrs. Hiram Root, Mercia and Minnie Richardson Weatherby, and standing Flora Root Richardson, four generations, 1910. (Collection of Rose June Feenaughty).

151. Flora Root Richardson with son Laurence on lap and standing Lewis, Ethel, and Mildred. (Collection of Rose June Feenaughty).

152. Children of Edward and Flora Root Richardson: Standing L to R: Ethel and Elizabeth; Seated: L to R: Lewis, Mildred, and Minnie. (Collection of Rose June Feenaughty).

153. Minnie Richardson Weatherby, husband Homer, and children; Mercia and Homer. (Collection of Rose June Feenaughty).

154. Howard and Mercia Weatherby. (Collection of Rose June Feenaughty).

155. Lewis Richardson. (Collection of Rose June Feenaughty).

156. Lois Cockle Richardson, first wife of Lewis Richardson. (Collection of Rose June Feenaughty).

157. Edward Richardson with sons: Stanley, Manley, and Lewis (Collection of Rose June Feenaughty).

158. Marjorie Seamans Richardson, second wife of Lewis Richardson. (Collection of Rose June Feenaughty).

159. Children of Lewis and Marjorie Richardson: Sallie, Jim, and Terry. (Collection of Rose June Feenaughty).

160. Doris Richardson June and husband Victor June. (Collection of Rose June Feenaughty).

161. Victor and Doris June Family: Standing L to R: Rose Mary, Beverly, and Inez Seated L to R; Dale, Dean, Gerald. (Collection of Rose June Feenaughty).

162. Dean's graduation day 1963: Dean, Dale, Jerry, Doris, and Victor June (back) and (front) Inez Une Pervorse, Rose June Feenaughty, and Beverly June Van Allen. (Collection of Rose June Feenaughty).

163. Stephen, Twannee, Beverly June, Gifford, and Heather Van Allen. (Collection of Rose June Feenaughty).

164. Jim and Tina Richardson. (Collection of Rose June Feenaughty).

165. Bill and Theo Richardson Dickerson. (Collection of Rose June Feenaughty).

166. Albert Hirliman, Ethel Richardson Hirliman, Dan Baker, Agnes Richardson Baker, Elizabeth Richardson Corcoran, John Corcoran, ?, ?, Margaret Baker Mink, Juanita Baker Cornell, two children, ?, ?, 1957. (Collection of Rose June Feenaughty).

167. Mary Elizabeth Richard Corcoran with husband John and son John, Jr. (Collection of Rose June Feenaughty).

168. Minnie Richardson Weatherby with daughter Mercia. (Collection of Rose June Feenaughty).

169. Frances Richardson Durfee, 1929 with her children: Rolland and twins Eloise and Eleanor. (Collection of the Vossler family).

170. Clifton and Effie Kathern Root. (Collection of Dr. William Paquette).

171. Children of Laphronia Root. L to R: Leah Isabell Root, Martha Root, Claude Root, Marvin Lambert, George Fox, Betty Root Lambert, Lillie Root Fox, Effie Smith Root, and Clifton Root. (Collection of the late James Fox).

172. Ernest Stanley Root and his second wife, Fayetta. (Courtesy of the late Fayetta Root).

173. Edwin C. Root grocery store, Main Street, Bolivar, 1914. L to R: Edwin, Hatti, Bertha, Gladys Root. (Collection of the late Gladys Root Nichols).

174. Gladys Root Nichols. (Collection of the late Gladys Root Nichols).

175. Rose Dugan Root, first wife of Edward A. Root. (Collection of the late Tracy Rose Root Martin).

176. Advertisement for Asa W. Root and E. M. Strayer businesses. (Courtesy of the 1900 Bolivar, New York Business Directory).

177. Advertisement for the Ira Root Shoe Store, Bolivar, New York. (Courtesy of BRAG).

178. Former Ira Root Shoe Store on left side of Hall's Department Store, Bolivar, New York. (Courtesy of BRAG).

179. State Bank of Bolivar, corner of Main and Boss Streets. (Courtesy of BRAG).

180. Boss Street residence of Asa P. Root, next to the State Bank of Bolivar. (Collection of Dr. William Paquette).

181. 1899 Check signed by James M. Curtiss, first President of the State Bank of Bolivar. (Collection of Dr. William Paquette).

182. 1898 check signed by J. H. Root. (Collection of Dr. William Paquette).

183. 1898 Account Book Page, J. H. Root and Son Store. (Collection of Dr. William Paquette).

184. 1898 Bankruptcy Papers for J. H. Root and Son Store. (Collection of Dr. William A. Paquette).

185. 1924 stock purchase by Jesse A. Withey for Standard Turbine Corporation, Wellsville, New York. (Collection of Dr. William Paquette).

186. 1924 stock purchase by Jesse A. Withey for Standard Turbine Corporation, Wellsville, New York. (Collection of Dr. William Paquette).

187. Four generations of Holly males: L to R: Lloyd, Judson, Fred, and Lloyd (Pete) in front. (Collection of Dr. William Paquette).

188. Minerva Holly (Joyce). (Collection of Sharon Joyce Cardwell).

189. George Edward Joyce in Pontiac, Michigan. (Collection of Sharon Joyce Cardwell).

190. George Joyce. (Collection of Sharon Joyce Cardwell).

191. Minerva and George Joyce in later years. (Collection of Sharon Joyce Cardwell).

192. Margaret with her mother, Minerva Holly Joyce. (Collection of Sharon Joyce Cardwell).

193. 1953, Charles and Sharon Joyce with Santa. (Collection of Sharon Joyce Cardwell).

194. Georgia Jo Joyce with husband Torrey Gomila. (Collection of Sharon Joyce Cardwell).

195. Jo and Margaret Joyce. (Collection of Sharon Joyce Cardwell).

196. Judson John Joyce, US Navy. (Collection of Sharon Joyce Cardwell).

197. Charles and Sharon Joyce, 1957. (Collection of Sharon Joyce Cardwell).

198. Judson and Betty Joyce, 1946. (Collection of Sharon Joyce Cardwell).

199. Edward Joyce. (Collection of Sharon Joyce Cardwell).

200. Jack and Betty Joyce. (Collection of Sharon Joyce Cardwell).

201. Edward George and wife Edith Joyce George. (Collection of Sharon Joyce Cardwell).

202. Edward, John, and Margaret Joyce. (Collection of Sharon Joyce Cardwell).

203. Joyce siblings: Charles, Sharon, Dixie, and Judson. (Collection of Sharon Joyce Cardwell).

204. Earles L. Root (Collection of Dr. William Paquette).

205. L to R: Merle and Lyman Root, their mother Maggie Snowdon Root Weaver, Allen Root, Mary Root Holland, and Stanley Root. (Collection of Dr. William Paquette).

206. Daughter of Isabelle Root Johnson: Standing L to R: Eloise, Buela, Marion, Gertrude; Center: Muriel Wilson Johnson; Seated: Evelyn. (Courtesy of the Alice Weatherell Moore).

207. Isabelle Lou Root Johnson. (Courtesy of the late Alice Weatherell Moore).

208. Olean, New York Lumber Company. (Collection of Reverend Joseph Weatherell).

209. Olean Lumber Truck, business of Richard and Nina Weatherell McMullen. (Collection of Reverend Joseph Weatherell).

210. Postcard Olean Lumber Company, South Main Street. (Collection of Reverend Joseph Weatherell).

211. Lola B. Root Weatherell with son Harold who died 1910 at six months. (Collection of Reverend Joseph Weatherell).

212. Lola B. Root with husband George Weatherell and son John. (Collection of Reverend Joseph Weatherell).

213. Claude, Laphronia, and Clifton Root. (Collection of Rose June Feenaughty).

214. Elizabeth Root Jewett Fistler in old age. (Collection of Rose June Feenaughty).

215. Helen Lockley Williams and her husband Wayne. (Collection of Richard Biggs).

216. Bob and Jane Williams Biggs. (Collection of Richard Biggs).

217. Ann Williams (Collection of Richard Biggs).

218. Ina Withey Burdick McEnroe in Grecian pose. (Collection of Molly Pike Riccardi).

219. Jesse Withey family at their Vosburg residence. Back L to R; Bessie, Sarah, Jesse, Ina; Front L to R: Charles, Harry, and Howard. (Collection of Molly Pike Riccardi).

220. Jesse and Sarah Withey at their Wellsville residence, corner of Maple and Madison. (Collection of Molly Pike Riccardi).

221. The Wellsville residence of the Jesse Withey Family at 135 Maple Avenue, Wellsville, New York. (Courtesy of Molly Pike Riccardi).

222. Barbara Fretts with her children: Duranna, Noelle, Greta and John III. (Collection of Barbara Fretts).

223. Fretts children: Duranna, Noelle, Greta, John III with daughter Gwenivere. (Collection of Barbara Fretts).

224. John and Lorie Biederwolf. (Collection of Lorie Biederwolf).

225. Delaney, Jesse, Marley, and Avery Biederwolf. (Collection of Lorie Biederwolf).

226. Sally Sweet. (Collection of Laine Pike).

227. Richard Sweet. (Collection of Laine Pike).

228. Sally Sweet and daughter Laine. (Collection of Laine Pike).

229. Melissa, Melinda, Molly, and Rodney Pike with Melissa's daughter Rhiannon. (Collection of Molly Pike Riccardi).

230. Ina Withey Burdick McEnroe at her Oak Street residence, Wellsville, New York. (Collection of Dr. William Paquette).

231. John and Helen Craig Weatherell. (Collection of Reverend Joseph Weatherell).

232. The Babcock Theater Orchestra, 1935 with conductor John Weatherell at the piano. (Collection of Reverend Joseph Weatherell).

233. Allen Root driving Coca Cola truck, Bolivar, New York. (Collection of the late Mary Root Holland).

234. Lola Root Weatherell Pilon with her second husband Charles Pilon. (Collection of Dr. William Paquette).

235. 1948 wedding of Elizabeth Marie Root: L to R: Elizabeth with her father Edward Albert Root and her step-mother, Margaret. (Collection of Anne Root Sale).

236. 1949 wedding of Tracy Rose Root to Richard Martin. L to R: Carson, Jessie, and Richard Martin, Rose, Margaret, and Edward Albert Root (Collection of the late Tracy Root Martin).

237. The four sons of Tracy Root and Richard Martin: Glenn, Richard, Paul, and James, 1981. (Collection of the late Tracy Root Martin).

238. Edward A. Root, Jr. (Collection of the late Tracy Root Martin).

239. Caroline Toner, sister of Emma Toner Root. (Collection of Anne Root Sale).

240. Edward Albert Root, Jr. in uniform. (Collection of Anne Root Sale).

241. Wiley and Anne Root Sale, 1950s. (Collection of Anne Root Sale).

242. 1943, Leo C. and Ethel Root. (Collection of Dr. William Paquette).

243. William E. Nichols, Gladys Root Nichols, and William G. Nichols. (Collection of the late Gladys Root Nichols).

244. Gladys Root Nichols at her Bolivar residence on her 80th birthday. (Collection of Dr. William Paquette).

245. Edwin Milford Root. (Courtesy of the late JoAnn Root Randall).

246. Huldah Jane Root, daughter of George and Elizabeth Root. (Courtesy of Lily Dale Museum, Lily Dale, New York).

247. Gold necklace given by Huldah Root Curtiss on her deathbed to great-niece Huldah Jane Root. (Courtesy of the late Jane Nulsen Bunse).

248. Alvya Root Richardson with daughter Patricia and granddaughter JoAnn. (Collection of Dr. William Paquette).

249. Ralph Cook, founder of Theatre Genesis. (Open Source).

250. Helen Ward Hulbert. (Collection of Barbara Tarantine Hulbert).

251. Helen Root Spargur and her husband Bill at their North Main Street residence. (Collection of the late Helen Root Spargur).

252. Helen Root Spargur at her Wellsville residence 1988. (Collection of Dr. William Paquette).

253. Alta Root Schwertfager and her husband Henry. (Courtesy of the late Alta Schwertfager).

254. Dr. Richard Kay Root. (Open Source).

255. Leona Root Ellis O'Grady Wellmon with her third husband, George, 1950. (Collection of the late Leona Root Gordon).

256. Terry Richardson. (Collection of Rose June Feenaughty).

257. Sallie Richardson Lowery and her husband Bill. (Collection of Rose June Feenaughty).

258. L to R: Siblings, Merle, Blanche, Theo, and Doris Richardson. (Collection of Rose June Feenaughty).

259. USS Presidential Yacht Sequoia, 1970s, with Enlisted Captain LeDale Feenaughty, second row, first on left. (Collection of Rose June Feenaughty).

The Photographs

#1 | Bolivar, New York, 1875, looking north up Main Street towards Richburg. This is the earliest known photograph of Bolivar.

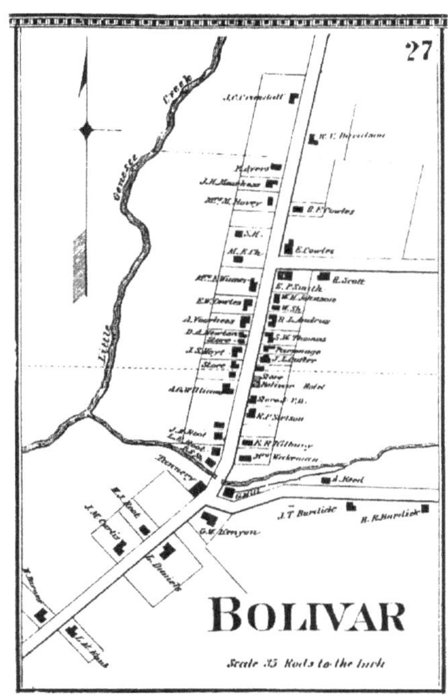

#2 | De Beers Insurance Map, 1879, Bolivar, New York.

#3 | Bolivar, New York, Main Street looking west, 1900.

#4 | Bolivar, New York, Main Street looking north, 1900.

#5 | Bolivar Methodist Church, Root family church.

#6 | Abel Root, Sr. farm across from Maple Lawn Cemetery, Bolivar, New York.

#7 | Abel Root, Jr.

#8 | Polly Scott Root, Mrs. Abel Root, Jr.

#9 | Maple Lawn Cemetery graves of Abel Root, Jr. and wife, Polly.

#10 | Union Cemetery, Fort Edward, New York grave of Frances E. Bancroft Root

#11 | David Cartwright Root.

#12 | Alceba Tyler Youngs and Marrieta Tyler Root (Mrs. David C. Root).

#13 | Maple Lawn Cemetery graves of David C. Root and wife Marietta.

#14 | Truman Bishop Root.

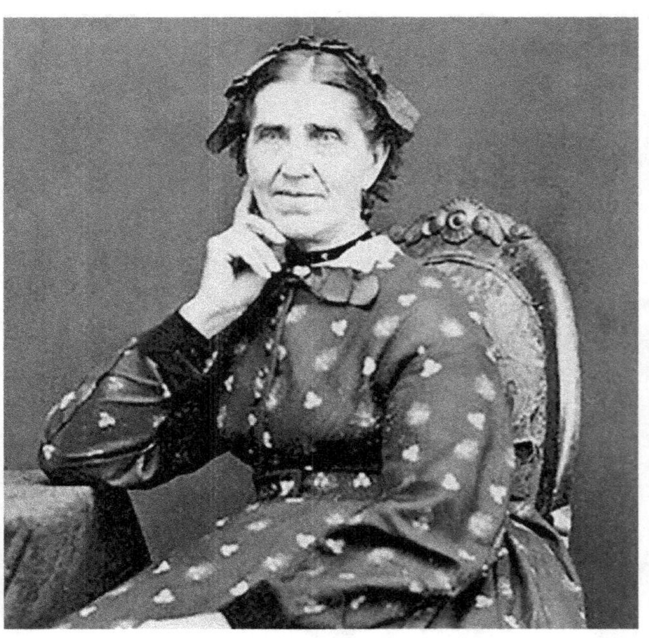

#15 | Polly Mead Root, Mrs. Truman Bishop Root.

#16 | Maples Lawn Cemetery graves of Bishop and Polly Root.

#17 | Maple Lawn Cemetery grave of Huldah Penelope Root Kellogg.

#18 | Maple Lawn Cemetery grave of Loring Grant Kellogg.

#19 | Until the Day Dawn Cemetery grave of Jane Voakes Root (and possibly of her husband, Franklin Root), Angelica, New York.

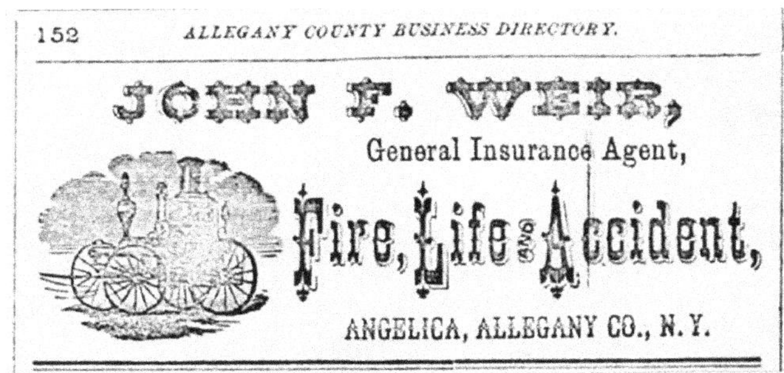

152 *ALLEGANY COUNTY BUSINESS DIRECTORY.*

JOHN F. WEIR,

General Insurance Agent,

Fire, Life and Accident,

ANGELICA, ALLEGANY CO., N. Y.

#20 | John F. Weir, Insurance Agent, Angelica, NY, son-in-law of Franklin Root.

#21 | Until the Day Dawn Cemetery, Angelica, NY grave of John Weir, first husband of Florence Root.

#22 | Desdemona Proctor Partridge Root, second wife of James H. Root.

#23 | Maple Lawn Cemetery grave of Mary W. Root, first wife of James H. Root

#24 | Charles A. Withey, second wife, Caroline Stebbins, and their son, William, 1865.

#25 | Maple Lawn Cemetery grave of Elizabeth Root Withey.

#26 | Richburg, New York Cemetery grave of Samuel Charles Withey, eldest son of Charles and Elizabeth Root Withey.

#27 | The children of Charles A. Withey, L to R: William, Ina, Emma, Jesse, and Clara.

#28 | The Jesse A. Withey family, Witheytown (Vosburg), July 10, 1910. L to R: Rufus Sawyer, Bessie, Harry, Ina, Charles, Sarah, Howard, Emma Withey Sawyer, and Jesse.

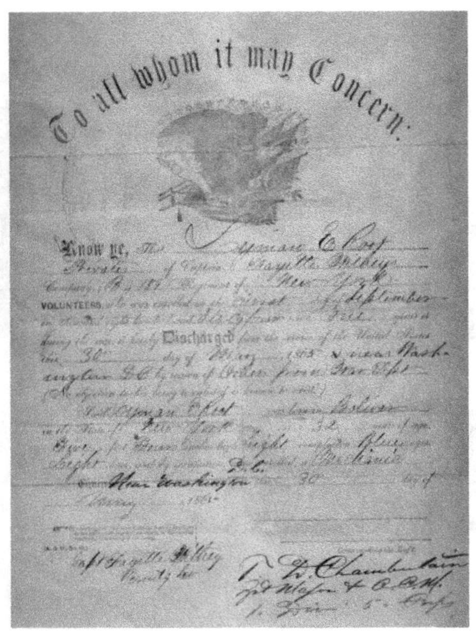

To all whom it may Concern:

Know ye, That

VOLUNTEERS

Discharged

#29 | *1865 Civil War Discharge Papers of Lyman E. Root.*

#30 | *Almyra and Lyman E. Root.*

#31 | *Jerome B. Reed and wife, Ruth Barber Reed.*

#32 | *Earles, Lola, and Libbie Root, Children of Lyman and Almyra Root.*

#33 | Lyman E. Root in later years.

#34 | Lyman Root Blacksmith Shop and residence, Main Street, Bolivar, New York.

#35 | Almyra Root in front of the family home, Main Street, Bolivar, 1910.

#36 | Almyra Reed Root and Maggie Granger Root.

#37 | The Paul Ennis, formerly Lyman Root, Blacksmith shop, Main and Leather Streets, Bolivar. L to R: Ward Rice, Bill Coon, Ted Macaane, Leo Root with his dog Spot, and Lester George, 1910.

#38 | The Paul Ennis residence, South Main Street, Bolivar. L to R: Maggie Granger Root and Libbie Root Ennis. The house was demolished in 1983.

#39 | Maggie Granger Root and her husband Earles Root.

#40 | Lola, Isabelle, and Harold Root with their uncle Bernard Root and cousin Dudley Root, 1893.

#41 | Isabelle Root, Dudley Ennis with their uncle Bernard Root.

#42 | Lola Root, daughter of Almyra and Lyman Root.

#43 | Ernest Jerome Root

#44 | Belle Fuller Root, Mrs. Ernest J. Root.

#45 | Leo C. Root.

#46 | Leo C. Root and sister Noria Root Wylie, 1910.

#47 | L to R: Jenny Cox and Belle Fuller Root, owners of a millinery and dress shop in Binghamton, New York.

#48 | Mary Jane Root Barber, Mrs. Elmer Barber.

#49 | Hiram and Mary Jane White Root with Flora, Laphronia, and Elizabeth.

#50 | Hiram Root standing in front of his residence and store, the Bee Hive, on Liberty Street after a hunting trip.

#51 | Flora Root Richardson.

#52 | Edward A. Richardson

#53 | Laphronia and Effie Meyers Root.

#54 | Laphronia and Effie Meyers Root with Clifford and Tina.

#55 | Laphronia Root and his second wife, Carrie Earl Root.

#56 | Elizabeth Root Jewett Fistler.

#57 | David Root.

#58 | Marietta Tyler Root.

#59 | *Huldah Root Curtiss as a young girl.*

#60 | *Back L to R: Albert Root and 2nd or 3rd wife, Addison Evans. Front L to R: Huldah Root Curtiss, James Curtiss, Elosica Root Evans.*

#61 | *Jane Huldah Root Curtiss.*

#62 | *Elosica Root Evans, as a young girl.*

#63 | Elosica Root Evans.

#64 | Albert Louis Root.

#65 | Asa W. Root, died Andersonville Prison, Georgia.

#66 | Grave of Asa W. Root, Andersonville, Georgia.

#67 | Asa W. Root, son of Albert Root, as a young man.

#68 | Asa W. Root, son of Albert Root, in later years.

#69 | Amina Root, daughter of Asa W. and Emma Toner Root.

#70 | Alice, Albert, and Agnes Evans at Lily Dale.

#71 | Alice and Agnes Evans as young girls.

#72 | Alice and Agnes Evans as teenagers.

#73 | Agnes Evans, 1895.

#74 | Alice and Agnes Evans.

#75 | Alice Evans.

#76 | Alice Evans in later years.

#77 | Jessie Evans, wife of Albert Evans.

#78 | Gladys, Bertha, and Milford Root, children of Edwin C. Root.

#79 | Milford Root as a young man.

#80 | Albert George Nulsen, son of Huldah and Albert Nulsen.

#81 | Albert L. Root with beard.

#82 | Armina Kilbury Root, Mrs. Albert Root.

#83 | Anna C. Moore, second wife of Albert Root.

#84 | Civil War sword and photograph of Colonel Edwin Kilbury of Bolivar.

#85 | Root/MacDonald Photo: L to R, Back Row: George Root, ?, Della MacDonald, Edwin C. Root; Center: L to R: Jane MacDonald, Elizabeth MacDonald Root, Charlie MacDonald, Harriet MacDonald Root; Front: Sadie MacDonald Hall.

#86 | L to R: Elizabeth MacDonald Root and Harriet MacDonald Root.

#87 | L to R: Gladys Root Nichols, Edwin C. Root; Edwin Milford Root, Bertha Root Osborne, Hattie Root.

#88 | Asa W. Root in formal attire.

#89 | Emma Toner Root, Mrs. Asa W. Root.

#90 | Edward A. Root and his sister, Armina.

#91 | Edward Albert Root as a boy.

#92 | Wilber P. Cook.

#93 | Bertha Root Cook.

#94 | Boss Street residence of Wilber and Bertha Cook, designed by Asa W. Root.

#95 | George and Elizabeth MacDonald Root.

#96 | Maple Lawn Cemetery Civil War Memorial listing E. C. Kellogg among the Civil War dead.

#97 | Christopher and Elizabeth Root Garthwait, 1907.

#98 | Emma Garthwait Hulbert.

#99 | Fred and Emma Garthwait Hulbert.

#100 | Emma, Gerry, Elba Hulbert, Elizabeth Root Garthwait, Margaret Hulbert.

#101 | Fred Hulbert family: Back L to R: Wayne and Gerald; Front L to R: Fred, Leta, Emma, Elba, Maude.

#102 | Hulbert family: L to R: Leta and Naomi Irvin, Emma Garthwait Hulbert, Elizabeth Root Garthwait, Helen and Margaret Hulbert, Maude and Virginia Hulbert.

#103 | Maple Lawn Cemetery gates and fence erected by Mr. and Mrs. Elmer Garthwait in memory of their son, Glen.

#104 | Maple Lawn Cemetery, Garthwait Mausoleum.

#105 | Erastus Root as a young man.

#106 | Erastus Root holding his granddaughter, Helen Root.

#107 | Asa P. Root.

#108 | Erastus Root family: Cora Root, Erastus Root holding Helen Root Spargur, Myrtie Root Strayer, Helen Prentice Root and Asa P. Root.

#109 | Myrtie Root Strayer holding her niece Helen Root.

#110 | Helen Morgan Root, wife of Asa P. Root.

#111 | Arthur Lew Root and his second wife, Ida Roberts Root.

#112 | Leona Root Ellis with her father, Lew Root, Salt Rising Road, Bolivar, 1900.

#113 | Leona Root Ellis with her first husband Ray Ellis, Deer Creek, NY.

#114 | Ray Ellis with his father-in-law, Lew Root, Titusville, Pennsylvania.

#115 | Leon Erastus Root.

#116 | James Curtis Root.

#117 | Seated: L to R: Burr LeRoy and Kate Root; Standing, L to R: their children: Howard Leroy, Coral Marie, Laurence, Ruth, and Dr. Raymond Root.

#118 | Mattie Ennis with her son Paul J. Ennis.

#119 | Paul Ennis with nephew, Leo C. Root, daughter-in-law Mattie Ennis and grandson Paul

#120 | Bernard and Maggie Snowdon Root at their home on Leather Street.

#121 | Leo C. Root, US Navy, 1916.

#122 | 1916 Wedding picture of Leo C. Root and Ethel Bernard Root.

INCORPORATED UNDER THE LAWS OF
THE STATE OF NEW YORK
Shares

VanCuren High Explosive Company

CAPITAL STOCK $20,000.00

This Certifies That

One Hundred Dollars

Van Curen High Explosive Company. Full Paid and Non-assessable

In Witness Whereof,

SHARES $100. EACH

#123 | Van Curen High Explosives stock certificate in the name of Leo C. Root.

#124 | Leo C. Root driving the Van Curen nitroglycerine wagon, Bolivar, 1920.

#125 | LeSuer House, State Historic Site, where the Leo C. Root family resided from 1930 to 1933.

#126 | Leo C. Root children, Clintonville, PA Top: L to R: Ernest and Fred; Seated: L to R: Eva, Lawrence, Nordica, and Dorothy.

#127 | L to R: Ethel, Dorothy, Eva, and Nordica Root, 1940, Clinton-ville, Pennsylvania.

#128 | Former Allentown, New York parsonage, residence of Leo and Ethel Root from1959 to 1976.

#129 | Leo Stanley Root and his wife, Barbara Lamson,

#130 | Children of Leo S. and Barbara Root: L to R: Jimmy, Bunny, Marleen, Debbie, Paul, and Dennis.

#131 | 1999 wedding of Melissa Coffey to Dan Root; L to R: Jamie Corson, Krista Root Corson, Nate Corson, Dennis and Janice Root, bride and groom, Jlene Root and daughter Hannah, Kim Root Monterio and Chris Monterio.

#132 | Paul, Barbara and daughters Daneille and Cheryl Root.

#133 | Nordica Root, high school graduation.

#134 | 1951 Wedding photograph of Nordica Root to Glen Anderson.

#135 | Diana Anderson LaFaro and her husband Jim

#136 | Sharon Anderson Wallace with husband Dave and son Andy.

#137 | Richard Anderson and daughter Dillon.

#138 | Eva J. Root, 1939.

#139 | Eva J. Root, 1960.

#140 | Lantern Lodge, Scio, New York, residence of Eva Root.

#141 | Fred Root, 1943.

#142 | Fred Root in Allentown Fire Department's Uniform.

#143 | Arthur C. and Dorothy Root Paquette, 1946.

#144 | Robert, Dorothy, Arthur, and William Paquette, 1951.

#145 | Hugh Daniel Root during military service.

#146 | Helga, Dan, Michael, and Angelika Root, 1963, Berlin, Germany.

#147 | Lawrence Leonard Root in Marine uniform.

#148 | Lawrence Root and his first wife, Margie, with sons Larry Wayne and Ronnie, 1951, Allentown, New York.

#149 | Betty Orvis Root, second wife of Lawrence Root.

#150 | Seated L to R: Mrs. Hiram Root, Mercia and Minnie Richardson Weatherby, and Flora Root Richardson, four generations, 1910.

#151 | Flora Root Richardson with son Laurence on lap and standing Lewis, Ethel, and Mildred.

#152 | Children of Edward and Flora Root Richardson: Standing L to R: Ethel and Elizabeth; Seated: L to R: Lewis, Mildred, and Minnie.

#153 | Minnie Richardson Weatherby, husband Homer, and children; Mercia and Homer.

#154 | Howard and Mercia Weatherby.

#155 | Lewis Richardson

#156 | Lois Cockle Richardson, first wife of Lewis Richardson.

#157 | Edward Richardson with sons: Stanley, Manley, and Lewis.

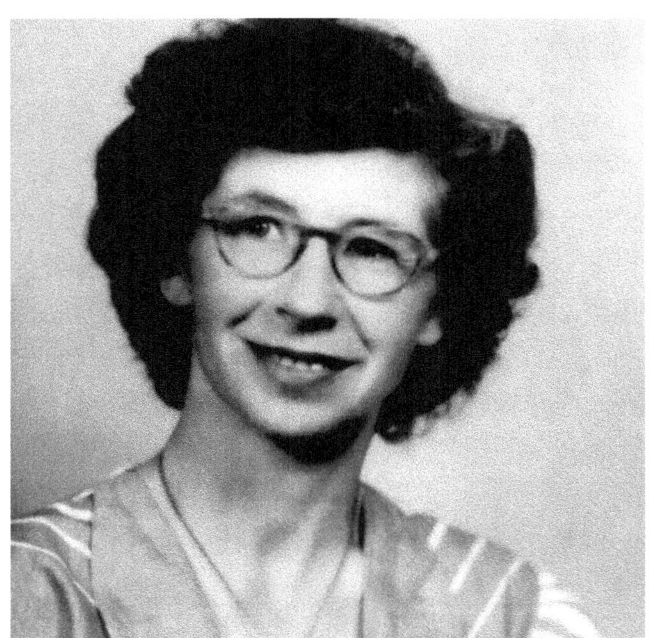

#158 | Marjorie Seamans Richardson, second wife of Lewis Richardson.

#159 | Children of Lewis and Marjorie Richardson: Sallie, Jim, and Terry.

#160 | Doris Richardson June and husband Victor June.

#161 | Victor and Doris June Family: Standing L to R: Rose Mary, Beverly, and Inez Seated L to R; Dale, Dean, Gerald.

#162 | Dean's graduation day 1963: Dean, Dale, Jerry, Doris, and Victor June (back) and (front) Inez Une Pervorse, Rose June Feenaughty, and Beverly June Van Allen.

#163 | Stephen, Twannee, Beverly June, Gifford, and Heather Van Allen.

#164 | Jim and Tina Richardson.

#165 | Bill and Theo Richardson Dickerson.

#166 | Albert Hirliman, Ethel Richardson Hirliman, Dan Baker, Agnes Richardson Baker, Elizabeth Richardson Corcoran, John Corcoran, ?, ?, Margaret Baker Mink, Juanita Baker Cornell, two children, ?, ?, 1957.

#167 | Mary Elizabeth Richard Corcoran with husband John and son John, Jr.

#168 | Minnie Richardson Weatherby with daughter Mercia.

#169 | Frances Richardson Durfee, 1929 with her children: Rolland and twins Eloise and Eleanor.

#170 | Clifton and Effie Kathern Root.

#171 | Children of Laphronia Root. L to R: Leah Isabell Root, Martha Root, Claude Root, Marvin Lambert, George Fox, Betty Root Lambert, Lillie Root Fox, Effie Smith Root, and Clifton Root.

#172 | Ernest Stanley Root and his second wife, Fayetta.

#173 | Edwin C. Root grocery store, Main Street, Bolivar, 1914. L to R: Edwin, Hatti, Bertha, Gladys Root.

#174 | Gladys Root Nichols.

#175 | Rose Dugan Root, first wife of Edward A. Root

ASA. W. ROOT,
Carriage and Wagon Repairing,
and General Blacksmithing, also Cabinet Work.
BOLIVAR, N. Y.

E. M. STRAYER,
Manufacturer and Dealer in
Light and Heavy Harness, and a Full Line of
HORSE FURNISHING GOODS,
Whips, Robes, Trunks and Grips.
Repair Work a Specialty. BOLIVAR, N. Y.

Root family owned businesses, Bolivar, New York

176_20200617 Root_190

#176 | Advertisement for Asa W. Root and E. M. Strayer businesses.

SEMI-ANNUAL SALE
OF RUBBER GOODS AND SHOES

will start Saturday, January 14, and continue for 15 days. During this time we will offer all rubber and felt goods at

10 PER CENT BELOW REGULAR PRICE

with the single exception of "Snag Proof" on which the manufacturers refuse to allow us to cut the price.

$3.50 Overs for Felts and Socks	$3.15
$3.25 Overs for Felts and Socks	$2.93
$2.50 Overs for Felts and Socks	$2.25
$2.00 Overs for Felts and Socks	$1.80
$1.75 Overs for Felts and Socks	$1.58
$1.40 Overs for Felts and Socks	$1.26
$2.00 Ball Band Lace Felt	$1.80
$1.50 Ball Band Overlap Felt	$1.35
$1.00 Ball Band Pressed Felt	.90c
$1.25 Ball Band Socks	$1.13
$1.00 Ball Band Socks	.90c
75c Ball Band Socks	.68c
Men's $2.75 four buckle arctic	$2.48
Men's $2.60 four buckle arctic	$2.34
Men's $2.00 two buckle arctic	$1.80
Men's $1.50 one buckle arctic	$1.35
Misses $1.40 two buckle arctic	$1.26
Childs $1.25 two buckle arctic	$1.13

Root's Shoe Store

No goods charged at above prices. BOLIVAR, N. Y.

Ira Root Shoe Store
Main Street Bolivar

177_20200617 Root_117

#177 | Advertisement for the Ira Root Shoe Store, Bolivar, New York.

#178 | Former Ira Root Shoe Store on left side of Hall's Department Store, Bolivar, New York.

#179 | State Bank of Bolivar, corner of Main and Boss Streets.

#180 | Boss Street residence of Asa P. Root, next to the State Bank of Bolivar.

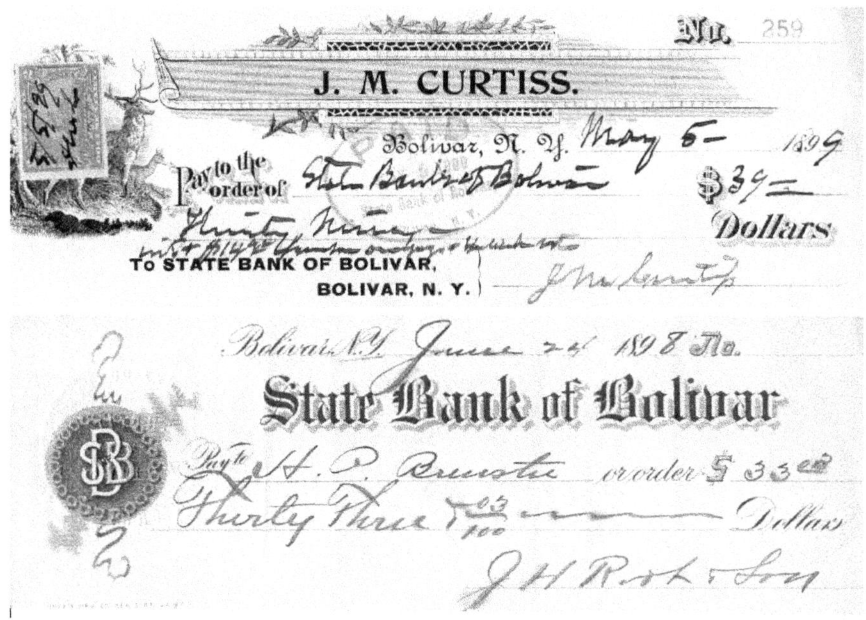
No. 259

J. M. CURTISS.

Bolivar, N. Y. May 5– 1899

Pay to the order of State Bank of Bolivar $39⁰⁰

Thirty Nine Dollars

TO STATE BANK OF BOLIVAR,
BOLIVAR, N. Y.

Bolivar N.Y. June 24 1898 No.

State Bank of Bolivar

Pay to H. P. Brewster or order $33⁰³

Thirty Three ⁰³⁄₁₀₀ Dollars

J H Root & Son

#181 | Top: 1899 Check signed by James M. Curtiss, first President of the State Bank of Bolivar.

#182 | Bottom: 1898 check signed by J. H. Root.

Bolivar, N. Y. 189

M

In account with J. H. ROOT & SON,

DEALERS IN

Dry Goods and Groceries. Boots and Shoes.

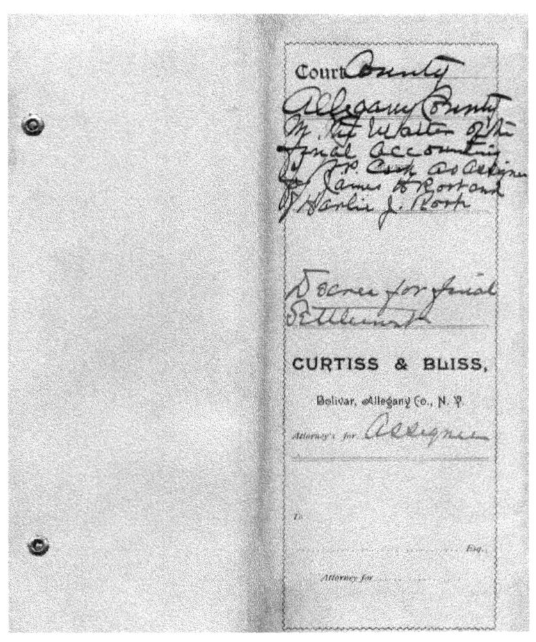
Court County

Allegany County

CURTISS & BLISS,

Bolivar, Allegany Co., N. Y.

Attorneys for Assignee

#183 | 1898 Account Book Page for J. H. Root and Son Store.

#184 | 1898 Bankruptcy Papers for J. H. Root and Son Store.

Incorporated Under the Laws of the State of New York

Number -40-

Shares -3 1/3-

Standard Turbine Corporation

Wellsville, New York

CAPITAL STOCK AUTHORIZED.
Preferred Stock 1,000 shares. Par value $100.
Common Stock 1250 shares. No par value.

This is to Certify, that J.A. Withey

is the owner of -3 1/3- Shares of COMMON STOCK of the **Standard Turbine Corporation** transferable only on the books of the Company by the holder in person or by Attorney on surrender of this Certificate.

The Preferred Stock, as more fully provided in Certificate of Incorporation, is entitled, in preference to Common Stock, to cumulative dividends at the rate of Seven (7) Per cent per annum.

In Witness Whereof, the said Corporation has caused this Certificate to be signed by its duly authorized officers and to be sealed with the Seal of the Corporation.

this 4th day of Jan A.D. 1924

Secretary-Treasurer. President.

Shares

No Par Value

#185 | 1924 stock purchase by Jesse A. Withey for Standard Turbine Corporation, Wellsville, New York.

Certificate

For 3 1/3 Shares

of the

Common Stock

Standard Turbine Corporation

Wellsville, New York

Issued to

J A Withey

Dated

Jan 4th 1924

#186 | 1924 stock purchase by Jesse A. Withey for Standard Turbine Corporation, Wellsville, New York.

#187 | Four generations of Holly males: L to R: Lloyd, Judson, Fred, and Lloyd (Pete) in front.

#188 | Minerva Holly (Joyce).

#189 | George Edward Joyce in Pontiac, Michigan.

#190 | George Joyce.

#191 | Minerva and George Joyce in later years.

#192 | Margaret with her mother, Minerva Holly Joyce.

#193 | 1953, Charles and Sharon Joyce with Santa.

#194 | Georgia Jo Joyce with husband Torrey Gomila.

#195 | Jo and Margaret Joyce.

#196 | Judson John Joyce, US Navy.

#197 | Charles and Sharon Joyce, 1957.

#198 | Judson and Betty Joyce, 1946

#199 | *Edward Joyce.*

#200 | *Jack and Betty Joyce.*

#201 | *Edward George and wife Edith Joyce George.*

#202 | *Edward, John, and Margaret Joyce.*

#203 | Joyce siblings: Charles, Sharon, Dixie, and Judson.

#204 | Earles L. Root

#205 | L to R: Merle and Lyman Root, their mother Maggie Snowdon Root Weaver, Allen Root, Mary Root Holland, and Stanley Root

#206 | Daughter of Isabelle Root Johnson: Standing L to R: Eloise, Buela, Marion, Gertrude; Center: Muriel Wilson Johnson; Seated: Evelyn.

#207 | Isabelle Lou Root Johnson.

#208 | Olean, New York Lumber Company.

#209 | Olean Lumber Truck, business of Richard and Nina Weatherell McMullen.

#210 | Postcard Olean Lumber Company, South Main Street.

#211 | Lola B. Root Weatherell with son Harold who died 1910 at six months.

#212 | Lola B. Root with husband George Weatherell and son John.

#213 | Claude, Laphronia, and Clifton Root.

#214 | Elizabeth Root Jewett Fistler in old age.

#215 | Helen Lockley Williams and her husband Wayne.

#216 | Bob and Jane Williams Biggs.

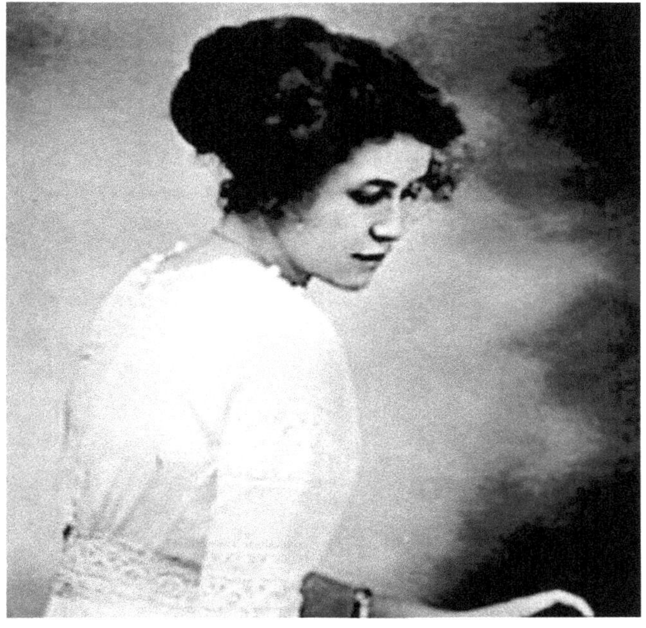

#217 | Ann Williams.

#218 | Ina Withey Burdick McEnroe in Grecian pose.

#219 | Jesse Withey family at their Vosburg residence. Back L to R; Bessie, Sarah, Jesse, Ina; Front L to R: Charles, Harry, and Howard.

#220 | Jesse and Sarah Withey at their Wellsville residence, corner of Maple and Madison

#221 | The Wellsville residence of the Jesse Withey Family at 135 Maple Avenue, Wellsville, New York.

#222 | Barbara Fretts with her children: Duranna, Noelle, Greta and John III.

#223 | Fretts children: Duranna, Noelle, Greta, John III with daughter Gwenivere

#224 | John and Lorie Biederwolf.

#225 | Delaney, Jesse, Marley, and Avery Biederwolf.

#226 | Sally Sweet.

#227 | Richard Sweet.

#228 | Sally Sweet and daughter Laine.

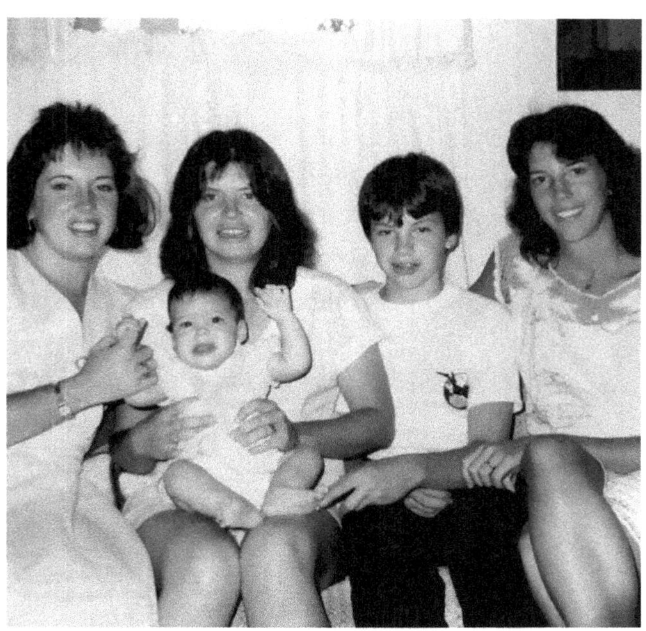

#229 | Melissa, Melinda, Molly, and Rodney Pike with Melissa's daughter Rhiannon.

#230 | Ina Withey Burdick McEnroe at her Oak Street residence, Wellsville, New York

#231 | John and Helen Craig Weatherell.

#232 | The Babcock Theater Orchestra, 1935 with conductor John Weatherell at the piano.

#233 | Allen Root driving Coca Cola truck, Bolivar, New York.

#234 | Lola Root Weatherell Pilon with her second husband Charles Pilon

#235 | 1948 wedding of Elizabeth Marie Root: L to R: Elizabeth with her father Edward Albert Root and her step-mother, Margaret.

#236 | 1949 wedding of Tracy Rose Root to Richard Martin. L to R: Carson, Jessie, and Richard Martin, Rose, Margaret, and Edward Albert Root.

#237 | The four sons of Tracy Root and Richard Martin: Glenn, Richard, Paul, and James, 1981.

#238 | Edward A. Root, Jr.

#239 | Caroline Toner, sister of Emma Toner Root.

#240 | Edward Albert Root, Jr. in uniform.

#241 | Wiley and Anne Root Sale, 1950s.

#242 | 1943, Leo C. and Ethel Root.

#243 | William E. Nichols, Gladys Root Nichols, and William G. Nichols.

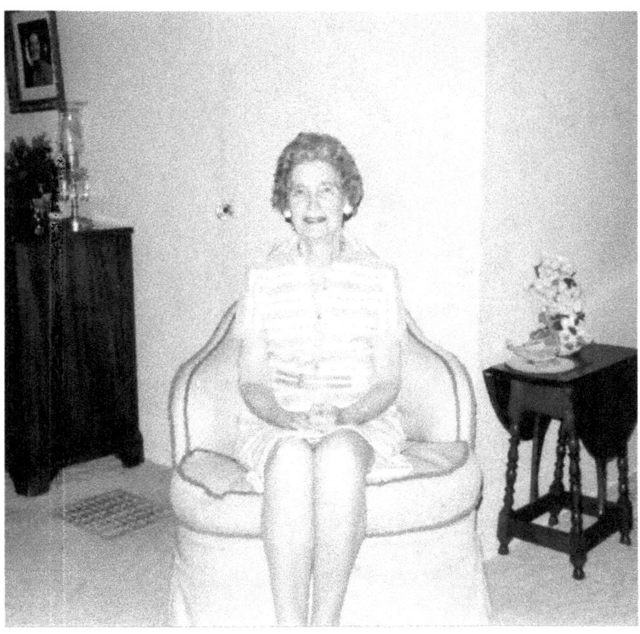

#244 | Gladys Root Nichols at her Bolivar residence on her 80th birthday.

#245 | Edwin Milford Root.

#246 | Huldah Jane Root, daughter of George and Elizabeth Root.

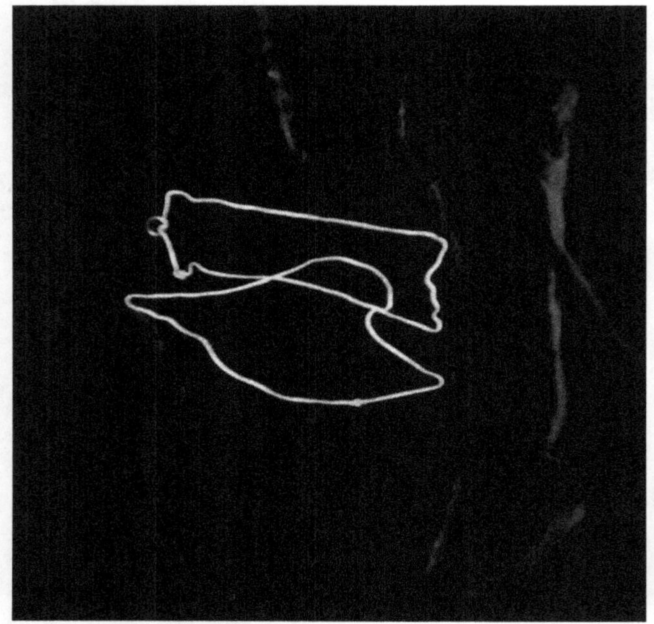

#247 | Gold necklace given by Huldah Root Curtiss on her deathbed to great-niece Huldah Jane Root.

#248 | Alvya Root Richardson with daughter Patricia and granddaughter JoAnn.

#249 | Ralph Cook, founder of Theatre Genesis.

#250 | Helen Ward Hulbert.

#251 | Helen Root Spargur and her husband Bill at their North Main Street residence.

#252 | Helen Root Spargur at her Wellsville residence 1988.

#253 | Alta Root Schwertfager and her husband Henry.

#254 | Dr. Richard Kay Root.

#255 | Leona Root Ellis O'Grady Wellmon with her third husband, George, 1950.

#256 | Terry Richardson.

#257 | Sallie Richardson Lowery and her husband Bill.

#258 | L to R: Siblings, Merle, Blanche, Theo, and Doris Richardson.

#259 | USS Presidential Yacht Sequoia, 1970s, with Enlisted Captain LeDale Feenaughty, second row, first on left.

Contributor Acknowledgments

I want to thank the members of the Root family listed below for their contributions to the 1990 edition of the family history and to the 2020 revised edition. Their assistance with genealogical information and family photographs was invaluable.

The Root Family History – 1990 Edition

The late Nordica Root Anderson
The late Jane Nulsen Bunse
The late Willard Cline
The late Wilber Cook
The late James Fox
The late Leona Root Gordon
The late Mary Root Holland
The late Tracy Root Martin
The late Doris Richardson
The late Evelyn Johnson LaFredo
The late Barbara Lambert
The late Eloise Johnson Leone
The late Martha Root Miller
The late Alice Weatherell Moore
The late Marion Noonan
The late Richard Osborne
The late Dorothy Root Paquette
The late Joann Root Randall
The late Alyva Root Richardson
The late Mrs. Harold Root
The late Dr. Richard K. Root
The late Edmund Root
The late Helen Root Spargur
The late Sally Burdick Sweet
The late Carolyne Williams
The late Jean Howard
The late Colletta Ennis Yehl
The late Jerry de Groff
June Sherri Nelson Jack
Dr. William Paquette
Anne Root Sale

Kathleen Root Abdo
Marleen Root Benoit
Raymond M. Berardi
Lorie Sweet Biederwolf
Richard Biggs
Sharon Joyce Cardwell
Elizabeth Windus Dinger
David Ennis
Timothy Ennis
Lisa Sweet Fountain
Barbara Windus Fretts
Rose Mary June Feenaughty
Timothy Hardy
Peggy Hinz Kohl
Barbara Tarantine Hulbert
Dale June
Dean June
Gerald June
Diana Anderson LaFaro
Sallie Richardson Lowery
Marsha Ennis Majors
Joan Root May
Jean Milliman
Ginger Root Mosher
Alexander Paquette
Dr. Natalie Paquette
Patricia Paquette
Dr. Robert Paquette
Dr. William Paquette
Inez June Pervorse
Molly Pike Riccardi
Dennis and Janice Root
Douglas Root
Gesa Haase Root
Leo James Root
Paul and Barbara Root
Richard Root
Ronald Root
Anne Root Sale
Tracy Barozzini Surdyk
Laine Sweet
Beverly June Van Allen
Sharon Anderson Wallace
Reverend Joseph Weatherell

Root | Roote – Last Name Index with Biography Numbers

Root Family Descendants – Last Name Index with Biography Numbers

A

B

C

D

E

F

G

I

L

N

Q

R

S

Y

Z

Author Biography

Dr. William A. Paquette

William A. Paquette, Ph. D., retired Professor of History, is the great-great-great-great grandson of Abel Root, Sr. Dr. Paquette can document lines of descent from Mayflower passenger Edward Fuller, his wife, and son, Samuel. Additional Mayflower lines of documented descent can be claimed from Governor William Bradford, Richard Warren, Dr. Samuel Fuller, and George Soule. Professor Paquette is a direct descendant of colonial Salem, Massachusetts leader Roger Conant and Henry Adams of Braintree, Massachusetts who is the ancestor of Presidents John Adams and John Quincy Adams. Dr. Paquette's descent from colonial minister Reverend John Lathrop allows him to claim collateral lineage with President U.S. Grant, Presidents George H. W. Bush, and George W. Bush, Mormon founder Joseph Smith, and Post cereals heiress, Marjorie Merriweather Post. Genealogical research has been a part of Professor Paquette's interests since childhood.

www.ingramcontent.com/pod-product-compliance
Lightning Source LLC
Chambersburg PA
CBHW081425270326
41932CB00019B/3096

* 9 7 8 1 7 3 3 1 2 9 2 5 1 *